YOUNG ADULT LITERATURE
BACKGROUND AND CRITICISM

YOUNG ADULT LITERATURE

BACKGROUND AND CRITICISM

Compiled by
Millicent Lenz and
Ramona M. Mahood

American Library Association   Chicago 1980

Library of Congress Cataloging in Publication Data

Main entry under title:

Young adult literature.

Includes bibliographies.
1. Children's literature—History and criticism—Addresses, essays, lectures.
2. Youth—Books and reading—Addresses, essays, lectures. I. Lenz, Millicent.
II. Mahood, Ramona.
PN1009.A1Y59   809'.89282   80-23489
ISBN 0-8389-0302-9

Contents

Part 4
Male and Female: Sexuality   169

Part 5
Free to Be: Liberation from Stereotypes   225

Part 6
Living in a Multicultural World   255

Part 7

Media in the Global Village   305

Part 8

Confession, Celebration, Illumination: Poetry Power   359

Part 9

Alternate Worlds and a Multiplicity of Futures   415

Part 10
Unshackling the Mind

Part 11
Turning Teens On to Books

Contributors

Preface

This book has grown out of a need for a collection of readings to use as a springboard for exploration into the fascinating realm of young adult literature. Its format reflects an existing course in young adult literature as it is taught at Memphis State University. The intended audience includes students of young adult literature (wherever they may be located, whether in schools of library science or education, or in departments of English), young adult librarians, secondary school media specialists and reading teachers, and any other adults who have a professional or personal stake in bringing teenagers and books together. In keeping with this assorted audience, the editors have attempted to represent the viewpoints of specialists in the aforementioned disciplines, plus those in medicine and psychology where the views of the latter can illuminate the topic. The editors hope this multidimensional perspective on young adult literature will stimulate and enliven interdisciplinary dialogue concerning it.

Knowledge, a wise man has said, is dialogue; that is, knowledge consists not in statements cast in bronze, but in the *process* of the interchange of ideas. In the belief that all perspectives have value (though all perspectives are limited and some are more valuable than others), the editors have endeavored to encourage questioning and discussion, rather than to supply definitive answers, and to stimulate original syntheses of facts and ideas. If this book raises more questions than it answers, that is in keeping with its intent.

The terms "adolescent" and "young adult," as applied to literature, have been used interchangeably, reflecting the editors' conviction that it is impossible to differentiate meaningfully between the two in their reading levels and interests.

No book comes to being in a vacuum, and this volume owes a debt to its trailblazing predecessors. For many years, *Books and the Teenage Reader* by G. Robert Carlsen has been a standard resource; unfortunately, the most recent edition (2nd rev. ed., Harper, 1980) was not available for examination at this writing. Planning for the present volume was well underway when *Young Adult Literature in the Seventies* (Scarecrow, 1978) by Jana Varlejs made its appearance. Just published, *Literature for Today's Young Adults* by Kenneth L. Donelson and Alleen Pace Nilsen (Scott, Foresman, 1980) provides an excellent framework for study, and promises to establish itself as the definitive basic text in the field. The present collection does not duplicate the content of these other works; the articles selected for inclusion are for the most part not reprinted elsewhere (two have not previously appeared in print), and further, we have brought them together in a unique topical arrangement.

It is hoped that this volume may add to the store of knowledge of the emerging field of young adult literature and that it may help to enlarge the company of those who find excitement and inspiration therein.

Part 1

Toward Self-Worth and Competence through Adolescent Literature

The emphasis on cooperation and group adjustment characteristic of modern life interferes specifically with the central developmental task of adolescence itself . . . *self-definition. Adolescence
is the period during which a young person learns who he is, and
what he really feels. It is the time during which he differentiates
himself from his culture, though on the culture's terms. It is the
age at which, by becoming a person in his own right, he becomes
capable of deeply felt relationships to other individuals perceived
clearly as such.*

Edgar Z. Friedenberg[1]

Of the herculean tasks facing the adolescent on the road to maturity, two
seem to be central. The first is the development of a positive self-image,
based on a secure sense of self-worth (what Bette Greene describes in
Summer of My German Soldier as Patty Bergen's perception of herself,
through Anton's love, as "a person of value"). The second is the achievement of a sense of competence—usually gained through what Eliot Wigginton has called "doing real work in the real world." The first two articles in this section are linked by their authors' belief in the importance of
self-worth and competence in the growth of young people toward adulthood. Until the young can affirm these two values within themselves, they
will continue to display a longing for the simplicity of childhood accompanied by separateness from the adult world. The adolescent's expanded
consciousness of self, heightened by a sense of the world perceived as indifferent, requires the forming of certain emotional strengths that literature can help to articulate. Books, therefore, as sources of "forms" for
interpreting human experience, have an important part to play in the establishment of the young person's readiness to affirm his autonomy.

Dana L. Farnsworth's "The Young Adult: An Overview" gives a multi-disciplinary perspective on the attitudes and behaviors of college students over the last two or three decades and thus provides an historical background for viewing today's young adults. Contrasting the radicalism of the sixties with the "new conservatism" of the seventies, he goes on to interpret changes in many aspects of their lives: counterculture life-styles, responses to the media, the use and misuse of drugs, new codes of sexual behavior. Citing evidence of a decline in personal integrity throughout society, he urges cooperation between young adults and their elders to bring about creative social change.

In "Understanding the Adolescent Reader," Armin Grams surveys the psychological development of the teenager and its part in determining his "reading needs." Central tasks are the development of a sense of identity, a perception of oneself as physically mature, resolving the conflict between dependency/independence, finding satisfying peer relationships, forming one special attachment with an individual of the opposite sex, and developing values. Added to all of these is the further task of adjusting to the idea of vocation (i.e., achieving a sense of competence).

Because adolescent literature cannot be discussed meaningfully in a vacuum, apart from some understanding of its audience, the first two essays have stressed adolescent psychology and the social pressures faced by adolescents today. Literature for teenage readers nonetheless needs to be considered for its literary qualities, for in addition to whatever socio-psychological or "coping" role it may play, it is also to be evaluated as literature. There is no reason why it should be judged by lesser standards than those of "adult" literature. The essays by Holland, Lystad, and Engdahl together suggest the problems encountered in formulating a definition of young adult literature. Holland poses the dilemma succinctly: does "adolescent literature" mean "whatever any adolescent happens to be reading at any time"? Or is adolescent literature a distinguishable genre, and, if so, what features differentiate it from "adult literature"? Stanek and Donelson explore the concomitant difficulties of the critical evaluation of young adult books.

Mary Lystad's "The Adolescent Image in American Books for Children: Then and Now," seeks not to define adolescent literature but to describe the kinds of books read by adolescents over the last 200 years. She identifies the uppermost concerns of the books, in historical order by periods—concern with life after death, with life after childhood, and with life in the present. One of the chief charms of her article is the collection of vintage quotations, which help to create an appreciation for how books read by adolescents have evolved over the centuries.[2]

"What is Adolescent Literature?" by Isabelle Holland addresses the question of definition from the viewpoint of a writer of fiction. She begins with a definition of the adolescent and describes the ways adolescents relate to books; she resists tendencies to categorize books rigidly by age or maturity level and deplores what she calls "trendy" thinking. We are encouraged, instead, to consider books as works of art and to worry less about trying to "wall off" adolescent literature from literature as a whole, as though it needed to be kept under quarantine. She manages to leave us with an appreciation of her respect for the "mysteriousness" of adolescence, a certain evanescent "je ne sais quoi" that, like fairy gold, turns to ashes when we try to possess it. We are left suspecting that there is something wrong-headed about an attempt to impose a definition upon adolescent literature.

But Sylvia Engdahl, also a creative writer, gives us still another outlook. Responding to some of the negative criticisms that have been levelled against teenage novels, she begins with an assertion of the raison d'être behind the decision to label a book "juvenile": the commercial realities of today's publishing world. She takes issue with Natalie Babbitt's contention that there is no need for teenage fiction and also points out recent changes in the nature of junior books. Finally she treats us to a negative definition of teenage novels and then identifies two factors that distinguish them from adult fiction: lesser complexity and "a fresh outlook on all cultures," a perspective "on the universe and the future" that is lamentably absent from books marketed as "adult." Without rigid categorizing, she succeeds in convincing us of the existence of a kind of book especially appropriate and appealing to teenage readers.

The next two essayists seem to assume that young adult literature is a recognizable literary type, and they concentrate on why certain books appeal strongly to teenagers and on assessing the quality of the YA novel. In "Real People, Real Books: About YA Readers," Lou Willett Stanek tells of her discovery of teenage books, identifies their stylistic features, and elaborates upon the purpose behind her research—to find why students read what they read. Kenneth L. Donelson also begins with personal experience in "Growing Up Real: YA Literature Comes of Age." Like Stanek (and many other English teachers) he found young adult literature only after his graduation from college. He traces the development of the young adult novel since the 1940s and reproaches those critics who condemn it wholesale without knowledge of the best productions of the seventies. Clearly conscious of the shortcomings of some of the books—the "social tracts" and "with-it" varieties—he nonetheless finds young adult books on the whole to be growing in literary stature.

Although the authors included herein emphasize different aspects of young adult literature, there seems to be a consensus that definitions are best kept flexible, that the books read by teenagers can be exciting fare (for them *and* for adults), and that whatever it is, young adult literature is still evolving and showing increasing literary worth.

A concluding note seems necessary to hark back to the two "tasks" that formed the theme of the opening. It seems self-evident to those familiar with young adult fiction and the commentaries upon it that the first task—

developing a "positive self-image"—receives much more "time" than the second—achieving a sense of competence. The novels that center upon a young person's growth toward a feeling of self-worth are legion, but where are the books that show a young person developing competence in his or her calling in life? A select few come to mind—Ursula Le Guin's *Very Far Away from Anywhere Else* and Nat Hentoff's *Jazz Country*.[3] Why do so few fiction writers attempt to give "a local habitation and a name" to this largely unarticulated need? Or can it be that this theme is more properly the province of the biographer?

NOTES

1. *The Vanishing Adolescent* (New York Dell, 1962), p. 29.
2. For a fuller history of more recent teenage books, see Margaret Hutchinson, "Fifty Years of Young Adult Reading, 1921–1971," *Top of the News* 30:24–53 (Nov. 1973).
3. (New York: Atheneum, 1976), and (New York: Harper, 1965) respectively.

The Young Adult: An Overview

Dana L. Farnsworth

Any discussion of the young adult must necessarily tell as much about the author as the subject; hence it seems appropriate that my own viewpoint emerge at the outset. My entire professional life has been spent in dealing with young people—conducting 4-H camps and teaching in high school before I went to medical school and serving as a college physician since that time, with a period of military service that was occupied with the care of psychiatric patients in naval hospitals and on a hospital ship. Interspersed in the last two decades were a year as acting dean of students at the Massachusetts Institute of Technology and six months as a house master at Harvard.

If I did not possess a natural fondness and respect for young people, I would have changed specialties long ago. However, I have not equated

Reprinted by permission of the author and the publisher from the *American Journal of Psychiatry* 131:845–51 (Aug. 1974). Copyright © 1974 by the American Psychiatric Assn.

that positive bias with acceptance and approval of everything they do. On one occasion of considerable and persistent strain an older colleague, noting my discouragement, pointed out that if young people were not ignorant and immature in varying degrees, teachers would have nothing to do, nor would schools and colleges be justified. This observation was just what I needed to get my perspective back into focus and was as valuable to me as several hours of psychotherapy.

This analysis will not be confined to a particular discipline but will instead look at the young adult from educational, psychological, physiological, sociological, psychiatric, and philosophical viewpoints—depending on which viewpoint is most appropriate to describing a particular phenomenon. I especially want to suggest some ways in which young adults, with the aid of trusted and competent older persons, can correct those conditions that distress them and that impair the ability of so many of their number to achieve up to the level of their potential.

Premonitions of Discontent

Although many people believe that the current discontent and low morale among the young is of quite recent origin, dating back only about ten years, a survey of the literature shows that numerous prodromal signs did exist in the attitudes and behavior of deprived groups and that these signs preceded the disenchantment of college students with their society. The findings of three comprehensive studies appear representative of what was going on when contemporary young adults were in their childhood.

One of the most perceptive and revealing of these studies was a report by former Senator R. C. Hendrickson of New Jersey when he was chairman of a Senate committee studying juvenile delinquency. For many months in the early 1950s his committee held public hearings in various cities, and the staff compiled a comprehensive report on the status of young people who were running afoul of the law.[1]

Among their principal findings were the following:

More than a million teenagers were in trouble, half of them seriously enough to warrant court action. This number had doubled in fifteen years, a growth rate much faster than that of the adolescent population as a whole.

Serious crimes were becoming common.

Urban decay was evident in many cities, leading to formation of young gangs involved in senseless violence.

A drug problem was emerging, with the major abused substances being alcohol, "goof balls" (barbiturates and beer), and "bennies" (amphetamines). It appeared to be spreading.

A style of life characterized by unrestrained impulse expression was being adopted by more and more young people.

Youngsters in trouble were often quite capable, but most of them were handicapped by broken or conflict-ridden homes, poor standards and role models in their homes, and very little impetus to character development.

Young people with "too much" were as likely to get into trouble as those with "too little."

Schools were boring to many youngsters since the schools were geared to academic achievement but neglected vocational interests.

Runaways from home were estimated at 300,000 yearly, and the number was increasing.

Consultants to the committee were nearly all convinced that examples set by older people were the greatest menace in the development of these antisocial trends. Speculation regarding other fundamental causes of delinquency also singled out horror comics and their television adaptations, which portrayed senseless violence.

Among Senator Hendrickson's final comments were:

> Many of our findings left me more shocked by the derelictions of our older generation than by the misdeeds of the younger. . . . The basic problem is not the behavior of the young so much as it is the ethical and moral standards of older people . . . any true and final solution to our problem lies in each home, in the resources of each community in America.

Meanwhile, what of the more privileged group who had survived their adolescence, mastered the academic orientation of the schools, and gone on to college? In an extensive study of the attitudes of college students in the mid-1950s, Jacob found that the values of American college students were remarkably homogeneous.[2] Students were gloriously contented with both their day-to-day activities and their outlook for the future. The great majority were self-centered and concerned about material gratifications; they expected to conform to the economic status quo and to achieve ample rewards for dutiful effort. Traditional moral virtues were valued, and most students expressed a need for religious belief and were dutifully responsive toward government.

The quality of teaching appeared to have little effect on the value outcome of general education. Some colleges, mainly private institutions with modest enrollments, did have a peculiar potency in creating a community of values. The personal magnetism and sensitivity of individual teachers was also highly significant in developing strong value commitments.

Immediately after Jacob's study, Eddy and his associates surveyed twenty colleges and universities in an attempt to delineate those influences of the institution which affected student character.[3] Again, the level of satisfaction was high, but in retrospect one finding was highly significant. At one college two observers, one of whom lived in a women's dormitory and the other in a men's dormitory, kept getting conflicting reactions to campus life. The men were enthusiastic about their work, but the women were often bitter and cynical. It became clear that the women's social life was sufficiently restricted to cause them to adopt a negative attitude toward nearly everything they did.

At another college a retired professor of philosophy sensed a change when he said, "When I first began teaching, practically everything I said shocked my students. Then came the time when nothing could make them move a muscle. Now I'm in the most distressing phase of all—everything they say shocks the life out of me."

Thus, when the campus explosion occurred, it was not without warning; however, because the symptoms of trouble had been buried under the fantasy of serene and unconcerned college life, the explosion took most people by surprise. Rather than attempt an abstract discussion of the causes and manifestations of worldwide student protest, I would like to concentrate on three institutions, in two of which I had prolonged personal involvement. The events at Berkeley, Columbia University, and Harvard are congruent with those at many other institutions.

Disaffection on the College Campus

Although student discontent began to become apparent in the early 1960s, the first major eruption occurred at the Berkeley campus of the University of California in September 1964. It continued for several months in its acute form, with lesser disturbances continuing intermittently for several years. The main issues centered around free speech, resentment of the governing bodies of the university, and the students' desire to have a greater voice in university policies. As the mass occupation of buildings became common and the administration attempted to retain control, many new disputes arose over the nature and extent of disciplinary measures taken against students. Local issues soon became entwined with national ones—the Vietnam war, treatment of minority groups, government-sponsored research, and many others.[4]

At Columbia the precipitating issue was the institution's relations with the urban environment around it; other prominent problems were classified government research, the Vietnam war, and administration and faculty remoteness and lack of response to criticism. Active and ingenious methods of harassment centering on the public aspects of these issues were pursued in a way that "radicalized" a considerable portion of both students and faculty members. The dominant mode of expressing dissatisfaction became occupation of buildings, which led to physical violence to persons and severe disruption of the usual educational procedures, while damage to offices and classrooms was extensive. Some administrators were made prisoners in their own offices, and sensitive files were ransacked. When officials in charge felt that evacuation of buildings was necessary, the resultant injuries to those who resisted (and some who did not) brought numerous charges of police brutality.[5]

At Harvard we had no widespread expectation that acute violence would occur, even after the Columbia uprisings in 1968. For many years numerous efforts had been made to improve faculty-student relationships and to make counseling services of all types readily available to those who wanted or needed them, at the same time maintaining an atmosphere of privacy and respect for each individual's life style. We had a house system, instituted by President Lowell in the early 1930s, with its provision of residential tutors; we had a Bureau of Study Counsel, a system of freshman advisors, and extensive health services, including a large psychiatric and psychological component. Mark Rudd, one of the leaders of the Columbia uprising, made an exploratory visit to Harvard in September 1968 to see what the chances for a similar outbreak might be, and he concluded that Harvard was hopeless because the issues for organizing disturbances were so few.[6,7]

Nevertheless, premonitory signs were plentiful, when viewed from the perspective of later events. Robert McNamara had received rude and forceful treatment when he visited the university for a lecture while he was Secretary of Defense. Objections to the Reserve Officers Training Corps (ROTC), recruitment for companies that manufactured supplies for combat use, investments in companies that had strong ties with agencies or countries of which students disapproved, and even the work of the Center for International Studies, which analyzed relations among various countries, resulted in various acts of discourtesy and violence.[8]

Finally a full year of intermittent violence erupted, with heavy destruction of property—not only within the university but also that of nearby commercial establishments as well. As at Columbia, a small group of hardcore extremists was able—especially by provoking police action—to radicalize large segments of the previously moderate student body and to spread confusion throughout the faculty.

The more I reflect on the behavior of young adults from 1960 to the present, remembering that this has been a constantly changing group (the young adults of 1960 are now in their mid-thirties), the more I am convinced that they were more perceptive than their elders in discerning the disintegrative elements in our culture and more willing to do something about correcting them. The Cox Commission was widely criticized at the time for statements such as these:

> The present generation of young people in our universities is the best informed, the most intelligent, and the most idealistic this country has ever known. This is the experience of teachers everywhere. It is also the most sensitive to public issues and the most sophisticated in political tactics. Perhaps because they enjoy the affluence to support their ideals, today's undergraduate and graduate students exhibit, as a group, a higher level of social conscience than preceding generations. . . . The ability, social consciousness and conscience, political sensitivity, and honest realism of today's students are a prime cause of student disturbances.[9]

After pointing out the irony of such students being unusually antagonistic to all forms of restraint and peculiarly violent in social or political protest, the commission asked, "May not the fault lie with the older generation?"

> Unless we are prepared to concede that ours is a sick society too corrupt to be saved, we must acknowledge that we have failed to transmit to many of the ablest young men and women either a sense of the values of reason, order, civility or an appreciation of the fact that freedom depends upon voluntary restraint.

The New Conservatism

The great majority of college students seem to have become more conservative in both their attitudes and behavior during the past two or three years. This change does not demonstrate that their idealism has diminished but rather suggests that they have become convinced that the tactics so widely used between 1964 and 1972 have proven to be not only ineffective but counterproductive. The rudeness, shouting, invectives, obscenities, and physical force turned out in the end not to get them what they wanted.

The young idealists who expressed their deep distress at the perceived injustices of society fell into the error of believing that drastic and even violent measures could effectively bring about desired reforms. It is quite true that violence has occasionally resulted in beneficial changes. But what they did not realize is that when violence becomes a way of life, when people believe that they are free to act as they see fit without regard for the safety of others, and when no one feels safe in the company of other people, a state of barbarism results. Winston Churchill once stated that "when war is itself fenced about with mutual extermination it seems likely that it will be increasingly postponed," and Walter Lippmann commented that if a détente between the two great powers could be achieved the world would be much safer but far more disorderly.[10,11] During the period of student uprisings the cold war had lessened, but its implications were continued in the seemingly interminable Vietnam involvement; this may well have given impetus to the dissatisfaction of the young even as it relieved them of the total commitment to national policy that a general war requires.

We have little evidence that basic attitudes of faculty members toward education have changed radically or even minimally. Faculty-student contact is still slight, and teachers still emphasize transmittal of facts rather than teaching students how to become increasingly curious and self-motivated as their knowledge grows. Counseling programs tend to have been curtailed for economic reasons, rather than being encouraged in order to help students become more aware of how personal values influence education. Education in the nature of the restraints that are essential to maintain maximum freedom for everyone is for the most part left to chance. The question is whether educators will continue to concentrate on resolving crisis after crisis or whether they will enlist the aid of students in using their energy, knowledge, and imagination to replace boredom and dissatisfaction with excitement and a sense of accomplishment.

In fact, the previous enthusiasm by students for courses in nontraditional subjects that emphasized tactics for forceful social reform has nearly disappeared. The pass-fail grading systems that students thought they wanted have been replaced in many institutions by traditional grading systems "so we know where we stand." We are witnessing a return to basic courses in the humanities, social sciences, and natural sciences, particularly courses that increase a student's chances of being accepted in a good graduate school or a satisfying job in business or industry. An increasing number of students are going into professions such as medicine, law, and research in the sciences or the humanities, which call for a high degree of preparation but can be quite effective in the solution of human problems.

Countercultural Life-Styles

In any analysis of youthful behavior we must remember the role of symbols and the way in which the meaning of symbolic objects and actions changes. During the height of the disturbances, protesting students were often instructed by their leaders to dress and act in ways that accentuated the differences between them and their antagonists. Demonstrators were encouraged to wear unconventional clothes, let their hair grow long, experiment with drugs, and publicize their unusual living arrangements and life-styles [Eichel]. Gradually some of these costumes and practices were adopted by other students and young people generally, without any relationship between their appearance and their views on social or political matters.

This tendency to dress and act alike, particularly those customs which seemed to simulate a romanticized poverty, contributed to the opinion of older and more conservative people that the young were irresponsible and discourteous. Many of these highly critical people were surprised to find that personal contact with young people of whose appearance they disapproved was friendly, courteous, and thoughtful. Little by little the various changes in costumes, manners, group behavior, and other characteristics listed under the common rubric of "counterculture expressions" lost their original meaning, and many of them have become solidly entrenched in the lives of older people who run our businesses and political and social life.

We all express our identities and our commitments through clothing and life-styles; these matters change, and the changes occur in cycles. Some of the photographs of members of the Harvard community in the mid-nineteenth century suggest that if they returned to Harvard Square today they would be quite inconspicuous.

At present the general appearance of most young people suggests an informality and lack of pride in appearance that goes beyond a desire for comfort and economy. When an improvement in the general morale and outlook of the young occurs, there may well be a concomitant change in their appearance. We should not be blind to the fact that our three-button suits reflect both our self-image and the expectations of our peer group. In any event, the issue to consider is not the details of the costume or life pattern but the person behind them.

Considerably more important in the development of these young people is the psychological upheaval that many of them experienced during this period of turmoil. Many became confused and dissatisfied with the aimless and unorganized lives that they were leading and sought, or were enticed into, activities that gave them social ties with others, a feeling of community and shared experience, and a sense of certainty.

These activities varied greatly. Some of the most publicized were a desire to live apart from modern technology, with involvement in organic gardening and "natural" farming and eating practices; macrobiotic diets; oriental religions; primitive Christianity; transcendental meditation; and astrology.[12] Rock festivals became common, serving as a means of providing intense shared experiences for large numbers at once—and incidentally providing excellent opportunities for exploitation on the part of those whose ideals had a more practical aspect. Experiments in communal living have been numerous, and though most have been short, they show a pattern of regrouping and continued existence.[13]

It is easy to identify individual cases where such responses are unsuccessful attempts to deal with feelings of isolation and uncertainty. More helpful is the encouragement of an attitude of experimentation with life structures, so long as these do not pose a threat to current or future well-being and are tempered with an individual's understanding of his own personality and needs.

Effects of the Media

A major change in the developmental influences on the ideas and ideals of young people, particularly in the more developed countries, has been the vast increase in rapid communication. Radio has been a factor for about fifty years, television for less than half that long. Newspapers and magazines have also increased in numbers and influence throughout this period, though not so spectacularly. The result has been that from a very early age most children have knowledge of events, cultures, and ideas not previously available to anyone of any age.

Although such instant communication has numerous advantages, it has also made possible the dissemination of attitudes that encourage instant gratification of appetites and desires through the use of thousands of products seemingly created to fill an artificial need. Anyone who views the programs and commercials designed for children can only wonder how parents can contend successfully with the demands of their children for products praised so indiscriminately. The emphasis on instant and continuous satisfaction of physical desires appears to have contributed to the greatly decreased impulse control that many psychiatrists have observed in young patients during the past decade. Whether the excellent media programs designed to help young people increase their sense of social responsibility are neutralized by irresponsible and offensive advertising is a question that should be continuously scrutinized by those who have the welfare of young people at heart.

Drug Use and Misuse

The tremendous interest among young people in drug use for nonmedicinal purposes had its origin in assertions that certain substances, usually referred to as psychedelic drugs, have the capacity to change people for the better by increasing their self-understanding and enabling them to use hitherto unused portions of their minds. Sometimes the analogy was made of exploring inner space, compared with the strong national interest in exploring the outer spaces of the universe. Vast efforts were expended to understand the nature and possible use of such drugs, including a wide variety of treatment experiments. Soon the fascination with drug use combined with the widespread social unrest and personal dissatisfaction to cause a virtual epidemic of nonmedicinal use of various psychoactive substances.

As a result of concern over this dangerous development and the many frustrations that resulted from trying to deal with it constructively, both the United States and Canadian governments established commissions to study the overall problem and make appropriate recommendations. Both commissions completed their comprehensive studies and submitted final reports in 1973.[14,15] To the surprise of many people, both reports emphasized the correction of youthful drug misuse by attention to questions of social issues, relationships with significant individuals, and general standards of value, concern for equal justice, and opportunity for everyone. The reports pointed out that the universal and irresponsible use of alcohol and barbiturates, under social and medical sanction, was a far greater problem than the use of psychedelic drugs.

Surveys sponsored by the National Commission on Marihuana and Drug Abuse indicated that the majority of people in the United States do not even consider alcohol to be a drug [*Drug Use in America*]. There was equally great confusion about the term "drug abuse." The commission recommended that this term be discarded and that increased emphasis be placed on learning how to use drugs appropriately rather than destructively. Thus the problem becomes one involving all segments of society and not primarily that of young people.

The National Commission on Marihuana and Drug Abuse conducted 200 student surveys involving more than 900,000 young people, which are summarized in table 1. Although definite proof is lacking, most observers at present do not feel that the overall use of drugs by young adults is increasing. Areas exist here and there of acute misuse of drugs, but throughout the country the use of drugs as a means of attaining peer group status has lost much of its influence.

TABLE 1: Mean Percent of Students Who Had Ever Used Drugs as of 1972			
Drug	Junior High Students	Senior High Students	College Students
Alcohol	56	74	83
Marijuana	16	40	50
Stimulants	9	19	24
Depressants	8	16	14
Hallucinogens	6	14	14
Opiates	4.75	5.2	6
Inhalants	11	9	2

In general, there has been wide acceptance of the U.S. commission's recommendation that the use of drugs not be emphasized as a separate problem but instead be considered along with all the other unproductive or self-defeating ways of solving personal quandaries.

Changing Codes of Sexuality

As I reflect on the problems of young adults as I saw them before, during, and after World War II and compare these with the problems encountered by the same age groups during the last two decades, it seems to me that the basic personal difficulties are very similar. These problems include family conflict, inconsistent or absent discipline, lack of appropriate role models, sexual conflict or confusion, and loss of a highly valued relationship that results in a degree of isolation. To these have been added increasing lack of impulse control and, above all, a sense of disillusionment with the behavior of older people and the standards of conduct of both private and governmental bodies.

Throughout history one can find denunciations of the young because of their sexual desires and behavior. For the most part, these complaints indicate not major changes in attitudes but the fact that sex is a more fundamental concern of the young adult than almost any other aspect of development and that youthful sexuality has rarely correlated with societal family structures. However, events of the past half century suggest that during this period profound changes have occurred in the sexual education of the young, public discussion of the problem, the use of sexual symbols in advertising and other commercial activities, and the development of freer social and sexual relations between the sexes during early adult years.

Adolescents are maturing at a significantly faster rate,[16] and with increased opportunities for learning in all fields, there has been a corresponding increase in the opportunity to learn about sexual activity. As social and commercial emphasis on sex increased, so did the tendency to discuss more and more of its aspects in a more open manner than previously. The awareness that civilization itself is threatened by overpopulation, coupled with the development of reasonably effective methods of contraception, has added tremendous significance to the ethical, religious, economic, and personal aspects of sex education and sexual practices. Recent changes in the public vocabulary of sexual discussion, altered attitudes about nudity and sexual relations outside marriage, and the intense concentration on sex in the mass media have caused the great majority of people to become quite confused about older concepts of right and wrong, proper and improper, constructive and destructive as they apply to adolescent and early adult development.

The only feasible answer lies in the development of free and comfortable communication between the young and their elders designed to work out customs and practices that will be as conducive as possible to development of responsibility in the broadest sense. Ways must be found to enable young people to make decisions in the light of their immediate needs as well as future obligations. The numerous pressures on young people toward early, intense sexual experiences in effect deprive many of them of the opportunity to make up their own minds as to what course of conduct they wish to pursue. These pressures prevent the "disciplined and devoted delay" Erikson described as so desirable while a couple is acquiring the psychological intimacy that should precede sexual intimacy.[17]

For parents, teachers, physicians (especially psychiatrists), psychologists, and all others who wish to influence the young in the direction of both individual and collective responsibility, the task of developing an ideal program of sex education is a formidable one. The choice is not between whether or not we should have such programs but whether we can or cannot use available information. Sex education proceeds inexorably, regardless of what families or schools or anyone else does. The problem is to prevent tragedy and promote happiness through the use of the intellect in modifying emotional responses that have ill effects.

Disadvantaged Young Adults

Any discussion of young adults is likely to overemphasize those who are in high school and college and who come from relatively affluent backgrounds, simply because they are more visible and have been studied more than others. Many young adults with marked ability but suffering from various deprivations could accomplish far more and attain far greater satisfaction in living if they had opportunities through which they could advance themselves. Many of them have come from broken or disturbed homes, live in economically deprived communities, or belong to minority groups that have been held back by circumstance or design for long periods. Among the latter are blacks, Chicanos, American Indians, residents of urban ghettos, and those living in isolated and deprived rural areas. Noteworthy exceptions have occurred; young people from these groups have succeeded in spite of their handicaps or in some instances because of them. Many others could do so if some support was given to them.

During the last decade particularly, multiple efforts have been organized to compensate for these handicaps: Head Start programs, equal opportunity projects, government and private pressures to employ and train higher percentages of minority groups, and special programs in schools and colleges for those with educational, social, and economic handicaps. Some progress has been made, but much more needs to be done. Possibly the most neglected and misunderstood of all young adults are those who for various reasons have fallen afoul of the law and have been sentenced to so-called correctional institutions. They are frequently treated according to customs and principles, basically unchanged over a period of centuries, that virtually ignore all that is known about how human beings respond to stress or kindness.

Enlisting the Young in Social Change

Perhaps the most disturbing problem we must face is the massive loss of confidence in our institutions and professions. National opinion polls show a steady decline in public confidence in our institutions of higher learning, military organizations, organized religion, major business corporations, and even the Supreme Court. Medicine, though at the top each year, shows a substantial overall decline. Television news, the press, and organized labor inspired little confidence to begin with and have suffered further losses. Most of the categories managed slight gains between 1972 and 1973, except for the executive branch of the federal government, which continued to decline sharply.[18]

Almost all organizations have experienced increasing difficulties in governing themselves, balancing their budgets, and learning how to deal with bitter criticism from people living and working in the communities surrounding them. Maintenance of standards has become increasingly difficult, even among religious organizations.

Lowered standards, lack of group cohesion, loss of confidence in institutions, and a general desire to express anger have combined to produce a situation approaching social anarchy. Petty thievery, crimes against persons and property, kidnapping, hijacking, sexual crimes, and murder have so increased in frequency as to become commonplace. In a [previously mentioned] survey conducted by the National Commission on Marihuana and Drug Abuse it was learned that one person out of three has been the victim or a close friend of a victim of violence. Periods of violence are nothing new in history, but violence has probably never before involved such vast numbers of persons in what is considered a civilized society.

Young adults must understand how and why public morality reflects the composite of many private moralities simply because it is to them that society must look for a revitalization of those principles and practices that make civilization possible. The great majority of young adults are indignant at much of what is going on around them, and the most hopeful sign is that they are rejecting the dramatic solutions of the demagogue or revolutionary and are trying to develop more solid and lasting ways of making equal opportunity and equal justice available to everyone. If older citizens and young adults could unite in marshaling their indignation at the affronts to human dignity that so disfigure our civilization, turning their energy into constructive channels, many of the problems in our major institutions could be solved.

It would be simpler if for every perceived shortcoming there were a specific individual or group that could be held responsible for it; the solution would then be to change the practices of the responsible agent or to eliminate the person from the system. Thus idealism often comes up against practicality, and for young people with much idealism but limited practical experience and power, their resources and determination are all too often not adequate for the task of reform. The idealist is then faced with the prospect of making serious personal sacrifice if he is to continue to strive for his ideals or modifying his zeal and making compromises in the quantity or quality of his work so as to ensure a living for himself or his family.

The central problem is how to retain one's idealism while working for the underprivileged, the handicapped, and the exploited groups in our society, while at the same time keeping personal abilities at a high level and enlisting the cooperation of like-minded people in correcting social and economic injustices. This task should also be a central one for the family; religious, social, and community organizations; professional associations of all kinds; business and industry; and all levels of government.

NOTES

1. Robert C. Hendrickson and F. J. Cook, *Youth in Danger* (New York: Harcourt, 1956), pp.291–300.

2. Philip E. Jacob, "Summary of Findings," in his *Changing Values in College* (New York: Harper, 1957), pp.1–11.
3. Edward D. Eddy, Jr. and others, *The College Influence on Student Character* (Washington, D.C.: American Council on Education, 1959), pp.150–51.
4. Seymour M. Lipset and S. S. Wolin, eds., "The History of a Student Revolt," in *The Berkeley Student Revolt* (Garden City, N.Y.: Anchor, 1965), pp. 99–200.
5. Robert Friedman, ed., "Introduction," in Jerry L. Avorn and others, *Up Against the Ivy Wall: A History of the Columbia Crisis* (New York: Atheneum, 1969), pp. 3–22.
6. *Harvard Crimson*, Sept. 20, 1968, p. 2.
7. *Harvard Crimson*, Sept. 28, 1968, p. 1.
8. Lawrence E. Eichel and others, *The Harvard Strike* (Boston: Houghton, 1970).
9. Fact-finding Committee on Columbia Disturbances, *Crisis at Columbia, The Cox Commission Report of the Fact-finding Committee Appointed to Investigate the Disturbances at Columbia* (New York: Vintage, 1968).
10. Winston S. Churchill, *Memoirs of the Second World War* (abridged ed.; Boston: Houghton, 1959).
11. Walter Lippmann, Personal communication, Harvard University Health Service, June 8, 1964.
12. J. J. Gill, "Religion and Psychiatry Today," *Psychiatric Annals* 1:44–59 (1971).
13. Rosabeth M. Kanter, "The Limits of Utopia," in her *Commitment and Community, Communes and Utopias in Sociological Perspective* (Cambridge, Mass.: Harvard Univ. Pr., 1972), pp. 213–37.
14. *Drug Use in America: Problem in Perspective: Second Report of the National Commission on Marihuana and Drug Abuse* (Washington, D.C.: Govt. Print. Off., 1973).
15. *Final Report of the Commission of Inquiry into the Nonmedical Use of Drugs* (Ottawa, Ont., Canada: Govt. of Canada, 1973).
16. T. E. Cone, Jr., *"Secular Acceleration of Height and Biologic Maturation,"* in James R. Gallagher, ed., *Medical Care of the Adolescent* (2nd ed.; New York: Appleton, 1966), pp. 45–55.
17. E. H. Erikson, "Growth and Crises in the 'Healthy Personality,'" in Milton J. E. Senn, ed., *Symposium on the Healthy Personality* (New York: Macy, 1950), p. 141.
18. *Chronicle of Higher Education*, Dec. 10, 1973, p. 4.

Understanding the Adolescent Reader

Armin Grams

No one who observes children will deny that in our culture the adolescent is concerned with achieving independence. Yet this tendency does not appear *de novo* with the onset of puberty. A child is characterized by strong strivings for independence in the preschool years (one of many interesting parallels between the adolescent and the toddler) and also during the later elementary school years. Nor are strivings for independence found exclusively in pre-adult years. They emerge strongly again in the middle-adult period.

The onset of puberty makes a considerable difference in the life experience of the youngster, even though a substantial part of the difference results from the changing reactions of others, rather than from sudden essential changes in the self. Within the limits of this article, we can include only certain assumptions about what is happening to personality during this time.

The emerging self. In many respects this period of personality development is analogous to the period of toddlerhood. Certainly the problem of identity again looms large. Much of the adolescent's concern is with himself, and while the years preceding puberty saw a heavy emphasis on personal achievement, the adolescent adds a highly personal dimension to the process of becoming an individual. One might say the adolescent rediscovers his world. During childhood he absorbs a great deal of information in rather blotterlike, indiscriminate fashion; he masters many skills and acquires many attitudes in a rather unconscious way. By the time he becomes an adolescent he has a large store of experience acquired over the years, but the process of acquisition has been uncritical and relatively impersonal. With the advent of adolescence a more individual and self-conscious regard for experience begins to emerge. What has been accepted thus far and incorporated into self is reexamined in the light of an emerging individuality. Uncritical acceptance of the ideas and attitudes of those who are older and presumably better informed decreases and there is an increasing tendency to scrutinize experiences and information.

The development of a sense of identity is considered a key issue in adolescence.[1] Questions like "Who am I?" and "What is my proper role?" although perhaps not consciously formulated in exactly those words are of central concern. To some extent such questions are both instigated and answered by the pronounced physical changes associated with puberty. There is, of course, something very final and irreversible about attaining one's mature physique. Young manhood and womanhood are undeniable facts, and their corresponding roles are now more than ever incumbent upon the individual. Our expectations of young people are influenced by their appearance. We revise them as soon as the rapid growth spurt begins. But these marked changes in physique do not automatically initiate more acceptable mature behavior.

Physical appearance influences an adolescent's self-perception in much the same way as it affects the evaluations which others make of him. He is quite concerned about his rate of development and its timing as well as the degree to which his new physique is of the approved sort for his sex. While space does not permit a lengthy treatment of this matter here, the reader who is especially interested may consult one of the more extensive studies of this matter.[2]

There is also the matter of accepting one's physique as it relates to one's sex membership. Both boys and girls may be somewhat confused about this, because the appropriate masculine and feminine sex roles in society are not as sharply defined as they once were. Rapid changes in our society have caused a marked shift in the roles of men and women, and in general the two are less sharply differentiated than they were in grandfather's generation. There is some difference of opinion among the experts regarding which of the roles is more difficult to learn to achieve, but all agree shifting societal expectations have complicated matters considerably. At this point, we are not so much concerned with the question "Who am I," for as we have already said, the answer to this question comes with unmistakable finality to the young adolescent whose sexual development no longer leaves this to his imagination. The question is rather one of "Now that I am what I am (young man or young woman), what kind of behavior is expected of a gentleman or a lady?" How dominant, how courteous, how aggressive, how understanding, how helpful, how domestic, etc., should I be? These are pertinent concerns of youth striving to achieve an appropriate masculine or feminine social role. These are some of the key issues in the task of sex role identification.

Changing relations with parents. This difficult and complicated problem of establishing oneself as a person in one's own right confronts the adolescent as a major conflict. In simplest fashion the emancipation conflict may be described as the drive to be free of parental control and domination; this is often coupled with the youngster's unwillingness and inability to shoulder the commensurate responsibility which such independence and freedom require. The first component in this conflict stems from rapid intellectual development and physical growth that tend progressively to blur the distinction between child and parent. In many ways the adolescent is becoming more like an adult with every passing year, and he is eager for any and all acknowledgment of this from the adult world. Hence the concern with his "rights" as a "grown-up." But only the unrealistic adolescent fails to recognize that although he is becoming more like an adult in many ways, he still is far from being their equal. Physical stature and intellectual acumen do not automatically supply vocational and economic security. Most adolescents recognize at some level their need for some shelter from adult responsibility and for a fair amount of support and guidance. These are, of course, dependency needs and they conflict, as we have said, with the need for independence. All of this causes conflict in the family and contributes to the tension which characterizes a segment of the parent-child relationship during this period.

Emancipation from parental domination is considerably more complicated today than in former years. In the first place, the adult role today is more involved and ambiguous. Technological progress and social change have created greater needs for training and preparation, and adolescents need additional time to acquire these. This situation, plus the fact that puberty is arriving earlier, has lengthened the period of adolescence and complicated the problem of emancipation.

Another complicating factor in the emancipation process is the attitude that parents take toward the child who is growing away from them. The principal function of parents *as parents* with regard to their children is to make themselves increasingly unnecessary. This means that there must emerge over time a new relationship between parents and their children. The process of becoming increasingly unnecessary *as parents* has been going on for some time, but during adolescence it is likely to become much more obvious.

If it happens that the parents' own security and self-esteem as individuals is linked primarily to their function as mother or father, rather than to their function as wife or husband, we can readily understand how they might resist rather than encourage the emancipation process. Before children can cease being children their parents will have to put aside the role of parents. This tests the parents' level of maturity. Are they able to say (as many of them are after twenty or more years of child-rearing) "We just can't wait to get the house all cleaned out so that we can just be alone again with one another?" Or do they secretly dread seeing the last child leave the nest, because with him goes the major source of their personal gratification?

Parental unwillingness to modify their relationship to their children is serious for yet another reason. The relationship which husband and wife have to each other serves as the child's most important model in learning appropriate sex role behavior. Youngsters reared in a home where mother and father have made it quite clear that they have a very special and different relationship are able to learn about the priorities and loyalties so fundamental to their own future happiness. Children who see that their parents are still very much in love with each other and desire frequently to be alone with each other, especially as their children's growth frees them from the necessity of spending many hours tending to their needs, are children likely to look forward with positive anticipation to an adult relationship with a spouse.

Learning "who and what I am" requires space and time and freedom to make mistakes. Certainly this is one reason the adolescent needs parents, although he would probably be the last one to admit it—at least publicly! He needs to try his wings in a sheltered place where he can afford to fall flat on his face without crushing embarrassment. His parents and his home are his sounding board and laboratory, and this, for parents, is a privilege, not a penalty. What better function could parents serve than to absorb the shock of early rebuffs and failures of a child's quest to establish his own identity? Since a certain amount of crudity, misbehavior, and emotional turmoil is inevitable at this time, it would seem better for the youngster to unload these at home than in settings where he is more visible and there is less freedom for error and greater likelihood of enduring or unfortunate consequences.

It is pleasant for parents to share the limelight with their children, and if there is ever a time when this is likely to happen, it is during their children's adolescent years. But such sharing means that the child can claim less of the accomplishment and sufficiency that parents should want to foster at this time. Thus, parents discover that at the time in their child's life when they might normally expect to receive considerable gratification from sharing in their children's achievements, they are for a number of reasons in a less advantageous position to do so.

Some parents may think they are being repaid evil for good. Even in the best of homes, friction between parents and children will intensify during adolescence. Commonly we find that adolescents are openly critical of their parents' shortcomings, and their remarks, insinuations, and attitudes may convey a lack of gratitude, to say the least. But youth's hypercritical attitude and behavior is usually a defensive reaction. The adolescent is aware that his parents have seen him at his worst. Because they know his weaknesses and frequently witness his lapses into dependency and immaturity, they represent a threat. Parents are at the same time his valuable allies and something of a nemesis! Small wonder, then, that ambivalence toward parents is a persistent corollary of the emancipation process.

Changing relations with peers. The high school peer group is a vital support or crutch on which the young adolescent leans for support when the going gets rough. It serves somewhat the same function as the home, in that it protects the young person from broadside attack by forces which hold an unfair advantage. The old saying that "in numbers there is strength" certainly applies. By identifying first with his peers he obtains temporary shelter while he works away at discovering what his true identity and function are. I think of the peer group as a large and leafy tree that protects adolescents from the elements of the adult world as they emerge from the shelter of the home.

Because the high school peer group serves this protective purpose, it of course receives high priority from the adolescent. Rejection from the peer group is dreaded by every adolescent fortunate enough to be a member of one in the first place. Those who are not in a group know the emptiness such exclusion brings. At this age, considerable conformity is understandable and even healthy. Thus appear the fads and fashions: the trademarks of the group. At the same time, this courting of the favor of the group must raise the question of the quality of leadership in the group. This is an impressionable age. Adolescents are rather easily influenced, and they respond enthusiastically to departures from "the old." Many a capable and responsible leader of young people has capitalized on this tendency and literally worked wonders with individuals and even with the group as a whole. On the other hand, certain ends and goals toward which eager adolescents have been steered by less responsible leaders are less desirable.

With increased maturity comes a recognition that liberty is not license and that the freedom of individuals in a society is limited by consideration for the freedom of others and by concern for the common good. Inherent responsibilities and the authority of the adult which youngsters find less and less tolerable must take on new meaning, and become more acceptable.

Adjusting to a worthy way of life. What is a "worthy" way of life? To answer the question requires a choice, a decision that one set of life goals is superior to another, that certain means to these ends are more desirable than others. The problem for the adolescent is to accumulate, organize, and evaluate enough ideas, beliefs, attitudes, and values to enable him to arrange these into a priority system uniquely his own, yet not entirely incompatible with the accepted standards and values of his society.

Studies of how children and youth develop moral and spiritual values, religious beliefs, moral character, and values during the developmental years tend to focus more on descriptions of existing circumstances than on the antecedent-consequent relationship. Certainly there has been no more widely used method in character education than that of informing children and youth of how they ought to behave. Our methods in religious education have been equally didactic. The emphasis placed upon conveying information reflects an implicit assumption that knowledge is likely to issue in action. Parents have long believed that their words will affect appreciably their children's deeds. Although verbalization may be an effective means of conveying ideas to children, most parents have their honest doubts at times about its efficiency. It is commonplace to find a child (or even an adult, for that matter) who knows very well what he ought to do, but seems unwilling or incapable of doing it.

Adolescents are given to reflection about ideas, to a critique of what has already been absorbed, to trying out this knowledge in vital everyday life. In order to make such evaluations the adolescent must be well supplied with facts, for he cannot think without them. To the extent that this information is true, his parents and others who have supplied him have nothing to fear from the "airing" it will receive at the hands (or better, the minds) of youth. If the verbalized beliefs are provincial and even prejudiced half-truths, they will, of course, be subjected to rather rude treatment by the questioning adolescent. The more he discovers the falsehood in elements of what he has been told to believe, the more he is likely to wonder how much—if any—of the information about moral and spiritual matters, which through the years has been implanted in him by others, deserves serious consideration.

Because most of us suspect that "preaching" has its limitations as a means of developing moral and spiritual values, we may well ask whether research can shed any light on how such development might be better nourished. Increasing numbers of social scientists are doing research in this area at the present time. Direct answers have not emerged in large numbers, but some interesting suggestions or guiding principles have. Unfortunately, the matter is further complicated by some of the evidence which does not point in the expected direction. Let us consider some of this briefly.

In the first place, adolescence is not marked by rejection of religious faith. Parents at times panic because they interpret the disinterest of youth in certain aspects of formal religious practice to mean that their faith is disintegrating. Gilliland[3] studied the attitudes of students toward God and the church and concluded that there seem to be very few atheists among high school and college students. At the same time it must be admitted that religious doubt reaches a high point in the teens, and a strong trend toward religious humanism is seen during the college years.[4]

The reexamination of ideas, which occupies much of the adolescent's time and serves to stretch his maturing intellectual powers, will include his religious beliefs and practices. One study reports three developmental trends which are normally associated with such reflections: (1) increasing uncertainty regarding certain issues, (2) shift from concrete belief to general and abstract concepts, and (3) increasing tolerance of the religious beliefs and practice of others.[5] Because these rumblings are such a universal characteristic of the mind coming of age, parents who are prepared for them might well interpret them as signs of intellectual and spiritual vigor rather than weakness.

Most of the evidence which is gradually accumulating from studies in this area indicates that example is more effective than any other single method. Living with people whose lives are meaningfully organized around a purpose which grows out of a firm religious faith profoundly influences the manner in which any of us relates his life to the world in which he lives. Recently two writers have stated it this way:

> The very little child will respond to our embodiment of virtue, but as he grows up he will find in us, we trust, a more complicated ethical pattern—that of strictly observing the best we know while we restlessly seek better understanding. This, too, the child will learn not as we verbalize the problem, but as he sees us actually living the double life of stability along with a questing mind. The verbalizations will mean relatively little to him without the concrete symbol of our doing this before his eyes.[6]

It appears that in quest for meaning in life and answers to basic issues, the adolescent is aided most by the patterns of action and relationships which persistently characterize the behavior of those with whom he is most intimately associated. We do not mean to imply, of course, that adolescents reared by parents whose value systems are rather clearly defined, coherent, and relatively consistently demonstrated will accept passively such attitudes and standards of behavior. Quite often the tests to which they put these parental convictions take them rather far afield. There are moments when most parents are tempted to despair of their efforts, since adolescent children occasionally appear to believe in and stand for ideas and philosophies which contrast sharply with those the parents have tried to model and reflect in their own lives.

It is encouraging at this point to recall that this period in personality development is normally characterized by vacillation and relatively extreme reactions. The "heresy" of which youth is so very capable is an integral part of their "limit testing." To some degree it may represent a deliberate attempt to shock parents or to bait them into argument. It is a fortunate adolescent whose parents, as we have already said, are good "shock absorbers" and who understand the need which adolescents, with their rapidly maturing intellectual capacities, have for discussion and debate.

There is also some evidence that although young people may occasionally espouse views which diverge substantially from those of their parents and teachers and often persist in behavior which is markedly discrepant from that which their elders might have hoped they would demonstrate, in the long run they tend to manifest attitudes, beliefs, and commitments which are strikingly similar to those which prevailed at home and in school during the developmental years. The return to the viewpoint of parents usually occurs during the young adult years when the matter of establishing one's own home and family life is receiving top priority. This is far more likely to happen where parents have resisted the temptation to be excessively dogmatic or authoritarian in their rearing of youngsters; such excesses are likely to create a rebelliousness which may smoulder on for years and for all practical purposes preclude the effective adoption of the very life philosophy they intended for their children to have.

Changing relations to the opposite sex. Boy-girl interaction is an important aspect of the trial and error activities which were referred to earlier. In part, early heterosexual behavior, as it is called, emerges as a response to cultural demand. Many young people display an interest in their age mates of the opposite sex because they feel called upon to do so. Such behavior is expected of youngsters who are growing up in our society. In part, of course, this behavior emanates from maturational sources, since newly acquired abilities force us to seek adequate settings and circumstances where they can be exercised.

Close friendships in early adolescence are still among members of the same sex. Only gradually during the college age do loyalties trend away from the same-sex clique to the opposite sex. This movement is accompanied by the growing identification with a new generation. It is in later adolescence that individuals come seriously to see themselves as those who have the responsibility of the future on their shoulders. It is only in these years that youngsters begin to understand the equal responsibility which is theirs in being entrusted with their heritage.

But with all this preparation, with all this self-aggrandizement, there is still a large gap in the system. Somehow, "it is not good for man to be alone." Independence, valued so highly in early adolescence—that goal with which our hope for the future was closely bound up—is now obviously a blind alley. Adolescents sought self-fulfillment in independence from older and wiser persons only to find that self-fulfillment is to be found only in self-emptying relationships. But with whom?

During the course of later adolescence the selective process goes on. The field is steadily narrowed; the number of truly intimate acquaintances diminishes until it stands at just a few, even just one. In order for this to happen, however, love is required. I do not mean here romantic love, although this certainly plays an important part in the selective process, but rather love in the sense of contribution and self-sacrifice. In the process of finding the mate with whom one may hope, in time, for personality completion, many demands are made upon the repertory of skills and abilities which has developed over the years. For the first time output is as important as, if not more important than, intake. But simultaneously, the gratifications which come from the giving of oneself within the framework of a complementary relationship are beginning to be realized. Once again some signs of things to come are seen in the developmental course.

Adjusting to the idea of work. Another major developmental task is that of adjusting to vocation. Not so much to *a* vocation as to *vocation,* or to the idea of work itself. We have witnessed in the past two decades remarkably rapid growth in the vocational counseling services in our high schools and colleges. I have no quarrel with these services, but I believe that we must provide more than appropriate and accurate information. There seems to be a need to counteract a growing attitude among people today that work is something to be avoided as much as possible.

Today many factors combine to reduce personal incentive, effort and dedication to the task, whatever its nature might be. Should this tendency dominate the thinking of increasing numbers of people, we are likely to see some rather unfortunate effects in the personalities of large segments of our working force.

We need to remember that work is not a curse. Man was made to work, and without the sense of well-being which he can derive from successful encounter with a variety of tasks, he can never hope to arrive at anything near the fulness of stature of which he is potentially capable. To the degree to which he disengages himself from work, he deprives himself of one of his chief sources of personal worth and ego integration.

There is, of course, a distinction between work and drudgery. One could scarcely contend that all forms of human activity are ennobling, and this is where vocational planning and guidance can be of considerable help. What may be basically toilsome and dissatisfying to one person may be a suitable form of activity for another. The important thing is the meaningfulness of the job for the individual worker. The consideration of a meaningful vocation is one of the characteristic adolescent decisions that must be considered by those who are attempting to fulfill the reading needs of young adults.

NOTES

1. Erik Erikson, "The Problem of Ego Identity," *Journal of the American Psychoanalytic Association* 4:56–121 (Jan. 1956).
2. The findings of the Adolescent Growth Study at the University of California at Berkeley are reported in numerous articles. Some of those which bear on the relationship between physical growth and the development of the self-concept are: Mary C. Jones and Nancy Bayley, "Physical Maturing among Boys as Related to Behavior," *Journal of Educational Psychology* 41:129–48 (Mar. 1950); Mary C. Jones, "The Later Careers of Boys Who Were Early- or Late-Maturing," *Child Development* 28:113–28 (Mar. 1957); Paul H. Mussen and Mary C. Jones, "Self-Conceptions, Motivations and Interpersonal Attitudes of Late- and Early-Maturing Boys," *Child Development* 28:243–56 (June 1957).
3. A. R. Gilliland, "The Attitude of College Students toward God and the Church," *Journal of Social Psychology* 11:11–18 (Feb. 1940).
4. Gordon W. Allport and others, "The Religion of the Post-War College Student," *Journal of Psychology* 25:3–33 (Jan. 1948).
5. Raymond G. Kuhlen and Martha Arnold, "Age Differences in Religious Beliefs and Problems During Adolescence." *Journal of Genetic Psychology* 65:291–300 (Dec. 1944).
6. Erwin R. Goodenough and Evelyn W. Goodenough, "Myths and Symbols for Children," *Religious Education* 57:172–77, 236–37 (May–June 1962).

The Adolescent Image in American Books for Children: Then and Now

Mary Lystad

The image of the adolescent in American books for children and youth has changed over the last 200 years. It reflects differing role definitions for adolescents and differing opportunities offered for their individual development. Through a study of children's books from 1776 to the present, one sees some of the hopes and values the country has placed on its young from time to time and some of the ways in which it has encouraged their participation and spirit. Mirrored, too, are the country's ongoing concerns with human relationships and human purpose.[1]

At the time of the American Revolution, and until about 1850, books containing adolescent characters and aimed at adolescent readers were written primarily to instruct young people in religious matters and other desired social activities. The religious behavior expected included piety, obedience, humility, and service to others, as well as prudence, hard work, and deference. By following such recommended behavior, a young man or woman would be prepared at any moment to die with a pure heart. Death occurred often and early, as reported in the following account of the death of fourteen-year-old Isaac Ball on August 2, 1799 *(A Memorial for Sunday School Boys,* Philadelphia, American Sunday-School Union, c.1825):

> The morning he died, his mother finding him so near his end, asked him if he knew he should be happy. He answered, "Yes; I know I shall go to heaven." His mother said, "Then thou knowest that God hath forgiven thee." He replied, "Yes; I know he has; I shall be happy! happy! happy!" which were his last words; for a short time after, his spirit took its flight into the realms of everlasting day.

Books offering instruction in social behavior, often imported from England, were also popular, with the definitions of "proper" conduct reflecting the concerns of the British upper classes. Many editions of Philip Dormer Stanhope Chesterfield's *Principles of politeness, and of knowing the world* were printed in this country. Among the subjects Chester-

Reprinted by permission of the author and the publisher from *Children Today* 6:16–19, 35 (July–Aug. 1977).

field discussed were modesty, lying, cleanliness of person, dress, elegance of expression, address, phraseology, and small talk. The express purpose of the instruction was "to complete the gentleman and man of fashion, to give him knowledge of life and to make him well received in all companies." The book focuses on the instruction of young men but points out that it is "yet not beneath the attention of any." Later versions did include instruction for young women.

The setting of these books was usually the home or other primary group environment, such as a neighborhood, classroom, or church. There was little interaction in large secondary groups. Life revolved principally around parent and youth, and the proper mode of behavior of the latter toward the former was often discussed.

The needs expressed were for salvation in heaven and also for strength and achievement on this earth, within a religious context. Biographies of Benjamin Franklin and George Washington became popular, and they showed adolescents who obeyed both the Commandments of God and of parents while at the same time becoming quite self-sufficient. Samuel Griswold Goodrich's work on Franklin (*The Life of Franklin*, Philadelphia, Thomas Cowperthwait and Company, 1848) shows Benjamin's teenage progression through various trades:

> At ten years of age he was taken from school to help his father in the business of a tallow-chandler; and was employed in cutting the wick for the candles, going errands, and tending the shop.
>
> Benjamin disliked the trade, and had a strong inclination to go to sea; but his father opposed his wishes in this respect, and determined to keep him at home . . . Benjamin continued employed in the business of his father . . . till he was twelve years old . . . As his dislike to the trade continued, his father was afraid that, if he did not put Benjamin to one that was more agreeable, he would run away, and go to sea, as an elder brother of his had done. In consequence of this apprehension, he used to take him to walk, to see joiners, bricklayers, turners and braziers at their work, that he might observe his inclination . . .
>
> His father at length determined on the cutler's trade, and placed him for some days on trial with his cousin Samuel . . . It was then usual to ask a sum of money for receiving an apprentice, and the cutler charged so much for taking Benjamin, that his father was displeased, and put him to the old business again . . .
>
> From his infancy Benjamin had been passionately fond of reading . . . This fondness for books at length determined his father to bring him up as a printer, though he had already one son in that employment . . . Benjamin liked this trade much better than that of his father, but still had a desire to go to sea. To prevent this step, his father was impatient to have him bound apprentice to his brother, and at length persuaded him to consent to it.

The family, the church, the school, and the work place were the principal locations of activity for youth of the period. In the family the adolescent usually spent time with both parents, but in those cases where only one parent took charge it was more likely to be the father. Boys, in particular, spent much time with their fathers in an apprentice relationship— they hunted with their fathers, discussed politics and economic affairs with them, sometimes helped in the family business, and certainly helped on the family farm.

Satisfactions were indeed attained by the adolescent—he died happy, or, if he were male and healthy, he went on to greater things in business or politics. With few exceptions, the young man was supposed to do this in the context of the established norms of the adults around him or the God above him. Social change was seldom encouraged.

There were differences in the ways young people of differing races and sex were portrayed. Very few minority youth appeared in books. When they did, they were usually depicted as lazy black slaves or warlike Indians. As for sex differences, boys and men worked hard and achieved in their professions and in the community—all the while avoiding drink, to which they were particularly prone. Girls and women practiced gentility at home or, like Goody Two Shoes, performed good works. Female docility, as in this tract by James Fordyce (*Sermons to Young Women,* Boston, Thomas Hall, 1798), was extolled:

> Your best emblem, beloved, is the smiling form of peace, robed in white, and bearing a branch of olive. Like the apostles and first christians, your highest glory is to conquer by benignity, and triumph by patience. Roughness, and even ferociousness, in a man, we often overlook, and are sometimes diverted with. In a woman we are always hurt by them. A loud voice, a bold gesture, a daring countenance, every mark of bravery, shall please in the former, when his courage is particularly called forth; but in a female we wish nothing to reign but love and tenderness; and where they do reign, they will produce very different effects.

By 1850 didacticism was still entrenched in books for adolescents, but there was more emphasis on social than religious behavior. The social behavior stressed involved the Protestant ethic of hard work, sobriety, and looking towards the future. It resulted in economic success and upward social mobility. The model related primarily to male behavior, and there were many book series detailing the rising fortunes of ambitious, diligent young men. Hard work was related as much to religion as to economic achievement, as seen in Mrs. A. K. Dunning's *Broken pitchers* (Philadelphia, Presbyterian Board of Publication, c.1887):

> God exempts nobody from work. A sense of responsibility is a brace to manhood and a developer of power; and because God wants work and responsibility to react healthfully on men, he wants them to work with a hearty, joyous spirit. When the joy and the enthusiasm have gone out of of work, something is wrong.

The setting of these books is often out of the home, at least for boys. The business world often transported a young man from his own town or hamlet to New York or other growing metropolises; other boys went to sea or to the West. Young men had a need to get away. For girls, however, the setting was more likely to be the home or, at best, a nearby campfire for an overnight outing.

In these books boys were shown to want adventure and achievement. Some girls wanted these things, too, but they were encouraged to be content with their lot. William O. Stoddard, in *Crowded out o' the Crofield; or, the boy who made his way* (New York, D. Appleton and Company, 1890) presents different expectations for brother and sister:

> "If they take away every cent I get, I'm going to the city, some time."
> "I'd go, too, if I were a boy," she said. "I've got to stay at home and wash dishes and sweep. You can go right out and make your fortune. I've read of lots of boys that went away from home and worked their way up. Some of 'em got to be president."
> "Some girls amount to something, too," said Jack. "You've been through the Academy."

Girls did work, as teachers or in the factories. Factory work, however, was not the road to success for a girl, as this quotation from Virginia Johnson's *Katy's Christmas* (New York, London and Paris, Cassell & Co., Ltd., 1885) shows:

> Katie was 12 years old, and her aunt considered it only right that she should earn something for herself, as there were many mouths to feed in the cottage.
> The little girl was sent to the factory, to begin at the lowest round of the ladder, which she would climb as the years rolled on, until she could control one of the looms of the upper story, like the older girls, guiding the whirling shuttles with nimble fingers, to weave bright-colored cloth.

Family and church, especially for girls, were very important institutions while the work place was important for boys. School was less significant for adolescents; in fact, adolescents were allowed to go to school only if the family could afford the luxury of their not working.

There was success in these stories—the male youth, in particular, made it to the top. He separated from the home easily and quickly. He had amazing adventures, like Huck Finn and Tom Sawyer, or he made good at his job like Horatio Alger's *The Young Salesman* (Philadelphia, The John C. Winston Company, 1896):

> Scott continues to prosper, and next year will become a partner in the firm of Tower, Douglas & Co. Harold is earning a good salary now, and his father's troubles are over. He gets more remunerative work at his profession, and, with his family, occupies a pleasant home in Bayonne.

The girls of the period were usually passive and stayed at home, moving only from the subordinate role of child to parent to that of wife to husband. Family relationships, as in Louisa May Alcott's *Little Women,* were stressed. Some girls, like Jo March, did rebel. But the rebellion did not take Jo out of the home. Nor did it take her out of a traditional professional role for women—teaching.

Blacks were rarely seen in books of this period, and when they appeared it was as caricatures—as if they were stunted people who did not grow and develop from childhood. Rarely were they treated as equal to whites.

In the early 1900s an increasing interest in the adolescent years was shown. More novels were being written for this age group and they included books set in foreign lands as well as in our own. Laura Ingalls Wilder's very popular series about the nineteenth-century Midwest gave a sense of the growth of our own country and also of the growth of a child into a young girl and then a young adult.

By the third decade of the twentieth century the purpose of books for adolescents had changed. The majority of these books were now being written for amusement rather than for instruction, although a substantial number were concerned with understanding—of people, of social groups, of cultures. The feelings of adolescents, both negative and positive, were discussed openly, as were social problems. Joseph Krumgold's *Onion John* (New York, Thomas Y. Crowell Co., 1959) discusses the age-old conflict between father and son. Here, the father wants his son to prepare for a career in science—first at the Massachusetts Institute of Technology, then on the moon, a desire prompted by his own youthful dreams of becoming an engineer. The son sees nothing wrong with the small town of Serenity and with working in his father's hardware store. The father finally realizes that his son is growing up and must be allowed to make his own career decisions. Here is the first response of the almost thirteen-year-old to such liberties:

> My father found the snow shovel and he handed it to me . . . I always get the coal shovel when we dig out after a storm. It's smaller. When he gave me the big one, it meant there wasn't any doubt that I was grown up.
> "And I'm the one to decide about myself?" I was halfway down the driveway, right behind him, cutting a narrow path alongside the house.
> He said, "Yes," same as the night before.
> "Well, I've decided," I told him when we reached the sidewalk out front.
> "No, you haven't." He heaved the shovelful he had and turned around. "You haven't had time to think about it."
> "All the way out here," I told him. "I've had the last ten, twelve minutes to think about it."
> "It's the rest of your life you're deciding on. Don't you figure you ought to give it a little more time?"
> "That's so!" I leaned on my shovel. "I suppose I ought."
> I gave it until afternoon, when I could get down to the hardware store.

A thirteen-year-old girl's feelings about her mother's proscriptions are described in Mary Rodgers' *Freaky Friday* (New York, Harper & Row, 1972):

> I can't stand how strict she is. Take food for instance. Do you know what she makes me eat for breakfast? Cereal, orange juice, toast, an egg, milk, and two Vitamin C's. She's going to turn me into a blimp. . . . She's also very fussy about the way I keep my room. . . . A few other things we fight about are my hair . . . and my nails which I bite.
> But the biggest thing we fight about is freedom, because I'm old enough to be given more than I'm getting. . . .

Settings are usually in or near the home. The adolescent character is likely to interact with both elders and peers; the tension of separation between adolescent and parent, and the fun between adolescent and his peers, are explored. Play is important, as are love, strength, and achievement.

There are satisfactions in the books. Problems get resolved—on a personal and a societal level—not in a pollyannish fashion but realistically, with the acknowledgment that there are responsibilities to be maintained and injustices to be dealt with. In William Armstrong's *Sounder* (New York, Harper & Row, 1969), the boy-child assumes a larger role in the family after his father's death, while still attending to youthful needs for learning and for making sense of his universe.

While sex stereotyping has not changed markedly, racial stereotyping has decreased considerably in the books of the last two decades. Gifted and determined black and Spanish-speaking writers are composing novels about their people and their culture, treating the individual characters with dignity and distinction.

Over a 200-year period, then, there have been definite changes in characterizations of and for adolescents. In the earliest period, until about 1850, the adolescent was seen as a person with one overriding duty: to cast off evil ways and engage in that religious and social activity which would merit him eternal life. The youth was born not to live but to die, and it was important that he die in a befitting manner. After 1850 the adolescent was encouraged to expand his horizons and to think not only about life after death but also about life after childhood. Ways of achieving in the world, especially for boys, were highlighted, and the adolescent was urged to think seriously about and to plan for adult roles, especially as they related to work.

In the books of the twentieth century there has been considerably less stress on future roles, either in this life or beyond. Rather, the adolescent's present feelings and values are explored. Negative feelings are seen as sometimes appropriate and certainly normal. Values are seen as relative rather than absolute. And the world presented offers choice—choice of lifestyle, career, family structure, artistic expression. Also at this time, adolescence as a legitimate growth period is acknowledged. Youth are no longer treated as potential celestial bodies, or as little adults, but as persons in transition from childhood to adulthood, with a need for adventure, for love, and for self-discovery.

The present role models are not applied equally to all youths and are more available to young men than to young women. Young men continue to separate easily and to succeed in sports and careers; girls are beginning to leave the home, but familiar settings are still the norm. Role models are more available to young whites than to the young of several minorities. The white models are more adventuresome, and they more often start out with stable economic and social situations. The careers of minority models usually involve struggle and oppression. Also relatively infrequent are role models which provide dignity for the handicapped, the sick and the poor. But inroads have been made. As our society moves in pluralistic and humanistic directions, one can predict that books too will change.

NOTE

1. For further historical analysis of adolescence in our society, see Joseph Kett, *Rites of Passage: Adolescence in America, 1790 to the Present* (New York: Basic Books, 1977). For a study of modern roles and values of adolescents in our country, see Mary Lystad, *As They See It: Changing Values of College Youth* (Cambridge, Mass.: Schenkman Publishing Co., 1973).

What Is Adolescent Literature?

Isabelle Holland

In discussing what is adolescent literature, I am coming more and more to the conclusion that adolescent literature is whatever any adolescent happens to be reading at any time. This, I feel, depends completely on the individual adolescent. An adolescent, depending on age, sex, and taste, can read Beatrix Potter, Henry Miller, John Knowles, Leo Tolstoy, Louisa May Alcott, the Bobbsey Twins, Arthur Clarke, Jane Austen, Philip Roth, or Tolkien—or all of them together within the same six months' period.

After all, what is an adolescent? An adolescent is a human being on

Reprinted from *Top of the News* 31:407–14 (June 1975).

a journey in that great, amorphous sea called adolescence. That is, he or she is somewhere between age twelve and ages eighteen or nineteen. In this period almost anything can happen to a human being—and usually does. There are adolescents who do little but work. There are adolescents who do nothing but play. There are adolescents of nineteen (as indeed there are adolescents of fifty-nine), while some young people of thirteen or fourteen seem, emotionally anyway, to have achieved a maturity and a sense of responsibility usually associated with adulthood in the most complimentary sense of the word. An adolescent, therefore, is a human being who is journeying from childhood to adulthood. He or she is learning, whether for good or ill, to do without certain things that were important to him or to her during childhood. He is also learning how to acquire certain qualities, skills, and defenses that will be important to him when he becomes an adult. But the adolescent is both a child *and* an adult, and his tastes in reading, as in everything else, reflect this fact.

I think, therefore, at the moment, I am really going to quarrel a little with the tendency to wall off various sections of a young person's life and along with that, to wall off the literature that is supposed to enlighten, entertain, and inform that period.

Most people here, I am sure, are familiar with the book *I'm OK, You're OK* by Thomas Harris, and have either read it or read about it. In it, the thesis of the author is that we all carry in us several voices, several tapes. There is the voice of the child we were. There is the voice of parental or other adult authority that fed into our early lives. And finally there is our own adult voice in which these previous voices blend or have been melded together. Now, in a sense, when we read, we read on these different levels. And an adolescent, more probably than at any other period in his life, will hop about among these levels from one minute to the next and will be entertained, amused, and informed by books of vastly different so-called reading levels. The child in him may delight in Beatrix Potter. The adult in him may read *Portnoy's Complaint*. The blending of the two may read *War and Peace*. He or she reads the comics. He or she reads *Playboy or Penthouse*. He or she reads *The Hobbit* and turns the same evening to *All the President's Men*.

Elsewhere I have talked about "The Walls of Childhood" and how they no longer exist in our sophisticated, permissive, and media-oriented society. A single paperback bookrack in a drug or candy store can—and often does—contain hardcore pornography, current best-sellers, assorted classics, and a modern-idiom edition of the Bible. If parents are old-fashioned and sticky about reading matter, then forbidden books can be kept in a school locker or in the home of a friend whose parents are not sticky. So how does the contemporary adolescent cope with this many-leveled, undifferentiated inflow of reading matter in contrast, say, to his or her grandmother, whose physical life may have been more demanding and difficult but whose reading was far more directed and protected?

I think today's adolescent deals with his and her multiple and (to me) bewildering options by receiving them, as I said, on different levels. And perhaps this facility is one of the most characteristic aspects of the teen-ager. Below the teens the reader is of necessity bounded and limited by lack of experience. Over twenty, the adult reader pretty much settles into the area of reading that he and she find comfortable at the end of a working day. And this, by the way, introduces a practical consideration that is often forgotten in studies of the reading habits of the human animal, but is of great importance.

Most adult readers, even compulsive readers, read in snatched moments of relaxation, usually when they are tired and bring to their reading only the attention and energy that is left over from everything else they have to do. Understandably, this is why most adults read what is comfortable rather than what is challenging or upsetting. At the other end of adolescence, it is the rare child below eleven who spends long hours in a book. Childhood, for the most part and for most children, is about other areas of life: playing, partying, eating, going, giggling, fighting. Of course, the adolescent does all these and more. But adolescence is probably the only time of life when a large proportion of its membership inhales books—all kinds of books—in huge, indiscriminate drafts at all hours of the day and night and at the full peak of the reader's energy. The adolescent is not only encouraged to do this, he is pretty much forced to do it, if he wants to keep up with his required reading. So he balances his assignment for English Lit. with his fancy from the nearest magazine stand, which could be *Popular Mechanics, Time* magazine, *Animal Life,* or various erotica. Most adults would find such drastic changing of gears discombobulating. Because apart from lacking time and energy for indiscriminate reading, the majority of adults, whether they are consciously aware of it or not, have evolved their own cosmologies. By that I mean that by the time an individual—whether he or she is an Archie Bunker, a Kenneth Galbraith, or a Margaret Mead—has reached adulthood, he or she has usually arrived at a philosophy, a set of values, a structure, whether consciously thought out or unconsciously felt, in which all aspects of life are related by a drawstring of meaning. And what that adult chooses to read, and how he reacts to it, is a reflection of what he believes about himself and the world around him, and he will seek out what is consistent with it. And this is true not only of so-called serious books, but of froth. Archie Bunker may put his feet up, turn off the television, and settle himself with that well-known paperback, *The Face on the Barroom Floor.* He will enjoy vicariously the blondes and the gore. But if he discovers that his hero is a secret member of the SDS, he will throw the book across the room with an expletive deleted. On the other side of town the professor of humanities at the local university may put down the *New York Review of Books,* pull down the shades, and settle himself with that masterpiece, *The Face on the Barroom Floor.* He, too, will enjoy the blondes and the gore and probably for the same reason, despite intellectual reservations about violence and sex exploitation. But when he discovers that his hero is a secret member of the CIA, he will throw the book across the room with an expletive deleted. This is what I mean by the adult tending to seek consistency of viewpoint. Another name for it is hardening of the attitudes, and the reading of adults, whether heavy or light, tends toward books that reenforce those attitudes.

Not the adolescent. Life for him is still a huge, unrelated, fascinating, frightening hodgepodge. He does seek meaning, but he looks for it everywhere with equal passion. So, free as Tarzan, he can swing from *Mad Magazine* to Kafka to Tolstoy and back with no dizziness.

So where does that leave the genre of books called young adult? I'm not even sure there is such a genre. As I said at the beginning, a young adult book is a book that is read and enjoyed by young adults. And that's just about it. If it deals with problems that are outside the experience of, say, ten-year-olds, then such a book is not suitable for ten-year-olds, but may very well be suitable for teenagers. But while it's possible to put a boundary or floor at the lower end of adolescence, it isn't possible to say of any book "this is too old, too mature for a young adult."

A young person may prefer *Romeo and Juliet* or *Hamlet* to *King Lear.* The anguish of young lovers caught up in a social system destructive to their interests, or the ambivalence of a young man torn by conflicting loves and loyalties is much more immediate to an adolescent than the agony of a parent. When I was fifteen and first taken to the opera by my opera-loving parents, my heart was wrung by *Madame Butterfly,* which is in essence the tragedy of young love, and I couldn't understand why my rather stoic father, who had sat dry-eyed through *Butterfly,* wept over *Rigoletto,* which is the tragedy of a parent. Holden Caulfield is a lot more comprehensible to the average teenager than Silas Marner. But while no book or play can, categorically, be called too old, books that touch the sensitive areas of adolescent life—sex, authority, schools, drugs, relationship to parents, relationship to adult society—are supremely young adult books, and are the staples of a young adult library.

So, let us see what these archetypical books are.

A recent survey made by secondary school English department chairmen produced two lists. The first list was the forty most commonly required novels in American high schools. The second list was the fifty novels most identified as favorites of high school youth. On this second list of favorites, the top ten listed in order were: *The Catcher in the Rye, Go Ask Alice, The Outsiders, To Kill a Mockingbird, A Separate Peace, Jonathan Livingston Seagull, Lord of the Flies, Of Mice and Men, Lisa, Bright and Dark,* and *The Exorcist.* Allowing for the fact that some of these titles were drawn from books recommended by the schools and that the list undoubtedly leaves out a lot of extraneous reading the students do on their own, outside, it is interesting to note that of the ten favorites, eight were published as adult books and became best-sellers among adults as well as teenagers. And when one remembers that such young adult classics as the Alcott books, *Jane Eyre,* and *Wuthering Heights* were published for adults, the categories become really blurred.

One of the reasons why I resist the increasing tendency to categorize according to age is that it becomes a form of pressure from the outside, telling a young person what he or she is supposed to be, or what stage he or she is supposed to be at. And the more this is done, the more, I believe, it is difficult for people—any people of any age, but particularly young people who are on this particular stage of the road of self-discovery—to know from within themselves who they are, where they are, and what they really like and want for themselves.

In a sense, this sort of reminds me of the adolescent who said he didn't know he was supposed to be having so many problems until he read what terrible problems adolescents have. This way, and with nobody's ill intent, an adolescent comes under subtle pressure to adhere to a stereotype of himself. This can be damaging to the teenager, one of whose main endeavors at this point of his development is to establish his own identity as an individual separate from not only his family, but his peers.

Another objection I have to categories too rigidly adhered to is that they are frequently inspired by what is generally called "trendy" thinking. C. S. Lewis once said that he had no opinion at all of fashionable attitudes, and I echo that brave statement. Occasionally in reviews and elsewhere I get more than a hint that novels for young people are praised or damned according to how they reflect a popular viewpoint— or the viewpoint of the reviewer—on various social problems of the day and not on the books' merits as pieces of fiction. Character, atmosphere, dialogue, writing, the magic of illusion—all basic elements in the ancient and honorable art of storytelling—are ignored or dismissed. What is important is the author's deduced attitude about such matters as protest, sexual liberation, racial equality. Now there are excellent books in all these areas—books that are sensitive and authentic and brilliantly written. But I get restless and uncomfortable when the only aspect of a book that is considered worthy of comment is whether or not the author is showing—in the reviewer's opinion—the correct orthodoxy in some controversial area. Perhaps I feel as strongly as I do about this because it has happened to some of my own books as well as to the books of authors I know and respect.

The trouble with this judgment-by-viewpoint, which is a kind of categorizing, is that it brings pressure on the writer and editor and becomes a form of censorship. Writers and editors are human. They like the books they have written and produced to be reviewed, if not always well, at least fairly as to whether or not their books succeed in what they set out to do. Writers do not write in a vacuum. They are part of their culture, whether they write in support of it or in opposition to it. No matter how independent, writers and editors are affected by what their peers and critics deem important. So when young adult novels are viewed as though their main purpose were to serve as slogans for right thinking—or what is held to be right thinking in any given year—and not primarily as works of fiction, then the novel as art form is dealt a lethal blow, and the teenager who, perhaps, has it in him or her to become a novelist is discouraged and misled.

And, of course, the irony is that trends behave like trends—they come and go. The crusading cry of last year has become this year's cliché. This leaves the adolescent trying to find out what he likes and considers important with no permanent standard or set of values with which he can appraise for himself a piece of fiction. And he is thrown back on having to read by category, by age, by subject, by what other people think, rather than by inner radar and his own God-given and quite unique intuition.

I used the word storytelling before. And this brings me to the second word of the general title of adolescent literature—that is, the word literature. I am very leery of that word. I do not, and have never, really considered myself a literary person. I've thought of myself much more as a storyteller. And the books that I have read and loved, all the way from the earliest to the most recent, are those where the stories and the people in them interested and held me. I'm not putting myself or what I write down. On the contrary, I feel that literature is rather a newcomer to the scene by comparison with storytelling. If the worst should happen and the bombs should fall and civilization should be wiped out and all the libraries and tapes destroyed, those who are left, when they assemble themselves and shiver beside the fire, will probably while away their gloomy hours by doing exactly what our ancestors did, which is to tell stories. I believe it to be the oldest and most honorable form of creative communication between people. I am sure—although I certainly have no proof—it probably predated those first drawings on the walls of the caves in France. This was undoubtedly the reason why, when I first went to university in Liverpool, England, I took history, not literature. I was always of the "and what happened next?" school and "why did he do that?" and "what made her react that way?" And for the person whose mind works in that fashion history is in many ways a much more satisfying study than literature. The truly literary person is much more preoccupied with form, with style and with criticism in the highest sense of the word. The true litterateur will find the evolution of techniques, the *way* something is said, as important, and many times more important, than *what* is said. The storyteller fundamentally cares very little about that, although some very great literary figures have been primarily storytellers. The first one who leaps to mind is Homer. Geoffrey

Chaucer was another. And I also claim among the storytellers the greatest of them all, William Shakespeare. Great as his poetry is, I think he is primarily a storyteller.

Some years ago Walter Kerr, in his book *Shakespeare and Breadbaskets,* commented that in the sixteenth century all the literary people and intellectuals went up to Oxford to watch the plays of John Lyly, and all the common people stayed down in London to watch the plays of William Shakespeare.

So, to return again to the question of adolescent literature, I really believe I interpret it as telling stories, of whatever kind, that will interest people within the ages of about twelve and nineteen, and this covers a good deal of territory. As I said at the beginning, it can be absolutely anything.

People ask me frequently, "How did you come to write young adult literature?" or "books for young adults?" as though it were a level of writing at which I had to take and maintain careful aim. The truth of the matter is that that is the way my books come out. My first book, *Cecily,* was published by the adult department of J. B. Lippincott. But the reason why it is still in print is that it was most highly praised as a young adult book and it is still found in the young adult section of libraries. I certain didn't try to write a young adult book. I wrote the kind of book that was natural for me to write, and it emerged at that level. My second book, *Amanda's Choice,* started as an adult book. This was also about a little girl. Cecily was thirteen. Amanda was twelve. It had been two years since the publication of *Cecily* and since that time I had written an adult suspense book which is one of the two unpublished orphans that I still have. Nobody ever took it. So I was feeling somewhat downhearted. And I started a third book about a little girl called Amanda. At this point I was working, most unhappily, as publicity director at a publishing house, and I bumped into Jeanne Vestal, then children's book editor at Lippincott, in the lobby of Lord & Taylor's. Jeanne said "How are things?" I said, "Terrible!" and I told her about the book that had been turned down. She said, "You know I've often thought you could write juveniles. Why don't you write me a children's book?"

So Jeanne and I had lunch and by this time I had dreamed up a whole category of nonfiction children's books—biographies of one kind or another—that I thought would be suitable. Jeanne listened to me very patiently and said, "Yes, that sounds like a good idea, but I don't think that's the kind of writing that you really want to do. What are you working on now?" So I told her about this horrible child called Amanda about whom I was writing. She said, "That sounds like the kind of book I'm interested in." So I said, "But I didn't think about this as a children's book." She said, "Never mind, finish it. And when you've finished it, bring it to me."

So I finished it and I took it to her. When she had read it she called me and said, "Now Isabelle, the one area where the fact that this is juvenile is going to make a difference is that your point of view must stay with the child. You can't go hopping around among all these adults." So she and I spent a day together, during which she indicated the cuts she wanted, which were where the adult characters were involved with one another, not with Amanda. Wherever they were involved with Amanda herself, or even if they were talking to one another *about* Amanda, the text stayed. In other words, I did not write a different book because I was writing a juvenile for Jeanne. I wrote exactly the same book as I planned to write, with the sole difference that I took out the parts where the child was not the main concern.

Many years ago, when I was trying to write short stories, I came to the realization that I would never write, or it would be most surprising if I would write, what is thought of today as an extremely adult, adult novel. Because, after all, a writer writes the kind of book that he or she likes to read. And I find an awful lot of serious, grown-up books—the kind that are gravely discussed by prominent reviewers on the front pages of leading book reviews—rather depressing. The ones I enjoy—*To Kill a Mockingbird, Red Sky at Morning,* for example—usually wind up on lists of young adult favorites, such as the one I quoted earlier. That is why I find categories like young adult literature misleading. As a technical convenience for grouping books in a library it is certainly valid, but not in creating a separate genre of novel.

So where does that leave us with adolescent literature?

It leaves us where I started, with the adolescent, a mysterious creature, as are all human beings, defying every attempt to classify, categorize, or pigeonhole him. Long may he and she remain elusive, guarding the secret places that only the adolescents themselves know and we have forgotten. The moment adolescence is precisely defined and we can say exactly what is of the adolescent, as opposed to what is of the child or of the adult, then, I suspect, adolescence will disappear, like the god Cupid did when his face was revealed. And then adolescence, like other endangered aspects of nature, over-examined, over-categorized, over-discussed, will be gone.

Do Teenage Novels Fill a Need?

Sylvia Engdahl

An author of novels for adolescents faces a problem not shared by other writers. I am sometimes confronted with the opinion that my profession fills no need—that the writing of fiction for today's teenagers is unessential, or even unwise. Those with some knowledge of the field are most prone to feel that it is a waste of time and talent. By the ignorant, the writer may be viewed with the perennial suspicion that a serious novelist, if good, would soon "graduate" to writing for adults—an assertion requiring no reply. A view less easily dismissed is that of experts on literature for youth who believe that an author who does not choose to write adult fiction should direct his or her books toward preadolescents. According to this view, there is no literate audience in between. Because it is a prevalent view, teenage fiction resides in a sort of limbo.

The question of whether teenage fiction is needed has received a good deal of attention during the past few years, primarily in journals read by librarians. Yet it seems to me that the controversy has been centered on side issues: issues that often obscure an information gap of which many teachers and librarians are unaware. Discussion about what is wrong with contemporary teenage fiction—and what is right with it—cannot be meaningful apart from clear understanding of *what* it is; and I find that people unfamiliar with publishing procedures have no such understanding. In debating the value of fiction for teens, most fail to define the category to which they are referring.

Just what is a teenage novel? The simplistic answer is obvious: a teenage novel is one intended for adolescent readers. To many people, however, the very words of this statement have connotations that exclude the better teenage novels of today. No truly adequate definition can be given except in terms of factors distinguishing teenage novels from adult ones. And when considering these, it is important to recognize that only one factor has bearing on the designation "teenage" (or "junior" or "young adult") as applied to a novel by the book trade and review media. That designation is determined solely by the structure of the publishing business. A novel suitable for adolescents is "teenage" if it is issued by the children's book department of a publishing house, and "adult" if it is issued by the adult department. From an organizational standpoint, these departments are wholly separate, and although many criteria may affect

Reprinted by permission from *English Journal* 64:48–52 (Feb. 1975). Copyright © 1975 by the National Council of Teachers of English.

the initial decision as to which will handle a given novel, once that decision is made the book is permanently categorized. The book's maturity, as judged by readers after publication, has nothing whatsoever to do with its classification, which is based mainly on marketing considerations.

This separation at the publishing level is more significant than it may seem, for it has far-reaching effects—some good, some bad—on the nature of novels made available to adolescents. Moreover, it is highly pertinent to the debate concerning whether or not a "teenage" category is worthwhile. The *raison d'être* of that category is not literary, but commercial. No one doubts that there is a need for books appropriate for teenagers to read. The real, underlying question is whether we need books to be read *only* by teenagers. And surely we do not. I cannot imagine writing a novel that I felt was of interest only to people within some particular age range; my books are enjoyed by ten- to twelve-year-olds of advanced reading ability, and also by quite a few grownups. But I direct them most specifically to readers of high school age, since they have characteristics which, in the climate of today's publishing field, mean that if they were not issued by children's book departments they would not be published at all.

I cannot deny that I say this with a tinge of regret, not because I see anything preferable about being an "adult" novelist, but because the outlook of modern teenagers seems to me in many respects healthier than that of their elders. Authors often find the children's book field less restrictive than the adult market in that it is less subject to the dictates of current fashion. As C. S. Lewis said, "They label their books 'For Children' because children are the only market now recognized for the books they, anyway, want to write."[1] The statement is perhaps even more applicable to teenagers; teenagers, having little regard for what is fashionable among adults, do not care that an optimistic view of the universe is not now in vogue. Their conception of "realism" is uncolored by the pronouncements of cynical critics—an issue that I have discussed in greater detail elsewhere.[2]

However, whether or not one shares my personal reasons for favoring a youthful audience (and many writers do not), it is indisputably true that adolescent readers need novels of a kind not presently being produced by publishers' adult departments. Natalie Babbitt writes, "Teenagers do not need a fiction of their own: They are quite ready to move into the world of adult fiction."[3] This might well be the case if contemporary adult fiction were more representative of the range of literate tastes than it has become; but the fact is that it does not even meet the needs of all older adult readers, let alone the youngest. Though worthwhile novels of past decades retain their value, suitable new ones are rare. Ms. Babbitt, wondering "if there *is* such a category as a teenage audience," cites partial reading lists for her sons' high school English classes consisting entirely of adult books—not one of which, I notice, was published within the last ten years.[4]

Publishing trends have undergone drastic upheavals during that period. The present adult market demands fiction of a kind that adolescents lack the experience and emotional maturity to cope with. Critically-acclaimed novels frequently treat themes in which adolescents are not even interested. But the nature of junior books has also been radically altered, a situation of which not all high school teachers are yet aware. Times have changed since publishers labeled insipid mysteries and school romances "ages 13 up"; both the old triviality and the old taboos are disappearing. Some of the books being issued by children's departments would have been published as adult a decade or two ago.

By no means do all such books qualify as literature. As Ms. Babbitt points out, they frequently suffer from deficiencies that would prevent their being considered true literature no matter what audience they were meant for. But hasn't it always been necessary to evaluate novels individually? The lowering of their age designation carries no implication that one should lower one's standards of judgment; nor, despite contentions of people who rate value in terms of "relevance," does increased maturity of adolescent fiction's subject matter necessarily imply sufficient maturity of presentation. Many teenage books that have appeared in the wave of enthusiasm for the "new realism" have been justly criticized for superficiality. One cannot argue with the reviewer who wrote, "You can't turn a bad novel into a good one by filling it with pregnancy, pot and the pill."[5]

Yet neither can one say that the existence of bad teenage novels tells against the need for good ones. In recognizing that shallow and superficial books are to be found among the newest fiction for adolescents, one must remember that shallow and superficial adult fiction also appears rather frequently. One might remember, too, C. S. Lewis's well-known statement: "No book is really worth reading at the age of ten which is not equally (and often far more) worth reading at the age of fifty. . . . The only imaginative works we ought to grow out of are those which it would have been better not to have read at all."[6]

Though Lewis was referring to books for preadolescents, the same principle applies to those directed toward adolescents. And it should be noted, before attempting to define adolescent fiction more fully, that there is no way to determine a particular novel's intended audience except through evaluation of the book itself or its reviews. Seekers of teenage fiction must bear in mind that for their purposes, any age or grade levels stated in the publisher's announcements, on the dust jacket, or at the heads of reviews are meaningless. These estimates apply only at the elementary school level, and even then they are inconsistent, since every publishing house has its own policy and the policies change from year to year according to sales experience. Thus one book's "10 to 14" designation may be the equivalent of another's "12 up," and the former may sometimes be given to a more difficult book by the same author.

This is a reflection of the uncertain status of teenage fiction at present. There was a time when most publishers set age level designations unrealistically high. Unfortunately, some over-corrected at the same time they were introducing books of increased maturity, and the result has been general confusion. Children's librarians are becoming wary of books marked "13 up," which may indeed be filled with pregnancy, pot, and the pill; while high school librarians who stopped buying—and reading—the output of children's departments before mature books began to appear retain the no longer reliable habit of automatically subtracting two or three years from the figures given. It is an ironic fact that some of the best new books for adolescents reach their intended audience mainly in public libraries large enough to have internal reviewing systems through which recommendations can be made to buyers for the adult collection; the more mature teens rarely visit children's rooms.

These novels are unheard of outside the specialized field of children's literature (though the new paperback trend may help the situation if current distribution problems can be solved). The hardcover editions of modern books for young people are sold almost exclusively to libraries. No attempt is made to market them to the general public, and few bookstores stock any but major award winners and the work of local authors. This, in fact, is the basis of the strict separation between fields in the publishing world, and its impact is great. It means that young people's books are advertised and reviewed primarily in publications read by librarians. It affects timing: Books are not published intermittently throughout the year, but are grouped into spring and fall lists for compatibility with school and public library ordering practices; children's editorial departments are organized around this schedule. Moreover, there is no expectation of producing instant best-sellers—the review procedures employed by libraries cause long delays between publication and shelving of teenage novels, which, unlike most adult ones, are kept in print for many years.

In most respects, this library orientation is a good thing for children's literature; it tends to preclude publication of books that will not remain valuable long past the current season. Furthermore, librarians are more discriminating buyers than the public at large, and they need not purchase young people's books merely to meet public demand, since the public does not even hear the titles of such books prior to seeing them—although this consideration is at times overridden by demand for novels of current topical interest. (Too often, these days, mere *topical interest* is confused with *contemporary theme,* as in the case where an author was advised by a librarian that young readers needed a novel about "a black adolescent unwed father on a Honda."[7]) On the whole, because the market is composed of professionals, editorial standards are apt to be higher in children's departments than in the adult departments where the prime aim is large, quick sales.

This is increasingly true now that funding problems are causing libraries to become more and more selective. And the more selective they are from the literary standpoint, the better off young readers will be—we do not need any more mediocre books. However, there is some danger that selectivity based upon insufficient funds will eliminate not only books of comparatively low quality, but also those of comparatively low readership. No one can afford to purchase—or to publish—novels that will not be widely read. Under present conditions, the best teenage novels will be the first to disappear, since they are not as widely read as those that can be appreciated by children of lesser maturity. Publishers have made an effort to bring out books appropriate for high school age readers of today, yet it is through the large public libraries, not the high schools, that they are being circulated. Though high school librarians often know of them, their funds are limited, too; they must give first priority to books requested by teachers.

It should therefore be asked whether teenage novels are worth teachers' attention, and if so, why. In defining what they have to offer, I can best begin by stating what they do *not* offer, for there are a number of prevalent misconceptions concerning their purpose.

First, few if any of the good ones are easier reading than the average adult novel considered suitable for younger high school students. Writers for teenagers do not limit vocabulary, nor do they use a less complex style than they would in fiction for adults (except in the case of stories specifically produced for "slow readers," which are not really "novels" in the literary sense). Some teenage novels are relatively short, but others—most of my own, for instance—exceed many adult novels in length. A serious novel for adolescents is distinguished from adult material by its conceptual and emotional levels, not by its reading level.

Second, novels of quality for teenagers do not preach. A writer who approaches young people in a condescending way receives short shrift from today's editors and reviewers. One can use a story to reflect one's views, just as an author of adult fiction can—but they must be views about life, not about how young people, as distinguished from other people, ought to look at it.

Third, teenage novels, if good, are not devoid of concepts worth pondering and worth discussing. Although fiction for the young ordinarily stays within the bounds of good taste, its themes are confined neither to traditional ideas nor to fashionable new ones. Thus it can hardly be called uncontroversial. An author cannot present honest opinions without evoking disagreement from some proportion of readers, and teenagers scorn books that are not honest.

A fourth thing novels for adolescents do not offer is shelter from the world as it is. Because of their honesty, such books cannot ignore the grimmer aspects of life any more than they can ignore aspects some adults consider shocking. The young do not want shelter. They know that people rarely live happily ever after; it is worse than useless for fiction to pretend otherwise. At the same time, however—and again for the sake of honesty—teenage books with true depth do not foster the notion that reality is uniformly grim. Even readers who have found it so are entitled to know that a bright side does exist.

Finally, contemporary teenage novels are not mere vehicles to provide reluctant readers with a fictional reflection of their own life-style and their own specific problems. It is true that many deal with settings and incidents familiar to the present teen generation; as Richard Peck says, young people "are liable to choose books as they choose friends, more as mirrors than as windows."[8] But he goes on to say: "Still, the best youth novels portray adolescence as a maturing process. Though the focus may be upon being young, there is a sense of the future—a sense of becoming, as well as being."[9] Relevance—real relevance—lies in this, not in a mirror image.

What, then, does distinguish teenage fiction from adult fiction, if not shallowness of a sort properly considered obsolete? It is largely a matter of two things, I think: complexity and viewpoint. These, at any rate, are the only allowances I make in my own writing for the youth of my intended audience.

Obviously, adolescents cannot absorb ideas of as great complexity as more experienced readers. They cannot follow as many interwoven threads, or perceive such involved interrelationships; nor do they possess the knowledge to make sense of allusions. This is not because they are "too young" for adult material; it is because they have had *too little time* to develop background. If a book is to be meaningful to them, it must be clearly focused. When it is based on complex ideas—as mine, which are set in hypothetical future worlds, usually are—the discussion of those ideas must be to some extent oversimplified. Lack of complexity, however, should not be confused with lack of profundity. In the words of one noted editor, "A book with good unity can have limitless depth. Only the circumference need be limited."[10] A teenage novel can and should have more than one level, and the deeper ones will be noticed by the most mature readers alone.

The other crucial factor that determines whether a book is meaningful to adolescents is viewpoint. This is more than a question of the age of the protagonist, though normally, the principal viewpoint character should be young. The real issue is the book's outlook. As everyone knows, teenagers neither share nor understand the outlook of adults with whom they are in actual contact; they cannot be expected to fathom the view of those for whom most contemporary adult novelists write. It is not merely that there is much in modern adult fiction the young do not comprehend—the reverse is also true. Fiction for teenagers is more than a watered-down version of adult literature with excess complexity screened out. I do not mean that it portrays the "youth subculture," although some of it may. In essence, outlook is independent of culture. Adolescents, not knowing this, tend to like adult books that reject our culture and dislike those that accept it. They need novels with a fresh outlook on all cultures: ours, theirs, others of this planet, and those of hypothetical worlds. Viewpoint concerns perspective on the universe and on the future, which is what I believe today's young people are seeking.[11] Too many adults have given up the search.

There are, of course, some fine adult novels with viewpoint and level of complexity suitable for today's high school students, novels that English teachers know well. These will be read for many years to come, and their worth will not diminish. But each year they become further removed from our time, and the supply of new material to supplement them is not growing noticeably larger—at least it does not appear to be if one discounts the publishing trend toward issuing books of substance as teenage books. As a result, adolescents are sometimes urged to attempt books beyond their understanding; from a real-life world that is complex and confusing enough, they are plunged hopelessly out of their depth into a fictional world of mature concepts and emotions. This is not a "realistic" world to the young—it is simply an incomprehensible one. It is unlike theirs, and asking them to enter it serves only to increase their alienation.

Lest teachers who agree immediately rush to the library with hope of finding a whole new body of literature appropriate for reading lists, it must again be emphasized that outstanding novels are the exception rather than the rule in the teenage field, just as they are in the adult field. Moreover, books of high quality for young adolescents are more plentiful than comparable ones for older adolescents. There is a good reason for this. Since the major market of children's book departments consists of children's librarians, publishers are understandably reluctant to bring out books that are too mature for sixth and seventh graders. Authors are therefore under pressure to oversimplify somewhat more than would be necessary if there were a large acknowledged high school market. Although many preadolescents have adult reading skills, their viewpoint and the level of complexity that meets their needs cannot also meet the needs of high school juniors and seniors. Until the status of teenage fiction is established, there must be a certain amount of compromise.

In the case of my own novels, this has not been as serious a problem as with some, since their interplanetary setting interests children who might otherwise find them difficult; furthermore, they can be read on several levels. They have been widely circulated among preadolescents, and I am very happy that this is so. Yet I would like them to reach the readers for whom they were intended, too. The most recent, *Beyond the Tomorrow Mountains,* is centered upon problems of deep concern to introspective older adolescents, but beyond the comprehension of most twelve-year-olds.[12] It thus strikes some people as a bit heavy. Reviewers whose aim is to evaluate usefulness in the upper elementary grades often either ignore aspects of a book perceptible only to more mature readers, or feel that they slow its pace—which for younger boys and girls is indeed true. Where fast action is sought, this is legitimately considered a defect; still it is my belief that today's teenagers want and need fiction that emphasizes the inner events of its characters' lives more than the outward ones.

Increasingly, the adolescents of our time are interested in questions: questions about life and its meaning, about the future of civilization, about man's place in the universe. No author can give them answers. But I feel that books directed toward the young can encourage them to go on looking for answers—which, surely, is one of the major goals of education. And if they can, teenage novels do fill a need.

NOTES

1. C. S. Lewis, "On Juvenile Tastes," in his *Of Other Worlds* (New York: Harcourt, 1966), p.41.
2. Sylvia Louise Engdahl, "Why Write for Today's Teenagers?," *The Horn Book Magazine* 48:249–54 (June 1972).
3. Natalie Babbitt, "Between Innocence and Maturity," *The Horn Book Magazine* 48:36 (Feb. 1972).
4. Ibid.
5. John Rowe Townsend, "It Takes More Than Pot and the Pill," *New York Times Book Review* 74:2 (Nov. 9, 1969, Pt. 2).
6. C. S. Lewis, "On Stories," in his *Of Other Worlds* (New York: Harcourt, 1966), p. 15.
7. Richard Peck, "In the Country of Teenage Fiction," *American Libraries* 4:204 (Apr. 1973).
8. Ibid., p.205.
9. Ibid.
10. Jean Karl, *From Childhood to Childhood: Children's Books and Their Creators* (New York: John Day, 1970), p.67.
11. See my article "Perspective on the Future: The Quest of Space Age Young People," *School Media Quarterly* 1:27–35 (Fall 1972).
12. (New York: Atheneum, 1973). A sequel to *This Star Shall Abide* (New York: Atheneum, 1972).

Real People, Real Books: About YA Readers

Lou Willett Stanek

University campuses are haunted by Pirandello characters searching not for an author, but for research topics. A sixteen-year-old girl in Tulsa, Oklahoma, unknowingly saved me from that fate. She also distracted my attention from what adolescents are *supposed* to read, refocusing it on what they read purely for pleasure. I think this anecdote has significance for those of us concerned about the reading interests of young adults.

In 1967 I was directing a demonstration center for students gifted in English. The center was at least democratic or liberal enough to allow students a voice in what they read, or more likely in what they thought they should read. They were reading Faulkner, Camus, Joyce, plays from theater of the absurd, *Hamlet* . . . a very impressive list. Then I heard the first version of what is becoming the Susan Hinton myth . . . I think I now know five, but originally I heard and told the students she was walking through a Tulsa park, saw a rumble, a young lad was killed, and Susan was so upset she ran home and started writing it out of her system. Whether Susan Hinton purged her soul in the manner of a Fitzgerald writing *Crack-Up* or simply was inspired to write a novel about kids she knew is interesting, but what *is* important is Velma Varner, then juvenile editor at Viking, being insightful enough to publish *The Outsiders*. Adolescent literature could never be quite the same—gangs, violence, poor kids had stolen the spotlight from mundane, middle-class Minnie.

The students at the center read it, loved it, and wanted more (as the earlier generation had wanted more *Seventeenth Summers*). And they were apologetic. These students had been labeled "gifted" and were very self-conscious. So they told me perhaps they should read these teenage books—even though they weren't *great literature*—because maybe some of them could write a novel like Susan Hinton. And they could get ideas.

I called Zena Sutherland, then children's editor at *Saturday Review*. She suggested wiggy titles—titles I'd never heard of—*The Pigman, Two Bad about the Haines Girl, My Darling, My Hamburger.* . . . The students waited in line for those books, wore them out, ripped them off. This had not been the pattern with Faulkner, Camus, Joyce, and company.

Reprinted by permission from *Top of the News* 31:417–27 (June 1975).

The teachers and I stood in line too. These books were different from those teenage books we had often sneered at—often causing our students to sneer too, I fear. They weren't just different; *they were better.* Nothing to challenge Beckett, but new to teenage fiction. There was experimentation in style:

1. First-person and multicharacter point of view
2. Stream of consciousness narration
3. Nonstandard English dialog
4. The setting had left virginal middleville and moved to Spanish Harlem, communes, Appalachia, the Village, and North Beach.
5. Anti-heroes, black kids, Indians, and fat kids were protagonists.
6. The old taboo subjects were themes: mothers had affairs, didn't get married, daughters got pregnant, daddies drank martinis, women went through menopause, girls reached puberty, sons rebelled against their fathers *and* a few loved other boys and older men.

There was intrigue here. Questions bobbing like corks—

Aesthetic and literary questions: Propaganda? Socializing tools? or art?

Sociological questions: Were these books barometers of our culture? values? reflecting a quasi-social revolution?

Psychological questions: Did these books aid in the maturation process, or stunt it?

Education and curriculum: Should they be taught or left under the pillow for pleasure?

Pondering these questions, I began to agree with T. S. Eliot when he said that "it is just the literature we read for amusement or purely for pleasure that may have the greatest . . . least suspected . . . earliest and most insidious influences upon us. Hence it is that the influence of popular novelists, popular plays of contemporary life, requires to be scrutinized." AND I HAD FOUND A RESEARCH TOPIC.

Previous studies indicated most adolescent reading lists had been compiled from data collected surveying librarians and English teachers. Seldom were kids polled and the rare cases were students geographically compatible with professors—university lab schools. I wanted a mixture of kids, so I sought my sample from the foothills of Illinois in a rural community to the Gold Coast of Chicago, stopping off at a blue-collar suburb, an inner-city ghetto, a parochial school, *and* the University of Chicago Lab School.

The study was limited to problem novels published specifically for young adults, and after several pretests I had a booklist of 150 titles ranging from a few such as Maureen Daly's *Seventeenth Summer,* published in the late 1940s, to several such as *Go Ask Alice,* with the publisher's ink barely dry. Since I was interested not only in *what* students read, but *why,* I read each book to determine the major fictional problem treated. My contention was that those (Dwight Burton, Robert Carlsen, and others) who thought the young read these books to help solve their personal problems were wrong. I had a hunch fat girls didn't want to read about other fat girls, but preferred the prom queen or a sleek ninety-pound female jockey.

Using Havighurst's developmental tasks of adolescents as the theoretical base for what concerns are significant at this age, I compiled a list of ten categories of real adolescent problems.[1] The students were asked to rank order both the books they most enjoyed reading and their most pressing personal problems as they perceived them. I tested the hypothesis that there was no significant correlation between the fictional problems they enjoyed reading and their perceived personal problems. The results supported my hypothesis so strongly the computer thought that I had cheated. The ten most popular books in ranked order were:

1. *Mr. and Mrs. Bo Jo Jones*
2. *Sounder*
3. *Fifteen*
4. *Island of the Blue Dolphins*
5. *Go Ask Alice*
6. *The Outsiders*
7. *My Darling, My Hamburger*
8. *Lisa, Bright and Dark*
9. *Jennifer*
10. *The Soul Brothers and Sister Lou*

Real problems rank ordered were:

1. Family
2. School
3. Personal
4. Appearance
5. Boy–girl
6. Concerns about future
7. Money
8. Moral issues
9. Recreation—leisure time
10. World tensions

The concerns that really hassled them were personal, private matters. But generally they read books about abstract, social, all-encompassing problems.

What flabbergasted me about the data was the popular booklist. This study was done in 1973. We were all talking about *Man without a Face; Sticks and Stones; Run Softly, Go Fast; Mom, the Wolf Man and Me; Dinky Hocker Shoots Smack.* But the kids were still reading *Fifteen* and *Jennifer.* They said they were least concerned about moral issues and world tensions. *But they were reading about pregnancy in high school, drugs, gangs, racial tensions, and ecology.*

However, if you could all ponder this list for a time, you would probably begin to see some patterns. Why *Go Ask Alice,* published only a few months before the study, and not *The Peter Pan Bag* (surely a better drug book)? NEVER UNDERESTIMATE THE POWER OF THE TELLY OR MOVIE HOUSE! I would hazard a prediction that Norma Klein's *Sunshine,* written from the television script, will be known to many kids before *Mom, the Wolf Man and Me,* published in 1972, and that twice as many teenagers know and read John Neufeld's *Lisa, Bright and Dark,* which has been televised, than the earlier *Edgar Allen,* which hasn't. Four of the first five choices in my study had either been movies or television shows before the survey.

Secondly—and this is discouraging—I surveyed the teachers and librarians in the sample schools. Their choices were significantly different from the students and were even less current. I checked card catalogs and found in some of the Chicago public schools that 1969 was the latest publishing date for a book in the teenage collection. *IT SEEMS THAT IT IS A LONG JOURNEY FROM PUBLISHING HOUSE TO SCHOOL HOUSE.* Perhaps this explains why kids are still reading *Fifteen* and *Jennifer.* Another contributing factor surely is that only three of the professionals in this study had taken a course in adolescent literature, and the majority of the English teachers admitted they did not read reviews of young adult fiction. Their formal educations not only didn't include a bibliography of the journals, most of their mentors had not legitimatized the study of this stepchild of literature, although both MLA and NCTE have recommended the course be included in English teaching programs.

The third trend is not nearly so obvious or significant, but two out of ten, *Sounder* and *Island of the Blue Dolphins,* were Newbery winners. Interviews revealed that even teachers and librarians having little respect for junior novels in general *will* promote award winners. Some kids reported having *Island of the Blue Dolphins* read aloud to them as many as four times in their short school histories.

The media, availability, and the awards accounted for outside influence, but told little about personal choice. Real insight came when I decided to look at adolescent literature as *popular culture.* Defining it in social terms rather than aesthetic, this was literature for a nonelite subculture—the young. The literary aspect of pop culture is that it crosses class lines. Perhaps a good comparison is with sports. Polo is a class sport; only the few can afford to play. It is high culture. Football crosses class lines; therefore, it is a part of our popular culture. *Finnegans Wake* is a class novel—only a few are adequately trained to comprehend [it]; *Gone with the Wind,* on the other hand, can be read by everyone.

Scholars of popular culture such as John Cawelti, University of Chicago, have been able to make inferences about groups by putting together their cultural products. They have also been able to isolate *forms* distinctive to types of popular literature. This is not a value judgment.

Sherlock Holmes stories are formula literature. The appeal of this formula literature seems to be:

1. People without training can learn how to react to the basic patterns; it becomes a game with all the rules known in advance.
2. Psychologically, it represents fantasy, dreams, or wish fulfillment—a search for gratification we can't get in our own lives.
3. It reaffirms the values of the culture. Less conventional—high culture—*Waiting for Godot, The Wasteland, Ulysses* QUESTIONS it.

Formula literature is *important* because it represents the way cultures have embodied both mythical archetypes and their own preoccupations in narrative form. These formulas of westerns, spy and mystery stories, best-sellers, science fiction . . . *adolescent literature* . . . represent a synthesis of several important functions in our modern culture taken over by the popular from religion. May I add that this view does not preclude judging the quality of writing, it just adds another dimension.

Barbara Martinec, University of Chicago researcher, using the four characteristic elements of the formula—type of situation, pattern of action, character roles and relationships, and setting—isolated the pattern of action in the adolescent novel. Use of this formula as a critical tool shed some light into three areas:

1. The novel's appeal for teenage readers
2. Adult concerns in our society
3. The development of the genre.

The appeal for teenage readers can perhaps best be understood by looking at the interrelated ideas suggested by the formula:

1. Immaturity (the basic problem of teenagers) is somehow to be equated with isolation from the group.
2. All problems can be solved and will be solved successfully.
3. Adults cannot help you much. They mean well but are ineffectual. True communication, true community is possible only with one's peers.
4. Solutions to problems are found gratuitously, either brought about by others or discovered by chance.
5. Maturity entails conformity. Acceptance equals happiness, and this is the true goal of life. The trick is to conform while maintaining one's own individual identity.

Perhaps these are not the ideas adults would choose to emphasize, but when compared with Havighurst's tasks of adolescent development, the value is more evident, so is the appeal. These tasks include learning new relationships with peers, achieving independence from parents, and acquiring self-confidence and a system of values of one's own. The adolescent novel formula is structured around these problems, and their apparent resolution in the patterned action of the formula helps to explain the popularity with young readers.

These books, in my opinion, don't solve kids' problems, but they offer a super means of escaping them for a couple of hours. The child whose parents don't trust her, hassle her about hours, clothes, keeping her room clean, can read *The Outsiders* and *Island of the Blue Dolphins* and identify with teenagers getting along on their own without adults at all. Or she can read *Lisa, Bright and Dark,* where the kids are all smarter and more capable than the adults. Or *Jennifer,* where it is the mother, not Jennifer, who has the problem. Or read *My Darling, My Hamburger,* where all the young character's problems are the fault of the adults. Or *Mr. and Mrs. Bo Jo Jones,* where a young couple go against their parents and make it. Or *Sounder,* where the young boy is better able to cope than his mother and father. If she's poor or black she can escape to quick and easy fame with Sister Lou and her soul brothers. If she doesn't have a boyfriend but would like one, *Fifteen* will confirm that eventually nice girls always win the "catch of the school." If she has to be home by ten, and the closest she's ever been to a commune or North Beach is a newsreel, she can trip with Alice through the counterculture, and when Alice dies from drugs, the young reader can be happy she was only a voyeur.

The second insight from the formula—*the adult social concerns reflected in these books*—seems to be a rich research area, hardly touched. In my more jaded moments I often felt my study probably revealed more of the adult's preoccupations than the kid's interest. At least they certainly do affect the form and development of the books. So I will discuss these issues jointly. From the 1940s to the 1970s the concerns moved:

1. from worrying about adolescents going steady and petting to fear of early pregnancy.
2. from concerns about cigarettes and alcohol to the fear of heroin, marijuana, and cocaine.
3. from concerns about materialistic status symbols—cashmere sweaters and convertibles—to fear of adolescents' rejection of most of our social systems.

I became interested in young adult fiction when the new realism had already been heralded. In 1969 George Woods, children's book review editor at the *New York Times,* said in spite of the new trend the books still plodded through the steps of the foxtrot—if not the minuet. But it wasn't the topics that were out of tune—all of those social issues of the sixties found their way into books about gangs, racial problems, and counterculture life-styles—it was the treatment. The book was still too often used to tell the young *how* to think. When we're fighting a popular war we push patriotism, pacifism when it isn't. Women are *the* minority of the seventies. Currently, it is difficult to find a female figure in adolescent fiction who gives a damn about the prom (even though a Skokie, Illinois, librarian recently told me *Cheerleader* was probably still the most popular [book] in her young adult collection). Their fictional mothers are plumbers, doctors, oil field roustabouts, most of them making it without daddy or his paycheck, while the majority of the readers probably still get their allowance from dad when he comes in on the 5:05—even if it isn't chic. Robert Peck's hero in *Millie's Boy* reverses the role and plans to work to send his Amy to medical school. Richard Peck's Super Doll rejects beauty contests, and the Cleavers' Littabelle Lee at six months survives a raging river flood, by sixteen proves she can bring home her own bacon, and finds a boy showing off his manhood a bit "tacky." Currently the women's issue in the genre resembles an adolescent girl's early experimentation with make-up—a bit heavy, applied rather thick, not yet artistic, but showing promise.

It almost seems an understatement to call Watergate a preoccupation. I wondered how this concern would appear in adolescent fiction. Perhaps I'm looking too hard, but the influence seems evident to me in *The Chocolate War* and *Some Sweet Day*. In both books evil is the strong force; the good are taken advantage of and evil is never really punished. If I'm correct this issue has affected the structure of the adolescent novel most dramatically. The racial issue changed the color of the protagonist, perhaps the setting, affected the dialog, but good deeds were still rewarded, evil characters punished. Not so in either *The Chocolate War* or *Some Sweet Day*.

I've been accused of being too harsh, too academic, my standards set too high. I come to you through a circuitous route—I worked my way through *Finnegans Wake, The Wasteland,* and *Waiting for Godot,* was and *am* excited by serious adult literature, but I'm equally excited by what is happening in young adult fiction and feel strongly that the standards must be high or too few teenagers will care enough about literature to ever wait for Godot. So let a convert—a late arriver—briefly summarize a long study. The results of my research indicate the following about reading interests of the young.

1. Adolescent literature written to interest the young generally reflects adults' social preoccupations. If we're lucky they come together—not always and *too* often the treatment is heavy. For example, the book I found universally loved by kids was *Mr. and Mrs. Bo Jo Jones.* I learned later it was originally written for adults and then marketed for kids.

2. Not all books written for the young follow the formula, but those that don't are the exception.

3. Kids aren't reading as much as they did a few years ago; girls are reading more adolescent novels than boys and the only ones indis-

criminately read by both are those adapted for the silver screen and cathode tube. And the readers are not generally twelve to sixteen; it's more like eight to thirteen. Teenagers are more often reading adult pop culture.

4. This is timely literature. The major breakdown in dissemination comes in two areas: English teachers, librarians, and parents are often uninformed about adolescent literature—a genre where more experimentation is probably taking place than in any other type of literature. Don't Tom Wolfe and his new journalism friends tell us the adult novel is dead? I don't believe him or them and I *know* junior novelists have not been intimidated. And I'm glad. But we need better hotlines to professionals influencing reading choices of the young. Finally, it takes too long for current books to reach the shelves.

But my study was completed a year ago, and this is timely literature. So I looked around for more recent studies, loaned current books to neighborhood kids and elicited their responses.

The most recent study I found was done by Hipple and Schullstrom, University of Florida, with an impressive sample of 308 schools. They also surveyed adults, but the lists are supposedly based on student feedback. Their categories were: Most Commonly Required Novels and Novels Most Often Identified as Favorites. The list of forty required novels contained three adolescent books—*The Outsiders, The Pigman,* and *Bless the Beasts and Children.* Nine on the fifty favorites list were adolescent; six of the nine were among the ten favorites in my study.

A few weeks ago I rounded up kids who hadn't escaped to The Cape, The Vineyard, or Lake Michigan, and asked them to read a few current books: *Watership Down, The Whys and Wherefores of Littabelle Lee, A Hero Ain't Nothin' but a Sandwich, The Chocolate War,* and *Some Sweet Day.* The books were current books that interest me. Admittedly these were University of Chicago Lab School kids and that might make a difference; however, I found in the more extensive study that geographic area didn't affect topic interest. Bo Jo Jones was as popular on the farms as the Gold Coast, but just read more often because fewer books were available. My recent sample of both kids and books was too small to be significant, but their responses were interesting:

> Littabelle Lee made them uncomfortable, but her Aunt Sorrow turned them on. Their comments included: Littabelle wouldn't have acted that way "way back" in Depression days. "They were trying to make us think a girl can do anything." These kids were so sophisticated. I tried to probe beyond what they thought they should say. Finally one fourteen-year-old professor's daughter said, "Boys would hate Littabelle and well, I couldn't identify much with her because she couldn't get married and feel as she did and I want to get married!"

Almost universally they liked *A Hero Ain't Nothin' but a Sandwich*

—not for the reasons I predicted, such as the unique multiviewpoint narration, but they liked Butler Craig, the stepfather who never really lost faith in Benjie, the drug addict. They all tuned in to Benjie's mother's thinking his friend was a better boy than he was, and all told stories about *their* friends their mothers thought were so nice, but *if they only knew*. All of my subjects just refused to talk about the adult sensuality. It was evident that this was too close to their parents' sexual relationships, which they didn't wish to discuss.

I expected and got a strong reaction to *The Chocolate War* and *Some Sweet Day*, especially to *The Chocolate War*, but again not where I had anticipated. They could accept adults' being evil with no problem, but they objected to kids' being evil. One girl kept saying three hundred kids would not have shown up to see that sadistic fight at the end of the book; some of the kids would have stopped it. Poor little Billy Budd. Wouldn't we like to think she is right, Golding wrong in *Lord of the Flies*, and that the young are basically innocent and good.

Watership Down was my real intrigue. When that book arrived— 426 pages about rabbits—I thought the entire Macmillan staff had lost their reason. When I realized it was being marketed for young adults, I was certain of it. No teenage hero, no obvious teenage problem, a multileveled plot, symbols, and *it was too long*. . . . But I read it, liked it, and found kids were reading it and liking it too. Macmillan asked me to write a teacher's guide for it, so I had the opportunity to talk to Richard Adams about his book. He said he wrote it for his teenage daughters, but wanted it to be a "proper" novel like *Wuthering Heights* was a proper novel, with character action growing out of personality. Everything he said sounded like a proper novelist writing a proper novel. But then I asked him if he thought it realistic for none of the characters—rabbits—to be killed in their freedom flight. He replied, "Yes, I know, but my daughter Juliet wouldn't hear of having any of the rabbits she loved die."

So kids in Chicago can't accept that teenagers could be evil and kids in England can't accept death of those they love. Perhaps the formula shouldn't change; perhaps young adult literature should remain escape literature, a way station, a super way to fantasize, dream, play a game, and be reassured. But it will . . . the question is how?

The evolution of a literary genre always seems so logical when viewed in retrospect. The piecemeal steps lock neatly into a crescendo. The gifted writers who took an avant garde tack are heralded for breaking into the new epoch and the second-rate writers who flirted with deviant styles or topics fall into convenient obscurity. But what of tomorrow in adolescent literature? Were the sixties and early seventies simply a watershed before the Watergate? Has our government perhaps created the first generation of European cynics in America's adolescent battalions? Will *Go Ask Alice* be yesterday's cold tea? What fiction, if any, will interest, delight, inspire, or shock those human beings invading their teens today? . . . I side for the moment with John Updike, who said in a recent interview:

"I have more faith than ever in fiction. I really think it's the only way to say a lot of things. To capture the mermaid live, it's the only net we have."
Mermaid beware!

NOTE

1. R. J. Havighurst, *Developmental Tasks and Education.* (University Committee on Human Development, Publications [Chicago: Univ. of Chicago Pr., 1949]).

Growing Up Real: YA Literature Comes of Age

Kenneth L. Donelson

I deeply believe in adolescent literature, with all its limitations and all its strengths. I did not come easily or early in my professional life to my enthusiasm for it. In fact I was a college-graduate snob about Literature. And why not? I had a B.A. in English and an M.A. in that most practical field for a would-be secondary-school English teacher, eighteenth-century English literature, with an even less practical master's thesis on an obscure late eighteenth-century English sentimental dramatist. Leaving college and heading for a small Iowa high school, I was properly sanctified, and I knew how to save all my students through great literature. Unhappily, I did not know how to reach any of my students with any literature.

I am enthusiastic about young adult books, but I believe we all need historical perspective to judge today's trends and themes. We need to recognize that adolescent literature did not begin a few years ago with Paul Zindel's *The Pigman,* nor did it begin with Mary Stolz's earlier *To Tell Your Love,* nor did it begin in the 1940s with Maureen Daly's *Seventeenth Summer.* Nor did it even begin in the early 1930s with the appearance of the first of the many *Nancy Drews.* To determine what changes, if any, in themes or trends have taken place in this literature over the course of the last few years, we might briefly note some of the popular or "good" young adult novels of the 40s and 50s.

Reprinted by permission from *Wilson Library Bulletin* 52, no. 3:241–47 (Nov. 1977). Copyright © 1977 by The H. W. Wilson Co.

Top of the Pops, 1940–60

In 1959 Steve Dunning reported on a survey of fourteen librarians who rated some "outstandingly popular" adolescent novels of the time.[1] The top ten were Maureen Daly's *Seventeenth Summer,* Henry Gregor Felsen's *Hot Rod,* Betty Cavanna's *Going on Sixteen,* Rosamund Du Jardin's *Double Date,* Walter Farley's *The Black Stallion,* Sally Benson's *Junior Miss,* Mary Stolz's *The Sea Gulls Woke Me,* Du Jardin's *Wait for Marcy,* James Summers's *Prom Trouble,* and John Tunis's *All-American.* The librarians ranked the most popular writers for young people as Betty Cavanna, Rosamund Du Jardin, Henry Gregor Felsen, Anne Emery, Mary Stolz, Maureen Daly, James Summers, John Tunis, and Amelia Walden, in that order.

In Dunning's doctoral dissertation that same year, the author rated thirty adolescent novels on qualities of style, structure, characterization, theme, and adult role/adult-adolescent relationships and determined the top eleven to be Maureen Daly's *Seventeenth Summer,* Mary Stolz's *The Sea Gulls Woke Me* and *To Tell Your Love,* Anne Emery's *Going Steady,* Henry Gregor Felsen's *Two and the Town,* Jessica Lyon's *This My Desire,* Betty Cavanna's *A Girl Can Dream,* Felsen's *Street Rod,* Don Stanford's *The Red Car,* Betty Cavanna's *Going on Sixteen,* and John Tunis's *All-American.*[2]

Only two years later Dorothy Petitt examined the qualities of literary excellence in her doctoral dissertation. She submitted a list of adolescent novels to twenty-eight reviewers, librarians, and teachers who selected what they believed was the best of adolescent literature. Their top twelve included Esther Forbes's *Johnny Tremain,* Marjorie Kinnan Rawlings's *The Yearling* (hardly an adolescent novel), Maureen Daly's *Seventeenth Summer,* Mary O'Hara's *My Friend Flicka,* James Street's *Good-Bye, My Lady,* Mildred Walker's *Winter Wheat,* Paul Annixter's *Swiftwater,* Carol Brink's *Caddie Woodlawn,* Eric Knight's *Lassie, Come Home,* Margot Benary-Isbert's *The Ark,* Mary Stolz's *Ready or Not,* and Iola Fuller's *The Loon Feather.*[3]

Given the tone and tenor of all but a few of these winners of the 1940s and 1950s—notably novels by Maureen Daly, Mary Stolz, Esther Forbes, and John Tunis—it would have been difficult to foresee the quality, subject matter or points of view of adolescent novels that were to appear in only a few years, and it would have been impossible to have predicted the literary and psychological achievements of writers for young people today.

By the 1950s certain taboos had been clearly established for adolescent novels—no early or forced marriages; no pregnancy outside marriage; no drugs, alcohol, or smoking; no profane or obscene language; no deaths; almost no ethnic references; no school dropouts unless as object lessons; no divorce; no sense of the ambivalent cruelty and compassion of young people; no alienation of young people from society or family; no sexuality or sensuality. Sometimes one or more of the above was used to point out a moral lesson. Some of the better writers worked their ways around the no-no's, but most authors accepted the taboos, perhaps because they approved, perhaps because they knew they would otherwise remain unpublished, perhaps because they were accustomed to working within the confines.

The values and moral stances of many earlier adolescent books do seem simplistic and unreal today, but the values are clear, moral, and always on the side of the angels. These books repeatedly emphasized that life is inherently good for the diligent worker who takes school and work and athletics seriously; that a virtuous life is not just its own reward, but certain evidence of psychological and perhaps financial riches to come here on Earth and later in Heaven; that adult interests like sex and marriage must be left to adults; that young people who hearkened to these tales will probably grow to be parents like those in Anne Emery's novels; that fast actions, fast driving, fast dates, and fast marriages will surely be regretted; and that good boys and girls will accept society's rules without question, for society is, in the final analysis, always right.

"Ain't She Sweet?"

A certain saccharine didacticism pervaded most adolescent novels of the 1940s and 1950s, often reflected in girls' books, with the young heroine pleading with her mother for permission to do something forbidden by the morals of the time. This might be dating a wild young man, befriending an old man, joining a high school sorority, or attending an all-night dance.

Mother clearly does not approve, and early in this type of book, she is almost sure to say, "Please, Honey, don't do ———. You won't like it, but I won't stop you because I love and trust you. Besides, I know you'll finally come to your senses. But you'll have to find out for yourself." Honey then proceeds to do what she wants anyway (if she didn't, there wouldn't be any book), and the plot complications unfold until by the end of the book Honey has repented and Mother is almost sure to say: "Now, Honey, you do understand what I meant, but I'm glad you found out for yourself. You've grown up, and I love and trust you even more."

Anyone interested in examining the kind of book popular then, but almost outlandishly out-of-date now, should read Emery's *Sorority Girl,* Du Jardin's *Senior Prom* (or anything else by Du Jardin, since they all look alike and read alike), Stanford's *The Red Car,* or Felsen's *Hot Rod.*

Unhappily, many of the criticisms leveled at adolescent literature were legitimate vis-à-vis these older novels. Worse, these criticisms are still being leveled, even though the novels have changed. Let me quote just two of the more celebrated comments about the so-called "trash" literature or "kiddie" literature.

> If I were asked for a list of symptoms pointing to what is wrong with American education and American culture, or to the causes for the prolongation of American adolescence, I should place high on the list the multiplication of books designed for readers in their teens. . . . The teenage book, it seems to me, is a phenomenon which belongs properly only to a society of morons.[4]
>
> At present, many junior writers are busily grinding out thinly fictionalized tracts on such subjects as brotherhood and the evils of teenage alcoholism. Tendentious, sentimental, stereotyped, and often wretchedly written, most junior fiction is literature only in the broadest sense of the term. Its chief *raison d'être* is that it offers reading to the young which their elders approve.[5]

I can be charitable and even sympathetic to critics of adolescent literature prior to perhaps 1965 or so, for much of it was third-rate or worse, although that charge can be leveled at most best sellers, science fiction, mysteries, translations, and whatever. I would be far more impressed by contemporary attacks on this genre if I had even the slightest feeling that critics had read Kin Platt's books or those of Laurence Yep, Rosa Guy, M. E. Kerr, or John Donovan. Either the critics judge adolescent literature as though it were still being written exclusively by Betty Cavanna *et al.*, or they subject it to that highest form of critical detachment: total and sublime ignorance.

Favorites of the Seventies

But what are the popular and good adolescent novels of our time, the 1970s? As former editor of the *Arizona English Bulletin,* I devoted two issues to adolescent literature, the first in April 1972, the second in April 1976. For both issues teachers were polled to determine what adolescent novels they would recommend for both literary value and appeal. The results suggest that a quite different kind of adolescent novel is being produced, a novel less worried about taboos, closer to touching the reality of young peoples' lives, less concerned with pandering to obvious and superficial needs, and rarely condescending to its readers.

The 1972 top ten were recommended by approximately one hundred English teachers and included Susan Hinton's *The Outsiders,* Paul Zindel's *The Pigman* (these two were far ahead of the other eight), Ann Head's *Mr. and Mrs. Bo Jo Jones,* Frank Bonham's *Durango Street,* Glendon Swarthout's *Bless the Beasts and Children,* Howard Fast's *April Morning,* Maia Wojciechowska's *Tuned Out,* Conrad Richter's *Light in the Forest,* Robert Lipsyte's *The Contender,* and Zindel's *My Darling, My Hamburger.*

The top ten in 1976 were recommended by nearly two hundred teachers and included Robert Cormier's *The Chocolate War,* Hinton's *The Outsiders,* Zindel's *The Pigman,* Robert Newton Peck's *A Day No Pigs*

Would Die, Alice Childress's *A Hero Ain't Nothin' but a Sandwich,* Swarthout's *Bless the Beasts and Children,* Bette Greene's *Summer of My German Soldier,* M. E. Kerr's *Dinky Hocker Shoots Smack,* Head's *Mr. and Mrs. Bo Jo Jones,* and *Go Ask Alice.*

To the 1976 top ten, I would like to add other widely recommended titles that seem to me at least slightly daring and even iconoclastic, titles like Isabelle Holland's *The Man without a Face,* Rosa Guy's *The Friends,* William Sleator's *House of Stairs,* Kerr's *Is That You, Miss Blue?,* Judy Blume's *Forever,* Norma Klein's *Mom, the Wolf Man, and Me,* Sandra Scoppettone's *Trying Hard to Hear You,* Paula Fox's *The Slave Dancer,* Kin Platt's *Headman,* and Jean Renvoize's *A Wild Thing,* books that with one exception I genuinely admire.

But what is a *good* adolescent novel? Today that is much the same question as what is a good *novel.* Obviously, they are not all of one piece. A good novel does not allow us to feel comfortable or complacent, although there may be moments of comfort or humor. It engages us and forces us to see ourselves and other people and the state and nature of humanity a little more perceptively. The good novel leads us to see truth or truths, and it may even, rarely, permit us moments of stark and naked revelation or epiphany, moments of honest and frightening awareness of ourselves, what is in us and outside us and even beyond us. A good novel respects its audience, neither condescending to it nor pandering to the lowest common denominator of taste or intelligence. It gives the reader a sense of satisfaction, not that all things are right or noble or good, but that the book is occupied with the honest and the real.

Four Essential Themes

I believe there are four themes in good adolescent novels today, all facets of reality and honesty, all themes of literature, adolescent or adult.

First, the theme of humanity's essential and eternal loneness. Each of us has an internal and lasting need to find out who and what we are, not to accept ourselves as we are (surely a first step, but a dishonest stopping place), but to enable us to aim at some higher level. We can be part of something with someone else, but we can never truly be with or of anyone else. That is a frightening concept to accept, we are all so willing to lean on others, but it is finally one we must accept. If this theme is treated in *King Lear* and *The Enemy of the People* and *Crime and Punishment,* so is it in fine contemporary adolescent novels like Kin Platt's *Headman,* M. E. Kerr's *If I Love You, Am I Trapped Forever?,* Mary Stolz's *Leap before You Look,* and Ronald Lockley's *Seal-Woman.*

Second, the theme of our need for love and companionship. Perhaps because we have faced our loneness, we are driven to relate to other human beings, possibly desperately, possibly selfishly, possibly because we may ennoble ourselves through loving and caring. And love can frighten us or threaten us as much as loneness, for in some ways we can protect ourselves through loneness. But love involves commitment and forces us to a state of vulnerability, a spiritual nakedness we fear and desire. If that theme has led to literature like *Romeo and Juliet, Pride and Prejudice,* and *The Assistant,* it has also led to some good contemporary adolescent novels: Honor Arundel's *The Blanket Word,* Rosa Guy's *Ruby,* Isabelle Holland's *The Man without a Face,* and Patricia McKillip's *The Forgotten Beasts of Eld.*

Third, the theme of our need for hope and our need to search for a truth or truths. Perhaps this theme is born out of both our loneness and our need for love and companionship, because humanity is perpetually searching for something to believe in, for some truth or truths, in effect challenging the universe for some reason, some purpose, some thing that gives point and validity to existence. As Susan Hinton reminds us,

> teenagers know a lot today. Not just things out of a textbook, but about living. They know their parents aren't superhuman, they know that justice doesn't always win out and that sometimes the bad guys win. They know that persons in high places aren't safe from corruption, that some men have their price, and that some people sell out. Writers needn't be afraid that they will shock their teenage audience. But give them something to hang onto. Show that some people don't sell out, and that everyone can't be bought.[6]

And as Frances Hanckel and John Cunningham say,

> but librarians and others evaluating YA literature should demand more than a cold rendering of reality. Honesty must be combined with hope, a hope that is life-affirming and encourages the reader to consider and develop a workable moral philosophy.[7]

Just as the theme of hope and truth-searching is basic to literature like *Don Quixote, The Divine Comedy,* and Ellison's *Invisible Man,* so much adolescent literature also focuses on this motif, for example, Robert McKay's *Skean,* Vera and Bill Cleaver's *Dust of the Earth,* Sue Ellen Bridger's *Home Before Dark,* and Robert Cormier's *The Chocolate War.* Cormier's book deserves some comment here, for all too many people seem to regard it as pessimistic or cynical. Iris McIntyre, one of my graduate students, argued in an unpublished paper that it is a moral and necessary book for all students:

> What Cormier shows us, once we stop to think about what the novel means, is that goodness in this world with its attendant qualities of hard work, clean living, honesty, and courage displayed by individuals can only hope to survive provided that everyone else supports that good person. Morality, for Cormier, is a collective duty. We all share in the responsibility of cooperating with others to withstand the forces of evil. I can think of no more moral theme for a book, nor of one more necessary for young people and adults alike.

Fourth, the theme of our need for laughter. Perhaps because we are essentially alone, because love or companionship may be denied us or may prove elusive, because we eternally hope and search, we need laughter—not the sardonic mocking of others (although that, too, we occasionally need), but the ability to laugh openly and heartily with others and at ourselves. One of the great writers of swashbuckling tales popular in the 1920s and 1930s was Rafael Sabatini. He opened his best work, *Scaramouche*, with these words describing his hero: "He was born with a gift of laughter and a sense that the world was mad." We need laughter to stave off madness. As great literature has used different kinds of laughter so well in books like *The Adventures of Huckleberry Finn, Dead Souls*, and *Catch-22*, so has contemporary adolescent literature used humor to lighten or enlighten novels like Bruce Clements's *I Tell a Lie Every So Often*, John Donovan's *Family*, John Ney's, *Ox: The Story of a Kid at the Top*, and Robert Newton Peck's *A Day No Pigs Would Die*.

If a considerable body of today's adolescent literature seems promising, one trend disturbs me deeply. The old taboos, maintained until around 1960 or even later, may indeed have taken their toll of potentially good books, and when publishers and librarians relaxed taboos, better writers took up the new challenge and followed their characters (sometimes) into areas earlier hedged in or forbidden. Other, inferior, writers seemed delighted to stake out previously taboo social problems and write fictionalized social tracts introducing the same old characters (albeit with different names) over and over and little more. I think particularly of Jeannette Eyerly, whose books seem to have little to do with life and much to do with social ills and breaking of taboos—witness pregnancy in *A Girl Like Me*, abortion in *Bonnie Jo, Go Home*, suicide in *The Girl Inside*, drugs in *Escape From Nowhere*, and political involvement in *Radigan Cares*.

Get on the Bandwagon!

Some contemporary writers for adolescents worry too much about what teenagers want in books or what they *ought* to want, or they worry about letting kids know what the writer wishes he/she had known when he/she was young. These writers usually become trendy, very much "with-it" writers. Thus the irritation I feel about some recent books. I am not especially disturbed that they include sexual scenes or four-letter words *if* the diction and situations and ideas are organic, intrinsic, and legitimate parts of the novel. But too much seems extrinsic, inorganic, illegitimate, and inserted only to shock or to prove how relevant the book is.

I'm appalled when a dust jacket refers to any book as "relevant," "meaningful," or "viable," or any other such cant or jargon. The with-it books plague the field of adolescent novels today, and I find myself growing more antagonistic toward most books about teenage pregnancies, dope, alcoholic mothers, divorce, the supernatural, and sexual experiences, for all too many novelists are all too willing to hop onto the latest teenage-worry bandwagon. Obviously, a good book can be written about a trite subject or a serious theme. And most bandwagon novels are so dismal they can be ignored for obvious literary reasons. But some are by writers I have genuinely respected for their earlier books.

Norma Klein's *Mom, the Wolf Man and Me* and *It's Not What You Expect* deserve wide readership. Unhappily, her two recent books have focused on social problems and not on life: *Taking Sides*, with its worries about divorce and possible lesbianism, and *What It's All About*, with its worries about divorce and Vietnamese orphans.

I admired Judy Blume's *Deenie, It's Not the End of the World* and *Are You There, God? It's Me Margaret*, but her recent *Forever* is something else. It may have been written to show that teenage sexual affairs need not be incredibly painful and inevitably result in pregnancies, but the book's sexual explicitness seems forced and mechanical, almost as if she loaded a hypodermic needle with four-letter words and then frequently and arbitrarily injected them into the story. Rather than being an honest novel about sex today, *Forever* is reminiscent of a creaky Betty Cavanna or Anne Emery novel, with four-letter words injected here and there to create a very much with-it book for a with-it generation of girls. (Coincidentally, I'd been rereading Dorothy Johnson's short story, "A Man Called Horse," at the same time that I read *Forever*, and I wondered for a moment why Blume hadn't titled her book *A Penis Called Ralph*.)

The best adolescent novels, the most honest and realistic ones, do not come from a publisher bearing the loud banner of "I Am Explicit, I Am With-It, I Am About THE Important Modern Problem, I Will Shock, I Will Open Your Eyes." The best books of our time for young people have worried about serious and depressing things like reality. They have frequently been concerned with social ills, but they have almost always been quiet books like Zindel's *The Pigman*, Donovan's *Wild in the World*, Platt's *The Boy Who Could Make Himself Disappear*, Mohr's *Nilda*, Lyle's *Fair Day and Another Step Begun*, and Mazer's *A Figure of Speech*. These books have not screamed out for attention. They are very much of our time, but they are equally about humanity's eternal problems. In the most complimentary sense, they are not with-it, relevant, meaningful, or viable novels. Instead, they are honest and real novels about real human beings caught up in the real dilemmas we all face.

Adolescent novels and writers come and go, but if I could play Jimmy the Greek for one moment and advise you to lay money on ten contemporary writers for young people who will last for several years to come, perhaps longer, I'd bet on these people: Nathaniel Benchley, whose novels demonstrate an incredible versatility; Vera and Bill Cleaver, whose books always ring true and show more compassion than almost any other writers I know; Susan Cooper, whose five-part trilogy, now four-fifths completed, made me enjoy fantasy again; John Donovan, whose books seem to get better and better; Rosa Guy, whose *Ruby* and *The Friends* seem almost perfect; Isabelle Holland, whose *The Man without a Face* I admire inordinately; M. E. Kerr, whose books demonstrate compassion and honesty mixed with delightful humor; Patricia McKillip, whose *The Forgotten Beasts of Eld* mixes fantasy with love and honesty with reality; Mary Stolz (my favorite writer for adolescents), whose books, first and last, seem to me always to be most sensitive, introspective, and perceptive; and Laurence Yep, whose *Sweetwater* and *Dragonwings* make him a writer of quality and the brightest young prospect in adolescent fiction.

Coming of Age

Adolescent literature has grown in literary value over the years, and 1976 saw no diminution in growth. Of the many books published, five stand out particularly. Ruth Nichols's *Song of the Pearl* is about death, dreams, reincarnation, and hopes; I found it persuasive and beautifully written. Robert Newton Peck's *Hang for Treason* is about the Revolutionary War, growing up, and the generation gap—the best book he's written since *A Day No Pigs Would Die*. Robert McKay's *Skean* is about death, life, immorality, and the perpetual battle between forces that would rule the world and humanity; it has elements of mysticism, theology, adventure, love, and science fiction and is the single most intriguing (and sometimes most perplexing) experiment in adolescent literature I've read in several years. John Donovan's *Family* is about the great ape escape; it is exciting and often funny, making perceptive statements about humanity today and tomorrow—a magnificent book. Finally, my favorite was Rosa Guy's *Ruby,* about loneliness, love, parents, sisters, lesbianism, being black, and, above all, being human and having human needs.

Adolescent literature has been around long enough to have its share of detractors, but over the last five or ten years it has begun to come of age. It has become more honest and sensitive to the reality young people face. Even more important, adolescent literature has become more sensitive to the reality we all face, old and young alike. It has accepted the responsibility that makes writing become literature, the responsibility to tell what it means to occupy space on this troubled planet in these troubled times, to tell about our nature and its humanity, our stupidity and cupidity, but also our spirituality and our potential nobility.

NOTES

1. "The Most Popular Junior Novels," *Library Journal* 84:3885–87 (Dec. 15, 1959).
2. *A Definition of the Role of the Junior Novel Based on Analyses of Thirty Selected Novels* (Ph.D. dissertation, Florida State Univ., 1959).
3. *A Study of the Qualities of Literary Excellence Which Characterize Selected Fiction for Young Adolescents* (Ph.D. dissertation, Univ. of Minnesota, 1961).

4. J. Donald Adams, *Speaking of Books and Life* (New York: Holt, 1965), pp.250–51.
5. Harvey R. Granite, "The Uses and Abuses of Junior Literature," *The Clearing House* 42:337 (Feb. 1968).
6. "Teen-Agers Are for Real," *New York Times Book Review,* Aug. 27, 1967, p.29.
7. "Can Young Gays Find Happiness in YA Books?" *Wilson Library Bulletin* 50:528 (Mar. 1976).

Part 2

The Search for Self-Transcendence and the Chimera of Certainty

The search is what anyone would undertake if he were not sunk in the everydayness of his own life.

Walker Percy[1]

The curious traveller, or tourist, desiring novel experiences, makes the journey itself the object of his travel; he stands in contrast to the pilgrim, who travels to reach a desired goal, a homeland, a blessed place that lies at the end of his journey. Most people experience life in the contemporary world as tourists rather than as pilgrims, for few could say where they are destined, though they relish the trip.

M. Primavera, unpublished manuscript

I don't like anybody who isn't unsure of himself.

Woody Allen

The quotations cited above speak of life as a search. To the questing individual, society is valued only for what the searching self can find in it. The searching adolescent finds society wanting because it is seen to hinder rather than to help in the quest for personal transcendence. On the other hand, society, including its libraries, offers the materials for this desired self-transcendence. For each stage in teenage development, resources appropriate to needs must be identified.

A need for finding one's self vis-à-vis religion is basic to the forming of the teenager's spiritual identity. Why else have young people in contemporary American society turned to religious cults in such unprecedented numbers? This is the question James S. Gordon explores in "The

Kids & the Cults," and the question has an especially urgent ring after the events in Jonestown, Guyana. Gordon points to the shortcomings in society, the vacuousness that causes young people to turn to counterculture cults to satisfy certain needs which are too often unanswered within mainstream religions—the need for transcendent experience (expanded consciousness), for "family," for leadership and authority, for community, for a sense of mission. He cautions against our tendency toward viewing the motives of the young as evidence of psychopathology or "childishness," when the quest "for deeper experience and a more meaningful way of life is one that we should encourage and guide. . . ." The "larger problem," he argues, is "with a society that prepares them so poorly for this quest and which provides so little guidance in it."

Authors recognize that cults may have a legitimacy derived from the natural limitations of any social order but are themselves subject to disorder. A persistent problem in the minds of many commentators is the difficulty of distinguishing "between exploitive or dangerous cults and genuine religious groups or benign alternative life-style communities"— really an old dilemma in a new guise: how to reconcile the sometimes contradictory claims of social order and individual freedom.[2]

With Lawrence Rakow's bibliographic essay, "Meditation and Spiritual Practice," the search for values expressed through exploration into drugs, the occult, and mysticism is related directly to books and reading for young adults. Rakow also brings into his discussion the recent scientific thought on the "bimodal theory of human consciousness"—or "right- and left-brain theory," as it is also called. (See also G. Lynn Nelson's essay, "Zen and the Art of English Teaching," in part 7.) Rakow brings out the positive dimension of exploration, via drugs, into "enhanced" states of consciousness, gives detailed attention to the writings of Carlos Castaneda and their influence on the young, and finally presents an annotated bibliography of nonfiction books on non-Western philosophy and religious teachings, an area of knowledge wherein many of us may need to expand our minds.

With "A Retrospective Look at *The Catcher in the Rye*," Gerald Rosen continues the theme of the influence of Eastern thought. He suggests that an underlying reason why *Catcher* was banned in some schools lies in its radical expression of "disappointment with American society." The parallels he draws between the story of Holden Caulfield and the story of the Buddha's life illuminate the deep level of spiritual concern in the novel. He also helps us to understand Holden's fear of sex (an aspect of his disgust with a society where human relationships are infected by the values of the "market place" as well as a symptom of his inability to accept time and change), and shows how his obsession with death, rot, and decay is a reflection of the repression of these realities in polite, middle-class American culture. The essay convincingly relates the truths of Buddhism to Holden's existential situation; since so many young people see themselves in Holden, we come away with a deeper appreciation of the reasons why so many of them have been drawn to Eastern thought.

Peter Scharf's "Moral Development and Literature for Adolescents" spotlights the stages of the adolescent's development toward maturity of moral judgment, drawing upon the theory of Laurence Kohlberg. Having carefully defined the stages, Scharf then identifies the kinds of literature that youths will appreciate at each step of their development. [Those familiar with the thought of Thomas Carlyle may see a certain parallel between the last two of Scharf's stages—namely the "relativism and nihilism of middle adolescence" and the final stage of "affirmation"—and the ideas of Carlyle's *Sartor Resartus* (1833), where the "Everlasting Nea" and the "Center of Indifference" are followed by the "Everlasting Yea."]

A nonconventional source for values is examined in Gordon Stevenson's "On Constructing Useful Realities: The Uses of Popular Culture in the Uncertain World of the Adolescent." He outlines possible approaches to popular culture, describes five possible perspectives on it, and then presents a series of "exhibits" that are meant to challenge our imaginations to consider the significance of the "multiple realities" implied in the bizarre reports of flying saucers, the "world" of Barbara Cartland's novels, the fantasies of working class girls about marriage, the fantasies inspired by Barbie dolls, and underwear portraying comic "super heroes." He asks us to compare all of these phenomena, in their "cultural functions," to the "books, magazines, films, and sound recordings" circulated by libraries. Stevenson's conclusion centers on the enormous importance of the librarian's awareness of the impact of the "popular culture environment" upon young adults. He implies, indeed, that popular culture is a wellspring of creativity, "of fantasy and experience," which can open up perspectives on "reality" that go beyond the confines of a person's "cultural heritage."

NOTES

1. *The Moviegoer* (New York: Knopf, 1961), p.13.
2. Another article devoted to explaining the popularity of the occult is "The Occult Today: Why?" by Gary E. Kessler [*Intellect* 104:171–74 (Nov. 1975)]. Pointing to the omnipresence throughout history of occultism, he identifies it with the " 'alternative reality' tradition of the West" and explains its essence as "the personal and immediate realization of the unity of opposites." Overall, his essay gives a positive outlook on occultism, articulating the element of "eschatological vision" (vision concerned with ultimate or "last" things) contained within it.

The Kids and the Cults

James S. Gordon

During the past eighteen months I have been a participant-observer in meetings of the new religious cults of the 1970s. I have attended a weekend workshop of the Unification Church, visited and eaten in the Ashrams, centers, coffee-houses, and communes of the Krishna Consciousness movement, the Divine Light Mission, the Love Family, and half a dozen other, smaller groups. I have met with young people in these groups, with parents who are deeply troubled by their children's membership, and with parents who are pleased by the changes they have seen in their children—their renewed sense of responsibility and their godliness. I have talked with young people who are very relieved to be out of these groups, and with young people who are puzzled or angered by their parents' attempts to coerce or cajole them into leaving. I have studied the theologies that these cults have constructed or adapted and considered the criticisms that have been leveled at them and at the cults themselves.

Historical Background

Many anthropologists and historians maintain that religious cults have always proliferated in times of social and cultural crisis, and in eras when the possibility of local or global destruction is or seems very real. It seems to me that the hundreds of thousands or, depending on who is estimating their numbers and what groups are included, the millions of people who have become involved in the religious cults of the late 1960s and 1970s *have* joined at just such a time.

Five years ago when I set out to understand the effects of the Vietnam war on junior high and high school students I was struck by an unexpected finding: again and again conversations about the war found their way back to the threat of world destruction. The devastation inflicted on Vietnam and the televised images of slaughter—especially the slaughter of children—insistently reminded my young friends of the possibility of their own destruction. It seemed to them that the mighty weapons unleashed on others—and the threat of still more powerful atomic ones—could and just might be turned on themselves.

Over the last fifteen years these kinds of fears and the sense of uncertainty they have produced have been continually stimulated. The debacle at the Bay of Pigs began, for the first time since World War II, to raise

Reprinted by permission of the author and publisher from *Children Today* 6:24–36 (July–Aug. 1977).

questions in the minds of America's young people about this country's military invincibility and moral authority. The Vietnam war threw these doubts and our vulnerability into bold relief. Enormous governmental effort could not convince a majority of the young that what seemed so obviously wrong to them was right.

The only movements to which young people could give their allegiance were those of opposition: an antiwar movement which perceived and condemned the United States as an imperialist monster, a counterculture which turned its back on all of our country's major institutions—schools, families, churches, businesses, professions—and sought to create a social system and world view apart from them.

A much publicized but nonetheless real gap grew between the older and younger generations. The nuclear families from which young people came, and to which they were supposed to look forward, felt tense, inadequate, and constraining. The schools—overcrowded and competitive— were experienced as irrelevant and oppressive and the goals for which they prepared the young—a career and social and financial success— seemed hollow.

With the end of the Vietnam war came the end of an era of unprecedented national prosperity. Too focused on one issue, too deracinated to grow beyond it, the antiwar movement evaporated. The counterculture, no longer able to draw nourishment from society's surplus, faded. But no new sense of national purpose or cultural community replaced these movements.

Many young people began to feel as disillusioned with their own collective action as with the society against which it was directed. Owing allegiance to no movement or guiding set of principles they, like their parents, became increasingly privatistic.

When they began to reach out from the isolation of their dormitory rooms and the insufficiency of their jobs to look for something more, for some way to make sense of their own feelings and the world around them, some of them wanted definite answers. Though many young people valued ideals and experiences of the 1960s, as expressed in the civil rights movement and certain social initiatives, they felt a need to inhibit their anarchistic questing with clear guidelines and firm structures. In the religious cults, which seemed to arise almost miraculously to meet their needs, they found both a confirmation of their private longings and a group structure which could help them overcome their isolation. In the web of exotic and highly rationalized theologies they discovered—and have tenaciously held onto—an unerring map, one that could guide them beyond the limitations and uncertainties of secular and political goals.

Needs and Answers

The search for transcendent experience. During the 1960s, psychedelic drugs opened what Aldous Huxley called "the doors of perception" to an unprecedented number of American young people. Aided by LSD, mescaline, peyote, psilocybin, and a host of other natural and chemical agents, and guided by such public figures as Timothy Leary, Richard Alpert, Allen Watts, Allen Ginsberg, and Carlos Castaneda, they began to discover what William James described seventy-five years ago as "potential forms of consciousness entirely different" from our normal waking consciousness. With the aid of psychedelic drugs they caught glimpses of a reality gorgeous and terrible beyond the routine of school or work, of a blissfulness which obliterated anxiety and aggression.

Parents, teachers, and the mental health establishment tended to dismiss these experiences as aberrant, drug-induced, or hallucinatory and in so doing they perpetuated the isolation and mistrust of those who had them. But the religious leaders of the 1970s and the ecstatic and prophetic traditions they drew on confirmed them. The rituals they practiced—prayer, mantras, abstinence—provided means to repeat and deepen these experiences; the organizations they created offered a context in which they could share and, in times of doubt, reinforce these experiences.

The search for family. The movements of the 1960s tacitly if not explicitly supplied a new kind of family to their members. The discredited authority of parents was replaced by a sense of brother- and sisterhood. Sometimes, as in the civil rights movement, it was difficult to achieve and hard to sustain; sometimes it seemed as easy to win as the smiles that long-haired youths, passing on the street, exchanged.

The religious cults of the 1970s have drawn on these feelings of fraternity and sorority, amplified them in the context of easily entered communal living situations, and reinforced them with emphatic ideological sanctions. The cults offer young people who are confused, troubled, temporarily homeless, or permanently drifting a welcome that is both unexpected and, in contemporary America, unprecedented.

If their attentions to potential converts seem synthetic to some observers, they nevertheless feel quite real and unaffected to lonely and searching young people. They are accepted—by saffron-robed, pigtailed Hare Krishnas, by smiling and conservatively dressed Moonies—in all their confusion and uncertainty. They are fed and housed without question or demand. At introductory *satsangs* or discussion groups their questions are patiently answered, their anxieties assuaged by sweet songs and enthusiastic testimony. In the houses they visit—and in which they may elect to live—they are taught to give and to receive solace, to share rather than to compete with one another.

Leadership and authority. During the last ten years, the failures of national political leadership and its abuses of authority have been mirrored in the absence of a guiding force or purpose in family life and in the shortcomings of religious, social, and academic leaders. Young people who were disillusioned with establishment leaders feared and mistrusted their own. The counterculture was suspicious of anyone who became too powerful or well known; the antiwar movement regularly cannibalized and calumniated those whom it had only recently followed; women resented men's dominance and men feared women's.

The young people who are joining the religious movements of the 1970s are in part reacting against this drift and seeking to fill the vacuum it left in its wake. Lacking experience of genuine leadership, increasingly fearful of an anarchy they sense as pointless and threatening, the young are easily attracted to those who manifest absolute conviction and certainty. In the cults, male-female relationships are generally stereotyped and dogmatically defined: women cook, clean, and care for children and they follow the men. The shifting uncertainties of relationships among equals are stabilized by patriarchal leaders who provide their followers with a never-ending stream of clear and generally divinely sanctioned directives.

The need for community. Contemporary sociologists have amply described the fragmenting effects of advanced industrial capitalism: the decline of the extended family, the radical separation between work and home life, the lack of contact among neighbors and the loneliness in our cities. One of the most obvious attractions of the cults is the sense of community they provide. Outside observers may find these communities to be artificial and jerry-built; they may argue that the price of their formation is too great, that the rules are too arbitrary, the living conditions too harsh, the customs inherently bizarre. However, for cult members these idiosyncrasies and hardships are a cement that binds and distinguishes them from "the outside world."

Cult members know that their personal and work lives form a seamless whole, that all the tasks they perform are at once personal and social. Every talent and chore—from cooking to child care, from postermaking to toilet cleaning and street solicitation—serves the greater good; the satisfaction of successful performance is amplified in the circle of communal appreciation.

In small cults this sense of integration is defined by a tight group of one or several neighboring houses. Members of larger religious cults are, in addition, part of a national or worldwide network: Unification Church members, followers of Krishna, or devotees of the Guru Maharaj Ji know that no matter where they may go they will never be alone, that in every large and many small cities they will find an open house and a warm welcome from coreligionists.

An overriding sense of mission. In addition to the feeling of belonging to a family and a community, each group offers its members the opportunity to take part in a uniquely valued, divinely sanctioned mission. This sense of mission dwarfs any disagreements and mutes ideological dispute and doubt. It gives cult members incentive to overcome personal hardship and the will to surmount attacks from the outside. Each obstacle is a challenge, a milestone which glorifies the journey; each attack is a reconfirmation of the group's correctness and of the outside world's lack of comprehension.

Some of the cults—like the tribal "Love Family" in Seattle—believe that their way of life is itself a witness. Members of tiny Christian fundamentalist communities feel that the way they live will bring grace and salvation to them and that it may also stimulate worshipful imitation by those who have "eyes to see and ears to hear." More actively proselytizing groups—the Unification Church is an obvious example although contemporary, nontheistic groups such as Erhard Seminars Training (est) and Transcendental Meditation (TM) exhibit some of the same messianic fervor—tend to see themselves as activist vanguards in the evolution of humankind, as divinely appointed healers of all the divisions which plague the earth.

Problems and Perspectives

Many of those who are opposed to the religious cults—parents of cult members, public prosecutors, mental health professionals, and leaders of traditional religions—have emphasized the innocence and naiveté of the young people who become involved with them, viewing them as victims of seduction and brainwashing by malevolent and acquisitive cult leaders. The parents' obvious concern, the strangeness of cult life and its profound and sometimes disturbing effects on young people all tend to make the critics anxious, arbitrary, and myopic. In public and private statements they call these young people "boys and girls" and continually speak of parental rights and responsibilities.

In so doing these critics obscure the fact that the overwhelming majority of young people in cults are past the age of eighteen and, thus, in our society, adults old enough to vote and marry and to fight and die in our wars. Even if we are concerned about their membership in cults, I think we must be wary of overemphasizing their youth and dependency and their parents' responsibility for them. Such descriptions lead too easily to a tendency to control all behavior that parents may deem unacceptable, irresponsible, or dangerous, and to institutionalization of that control.

Young people who are uncertain about their membership in cults or who want—but do not know how—to leave them, and parents who are concerned about their children, certainly deserve our attention. But if this attention is to be more than reaction, it must be tempered by a deep and respectful understanding of the needs that young people have, of the religious experiences they seek, and of the limited alternatives available to them in our society.

Anyone who wants to be helpful to these young people—and their parents—must also understand the family dynamics of which disagreements over cult membership may be but a part. The concerns of parents who want their child out of a cult are real and their opposition to the cult may be well founded, but these concerns and this opposition are also part of an ongoing series of interactions among family members. Removing an unwilling young person from a cult is sometimes a move in a continuing battle for control of that person's life. In the context of working with a family, the young person's choice can be understood as a step toward independence, as a covert expression of resentment against parents, or simply as an assertion of genuine religious commitment—or all of these, or none.

Many psychiatrists tend to focus on the pathological vulnerability of young people who have become involved in religious groups. They use such terms as "ego defects," "narcissism," and "schizophrenia" and hint at profound and generally pernicious neurophysiological changes that young people undergo, as a result of diet, prayer, and abstinence, in the course of their indoctrination. I think that emphasizing psychopathology is as much a mistake and is as demeaning to young people as dwelling on their "childishness."

Young people often do come to these religious groups during a period of heightened uncertainty, in a period of life characterized by anxiety about career, sexuality, intimacy, and the "meaning of life." But this uncertainty is a product of our society and an integral part of the extended period of youth that we in the industrialized West offer to people in their late teens and twenties. Our young people's search for deeper experience and a more meaningful way of life is one that we should encourage and guide, not diagnose and restrict.

I have met some young people who seemed profoundly, clinically, disturbed before they entered religious cults, as well as during their membership and after their departure. In some cases, membership in these groups has provided the young with a social context in which to resolve or transmute this disturbance. They feel, and to all appearances have become, more loving, productive and happy. In other cases, the belief systems and structures of these groups seem to have exacerbated the rigidity and defensiveness of these young people, to have made them ever more fearful and contemptuous of those with whom they disagree. But even in such instances I think that we must be extremely wary of treating young people as "cases," of insisting that we, whether parents, "deprogrammers," clergymen, lawyers, or mental health professionals, know better than they what is good for them. By what right, moral or legal, do we turn people who are content with what they are doing—if they are harming no one else—into prisoners of deprogrammers or patients in mental hospitals?

Critics argue that the cults pursue and proselytize young people who are in a state of heightened vulnerability—lonely people in restaurants, students just entering or leaving college or about to take exams, solitary travellers in bus stations. Cults are accused of not telling prospective members that they are a religious group or that members may eventually have to submit to strict discipline. It is said that their intense indoctrination—long hours of lecture, prayer, meditation, strenuous physical activity, and continual group pressure—is a form of "brainwashing" and coercion, that drugs are used to restrict members' freedom, and that a cult's purpose is basically financial or political, not religious.

Some of these characterizations are true of some cults some of the time, but none of them is true of every cult and all of them should be looked into far more thoroughly before our attitudes toward and responses to cults become fixed by pejorative stereotypes. Unorthodox, heretical, and antiestablishment religious groups have always been an easy prey to irresponsible inquisitions and persecutions. Too often those who have charged the new religious cults with these abuses—and those who order "legal conservatorship" and mental hospitalization for young people belonging to cults—have no firsthand knowledge or solid evidence about what a particular cult is really like and what its actual practices are.

Legal redress already exists for the most flagrant abuses. A young person held against his or her will can charge a cult with kidnapping; cults which use their tax exempt status to engage in political activities can be investigated; those which drug unwilling members may be prosecuted for assault, and those which solicit funds for nonexistent projects for fraud.

Other practices which are condemned in cults have gone unremarked in traditional religious organizations, which, of course, were themselves once cults. Some of these traditional organizations have acquired far more property and influence and they have at times used them for more destructive purposes than today's cults may ever accomplish. The proselytization that even the most intrusive cults do is only a shadow of that which American missionaries abroad have engaged in.

Still other practices presently fall into a borderland between the illegal and the immoral. People should be protected—perhaps by more stringent application of fraud laws—from deceptive and incomplete information about a cult's aims, methods, and expectations and its connections to other, nonreligious groups. But in making or applying such laws, we have to remember their limitations.

It is hard to see how the indoctrination that prospective cult members voluntarily submit to can be called brainwashing—a term with connotations of imprisonment. And it is harder still to imagine what kind of law can be applied to those who believe that they will receive "knowledge" in a single afternoon with one of the Guru Maharaj Ji's mahatmas or "get it" in two weekends of Erhard Seminars Training. We can hedge the quest of the young, and the not so young, with legal sanctions, but these sanctions will only protect not strengthen or guide them.

I think that if we are really concerned about our young we should devote the greater part of our energy to learning from the choices they are making. We should regard their disagreements and disaffections from us as a critique of the way we—as families, communities, and a society— are. If so many young people believe that salvation can be mass produced, merchandised, and franchised, then we can only conclude that our society has predisposed them to believe it. If so many join the first group that promises them "a family," then perhaps we ought to reexamine the way we, as family members, live. If the cults they join are dogmatic and Manichaean—splitting the universe into the good cult and the evil world —if they offer rigid and simple solutions to problems that seem complex and subtle, we must ask where our young people have acquired a habit of mind that makes this so attractive.

The larger problem is not with the young people's quest for meaning or transcendence or community or even with the cults that have arisen, for the time being, to satisfy it, but with a society which prepares them so poorly for this quest and which provides so little guidance in it. In a nation which provided a sense of community and purpose to its young, it would hardly be necessary to find a sense of mission elsewhere. In a society that regarded all life as sacred and encouraged the deep inwardness of prayer and meditation that are not simply rote or narcotic, neither young nor old would be so naive about enlightenment nor so slavish to those who promise to bring it to them.

Meditation and Spiritual Practice: A Selective YA Bibliography

Lawrence Rakow

Drugs, the Occult, and Mysticism

What is the role of the school or young adult librarian in answering the most basic of human questions: Who am I? Why was I born? Why must I die? Spurred on, perhaps, by the 1962 Supreme Court decision forbidding prayer in the public schools, many administrators and teachers have opted to reject the entire concept of religious studies in the classroom or, as a concession to the students interested in this area, offer such fare as

Reprinted from Top of the News 33:352-57 (Summer 1977).

"The Bible as Literature." While the promotion of any specific religious practice or system of thought in a public school setting is considered an infringement of the rights of all students, *spiritual* education goes beyond standard religious, philosophic, or materialistic values and investigates that which is the basis for them all: the nature of human existence.

Recently we have witnessed a progression in young adult interest from the drug experience, through the occult, to Eastern religion, mysticism, and meditation; each step in this process is a logical progression from the preceding stage of development. The first of these, the drug revolution of the mid-sixties, was a manifestation of the inborn need to change our consciousness, to strive for enlightenment. Altered states of consciousness, whether achieved through drugs or meditation or mysticism, and the natural and artificial methods used to induce them are neither new nor unique to this culture. Every society throughout history has discovered these tools and claimed them as its own, integrating them into its own religious and secular environment.

Rationalists may attack these enlightened states as socially unproductive flights from reality, yet contemporary scientific inquiry tends to substantiate and validate the existence of nonordinary levels of awareness. Robert Ornstein, a research scientist at the Langley Porter Neuropsychiatric Institute and editor of *The Psychology of Consciousness,* has gathered evidence which indicates a bimodal theory of human consciousness in which the right and left hemispheres of the brain are related to different kinds of thought processes. Ornstein's investigation has led others to comment that:

> Rational thinking, associated with the left hemisphere of the brain, is characteristically verbal, logical, analytic, and linear. Intuitive thinking, associated with the right hemisphere, is creative, holistic, visual, and pattern-oriented. . . . Philosophies of education which do not recognize the importance of developing right-brain hemisphere potentials are seriously underestimating the human capacity for learning.[1]

The widespread use of psychotropic drugs provides empirical evidence to countless young people that human consciousness is a variable and not a fixed condition. The expression of that realization is subject to change; proper guidance can lead to the discovery of alternative, nonchemical methods of consciousness enhancement. Repression and denial of the drive to enhance consciousness could be devastating, as Andrew Weil points out in *The Natural Mind:*

> To attempt to thwart this drive would probably be impossible and might be dangerous. True, it exposes the organism to certain risks, but ultimately, it could confer psychic superiority. To try to thwart its expression in individuals and in society might be psychologically crippling for people and evolutionarily suicidal for the species. I would not want to see us tamper with something so closely related to our curiosity, our creativity, our evolution, and our highest aspirations.[2]

Not all drug experimentation is motivated by such lofty ideals as enhancing consciousness; much of it is characterized by excess founded in the lack of respect for hallucinogenic substances and the absence of a firm theoretical base upon which to interpret the drug-induced experience. Simple criticism of contemporary drug usage, however, misses the point; it is the initial drive, the innate desire to alter consciousness, rather, that deserves our attention.

The psychic powers displayed by devotees of the occult are natural areas of investigation for those who have experienced similar levels of awareness through drug use. Such interest on the part of young adults is usually satisfied vicariously; while large numbers of young people actively engage in drug experimentation, their interest in magic, witches, ghosts, exorcism, sorcery, et al., is almost exclusively confined to their reading, film viewing, and talking about the subject. Whatever the reasons for this, the occult sciences have failed to offer a practical means of liberation to very many young people; the continuing interest in the field is probably more flash than substance. The supernatural offers adventure and a search for personal power through a nonchemical vehicle, but it lacks the sense of "community" that young people find in the drug subculture. Both the adventure of the search for personal power and the sense of "community" are found, even transcended by many, in mysticism and meditation at the spiritual stage of development.

Why has this quest for self-knowledge been such a basic theme in human history? Three reasons have already been touched upon. First, the search itself, whatever its goal, offers a unique experience in itself, in which the extraordinary effort and determination required of the aspirant are universally regarded as beneficial and growth-enhancing. Second, the spiritual community meets social needs by providing both companionship and assistance on the way. Third, if, as Andrew Weil suggests, the desire for self-realization represents an inborn, uncontrollable drive, its presence may have less to do with will or desire than with biology or evolutionary readiness.

Enlightenment and Inner Development

Enlightenment is at the core of the spiritual experience, the essence of which remains unaltered from culture to culture. Variously referred to as the Void, the Clear Light, Suchness, Wholeness, being One with the Universe, or Egolessness, the enlightenment experience transcends such words, and any attempt to describe it in a word or two usually fails. Yet we know of its existence from the writings and sayings of the great religious teachers, and from the experiences of students who have taken their teachings to heart:

> In my own search for that which matters, I found . . . so many years ago, a full confirmation of my intuition that I, like every other human be-

ing, contain a hidden but incorruptible core. It is hidden underneath immense layers of confusion, neurosis, and delusion. Yet it is our true center. When they speak of enlightenment, satori, awakening, liberation, the masters refer to the breakthrough, the full awareness, the realization of this hidden core, this mysterious ingredient that I share with all beings, but that is unattainable by intellectual effort.[3]

No contemporary student of inner development has captured the attention of the young adult audience as has Carlos Castaneda. Little is known about Castaneda's life prior to 1960, the result of a deliberate attempt on the part of Castaneda to (in his teacher's words) "erase personal history." In 1960, Castaneda was an anthropology student at the University of California. While gathering information on native American use of medicinal herbs, he was introduced to Juan Matus, a Yaqui Indian from northern Mexico, who knew a great deal about ritual use of peyote. After meeting Matus, Castaneda began an eleven-year period of apprenticeship to Matus in which Matus instructed Castaneda in the art of sorcery and taught him the way of a "man of knowledge."

The author's experiences during those years are related in Castaneda's four books: *The Teachings of Don Juan: A Yaqui Way of Knowledge* (1968): *A Separate Reality: Further Conversations with Don Juan* (1971); *Journey to Ixtlan: The Lessons of Don Juan* (1972); and *Tales of Power* (1974). The books' initial popularity among many young adults must have been due in large measure to the author's descriptions of drug-induced states of nonordinary reality. Ironically, Castaneda's insistence upon rational interpretation of his drug experiences led him to misinterpret the real meaning of Don Juan's teachings and to place greater emphasis upon the role of hallucinogenic drugs than they rightly deserved:

> It became evident to me that my original assumption about the role of psychotropic plants was erroneous. They were not the essential feature of the sorcerer's description of the world, but were only an aid to cement, so to speak, parts of the description which I had been incapable of perceiving otherwise. My insistence on holding on to my standard version of reality rendered me almost deaf and blind to Don Juan's aims. Therefore, it was simply my lack of sensitivity which had fostered their use.[4]

Only after several years of rigorous study did Castaneda reexamine the teachings in light of an extraordinary nondrug experience which brought him to the verge of seeing and the end of his apprenticeship. Then he realized that drugs at best represent an incidental aid to perception but are an unreliable method of self-discovery. This coincided with a similar realization among many young people who abandoned chemical experimentation and began to seriously study traditional Eastern disciplines as an alternative to drugs, a movement which continues to grow in the late 1970s.

Notes on the Bibliography

The bibliography is limited to books on non-Western philosophical and religious teachings; teachings of several important fundamentalist Christian and Jewish sects are not included. I encourage others to develop additional bibliographies in these areas of interest; they are sorely needed by those serving young adults.

The recent glut of titles in the field has led to some confusion for those involved in the book-selection process. To clarify matters, a book's practical rather than theoretical emphasis was a primary criterion for inclusion in the bibliography. For example, while Pirsig's *Zen and the Art of Motorcycle Maintenance* is an extraordinary autobiography popular with young adults, its emphasis upon philosophy rather than practice is one of the reasons it does not appear in the bibliography. Primary sources and works by recognized authorities account for many titles: introductions to various traditional disciplines and current spiritual movements account for others. A few materials designed specifically for teachers and librarians are included.

Young adult patrons often indicate their confusion concerning spiritual paths in their requests for assistance. For example, Yoga, TM, Zen, and Sufism are all examples of movements that use "meditation." To which do we direct the young adult who wants to learn about meditation? We owe it to those we serve to investigate these very different areas in sufficient depth to be able to guide them to the materials they need. As librarians, we have an opportunity to play a central role in what many persons believe is a pivotal evolutionary act of development. With due respect to Mr. Kipling, East and West may well first meet on our shelves and in the minds of our patrons.

Books

Akins, W. R., and Nurnberg, H. George. *How to Meditate without Attending a TM Class.* Amjon/Crown, 1976.
For most people in this country, meditation means "Transcendental Meditation," or TM, a method popularized by Maharishi Mahesh Yogi. Until recently, all books which purported to teach the TM method (including some that achieved best-seller status) have been thinly veiled ads for the costly TM program; each has stopped short of disclosing *how* to meditate. This book does what its title spells out. The question-and-answer format includes instructions for selecting a personal mantra, how to master the TM technique, and chapters on the physical and mental benefits of meditation.

Christensen, Alice, and Rankin, David. *The Light of Yoga Beginner's Manual.* Simon and Schuster, 1974.
Without an instructor, even the most preliminary Hatha Yoga exercise *(asana)* seems difficult as described in most books. This inexpensive, spiral-bound instruction booklet has clear sequential line drawings which illustrate each step of many *asanas.* A best bet for areas in which no formal instruction is available.

Farzan, Massud. *The Tale of the Reed Pipe: Teachings of the Sufis.* Dutton, 1974.
Historically, Sufism is identified with mystical Islamic thought, though some modern Sufis would include all systems of self-discovery under the Sufic umbrella. The author is a member of the faculty of Pahlavi University in Shiraz, Iran, and has written and lectured extensively on Sufism. *The Tale of the Reed Pipe* is an introduction to Sufic thought and practice including the remarkable teaching stories of Jala ud-Din Rumi and others and a description of Sufi dance and music.

Hendrics, Gay, and Wills, Russel. *The Centering Book: Awareness Activities for Children, Parents, and Teachers.* Prentice-Hall, 1975.
Eastern spiritual traditions provide the source for meditative exercises designed to enhance the standard school curriculum. Basic centering, relaxing the mind and body, dream work, imagery, movement, dance, and storytelling are among the subjects covered by the authors, who refer to their approach as "transpersonal education." Highly recommended reading for students and teachers.

Kapleau, Philip, ed. *The Three Pillars of Zen: Teaching, Practice, Enlightenment.* Beacon Press, 1975.
Kapleau is the spiritual director of the Zen Center at Rochester, New York, and one of the first Westerners to receive full training in a Japanese monastery. *The Three Pillars of Zen* is an excellent introduction to Zen practice and includes Yasutani Roshi's lectures and private instruction to Western students, passages from masters Bassui and Dogen, accounts of ten contemporary enlightenment experiences, illustrations of Zazen (meditation) postures, and a glossary of Zen and Buddhist terminology.

Lao Tsu, Gai-Fu, and English, Jane, (tr.). *Lao Tsu: Tao Te Ching.* Random, 1972.
The Tao Te Ching has been translated into more versions than any spiritual book except the Bible; more commentaries have been written on it than on any other Chinese philosophical text. Within its framework lies the embodiment of classical Chinese philosophy, religion, art, government, and social conduct. Again and again, its poetic, epigrammatic teachings remind the reader to observe nature and attune one's life and action to the natural order. The Random House edition is graced by beautiful photographs and Chinese calligraphy and is one of the best available.

Menen, Aubrey. *The Mystics.* Dial, 1974.
Beautifully illustrated in color and black and white, *The Mystics* is an easily accessible introduction to Hindu mysticism. Beginning with the Upanishads, a central Hindu scripture recounting the religious experiences of past sages, *The Mystics* examines the outgrowths of Hindu thought: Yoga, Tantrism, and modern mystical teachers and groups, such as Krisnamurti, Vivekananda, and Krishna consciousness.

Needleman, Jacob. *The New Religions.* Doubleday, 1970.
The author, chairman of the department of philosophy, San Francisco State College, examines the reasons why Western religions have failed to capture the enthusiasm of young people. A number of popular Eastern alternatives are described, among them Zen, Meher Baba, Subut, TM, and Tibetan Buddhism. Portraits of spiritual leaders and experiences of contemporary aspirants are included in the text.

Popenoe, Cris. *Books for Inner Development: The Yes! Guide.* Random, 1976.
This comprehensive, annotated catalog of books and materials on every
aspect of spiritual and religious practice and thought is the most complete
general bibliography currently available. More than 8,000 entries in seventy-
six fields list and critically examine the literature. Yes! is a bookstore in
Washington, D.C., that stocks every title listed in the guide; order forms are
printed in the back. Access is through subject headings and author index.
No title index.

Prabhavananda, Swami, and Isherwood, Christopher, (tr.). *The Song of God,
Bhagavad Gita.* Vedanta Press, 1944.
The Bhagavad Gita is India's epic spiritual poem. The eternal war between
the higher and lower aspects of the human personality is enacted on a
symbolic battlefield; in fact, the Gita is a statement concerning right action
and universal law. This highly readable interpretive translation features an
introduction by Aldous Huxley.

Ram Dass, Baba. *Be Here Now.* Crowell, 1971.
If any single published work marks the revitalized interest in spirituality
among the young, *Be Here Now* is surely it. The book chronicles the transformation of Richard Alpert, a Harvard professor who, with the help of
Timothy Leary, was responsible for much of the mid-sixties LSD craze, into
Baba Ram Dass, counterculture guru and lecturer. Sections include an
account of the transformation, transcriptions from Ram Dass' talks, and a
brief survey of his spiritual practices, books, and sayings. Variously described
as "a blessing in book's clothing," a "printed friend," and "a magnificent
document," *Be Here Now* has been appreciated by hundreds of thousands of
readers.

Spiritual Community Guide for North America, 1975–76. Spiritual Community Publications, 1974.
Teachings and teachers for a new spiritual age are identified in more than
3,000 city-by-city listings of yoga and meditation centers, ashrams, natural
food stores, bookstores, etc., plus brief descriptions of some 100 major
spiritual groups. This guide provides a link between library print resources
and actual practice.

Wetering, Jan Willem. *A Glimpse of Nothingness: Experiences in an American
Zen Community.* Houghton, 1974.
As Zen continues to spread, we can expect to see more accounts by Western
students. Mr. Wetering described his experiences at a Japanese monastery in
a previous book, *The Empty Mirror.* In *A Glimpse of Nothingness,* the
author participates in a two-week intensive retreat *(sesshin)* at an American
Zen center. His story is vividly written and will reach readers not yet ready
to tackle more profound materials.

Wilhelm, R., and Baynes, C. F., (trs.). *I Ching or Book of Changes,* 3d ed.
Princeton Univ. Pr., 1967.
The *I Ching or Book of Changes* is a 3,000-year-old Taoist oracular tool.
Manipulation of yarrow stalks or, more recently, throwing of coins yields
sixty-four permutations of symbolic hexagrams. Each set of the six resultant
broken or unbroken parallel lines answers specific questions or explicates a
current situation. The Wilhelm/Baynes translation is without peer and features a glowing introduction by Carl Jung.

Yogananda, Paramahansa. *Autobiography of a Yogi.* Self-Realization Fellowship, 1972.
Paramahansa Yogananda was the first Indian spiritual master to live and teach in the West. In his autobiography, he explains the laws by which Yogis perform seeming miracles and attain self-mastery. This remains one of the few full-length accounts of traditional yogic training written not by a journalist, but by an acknowledged modern master.

NOTES

1. Thomas B. Roberts and Frances V. Clark, "Transpersonal Psychology in Education," in Gay Hendricks and James Fadiman *Transpersonal Education* (Englewood Cliffs, N.J.: Prentice-Hall, 1976), p.23.
2. Andrew Weil, *The Natural Mind: A New Way of Looking at Drugs and Higher Consciousness* (Boston: Houghton, 1972), p.37.
3. Frederick Franck, *The Book of Angelus Silesius* (New York: Vintage, 1976), p.15.
4. Carlos Castaneda, *Journey to Ixtlan: The Lessons of Don Juan* (New York: Simon and Schuster, 1972), p.13.

A Retrospective Look at
The Catcher in the Rye

Gerald Rosen

Now that over a quarter century has passed since the publication of *The Catcher in the Rye,* it is possible to see the book in the light of the enormous body of writing that has been done on it. There are collections of articles and bibliographies to aid the person who wishes to do this.[1] It is also possible to see the book in the context of Salinger's other work, especially the writings about the Glass family, most of which were published after *Catcher.* These stories reveal themes not immediately apparent in a reading of *Catcher* and stem from a side of Salinger that has been of less importance to his critics than to Salinger himself. I refer to the importance of Eastern thought and religion to Salinger, and of Buddhism in particular, especially the form which we in the West refer to as Zen.[2]

Reprinted by permission of the author and publisher from *American Quarterly* 29:547–62 (Winter 1977). Copyright © 1977 by the Trustees of the University of Pennsylvania.

The Zen masters have a saying, "Sometimes we go east, sometimes we go west," and it appears that Salinger, after a brief attempt to "go west" in the American army during World War II, became disillusioned with his native culture and society and turned to a study of Eastern thought. This disillusionment can be seen in Holden's approving remark about his brother D.B.: "My brother D.B. was in the Army for four goddam years. He was in the war, too—he landed on D-Day and all—but I really think he hated the Army worse than the War. . . . He said the Army was practically as full of bastards as the Nazis were." Of course I don't mean to identify Salinger with D.B., but like D.B. Salinger himself participated in the Normandy invasion and his story, "For Esme—with Love and Squalor," embodies the vision which Holden attributes to D.B.

In Buddhism one is asked to give up one's illusions. *Catcher* was given final shape in the postwar period, and it is basically a novel of disillusionment. The radical nature of Salinger's portrayal of disappointment with American society, so much like Twain's in *Huck Finn,* was probably as much of the reason that *Catcher* (like *Huck*) was banned from schools and colleges as were the few curse words around which the battle was publicly fought.

After this novel of the death of belief in America, Salinger turned to wrestling with the problems of Eastern thought in the Glass books. In particular, Franny (who is, in many ways, an older female Holden, suffering from the same alienation-nausea of the seer) and Zooey are faced with the problem of reconciling their interest and training in Eastern thought (embodied in the influence of their brother Seymour upon them) with their deep conditioning and tangled loyalties to Western culture and perceptions and to their personal histories as Jewish-Christian Americans from the Upper West Side of Manhattan. "I was *born* here. I went to *school* here, I've been *run over* here—*twice,* and on the same damn *street*," Zooey lectures Franny (and himself as well).

Since Salinger seemed to achieve instant success with the appearance of *Catcher* in 1951, it is important to remember that he was already in his early thirties by this time, had been publishing stories in slick magazines like *Saturday Evening Post* for ten years, and had been working on *Catcher* through much of this decade during which time he was studying Buddhism and working on the beginnings of the Glass family saga as well. ("A Perfect Day for Bananafish" and "Down at the Dinghy" were published before *Catcher*).

The Buddha, like most great ancient religious teachers, now exists at the point where the lines of history and legend cross. But as Christmas Humphreys observes in his study of Buddhism, "Legend is often a poetic form of history. . . ."[3] A Raja of the Sakya clan (he is sometimes referred to as Sakyamuni—the sage of the Sakyas), the Buddha, according to tradition, was born in what is now Nepal in 563 B.C. His name was Siddhartha Gotama. Raised in a protective, affluent environment, the young prince was shielded from the suffering of the world and not taught to deal with it. The turning point in the story of the Buddha's life occurs when he is confronted with old age, sickness, and death. They so shake him he decides to leave the shelter of his surroundings and the distractions of his involvement in his everyday life in order to wander in the world in search of a guide who will teach him to come to terms with old age, sickness, and death. He doesn't find one, is forced to work out his salvation on his own, persists in his detachment and alienation, has a vision of the truth, and returns to the world out of compassion for his fellow living suffering beings.

I would suggest that, in rough outline, and without the Buddha's final conscious mature understanding, this is the form of the story of Holden Caulfield. When we first meet Holden in the affluent, protective environment of a prep school, we are prepared for his lonely journey by immediately being given a picture of his alienation from the nonseeing groups of people around him. (Alienation is the negative side of detachment or nonattachment which the Eastern religions see as a virtue.) Salinger presents us with our first glimpse of Holden on the day of the big football game. Holden's detachment from the game is emphasized by having him view the stadium from a distance where the excitement and involvement of the crowd over "the two teams bashing each other all over the place" appears ridiculous. Holden comments, "The game with Saxon Hall was supposed to be a very big deal around Pencey. It was the last game of the year and you were supposed to commit suicide or something if old Pencey didn't win."

The reference to suicide is not fortuitous for we soon come to see that it is precisely a continuing preoccupation with death that keeps Holden from participating in the games of those around him. It prevents him from concentrating on those activities like day-to-day school chores which we don't ordinarily think of as games but which, in the presence of death, tend to recede toward the unimportance we usually ascribe to games.

And, in fact, just as in the story of the Buddha, it is sickness, old age, and death, which we the readers, along with Holden, encounter when we begin our journey through the pages of *The Catcher in the Rye.* We meet sickness and old age in the form of Mr. Spencer, Holden's teacher:

> The minute I went in, I was sort of sorry I'd come. He was reading the *Atlantic Monthly,* and there were pills and medicine all over the place, and everything smelled of Vick's Nose Drops. It was pretty depressing. I'm not too crazy about sick people, anyway. What made it even more depressing, Old Spencer had on this very sad, ratty old bathrobe that he was probably born in or something. I don't much like to see old guys in their pajamas and bathrobes anyway. Their bumpy old chests are always showing. And their legs. Old guys' legs, at beaches and places, always look so white and unhairy.

Holden explains to Mr. Spencer that his problem relates to the idea of life as a game. "He [Dr. Thurmer—the headmaster] just kept talking about life being a game and all." To which "old" Spencer responds, "Life *is* a game, boy." Holden agrees with him outwardly, but he tells us, his confidants, "Game my ass. Some game." At this point Holden believes his objection to life as "a game" is that it's only fun for the winners. But he has deeper, unconscious objections to life, since ultimately in life there are no winners, only corpses. And immediately after introducing sickness and old age, Salinger presents us with the third member of the Buddha's problematic triad—death.

Holden, like the young Buddha, is obsessed by death, and by its corollaries, time and change. He has turned Spencer's exam question about ancient Egypt into a short essay which Spencer cannot see as springing out of this obsession: "Modern science would still like to know what the secret ingredients were that the Egyptians used when they wrapped up dead people so that their faces would not rot for innumerable centuries." And Holden flunks, because on this exam, as in his life, no one has ever taught him how to get beyond this primary question, in the shrill light of which all secondary questions are obscured.

From the start, Holden's mind has been filled with images of rot and decay. (Besides "old" Spencer himself, we have also met his rotting bathrobe.) And it is this obsessive concern of Holden's which accounts for the concentration of his narrative upon details of bodily functioning, dirt, and decay—filthy fingernails, mossy teeth, smelly socks, a rusty, filthy razor—which our institutions attempt to repress or deny.

Disgust is our culturally conditioned response to these natural data, and when the book appeared many teachers and reviewers—people who are successfully functioning within the culture's institutional system—did, in fact, respond to the mention of these matters in the text with disgust. Holden is also disturbed by much of this. He, too, has been raised in this culture (many critics have pointed out that he still holds some of the middle-class values he attacks) and he is sickened by their presence. Yet he cannot sweep the evidence of decay and death under the carpet of his mind into his unconscious. He doesn't like what he sees, but he can't help *seeing* it, just as he can't avoid the presence of the central fact of his life, his brother Allie's death, which ultimately sets him off on his quest for an adult guide.

Salinger himself has his present narrator, Buddy Glass, define the artist as seer, and Buddy too seems determined to wrestle openly with death; not only Holden, but the Glass children as well are obsessed by the death of a brother. It was probably a fight against allowing the facts of death and change to get out of his sight and become unconscious that led Salinger to his postwar studies of such philosophies as Taoism and Buddhism, which begin with the primary fact of impermanence and change and attempt to teach us to see and accept this central datum of our experience.

Holden has no one to teach him how to cope with death. In a stable culture, one would ordinarily turn to the oldest people for this kind of wisdom. They've been around the longest and presumably would have had the most experience with these matters. But in a rapidly changing culture like ours, the old people and their knowledge appear obsolete to the young. To Holden, the older people he meets are generally all right, but they seem "out of it": "I have this grandmother that's quite lavish with her dough. She doesn't have all her marbles anymore—she's old as hell . . ." and in "old" Spencer's case, "he was a nice old guy that didn't know his ass from his elbow."

Seeking protection himself, Holden is forced to protect the adults he encounters. He forgives Spencer in advance for failing him, writing on his exam, "It is all right with me if you flunk me. . . ." Several critics have noted the contradiction between Holden's hatred of phoniness and his lying to Ernest Morrow's mother when he meets her on the train on his way to New York from Pencey. Yet he lies to her to protect her from having to face the fact that "Her son was doubtless the biggest bastard that ever went to Pencey. . . ." And it is interesting that when he lies to her about his name, he doesn't do it for the usual reason one lies—to aggrandize oneself—but rather he takes on the name of Rudolph Schmidt, the dorm janitor.

After he fails to get the guidance he needs from his teachers or from the other adults he meets, one would expect Holden to turn to his parents. But in the entire novel, his father never appears and his mother appears once and then only speaks to Phoebe as Holden hides in the closet. The absence of Holden's parents (along with the absence of real religious guidance in the form of a school chaplain or family minister) is so important it amounts to a presence. On the failure of religion, Holden tells us, "my parents are different religions, and all the children in our family are atheists. If you want to know the truth, I can't even stand ministers. . . . They sound so phony when they talk." And, about his family, in the first paragraph Holden explains, "my parents would have about two hemorrhages apiece if I told anything pretty personal about them." Here is the genesis of his hatred of phoniness. His parents live in two worlds: the real world and the world of appearances. The surface does not reveal the underlying reality and Holden has been taught not to talk about what lies beneath. Yet, at times, indirectly, he does. When Phoebe suggests he become a lawyer like their father, he says, "Lawyers are all right, I guess —but it doesn't appeal to me. . . . All you do is make a lot of dough and play golf and play bridge and buy cars and drink martinis and look like a hot-shot." This occurs right after Phoebe asks him to replace their father at her play (the father will be in California on business).

Holden's mother, though well-meaning, won't be of much help either. "She still isn't over my brother Allie yet," and, "She's nervous as hell. Half the time she's up all night smoking cigarettes." Like the other adults, parents can't be relied upon to see, much less give good advice. Holden says of insensitive Stradlater, the secret slob, "he was mostly the kind of a handsome guy that if your parents saw his picture in your Year Book, they'd right away say, 'Who's *this* boy?' "

Holden sorely misses being able to turn to his parents in his time of trouble. He doesn't say this, but he reveals it obliquely in his movie-fantasies of being shot by the mob. In the first, he pulls the peak of the hunting cap over his eyes and shouts about being blind. (This is the reverse of the baseball catcher's hat position, in which the peak is *back,* implying the catcher *must* see, and Holden has chosen to be a "catcher.") Then Holden shouts, "Mother darling, everything's getting so *dark* in here," and "Mother darling, give me your *hand.* Why won't you give me your *hand?"* This seems like clowning, but in fact it is a revelation of his terrible anguished isolation from his family. In a later fantasy, Holden reveals, "I didn't want anybody to know I was even wounded. I was *concealing* the fact that I was a wounded sonofabitch." Then he calls Sally and explains the source of his wound: "They got me. Rocky's mob got me." This is clarified three pages later, when he refers to his family at Allie's funeral as "a mob," thereby revealing the source of his wound and the traumatic occasion when he first really felt the pain of it. And he begins to speak of Allie as if he were alive but underground: "I certainly didn't enjoy seeing *him* in that crazy cemetery" [italics added].

So Holden cannot get advice on how to leave the world of childhood from the adults around him. Nor can he find suitable models to emulate. The two Pencey alumni we encounter are Ossenburger, a phony under-taker, and an old guy who appears on Veteran's Day and tells Holden that Pencey will prove to be the best years of his life. This does not increase Holden's hope for the future. And as for Ossenburger, "he started these undertaking parlors all over the country that you could have members of your family buried for about five bucks apiece. . . . You should see old Ossenburger. He probably just shoves them in a sack and dumps them in the river." (Again, Holden can't stay away from the subject of the death of family members and the decay of the corpse. Even when he later goes to the Museum of Art, he winds up in the mummy room explaining about preserving the dead to two boys and then getting sick and "sort of" passing out.)

Holden possesses the necessary but painful gift of the novelist—the intuitive ability to perceive that words are instruments used to create effects and have no necessary attachments to nonverbal reality. So he needs more than even good advice, he needs a living adult, a mature person within the culture who, by his or her living presence, will *demonstrate* a possibility that Holden might achieve if he gives up the non-defined personality of his childhood and accepts a role as a mature member of the society. Holden's brother D.B., who once offered this possibility, has sold out to Hollywood, which produces images such as the great lover with the violin and the courageous guy with romantic wounds. Since the viewer can't hope to live up to these images, they contribute to making him feel small and uncourageous and add to his wounds. As Holden notes, "The goddam movies. They can ruin you. I'm not kidding." And he isn't. And Mr. Antolini, who gives Holden what might seem to be good advice, cancels any effects his words might have had by his actions and his mode of life.

Americans have always found it difficult to accept limits. Even if the chance to head for the frontier was largely mythic, its significance as myth was its denial of limits in the imaginations of those Americans who were stuck in the East. Of course death is the ultimate limit, and Jessica Mitford has shown to what lengths Americans will go to deny its reality. Institutional roles are limits, too, and Holden, in his extended adolescence, is in the position of one who has been left outside the house of the culture's institutions for too long, and has become taller than the ceiling. Everyone in the house appears to him to be unconscious of the fact that they are stooping to fit inside because this posture has become habitual to them. They have grown into it. Holden is asked to stoop consciously— to enter the house at a time when, so to speak, he has become too tall for it.

In reaction to this, Holden fantasizes a Thoreau-like existence in the country, outside of the limits of institutional roles and of social norms and manners. He tells Sally, "we could drive up to Massachusetts and Vermont, and all around there, see. It's beautiful as hell up there . . . we could live somewhere with a brook and all . . . I could chop all our own wood in the wintertime. . . ."

Sally, who has been successfully acculturated, explains to Holden about his obligation to fulfill the traditional male role of husband and provider, and then she promises, "There'll be oodles of marvelous places to go." In responding to Sally, Holden gives us the novel of his future which haunts him and which is one more factor preventing him from accepting an adult role and "growing up" into the society:

> I said no, there wouldn't be marvelous places to go to after I went to college and all. Open your ears. It'd be entirely different. We'd have to go downstairs in elevators with suitcases and stuff. We'd have to phone up everybody and tell 'em goodbye and send 'em postcards from hotels and all. And I'd be working in some office, making a lot of dough, and riding to work in cabs and Madison Avenue buses, and reading newspapers, and playing bridge all the time, and going to the movies. . . .

It is important to note here that Holden's rejection of an adult role is not a case of sour grapes. He believes he *will* succeed and it is the successful life he fears. And this passage, in which he tells Sally to open her eyes and ears, "Open your ears. . . . You don't see what I mean at all," further highlights his desperate isolation. Like the adults, his contemporaries don't see what he sees or hear what he is saying either.

With such a dead-end vision of the trap of adulthood and marriage, it is no wonder that Holden fears initiation into that most adult and most involving and nondetached form of relationship—sex. In a society in which human relationships are infected by marketplace values of competitiveness and surface appearance, and humans are measured in terms of social status and money income, Holden is seeking a deeper, more real relationship with someone—a more human relationship. Holden is against many things, but he isn't nihilistic. "Human" is one of his values, as he reveals comically in his preference for the horse over that sacred American object, the automobile: "A horse is at least *human* for God's sake."

Another positive value of Holden's is that it is wrong to hurt people. He reveals this when he says, in attempting to forgive bores, "They don't hurt anybody, most of them. . . ." So Holden is very careful not to use people as a means for his own ends, to try to be certain that he treats each person as a human being and not as a commercial object available for his use in the manner sanctioned by his culture. Yet he is a member of his culture to a degree, so it is not surprising that when he is offered the teenage dream of being indoctrinated into sex in a nonresponsible situation, in which all he has to pay is money, he jumps at the chance, and then, when he is confronted by the human reality of the situation, his tremendous empathy surfaces and he feels sorry for the girl. Of course, Maurice victimizes him here, because Holden allows himself to be victimized by virtually everyone who tries; the culture's emphasis on "winning" in encounters with other people is so threatening to him that he plays it safe by always losing—his scissors to Ackley, his coat to Stradlater, his sweater to James Castle, and so on.

Pure sex, like the myth of rural peace, is a romantic good place Holden is struggling to hold onto in the face of the urban-commercial society determined to pollute both. But Holden's mistrust of sex goes deeper than the merely social level. For Holden, sex is the ultimate involvement in the world; it is the final entry into time. Holden cannot accept change and time is the measure of change. Time is the medium in which change lives. Time is the silent partner of death. And sex is the passageway through which one is seduced into entering time. Salinger makes this connection clear when Sunny, the prostitute, first comes to Holden's room and asks him, three times, whether he has a watch. Of course, he doesn't. He is still a virgin. He has not yet left the timeless world of childhood.

At Pencey, Holden equates sex with time when referring to Stradlater's date with Jane Gallagher. At first, he virtually equates sex with perversion when he calls Stradlater "a very sexy bastard" because of his interest in the details of Jane's stepfather running around naked in front of her. And then, obsessed with the idea of Stradlater's copulating with Jane, whom Holden remembers as a young girl, he begins to talk of Stradlater's "giving her the time." The fact that this was a popular expression does

not reduce the significance of Holden's repeated use of it—rather it gen-
eralizes Holden's identification of sex with time.

Thoughts of sex seem to lead Holden to thoughts of death. After the
fight with Stradlater over Jane, Ackley asks Holden what the fight was
about, and Holden tells us, "I didn't answer him. . . . I almost wished
I was dead." In his New York hotel room, when he is thinking about
sex and then considers calling Jane at college, an excuse for the late-night
call pops into his mind: "I was going to say her aunt had just got killed
in a car accident. . . ." And after Sunny, the prostitute, leaves his room
he begins to talk out loud to his dead brother Allie.

In both Holden's mind and in his culture, besides the link between
sex and death there is a connection between sex and aggression, and
aggression is an extremely negative quality to Holden. As in his reaction
to the culture's emphasis on winning, Holden is so anxious to avoid
aggression that he makes himself defenseless. He fights Stradlater, but
loses and tells us, "I'd only been in about two fights in my life, and I lost
both of them. I'm not too tough. I'm a pacifist, if you want to know the
truth."

One reason he loses the fight is that he can't make a fist, and it is
interesting to note that he injured his fist, and thereby partially rendered
himself incapable of aggression, by punching it through a window after
Allie died. Aggression, at its extreme, will lead to someone's death and,
as Holden comments about the death of Mercutio, "it drives me crazy
if somebody gets killed . . . and it's somebody else's fault." Here we have
a clue as to why Holden has crippled himself—he has been so shocked
by Allie's death that he is afraid to act in the slightest manner that might
implicate him in the injustice of it. At bottom, beneath Holden's quarrel
with his culture, there is always his quarrel with God whom Holden can't
forgive for killing his brother.

Although his swing at Stradlater would seem to violate his anti-aggres-
sive stance, it is in the name of protecting a nonaggressive person that
Holden attempts it. What he especially liked about Jane was that she
kept her kings in the back row in checkers. This has intrigued the critics,
but what it seems to me to represent is a holding back of one's aggressive
powers and an unwillingness to enter the competitive game and use them
against other people; this is one of Holden's cherished values and, in his
own case, his bane as well.

The connection between sex and death in the culture surfaces in the
famous scene near the end of the book where Holden attempts to erase
the "Fuck You" signs in Phoebe's school. The culture uses the same word
for its highest aggressive insult and for its term for sexual intercourse.
In the culture's mind and in Holden's, sex is something men *commit* on
women and it is clear that this view of sex, built into the culture's language and value system, has poisoned it for Holden.

So here we come full circle: Holden fears aggression because it may lead to death, sex is equated with aggression, and, once again, sex is thus connected with death and with its agent, the grim-reaper Time.

In opposition to this vicious circle, Holden dreams of an Edenic world, outside of time, beyond aggression: a world prior to the anxiety caused by the Fall. In his romantic imagination, this world is equated with the prepubescent world of childhood. No one in Holden's world understands natural forces (no adult ever *does* tell him what happens to the ducks in the winter) and puberty resembles death in the way it places man at the mercy of tremendous natural forces which come with one's body and are the price one pays for living in the changing material world. The Hindus, wrestling with these same problems, define this material world as Maya, the veil of illusion, which supposedly keeps one from seeing his ground in the eternal, unchanging, One. The Buddhists see the notion of the unchanging One as one more concept of stability which we manufacture and hold on to to keep from dealing with the reality of change.

Holden holds on to many things to keep from dealing with the reality of change. In the museum, there is glass which keeps things out of time and decay. Holden especially likes the museum for this reason. "The best thing, though, in that museum was that everything always stayed right where it was," and "Certain things should stay the way they are. You ought to be able to stick them in one of those big glass cases and just leave them alone." It is at Allie's funeral that Holden is jolted out of this time-less world that he has seen preserved behind the glass, and, as if in revenge against this fraud, his response is to punch his fist through a window, breaking the glass which has deceived him. Later in the book, be-neath the glass in the wall in the Museum of Art, he sees a "Fuck You" scrawled in red crayon and this verbalizes the traumatic insult the time-less world gave him when it broke with Allie's death.

The presence of these "Fuck You" signs in the book points to a crucial difference in attitude between Salinger and his young narrator. The close-ness of Salinger and Holden in terms of certain values and aspects of vision is emphasized by Salinger's use of Holden as a first-person nar-rator. Any distance between them tends to be obscured by Salinger's obvious sympathy for Holden, and by the tone of his writing which succeeds in its scrupulous efforts to get Holden's speech down exactly, creating an intimate effect which is almost like having Holden in the room, telling the reader his own story.[4]

Yet, to ignore the distance between Holden and his creator is to do a disservice to Salinger. In the instance of the "Fuck You" signs, Salinger is doing precisely the opposite of what Holden is attempting to do. Quixotically, Holden attempts to erase the "Fuck You" signs, thereby trying to keep children from learning about sex in this misguided (and even aggressive) context. He is trying to be the catcher who keeps chil-dren in their Eden before the Fall. Yet Salinger, by *including* these "Fuck You" signs, is actually scrawling them on the walls of his book, forcing the reader to acknowledge their presence and deal with them. At the time the book was published this caused a controversy and was one reason the book was deemed "dirty" by many readers and was taken from libraries and the reading lists of high school courses. Salinger here is not playing the catcher at all, but is asking the reader to grow up and accept the fallen world in which he finds himself.

Interestingly, the readers who attempted to ban the book from libraries and from the schools of their children were acting in exactly the immature manner which causes Holden so much pain and which Salinger is trying to diagnose and prescribe for in the novel. Yet here we see what must be a conflict in Salinger's own mind: after 1947, he has identified himself with the *New Yorker* magazine, publishing almost all his stories in its pages. *Catcher,* however, was not published in the *New Yorker,* and it is clear it couldn't have been published there because of these same "Fuck You" signs.[5]

Brendan Gill tells us, regarding Harold Ross, the founder of the *New Yorker* and its editor at the time *Catcher* was published, that Ross had "a puritanical determination to exclude even the mildest sexual innuendoes. He said it was his intention to publish nothing that would bring a blush to the cheek of a twelve year old girl. This was a peculiar standard to set for a magazine universally acknowledged to be among the most sophisticated in existence—a magazine that Ross had founded, moreover, with the stipulation that it was not to be edited for the old lady in Dubuque." As for William Shawn, the editor who succeeded Ross and who was in charge during the publication of the Glass stories which came after *Catcher,* Gill comments, "the harshest expletive I ever heard him utter is a whispered, 'Oh God!' "

Thus, by serving up a fare that includes "Fuck You" signs, Salinger is rebelling against his literary parents at the *New Yorker,* giving them a dish they can't chew and thereby, by implication, putting them in the position of poor immature Holdens, trying to serve as catchers for their readers. And, by the way, perpetuating the same standards of sex and language which are causing Holden so much of his pain. Brendan Gill tells us, "Ross believed in a double standard of language—one for the publicly printed word, the other for private speech."[6]

"Life is suffering." This is the first "Noble Truth" of the Buddha, and it stands like a neon sign over the entrance to Buddhism, acting like a filter that only lets in those who are willing to accept this premise as the price of admission. By the time Holden goes to see his sister Phoebe, one can certainly say that *his* life is suffering in the true Buddhist sense. (Another translation of "suffering" would be "continued irritation" or "anxiety.") The other of the four Buddhist Noble Truths say there is a cause for suffering and a cure. The cause, most briefly termed "desire" or "selfish craving," is said to stem from the failure to accept change (and the failure to deal with sickness, old age, and death) and the concomitant attempt to avoid change by holding on to things, grasping at false possibilities for stability and illusions of permanence. The cure is to let go of desire and selfish craving for ways out of time, be they promised by public gods or private fantasies.

Holden is holding on to many things besides his virginity. He is holding on to his old character patterns which lead him to be unable to let go of saying yes to virtually everything anyone asks him for, and to losing in almost every encounter with other people (especially where money is concerned). He also holds on to objects, such as Allie's glove, and the broken pieces of Phoebe's record (symbolically so like a corpse—the matter is still there, but not the music). He holds on to old opinions as well, such as his (and Allie's) veneration of the kettle drummer at Radio City Music Hall. By avoiding a meeting or a telephone conversation with Jane Gallagher, he holds on to his old image of her which is clearly no longer applicable since she is dating Stradlater; apparently Holden has been defending this image and avoiding her present reality for quite a while since he doesn't even know which school she goes to.

The Buddha said the greatest source of suffering is the belief in a single, continuous, unchanging personality, and the attempt to hold on to it. By not letting go of his old character traits and images of the world, Holden is doing precisely this. Of course, Holden is most strongly holding on to (is most attached to) Allie. When Phoebe challenges Holden to name one thing he likes, he appears to be at a loss for an answer at first, getting stuck on thoughts about James Castle, the boy who committed suicide. Holden is identified with Castle by Castle's having killed himself while wearing Holden's sweater and by Castle's appearing just before Holden on the roll call at school. This carries the implication that Holden may be next in line for Castle's fate. (The fact that Mr. Antolini attempts to help Castle, but is too late, prefigures Holden's experience with Mr. Antolini.) From this image of the dead James Castle, when Phoebe again challenges him, Holden's mind moves back to the image of his dead brother, which he carries with him wherever he goes, and he responds, "I like Allie."

Many people equate Eastern religions with mysticism, and mysticism with pure subjectivity, but Buddhism, at its highest levels, is empirical and asks one merely to be awake to one's real situation and not to believe anything one hasn't experienced. When the Tibetan Buddhist teacher Chogyam Trungpa was talking about finding "a spiritual friend," he was asked by a student, "Is it absolutely necessary that the spiritual friend be a living human being?" to which he replied, "Yes. Any other 'being' with whom you might think yourself communicating would be imaginary."[7]

After Holden says he likes Allie, he immediately turns to the real world and gives us a hint of what will occur at the end of the book at the carrousel. After Phoebe objects, "Allie's *dead* . . ." he adds, "Anyway, I like it now . . . sitting here with you. . . ." What Phoebe has done here is to pull Holden out of his obsession with the sorrows of his past and direct his attention to the existential situation he is in at present.

Right after this, Salinger directs our attention to the Buddhist under-pinnings of the novel by having Holden inform us about Phoebe, "She was sitting smack in the middle of the bed, outside the covers, with her legs folded like one of those Yogi guys." This is the lotus position of meditation, the traditional posture of the Buddha, and if Holden doesn't know it, Salinger certainly does. To quote Chogyam Trungpa on the Buddhist idea of psychotherapy:

> Once you begin to deal with a person's whole case history, trying to make it relevant to the present, the person begins to feel that he has no escape, that his situation is hopelesss, because he cannot undo his past. He feels trapped by his past with no way out. This kind of treatment is extremely unskilled. It is destructive because it hinders involvement with the creative aspect of what is happening now, what is here, right now.[8]

Holden's meeting with Phoebe is the turning point of the book. For the first time he admits, "I just felt good for a change." And the reason he feels good is clear. He is with a person who sees. He tries to lie to her about his getting kicked out of school and she sees through his lie immediately. He tells her, "I'll probably be in Colorado on this ranch," and she responds, "Don't make me laugh. You can't ride a horse." She isn't easy, but she *sees*. And Holden quickly begins to pour out what is bothering him, as if she were a little doctor. When her mother returns with a headache, she prescribes a few aspirin. And she lies to protect Holden, taking the blame for his smoking. These upside-down situations, in which the younger person protects the older ones and gives them ad-vice, are in line with the whole pattern of the book. And the failure of the older people to protect and guide the young not only results in botched initiations like Holden's, it also leads the younger people to try to be their own parents, forcing them to act older than they are by cursing, affecting a false cynicism, lying about their age, drinking, and wearing falsies.

The Zen masters say, "Cold eye, warm heart," and besides seeing, Phoebe is also compassionate. The *Dhammapada* says, "Let us live hap-pily then, we who possess nothing," thereby defining Buddhists. Holden includes Phoebe within this definition when he says, "She says she likes to spread out. That kills me. What's old Phoebe got to spread out? Noth-ing."

But Phoebe does have a small amount of money, her Christmas money. Eight dollars and sixty-five cents. It isn't much, but it's all she has and she gives it to Holden. And this *act* of compassion breaks through the shell of Holden's fearful isolation: "Then, all of a sudden, I started to cry."

What we have here in miniature, in 1951, is the prescient portrait of an attempt to create a counterculture. The children, unable to connect with the prevailing culture, begin to separate from it and to attempt to care for each other. As the Buddha said, "Brothers and sisters, you have no mother and father to take care of you. If you will not take care of each other, who else, I ask, will do so." We also have the reason for the failure of the counterculture. Holden and Phoebe have charge accounts. The money they give away so freely still comes from their parents and their parents' culture.

Culture is a form of hypnosis and it dies hard. Holden makes one last try to connect. He leaves Phoebe and plays his ace-in-the-hole: Mr. Antolini. Mr. Antolini is full of advice, much of it good, but he is blind to the existential reality of Holden's condition. Once again, when Holden needs a guide, he gets words. They aren't enough. Phoebe remains the only person who has *seen* where he is and who has *acted* truly in his behalf.

So he returns to Phoebe and, in opposition to Antolini's treatment of himself, Holden *watches* the situation and doesn't chase her away, explaining, "I didn't put my hands on her shoulders again or anything because if I had she *really* would have beat it on me. Kids are funny. You have to watch what you're doing." And he accompanies her to the carrousel in Central Park where he gives up his desire to be a catcher and his craving for an Edenic world and accepts the world in which he finds himself at present: "The thing with kids is, if they want to grab for the gold ring, you have to let them do it, and not say anything. If they fall off, they fall off, but it's bad if you say anything to them."

In a scene which parallels the one in his parents' apartment when Phoebe gave him her money and his body responded by beginning to cry, here Phoebe gives him a kiss and nature itself seems to respond as it begins to rain. Holden, who has been obsessed with Allie's being out in the rain, stays out in the rain himself, accepts the rain, thereby identifying himself with Allie and Allie's fate, accepting his own death and vulnerability to natural forces. He turns away from what he has lost, letting go of his obsessive hold on the vision of the dead Allie, and turns toward the happiness which comes in seeing what he still has—a living Phoebe, with him, right there in the present. When Holden says, "God, I wish you could've been there," he isn't just talking to us. He is talking to God.

One suspects that this resolution is merely a temporary respite for Holden; that he has a long way to go before he'll be able to extend his acceptance to include the new phonies he meets. But he has survived to tell his story, and in this respect he is more fortunate than Salinger's other "seer," Seymour Glass. After a similar "perfect" encounter with a young girl, Seymour has shot himself through the head.

For the epigraph of his *Nine Stories,* Salinger has chosen the famous Zen koan, "We know the sound of two hands clapping. But what is the sound of one hand clapping?" A koan has no "right" answer. A particular koan is given to a particular student to see from many sides and learn from, but ultimately it is something that, however fascinating, must be let go of. I would suggest that this first Glass story, "A Perfect Day for Bananafish," is a kind of koan, one whose meaning the Glass children will be meditating on and wrestling with for years to come. Ultimately, the problems faced by Holden and the Glass children have no "answer" that *we* can hold on to. But we must be careful not to ask Salinger or anyone else to provide us with this illusory "answer." As Salinger certainly knows, tradition has it that when the Buddha was dying he was asked for one final piece of advice and he replied, "Work out your own salvation with diligence."[9]

NOTES

1. See the articles in Henry Antole Grunwald, ed., *Salinger* (New York: Harper, 1962) and Marvin Laser and Norman Fruman, eds., *Studies in J. D. Salinger* (New York: Odyssey, 1963); the articles and bibliography in Harold P. Simonson and Phillip E. Hager, eds., *Salinger's "Catcher in the Rye"—Clamor vs. Criticism* (Lexington, Mass.: Heath, 1963); and the bibliography in Warren French, *J. D. Salinger* (New Haven: College and University Pr., 1963).
2. Several critics touch upon this briefly, some with condescension. There are exceptions however, one of which is Tom Davis, "J. D. Salinger: 'Some Crazy Cliff' Indeed," *Western Humanities Review* 14:97-99 (Winter 1960).
3. Christmas Humphreys, *Buddhism* (Harmondsworth, England: Penguin, 1951), p.30.
4. The assumption which is often made, that Holden is relating his experiences to a therapist while he "rests" at a California sanitorium—like Charlie Parker "Relaxing at Camarillo"—is belied by the first sentence of chapter 19: "In case you don't live in New York, the Wicker Bar is in this sort of swanky hotel, the Seton Hotel." It is hardly likely that Holden would address this to a California psychotherapist. Holden seems to be addressing *the reader* here, and this is interesting in that it hints at Salinger's own solution to the problem of growing up in America without accepting the limits and blindnesses of an institutional role—becoming a writer. A writer is supposedly paid to see, and "author" tends to be one of the least constricting roles in our society.
5. For example, in *Catcher,* when Sally tells Holden to be reasonable and not run away, he responds, "You give me a royal pain in the ass. . . ." In the original version of this, which was published in the *New Yorker* as "Slight Rebellion Off Madison," 22:86 (Dec. 21, 1946), Holden's reply is amended to the less accurate, "You give me a royal pain."
6. Brendan Gill, *Here at the New Yorker* (New York: Berkeley Medallion, 1976), pp.34, 35, 70-71.
7. Chogyam Trungpa, *Cutting through Spiritual Materialism* (Berkeley: Shambhala Publications, 1973), p.88.
8. Ibid., pp.88-89.
9. Humphreys, *Buddhism,* p.40.

Moral Development and Literature for Adolescents

Peter Scharf

Introduction: Literature and Adolescents

Until recently, there has been little investigation of the precise role played by literature in adolescent development.[1] This paper offers that a clue to the relationship of literature to adolescent development may lie in an understanding of the adolescent's evolving moral conscience. We will suggest that as the adolescent matures in terms of moral thinking, the meaning of particular literary experiences may shift dramatically. By understanding changes in adolescent moral thinking we may be able to better understand how literature affects the adolescent at different development stages.

Kohlberg's Theory of Moral Judgment

Our approach requires an explanation of Kohlberg's theory of moral judgment. The theory was developed at Harvard University by Kohlberg and his associates.[2] It argues that there is an invariant sequence in moral judgment. Longitudinal studies indicate that individuals in a number of different societies move sequentially through each of six moral stages. Moral development occurs through age twenty-five; however, individuals progress at different rates, and some people become fixated at primitive stages of moral thought.

The six stages are divided into three levels: the preconventional (stages one and two), the conventional (stages three and four), and the post-conventional or principled (stages five and six), as shown in table 1.

The preconventional mode of moral problem-solving is typically associated with preadolescent children (ages ten to twelve) and morally fixated adults. At stage one there is an orientation toward punishment and obedience, toward superior power. The physical consequences of human action determine right and wrong regardless of their human meaning. Stage two assumes that right action becomes that which satisfies one's own needs. Human relationships are viewed in terms of the marketplace: "You scratch my back and I'll scratch yours."

The conventional level becomes dominant in late preadolescence

Reprinted from *Top of the News* 33:131–36 (Winter 1977).

Table I. Classification of Moral Judgment into Levels and Stages of Development	
Levels	Stages of Development
Level I. Preconventional	Stage 1: Obedience and punishment orientation
	Stage 2: Naively egoistic orientation
Level II. Conventional	Stage 3: Good-boy orientation
	Stage 4: Authority and social-order maintaining orientation
Level III. Postconventional	Stage 5: Contractual legalistic orientation
	Stage 6: Conscience or principle orientation

Source: Adapted from Lawrence Kohlberg, "Stage and Sequence," in Goslin, ed., *Handbook of Socialization* (New York: Russell Sage, 1967).

(ages twelve through sixteen). At stage three we have what we call the good boy/good girl orientation. Good behavior is what helps others and is approved by them. One gains approval by being "nice" or exhibiting behavior which will be approved by others. At stage four there is a shift toward fixed definitions of social duty and concern with firm social rules and a respect for formal authority.

The postconventional (or principled) level first appears in late adolescence (late high school or early college years). Stage five is a legalistic contract orientation, generally with utilitarian overtones. Laws which are not constitutional, that violate human rights or are not in the general interest, are judged to be invalid at stage five.

The transition from stage four to five is often stormy. Before moving to stage five, the adolescent often rejects the conventional moral categories of teachers and parents while declaring that all values are relative and meaningless.

At stage six, Kohlberg postulates there is a basis for rational agreement to moral principles. There are universal principles of justice, of ideal reciprocity, the equality of human rights, and the respect for the dignity of human beings as individual persons.

Moral Maturity and Literature

At each stage of development, particular literary issues are especially salient. While, clearly, great literature has an impact upon almost any age or developmental level (for example, Dostoevski's *Crime and Punishment* can be read at age thirteen as a mystery story and at age twenty as a complex study of human morals), it may still be argued that the moral focus of particular literary works may be especially psychologically significant at specific stages of development.

For example, certain novels of style and manners are of great appeal to conventionally reasoning early adolescents. *Ivanhoe* by Scott, concerned with courtly attitudes and romantic love, is of continuing appeal to early adolescents seeking to discover the rules and mores of social interchange in their own society. In contrast, Ibsen's *Enemy of the People* only makes sense much later when the adolescent is able to differentiate his or her own moral principles from community norms. Similarly, complex novels of social responsibility such as Camus' *The Plague* and Melville's *Moby Dick* only become psychologically meaningful when the late adolescent has acquired the ability to clearly weigh in his or her own mind the rights of the community with the legitimate moral claims of the individual.

These differences in moral concerns of literature may be described in terms of three distinct "types" of literature:

1. The literature of social expectations: significant in attaining conventional moral orientations, that is, stages three and four.
2. The literature of social revolt: significant in the rejection of conventional moral thought.
3. The literature of affirmation: significant in the acceptance of postconventional moral principles.

The Literature of Social Expectations

One of the key developmental tasks of early adolescence involves the adolescent's anticipating and accepting the legitimate expectations of his social world. This is the core of Kohlberg's third and fourth stages (the conventional level). In any historical era, the content of conventional moral thinking may differ. The Amish adolescent may be socialized into a highly prescriptive, regulated set of norms and role expectations. For the suburban youth, the norms will be more humanistic and open-ended. Still, in each milieu, the adolescent grapples with a key developmental question: What does this society expect of me?

When the literature of social expectations is critical of society it poses an alternative set of conventional norms to those which are attacked. For example, one fourteen-year-old black student suggested after reading Claude Brown's *Manchild in the Promised Land* that the book "showed how if a black man tried hard he could be accepted, even if the whites were prejudiced and didn't want you." A young Jewish girl in the same class suggested upon reading Herman Wouk's *Marjorie Morningstar* "that the book showed how people are not nice to Jewish girls and make them feel bad, no matter what they do to convince people they are really trying to belong."

This literature of social expectations stimulates a sense of moral conventionality by praising "appropriate" social attitudes. Often protagonists will represent heroic values which are reflected and emulated by young readers. Villains are frequently portrayed as "unfeeling" or "cruel" in often one-dimensional, somewhat stereotyped ways. Good literature of this type presents a coherent moral universe in which good and evil are polarized and defined. This provides a platform of social conventions upon which the early adolescent can differentiate his group's social ideology from other philosophies. While this type of literature may seem "corny" or "sentimental" to adults, it is a necessary stage toward the learning of more complex personal moral philosophies.

Much of the literature popular in early adolescence deals with the social expectations theme. Biographies are especially rich in information on the appropriate social expectations of society. One youngster may be drawn to a biography about Martin Luther King; for another, it will be the narrative of Joe Namath's career; for another, a novel about Susan B. Anthony might be significant. Usually, novels popular through age thirteen deal with themes which are moralistic in the sense that characters are defined as either good, bad, heroic, or cowardly in a given society. Historically based fiction has a similar impact in its detail about a tradition and its expectations.

The Literature of Social Revolt

Typically in the middle adolescence, many adolescents come to increasingly question the moral order of their society. In any historical era this may take a unique form. Youth will become Freedom Riders, Skinheads, LSD "freaks," or Klansmen. They will join S.N.C.C. (Student Nonviolent Coordinating Committee), Y.A.F. (Young Americans for Freedom), the Hare Krishna, or the Communist Party. They will follow people as diverse as Martin Luther King, Gandhi, or the "fifteen-year-old perfect master." The key to any such commitment is the youth's critique of society as it stands. The youth rejects the conventional moral order and seeks to find his own.

Needless to say, this questioning is disturbing to many adults, including librarians. They fail to see that such a rejection of conventional societal truth is a critical step in the adolescent's defining for himself an autonomous value base. Of course, some youth will become fixated in one rigid ideology or another (Hitler and Abbie Hoffman may be good examples of permanent nihilistic fixation). For most, however, the beginning of social doubt and questioning is a necessary developmental step toward finding a set of autonomously chosen, universal moral principles.

The surfacing of doubt requires a new literature. A key to this type of literature is the rejection of social conventions. Salinger's *The Catcher in the Rye* is a good example of such a critique. As the protagonist, Holden Caulfield sees his world as hypocritical and shameful. Adults lie to adolescents and to each other. Nobody really believes in any of society's expectations and roles. Success is mere conformity. Love is a bourgeois excuse to become respectably "settled."

The adolescent reading *The Catcher in the Rye* strongly identifies with Holden Caulfield's rebellion. Most adolescents by age sixteen have begun to have strong doubts about the perceived moral propriety of their parents and teachers. Their initial questioning is no doubt stimulated by the vivid images in *The Catcher in the Rye* and through similar picaresque novels. For example, one suburban high school student noted:

> The character in the novel *Catcher in the Rye* showed me how screwed-up things are in society. It shows that the morality of people is really old-fashioned and out of date. It really gets you thinking about what SOCIETY is like. . . .

Similarly, in one discussion about Heller's *Catch-22* with some bright high school seniors, a seventeen-year-old boy offered that the book showed how "in an upside-down world, you gotta be upside-down to see things right-side-up." The popularity of Castaneda's books on Don Juan among adolescents may be understood in terms of contemporary adolescent questioning of Western notions of rationality, science, and progress. Such works clearly stimulate a process of moral doubt which has roots in both the polarization of the youth and adult cultures and the pluralism of American values. While such doubt is threatening to some adults, it should be seen as a necessary (but not final) step toward attaining truly principled values. Unless the adolescent rejects what is arbitrary in conventional social norms he cannot seek to move toward values which are truly internal and universal.

The Literature of Affirmation

In *The Rebel,* Albert Camus writes:

> Who is the Rebel? A man who says no, but by saying no does not imply renunciation. . . . To say yes, by saying no. . . . (p.6)

As in Camus' statement of moral rebellion, Kohlberg argues that beyond a rejection of social morality comes an affirmation of universal principles. Much literature involves a quest for universal moral and metaphysical meaning. This literature becomes increasingly important in early adulthood.

Much of the world's great literature deals with these ultimate human values. In the realm of ethics, Buber, Camus, Orwell, Dostoevski, Melville, and others all attempt to pose ethical principles which provide moral limits to human conduct. Such writers as Hesse, Nietzsche, Castaneda, and De Chardin powerfully explore the question of the metaphysical meanings underlying daily experience. Much great poetry moves toward finding an ultimate standard of beauty and truth.

In these works of affirmation there is some kind of ultimate human meaning or value. The works move toward some moral, metaphysical, or aesthetic truth which is seen as nonrelativistic and ultimate. They offer that there are some values which are worth affirming, something positive to live for.

The literature of affirmation, though critical for later development, is probably the least accessible to most adolescents. On reading Hesse's *Siddartha,* one high school senior offers in a paper: "I didn't understand it but I think it made me think that there was some purpose in experiencing life as it comes." Another student commented on Camus' *Plague,* "that it raised the question of when it is right to let people die, and what one might die for."

The final stage is psychologically quite distinct from both an early adolescent conformity as it is from the relativism and nihilism of middle adolescence. The search for transcendent values through literature offers a bridge to a full adulthood where, in Erik Erikson's terms, the young adult seeks to make meaningful and self-determined choices in the realms of love, work, and meaning.

This movement toward a mature adulthood has special meaning in a world of cultural change and conflicting value systems. Only adults who have reflected upon and developed a clear set of inner values can hope to cope with the flux of the last quarter of the twentieth century. In this search for values, books and libraries have a unique task. If libraries can encourage meaningful personal searches among young people, they can play a vital role in the process of moral development. To do this, they must create a climate of openness toward the exploring youth and gear their offerings to the developmental concerns and interests of the emerging adolescent.

NOTES

1. Lawrence Kohlberg, "Moral Judgment, Tragedy and Pathos" (Cambridge, Mass., Harvard Univ., n.d.).
2. Lawrence Kohlberg, "Stage and Sequence," in David A. Goslin, ed., *Handbook of Socialization* (New York: Russell Sage, 1967).

On Constructing Useful Realities: The Uses of Popular Culture in the Uncertain World of the Adolescent

Gordon Stevenson

> *Social life is dubious enough and ludicrous enough without having to wish it further into unreality.* (Erving Goffman[1])

I suppose a lot of learning goes on in the American high school, but not all of the teaching is done by the teachers. And what is taught is surely not all that is learned. Nor is it all that a maturating young person needs to learn, would like to learn, and indeed must learn. Some of the non-curriculum-based learning has to do with the development of mental constructs, fundamental ways of looking at oneself and the world in which one finds oneself. What does one really believe in? What values are to guide one in dealing with other people? The adolescent asks: "Who am I? Where am I going? What is it all about? What a shock it must be to face these questions for the first time. I suspect that in the growth of the individual (somewhere between childhood and adulthood) there is a point where answers to these questions cannot be taught—but can only be learned.

It is for this reason that adolescents have developed their own systems of learning about and exchanging information about the world and about life. They all know that there are things, secret and exciting things (even grim and terrible things), that they are not supposed to know about, things that are never mentioned in school, and about which they never, ever ask their parents. They sit in classrooms, playing out their outrageous little roles—acting innocent, bored, ornery, perverse, indifferent, interested, or whatever. They put up with teachers as best they can, and surely this is not always an easy thing to do. But when school is out, there is a different curriculum to attend to. It is, for the most part, a nice curriculum because it consists entirely of "electives," you don't have any assignments, you don't have to study, and it's a lot of fun. You also learn a lot of very important things which are useful to know. The warp and woof of this

Reprinted by permission of the author and publisher from *Voice of Youth Advocates* 1:7–11 (Oct. 1978).

curriculum is that confusing melange of media and messages which we call popular culture.

For all practical purposes, the culture of adolescents *is* popular culture. It is the culture of their parents, of most of their teachers, and probably all of their friends. It may not be the most important aspect of the life of the typical adolescent, but—as they say—if it isn't, it runs a close second.

It cannot be an easy job for young adult librarians to decide what to do about popular culture. There is too much we don't know about it; it offers innumerable potentials for serious conflicts with the value systems which many parents swear by (but may not themselves live by); and the folklore of our profession tells us that we should avoid it. But it should now be obvious to everyone that we can't avoid it. And since we can't avoid it, we ought to try to understand it. I certainly do not understand it. I do not think that anyone else understands it either. What follows is an attempt to suggest some ways of understanding it.

Approaches

When we examine popular culture as a series of individual books, sound recordings, spectacles, television shows, or whatever, it would appear that it can be understood (or explained, or interpreted) without too much difficulty. Reviewers of books and sound recordings do this all of the time. But the "understanding" we get from such an approach—useful though it may be—has serious and obvious limitations. For one thing, such exercises frequently tell us as much or more about the point of view (the biases, prejudices, class origins, etc.) of the person who is doing the reviewing or the explaining than they do about the works in question. Therefore, we should also consider popular culture from some larger perspectives. For example, we could explore the possibility that popular culture is a way of life, or at least an important part of a way of life. Or, better yet, we could say that it is a human environment of images, symbols, rituals, styles, secular liturgies, games, and stratagems which, to some extent, defines the nature of modern life and even makes the living of life more or less possible. Perhaps not only possible, but also sad, happy, meaningful, meaningless, beautiful, or ugly. Thus, we could say that popular culture may be looked upon as:

1. a series of interrelated events or activities (some of which are random and some of which are carefully planned)
2. which involve artifacts (such as books and movies—with all of their infinite varieties of content)
3. which are *experienced* by individuals (all of whom are different in complex psychological ways)

4. who have histories (that is, they have accumulated and stored experiences, consciously or subconsciously)
5. and who also have futures which, in the case of adolescents, are likely to be somewhat uncertain and even frightening
6. and whose lives are connected (in wonderfully complex networks) with the lives of other people whom they may or may not know
7. in a changing social environment.

And all of this is taking place late in the twentieth century—not ten years ago or one hundred years ago, but today and tomorrow.

Looked at in this way, discussions of "quality" versus "popularity" which juxtapose popular culture with elite, academic, traditional, or high culture are not particularly useful or even germane to our problem.

Five Perspectives

It seems to me that we should look for an approach which places the individual at the center of the popular culture process (which is what some young adult librarians are now doing). In thinking about this problem, there are at least five perspectives (or concepts, or points of view) which seem to be relevant:

1. Functionalism: The idea that popular culture is "functional," which is to say that any popular culture event or experience takes place for a purpose. This seems obvious. People are motivated to attend to popular culture of one sort or another because they have "needs." For example, when we say that a popular Western or gothic novel is "escape fiction," we are using a functionalist concept. In a Western novel (if it is typical of the genre), in addition to escape, the reader will find a vision of an orderly world run by men and in which good eventually dominates evil in an environment free of the burdens of modern urban life. Presumably, some people have a "need" to experience life in such terms. It is not for you or me to say whether this be good or bad.
2. Identity: Although people are clearly subject to many influences which are beyond their control, we like to think that they retain a degree of freedom in deciding who they are and what they want to be. This imagined "self" may be, to some extent, a fiction, but it is real to the individual. The "search for identity" is thought to be one of the most important dimensions of human development, and a particularly crucial one for the adolescent.
3. Role theory: Whatever the private "self" may be, the public self is generally all we see of other people and all they see of each of us. It is an interesting theory that in human development we play

roles, we try to define for other people who we are. We wear masks and we play games.

4. Reality: What is real and what is not real are frequently beyond dispute. Nevertheless, it is a fact that it is in the nature of human perceptual systems that reality, for each of us, is to some extent subjective.

5. Persuasion: Some communications theorists have argued that all communications are attempts to persuade. Advertising, public relations, and almost all political rhetoric are obvious examples of this. But it seems that almost from the beginnings of consciousness in childhood, people are subjected to a massive stream of persuasive messages (most of all from parents and teachers) which do not end when they leave school and leave home. Other people want to tell adolescents who they are, how to act, what to think, what not to think, what to do, what they should like and dislike, et cetera. It must become an awfully tiresome experience.

The relationship of these perspectives to popular culture cannot be fully explored here. But in order to suggest a frame of reference, I have assembled a series of "exhibits." If some of these strike you as a bit absurd, I must admit that that's what I have in mind.

Exhibit 1: Flying Saucers

Alamasco, Col.—An autopsy on a horse *believed by its owners to have been killed by inhabitants of a flying saucer* has revealed that its abdominal, brain and spinal cavities were empty.

The pathologist, a Denver specialist who wished to remain anonymous, said that the absence of organs in the abdominal cavity was unexplainable.

. . . "There definitely should have been a good bit of fluid in the brain cavity," the pathologist said. *(San Francisco Chronicle,* October 10, 1967. Emphasis added.[2])

This little snippet from the passing parade (typical of many such anomalies and quirky events that the media love to report) raises some interesting questions. The phenomenon as a physical event defies a natural explanation. But one can attempt to explain the behavior of those who are convinced of the reality of the bizarre incident. In their study of the modern "subculture" which comprises the audience for popular literature about flying saucers, David Stupple and Abdollah Dashti found their theoretical perspective in the work of William James:

In 1893 William James pointed out that we live in several different mental worlds. In addition to the "paramount reality" of common sense built up around everyday experience, there are five mental subuniverses: the world of science, the world of abstract and logical truth, the world of collective illusions and prejudices, the world of supernatural thought, and various worlds of sheer madness and vagary. Each reality is "real" when attended to but the subuniverses are temporary dwelling places and must ultimately terminate into common sense.[3]

I have not been persuaded that everyone's mental dwelling places "ultimately terminate into common sense." However, the concept of "multiple realities" is useful in explaining human activities much more ordinary than the contemplation of flying saucers.

Exhibit 2: They Lived Happily Ever After

> "I love you Sebastion," she whispered. "I love you as . . . a man!" Then, with his lips against hers, he murmured hoarsely: "I love you, my darling, my sweet, my woman—and my wife!" (*The Unknown Heart*, Barbara Cartland.)

This is the very last sentence of an eighty-thousand word saga. And in this sentence we see a way of life, a purpose in life, a system of social organization, a set of personal values. Are these values good or bad? How can we decide? What are their consequences? Their origins? Do they have anything to do with the real world? Does it really matter? Does it have anything to do with libraries?

Exhibit 3: Or Did They?

In her book, *Worlds of Pain: Life in the Working-Class Family,* Lillian Breslow Rubin examined the hopes and dreams and realities of life in the contemporary working-class family. She wrote that "for most young working-class girls . . . getting married was—and probably still is . . . the only way to move from girl to woman." The women Rubin interviewed were in their teens between ten and fifteen years ago. One of these women told her:

> When I think about it now, it sounds crazy, but honestly, the worse things got at home, the more I used to dream about how I was going to marry some good, kind, wise man who would take care of me; and how we'd have beautiful children; and how we'd live in our nice house; and how we'd love each other and be happy.[4]

Of course, it didn't work out that way for any of these women. " 'He's a steady worker; he doesn't drink; he doesn't hit me'—these are the three attributes working-class women tick off most readily when asked what they value most in their husbands."[5] This, Rubin found, was a function of social class (wives of middle-class professional men did not respond with such dark pessimism).

Exhibit 4: "The Mattel Corporation's Wonderful Doll"

In an essay on the cultural significance of Barbie dolls, Don Richard Cox wrote that "the girls who screamed for Elvis in the fifties were seventeen;

those who now swoon at Donny Osmond are eleven."[6] This phenomenon, Cox believes, is somehow related to the wide popularity of little plastic Barbie and her plastic world. These toys redefine a "feminine role," they "alter a child's basic attitudes toward sex, marriage, or a career." Judging by the fate of the women Rubin studied (or some of them), such a redefinition is long overdue.

In any case, whatever is happening here, whatever complex cultural chemistry we are dealing with, it is certain that there are technological and economic elements involved (the plastics industry invented Barbie). Business interests played a part in inventing the American teenager, and are now cultivating an even younger audience as a "potential market for cosmetics, magazines, and phonograph records," as Cox points out.

Exhibit 5: Dreams for Sale

I now believe that there are, quite literally, no limits to the surprises which await us as the manufacturers of consumer culture explore new vistas of human needs. What is one to make of the following incident?

> It is just possible that the next youngster you meet may be either Superman, Spiderman, or Wonder Woman or at least be wearing the proper secret uniform of same.
> And if the youngster is just so secretly garbed, it is probably because mommy is proving the Union Underwear Company right in its decision to branch out from plain white underwear for men and boys . . . into underwear wearing for youngsters of both sexes. (*New York Times,* June 29, 1978, p.71)

What a stroke of marketing genius: underwear designed to resemble the costumes of the great comic book super heroes (forty-five characters will soon be available). But, perhaps, a mixed blessing for parents, since the new product will sell for $4.79 whereas ordinary underwear sells for $2.25. At stake is a $600 million market. The manufacturers are extremely optimistic of success because "for the first time" they have been able to add the influence of children to the purchasing decision for underwear. A spokesman for the company said: "Advertising is not necessary to sell the product, but advertising is necessary to establish it as a *permanent part of the children's culture*" (emphasis added).

Advertisers learned a long time ago that many consumer products are not easily sold on a competitive market unless they can somehow be related to some basic human need. And so they sell dreams, hopes, fantasies, and promises. They give us a version of reality that has some order and meaning. They lie to us.

Exhibit 6: Barbie's Life-style

When parents buy Barbie dolls, they buy images of a way of life. Cox tells us that Barbie gives us her "version of the American dream":

> Barbie's life is that of the ultimate swinging single. Although she has no parents to cast shadows into her life of constant boating, skiing, and camping, she also does not seem to have a need for them. Total independence is a central characteristic of Barbie. Although she owns an extensive amount of sporting equipment Barbie seemingly has no need for employment that allows her to purchase this merchandise . . . although Barbie might be in high school or college there are no accessories that hint at her having to endure the boredom of education.[7]

There are two dimensions to this. The first is the Barbie phenomenon itself. The second is the idea of taking it seriously, as Cox does. You may find the whole business funny or you may find it pathetic. Or trivial. Or sad. Or perhaps even good news. It is all absolute nonsense (this and my other exhibits), or it is very, very important. I am inclined to assume that childish games and fantasies have something rather important to do with what one learns to expect from life. The fantasies that the child acts out with Barbie (or with toy trucks, or with plastic machine guns) may not be real, but their consequences surely are real.

As far as I know, libraries do not circulate Barbie dolls. But they do collect and circulate books, magazines, films, and sound recordings, some of which—I will argue—have cultural functions generally similar to those of the Mattel Corporation's wonderful toy. It is obvious (isn't it?) that games and fantasies do not end with the onset of adolescence.

"All the World's a Stage," etc.

When fantasizing with Barbie (or with toy trucks, or plastic machine guns), the child is for a brief time an instant dramatist, a playwright who prepares a "script" and then acts out the leading role. The outcome of the "play," one assumes, is a happy ending. But these little girls and these little boys are soon marched off to school, and there they learn to play other roles and other games; they interact with other actors; and within the confines of a script they never wrote, they must come to some accommodation with the world. The setting for the last few acts of this game of learning is what strikes me as one of the more bizarre institutions of modern times: the American high school.

Fictions and Conflicts

In one of his studies of popular culture, Lawrence Chenoweth wrote:

> To achieve a sense of control over oneself and one's environment, the individual, as Alfred Adler posited, uses a fiction—or set of values, goals and self-conception of one's potential power—through which he can direct his life.[8]

There are inevitable tensions and paradoxes which emerge from the nature of the modern environment in which the adolescent seeks to "achieve a sense of control" over life. At least three worlds are potentially in serious conflict:

1. The personal world of the adolescent. This is the world of values, goals, and self-conceptions which Chenoweth spoke of. It is one's image of what one wants to be. It is the "self" one has to live with.
2. The "real world," which is the one we all recognize by common sense. It is the objective world we can learn about, the one we can see, the one we live in.
3. The world which the "system" (or some "system") wants to impose on the adolescent. Parents, members of school boards, the clergy, government officials, and business interests have sort of an "official" version of the world which is somewhat sanitized. It includes certain democratic myths and ideologies. In this world there are certain things boys and girls don't do. Some things are never said and some thoughts never thought. Even those who insist that it be perpetuated know it is not true to life.

Young adult librarianship is "subversive" (perhaps even "revolutionary" to a certain extent) insofar as it does not support the idealized version of the parent/school board member/clergy/etc. Formal public school education has always had among its goals the perpetuation of the most widely accepted public myths and ideologies. There is every indication that there are limitations on the extent to which parents want a true and complete version of the real world examined in the public schools.

In the real world there are madmen designing automobiles; there are deranged businessmen selling breakfast food and candy; there are cynical public relations experts trying to invent new ways to lie to us; there are advertising agencies with behavioral scientists who want to teach us to fear and then want to exploit our fears; there are corrupt government officials at all levels. A lot of things people do are not very nice—there are rapists, thieves, whores, and murderers abroad. A few years ago, Martin Pawley wrote that "the massive public outcry in favor of Lieutenant Calley, convicted by a military court of killing over 20 unarmed civilians, reflects not so much the lurking savagery of the average American suburbanite as his refusal to be dragged out of the theatre and into the world."[9]

You may, of course, prefer to look at the brighter side of things (that is, construct a different reality), but this "negative" point of view serves my purpose here. In any case, to a reasonably sensitive and intelligent adolescent, the world must seem somewhat schizophrenic. But this world is the only one they will know, and it is the one in which they must find some sort of meaning.

A Point of View

The title of this paper and its sundry exhibits suggests my point of view. I am not irrevocably committed to [it], but it seems to make sense and is useful: Given that there is a reality "out there" which we all share, it is a fact that the only realities any of us can know are the ones which are in our own heads (fluid and all). And this is as true of librarians (and of you, and of me) as it is of the people librarians serve or would like to serve.

These "inner realities" are, in a very real sense, constructed by ourselves. Some constructed realities work (and one can survive to live and sustain some sort of meaningful life), and others may not work (resulting in despair, unhappiness, and in some cases in self-destruction). I should imagine that one of the traumas of the life passage we call adolescence is in dealing with the perception of some useful reality. The following two quotations seem to suggest a relationship between the cultural environment of young people and the problems (or some of the problems) with which they must deal:

> Culture must first of all be seen as a set of practices, a mode of human activity, a process whereby reality is created, maintained, and transformed.[10]

> The world is essentially without meaning . . . all systems of belief, including that of the conventional sociologists, are arbitrary. The problems previously supposed to be those of the sociologist are in fact the everyday problems of the ordinary man. It is he who must carve out meanings in a world that is meaningless.[11]

In the context of my argument, the point is not whether the world is arbitrary or meaningful. The point is that adolescents must themselves decide what it means and what it means to them as individuals. And I am inclined to believe that formal public school courses contribute only minimally to this process. For my part, I would not have it otherwise.

Conclusion

If the reader agrees with some of the things I have written, then the whole area of the popular culture environment (about which we know very little) has to be of enormous importance to the development of young adult librarianship which goes beyond the support of what is taught in the American high school. The library may "pass on a cultural heritage" (as we have so often claimed), but if it does *only* this its educational functions will be quite limited and removed from that "real world" which we all have to deal with.

I am now convinced that people are born into a world—into a culture

—which is not a "heritage," a culture which did not exist twenty years ago. And this is the one which, above all others, they should learn about. I want adolescents to *experience* popular culture extensively—in fact, most of them experience only a very small part of it. But I also want them to *reflect* on some of it sometimes, to ask themselves what it means, what it is saying to them. They should have a chance to learn about the really rich sources of fantasy and experience which are available in popular culture. Carey and Kreiling said it better than I can: Popular culture is "a cultural process in which persons create shared expressive and conceptual models that supply common identities and apprehended realities."[12]

NOTES

1. Erving Goffman, *Frame Analysis* (Harper, 1974), p.2.
2. *Chronicle* story quoted from Goffman, *Frame Analysis,* p.29.
3. David Stupple and Abdollah Dashti, "Flying Saucers and Multiple Realities," *Journal of Popular Culture* 11:480 (Fall 1977).
4. Lillian Breslow Rubin, *Worlds of Pain* (New York: Basic Books, 1976), p.41.
5. Ibid., p.93.
6. Don Richard Cox, "Barbie and Her Playmates," *Journal of Popular Culture* 11:307 (Fall 1977).
7. Ibid., p.305.
8. Lawrence Chenoweth, "The Rhetoric of Hope and Despair: A Study of the Jimi Hendrix Experience and the Jefferson Airplane," *American Quarterly* 23:27 (Spring 1971).
9. Martin Pawley, *The Private Future* (London: Thames and Hudson, 1973), p.168.
10. James W. Carey and Albert L. Kreiling, "Popular Culture and Uses and Gratifications: Notes Toward an Accommodation," in Jay G. Blumler and Elihu Katz, eds., *The Uses of Mass Communications* (Sage Annual Reviews of Communication Research, vol. 3 [Beverly Hills: Sage Publications, 1974]), p.243.
11. Stanford M. Lyman and Marvin B. Scott, *A Sociology of the Absurd* (New York: Appleton, 1970), p.1.
12. Carey and Kreiling, "Popular Culture and Uses and Gratifications," p.246.

ADDITIONAL REFERENCES

Arnstine, Donald. "Learning, Aesthetics, and Schooling: The Popular Arts as Textbook on America." *Educational Theory* 27:261-73 (Fall 1977).
Chaffee, Steven H., and Tims, Albert R. "Interpersonal Factors in Adolescent Television Use." *Journal of Social Issues* 32:98-115 (Fall 1976).
Clarke, Peter. "Teenagers' Coorientation and Information-Seeking About Pop Music." *American Behavioral Scientist* 16:551-66 (Apr. 1973).

Faber, Ronald, F.; Brown, Jane D.; and McLeod, Jack M. "Coming of Age in the Global Village: Television and Adolescence." In Ellen Wartella, ed., *Children Communicating* (Sage Annual Reviews of Communication Research, vol. 7, pp.215-49). Beverly Hills: Sage Publications, 1979.

Gentile, Lance M., and McMillan, Merna M. "Why Won't Teenagers Read?" *Journal of Reading* 20:649-54 (May 1977).

Johnstone, John W. C. "Social Integration and Mass Media Use among Adolescents: A Case Study." In Jay G. Blumler and Elihu Katz, eds., *The Uses of Mass Communications* (Sage Annual Reviews of Communication Research, vol. 3, pp.35-47). Beverly Hills: Sage Publications, 1974.

Mertz, Maia Pank. "Popular Culture and the Social Construction of Reality." *English Education* 8:12-21 (Fall 1976).

McLeod, Jack M., and Chaffee, Steven H. "The Construction of Social Reality." In James T. Tedeschi, ed., *The Social Influence Processes,* pp.50-99. Chicago: Aldine-Atherton, 1972.

McLeod, Jack M., and O'Keeje, Garrett J., Jr. "The Socialization Perspective and Communication Behavior." In F. Gerald Kline and Philip J. Tichenor, eds., *Current Perspectives in Mass Communication Research* (Sage Annual Reviews of Communication Research, vol. 1, pp.121-68). Beverly Hills: Sage Publications, 1972.

Seltzer, Shirley. "Quo Vadis, Baby?: Changing Adolescent Values as Reflected in the Lyrics of Popular Music." *Adolescence* 11:419-29 (Fall 1976).

Part 3

The Family Circle, the Life Cycle, and the Human Condition

Researchers in this field [family systems health research] agree that the family is the unit of health and/or disease. Psychologically healthy young people live in families where the parents have attained a degree of emotional stability in their own lives and work to create the conditions under which their children will grow to be autonomous adults.[1]

The life so short, the craft so long to lerne. . . .

Geoffrey Chaucer, The Parliament of Fowls

O terminality, where is thy sting!

Edwin Newman, speaking on the topic of euphemisms

Throughout recorded history, families have been a rich source of stories, from the family of Sophocles' *Oedipus Rex* to the family of Puzo's *The Godfather*. It was Aristotle who urged poets to seek out horrible or piteous deeds within families as the basis for their dramas, the better to evoke tragic pity and fear in the audience.[2] Tolstoy incorporates a similar idea in the opening of *Anna Karenina* when he writes, "All happy families are alike. Every unhappy family is unhappy in its own way." It ought not to surprise anyone that the families of many novels read by young adults are also "born to trouble as the sparks fly upward." How true-to-life are these troubled fictional families?

That question is perhaps impossible to answer, but it is nonetheless enlightening to probe into factual information on the family in late twentieth-century America, if only to clear the mind of assorted misconceptions. Marvin B. Sussman, in "The Family Today: Is It an Endangered Species?," lays a factual foundation for an understanding of fictional families as reflective of "the diversity of family forms" in the United States today. He presents and interprets statistics on types of households and climaxes with an appraisal of "the strengths and weaknesses of six different family forms. . . ." Recognizing the diversity of actually existing family forms should help us better to appreciate the "alternative families" encountered in today's literature.

James T. Henke, in "Six Characters in Search of the Family," interprets three of the novels of Paul Zindel, tracing the theme of teenagers seeking "to create their own families in order to successfully fulfill the role of parent," a role at which their own stereotypically bad parents have miserably failed. Readers may also wish to see "Family Relationships and the Growing-up Task in Four Recent Novels for Adolescents" by Eleanore Braun Luckey and Lee Hadley's exploration of " 'Ordinary People': Extraordinary Lives" for related discussions of families in current fiction.[3]

In "The Novel of Crisis: Contemporary Adolescent Fiction," Steve Roxburgh coins, by analogy, a new critical term, *crisotopia,* to describe many of today's novels for young adults. He explains their relationship to an historical tradition but also identifies their divergence from novels of earlier centuries as symptomatic of "a significant shift in consciousness over the last century." A special contribution of his essay is his critical rationale for distinguishing the "best" from the "worst" books in this genre.

Normally, young people develop and grow, becoming progressively independent of the family circle. Schools have served traditionally as avenues through which the young achieve social maturity and finally commence their lives as independent adults, who then go on to establish their own families. Schools and colleges, then, could be seen as extensions of the family (an idea implicit in the old view of the teacher as serving *in loco parentis*). A young person's success or failure in school has inestimable impact upon the shape of his or her subsequent life, yet curiously little literary criticism or interpretation focussing upon "academe" as depicted in literature can be found. Many books come to mind that incorporate a school setting, as for example the settings of Cormier's *The Chocolate War* and Salinger's *The Catcher in the Rye,* yet for whatever reason, essays on these works rarely come to grips with the images of school and college which are presented. Can it be that literary critics and reviewers, who are largely immersed in the academic world, prefer not to examine it too closely? One insightful article, George Watson's "Fictions of Academe: Dons and Realities," takes a penetrating look at the subject from an English perspective and identifies three "plausible charges" against universities: "the sin of Pygmalion," "hypocrisy," and "righteousness," but the novels discussed are not widely read by young adults in the United States.[4] Short stories relating to "Schools, Students, and Teachers" can be found in Thomas West Gregory's *Adolescence in Literature,* with a valuable brief introductory commentary.[5] However, virtually no sustained discussions exist of this topic in the novels familiar to most young people; critical exploration of it is sorely needed.

The remaining essays in this section are devoted to critical points in the lives of young people, probing into the human condition in a world devoid of the traditional certainties and lacking in secure familial bonds. The family and the schools provide arenas wherein the young succeed or fail in satisfying their needs for relatedness; the denial of these needs can trigger severe alienation and result in tragedies such as mental illness and suicide. The essays by Kary K. and Gary K. Wolfe and Joanne Bernstein discuss mental illness and suicide as manifested in popular literature. The Wolfes, in "Metaphors of Madness: Popular Psychological Narratives," identify the characteristic features of a relatively new literary genre—the psychological narrative, citing reasons for its popularity, identifying its literary "relations," and concluding with a lucid and detailed interpretation of *I Never Promised You a Rose Garden,* a book which established a link "between practicing psychology and popular culture."

Joanne Bernstein's "Suicide in Literature for Young People" provides concise reviews of a variety of fiction and nonfiction books relating to this topic. Bernstein also highlights the need for informational literature on suicide prevention and intervention. She succeeds in combining her implied belief in the "coping" value of books (the assumption basic to the approach of bibliotherapy) with her recognition that writing of "competence and beauty" stems from the writer's truth to an inner compulsion to create—not from trying to write in response to "societal need."

For an informative approach to the topic of suicide, the reader is referred to "Cries for Help: Adolescent Suicide" by Mary Susan Miller, which gives a factual treatment, explaining reasons why adolescents are prone to depression, demolishing some myths about suicide, identifying actual factors leading to suicide, danger signals, and ways to help in suicide prevention.[6]

Suicide unquestionably is linked to a life crisis; death may or may not be categorized as a "crisis," depending on the larger cultural context in which death is abstractly viewed and the personal context in which a particular death occurs. Space limitations have not allowed the inclusion of articles treating the topic of death in young adult literature, but the student may wish to see Mary Langer Thompson's " 'Symbolic Immortality': A New Approach to the Study of Death," which describes literature and

films that provide springboards for discussions aimed at finding significance in our experiences with death.[7] Further information on fiction and
nonfiction books on death and death education may be found in "A
Bibliography for Young Adult Education Programs" by Sister M. Frances
Loretta Berger, wherein the annotations relate each item to one or more
of the "stages in attitudes toward death as described by Kubler-Ross."[8]

NOTES

1. Dorothy M. Broderick, "Censorship: A Family Affair?" *Top of the News*
   35:223 (Spring 1979).
2. *Poetics,* chapter 14. See *The Rhetoric and the Poetics of Aristotle,* trans.
   by W. Rhys Roberts and Ingram Bywater (New York: Modern Library,
   1954), p.240.
3. *Children's Literature* 4:176-78 (1975); *Media & Methods* 14:75-76, 84
   (Oct. 1977).
4. *Encounter* (England) 51:42-46 (Nov. 1978).
5. (New York: Longman, 1978), pp.205-7.
6. *Independent School* 37:26-32 (Dec. 1977). An earlier version, under the
   title "Teen Suicide," appeared in the Feb. 1977 issue of *Ladies' Home
   Journal.*
7. *Media & Methods* 13:60-64 (Feb. 1977).
8. *Catholic Library World* 49:107 (Oct. 1977).

The Family Today:
Is It an Endangered Species?

Marvin B. Sussman

Is the family an endangered species? Future historians may label the
1970s as the decade of "The Great Family Debate." The question is: Can
the traditional nuclear family created by the legal act of marriage survive? In discussing this concern I would like to examine what constitutes
a family and consider the variety of family forms, including the dual

Reprinted by permission of the author and publisher from *Children Today*
7:32–37, 45 (Mar.–Apr. 1978).

working, single-parent and childless family, and their dealings with societal institutions and agencies. The debate over the family's future is by no means academic but one which has gripped all segments of the body politic.

Recently a member of the religious sect, Jehovah's Witnesses, came to my door with a pamphlet entitled "The Family—Can It Survive?" The booklet suggested that the existence of the family unit is threatened because we have a high divorce rate, increased inflation is forcing mothers to seek outside employment and thus give up their traditional parenting roles and violence in the family is increasing, as reflected by the higher incidence of battered wives and abused children. Increasingly, more and more families are no longer eating, working, or praying together.

The group's position on these issues was that higher income would not solve these problems and that while education and counseling might offer some help, one should seek wise counsel in the Holy Bible, which provides answers to such questions as "What relationship should exist between a husband and wife for real happiness? How can differences be resolved so that love is kept or restored? What can help the generation gap between children and parents? and How much discipline do children need and how should it be given?"

Such social scientists as Amitai Etzioni and Urie Bronfenbrenner, using more scientific arguments, have reached similar conclusions about the family's future. They assert that the family is becoming increasingly obsolete, with some of its essential and traditional functions under attack. They point to the availability of unlimited sex outside of marriage, the increase in singlehood with a consequent downgrading of the parenting role, the increasing dependence of people upon a complex and bureaucratized work system to meet such primary needs as shelter, food and maintenance, and such secondary needs as education, leisure, work, social services and religion. The hamburger phenomenon of the 1970s—the growth of the fast food chains—threatens the traditional homemaker's role and there is increasing dependence on such specialized institutions as schools and social agencies in the socialization of children. Professor Etzioni predicts: ". . . if [the] increase in divorce and single households continues to accelerate as it did the last ten years, by mid-1990 not one American family will be left."[1]

Dr. Bronfenbrenner's posture is equally pessimistic. There is a touch of nostalgia to his stance. He recognizes the need for families to be formed and procreation to occur and that, in accordance with modern thought, it is necessary that couples have a relationship of shared partnership in regard to household and parenting tasks and responsibilities.

Not all behavioral scientists are taking the postures of Etzioni or Bronfenbrenner, however. Sociologist Mary Jo Bane, for example, believes that proponents of the family's demise have made selective use of demographic and historical data. The nuclear family consisting of husband, wife, and offspring living in a separate household apart from either set of parents has existed side by side with extended households since historic American times. In 1870 the average household had 5.8 people, a very small family compared to the traditional extended family currently found in India and Pakistan, for instance, and in pre-World War II Japan.

Despite the alarming views presented by Etzioni, Bronfenbrenner, and others, based on such parameters as the high divorce rate, we find that the rate of remarriage is equally high. This indicates that it is not marriage as an institution that is being rejected but only that specific marriage relationships are not all that people would like them to be and that the dictum that marriage is for life is no longer accepted. Most people want to be married but they do not want to stay in an unhappy marriage relationship.

The current concern regarding the increasing incidence of the single-parent family—16 percent of all households in the United States today—ignores the fact that there have always been single parents in the United States. The assumption that in early colonial times nearly all children lived with both of their parents during their formative years is more myth than fact. High death rates and the mobility of the breadwinner, seeking an improved livelihood by westward migration, meant that more children in early America had fewer parental surrogates than today. Most children born in the 1970s have at least one parent living with them and there are no hard empirical data proving that two parents are better than one in performing the roles necessary for appropriate socialization of a child, to help him or her become a vital, creative person.

Family Survival

The years following the 1970 White House Conference on Children and Youth saw a growing recognition that the structure of the family varies extensively and that concern for the well-being of families should include consideration of both the traditional nuclear family—consisting of husband and wife created by the act of marriage and living with offspring in a residence apart from either set of parents—and other family forms—created by conditions in the larger society or by individual desire and motivation. The report of Forum Fourteen, "Changing Families in a Changing Society," in the *Report to the President: White House Conference on Children (1970)* highlighted the diversity in family structure and functions.

It begins: "Our pluralistic society of varying family forms and a multiplicity of cultures is a fact." Referring to the diversity of family forms in the United States, and the range of ethnic and racial variations within each one, it defines family functions:

> The family functions as a facilitating, mediating, adapting, and confronting system for its members who have differing aspirations, capa-

bilities, and potentials. Families both adapt to, and simultaneously influence, the development, structure, and activities of today's complex urban and industrial institutions. But families differ in their adaptive capabilities largely because of variations in form, and they differ in their efforts to mitigate the demands of non-family groups and influence the behavior of outside organizations such as the school, welfare agency, or factory. *The primary tasks of families are to develop their capacities to socialize children, to enhance the competence of their members to cope with the demands of other organizations in which they must function, to utilize these organizations, and to provide the satisfactions and a mentally healthy environment intrinsic to the well-being of a family.*

The report emphasized the need to recognize variations from the traditional ideal family form, the implications that such recognition has for parenting, socialization, mental and family health, public policy and legislation, and a need to examine policies and programs in order to see whether they support or constrain the behaviors of members of different family forms in maintaining and expressing themselves.

Since 1970 the federal government has provided increasing support for research and demonstration programs relating to family problems and issues. This indicates the seriousness of its concern over the family's current functioning and future. One expression of its interest is the proposed welfare reform legislation being developed by the Carter administration. Another is that in 1977 the Office of Child Development (OCD) was replaced by the Administration for Children, Youth and Families, which administers all programs formerly in OCD as well as the Youth Development Bureau (formerly the Office of Youth Development) and the Title IV-B Child Welfare Services Program.

Variant Family Structures

There are several ways to perceive the pluralistic structure of families in the United States. One major approach to developing a useful typology is to consider the strengths and weaknesses of different kinds of families, the issues and problems that must be solved by their members. Another way is to look at household distribution. One researcher, J. Ramey, compiled recent Bureau of Labor statistics and arrived at the pattern of household distribution shown in the accompanying [table].[2]

As shown, all but 1 percent of households have breadwinners and the number of nuclear families with two breadwinners (16 percent) is higher than the number with only one (13 percent). Childless households are in the plurality, reflecting the small-size family norm, zero population growth values, and persistence of the pattern that after children are launched into college, jobs, or marriage they establish households independent of the family in which they were reared. The single-headed households include an increasing number of individuals who are post-

Table 1. Distribution of Adult Americans by Type of Household	
(Household Type)	(Percentage of all Households)
Heading single-parent families	16
Other single, separated, divorced or widowed	21
Living in child-free or post-childrearing marriages	23
Living in extended families	6
Living in experimental families or cohabiting	4
Living in dual-breadwinner nuclear families	16
Living in no wage-earner nuclear families	1
Living in single-breadwinner nuclear families	13

poning or rejecting marriage or are between marriages or widowed. Even if early (teenage) marriage should once again become the predominant choice among young people, it is likely that the increasing number of widowed persons (whose life span is increasing) will sustain the percentage of this household form in future years.

A fundamental catalyst behind the development of pluralism in family forms is the movement toward a more equitable distribution of tasks within the household and parity in marital relationships, decision making, parenting, responsibilities for gainful employment, and uses of income. In the prerevolutionary war period there were calls for egalitarianism in marriage and family life. Women of elite colonial families such as Abigail Adams and Mercy Warren found a measure of equality with their spouses as they worked with them to rid the colonies of an English crown and called upon their husbands and leaders of the Constitutional Assembly to consider the human rights of women. But along with all other colonial women, they were subject to the common law of England, which was transported along with other baggage to the New World.

Inequality in marriage continued after the successful American Revolution and passage of a Declaration of Independence and Bill of Rights which provided unprecedented freedoms for the people of the new nation. Urbanization and industrialization had not reached the critical level of development necessary to provide education and occupational options for women of all social backgrounds.

The state marriage laws which came into existence followed the common law patterns. They denigrated the roles of women and perpetuated a chattel relationship between men and women by their emphasis upon marriage as a status rather than a contract. If marriage is viewed as a contract, it can be dissolved like any other contract when parties find it is not to their benefit and contractors do not live up to expectations. As a status, marriage is a matter of "public interest" to be dissolved only by the state, a procedure which contributed to continued male domination within the family. On the premise that women were incompetent, or at least incapable of providing for themselves, the adopted English common law, reinforced by numerous court decisions, stipulated the man's responsibility for providing for the family. In exchange, his wife carried out his wishes, bore and raised his children, and followed him to wherever there was the best opportunity for a job.

Historians, family watchers, and other experts will undoubtedly continue to debate the exact causes which have led to recent and continuing changes in gender roles. One explanation is that such situations and events as rapid urbanization and industrialization and two world wars have made women's labor critical to the national effort and so gradually increased the base of economic and political power to include an increasing number of women.

More educational options for all members of society have led to less contentment with the status quo. The strong social movements of minority and youth groups in the 1950s and 1960s, legislation since the historic 1954 court decision on school desegregation, and the development of mass communication networks have all helped push society toward gender role equality.

At the same time, changes in basic values have occurred within society as well as the family. The right to separate and file for divorce to dissolve a marriage is an accepted new value. Thirty-one states now have "breakdown of the marriage" and thirteen others invoke separation—usually for one year—as a ground for divorce.[3] The fact that forty-four of the fifty states have some version of a no-fault divorce law reduces the legal posture of divorce as an adversary process in which one partner must be found guilty and the other innocent.

Another critical value change has been the increased openness regarding human sexuality—and the distinctions made between sexual behavior for its intrinsic value and for procreation. As a result, there is widespread use of contraceptives, with voluntary sterilization now the most used and preferred technique for fertility control by couples who have been married more than ten years or by those who have had all the children they want.

The current emphasis on the sharing of responsibilities and parity in couple relationships within the family has led to the emergence of the personal marriage contract.[4] Within the context of a society that supports partnership agreements or contracts and which has accepted the norm of zero population growth, there is also an increasing sense of individualism.[5] The family exists for the benefit of the individual, rather than the individual existing for the benefit of the family.

Concomitant with the emphasis on the individual is a view that parents as well as children have a right to live a full life and that attention should be given to the marital health of a couple.[6] There is a definite shift from viewing one's good work for future gains and rewards and to pass on a legacy to one's issue to viewing life in the present, in terms of

one's own existence. Life should be experienced and activities and relationships judged for their intrinsic qualities—joy and satisfaction. It is in
this changed time perspective—to consider the present rather than the
past or the future—that human rights' movements, including the movement for sexual equality, have their ideological roots. The corollary is a
reduction of faith in traditional family forms and institutions, together
with an increased suspicion of authority.

Other shifts in values and perspectives result in less reliance for help,
information, and intimacy upon traditional organizations and institutions
such as the church and school and more dependence upon one's peers for
response and interest. As a consequence, ideologies and values long identified with established institutions are being rejected as sources of truth.
The solution is to rely upon oneself, to take responsibility and do what
is required, working with those few with whom it is possible to identify
and communicate. Implicit is the assumption that an individual today can
choose his or her own living pattern, pursuing the lifestyle and family
form which promises the greatest self-actualization.

Problems and Issues

Endemic to changes in family and household organization and intra-
family relationships are a diminished quality of parenting and increased
unpleasantness in the way family members treat one another. Many
studies suggest that the incidence of family violence—most often in the
form of child abuse and wife-beating—is increasing. In reviewing the
research on the extent of marital violence in the United States (and inter-
polating from three studies which used large samples of the population),
S. Steinmetz reports that of the forty-seven million couples, possibly
more than three million wives—and a quarter of a million husbands—
experienced severe beatings from their spouses.[7]

The true incidence of child abuse and neglect is also difficult to determine. The National Center on Child Abuse and Neglect in the Children's Bureau, ACYF, estimates that it may be as high as one million
cases a year. In one sample of intact families, a researcher discovered that
in one of five families parents hit their children with some object as a
routine aspect of child-rearing and that more than 4 percent thrashed
their children and over 2 percent threatened them with such bodily
harm as stabbing or shooting. And these are "normal" families![8]

Unwanted births and teenage pregnancies are other pressing problems
for families, agencies, and society.

One development of the 1960s, the Forum Fourteen Report notes, "was
the emergence of the client-centered society" and another critical problem
is the conflict between the self-help efforts of family members in their roles

as clients, patients, consumers, workers, pupils, or victims and the organizational bureaucracies and professionals which provide services. Family-centered organizations are demanding reciprocity in their relationships with bureaucracies and are working to effect change in policies and allocation of resources. However, many efforts are being coopted by well- and some not so well-intentioned agencies and their staffs.[9] The professionals have resources and knowledge and the best that most families can do is to develop competencies to use and deal with the bureaucratic procedures and workers in these human service agencies.

Battered spouses, abused children, unwanted pregnancies, and individuals unprepared for handling the daily exigencies of survival are phenomena endemic to highly complex and differentiated societies; they occur among all family forms in varying degrees. A change in their incidence will only take place if basic modifications are made in our present social structures and in the allocation of economic resources and human services. This important issue cannot be treated in a short essay. What can be discussed here are some of the difficulties and some of the advantages encountered by individuals living in different types of households, as viewed by this family watcher. In so doing, I pass on to the reader responsibility to make an overall judgment of the strengths and weaknesses of American families.

My appraisal of the strengths and weaknesses of each of six different family forms, based on a review of empirical studies, clinical reports, and my own research activity, follows.

The single career family. Intact nuclear family consisting of husband, wife, and offspring living in a common household where one partner, usually the husband, is the provider. (Represents 13 percent of all households.)

Strengths

Maintains its position as the primary structure for potential socialization of members over the life cycle.

Is the primary unit for taking care of disabled, deviant, and dependent members.

Is among the best adapted in terms of fitting the demands of the corporate economic structure.

Weaknesses

Is easily broken, with increasing intervention of organizations and expenditure of monies to maintain individuals of broken marriages and new family forms.

The single breadwinner of the working class is unable to provide adequately for its maintenance. Among the middle classes, there is difficulty in providing an expected quality of life.

The dual career family. Intact nuclear family consisting of husband, wife, and offspring living in a common household where both partners work. (Represents 16 percent of all households.)

Strengths

Competent structure to provide maximal income for maintenance and to achieve quality of life aspirations.

Highly adequate form for effecting goals of gender equality. It provides work options for both marital partners and opportunity to share household tasks and marital responsibilities.

Weaknesses

Dependence on kin and institutional support systems for effective maintenance and functioning.

Developing but still noninstitutionalized values and means to harmonize the career activities and ambitions of both partners and the roles concerned with marital relationships and parenting.

The single parent household with children under age 18. (Represents 16 percent of all households.)

Strengths

Many adults who can function as socialization models for children are potentially available. Adults other than parents may be more effective in teaching and socializing children.

If supported appropriately, the single parent can achieve greater self-expression than a married counterpart; accountability is limited to children.

For a significant number of single-parent families, which result as a consequence of separation and divorce, the removal or absence of a violent parent results in a nurturant and liveable family form.

Weaknesses

Need for support systems for parenting, economic and health maintenance, and social relationships—often scarce or unavailable in particular communities.

The insufficiency of finances endemic to this family form often results in higher morbidity and expenditure of third party monies for maintenance and survival. Another consequence of economic deficiency is the pressure for some to remarry in order to obtain such support, with increased probability that the previous marriage experience will be repeated.

For some families, when the single parent is gainfully employed and substitute parents are unavailable or ineffective, the socialization is done by peers, and the behavior of children may be viewed as deviant and delinquent.

The remarried nuclear family. Husband, wife and offspring living in a common household. (Represents 11 percent of all households.)

Strengths

Previous marital experiences may result in an increased number (actual incidence unknown) of stable marriages.

Parenting, which may formerly have been the function of a single adult, may be shared with the new partner and his or her older children.

For some, there is improved economic status as a consequence of shared income.

Weaknesses

The difficulties in blending two formerly independent households into one functioning unit may result in extreme psychic stress for some members.

Formations consisting of two large-size families may require substantial economic help, counseling and other supports in order to survive.

Economic and social commitments to individuals of previous marriages may restrict the development of adequate, stable relationships in the new marriage.

The kin family. Consisting of bilateral or intergenerational-linked members living in the same household. (Represents 6 percent of all households.)

Strengths

Maintenance of familial values and transmission of accumulated knowledge and skills are likely occurrences.

Multiple adults are available for socialization and shared household and work responsibilities.

Weaknesses

Demands for geographical mobility are not easily met.

From one perspective, the resistance to changes which threaten the maintenance of this family form can reduce the motivation of individuals to achieve in the society.

Experimental families. Individuals in multi-adult households (communes) or cohabitating. (Represents 4 percent of all households.)

Strengths

In communal forms, a large number of individuals are available to form a support system to meet individual needs, a situation especially important to individuals in transition from one family form to another, such as recently divorced women with small children.

Individuals not ready or unwilling to make a commitment to a long-term partnership can experience economic and social sharing, psychic growth and open communication and interpersonal relationships.

Weaknesses

Few of these forms have developed strategies, techniques or economic bases to sustain their activities or achieve their goals.

In a large number of experimental family forms, role responsibilities are not clearly delineated or articulated, with consequential difficulties in implementing parenting, economic, household, and other functions.

Notes

1. A. Etzioni, "The Family: Is It Obsolete?" *Journal of Current Social Issues* 14 (no. 1, 1977).
2. J. Ramey, "Experimental Family Forms—The Family of the Future," *Marriage & Family Review* (Jan./Feb. 1978).
3. D. J. Freed, "Divorce Laws Coast to Coast," in *Family Law Reporter,* 4, 1, text section #1, 1977.
4. M. B. Sussman, Plenary Address, "Marriage Contracts: Social and Legal Consequences," 1975 International Workshop on Changing Sex Roles in Family and Society, Dubrovnik, Yugoslavia.
5. J. Ramey, "Experimental Family Forms."
6. C. E. Vincent, "Barriers to the Development of Marital Health as a Health Field," *Journal of Marriage and Family Counseling* (July 1977).
7. Susan Steinmetz, "Violence between Family Members," *Marriage & Family Review* 1:1-16 (May-June 1978).
8. M. A. Straus, "Violence in the Family: An Assessment of Knowledge and Research Needs," in Mary Van Stolk, ed., *Child Abuse: Its Treatment and Prevention: Interdisciplinary Approach* (Toronto: McClelland and Stewart, 1977).
9. J. Lawton, " 'Control' Is a Dominant Motif in Social Work Motivation," *Behavior Today* 8:3 (Oct. 24, 1977).

Six Characters in Search of the Family: The Novels of Paul Zindel

James T. Henke

Since the appearance of *The Pigman* in 1968, the novels of Paul Zindel have been the objects of a good deal of contradictory discussion and evaluation. These works, *The Pigman, My Darling, My Hamburger,* and *I Never Loved Your Mind,* have been hailed as delightfully humorous, refreshingly honest attempts to deal with a number of the classic themes of modern literature. On the other hand, they have been condemned, with

Reprinted from *Children's Literature* 5:130–40 (1976) by permission of *Children's Literature: An International Journal,* Inc. Copyright © 1976 by Francelia Butler. Versions of this essay were presented at Youngstown State University's first annual Children's Literature Workshop (Nov. 1974) and at the seventeenth annual meeting of the Midwest Modern Language Association (Nov. 1975).

equal fervor, as squalid pieces of trash, as slick "con jobs," and as simple-minded hack work.[1]

Obviously, the resolution of such controversy, if indeed any resolution is possible, is an undertaking far too ambitious for a single essay. Therefore, in this discussion my goals will be much more modest. First, I will sketch one thematic approach to Zindel's novels and then attempt a brief evaluation of the literary worth of each. In so doing, I anticipate that, rather than providing a resolution, this discussion will intensify the Zindel debate.

In any case, for the moment we will put aside the problem of the literary quality of Zindel's novels and turn instead to the ideas contained in those novels. Better yet, we will focus upon one idea that, with varying degrees of clarity, informs all three of the author's books. The tracing of this major theme may possibly prove rewarding regardless of the merits of the works themselves. So, let us turn first to *The Pigman*.

The hero of Zindel's first novel is John Conlan, sixteen years old, a bright, imaginative, rebellious high school sophomore. The heroine is Lorraine Jensen, sixteen years old, a bright, somewhat less imaginative, and somewhat less rebellious high school classmate. John and Lorraine are friends, and the novel is their collaboration on a first-person, reflective account of their experiences with Mr. Pignati, the Pigman.

By page eleven of the book the reader has been introduced to the respective parents of the protagonists. John's father, whom he calls the "Bore," is a reformed alcoholic and a thorough-going materialist, a preoccupied commodities broker who cheats on his income tax. John's mother is a compulsive housekeeper who will not allow the boy to use her spotless living room. Lorraine is a bit better off. She has only one parent, a divorced mother, a private nurse who specializes in terminal cancer cases so that she can sell the dying patient to the highest-bidding mortuary. The reader can easily understand, then, why both John and Lorraine are lonely and why, as Beverly Haley and Kenneth Donelson note in a recent article, they attempt to escape the loveless reality of their existences by guzzling beer and playing mischievous games.[2] That is, until they meet the Pigman.

Angelo Pignati, the third major character of the novel, is a sixtyish widower who is attempting to escape his own unfaceable reality: he cannot admit to himself that his wife is dead. Rather, he insists upon pretending that she is visiting a sister in California. Obviously, like the children, he lives a life without love; like the children, he yearns for something, for someone.

When these three meet quite by accident, their lives are changed, but not in the way critics generally assume. For instance, Haley and Donelson write: "Then they [the children] find a substitute parent in Mr. Pignati, a childless widower, who becomes the parent neither has ever known, as they become the children he has never had."[3] Although close, this is not quite on the mark. None of Zindel's heroes and heroines is seeking a surrogate parent. Quite to the contrary, all of Zindel's paired protagonists (and the reader encounters these boy-girl teams in all three novels) have rejected the subordinate role of child and are seeking to assume for themselves the dominant identity of parent. In other words, what they attempt to do is in various ways to create their own families in order to successfully fulfill the role of parent, a role at which their own parents have failed so miserably.

Thus, in *The Pigman* John and Lorraine are not searching for a substitute father. Without the remotest awareness on their part, they are searching for a surrogate child, and Mr. Angelo Pignati, the aging widower, becomes that child.

Indeed, the thing about the old man that first strikes John and Lorraine is his childlike openness and his youthful enthusiasm for fun and games. Five minutes after they first meet, he offers to teach the children a memory game. "Do you know the secret of how to memorize ten items?" he asks eagerly. John remarks: "I looked at him, and I had to bite my tongue because I was going to burst out laughing. He looked just like a great big kid—so happy we were there" (p. 41).[4] Lest the reader miss the significance of the Pigman's incongruous youthfulness, then, Zindel helpfully allows John to underline that significance for him. And just to make doubly certain that he recognizes Mr. Pignati's symbolic role, when with a great deal of pride the Pigman successfully demonstrates his skill at the memory game, Zindel once again allows John to note: "Then he said the items, starting with girl and working back to cockroach, and I swear he looked just like a great big baby that had just made a super-duper mud pie" (p. 42).

Certainly, the reader must view John's evaluation of Mr. Pignati's character and conduct with some suspicion. The trustworthiness of the solitary, first-person narrator must always be suspect. Lorraine, however, shares some of the narrating duties in this novel. Though somewhat less imaginative than John, she seems the more sensitive of the two and her evaluation reinforces his.

Note her account of a "family" shopping spree. No sooner do the three enter the department store than Mr. Pignati, the avid zoo fan, pleads, "Can we look at the pet shop?" Like the much-put-upon father, John groans, but Lorraine, scowling at John, and humoring the Pigman, assures him, "Of course we can" (p. 85). A bit later, the role she is playing is clarified for the reader. The three are in the sporting goods department, and Mr. Pignati wants to buy them all roller skates. Lorraine, shocked at the extravagance, shows her displeasure. But Mr. Pignati wheedles, "Please let me get them." The girl remembers that the old man had been "practically asking for my permission" (p. 87).

Here she is clearly the surrogate mother and the old widower her child, and although she never seems completely to grasp this psychological reality, she is at least partially aware of it. Later, just before the Pigman's first heart attack, she reflects on the significance of her and John's relationship with the old fellow: "The longer he knew us, the more of a kid he became. It was cute in a way" (p. 108).

But it is not really cute; it is tragic. Mr. Pignati's regression indirectly costs him his life. While he is in the hospital, John and Lorraine take over his house and, *sans* sex, act out the role of man and wife. They masquerade in adult clothes, enjoy a candlelight dinner, and even throw a cocktail party. The fantasy is shattered, however; for at the party John gets drunk, the guests become unruly, and Mr. Pignati's cherished collection of pig figurines is smashed—just as Mr. Pignati returns home unexpectedly from the hospital.

The Pigman forgives John and Lorraine. He forgives them as only the adoring child can forgive those parents who have inexplicably caused him pain. Yet they know and the reader knows that their betrayal is partially responsible for the death of their surrogate son. The following day, Pignati is stricken by a second, and this time fatal, heart attack.

In Zindel's next novel, the theme of adolescent aspirations to parenthood is once again traceable, but, perhaps because *My Darling, My Hamburger* concerns two teenage couples instead of one, the idea is less central than in *Pigman*. In *My Darling,* the story focuses as much upon the maturation of Maggie and Denis as upon the young lovers Sean and Liz. Moreover, in this second book the author seems to get tangled in a rather superficial examination of such fashionable topics as teenage premarital sex, illicit pregnancy, and abortion, and in so doing partially to slight the theme he first introduced in *The Pigman*. Nevertheless, the idea is there and merits examination. But we will shorten that examination by ignoring the stories of Maggie and Denis and by noting that, for the parents of Sean and Liz, Zindel once again creates stereotypically "bad" parents, not unlike those which appear in *The Pigman*.

In this second book, then, the reader again encounters a teenage couple attempting to escape the harshness of their respective family lives by creating a third family in which they assume the parental roles. Now, however, the protagonists are older and are no longer content to "beget" surrogate children. Sean and Liz, high school seniors, become lovers and soon Liz becomes pregnant.

Like John and Lorraine in *The Pigman,* these young people also botch their new parental roles. With a premeditation lacking in John and Lorraine, they kill the life that they have created. Sean, who had promised to marry Liz, reneges under pressure from his father and the girl gets an abortion.

What is interesting here is not the love story itself, but the elaboration upon a Zindel stance not fully developed in *Pigman*. In *My Darling* the author suggests the reason why these adolescents fail in their prematurely assumed parental roles is that contemporary society is so brutal and so sterile itself that it deliberately seeks to corrupt the greatest parental duty, which is not simply to create life, but to cherish it.

Indeed, in this book Zindel goes even further. Contemporary society corrupts Sean and Liz by forcing them to sacrifice the life they have created. In Sean's essay "The Circus of Horrors," which he writes for an English honors seminar and which is inserted toward the end of the novel, it becomes clear that society has forced the children to murder their baby. Sean describes a circus performance in which a naked boy and girl, standing on a huge wagon, are pulled into a large tent to confront a savagely howling audience. With them they have a baby. To the delight of the mob, the ringmaster, assisted by a male acrobat and female witch, forces the young couple to submit the baby to a guillotine. Obviously, the mob is society, and the male acrobat and female witch represent parents.

Now surely, the sensitive reader must see that this is, in part, Sean's attempt to shift guilt. Yet Zindel's third-person narrator never clearly points out this fact. Thus, the reader is justified in interpreting Sean's unconscious rationalization as Zindel's conscious condemnation.

That Zindel does indeed share with his adolescents their view of contemporary society becomes even more apparent in his last novel, *I Never Loved Your Mind*. In this first-person narration by Dewey Daniels, the seventeen-year-old high school dropout, the family, which in the earlier novels stood as the chief symbol of a sterile society, has all but disappeared. On one occasion when Dewey asks Yvette Goethals, the heroine of the book, why she does not live with her parents, she responds: "Because they're bastards. My mother's a dumb one. My father's a mean one" (p. 29). But this is virtually the only time they are mentioned. To Yvette, they seem to be merely a part of the general corruption and brutality of society, a society for which her own neighborhood becomes a kind of malignant biopsy sample blighted by such as a crooked judge, a cheating doctor, a thieving cop, and a host of other parasites. As Yvette herself says, "practically every house has some type of lousy, sneaky, illegal, bloodsucking scrounger in it" (p. 62). Nor, indeed, do Dewey's parents play a more prominent role in the story. As with Yvette's, the reader never sees them, but Dewey does say: "My folks happen to be plain, nice, detached, insignificant people, and nobody has the right to pin any rap on them" (p. 33). Rather than parents, then, in this last novel, the principal symbol of a degenerate society is the hospital in which both Dewey and Yvette work, a hospital steered by a vacuously authoritarian administrator, staffed by indifferent nurses, and stocked with deformed or dying patients.

In the midst of this pain and despair, Dewey discovers Yvette, another high school dropout. The girl, who once waged a futile battle with bulldozers to save a plot of woods in her old neighborhood, becomes a symbol of new life. In fact, Yvette Goethals appears to be a twentieth-century, adolescent reincarnation of the Greek goddess Demeter, the Earth

Mother and Goddess of Grain. Consider that throughout the narrative, Dewey, with what appears to be unconscious intuition, speaks of her in such a way as to link her with all things natural. For instance, when he first meets her, she appears to him to "look like an owl with a thyroid condition" (p. 3). On their first date Yvette wears a huge, furry mouton coat which, Dewey tells the reader, makes her look like a grizzly bear, a "wolf-woman" (p. 46), and a "koala cub" (p. 58). When she runs and the wind catches the coat, she reminds him of a pterodactyl, spreading its wings (p. 59). At the end of this first date, he walks her to Clove Lakes Park, but she will not allow him to take her home. As Dewey describes it: "She just took off into the brush, like a bear at Yellowstone National Park . . ." (p. 67). Probably, she is headed for her house on "Van Pelt" street. This house Dewey will later see and will describe as being surrounded by "landscaping that resembled an acre of overfertilized rain forest" (p. 75).

Even more than the narrator's intuitive descriptions, however, the actual events of the story suggest that Yvette is a twentieth-century version of the Earth Mother, who, in addition to her role as fertility goddess, is also a goddess of rebirth. That Zindel does indeed intend to endow the girl symbolically with the Goddess' power of rejuvenation is apparent in the fact that Dewey first actually meets his love in the autopsy room, as he awakens from a fainting spell to see her bending over him. The symbolic significance of this episode is underscored some eight chapters later when Dewey describes his thoughts and emotions on the morning after he and Yvette have made love: "When I woke up in my own room on Saturday morning, I felt like I had just been born. . . . I kept myself in a luxurious somnolent state, trying to relive everything all over again. . . . I remembered her gently nursing me back to health in the autopsy room" (p. 91).

This, then, is symbolic rebirth, but before complete rebirth Dewey had had to ply his Demeter with "sacrificial offerings." When he first courts Yvette, he gives her flowers and candy. However, she tells him that instead of these she would prefer bags of seed, especially wheat and barley (both grains are traditionally associated with Demeter). Moreover, on the night they make love, Dewey brings her a fifty-pound bag of Burpee radish seed.

Nevertheless, even though he thinks himself born anew, the goddess ultimately rejects him. Although she loves him, she feels that he has been corrupted by society, and she flees with the Electric Lovin' Stallions, a rock music group with whom she has been living. Now, Dewey and the reader discover the literal reason for the girl's bizarre taste in gifts; she and the Stallions are leaving in a horsedrawn covered wagon for New Mexico, there to establish a commune.

Does Dewey follow? Zindel does not tell the reader. He lets him see only that Dewey has indeed undergone a rebirth of sorts. In the final pages of the novel, having learned the address of Yvette's commune, the hero resigns his position at the hospital and closes his story: "I don't really know what I'm going to do. . . . I'm not going to give civilization a kick in the behind, because I might need an appendectomy sometime. But I'm going to do something, and I have a strange feeling it's going to be phantasmagorically different" (pp. 134–35).

Zindel's final novel, then, presents a mythically translated and exalted treatment of the theme of the adolescent aspiration for parenthood. After all, while John and Lorraine become surrogate parents and while Sean and Liz almost become real parents, Dewey may have the chance to embrace the family of the Earth Mother. And because, as Yvette has told him several times, her relationship with the Stallions is platonic, if the hero is accepted as being worthy of the honor, he will become the goddess' consort and patriarch of the communal family.

But Zindel may be hinting at much more here. Should the Earth Goddess mate, the result would be a general rebirth of nature. Thus, the author may be telling the reader that from the zest for life, from the compassion for nature of such young people as Dewey and Yvette, a new order is possible. Such vital young parents may beget not just children, but a whole new world.

The question is whether or not one must turn his back on contemporary society to create this world. Here, perhaps, Zindel's attitude toward contemporary society may soften. Although Yvette has fled, Dewey has resolved not to do so completely. He is not, as he says, "going to kick civilization in the behind." Maybe this is just a cowardly evasion on Dewey's part. Or maybe Zindel is saying that society can be rejuvenated and purified by the union of the hero, who will not forsake it, and the goddess: the one representing the rebirth of civilized humanity's love for nature, the other representing the lifegiving forces of nature itself.

Is this a Pollyannic interpretation of Zindel's meaning? Perhaps. But before we dismiss it, we ought to remember that in the hospital, that symbol of a dying society, both Dewey and Yvette worked in the inhalation section. Their jobs were to resuscitate patients with oxygen, literally to revive them by providing a breath of fresh air. We ought to remember, too, that when Yvette leaves the hospital and heads for the covered wagon that will take her to a new world, Dewey tries to stop her. In the struggle, her mouton coat flaps open, and Dewey sees that the girl has strapped a "Byrd" machine to her waist. At first, this detail may seem insignificant, since Yvette previously has pilfered medical supplies from the hospital. Still, on second thought, we must wonder: after all, the function of a Byrd machine is to resuscitate patients dying of asphyxiation. In other words, literally and symbolically Yvette has the means to revive and restore life; all that remains now is for Dewey to have the courage to go after her and teach her how to use it.

This, then, is a sketch of the treatment of one of Zindel's themes, an overview which we can use as background for a rough evaluation of the author's individual works. So, let us return to *The Pigman*.

Paul Zindel's first novel is rich in provocatively suggestive metaphor and symbol, only a small part of which is noted in our previous discussion. For instance, Mr. Pignati's beloved zoo is a symbol of the plight of modern man in our impersonal society. Each of us, so Zindel says, lives in his own cage of indifference, boredom, or self-absorption. As do the creatures in the zoo, we may live in close proximity, but we do not live together. At the zoo, Mr. Pignati delights in tossing peanuts to Bobo the gorilla, and John delights in teasing Bobo by attempting to "speak" like an ape. Both acts, one pathetic, the other comic, are symbolic of modern man's need to communicate with someone, something, anything. Lorraine suggests yet another symbolic significance of the zoo. Both she and John have cut classes and she is waiting for him at the sea lion pool. She broods over the indifferent, unimaginative way a zoo keeper feeds the sea lions: "I mean, if you're going to feed sea lions you're not supposed to plop the food into the tank. You can tell by the expressions on their faces that the sea lions are saying things like 'Don't dump the fish in!' 'Pick the fish up one by one and throw into the air so we can chase after them.' 'Throw the fish in different parts of the tank!' 'Let's have fun!' 'Make a game out of it!' " (p. 54). This may be simply a comment on man's inhumanity to the animals. But is it not far more likely that the character's observations are a metaphoric indictment of what the author considered to be the stifling sterility of our modern schools?

In *The Pigman* even stereotypes are functional. Although John's and Lorraine's parents may remind the reader a bit of Cinderella's stepmother, the author puts their stereotypical nature to good use as a yardstick against which to measure the final actions of their children. Consider, for instance, the drunken cocktail party which wrecks Mr. Pignati's house. Inadvertently, without malice, John and Lorraine betray the trust of their "child." Surely, the reader is meant to compare their selfish thoughtlessness with that of their own parents. They have failed their "child," as they themselves have been failed. Thus, the stereotyped parents stand as an indictment of the actions of their children, while at the same time the stereotype of the "bad" parent is given greater depth by those actions, which suggest that John's and Lorraine's parents abuse their children, not out of brutality, but out of thoughtlessness. Finally, the rigid parental stereotypes, when compared with the protagonists' final contrition, serve to emphasize John and Lorraine's moral superiority: they are capable of moral growth; their parents are not.

About Zindel's second novel, *My Darling, My Hamburger*, I wish I could be as enthusiastic. This appears to have been a hastily written book whose stereotypical characters and actions manifest little of the functional utility of those in *Pigman*. With minimal injustice, the love story of this novel can be summarized as follows: Liz, the most beautiful girl in the senior class, and Sean, the handsomest boy, have an affair which culminates in an illicit pregnancy. The pregnancy is aborted in an operation arranged by a slimy hospital technician. Liz's future, rich in promise,

is destroyed; Sean's is forever blighted by his sense of guilt for having rejected Liz. Moreover, in this story the reader also encounters parents
whose wickedness is as unmotivated as is that of Cinderella's stepmother.
In fact, Liz's father, a particularly vicious and insensitive type, is really
her stepfather, *à la* Cinderella. The story reads like a mushy episode from
Peyton Place.

Still, *My Darling, My Hamburger* does have interest as a transitional
link between *The Pigman* and *I Never Loved Your Mind.* Indeed, *My
Darling* could prove very useful in the classroom. Paired with *The Pig-
Man,* for instance, it could be used to demonstrate to young readers the
limitations of slick, pat literature, and at the same time, to demonstrate
the provocative richness of the other work.

Finally, Zindel's last novel, *I Never Loved Your Mind,* is both his most
ambitious and his most difficult. The craftsmanship here is painstaking,
but it is often obscured by the narrator Dewey's cloyingly fatuous prose
style, perhaps best described by his own favorite adjective "puerile."
Nevertheless, Zindel clearly intends the style to be functionally suggestive.
The overused technique of alliteration, the often-inappropriate diction,
and the generally inflated rhetoric suggest both the immaturity of Dewey's
intellect and the fact that he does possess a vigorous, perceptive intellect
capable of growth.[5] In one sense, we should see Dewey as an embodiment of the intellect, of the mind paired with but at the same time con-
trasted to the unbridled spirit of the flesh, Yvette Goethals.

The danger with this novel is that because Zindel chooses to tell the
story through the limited, first-person narration of a hero who does not
yet understand either his own or Yvette's role, the inexperienced reader
may confuse the story's meaning and accept the girl's flight from society
as the intelligent way to deal with evil. But this is not Zindel's meaning.
The phoniness of the Loveland commune, to which Zindel devotes an
entire chapter, and Yvette's illiteracy, evidenced in the note which Zindel
inserts toward the close of the story, suggest both her own very limited
intelligence and the impossibility of realizing the pastoral dream. This
impossibility is further emphasized by the plight of Irene. In the hospital
Irene, eighty years old and dying of emphysema, writes a poem entitled "Let's Go Back." But just as she cannot return to childhood, so
neither can society return to an agrarian Eden.

As her covered wagon pulls away from the hospital gate, Yvette
screams at Dewey: "I never loved your mind." Certainly. The business of
the Earth Goddess is not the intellect, but the spirit and the flesh. Zindel
seems to be telling his youthful readers that only by a combination of
common-sense intelligence (one that appreciates the virtue of civilization
represented by the appendectomy Dewey may some day need) and passionate spirit can society be saved.

The final evaluation, then? Paul Zindel is a fine craftsman, a genuine
literary artist. Whether, as many have questioned, his novels are appropriate for the adolescent audience, I will leave to others to decide. I am

certain of one thing, however: I will not be the last critic to attend to those novels.

NOTES

1. For a sample of this discussion, see, among others, review of *The Pigman* in *Best Sellers* 28:327 (Nov. 1, 1968); Diane G. Farrell, review of *The Pigman* in *Horn Book* 45:61 (Feb. 1969); E. M. Graves, review of *My Darling, My Hamburger* in *Commonweal* 91:257 (Nov. 21, 1969); Margot Hentoff, review of *I Never Loved Your Mind* in *New York Review of Books* 15:11 (Dec. 17, 1970); Josh Greenfield, review of *I Never Loved Your Mind* in *New York Times Book Review* pt. 2:14 (May 24, 1974).
2. Beverly A. Haley and Kenneth L. Donelson, "Pigs and Hamburgers, Cadavers and Gamma Rays: Paul Zindel's Adolescents," *Elementary English* 51: 941-45 (Oct. 1974).
3. Haley, p.943.
4. Quotations from Zindel's novels are taken from *The Pigman* (1968; reprint ed., New York: Dell, 1970) and *I Never Loved Your Mind* (1970; reprint ed., New York: Bantam, 1972).
5. For an interesting treatment of Dewey's style, see Lou Willett Stanek, "The Junior Novel: A Stylistic Study," *Elementary English* 51:947-53 (Oct. 1974). Stanek notes that Dewey's language is not "authentic teenage speech" and suggests that this lack of authenticity may be due to the fact that Zindel is using the style to parody other writers such as Salinger.

The Novel of Crisis: Contemporary Adolescent Fiction

Steve Roxburgh

Forever, by Judy Blume. New York: Bradbury Press, 1976.
I Am the Cheese, by Robert Cormier. New York: Pantheon, 1977.
Year King, by Penelope Farmer. New York: Atheneum, 1977.
Hitchhike, by Isabelle Holland. Philadelphia: J. P. Lippincott, 1977.
Hiding, by Norma Klein. New York: Four Winds Press, 1976.
Pardon Me, You're Stepping on My Eyeball, by Paul Zindell. New York: Harper & Row, 1976.

Reprinted by permission of the author and publisher from *Children's Literature* 7:248-54 (1978). Copyright © 1978 by *Children's Literature: An International Journal,* Inc.

In his landmark discussion of pornography in mid-Victorian England, Steven Marcus constructs an abstract paradigm of the form, based on Max Weber's assumptions concerning "ideal type." Marcus' "pornotopia" is a descriptive model—no actual example exists—derived from significant aspects of individual manifestations of the form, and its purpose is descriptive, rather than judgmental. A similar model can be imagined for one kind of contemporary adolescent literature.

Certain attributes are shared by much of the fiction written for young adults today. Most of it is, in the broad sense of the word, mimetic; that is, imitative, rather than fantastic. The setting is the contemporary world. The main characters are, in the ambiguous language of age groups, neither children nor adults, but, rather, adolescents. Situations arise out of home and school life, generally, and involve family and peers. We see the world through the eyes of the youthful protagonists. Perhaps the most significant aspect of contemporary adolescent fiction is its focus on the moments of crisis that are typical of the transitional stage between childhood and adulthood. This focus so informs the fiction that it can appropriately be called, following Marcus' lead, "crisotopia," the novel of crisis.

The crises that are the *raison d'être* of the form are, as mentioned above, typical, and they are traditional in literature written for youth. The confrontation between parent and child, peer relationships, and crises of identity are as apparent in the literature of the eighteenth century as they are in that of the twentieth century; only the treatment changes.

The "ideal type" of contemporary adolescent fiction focuses on two kinds of crisis, although many related crises are tied to those. The recognition by youth of the breakdown of the traditional values and institutions of the adult world, be it the family, marriage, or parenthood, translates itself into novels about divorce, runaways, and unwanted pregnancy, Related to this, but distinct from it, are novels that deal with growth and burgeoning self-awareness, specifically, consciousness of sexuality. Neither of these foci are new; Crusoe rejected his father's much-praised middle way and ran away to sea, while Pamela—not to mention Clarissa —suffered considerably from her forced awareness of her sexual nature. What *is* new is the radical resolutions that our culture allows and the explicit treatment of all aspects of the crisis.

As mentioned above, the most frequent setting for the adolescent novel of crisis is the home or the school. Louisa May Alcott's domestic stories and the school stories typified by Thomas Hughes's *Tom Brown's School Days* testify to the fact that the tradition has roots in the Victorian period. Two major differences between the nineteenth- and twentieth-century manifestations of the tradition indicate a significant shift of consciousness over the last century. Almost without exception, the earlier works are told by an omniscient narrator, who freely comments on the moral significance and probable consequences of the characters' actions and thoughts. Such narration rests on the assumptions that actions have clearly discernable moral significance and far-reaching, almost inevitable, consequences. Most modern manifestations of the form are, in effect, if not in fact, presented from the viewpoint of the young protagonist. From this limited perspective life is less continuous, and not at all like the rigorously sequential lives of Jo March and Tom Brown. Any given incident is altogether less significant as a causal factor in a person's life. Meaning is to be found in the immediate consequences of an action rather than in its far-reaching effects. No moral value is assigned to actions; at best, the character subjectively evaluates the situation, and the reader is left with that. Generally, the shift is from an outer to an inner view, the consequences of which are a personalization and fragmentation of experience that characterizes the modern age and the modern novel of crisis. In this respect, the adolescent novel parallels in its development the mainstream novel.

The novel of crisis has, appropriately, utopian and dystopian extremes. In the former a single experience, apparent in every aspect of life, or, at least, the protagonist's consciousness, informs the fiction. In the latter, the main character is involved in a number of crises simultaneously, or is involved in them sequentially, like Hercules undergoing his twelve labors. In both, the fiction begins with the inception or perception of the crisis, climaxes at its culmination, and ends with its resolution or passing away. In the utopian visions, far and away the majority, the character manages to live through the crisis; in the dystopian vision, the character succumbs. The character need not learn anything from the experience, but need only survive it. (A comparison of *Tom Brown's School Days* and *Eric, or Little by Little* shows these two extremes in the Victorian forerunners of the modern form.) Given these dominant characteristics, individual examples of the genre can be distinguished against a common background.

One of the simplest examples of the novel of crisis to be found in the fiction published in the past few years is Judy Blume's *Forever*. The book focuses on a young woman's first intimate sexual relationship. The plot climaxes (literally and figuratively) at the consummation of the sexual relationship, after which the relationship and the plot dissolve. Incident serves either to facilitate or interfere with the consummation. The story is related through the eyes and mind of Katherine, the main character, who is idiosyncratic enough to be the roundest of a host of flat characters, yet innocuous enough to permit vicarious identification. Several typical characters and current crises embellish the main event of the book, including an attempted suicide by a token homosexual, the birth of an illegitimate and unwanted child to a girl who had the baby just for the experience, the death of a favorite grandparent, and an inconvenient bout with the flu.

Convenient is an appropriate way to describe the world in which the characters posture. Katherine's parents are mindlessly liberal, her house is a veritable pleasure dome, her circumstances are comfortable to the nth degree. Michael, the *object* of her desires, is similarly well-situated. Katherine, fixated on genital intercourse, is virtually oblivious to anything else, and the presentation of sexuality is, at best, partial. The book, finally, is analogous to a television "dramatization" in which viewers, or, in this case, readers, realize that the actors are insignificant and that the message, the information conveyed, is all important. From the heavy-handed subtlety of the title to the equally crude suggestion that life goes on in the final brief sentence, the book is written to tell the reader about sex and "love." *Forever* is not literature and cannot be evaluated by literary standards. It is an information book and stands, or falls, finally, on the accuracy of the information it attempts to present. It has the form of the novel of crisis, but lacks the substance.

A less crude treatment of sexuality and its relation to aspects of identity is Norma Klein's *Hiding*. Again we see the action through the eyes of a young woman experiencing her first intimate relationship with a man. In this book, however, sex is not an obsession. It is, rather, one of several aspects of the character's identity that seem to be dissociated and the cause of confusion. Eighteen-year-old Krii travels to England, ostensibly to attend ballet school, but, actually, to seek anonymity. There, to her dismay, several crises are precipitated in rapid succession. She becomes involved in a relationship with a young man who tries, using methods that inflict varying degrees of pain, to draw her out of her shell. At the same time she discovers that her parents' unconventional marriage arrangements have served to mask her father's extramarital relationships, which she, following this accidental discovery, is expected to accept, understand, and keep to herself. Her discomfort with her own sexuality and the dissolution of her relationship with Jonathan coincide with the discovery of her father's infidelity and cause her to withdraw from the social world into herself. Succumbing to the confusion, she hides in the attic of her parents' home for several days. In the limbo of mental and emotional exhaustion, she gradually heals, and on reentering the world is able to begin to sort out her life and to act again. No answers are offered; no information is relayed. Krii decides to return to the States, giving up dancing as a career in favor of going to college. Although seen from the outside, Jonathan moves through the story as a complex, albeit unknown, personality struggling in his own way with his own problems. The story ends with the two characters, as survivors, beginning a new relationship on the rubble of the old.

Penelope Farmer's *Year King* shares with *Hiding* a common treatment of identity and the relation of sexuality to identity. It is substantially more complex in its treatment, however, and it lends itself to (that is, will sustain and reward) critical attention. Working from the unlikely situation of a young man's intermittent and unexpected transfer of consciousness into his twin brother's body, the novel deals with problems of identity in psychological and, finally, archetypal terms. Through the eyes of Lan, the West Somerset countryside takes on human characteristics; the landscape reflects his emotional condition. In the midst of his struggle to free himself from the domination of his mother, and to sever his self-negating attachment to his popular and successful brother, Lew, Lan meets an American girl, Novanna, who introduces him to an entirely different vision, symbolized by strangely alluring pictures and tales of the American deserts and their inhabitants. Novanna teaches him about his sexuality, and he finds in it mindless release from his struggles. The culmination of his conflict with his brother is presented in a way that is comparable to certain scenes in the novels of D. H. Lawrence. Everything comes across as larger than life; emotions are world-transforming. Sexuality is the prevailing metaphor of the novel, and it is dealt with both evocatively and explicitly. *Year King* tries to present universal human conflicts and errs, perhaps, in being too self-conscious an attempt to do so. The author is constantly pointing out what she is doing. The book is overwritten, yet it does succeed in translating the novel of crisis into mythological terms.

Isabelle Holland's *Hitchhike* departs from the model of the novel of crisis presented above by harking back to a much different and older form, the exemplum or cautionary tale, yet its concerns are those common to the contemporary fiction already discussed. A sixteen-year-old who is miffed at her father for allowing a business deal to interfere with a long-anticipated camping trip decides to buy a coat with the money sent for her plane fare and to hitchhike home instead. She picks up a stray dog along the way and so complicates things. (Not since Toto got Dorothy caught in a tornado has a dog caused a heroine so much trouble.) Forcibly detained by a man seeking answers from her about why his daughter ran away and never contacted him, Pud escapes only to be kidnapped and very nearly raped by a group of teenage hoodlums. She manages to escape (with the dog) and so survives the crisis relatively unscathed. Her escapades may have left her a little less certain that she has life figured out, but for the most part they are just an adventurous interlude. At the end of the story she is awaiting the inevitable quarrel with her father with something akin to eagerness. The incident is realistically and convincingly portrayed. Its only apparent significance is to verify the warning, "don't hitchhike."

The first-person point of view that characterizes the adolescent novel of crisis is discarded for an omniscient narrator in Paul Zindel's *Pardon Me, You're Stepping on My Eyeball,* in order to present the perspectives of two characters, "Marsh" Mellow and Edna Shinglebox. (In his earlier novel, *The Pigman,* Zindel retained the first-person narration even though he dealt with two characters, by the simple device of alternating chapters in a chronicle they are jointly writing describing the events.) Each is struggling with his/her own identity against the backdrop of parental relationships. Marsh is trying to deal with the fact of his father's death and an alcoholic mother. Edna must exorcise the negative self-image that her misguided parents have foisted on her. These two meet in a special therapy class for disturbed students at their high school and discover that they are drawn to each other. As they come to know each other better, a bond grows between them that enables them to escape for a while from their problems at home. With Edna's active companionship Marsh is finally able to admit to himself and to her that his father is dead, and Edna, in committing herself to help her friend, is able to initiate an action on her own and accept the responsibility for that action.

The story is set in the almost surrealistic world of adolescence. It is a nightmare world, an exaggerated world. It is the world seen through the eyes of adolescence. The language is that of the hip underground, alien to child and adult alike, which serves to mark the alienation of the adolescents who speak it. The climax of the novel is cataclysmic, involving the destruction of a glass mansion by a fire caused by the orgy of the followers of a cult hero. Running from this, Marsh and Edna embark on a journey to find Marsh's dead father which ends when their car crashes. Seeking refuge in a cemetery, the two set off a rocket that marks their ritual and symbolic liberation. *Pardon Me, You're Stepping on My Eyeball* brings the novel of crisis as close to fantasy as it can go without sacrificing its basic form.

Perhaps the most dystopic of the novels of crisis under discussion is Robert Cormier's *I Am the Cheese*. (His very popular novel *The Chocolate War* is the best example of the continuity of the tradition of school stories mentioned above.) It is the story of a victim. Its informing crisis precedes the action of the novel. A young boy's parents are assassinated by underworld criminals against whom the boy's father, an investigative reporter, had testified. With the help of psychological therapy sessions, the boy attempts to remember that event which he witnessed. Transcripts of the sessions are counterpointed by the stages in an imagined bicycle trip the boy is making to see his father. The two stories converge when the odyssey ends on the grounds of the institution where Adam is being held, and all his adventures are seen to be the fantasy creations drawn from his surroundings and companions in the sanatorium. The boy's nagging fear that his psychiatrist is after information that he might have about his father's activities is realized at the end of the book which finishes with the sparse, codified memorandums to the effect that Adam is incurable, that he is withholding no information, and that he should be held until "termination procedures are approved" or until he "obliterates." *I Am the Cheese* shows the novel of crisis expanded to include a very contemporary political and cultural phenomenon, and its vision is bleak.

These examples suggest some of the variations of the form that is generally characterized at the beginning of this discussion. Coming to grips with crises of identity, be they social, familial, or personal, informs each of the books. Adolescence is a time of rapid and confusing change in a person's life. What the novel of crisis has to offer, at its best, is the assurance that one can live through the changes, that they are shared by us all, even though they take on different forms. When poorly handled, the novel of crisis is a clumsy and patronizing medium for crudely constructed stories offering simplistic solutions or rendering misinformation. The best asserts the complexity and poignancy of the transitions that have to be lived through; the worst reduces life to categories of experience and treats them as if they can be dealt with separately. As long as cultures develop, the novel of crisis will assume new forms. Previously taboo subjects will serve as the focus of new stories. Presently "relevant" themes will become outdated and heretofore unimagined situations will replace them. The changes in treatment do not matter, as long as at the core of the vision is the realization of and concern with those crises that are typical to youth and that transcend all topical limitations.

Metaphors of Madness: Popular Psychological Narratives

Kary K. and Gary K. Wolfe

Movements and genres in popular literature, emerging as they do from a variety of media and often over an extended period of time, sometimes have the effect of "sneaking up" on scholars of the genre, of developing quietly over a period of years and then seeming to spring full-blown upon the consciousness of the reading public. Such was partially the case with science fiction, which grew almost unnoticed for decades before being "discovered" by critics during the last ten years or so. Such is also the case with the genre we propose to discuss today, a genre which has its roots in the literature of mental abnormality stretching back to classical times, but which has emerged as a genre in itself—drawing on the novel,

Reprinted by permission from *Journal of Popular Culture* 9:895-907 (Spring 1976). Copyright © 1976 by Ray B. Browne.

memoirs, autobiography, and psychological case history—only during this century. Psychologists have long been aware of these works as a sub-genre of psychiatric literature, but it shall be the contention of this paper that such works have in recent years transcended in popularity and form the rather narrow scope of "professional literature" and become a profitable genre of popular writing (and to a lesser extent, of film and television). Such works not only enjoy an appeal that goes well beyond people professionally interested in psychology, but they also have evolved recognizable formulaic elements in structure and imagery. We propose to treat these works, then, not from the point of view of the psychologist so much as from the point of view of popular culture: specifically, what are their characteristics and what might be the reason for their popularity?

Robert Coles, in his introduction to Barbara Field Benzinger's *The Prison of My Mind,* remarks that the book "shares a tradition that goes centuries back" and even cites Augustine's *Confessions* as a precursor.[1] While this statement is undoubtedly true in the broadest sense, and while the list of autobiographical accounts of mental illness includes such illustrious figures as Strindberg, Nijinsky, Boswell, de Maupassant, Arthur Symons, and others,[2] a more immediate source for works such as Benzinger's can be found in the works of "muckraking" novelists, reporters, and autobiographers. Perhaps the most significant of these, and perhaps the seminal work in this genre in the twentieth century, is Clifford Beers's *A Mind that Found Itself* (1908), both a moving account of a severe manic-depressive's years of illness and recovery and powerful indictment of the treatment of mental patients at the beginning of this century. The muckraking theme is a recurrent one in later works as well, and what is probably this genre's first major best-seller, Mary Jane Ward's (1946) *The Snake Pit,* is less concerned with the structure of mental illness or the process of therapy than with the nightmarish conditions of the asylum itself. More recently, a similarly social-minded concern with the manipulative aspects of mental treatment is expressed in Ken Kesey's *One Flew over the Cuckoo's Nest* (1962) and Elliott Baker's *A Fine Madness* (1964), and in such related nonfiction studies as Thomas Szasz's *The Myth of Mental Illness* and Phyllis Chesler's *Women and Madness* (which curiously demonstrates little awareness of this genre, whose major figures are all women).

The Snake Pit was not the first novel in the 1940s to deal with mental illness and recovery; it had been preceded by several years by Millen Brand's *The Outward Room* (1941), and it came at a time of extensive interest in psychological topics in the popular media, especially films (more about which in a moment). But it established as no other book had the market potential of this subject, and for the next twenty years the genre developed steadily, with narratives told not only from the patient's point of view, but from the doctor's as well. In 1955, Max Lerner could write, "One of the byproducts of the post-Freudian age has been the emer-

gence of a new genre of American writing—the work of the writing psy-
choanalyst or psychiatrist, who applies his insights to the problems of
the day or tells of some of his adventures with his patients."[3] Lerner was
writing in the introduction to Robert Lindner's *The Fifty Minute Hour*,
itself one of the more successful collections of case histories published
during the 1950s. It was followed in 1957 by a similar collection, Joseph
Anthony's *The Invisible Curtain*, as well as Corbett Thigpen and Hervey
Cleckley's *The Three Faces of Eve* the same year. In 1962 appeared *Lisa
and David*, the best-known of Theodore Isaac Rubin's series of novelized
case histories.[4]

None of these works from the therapist's viewpoint ever achieved the
resounding success of a 1964 novel told from the patient's viewpoint,
however. Joanne Greenberg's *I Never Promised You a Rose Garden*,
published under the pseudonym "Hannah Green," remains the most famous and influential book in this genre, with sales of nearly four million
copies in its first decade of publication. Its success is almost certainly a
key factor in the present growth and popularity of the genre. Following
I Never Promised You a Rose Garden, booksellers began to set up displays of popular psychology paperbacks; publishers began to reissue
earlier works, citing similarities to the Greenberg book in an effort to
increase sales, and in some cases even changing the titles in order to point
up similarities: Margaret Wiley Emmett's *Satan Have Pity*, originally
published in 1962, was reissued in paperback in 1971 under the title *I
Love the Person You Were Meant to Be*. Characteristic paperback blurbs
would read "A book to equal *I Never Promised You a Rose Garden*"
(Autobiography of a Schizophrenic Girl); "Not since *INPYRG* [which
we shall henceforth abbreviate thus for convenience] *"(I Love the Person You Were Meant to Be);* A novel in the poignant tradition of
INPYRG" *(Lisa, Bright and Dark);* "As haunting as *INPYRG* *(The Eye
of Childhood);* "A novel with the poignancy of *INPYRG"* *(The Better
Part);* or "A novel for those who enjoyed *INPYRG"* *(Crown of Flowers)*.
"I Never Promised You a Rose Garden," bizarrely, even became the title
of a country and western song in 1971 that had nothing to do with mental
illness. The genre, at least as far as the marketing departments of publishers were concerned, was established—and highly lucrative.

The sudden flowering of sales of these books also brought renewed
attention to such writers as Mary Jane Ward, Lucy Freeman, and Vera
Randal, each of whom has published more than one book in the genre
since the late forties, with Freeman at least (whose first book, *Fight
Against Fears*, appeared in 1951), making a successful career out of such
writing. Writers with more serious literary ambitions also found the genre
attractive during this period. J. R. Salamanca's *Lilith* (1961) enjoyed
some critical success, as did the Robert Rossen film later adapted from it.
Both Ken Kesey's *One Flew over the Cuckoo's Nest* (1962) and Sylvia
Plath's *The Bell Jar* (1963) gained wide audiences and critical attention,

and both have become "cult" books of a sort, reflecting as they do the values of the counterculture and the women's movement, respectively.

At the same time, the genre has grown in popularity in the movies and on television. Psychiatry in general, and amnesia in particular, became a common theme in films of the forties, most notably in such films as Hitchcock's *Spellbound* (1945) and the film adaptation of *The Snake Pit* (with a screenplay co-authored by Millen Brand, 1949), but also in films from other popular genres, such as *Pride of the Marines* (1945).[5] The fifties followed with film adaptations of William Gibson's *The Cobweb* (1955), Jim Piersall's *Fear Strikes Out* (1957), and Robert Lindner's *Rebel without a Cause* (1955), the latter, as Gene and Barbara Stanford have observed, turning a psychopathic case study into "the cultural hero of the fifties."[6] *The Three Faces of Eve* won an Academy Award for Joanne Woodward in 1957, and *David and Lisa,* an adaptation of Rubin's *Lisa and David,* brought director Frank Perry to prominence in 1962. This is not to mention the flood of psychological horror stories following Hitchcock's *Psycho* (1960), Robert Aldrich's *Whatever Happened to Baby Jane* (1962), and Samuel Fuller's *Shock Corridor* (1963).

Television also entered the arena briefly in the early sixties, with two series, "The Eleventh Hour" and "The Psychiatrist," dealing on a weekly basis with mental problems. Mental illness remains a frequent theme on such programs as "Marcus Welby, M.D." and "Medical Center," and John Neufeld's "Lisa Bright and Dark" recently appeared as a television movie. As far back as 1955, Max Lerner castigated television and motion picture exploitation of mental illness in terms that are still applicable today:

> They have usually taken the cheap-and-easy way of starting with some highly dramatic event and, with psychiatric help, working back to infancy and mother-fixation. Although the psychiatric play or movie is still young it is already so threadbare as to be vulnerable to caricature. The trouble with most of them is that they start with a prefabricated drama rather than with a given personality. It takes honesty to avoid the temptation of this kind of synthetic pattern, where everything is untangled neatly and tied together again just as neatly.[7]

Before proceeding to a fuller discussion of the popularity of this genre, and to a more detailed analysis of *I Never Promised You a Rose Garden* as an example of the genre, it is necessary to outline briefly just what it is that justifies lumping all these works together, beyond a common concern with psychology. The more familiar genres of popular writing— westerns, detective stories, gothics, and the like—may be characterized and identified by a number of structural and conventional elements involving style, atmosphere, setting, and characterization, as well as plot. Largely through the cross-influence of writers within the genre, certain formulae are evolved, and popular writers who most successfully make use of these formulae become, in John Cawelti's sense of the term, *au-*

teurs.[8] In our psychological narratives, such cross-influence seems relatively sparse, and while easily discernible formulae may not yet have completely evolved, there are noteworthy recurrent elements. We shall attempt to characterize the genre in terms of these elements, specifically in regard to imagery and metaphor, structure, point of view, and characterization.

Our first area of concern is imagery and metaphor, and in some ways this is the most important. A striking feature of many of these narratives is their organization of a deliberate metaphoric pattern, guided or controlled by one or two central metaphors that set the tone and attitude for the entire work. Many of these controlling metaphors are evident in the titles of the works: *The Snake Pit, The Prison of My Mind, Labyrinth of Silence, Halfway through the Tunnel, The Invisible Curtain, The Bell Jar*. Most of these are simple metaphors of madness, although some, like the snake pit, serve the dual function of representing both the patient's state of mind and the horrors of the mental hospital itself. The central importance of the controlling metaphor in these works stems in part from the fact that many of the works tend to be autobiographical, and, as James Olney writes in his study of metaphor in autobiography, "By their metaphors shall you know them."[9] In other words, the power of metaphor becomes the central link between the experience of the reader and the experience described by the author in an autobiographical work. On the most basic level, it represents an attempt at communicating the incommunicable; Frank Conroy writes of the anonymous author of *Autobiography of a Schizophrenic Girl* that she "attempted to re-create through metaphor . . . sensations in the mind of the presumably sane reader that were in her mind while she was insane."[10] Another reason for the importance of such metaphor is the significance of metaphor and metaphoric language in the structure of many psychoses. The personal mythology of Deborah in *I Never Promised You a Rose Garden* is guarded from the outside world by an artificial language based on metaphors; an exchange with Deborah's doctor in therapy illustrates the complexity of this metaphoric structure:

> "There must be some words," the doctor said. "Try to find them, and let us share them together."
> "It's a metaphor—you wouldn't understand it."
> "Perhaps you could explain it then."
> "There is a word—it means Locked Eyes, but it implies more."
> "What more?"
> "It's the word for sarcophagus." It meant that at certain times her vision reached only as far as the cover of her sarcophagus; that to herself, as to the dead, the world was the size of her own coffin.[11]

Metaphors, then, often represent not only an attempt to communicate the emotional quality of the illness, but to some extent its structure as well. It is not surprising that the most common metaphors are metaphors of darkness and confusion: fog, mazes, labyrinths, tunnels, pits, water, caverns, fire and ice.

Many of these metaphors suggest the classical journey to the underworld, and indeed this is a useful analogue to the structure of many of these works. The pit, among the most common of metaphors, is readily analogous to the pit of Hell, as the less common but occasional mountain metaphor is analogous to Purgatory. Most of the narratives involve some sort of chaotic, metaphoric journey within the hospital, from ward to ward and in some cases from hospital to hospital, with certain wards representing relative health and others representing the "forgotten," the hopeless cases whose screaming isolation seems like nothing so much as the condition of the damned in the lower circles of Dante's Hell. Janet Frame, in *Faces in the Water* (1961), gives evidence of the extreme importance of particular wards to patients in these stories:

> What is Ward Seven but a subaqueous condition of the mind which gave the fearful shapes drowned there a rhythmic distortion of peace; and what if, upon my getting up from my bed, the perspective was suddenly altered, or I was led into a trap where a fire burning in the walls had dried up the water and destroyed the peace by exposing in harsh daylight the submerged shapes in all their terror?[12]

The ward becomes like the unconscious mind itself, hiding "fearful shapes" in a labyrinthine distortion of space and perspective. This distortion of perspective is also mentioned by Mary Jane Ward in *The Snake Pit:*

> The nurse led her to a door she had never seen before. Naturally. The door was not there before. Just as the washroom was at one end of the corridor one day and at the other end the next day. Entirely new doors were created in order to insure perpetual confusion.[13]

Labyrinthine chaos such as that described in these passages, followed by emergence into some sort of an ordered universe, seems to be the central dramatic movement of many of these narratives: a movement from disorder to order, or at least the promise of order. The movement is highly— and literally—cathartic, and as we shall see later, this catharsis may be a strong reason for the popularity of this genre.

A third element worth noting in these narratives, along with metaphor and structure, is point of view. The autobiographical element again becomes important here, for in most of the narratives we find that the point of view is confined narrowly to the narrating patient or doctor, with perhaps an occasional shift back and forth, but almost never shifting to the point of view of another patient. Within these limits, point of view might further be categorized fourfold: (1) the patient, describing her or his own illness and internal conflicts *(I Never Promised You a Rose Garden; The Prison of My Mind);* (2) the patient, describing hospital conditions and the outward appearance and character of other patients *(Faces in the Water;*

The Snake Pit); (3) the therapist, describing a particular case history *(The Fifty Minute Hour; My Language Is Me);* and (4) the therapist or doctor, describing a number of patients and/or conditions in a hospital *(Labyrinth of Silence; Savage Sleep).* In addition to these most common points of view, a few narratives may be told from the perspective of someone outside the therapist-patient relationship, usually a relative *(In a Darkness; This Stranger, My Son),* and some may contain more than one perspective on the same case, such as Mary Barnes and Joseph Berke's *Two Accounts of a Journey through Madness* or Marguerite Sechehaye's interpretation appended to the narrative of *Autobiography of a Schizophrenic Girl.* But the prevalence of the four major points of view, with their concentration on the process of therapy or the conditions of therapy and with their clearly defined narrative scope, offers some evidence for the didactic nature of this kind of narrative—and this didacticism may be yet another reason for the genre's popularity.

Finally, there is the element of characterization, and in this area the genre begins more to resemble conventional characteristics of other genres of popular fiction. As we have already noted parenthetically, the vast majority of these narratives concern women, and most of the autobiographical narratives are written by women as well. Furthermore, it seems evident that the majority of readers are women. Much is done, then, toward the development of identification with the central character or characters, who are usually presented as highly intelligent, witty, articulate (within the bounds of their illness), and yet vulnerable and perhaps above all, passive. The narrator's wit is a distinguishing mark of the style in *The Snake Pit* and Sylvia Plath's *The Bell Jar;* it is described as a psychotic defense in *I Never Promised You a Rose Garden.* Yet the protagonists of each of these novels, as well as many others, hardly could be called protagonists in the real sense at all: they simply don't make much happen. They tend to be presented as passive victims, buffeted about by family, friends, other patients, doctors, nurses, orderlies, strangers, society in general, and their own internal disturbance. Furthermore, they tend to be creative, usually as artists *(Two Accounts of a Journey through Madness; I Never Promised You a Rose Garden)* or writers *(The Snake Pit).* This dual aspect of the central character—the creative, intelligent woman victimized by roles she is forced into—probably accounts for a large measure of the popularity enjoyed at least by *The Bell Jar* among feminists.

What villains there are in these narratives tend to be unwittingly played by family and friends who mean well but simply "don't understand." Usually, however, the only major figure to recur in a number of the books is a variation on the wise old person, the wizard or wise woman of fairy tales. This role is generally occupied by the therapist, who often represents the first benevolent authority figure the patient encounters during the illness. Advocates of the women's movement may rightly question the frequency with which this figure is a strong male character, but

not infrequently the figure is a woman therapist—such as Dr. Fried in
I Never Promised You a Rose Garden.[14]

Having surveyed thus all too briefly the genre in terms of imagery,
structure, point of view, and characterization, we should look back over
these elements and try to see what in them, if anything, might account
for the growing popularity of this kind of writing. Max Lerner contends
that much of this popularity may derive from certain similarities to the
detective story, with the process of unravelling the past even more ingenious than in most mysteries, because all we have to begin with is a
victim who, with the aid of the doctor, must discover not only who the
villains are but indeed if any "crime" was committed at all.[15] Frank Conroy, writing of *Autobiography of a Schizophrenic Girl,* describes the
book in terms of another genre: to him the book is "clearly a triumph
of faith. . . . As a human document Renee's book is without doubt in-
spirational."[16] Gene and Barbara Stanford offer yet another explanation:

> Part of the fascination seems to be the sense of strangeness and horror
> that some of the books convey. In our modern world, where fierce beasts
> and uninhabited continents have all been conquered, the frontiers of the
> mind are about the only places where adventures are still possible. This
> interest in the strange world that lies beyond the borders of the rational
> mind may partially account for experimentation with drugs as well as for
> an interest in mental illness.[17]

This "adventure into the unknown" aspect of the books, we might add,
also would seem to relate their popularity to the resurgence of interest in
witchcraft and occultism, and to the popularity of fantasy and science
fiction, particularly the artificial cosmologies of such writers as H. P.
Lovecraft or J. R. R. Tolkien.

Certainly all these factors are involved in the popularity of these
books, but we might also find clues to popularity from the characteristics
we have already mentioned. In terms of structure and imagery in particular, and characterization to a lesser extent, we might regard these works
as a variety of romance, which uses the interior landscapes of real mental
illness in much the same way that the interior landscapes of the poetic
imagination have functioned in romances from the Middle Ages to the
present. We may use the term "romance" in a fairly broad sense here,
since we are speaking primarily of the manner in which these works are
received by a popular audience rather than the manner in which they are
deliberately conceived by their authors. We have already noted how these
narratives are often structured as a journey into a kind of inferno or
wasteland in search of a mysterious goal or boon; this quest element certainly calls to mind heroic romance of the Arthurian sort, and indeed
Erich Neumann has already demonstrated at some length the manner in
which such quest romances can represent, in Jungian terms, the evolution
of consciousness from the unconscious—a process which is often recon-
structed in therapy with psychotics.[18]

On another level, these journeys also represent a consciously educational process of self-discovery, and this factor, coupled with the frequently youthful or adolescent protagonists, suggests thematic relationships with the *bildungsroman* of Romantic narrative art. Still a third literary relation, mentioned above, may be found in fantasy and science fiction, whose artificial systems and fantastic imagery are echoed in the detailed fantasies of many psychotics.[19]

Finally, yet another variety of romance that is of perhaps even greater interest than the others in explaining the current popular appeal of the genre is the Gothic romance. We have already noted the passive "victim" aspect of many of the heroines, and this is certainly an element shared with the popular "modern Gothics" that grace newsstands with endless cover paintings of ladies in nightgowns fleeing dimly lit mansions. But many of our protagonists also share the dark obsessions and compulsions of a Heathcliff, thus partaking of the Gothic villain as well as the Gothic heroine and becoming romantic figures in themselves. Janet Frame demonstrates awareness of this aspect of popular psychological fiction in *Faces in the Water:*

> There is an aspect of madness which is seldom mentioned in fiction because it would damage the romantic popular idea of the insane as a person whose speech appeals as immediately poetic; but it is seldom the easy Opheliana recited like the pages of a seed catalog or the outpourings of Crazy Janes who provide, in fiction, an outlet for poetic abandon. Few of the people who roamed the dayroom would have qualified as acceptable heroines, in popular taste; few were charmingly uninhibited eccentrics. (p. 115)

But even Frame's own prosaic narrator is capable of wildly "poetic" outpourings and images. Add this aspect of the protagonist to the presence of the very real "ghosts" and "demons" of mental illness and the labyrinthine settings of huge, shadowy institutions—a modern equivalent of the Gothic castle—and the narratives seem even closer to the more familiar Gothic romance.

To illustrate these various points in a more unified manner, we should now like to examine in greater detail one of these works, analyzing it for the characteristics of the genre, its specific relations to romance, and the reasons for its popularity. The work we have chosen is one which by its huge popular success and influence has become virtually the archetype of the genre, Joanne Greenberg's *I Never Promised You a Rose Garden.* Published in 1964 under the name "Hannah Green," the novel is a fictionalized account of Joanne Greenberg's own illness and her therapy at Chestnut Lodge under Dr. Frieda Fromm-Reichmann.[20] While the novel was generally received well critically as a didactic work concerning mental illness, many reviewers had reservations about its value as fiction. Frank Haskel, writing in *Saturday Review,* complained that "the two-steps-forward, one-step-backward progression of Deborah's surfacing to life lacks that tightness which fiction requires."[21] R. V. Cassill, while generally lauding the book in his *New York Times Book Review* review, observed that it is not wholly "fictionally convincing" and that "it is as if some wholly admirable, and yet specialized, nonfictional discipline has been dressed in the garments and mask of fiction."[22] The *Times Literary Supplement* reviewer noted what is probably the book's chief defect as a novel by pointing out that the "real" world to which Deborah must return is never made nearly as convincing or attractive as her fantasy world: "her normality is perilously close to dullness."[23] And Brigid Brophy in *The New Statesman* declared flatly that "should it turn out to be a work of fiction, its value would vanish overnight."[24] It soon became publicly known that the novel is *not* entirely fiction, of course, and in the years following these initial reviews, as the book phenomenally grew in popularity, relatively little attention was paid to it as anything other than a highly readable case history. And yet there is much evidence, both from the novel itself and from Greenberg's other works, that the book is an attempt at a coherent novel and not merely fictionalized autobiography.

In *Rose Garden,* Greenberg has tried to portray the often chaotic imagery of schizophrenia and the often uneven process of therapy, and to impose upon these realities of her own experience the order and structure of a unified narrative. This is not to suggest that she has deliberately misrepresented either her illness or her therapy for the sake of novelistic expediency; rather it is to suggest that the aesthetic elements of the book exist on two principal levels. For example, the imagery of mountains, which serves a number of complex functions in the context of Deborah's own schizophrenic world, is introduced into the narrative late enough so that it can also function in aesthetic terms as an image of the struggle toward sanity, toward resolution of conflict: "All Deborah heard were the sounds of her own gasps of exhaustion as she climbed an Everest that was to everyone else an easy and a level plain" (p. 211). Similarly, the imagery of the underworld ("the Pit"), which seems to appear more or less at random within the context of the illness, is for the sake of the narrative organized into the more familiar aesthetic pattern of the underworld journey: descent, chaos, and purifying ascent. The danger of this kind of dual use of imagery, of course, is that it tends to lead the reader to confuse the structure of the novel with the structure of therapy, and the pattern of aesthetic imagery with the pattern of schizophrenia. Such confusion is furthered by the commonplace belief that there is some sort of *de facto* relationship between insanity and art, and one must wonder if in fact such works as *Rose Garden* are popularly read as novels *about* schizophrenia, or as vicarious schizophrenic experiences; the word "seductive" appears prominently twice on the cover blurb of *Rose Garden.* But this question is merely another way of asking the reason for the popularity of these books, and perhaps it can be in part answered by looking at the four key aspects of *Rose Garden* itself: characterization, structure, style and imagery, and rhetoric.

The central element in characterization, as we have already noted for the genre as a whole, is the nature of the protagonist herself. The protagonist in *Rose Garden* is sixteen-year-old Deborah Blau, a plain but highly intelligent and witty girl whose psychosis involves an elaborately imagined, almost Blakean universe called Yr, with its own pantheon of gods, its own language, and its own landscapes. During the course of the novel, Deborah moves in both the real world and this world of her own creating. But the "real world" in this novel is the world of the mental hospital and its surroundings, a world that is in its own way as artificial as the one Deborah has created. The arbitrary and sometimes hostile nature of this reality is what provides the book's title; in warning Deborah that reality is not necessarily more rewarding than the world of Yr, and in arguing that Deborah's choice must be based on deeper criteria than mere comfort, the therapist Dr. Fried says, "I never promised you a rose garden. I never promised you perfect justice . . ." (p. 106). And in making this statement, Dr. Fried herself is reminded of her days in Nazi Germany, as if to underline to the reader the point that "reality" is not necessarily morally superior to the world of the psychotic. In fact, it is this real world, the "outside," represented initially in the novel by the almost mythic figure of Doris Rivera, a patient who has apparently successfully "gone outside," [that] is the mystery. The artificial worlds of the hospital and the psychosis itself are clearly delineated; the world outside is presented only slightly near the end of the novel.

Deborah must somehow learn to function in all three worlds: her own mind, the hospital, and finally the outside. Each world has a different landscape, a different set of rules, even a different language, and in each world the character of Deborah is developed along certain lines congruent with the fictional reality of that world. And in each world, she must pass from a stage of passivity to one of self-determination and control. Put another way, Deborah must undergo a process of education on three levels: first mastering the workings of her own mind, then mastering the fairly simple rules of life with the other patients in the hospital, and finally mastering the more complex rules of life on the outside. This multifaceted educational process, together with Deborah's adolescence and her relative innocence in each situation, suggests the kind of education undergone by the adolescent protagonists of the *bildungsroman*. It is also, of course, a stylized version of the process of socialization in the development of any personality, and it may be for this reason that it is easy to identify with Deborah's problems, stated as they are in such bizarre terms.

Deborah is also appealing because she is essentially an heroic figure, and her Kingdom of Yr is an heroic, even mythopoeic, world. In that world, she initially seems to identify with Anterrabae, "the falling god," who is later revealed to be her own version of Milton's Satan (p. 252), with all its associations of heroic defiance, eternal punishment, and the underworld. She must endure the derision and hostility of the Collect, "the massed images of all the teachers and relatives and schoolmates standing eternally in secret judgment and giving their endless curses" (p. 22). She is often referred to [by] her gods as "Bird-One," with its suggestion of Icarus, of pride and freedom. Finally, she must declare her self-mastery by renouncing all her gods and the Kingdom of Yr itself—an act which dramatically parallels the myth which gave rise to Anterrabae in the first place, and which in itself represents a kind of Promethean defiance. Deborah renounces her own security in favor of knowledge of the world and freedom; such an ideal is not uncommon in Romantic poetry and fiction.

Another reason for Deborah's success as a popular heroine is her appeal to our own fantasies of irresponsibility. Almost anything she does is excusable in the context of the fiction, and as such she represents, however perversely, a kind of absolute behavioral freedom. She doesn't necessarily get away with all her actions, but she isn't entirely responsible for them either, and it is likely that this freedom is, on a rather basic level, an example of the sort of wish-fulfillment that characterizes much popular literature. The freedom has its limits, however, and these limits seem at least in part defined by the necessity of maintaining reader sympathy. None of the violence on Deborah's part is directed at anyone other than herself, and the general absence of sexual motives and experience from her story—even though it seems likely that such experiences would comprise a significant element of her psyche—give her the aspect of the "innocent." Not even her most repulsive actions, such as her continued self-mutilation, are sufficient to remove our sympathies from her, and in this respect she is not unlike many other adolescent heroines in popular fiction.

The structure of the novel also may be a contributing factor to its popularity, for despite all its images of doom and confusion, *Rose Garden* is essentially comedic. There is from the outset a feeling of imminent resolution and hope; like the traditional fairy tale, elements of horror may be introduced as long as there is no overall feeling of despair. Part of this may be due to the journey motif; the suggestion of a journey naturally implies that the journey will have an end, and in the case of Deborah, this end is relative sanity (the alternative end, death, is only suggested slightly in the novel in brief references to her earlier suicide attempt). *Rose Garden* begins literally with a journey—the trip to the mental hospital—and continues with Deborah's movement from ward to ward and finally back out into the world. This movement, though not effortless, seems inevitable, and its inevitability is reinforced by the time sequence of the book. Deborah is in the hospital for three years, and in each of these years, springtime represents a progression towards sanity. The first spring arrives when Deborah first secures her relationship with Dr. Fried by learning that she is of value to the doctor: " 'If I can teach you something, it may mean that I can count at least somewhere' " (p. 147).

The second spring is characterized by Deborah and her friend and co-patient Carla declaring their friendship and running away from the hospital in a show of self-assertion and fun, prompting the doctor in charge to comment, " 'I'm kind of proud of you' " (p. 220). The third spring, coming at the conclusion of the book, includes Deborah's successful passing of the high school equivalency exams—an act which symbolically certifies both her maturity and her sanity. The three episodes taken together constitute Deborah's learning about the value of her person to others, then asserting that value, and finally proving it with the socially accepted measure of the high school exams. She finally emerges from her private world and prepares to leave the hospital in springtime, just as she had entered it, three years earlier, in the autumn. The three years become metaphorically compressed into one cycle of the seasons, and the inevitability of this cycle—the inevitability of spring—lends to the novel an overall tone of hope.

Yet another source of popularity may be the book's imagery. The idea of the "secret garden"—the private respite from the world that is known only to the child—has long been popular in children's and adolescent literature, and it is not unlikely that Deborah's Kingdom of Yr is just such a garden to many readers. Though on a more intense level, it is not unlike Frances Hodgson Burnett's secret garden in her book of that title, or C. S. Lewis's Narnia. Its landscape is a wildly romantic, exciting one of fire and ice, and its language bears resemblance, though on a much more complex level, to the "secret codes" popular among children. In other words, Yr, though the myth of a psychotic mind, is still a myth, and as such bears strong attraction for the imagination. Thus, as we have mentioned earlier, some of the attraction that readers feel for the novel may be akin to the attractions of Blake, or Lewis, or Tolkien.

Finally, and probably most importantly to the novel's professional audience, there is the didactic element. *Rose Garden* has been used as a supplementary text in many university psychology courses because of its accurate dramatization of facts about psychosis and therapy. Karl Menninger wrote of the book, " 'I'm sure it will have a good effect on lots of people who don't realize that this sort of exploration can be done and this sort of effect achieved' " (*Rose Garden*, p. 1). Robert Coles reacts in a similar manner: "If I were upset, in despair, worried about whether there will be many days left, I would be grateful to people like Clifford Beers or Hannah Green or Barbara Benzinger."[25] It appears, then, that the book is widely read as an object lesson in mental illness, and that for many its value as fiction is secondary to its value as case history. And it seems likely that a didactic motive was one of the major reasons the book was written in the first place; a number of novelistic decisions seem to be made on didactic (i.e., what will teach most effectively) rather than aesthetic (i.e., what will work best as fiction) grounds. We learn a great deal more about Deborah's psychosis than we do about her actual personality, for example. Such didacticism may occasionally weaken the novel as fiction, but it probably adds to its popularity.

Rose Garden, then, brings together in a single book many of the elements that have gone into the making of a popular narrative genre. And in terms of the popular audience, it is the book most responsible for the present ascendance of that genre. Part autobiography, part fiction, part educational tract, it is in many ways one of the most significant popular books of the last twenty years. It and the other books in its genre may represent the most broad-based connection yet established between practicing psychology and popular culture. As such, it is worth studying, and the genre is one whose development is worth watching, not only for what it may tell us about how popular genres evolve, but also for what it may tell us about changing attitudes of a mass audience toward issues in psychology and mental health.

NOTES

1. (New York: Pocket Books, 1970), pp.13-14.
2. For a synoptic account of these and many other autobiographical narratives, see Walter Alvarez, *Minds that Came Back* (New York: Lippincott, 1961). Written before the current flood of paperbacks in this genre, Alvarez's book remains the only full-length study of the subject; it is written with an eye to the didactic value of the narratives rather than to their value as literature or popular culture.
3. "Introduction" to Robert Lindner, *The Fifty Minute Hour* (New York: Bantam, 1955), p.vii.
4. This very brief account of the development of the genre from 1946 to 1964 is of course by no means exhaustive, but rather it is an attempt to point out some of the more significant such works during the period. Certain of the more sensational treatments of the fifties, such as Dariel Telfer's *The Caretakers* (1959) are, for reasons that will become clear later, marginal to the central focus of this study, while others are discussed in the following paragraph.
5. We are indebted to Professor Carol Traynor Williams for calling our attention to the significance of this theme in popular films of the period.
6. "Foreword" to *Strangers to Themselves: Readings on Mental Illness* (New York: Bantam, 1973), p.ix.
7. "Introduction," *Fifty Minute Hour,* p.viii.
8. "Notes Toward an Aesthetic of Popular Culture," *Journal of Popular Culture* 5:255-68 (Fall 1971).
9. *Metaphors of Self: the Meaning of Autobiography* (Princeton: Princeton Univ. Pr., 1972), p.35.
10. "Foreword," in Marguerite Sechehaye, ed., *Autobiography of a Schizophrenic Girl* (New York: New American Library, 1970), p.ix.
11. (New York: New American Library, 1964). Future references to *Rose Garden* will be by page number in the text.
12. (New York: Avon, 1971), p.73.
13. (New York: New American Library, n.d.), p.67.

14. It should perhaps be noted that in certain peripheral books to the genre, doctors and nurses are treated openly as villains. Most notable of these are Nurse Ratched in Kesey's *One Flew over the Cuckoo's Nest* and Dr. Massey in Elliott Baker's *A Fine Madness.*
15. Lerner, p.vii.
16. Conroy, pp. xi, xii.
17. *Strangers to Themselves,* p.ix.
18. *The Origins and History of Consciousness* (New York: Harper Torchbooks, 1962).
19. Linder, in *The Fifty Minute Hour,* details a case history in which the psychosis was wholly based on an elaborate science-fiction universe very similar to those depicted in "pulp" science fiction, and even notes that the therapist's own interest in science fiction almost led him to join the patient in his fantasies ("The Jet-Propelled Couch").
20. Helm Stierlin, *Conflict and Reconciliation: A Study of Human Relations Schizophrenia* (New York: Doubleday, 1969), p.235.
21. "Alone in the Kingdom of Yr," July 18, 1964, p.40.
22. "A Locked Ward, A Desperate Search for Reality," May 3, 1964, p.36.
23. "Calling Mad Mad," Aug. 13, 1964, p.721.
24. "An Yri Story," Aug. 14, 1964, p.221.
25. "Introduction," *The Prison of My Mind,* p.16.

Suicide in Literature for Young People

Joanne Bernstein

More people die at their own hands than is commonly realized. Motivated by great unhappiness, twice as many people kill themselves as kill others. The situation is even more alarming because the actual rate of self-inflicted death is believed to be much greater than actuarial figures indicate. The suicide phenomenon is even larger when one realizes that attempts at self-destruction outnumber successful suicides by the fantastic ratio of 100:1!

With suicide a brutal societal problem, it is appropriate to examine its treatment in the literature of youth. The literary portrayal of suicide is of

An earlier version of this article appeared in *The ALAN Review* 6:5-13 (Winter 1979). Some of the material was adapted from Bernstein's *Books to Help Children Cope with Separation and Loss* (New York: Bowker, 1977). Reprinted by permission of the author and *The ALAN Review.*

interest to teachers, librarians, counselors, and parents, for it is one aspect of death imagery which will have impact upon youngsters.

There are at least two different categories of death by suicide, both of which appear in books for young people. One form takes place when an individual seeks to escape what seems an intolerable situation. For an adult, this might occur after a dreadfully long period of defeat, or when a scandal threatens to "ruin life." For a young person, the draw toward extinction might be caused by unwarranted academic pressure, threats by a gang, great anxiety over sex and love, or excessive guilt. In all these instances, to the victims there seems to be no workable solution to problems.

The second type of suicide has been called instrumental. In dying, the victims wish magically to influence someone else. Be they adults or youngsters, they are communicating "do something." Often this group does not seek death, but searches for new hope instead.

Suicide undertaken in order to relieve insurmountable despair is the form which appears most often in the literature. That hopelessness derives from several sources.

War is a unifying theme. Highly respected and widely read novels depicting World War II feature suicide. Among them are *Till the Break of Day* (Wojciechowska), *When Hitler Stole Pink Rabbit* (Kerr), and *The Endless Steppe* (Hautzig). The suicide committed by a woman in the last book is typical of the portrayal of self-destruction in all three books— in fact, of suicide in many books for young adults. Most of the time, the character is an adult. Suicide is a secondary issue in the plot, decided upon by a supporting, often minor, character. It affects the thoughts of the more youthful protagonist, but does not fully determine his or her actions. The act cannot fail to be memorable; occasionally it haunts, as in Hautzig's penetrating factual story of exile in Siberia. Therein, upon being ordered by the Nazis to leave her home, an adult relative of the main character simply lies down on her bed, literally wills her life away, and swiftly dies.

In facilitating her own death, the protagonist's great-grandmother actually refuses to yield to despair, expressing her wish to live—with dignity. Says Hautzig, " 'It is time for me to die and it is for me to say when and where. Not them. So I will die today, here, in my own house.' And so she did: she lay down on her own bed, in her own black silk and pearls, in her own house, in her own beloved city, and picked the moment for dying herself. It was not suicide; by a supreme act of will, this old woman cheated the Nazis of her death."[1]

The Great Depression is another cause for utter despondency. The spate of recent books about this period in American history is not without its portrayal of suicide. Representative of this mode are *Pistol* (Richard), *The Dark Didn't Catch Me* (Thrasher), and *Nothing Rhymes with April* (Karp). In each, joblessness and its concomitant poverty (in an era preceding unemployment insurance) are adequate to send adult relatives or neighbors of literary protagonists over the edge. *Nothing Rhymes with April* is noteworthy because it is one of the few books for the 8-12 group in which suicide is part of the action. Nevertheless, the pattern found in the war books remains the same.

Depression is a continuous state on most Indian reservations. In *The Owl's Song* (Hale), a Native American cousin of the protagonist takes his own life when on the threshold of adulthood, feeling there is nothing to look forward to in coming years. In this case, suicide of a younger member of the population reflects reality, for suicide, along with alcoholism, is a route often taken to flee the circumstances of reservation life.

Other difficulties regarded as insoluble by suicidal literary characters are varied. They include the problem of being a "greaser" (*The Outsiders,* by Hinton), the problem of aging *(A Figure of Speech,* by Mazer), and the problem of guilt arising from thinking one has killed *(The Mills of God,* by Armstrong). The problem of physical and verbal abuse in a foster institution and the shame of rape are also causes, respectively seen in *Fly Away Paul* (Davies) and *Listen for the Fig Tree* (Mathis).

Instrumental suicides are depicted in novels for young people, although much more sparsely. In contrast to the books about insurmountable problems, stories of instrumental suicide tell of youth. Their dilemmas constitute the central problems of their books. This is not a surprise, for instrumental suicide is a specialty of the young.

Jenny's Corner (Bell) is an unusual book, one based loosely on fact. Aimed at very young children, ages 5-9, it tells of a girl so sensitive that the hunting which takes place on property near her home causes her intense grief: She becomes ill and loses all desire to live. Her self-imposed near starvation leads to the establishment of a reserve on the land. This type of instrumental suicide was called altruistic by Emile Durkheim, taking place when a "group's authority over the individual is so compelling that the individual loses his own personal identity and wishes to sacrifice his life for his community."[2] Readers might also infer from the imagery that grief can kill. The question of whether bereavement can indeed precipitate illness and death is one currently being investigated by thanatologists.

Instrumental suicides sometimes take place for less lofty causes than animal protection. Whatever the motivation, the victims envision new beginnings which would presumably come from a helping reaction of those surrounding them, as did happen in *Jenny's Corner*. Unfortunately, however, if those attempting suicide leave no mechanism for rescue, the message may go unheeded. Lucky in this regard is Lisa of *Lisa Bright and Dark*. The unsuccessful suicide attempt of Neufeld's mentally ill character is the climactic act which brings Lisa's parents to come to terms with what is evident to everyone else: their daughter needs psychiatric care.

Several major issues remain largely unconfronted. Traumatizing psychological aftermath is depicted rarely in fiction. The books *Grover* (Cleaver), *Wild in the World* (Donovan), and *Chloris and the Creeps* (Platt) are three titles which are exceptions, treating in depth families' shame and confusion, as well as reactions of neighbors and friends. All three concern the death of a parent, and all touch upon identification with the victim, treating survivors' ambivalent struggles to keep from joining the loved one in death.

Grover is additionally noteworthy because of its mention of another aspect of suicide rarely handled in fiction for youngsters: Grover's mother has ended her life because of the ravaging prospects of terminal illness. In today's society, such decisions are viewed increasingly with compassion. In time, Grover and his father come to terms with their relative's need, pick up the pieces, and go on with their lives. It is interesting to observe that of the very few stories now in existence which go beyond casual analysis of self-willed death, two (*Chloris* and *Grover*) attract preteens.

Psychiatrists indicate that many adults and children who suffer frequent serious accidents may be veering toward suicide. To this author's knowledge, the purposeful accident is rarely a central event in novels for youngsters. One occurs in *Twyla,* by Pamela Walker. Here, the reader follows one young girl's misery step by step. In lovelorn letters to a college student, Twyla pours out the only partially understood rejected feelings of a slow learner and high school misfit. The dream of her long-absent father's return fails to come to pass; the target of her affection fails to correspond to her letters; finally, her mother, in great frustration, makes plans to send Twyla away to a trade school where she will board. Hopeless and unable to cope, Twyla crashes a car into a tree. Few realize the true nature of her death.

It is evident that few authors have felt the need to write fiction in which suicide is treated in depth from a youthful protagonist's point of view, be that protagonist either one who ends life or one who goes on as immediate survivor. This may be as it should. Good stories do not come forth when fiction is written to order, keeping with societal need. It is not the purpose of this article to recommend that more fictional suicide books appear on the scene. It is better to wait until writers who manage their craft with competence and beauty see cause to pen their stories because they are compelled to do so.

A fine example of such a novel is Richard Peck's *Father Figure,* concerning a high school boy whose mother has taken her own life, or what is left of it, for she will soon succumb to cancer. With her death, Jim must provide the major care for his younger brother Byron. He acts as the father until their long absent real father comes forth to transport them from a chic section of New York City to a shabby section of Miami. The adjustment everyone makes is realistic, lively, and sometimes quite funny.

What other literary avenues exist for adolescents and preadolescents to learn about suicide? While novels are pursued for enjoyment, in their seriousness of perception they also constitute a way of knowing. Where can young people read of the vengeance suicide? "Let this be a lesson to you" is a type of instrumental suicide which adolescents who feel inferior sometimes fantasize, attempt, and succeed in accomplishing. In evoking sympathy, the victims try to get back at those who deprive them of self-worth (Grollman, p. 35). This type of suicide is missing in today's fiction.

Youth might logically search in fiction to understand anomic suicide. Anomie is caused by failure to adjust to social change. One sees reactions to business crisis and war depicted in fiction, but what of anomic upheaval felt in families who have moved sharply *upward* economically, nevertheless suffering severe dissatisfaction?

Where in fiction can young people seek knowledge of the slow forms of suicide, accomplished by those who Grollman says participate in life-shortening activities? Death by drugs has been explored, in such books as *Go Ask Alice* (Anonymous), but other forms have yet to be examined. Anorexia nervosa, dieting compulsively to the point of malnutrition or starvation, a condition increasing in frequency among teens, is an example of a problem indicating subintended suicide.

Where can young people search for balanced points of view? Is suicide self-murder, or is it a civil right? Is it a final, acceptable reassertion of control over one's direction? Most important, what are the literary ways for young people to know about suicide prevention and intervention?

For now, those seeking answers to these questions may be best guided to the nonfiction books about death which have become recent additions to young people's library collections.

Suicide is discussed briefly in *Learning to Say Goodbye: When a Parent Dies* (LeShan), *Houses for the Dead: Burial Customs through the Ages* (Turner), *Living and Dying* (Lifton and Olson), *Living with Death* (Segerberg), and my own *Loss: And How to Cope with It*. Working from differing perspectives, each tries to offer an understanding of the emotions and beliefs behind self-destruction.

Four nonfiction volumes treat suicide in greater depth. *Death: Everyone's Heritage* (Landau) includes a chapter on the subject. The chapter offers statistics and information concerning many aspects of suicide, including slow self-destruction. The author dispels myths, such as the folly of suicide as a luxury reserved for the rich. Landau thoughtfully asks readers to decide for themselves if suicide is more than a personal decision. In advice for prevention, she teaches readers how to be normalizing listeners.

Death Is a Noun also devotes a chapter to suicide. Author Langone appreciates an historical outlook, revealing that Samson was among several heroes who took the suicide route. One valuable aspect of Langone's chapter is an investigation of many forms of violence, such as shootouts, as hidden suicides. Langone quotes many recent studies, including one which concludes that the suicidogenic seed is sown during a critical period when a child is between six and eighteen months old. Presumably, a child who has not been physically or emotionally abandoned during this period is protected against suicide. This finding has implications for intervention in families and should be made widely known. Langone presents Dr. Avery Weisman's observation that many suicides have much in common with the terminally ill—both have come to see death as acceptable for themselves and eventually yield to it, refusing help. For readers who identify with this and many other insights, the book can be invaluable.

A most comprehensive book available today is *Too Young to Die: Youth and Suicide,* by Francine Klagsbrun. Written for youngsters twelve and up, it reaches a wider age group, having been featured in condensed form in newspapers throughout the country. No wonder. Through use of interesting case histories, the author suggests numerous causes for suicide. She examines all the questions asked in this article, and more. Her sections on depression and slow suicide go further than any other, including mention of types infrequently noted, such as diabetics who "forget" medication.

Devoting an entire book to the subject allows Klagsbrun to spend adequate time on the plight of survivors. No punches are pulled. Klagsbrun analyzes the higher rate of suicide among survivors, explaining that it is not biologically based. Instead, survivors bear the burdens of guilt, anger, and doubts of self-worth. These are the factors which may start a suicide cycle. Klagsbrun opens new doors. Many readers may identify with her discussion of parents who unconsciously want their children dead. Realizing their parents feel most at ease with lifeless beings who cause no trouble, the youngsters of such parents soon learn to deaden their emotional capacities. Actual suicide becomes a possibility.

Meticulous research is the underpinning of *Too Young to Die.* An extensive bibliography and listing of suicide referral agencies are included. In its scope and fair-mindedness, the author has offered readers an eloquent assertion which fosters celebration of life.

Also highly worthwhile is Arnold Madison's *Suicide and Young People.* Special emphases here include discussion of suicide in other countries, suicide and minorities, and suicide equivalents. Readers will be fascinated to learn about monkeys who engage in self-biting, suicidal aspects of voodoo, and events during a typical day at a suicide prevention center. The author's historical viewpoint offers perspective.

NOTES

1. Esther Hautzig, *The Endless Steppe* (New York: Crowell, 1968), pp.24-25.
2. Earl A. Grollman, *Suicide: Prevention, Intervention, Postvention* (Boston: Beacon, 1971), p.40.

SELECTED BIBLIOGRAPHY

Anonymous. *Go Ask Alice*. Englewood Cliffs, N.J.: Prentice-Hall, 1971.

Armstrong, William. *The Mills of God*. Garden City, N.Y.: Doubleday, 1973.

Bell, Frederic. *Jenny's Corner*. New York: Random, 1974.

Bernstein, Joanne. *Loss: And How to Cope with It*. New York: Seabury, 1977.

Cleaver, Vera, and Cleaver, Bill. *Grover*. Philadelphia: Lippincott, 1970.

Davies, Peter. *Fly Away Paul*. New York: Crown, 1974.

Donovan, John. *Wild in the World*. New York: Harper, 1971.

Hale, Janet. *The Owl's Song*. Garden City, N.Y.: Doubleday, 1974.

Hautzig, Esther. *The Endless Steppe*. New York: Crowell, 1968.

Hinton, S. E. *The Outsiders*. New York: Viking, 1967.

Karp, Naomi. *Nothing Rhymes with April*. New York: Harcourt, 1974.

Kerr, Judith. *When Hitler Stole Pink Rabbit*. New York: Coward-McCann, 1971.

Klagsbrun, Francine. *Too Young to Die: Youth and Suicide*. Boston: Houghton, 1976.

Landau, Elaine. *Death: Everyone's Heritage*. New York: Messner, 1976.

Langone, John. *Death Is a Noun*. Boston: Little, 1972.

LeShan, Edna. *Learning to Say Goodbye: When a Parent Dies*. New York: Macmillan, 1976.

Lifton, Robert Jay and Olson, Eric. *Living and Dying*. New York: Praeger, 1974.

Madison, Arnold. *Suicide and Young People*. New York: Seabury, 1978.

Mathis, Sharon Bell. *Listen for the Fig Tree*. New York: Viking, 1974.

Mazer, Norma Fox. *A Figure of Speech*. New York: Delacorte, 1973.

Neufeld, John. *Lisa Bright and Dark*. Chicago: S. G. Phillips, 1969.

Peck, Richard. *Father Figure*. New York: Viking, 1978.

Platt, Kin. *Chloris and the Creeps*. Philadelphia: Chilton, 1973.

Richard, Adrienne. *Pistol*. Boston: Little, 1969.

Segerberg, Osborn, Jr. *Living with Death*. New York: Dutton, 1976.

Thrasher, Crystal. *The Dark Didn't Catch Me*. New York: Atheneum, 1975.

Turner, Ann. *Houses for the Dead: Burial Customs through the Ages*. New York: McKay, 1976.

Walker, Pamela. *Twyla*. Englewood Cliffs, N.J.: Prentice-Hall, 1973.

Wojciechowska, Maia. *Till the Break of Day*. New York: Harcourt, 1972.

Part 4

Male and Female: Sexuality

O western wind, when wilt thou blow,
   that the small rain down can rain?
Christ, if my love were in my arms,
   And I in my bed again!

Anonymous

"To be human is to be sexual. . . . ," observes Mary S. Calderone, and sexuality is "one of the great human endowments, comparable to the intellect in its importance, universality, and depth of concern for every person." Yet human sexuality in American society is freighted with problems, and these problems are dramatically rising among teenagers.

W. Cody Wilson brings to his discussion of "Adolescent Moral Development and Sexual Decision" the perspective of a professor of behavioral sciences. The statistics he cites on teenage sex are depressing, especially when we consider the human beings behind the figures, and the devastating impact of teenage pregnancy and teenage parenthood upon the lives of so many young people. To analyze the serious social problem of teenage parenthood, Wilson identifies the alternative "action paths" or options open to sexually active young people, reports the results of various scientific studies, and examines how different behaviors, whether consciously chosen or not, relate to the individual's level of moral development as defined in the theory of Lawrence Kohlberg. He leaves us with a challenge: recognizing the relatively immature level of moral reasoning about sex displayed by most teenagers, what can we do to communicate with them more effectively on their own levels and, further, to provide them with meaningful dialogue that will help them to reach "a higher, more principled, perhaps more responsible, level?"

The next three essays address this challenge as it must be faced by library professionals working with youth. Libraries, most especially school libraries, do not sufficiently reflect the centrality of human sexuality to human experience; despite the wealth of material available, much of it "remains fearsomely forbidden or totally absent, both on the shelves and in the minds of school librarians." To the public libraries, then, falls the task of, in Mel Rosenberg's words, "Filling the Gap" in knowledge about sexuality. But all of us, whether professional librarians, educators, health-care professionals, parents, teenagers, etcetera, need to ponder the schizoid attitudes of our society towards sexuality. As Calderone points out, we send the young contradictory signals. On the one hand, the media betray an obsessive concern with sexual pleasure and promote the pursuit of sex as happiness; yet, on the other hand, we try to tell young people to "forget sexual pleasure until you are ready to reproduce —which won't be until after education and job-finding and marriage." And yet we are aware that young people are reaching reproductive maturity at an ever earlier age. It follows, surely, that they need sex education at even earlier ages as well.

Few people can speak more knowledgeably and persuasively in favor of educating the young about their sexuality than Calderone, whose name is virtually synonymous in many people's minds with the Sex Information and Education Council of the U.S., Inc. Addressing herself particularly to librarians, she makes a clear case for the importance of the role of public librarians, in particular, in meeting the sex education needs of the young and their parents, since parents are, for better or worse, "the most important sex educators of their children." Her "sweet reasonableness" on this topic that is all too often distorted by fears and biases stands as exemplary. Let us hope her clear-eyed vision, with its recognition of the dignity and life-enriching power of sexuality, will be the "norm" of the future.

In "The Librarian's Role in Young Adult Sex Education," John Cunningham and Frances Hanckel speak to the same topic as Calderone, but their discussion incorporates the perspective of the professional librarian. Their practical, direct comments—such as their hints on procedures for referral service and their ideas for programming—round out the discussion, and their bibliography of source materials adds to the usefulness of their essay.

Mel Rosenberg's personal experience as a young adult librarian in a public library gives special interest to his brief article, "Filling the Gap," wherein he spotlights the need for cooperation between public and school librarians to answer the demand of youthful readers for nonfiction books on sex.

The topic of sex in fiction books for the young is broached by Pamela S. Pollack in "Sex in Children's Fiction: Freedom to Frighten?" (The "Children's" of the title may be misleading; almost all the books discussed are for teenagers.) She begins with the admonition that the new freedom to explore formerly "taboo" subjects can become a "license to exploit"—"to cash in on every titillating theme and call it 'bibliotherapy.'" She also alerts us to the presence of the old stereotypes in some of these "new" books dealing with sexuality. Her insight concerning the "joyless"-ness of sex in some of these books is well worth pondering. However, some readers will take exception to her judgments of particular novels (e.g., *Diving for Roses* and *The Terrible Love Life of Dudley Cornflower* deserve a more sympathetic reading), and others may disagree with her apparent assumption that authors of books for the young should present characters who behave in exemplary fashion, to avoid "terrifying readers already fearful about sex and its consequences." The basic question must be, do these books portray reality in truthful, sensitive, emotionally involving terms? Or do they distort that tenuous thing we call "reality," tending towards melodrama, as too often happens in young adult books? To answer these questions, readers will have to exercise their own critical powers, but it is important to analyze the books in terms of their literary as well as their therapeutic value.

Hanckel and Cunningham's second article, "Can Young Gays Find Happiness in YA Books?" opens up the topic of homosexuality in teenage fiction. Immediately following it is a previously unpublished response, W. Bernard Lukenbill's "Homosexual Conflicts and Their Resolutions in Five Adolescent Novels: A Psychosocial Inquiry." Hanckel and Cunningham make a strong case for materials supportive of homosexuals and offer critiques of "the handling of the gay experience in YA fiction as a whole"; Lukenbill in turn presents thoughtful replies, questioning whether truth to "social reality" permits a realistic author to be as supportive of the homosexual characters as our first two authors wish, and presenting his own interpretations of the novels considered, plus one other, more recently published. It is hoped that the juxtaposition of these two articles, on a topic that has received little critical attention, will encourage more dialogue and lead to a clarification of the values at issue.

The differences in perspective between the Hanckel and Cunningham article and the article by Lukenbill imply another, more basic debate about the nature of literature, one upon which we can only speculate, since it is ultimately unanswerable. Since Aristotle, it has been assumed that "art imitates nature": Oscar Wilde jestingly expressed the paradoxical inversion of this dictum, that "nature imitates art." To what degree does art (fiction in this case) offer models for imitation (role models, in this case, for homosexuals) and thus actually *shape* human nature? And to what degree, on the contrary, is nature (human nature) a constant, a "model" for the artist's representation? It is clear that the two views cast the artist or author in quite different roles, and imply quite different expectations of literature.

Young People, Sexuality, and Librarians

Mary S. Calderone

In the burning and pillaging of libraries in historic times, much knowledge is considered to have been lost. If our own public libraries were destroyed today, we could claim the same, except for one subject: human sexuality. In the past fifteen years this has become an area of knowledge that is exploding among researchers and professionals. There are now no less than twelve professional journals in the field, as compared to one in 1964 when SIECUS [Sex Information and Education Council of the U.S., Inc.] was formed. Some of the knowledge gained during this period is beginning to percolate through the public—the adult public, that is. But is it reaching our children and young people? Certainly not where they need it—not in their homes, not in their schools, nor in many of their school libraries, where for the most part it remains fearsomely forbidden or totally absent, both on the shelves and in the minds of school librarians. So the hope must lie for the moment in the public libraries—and especially in the courage and wisdom of their staffs.

What should be on those public libraries' shelves? The truth, that's what. There has been enough of myths and falsehoods, of opinions given as facts, of statements trumped up to serve wily but transparent adult ends. "The trouble with grownups," said one high school girl to me, "is that they really don't want to educate us about sex, but just to control our behavior." True enough, and this backfires so that, in the sexually silent ignorance carefully imposed by the adult world, youthful sexual behavior goes underground, to surface only in adolescent pregnancies—almost twenty thousand *every week,* one million *every year* in this country; one in ten of these pregnancies occurs in girls fifteen to nineteen, and in girls *under* fifteen, thirty thousand pregnancies occur every year, and the rate is rising. How can we have been so blind, stubborn, stupid, and fearful as to have let this happen?

But it has, and is now epidemic in the U.S. and pandemic across the world. What kind of knowledge, of truth, might serve to help young people themselves stem this tide? Even if only they can do so, they will still need our help. Therefore this is the kind of information we must give them.

Reprinted from "Sex and Youth: A Symposium," *Top of the News* 34:125-30 (Winter 1978).

Basic Knowledge about Human Sexuality—the Sexualization Process

Gender identity. To be human is to be sexual; to be sexual is to be human. We come into the world sexual—and instantly our parents, and the world around us, begin to treat us differently depending on our gender. The first question asked is, "Is it a boy or a girl?" Why is this the first question? Because no one knows how to respond to an *it;* "it" makes us uncomfortable. Try it!

As a result, through the cues, actions, and words of those around the tiny baby, "it" eventually learns whether he is a boy or she is a girl, and sex research shows that it learns this indelibly by two years of age—no later—from the myriad clues furnished constantly by those closest to it.

Gender role behavior. What kind of boy or girl? That is, what behaviors are considered appropriate to each gender? These too must be learned, differently in each society or in different areas of each society. They are learned by observation, copying, practice, admonition or rules, by inference, and, of course, from television. Television is immensely powerful and sometimes manages to impose gender imagery on a child that goes quite contrary to what that child's family is trying to teach it. Today, of course, gender roles that used to be fixed are in a state of flux. "The times they are a-changing," and so are male and female *roles.* As to the nature of male-female *relationships,* these are also absorbed from parents and television. "Tune in tomorrow and see what else men and women can do to each other!"

The erotic aspects of sexuality. This area is what the fear is all about. Most people are not aware that the erotic is part of us throughout the entire life cycle. Boy babies have erections, girl babies derive pleasure from self-caressing, and their vaginas lubricate as they will in adult sexual arousal. To deny this, or to try to interfere with it, is to do violence to something that is deeply fundamental to being born human. It is, indeed, now looked upon as part of rehearsal play for adult life, just as the young of other animals and of primitive tribes show it. However, other animals do not share the erotic feelings of humans; their sexual behavior is really reproductive behavior, governed by external seasonal factors such as climate, length of day, state of nutrition. Animals do not fall in love nor do they have the capacity to postpone, to plan, to identify and exercise options. Those are human attributes, and they too, like our total sexuality, are learned.

We have learned too, how to separate the two goals of eroticism: pleasure and procreation. Both of these goals are natural and valid, the first being designed to lead to the second. In modern societies we have learned that both must be pursued with a sense of responsibility and appropriateness as to time, place, purpose, partner, and effects on others—from the partner to the possible offspring, to the future life of the self, and to the society. But the only way that we have found for getting over this message to the young is to say, in effect, "Forget sexual pleasure until you are ready to reproduce—which won't be until after education and job finding and marriage." This is unrealistic: reproductive maturation has been arriving earlier and earlier, in the same period that education is taking longer and longer. So what the young are saying is, in effect, "Hey, we're sexual people *right now*. You've just forgotten what it's like—and anyway, you've made it clear, through magazines and ads and movies and TV, that sexual pleasure is part of life, *the younger the better!* We've got the message, so forget trying to stop us from acting on it." This is why saying no doesn't work; what is there left for us to do in this societal dilemma in which that whirling sawblade of sexual and reproductive disaster approaches ever closer to our children, while *they* are still children?

Consequences of Increasing Teenage Births

At this very moment research is showing that approximately 50 percent of girls fifteen to nineteen are sexually active, and about one in ten has a baby as a result of this. An unknown number get pregnant and have natural miscarriages or have been having abortions. With the changes in abortion laws we can expect a larger number of teenage births to result. But pregnancies in women under eighteen have higher rates of prematurity (and its consequences—birth defects and mental retardation); of illness and death to both mother and baby; of maternal suicide; and of permanent welfare dependency, than do pregnancies in women over eighteen. That's where we are today—a bad place to be.

What Librarians Can Do

Public librarians can have a vital role to play in educating the public to all of these established facts, but given the complexity of the subject and the way it touches every single human being who walks into a library or works in it in a very personal way, such education really depends on three vital steps:

Librarians need first to educate *themselves* about human sexuality if they are to exercise good judgment in what materials to offer to which part of their public.

They need to educate the *parents* of children and young people.

Concurrently, they must exercise skilled judgments about *their role* in the sex education of children and young people who come to the libraries.

How can they accomplish these three tasks?

Educating Themselves

1. All of us must work toward broad acceptance of human sexuality as a universal and valid part of each human being at every age. It follows that all of us, including librarians, must be understanding and accepting of our own sexuality.
2. Librarians need to go as far as they can to inform themselves of the rich store of knowledge about human sexuality that has emerged from intensive research in the past fifteen years.[1]
3. They can take advantage of the many opportunities now becoming available for training in knowledge, skills, attitudes. At least one person in each library should take some training in order to develop judgment about what is "good" in published materials.[2]

Educating Parents of Young Children, Preadolescents, and Adolescents

1. Everyone, parents included, must understand that parents are, willy-nilly, the first and therefore the most important sex educators of their children. In fact, by the time a child reaches kindergarten his or her primary sex education has already been accomplished—for good or ill.
2. Libraries can be leaders in developing local opportunities for parents to better their attitudes and performance in this role.[3]

Educating Preadolescents and Adolescents

This is the age at which young people begin to exercise independent judgment on what books they would like to read. But a word of caution here: it is a mistake for libraries to get too far ahead of the community in this, for only by bringing the community along with the library can community acceptance through education avoid some of the wasteful and damaging flare-ups that result in book-burning attitudes.

1. Libraries can provide programs and reading materials that promote sexual values as part of all values clarification.
2. They can develop programs and reading materials that support the development of sound attitudes and options about sexuality.
3. And there must certainly exist programs and reading materials that are based on communication of sexual facts that preadolescents and adolescents need to know.
4. Reading materials can be collected and listed for discussion around various social issues that are basic today, to which we bring points of view different from those held in other epochs. Some examples that combine all three of the above desirable activities (1, 2, and

3) are: Hawthorne's *The Scarlet Letter,* which highlights extramarital sex and out-of-wedlock pregnancy and how we ourselves treated this at a certain period in our history; Shakespeare's *Henry the Eighth,* with his multiple serial marriages (and the magnificently produced British television series on these marriages); Dreiser's *An American Tragedy,* the tragedy of teenage pregnancy; Shakespeare's *Romeo and Juliet,* the epitome of romantic teenage love. However, you, as librarians, can extend this list far better than I can.

High on the list of recommended activities, I would place discussion groups with parents, both mothers and fathers—any who might be enticed to talk about what they would like their children to read that might protect them from the unwise and premature engagement in total sexual activity that is proving so disastrous. Parents have a tendency, quite natural, to think that this cannot happen to their children, only to *someone else's* children! A reading of Judy Blume's *Forever* by the parents themselves might help them understand how naturally such sexual activities that Blume describes do come about under present-day social conditions. If they feel that this book seems like advocacy, or implies "getting away" with something, help them remember that their daughters and sons are daily in contact with other young people who are actually going through the same kinds of experiences. What a book can do is give people *insight,* once they have had a chance to discuss it in a group and in the context of their own lives. If parents can read Eric Johnson's *Love and Sex in Plain Language* before their children reach junior high, they can be given the words with which to open the topic of sexual activity with their children, and to discuss the values by which the children are governing their lives in preparation for greater maturity. Waiting for such discussions until the children are already in the throes of adolescence is far too little and too late, as was shown in the classic study by the Connecticut State Health Department in which five thousand children, kindergarten through twelfth grade, asked some of the questions that they really wanted to know about sex.[4] This study should be in every public library that undertakes an intensive program of orientation in the field of human sexuality, for it is invaluable for parents and for librarians themselves.

Conclusion

Sexuality has, at long last, been identified for what it is: one of the great human endowments, comparable to the intellect in its importance, universality, and depth of concern for every person. It is coming to be looked upon more and more by religions and by professionals as a kind of sixth sense, by which we come to know, understand, and communicate with others. The World Health Organization has identified human sexuality as integral to the well-being of every person, and a special WHO committee has recommended that sexual health services become a part of all health services. This special committee defined sexual health as follows:

> Sexual health is the integration of the somatic, emotional, intellectual, and social aspects of sexual being, in ways that are positively enriching and that enhance personality, communication, and love. Fundamental to this concept are the right to sexual information and the right to pleasure.[5]

Library science and services are in the truest sense part of the health sciences, and librarians can look upon themselves in the truest sense as health personnel, with an enormous potential for adding to the "physical, mental, and social well-being" of people, as defined by the World Health Organization at its establishment in the 1940s. Librarians perhaps cannot be therapists, but they *can* add their weight and skills to preventing the *need* for therapy, thereby contributing greatly to the future well-being of countless individuals and their families.

NOTES

1. *SIECUS Report* (bi-monthly) reviews current important books in the field of sexuality and contains lead articles on important issues in the field as well as lists of resources that are obtainable. *SIECUS* also publishes a *Professional Book List* and a list of *Books for Everyone* (by age levels), which are revised every two years.
2. The March (Education) issue of the *SIECUS Report* lists forthcoming summer workshops in universities all over the United States to which professionals can go for training. The state of California, in September 1976, passed a law requiring health and caring professionals to obtain training in human sexuality, whether in preparation for their degrees or as postgraduate continuing education.
3. Family Sex Education Week takes place in early October and 1977 was its third year. Communities and community libraries can use this as an opportunity to draw to the attention of parents that theirs is the primary role in the sex education of their children. For information contact Joseph Fanelli, Institute for Family Research and Education, 760 Ostrom Ave., Syracuse, NY 13210.
4. Ruth Byler and others, *Teach Us What We Want to Know* (New York: Mental Health Materials Center, 1969).
5. *Education and Treatment in Human Sexuality: The Training of Health Professionals* (Geneva: World Health Organization, 1975).

Adolescent Moral Development and Sexual Decision

W. Cody Wilson

Teenage Parenthood and Decision Making

Approximately 2 million teenagers engage in sexual intercourse in the United States each month; approximately 8¼ million instances of teenage sexual intercourse occur in any given month; more than 1 million teenage pregnancies occur each year; and approximately ¾ million teenage females give birth in the United States each year. The consequences of teenage parenthood in the medical, economic, social, and psychological realms are generally valued negatively in our present society; and teenage parenthood is generally viewed as a serious social problem.

For purposes of analyzing the problem, teenage parenthood may be considered as the end point of a series of "decisions": the first decision is to have or not to have sexual intercourse; if one has sexual intercourse, the second decision is to use or not use effective contraception; if one does not use effective contraception and becomes pregnant, the third decision is to have or not have an abortion; if one does not have an abortion, the fourth decision is to keep or not to keep the child. This series of decisions leading to parenthood may be expressed pictorially as a decision tree (figure 1.).

Note that one can "get off the path" to teenage parenthood at several different points. Some of these "decision points" for departing from the path leading to teenage parenthood are more positively valued and others are more negatively valued by our society: e.g., "not having intercourse" is perhaps more positively valued (especially by adults for teenagers) in our current society; having intercourse using an effective contraception is less positively valued; and having an abortion is yet more negatively valued. Further, different segments of our society may value a given "decision point" quite differently; consider the lack of consensus on the issue of abortion in our country today.

Note also that although these are called "decision points" and "decisions," there is no implication that "deliberate," "explicit," "rational," or "conscious" *decisions* are made at these choice points. Rather, we simply mean to indicate that there are alternative behavioral or action paths

Reprinted by permission from "Sex and Youth: A Symposium," *Top of the News* 34:145-53 (Winter 1978).

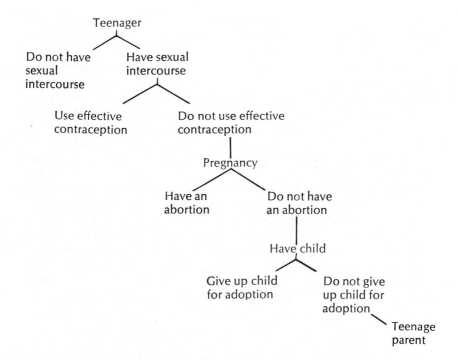

Fig. 1. Decision tree leading to teenage parenthood

that may be taken at each point and that some individuals "take" one path while other individuals "take" the alternative path.

There now exists quite good information that enables us to describe the distribution of "decisions" made by teenage women at these various "decision points" on the path to teenage parenthood, and to state the probability with which each choice will be made.

Zelnik and Kantner (1972) conducted an interview study of 4,611 teenage women selected in such a way that they were representative of all the females aged fifteen to nineteen years who live in the United States. The results of this study have been reported in considerable detail in several articles in *Family Planning Perspectives* (Kantner and Zelnik, 1972; Kantner and Zelnik, 1973; and Zelnik and Kantner, 1974). Many of the figures reported in this paper are quoted from their study or derived from their data.

Consider the first decision point on the path to teenage parenthood—to have or not to have sexual intercourse. About one-third of all females age fifteen to nineteen have had sexual intercourse (Zelnik and Kantner, 1972). This single figure is somewhat misleading, however, in two ways: first, there is considerable variation among the several age groups in the proportion having intercourse; and second, having had intercourse once does not necessarily usher into being a regular pattern of relatively frequent intercourse.

Only 14 percent of fifteen-year-old girls, 27 percent of seventeen-year-old girls, but 50 percent of nineteen-year-old girls report having had sexual intercourse. Thus as a girl grows older during the adolescent period, she is more likely to have had intercourse; indeed, half of women have their first experience with sexual intercourse as teenagers (Zelnik and Kantner, 1972). Moreover, this figure has not changed since the generation of women who were teenagers during the period of the Second World War (Wilson, 1973).

The probability of a teenage girl having had sexual intercourse does not vary significantly with the region of the country in which she lives, with the type of community in which she lives, or with her family's socioeconomic status. The probability of having had sexual intercourse does vary with other characteristics, however. We have already seen that the probability approximately doubles from age fifteen to age seventeen, and roughly doubles again from age seventeen to age nineteen. Black girls have intercourse earlier than white girls; girls who attend church more often are less likely to have had intercourse; girls who confide in their parents are less likely to have had intercourse; girls who live alone are more likely to have had intercourse than are girls who live in groups or in mother-headed households, who in turn are more likely to have had intercourse than are girls who live in father-headed households. That is, living in a father-headed household, having a confiding relationship with parents, and attending church tend to inhibit the initiation of sexual experience by teenage girls, and belonging to the black ethnic group and living alone tend to facilitate the initiation of sexual experience by teenage girls (Kantner and Zelnik, 1972).

The probability of using some form of contraception on the part of teenage women is *not* related to ethnic group membership, religion, family income, where the person lives, or living arrangements. The probability of using some form of contraception is greater, however, on the part of girls whose mothers attended college, girls who have been having intercourse for a longer length of time, and girls who have intercourse more frequently.

The consequence of sexual intercourse without effective contraception is pregnancy. More than 10 percent of all females aged fifteen to nineteen have experienced a pregnancy (Zelnik and Kantner, 1974; Tietze, 1977). Nearly one-third (29 percent) of sexually active females aged fifteen to nineteen have had a premarital pregnancy (Zelnik and Kantner, 1974). Although direct data are not reported, it is possible to combine information from several sources (Zelnik and Kantner, 1974; Sklar and Berkov, 1974; and Tietze, 1977) to estimate that between one-quarter and one-third of all nineteen-year-old women have been pregnant at least once. Since half of women have had sexual experience by age nineteen, this means that more than half of women who are sexually experienced as teenagers will become pregnant before leaving the teenage years.

The third decision point on the path to becoming a teenage mother is: if one gets pregnant, to have or not to have an abortion. Approximately one-quarter of teenage pregnancies end in induced abortion (Zelnik and Kantner, 1974; Tietze, 1977); another nearly 10 percent end in spontaneous abortion (Zelnik and Kantner, 1974). But two-thirds of teenage pregnancies result in live births.

The final decision point on the path to becoming a teenage mother is: if one has a child, to give it up for adoption or not to give it up for adoption. The best estimate is that about 15 percent of illegitimate children are given up for adoption in the 1970s (Sklar and Berkov, 1974). Thus, the vast majority of teenage women who bear a child do become teenage mothers.

These various figures on the results of teenage "decisions" at the several "decision points" on the path to teenage parenthood may be summarized as follows:

Among fifteen-year-old girls, 14 percent have had intercourse at least once and 3 percent have a pattern of regular relatively frequent intercourse; the vast majority (85 percent) of those who are sexually experienced do *not* use a generally effective method of contraception at a given instance of intercourse.

Among seventeen-year-old girls, 27 percent have had intercourse at least once and 9 percent have regular frequent intercourse; nearly three-quarters (73 percent) of the sexually experienced do *not* generally use an effective method of contraception.

Among nineteen-year-old women, 50 percent have had the experience of sexual intercourse and 25 percent have regular frequent intercourse; more than half (55 percent) of these sexually experienced women do *not* typically use a generally effective contraceptive action.

Nearly one-third of all nineteen-year-old women have been pregnant at least once; more than half of women who are sexually experienced as teenagers become pregnant before leaving the teenage years.

Approximately one-quarter of teenage pregnancies end in induced abortion and another 10 percent in spontaneous abortion; but two-thirds of teenage pregnancies result in live births—indeed, ¾ million each year.

Piaget's Approach and Adolescent Decision Making

Only a small percentage of these babies are given up for adoption; the vast majority of teenage women who bear them become teenage mothers. Unfortunately, we have almost no reliable empirical knowledge to undergird an attempt to understand *why* these decisions are made—what influences the decisions and how the associated probabilities can be changed at each decision point. Indeed, we have few theoretical ideas that have sufficient power and scope to provide the needed illumination in these areas. The developmental psychology of Jean Piaget, however, seems to hold considerable promise for understanding a wide range of significant aspects of adolescent functioning, and I would like to describe one approach that is derived from his ideas and is just recently being applied to thinking about adolescent sexuality and adolescent decision making about sex.

First, however, I would like to make a brief comment on the apparent "sexism" involved in the previous description of the decisions leading to teenage parenthood—in which the focus was entirely on females. The reason for this focus is that we have information on females and do not have it on males. The likely reason for this fact is that the locus of conception and gestation is the female body, and the consequences of the various decisions directly affect the female physiologically; further, because of the period of gestation in the female body, the baby is, in our society, perceived as "belonging to" the female. The female is, therefore, the "focus" of societal interest, concern, and research.

The decision processes on the path to teenage parenthood, on the other hand, involve males in varying degrees. The first decision point, to have or not to have sexual intercourse, is necessarily a joint decision involving both male and female. The second decision point, to use or not to use contraception, may be, and often is, a joint decision with both male and female actively participating; but it is possible for the female to reserve this decision entirely to herself. The third decision point, to have or not to have an abortion, may sometimes be a joint decision, but the male is less directly involved and the locus of the issue is directly the female body; thus the female interest far outweighs that of the male.

The ideas about human development formulated by Piaget apply to males as well as females. Piaget focuses on the cognitive processes and suggests that cognitive structure, or the manner in which an individual organizes experience, is a major determinant of social behavior. The overall direction of development of cognitive structure is from "concrete" (in childhood) to "abstract" (in adulthood). Indeed, during the teenage years there begins to develop a comprehensive abstract cognitive structure that changes radically the way an individual thinks about his/her world and organizes his/her experiences, and therefore, the way he/she makes behavioral decisions (Inhelder and Piaget, 1958).

Kohlberg's Moral Developmental Theory

A Harvard psychologist, Lawrence Kohlberg, has applied these ideas of Piaget's to the study of the development of moral judgment during adolescence. His technique is to pose, in an interview situation with an adolescent, a hypothetical moral dilemma and ask the individual not only what he or she would do in that situation but also *why* he or she would take that particular action. He analyzes the reasoning that is used to justify the action taken. People at different ages in adolescence tend to use quite different and distinctive modes of thinking about the same problem, with older adolescents using more differentiated and integrated modes of thought organization. These modes of thought are organized into six stages that appear to form a hierarchical sequence (Kohlberg, 1969); i.e., each "higher" stage builds on a preceding "lower" one and grows out of it.

Stage one—the lowest stage of moral reasoning—is called by Kohlberg the *punishment and obedience orientation*. In this stage the physical consequences of an action determine its goodness or badness. Avoidance of punishment and unquestioning deference to power are valued in their own right (not in terms of respect for an underlying moral order that is supported by punishment and authority—which is a higher level of reasoning).

Stage two is labeled the *instrumental relativist orientation*. Right action consists of that which instrumentally satisfies one's own needs. Human relations are viewed in terms like those of the marketplace. Reciprocity is a matter of "you scratch my back and I'll scratch yours"—not of loyalty, gratitude, or justice, which represent higher levels of reasoning.

Note that these first two stages of moral reasoning are very *egocentric*; the focus is on the physical or hedonistic consequences *for one's self* of an action.

Stage three is the *interpersonal concordance* (or good boy-nice girl) *orientation*. Good behavior is that which pleases or helps others and is approved by them, and there is much conformity to stereotypical images of what is majority or "natural" behavior.

Stage four is the *"law and order" orientation*. The focus is on maintaining the social order by supporting established authority and obeying fixed rules. Right behavior consists of doing one's duty, showing respect for authority, and actively maintaining the given social order for its own sake.

Note that stages three and four are *sociocentric* as opposed to the earlier and more primitive egocentric orientations. The focus at these *sociocentric* stages is the expectations of others—one's family, group, or nation. Loyalty to the established social order and identification with the people involved in it take precedence over the immediate personal needs and concerns in judging the consequences of action.

Stages five and six move on to a *principlecentric orientation*—an attempt to define moral values in terms of principles that have validity and application apart from the authority of a specific group or society and the individual's own identification with that group.

Stage five is labeled by Kohlberg the *social-contract legalistic orienta-*

tion and it has some utilitarian overtones. Moral action is defined in terms of general individual rights and in terms of standards that have been critically examined and agreed upon by the participants. There is awareness of the relativism of personal values and opinions and a consequent emphasis upon procedural rules for reaching consensus. Existing law or rules are not "fixed" but are subject to change, by general agreement, for rational consideration of social utility. Free agreement and "contract" is the binding element of obligation.

Stage six, the highest level of moral reasoning, is the *universal ethical principle orientation*. Right is defined by the decision of conscience in accord with self-chosen ethical principles appealing to logical comprehensiveness, universality, and consistency. Behavior should conform to abstract principles, of reciprocity, justice, and equality of individual persons (e.g., the Golden Rule) rather than to concrete moral rules (e.g., the Ten Commandments).

Kohlberg (1969), in extensive longitudinal and cross-cultural research, has found these six stages of moral reasoning to constitute an invariant, cultural, universal, developmental sequence; i.e., every individual, in order to reach a "higher" stage of moral reasoning, necessarily passes through, in sequence, each of the lower stages. However, not every individual (or culture) necessarily reaches the highest stage of moral development; one may be fixated at, or not develop beyond, one of the lower stages.

Kohlberg's Theory and Adolescent Sexual Decision Making

These several stages of moral reasoning are manifest in adolescence in dealing with general social, political, and economic issues. The thinking of younger adolescents is limited to the lower levels of moral reasoning, but older adolescents utilize higher stages of moral reasoning in thinking about such issues.

How do these stages of moral reasoning apply to sexual decision making?

Two small studies have been made applying the concept of stages of moral reasoning to the realm of sex.

A colleague of Kohlberg's (Gilligan and others, 1971) adapted his procedures to deal with sexual dilemmas (e.g., premarital sex, late adolescent marital sex, and premarital pregnancy) and studied the moral reasoning about sex of eleventh-grade high school students, both boys and girls.

These eleventh-grade students—sixteen and seventeen years old—used predominantly stages 2, 3, and 4 of moral reasoning in discussing these sexual issues. You will recall that stage 2 (which instrumentally satisfies one's own needs) is still at the primitive *egocentric level*. Stages 3, interpersonal concordance orientation (i.e., good behavior is that which pleases others and is approved by them), and 4, the "law and order" orientation (i.e., obeying fixed rules and maintaining the given social order for its own sake), are the *sociocentric levels*. Approximately one-quarter of these sixteen- and seventeen-year-old adolescents used stage 2 moral reasoning, one-half used stage 3, and one-quarter used stage 4 reasoning when dealing with sexual issues. Very seldom did the level of moral reasoning about sex reach the abstract principled level.

These levels of moral reasoning about sex were lower than one would have expected from people of this age. Indeed, the level of moral reasoning about sex was lower than that manifested by these same adolescents when dealing with nonsexual social, political, and economic issues.

Why does the level of reasoning about sex lag behind the level of reasoning in other areas? Three possible explanations immediately rise in my mind. First, sex is a highly affectively charged area in our society, especially for adolescents, and this affective involvement may depress the reasoning ability in this area. Second, sex is not supposed to be discussed explicitly by adolescents and so they have little opportunity to practice moral reasoning about sex and there is a consequent developmental lag in this area. And third, adults in our culture prefer that sexual dilemmas be resolved by adolescents in terms of the lower levels of moral reasoning and both expose them primarily to lower-level arguments and reward low-level reasoning.

The two latter explanations certainly seem reasonable if we examine the precept regarding sex that has in the past dominated in our society and still prevails today in many quarters: In childhood and adolescence an individual should know nothing about sex, should have no interest in sex, and certainly should have no experience with sex. When the individual becomes an adult and marries (typically sometime during the decade of the twenties), an official representative of the society will issue a permit and utter an incantation at a ritual, the individual will go with a partner to a private chamber, and, without even a perfunctory education into the mysteries, will become a fully and adequately functioning sexual being from that point on.

I have recently begun further research into moral reasoning about sex in adolescence. Using interview procedures similar to those used by Kohlberg and his associates, I have confirmed the generally low levels of moral reasoning about sex in adolescence and have confirmed that the level of reasoning increases with age in adolescence: eighth-graders are just beginning to move from stage 2 to stage 3; tenth-graders use predominantly stage 3 reasoning; and twelfth-graders are well into stage 4.

Unfortunately, the interview technique of eliciting level of moral reasoning is quite time consuming; it requires one-half to three-fourths of an hour to interview one adolescent and another three-fourths to one hour to score the interview protocol for level of reasoning. Thus, about 1½ hours is required for each person studied. It is obviously quite unwieldy for studying how level of moral reasoning about sex affects sexual decision making during adolescence.

However, I am now working on the development of a paper-and-pencil, self-administered instrument for measuring level of moral reasoning about sex. If I am successful, this will make feasible a wide range of studies that will undoubtedly illuminate sexual decision making in adolescence and help us to identify girls who are at risk of becoming teenage parents and to help them to make more appropriate decisions at the various decision points.

Meanwhile, those of us who are working with adolescents who are at the various decision points on the path to teenage parenthood need to recognize that the level of moral reasoning of many of these adolescents, especially in the sexual realm, is still relatively primitive. Recognizing this fact, we can do two things. One, we can modulate our level of discussion to be more congruent with the levels they use and thus be more effective in communicating with them. And two, we can give them an opportunity to practice explicit discussion of sexual dilemmas and encourage and reward their reasoning at a higher, more principled, perhaps more responsible, level.

The Librarian's Role in Young Adult Sex Education

John Cunningham and Frances Hanckel

A degree in library science certainly does not qualify anyone to become a sex educator. Librarians are not professionally trained to be experts on human sexuality or to do counseling in this area. Nevertheless, within the framework of traditional library services, librarians can play an important role in educating young adults about sexuality by incorporating a strong commitment to effective sex education into book selection, collection development, reader's advisory, referral services, library programming, and staff development. Before elaborating on the implementation of such

Reprinted by permission from *Drexel Library Quarterly* 14:53-64 (Jan. 1978). Copyright © 1978 by the Graduate School of Library Science, Drexel University.

a role, we would like to review the current situation regarding adolescent sexuality.

The Current Situation

There is a multitude of statistics on the contemporary mores of American teenagers which underscore the need for increased emphasis on sex education by all agencies which serve youth. A total of eleven million teenagers, over half of all those between fifteen and nineteen, are sexually active.[1] One million teenagers, including thirty thousand younger than fifteen, become pregnant each year, resulting in six hundred thousand births, more than a third of them born out of wedlock.[2] The rate of teenage abortions has almost doubled in the past five years and now accounts for almost four hundred thousand legal abortions annually.[3] Recent figures on venereal disease among teenagers between fifteen and nineteen show that for both males and females one in every hundred contracts gonorrhea annually.[4]

Despite the magnitude of the consequences of adolescent sexual activity, only six states and the District of Columbia mandate sex education curricula in public schools, and only a third of the remainder teach anything about human reproduction and sexuality. Other social agencies, such as Planned Parenthood, local medical clinics, and a few church-related groups, have tried to fill this gap. In these circumstances, young adult librarians in both school and public libraries have the opportunity and the obligation to provide sex education services to young men and women. An excellent example of the support a library can provide was described in the journal of the American Public Health Association.[5]

In defining the direction and priorities of library service, librarians should be guided by the needs of their patrons. Some knowledge of the psychology of adolescence will assist librarians in providing services appropriate to young people's needs. Among the greatest challenges faced by all adolescents is the need to integrate their developing sexuality into the framework of their personal value system. Young women and men struggle with sexual awakening through fantasies and masturbation; they have questions about sex role expectations and sexual orientation. Peer group pressures influence dating and often encourage early sexual experimentation. Sex-related concerns often seem to dominate adolescence.

Unfortunately, sex education is frequently limited to talk about sperm and eggs. Not only is this focus on the process of conception boring to most teenagers, it misses the point. A wide range of topics which will directly influence individuals' lives and happiness must be included, particularly those relating to the effects of teenage pregnancies. Most teenage girls do not realize the social handicapping which occurs to young mothers: many do not finish high school; most must stay at home due to lack of child care facilities, thus severely limiting their future employment or career opportunities. Equally important, girls are generally ignorant of the higher risks to both mother and child during a teenage pregnancy; adolescent mothers frequently receive little guidance on nutritional needs before and after delivery. Further, young men and women are taught virtually nothing about parenting and family relations. Good sex education programs must help adolescents comprehend the physical, moral, and social aspects of intimate relationships.

Building an Information Base

Facts about sexual development and orientation, sex, conception and contraception, pregnancy, childbirth and child rasing, and venereal disease can form the information base necessary for understanding the implications of a particular course of action. However, most of the problems people of all ages encounter with respect to sex are not physical, but are due to difficulties in personal development and the skills required to initiate and sustain a loving relationship. Thus the emotional ramification of sexuality, orientation, sexual and social roles must be given more attention than that devoted to anatomy and physiology. Communication and responsibility are perhaps the most important of the topics which should be included in sex education materials.

Building a collection of resources which meets the sex education needs of teenagers is clearly within the confines of established library service. Young people bring certain age-specific skills and attitudes to their search for information, and YA librarians routinely take this into account during book selection through attention to factors like young adult appeal, style, literary merit, and reading level. All sex education materials merit informed, thorough reviewing because sexuality information is sometimes controversial, often biased, and quickly dated. (This also means that materials already in the collection require periodic reevaluation as part of an active weeding program.) Standard commercial and professional reviews may serve as good initial indicators of a material's utility to a given collection but are usually of limited length. In-house assessment allows examination to determine contribution to a specific collection serving a known user-group. In-house reviews can also alert librarians to potentially problematic selections and suggest appropriate ways to manage reader's advisory or adverse patron reaction.

Accuracy of Materials

In examining sex education information, accuracy should be the first consideration in deciding whether or not to acquire any material. This criterion should be applied to the entire spectrum of legal, medical, and social topics associated with sexuality and human relationships. Is the availability of abortion presented in the material consistent with current laws both federal and state? Are male options and responsibility included in discussion of birth control? Does the discussion of contraception for women point out the potential long-term hazards of common methods? These three examples alone demonstrate the changes in knowledge and attitudes which are occurring over time. Reprinted titles or new works prepared without adequate investigation may be inaccurate on accessibility of abortion or misleading about the safety of certain contraceptives. Sexism in some materials may perpetuate myths like the one that only women can and should practice birth control.

Contribution to a Healthy Attitude

Beyond accuracy, materials must be evaluated for their contribution to development of a healthy, comfortable attitude toward sexuality. Is sex assumed to be an integral part of a whole life? Are the responsibilities inherent in a sexual relationship discussed in a way which will encourage adolescent readers to incorporate love, respect, and sharing into their value systems? Are controversial topics like abortion and homosexuality handled in the same way as other topics in the book? Are all the options in a given course of action, such as contraception, outlined clearly so that young people can consider their own choice? The tone of a book for young adults is also critical to its acceptance and usage. Does it address the concerns and questions of teenagers in a noncondescending, unprejudiced manner, yet include the range of consequences to sexual behavior choices? The material should promote adolescents' understanding of themselves and their situation and avoid scare tactics or limited perspectives to promote "preferred" behavior.

Formats

Quality sex education materials are available in a wide range of formats. In building a collection of these resources, librarians should consider the relative merits of print and other media. Audiovisuals can be especially useful to adolescents who are poor or reluctant readers. Current films, filmstrips, video and tape cassettes and recordings have a valuable place in library programming. However, since many young women and men are hesitant about publicly requesting or viewing sex education material, books continue to be a prime source of information since teenagers can usually locate and use them without the direct intervention of a librarian. Teenagers are often surprised by the availability of books and pamphlets relating to their concerns about sexuality. Advertising these resources by regularly integrating them into displays can dispel the myth that librarians will not touch this subject. Adolescents who are hesitant to ask for sex education materials may likewise decline to borrow them in the traditional manner. Sex education books and pamphlets disappear from most collections with predictable regularity. Under these circumstances, paperbacks are preferable to hardcovers not only for their popularity with young people, but also because their low cost makes continued multiple-copy replacement possible. Routine periodic purchases will assure continuous availability of material. Where ordering practices permit, librarians may develop quarterly high-casualty replacement lists to compensate for anticipated regular losses.

Responsibility for an Advocacy Role

Young adult librarians should not shy away from their responsibility to assume an advocacy role on behalf of their patrons. School and public librarians seeking to fulfill their role in sex education may have to confront an administration openly hostile about the subject. Parent groups or religious organizations in the community may be similarly unsupportive. In such cases, collection development activities carry with them the responsibility to support the intellectual freedom rights of young people by helping to educate superiors and the general public about the real need for sex education materials. To achieve the goal of good collection development some nontraditional activities may be required. Assuring the availability of good information on sexuality also obliges young adult librarians to advocate patrons' rights to good materials on controversial issues; an obvious example is the provision of information on homosexuality comparable in quality to that on heterosexuality. Leah Stenson has effectively clarified this issue in *School Library Journal*.[6] Communicating with authors and publishers is yet another area of advocacy too often overlooked by librarians. Those of us working with young people have a special responsibility to make the publishing industry responsive to the needs of these patrons who have little direct leverage themselves. If current materials are inadequate, we need to report this to those responsible for their production. A few well-written letters can have a big impact.

The Librarian's Attitudes

A library's resources come alive to young adult patrons through the active intervention of the librarian performing traditional patron-centered services like reader's advisory, information and referral, and programming. Within the librarian's role in sex education, the quality of interaction with young adult patrons will be in large part determined by the librarian's own attitudes and knowledge about sexuality. Those working with youth should strive to inform themselves about sexuality and be in touch with their own feelings and values. Developing active empathetic listening skills is equally important. Openness and a nonjudgmental approach to individual adolescents do not mean that a librarian is neutral on a specific subject. Rather, it indicates a willingness to help a young person arrive at her or his own sexual understanding and values.

Referral

The library is a community resource center with a duty to provide information on agencies which help people with specific problems. Teenagers may on occasion directly request a referral for more immediate help with a sexual problem than reading a book can offer. Counseling and medical or legal assistance are areas where referrals are frequently requested. Librarians working with young people need to be aware of the network of institutions which service the needs of adolescents. On the other hand, young adults unfamiliar with the programs of community agencies may not request help, believing that none is available. Here sensitive librarians engaged in reader's advisory may mention the services of an appropriate agency. Sexual concerns are, of course, very personal; when adolescents come to a librarian with matters about sexuality, they have a right to expect that the discussion is confidential.

Just as librarians have traditionally been concerned about the quality of recommended books, comparable concern about the quality of referral services must be developed. When teenagers ask for books, pointing to a shelf would hardly be considered the full exercise of professional responsibility. Giving agency name, address, and telephone number when a patron requests counseling or assistance with a sex-related problem is likewise inadequate. Young people are sometimes fearful of approaching unfamiliar situations and can be greatly reassured if additional information can be offered about types of services, application procedures, attitudes of agency staff, and confidentiality. Specific contact names at the referral agency can often be very helpful. Formal follow-up procedures to determine how a patron was assisted are not part of the general pattern of librarian-patron interaction. Nevertheless, to benefit future referrals, some effort should be made to encourage the library patron to report on the quality of service received.

Programming

Occasional library programs for young adults which touch on sexuality should be carefully considered, planned, and implemented. Such programs are visible public statements of concern with the issue of adolescent sexuality. Much of the potential for controversy can be minimized through cooperative sponsorship with responsible agencies and individuals active in counseling youth on sexuality. Such agencies are often looking for ways to present their programs to the public and may welcome the opportunity to use the library as a way of reaching out to the community. Groups like Planned Parenthood or Family Services, as well as professionals from the fields of social work, mental health, or medicine, are all potential co-sponsors. Controversy can also be lessened by integrating programs on sexuality into a broader framework like dating or personal development. Programming on adolescent sexuality need not be exclusively directed to teenagers. Workshops for parents or community agencies serving youth are yet another way in which the young adult librarian may approach the topic.

Staff Development Programs

Staff development programs can educate librarians on the need for a commitment to serving youth by providing traditional library services around sex-related topics. Equally important, however, is the need for such forums to explore how library policy will support librarians should a controversy develop. The overwhelming majority of censorship problems faced by both school and public libraries involves complaints about the availability of materials or programs for young people; many of these censorship attempts stem from concern about sex-related issues.[7] Under these circumstances, it is important that librarians and library administrators clearly recognize the potential for controversy and plan in advance how difficulties should be handled.

Staff development programs can create a local base of support. In addition, young adult librarians should encourage national and state library associations to write policy statements on providing information and programming on sexuality for youth. Planned Parenthood has published *The Positive Policy Handbook: Organization Statements to Support Sexual Health and Education Service for Youth*. The handbook contains supportive statements from many organizations, including the American Medical Association, the American Nurses Association, the American Public Health Association, the American Bar Association, the American Parents Committee, the National Congress of Parents and Teachers, the National Urban League, and the United Methodist Church. Library associations and their youth divisions need to be counted among the committed.

Awakening interest in sexuality is a hallmark of adolescence. How young people deal with their developing sexuality is strongly influenced by their degree of understanding of both the physical and emotional components of sex. Young adult librarians, while not sex educators, can play an important role in the sex education of youth through traditional library services. While young adult librarians should be prepared for potential controversy, they nevertheless owe their primary allegiance to the rights and needs of their patrons. Access for teenagers to quality information on sexuality should receive top priority in both school and public libraries.

NOTES

1. Alan Guttmacher Institute, *Eleven Million Teenagers: What Can Be Done about the Epidemic of Adolescent Pregnancies in the United States* (New York: Planned Parenthood Federation of America, 1976), p.9.
2. Ibid., pp.10-13.
3. Ibid., p.49.
4. National Center for Disease Control, "Annual Supplement Summary 1975," *Morbidity and Mortality Weekly Report* 24:54-55 (Aug. 1976).
5. Joseph A. Walsh, "Dr. Seuss Meets Dr. Freud: Primary Prevention in the Community Library," *American Journal of Public Health* 67:561-62 (June 1977).
6. Leah D. Stenson, "Playing Favorites: The Trouble with Sex Ed Guides," *School Library Journal* 23:34-35 (Nov. 1976).
7. Bruce A. Shuman, "A Geography of Censorship: A Regional Analysis of Recent Censorship Cases," *Newsletter on Intellectual Freedom* 29:3 (Jan. 1977).

RESOURCES

The items listed below by no means constitute a complete survey of all the current materials about sexuality with a focus on young adults. They do however give an indication of the tremendous amount of such information and provide assistance in collection development. We consider all of them to be good, reliable sources.

Chiappa, Joseph A., and Joseph J. Forish. *The VD Book.* New York: Holt, 1976.
An official publication of the U.S. Alliance for the Eradication of Venereal Disease which reviews the eighteen venereally transmitted diseases.
Consortium on Early Childbearing and Childrearing. Suite 618, 1145 Nineteenth Street, N.W., Washington, DC 20036.
A federally funded information-sharing project to help U.S. communities establish and improve services to school-age pregnant girls, young fathers, and their infants.
Eagen, Audrey. *Why Am I So Miserable if These are the Best Years of My Life?* Philadelphia: Lippincott, 1976.
An excellent sex education book for young adults which emphasizes the social and emotional aspects of emerging sexuality.
Eleven Million Teenagers: What Can Be Done about the Epidemic of Adolescent Pregnancies in the United States. New York: The Alan Guttmacher Institute, 1976.
A complete survey of the current situation with a review of available resources and suggestions for future social responses. Available for $2.50

from the Guttmacher Institute, 515 Madison Avenue, New York, NY 10022.

A Gay Bibliography. Chicago: Task Force on Gay Liberation, Social Responsibilities Roundtable, American Library Association, n.d.

Includes nonfiction books, current gay male and lesbian periodicals, pamphlets, and audiovisuals and lists additional bibliographies. Revised annually. Available from Barbara Gittings, Box 2383, Philadelphia, PA 19103, for $.25 a copy. Bulk rates available.

Gordon, Sol. *The Sexual Adolescent: Communicating with Teenagers about Sex.* Belmont, California: Duxbury Press, 1973.

Written as a guide for those who are concerned with helping adolescents to resolve or avoid sex-related problems.

_____. *You: The Teenage Survival Handbook.* New York: Quadrangle, 1975.

Includes many pamphlets on venereal disease, parenting, etc., in an informal format popular with teenagers. Good discussion of values development.

Gordon, Sol, and Wollin, Mina. *Parenting: A Guide for Young People.* New York: Oxford, 1975.

Designed as a text for courses in parenting for teenagers, this book covers topics from child development to the women's movement and marriage.

Hanckel, Frances, and Cunningham, John. "Can Young Gays Find Happiness in YA Books?" *Wilson Library Bulletin,* March 1976, pp.528-34.

Reviews four young adult novels with gay themes and includes guidelines for librarians in evaluating gay fiction for teenagers.

Improving Family Planning Services for Teenagers. San Francisco: Urban and Rural Systems Associates, 1976.

A study of ways to improve family planning clinic services with implications for library services in the same area. Available free from Clara Schiffer, Room 441-E, HEW, South Portal Building, Washington, DC 20201.

Johnson, Eric. *Love and Sex in Plain Language.* 3rd rev. ed. Philadelphia: Lippincott, 1977.

An excellent, basic sex education book for teenagers.

Kappelman, Murray M. *Sex and the American Teenager.* New York: Reader's Digest Press, 1977.

A book written for parents by a physician who has had many adolescents in his practice.

Kelly, Gary F. *Learning about Sex: The Contemporary Guide for Young Adults.* Woodbury, N.Y.: Barron's Educational Series, Inc., 1977.

A well-written book which contains exercises in values clarification, reading lists after each chapter, and scripts showing communications problems in sexuality.

Kirkendall, Lester A., and Adams, Wesley J. *The Students' Guide to Marriage and Family Life Literature.* 7th ed. Dubuque, Iowa: Wm. C. Brown Publishers, 1976.

Includes an extensive bibliography and list of organizational resources and newsletters with a master index.

Lieberman, E. James, and Peck, Ellen. *Sex and Birth Control: A Guide for the Young.* New York: Schocken, 1973.

Goes far beyond the title and covers most aspects of sexuality in better detail than any other book for young adults.

Lukenbill, W. Bernard, ed. *Media and the Young Adult: A Selected Bibliography, 1950-1972.* Chicago: Research Committee, Young Adult Services Division, American Library Association, 1977.

Includes abstracts of many sources dealing with adolescent sexuality and sex role identity.

Multi-Media Resource Center, 1525 Franklin Street, San Francisco, CA 94109.

Distributor of films and print materials on all aspects of sexuality which may be used in sexuality workshops and counseling for adults. Librarians might find this source helpful in self-education as preparation for working with young adults.

National Alliance Concerned with School-Age Parents, 7315 Wisconsin Avenue, 211-W, Washington, DC 20014.

An annual membership of $20 includes subscription to the organization's newsletter. They also publish a *National Directory of Services for School-Age Parents.*

National Film Board of Canada, 1251 Avenue of the Americas, New York, NY 10020.

Produces many films on sexuality which are distributed free in Canada and at low cost in the United States.

Planned Parenthood Foundation of America, Inc., 810 Seventh Avenue, New York, NY 10019.

The Youth and Student Affairs section issues a bi-monthly newsletter for $4 which includes articles, service reports, notices of conferences, etc. Other excellent publications of the YSA are *A Guide to Sexuality Handbook* and *The Positive Policy Handbook.*

Personnel and Guidance Journal. Monthly, September to June. Subscription, $20.

Published by the American Personnel and Guidance Association, 1607 New Hampshire Avenue, NW, Washington, DC 20009. Includes many articles on adolescent sexuality from the perspective of the guidance counselor; helpful to all those working with adolescents in this area.

Sex Is a Touchy Subject: A Select Bibliography of Books, Pamphlets and Films on Sex and Sexuality for Young Adults. Bay Area Young Adult Librarians, 1976.

This extensive list is divided into sections ranging from "Plumbing" to "Love and Romance" and is a good tool for collection development. Available from Richard Russo, 2343 San Juan Avenue, Walnut Creek, CA 94596. Cost is $2; $2.50 if billed.

Sex News. Monthly. Subscription, $4.50.

A four-page digest of books, articles, conferences, etc., which deal with sexuality; all entries annotated by the editor. Order from P. K. Houdek, Editor, 7140 Oak Street, Kansas City, MO 64114.

SIECUS Report. Bi-monthly. Subscription, $10.

Published by Human Sciences Press, 72 Fifth Avenue, New York, NY 10011.

Newletter of the Sex Information and Education Council of the United States, containing book reviews, articles, resources, etc.

Silverstein, Charles. *A Family Matter: A Parent's Guide to Homosexuality.* New York: McGraw-Hill, 1977.

An excellent reference for both parents and young people which describes how to handle the discovery that a family member is gay.

Sussman, Alan N. *The Rights of Young People: The Basic ACLU Guide to a Young Person's Rights.* New York: Avon, 1977.
Legal aspects of sexuality are rarely mentioned in any sex education material, but this volume presents current legal rights for minors, including marriage, contraception, abortion, and other sexuality-related laws.

Filling the Gap

Mel Rosenberg

A main educational thrust in Los Angeles this past year has been improved cooperation between schools (public, private, and parochial) and the public library. Briefly, it was an attempt to inform teachers of the various services provided by the public library, specifically to teachers, that they may not be aware of or are not availing themselves of. The almost missionary zeal on the part of many public librarians, who were the host group, and the receptiveness and informativeness of many teachers has been especially notable in these socially and fiscally tough times.

As might be expected, the teachers were supplied with booklists, some of them generated for the occasion. My own office prepared one, highlighting books that we think are popular with Los Angeles teenagers now; included were fiction, nonfiction, books of special interest to minority youngsters, and materials that are engrossing but easy to read. Among these many titles there were almost no nonfiction books on sex. This was not a matter of conscious policy; it came out that way because we do not find that books on sex are really popular with teenagers, even those (maybe especially those) written for them. We know they are used because they are often off the shelves, but they aren't often requested.

Though there was no direct connection, but in the same spirit and in the midst of the series of meetings described above, I was asked to address the assembled public junior high and senior high school librarians (on separate but equal occasions), mainly to discuss the problems of *selection* of materials on sex for teenagers, ages twelve to eighteen. Note the emphasis, because it betokens an historical change, at least in most big-city libraries. External pressures have decreased almost to the zero point in the area of nonfiction books on sex. (Fiction is a different matter, and I won't touch on it here.) But the internal pressures have increased.

The feminist and gay rights movements have made sex a touchy subject in a new way. Females, predominating numerically in the library profession, have been very influential in the area of "correct" book selection, ultimately influencing publishing (along with the general population, of course) of materials on sex. Consequently, the selection of books on sex for teenagers requires more than usually careful reading, much discussion, and an awareness of the shifts in values and emphases that keep manifesting themselves in sometimes surprising ways.

That the pressures on school librarians are both external and internal was expressed on both occasions. The internal pressures are not entirely the same as those for the public library, but emanate mainly from regulations and understandable administrative conservatism. The external pressures are the traditional ones of course, from parents and public opinion in general. Many of our schools have developed their own instructional materials for sex education, and, while I have not examined them, I would guess that they do not resemble closely the language and comforting intent of some commercially published material for teenagers. The best recent example [is] Sol Gordon's *YOU,* with its youthfully appealing mixture of playfully vulgar farce and avuncular warmth, a book I feel certain has not easily found a place on school-library shelves, but which has been embraced cordially by many public librarians. (It was selected a Best Book for Young Adults by the Young Adult Services Division of the American Library Association in February, 1977.)

It became clear after my talks that the problem school librarians have is not what to select (good books are plentiful, and there is good guidance for that) but that they really cannot select sex education books at all. This is the ultimate professional frustration for librarians [since] a principle basic to library education is to bring the reader together with the right book, for librarians something tantamount to the Hippocratic Oath. I was faced with a roomful of frustrated librarians and my refrain was: "Send them to us," meaning the public library where the material is available. As soon as I said it, it struck me as smug and self-satisfied but it was all I could offer, and it wasn't good enough. Later, thinking about it, I kept hearing in my head a paraphrase of Emma Lazarus's famous lines: "Send us your uninformed, inquisitive young muddled masses, yearning to read free," small comfort for a large frustration.

I don't want to imply that there are no courageous and dedicated school librarians. I know many of them. After my talk to high school librarians one of them told me that she keeps *Our Bodies, Ourselves* in her desk, that she would supply it if it were asked for, but that she could be laying her career on the line if she did so.

Meanwhile the material proliferates. Next up, the first book on homosexuality written especially for teenagers, according to the publisher for junior high age up, is called *Gay: What You Should Know about Homosexuality* by Morton Hunt (New York: Farrar, 1977).

Some wise person has said that on any subject the only book that counts is the first one and the best one. Since it's the first we'll have to pay special attention to Hunt, but it will be a while before all the results are in, something that is both frustrating and enlivening to librarians who have to keep revising their judgments of material on sex. I look forward to the day when sex education materials can appear on the shelves of both public libraries and public school libraries, when school librarians can join us in our search for the best sex-related materials to meet the reading needs of young people, when they will no longer have to act mainly as go-betweens while we public librarians fill the gap.

Sex in Children's Fiction: Freedom to Frighten?

Pamela D. Pollack

Children learn about themselves and their world primarily from living—from their experiences and relationships with people and things around them. And this is as true of sexual learning as any other kind.

However, they also learn from the mirrors of reality—movies, television, books—both of the documentary/nonfiction variety, and of fiction. Not too long ago, if sexual matters were mentioned at all in children's fiction, a single standard of abstinence-or-else was applied unilaterally to the unmarried and underage.

In the last few years, society as a whole has begun to accept sexuality —even children's sexuality—as a natural part of life and living, and this has led to a new openness in dealing with sexual themes in the movies, television, and books. The November, 1972, issue of the *SIECUS Report* featured a look at the children's fiction of the late 1960s and early 1970s, just beginning to deal with young people's sex-related concerns.

Children's books are now freer to deal with formerly taboo subjects. If anything stands out from a sampling of fiction and picturebooks with sex-related themes published in 1976, it is that all shades of the sexual spectrum are presented. Yet with this freedom has come license to

Reprinted by permission from *SIECUS Report* 5:1-2;15-16 (May 1977). Copyright © 1977 by Sex Information and Education Council of the U.S., Inc.

exploit—a calculated bid by publishers to cash in on every titillating theme and call it "bibliotherapy." Unfortunately, these new books are not free of old stereotypes about male/female relationships or misbegotten ideas about sexuality.

The presence of three books in a single year on the most violent sexual act—rape—represents a turning toward the pathological aspects of sexuality. Dizenzo's *Why Me? The Story of Jenny* and Peck's *Are You in the House Alone?* depict two of the most common rape attacks—Jenny is sexually assaulted while hitchhiking; Gail knows her "sickie" assailant —and in neither case does the rapist take the rap. That's the extent of the similarity: one is uncommonly good while the other is uncommonly bad.

Why Me? is merely an object lesson in what not to do. Jenny accepts a ride from a stranger she has a "funny feeling" about; doesn't report the rape right away; chooses as a confidante a flaky teenage runaway. More- over, it's a no-win situation: no matter what Jenny does, all avenues lead to dead ends. When she finally unburdens herself, a doctor tells her never to darken his door again; dad blackens her eye; and the kids at school besmirch her reputation.

Dizenzo's commiserating (she has Jenny wail on and on about how "filthy" she feels) is not nearly as supportive of the character as the indignation Peck projects in *Are You in the House Alone?* Peck treats rape as a serious issue, effectively dramatizing it in the style of a Hitch- cock thriller, with the heroine hounded by obscene notes and heavy- breather phone calls. The book is a page-turner at the same time that it is a rallying cry against antiquarian, antiwomen rape laws; but, most im- portantly, Peck creates a character with the grit and determination not to be permanently scarred by her scarifying experience.

Another chiller, Bawden's *Devil by the Sea* is a homicidal pedophile who terrorizes a British coastal town. Playing atmospheric effects to the hilt, Bawden is nonetheless compassionate in portraying a pathetic child molester. Adults, for whom the book was originally published in 1958, will respond. But, the book has now been reissued as fitting fare for children. It isn't. Once again the financial exigencies of publishing push a book where it shouldn't go—perhaps to the detriment of kids.

It's expected that books on sexual assault convey a sense of coldness and alienation. Disturbingly, so do the books on normal sexual relation- ships. It's not necessary in this day and age to make love a prerequisite for sex; it may not even be advisable to do so since teens tend to convince themselves they're in love in order to have sex anyway. What is necessary is some notion that sex should be a satisfying experience shared by people who care about each other. That's precisely what's missing from the books discussed below, and it is why the descriptions of sex in them are so joyless.

In Klein's *Hiding,* Krii agrees to go to bed with Jonathan for the first time and feels "like someone going to their execution." She remains unaroused and when, in rapid succession, Jonathan ditches her, gets hitched, and fathers a baby, Krii retreats to her parents' attic for a week.

In Krii's case, premarital sex is a prelude to a mini-breakdown. Other books present less extreme repercussions from first sex, but are negative and misleading in characterizing boys as being at the mercy of their hormones and girls as being at the mercy of boys. Although this is certainly true in some cases, it's not always the case—as these books would have readers believe.

In Rosen's *Cruisin for a Bruisin,* set in the 50s, an uninvolved and uncomfortable Winnie doesn't call a halt to a session of "everything but" with her boyfriend because "it's supposed to be painful for him not to have an orgasm." Better, Winnie decides, that she forgo her enjoyment.

It's not just a question of 1950s mores. In another novel, set in the 1970s, when *Marcia*'s boyfriend takes up with her rival who "puts out," it's no more than she expects ("I guess Danny had to get something off his chest, well not his chest . . ."). The will-she-or-won't-she question is settled by author Steptoe—Marcia decides to "get me some damn pills . . . before he leaves me"—but it is unsettling that the value of the shallow relationship thus preserved is never questioned.

However it misfires, *Marcia* is at least well intentioned in trying to show pressures on teenage girls. Not so Platt's sleazy *The Terrible Love Life of Dudley Cornflower,* which is aggressively harmful to young readers. A "young adult" novel, it was ostensibly published for adults but heavily promoted for the youth market—a marketing device which serves publishers in getting books too hot to handle through ordinary juvenile publishing channels into the hands of teenage readers. The compulsive nature of ninth-grader Dudley's scramblings to "get laid" (he is self-diagnosed as suffering from "gynecomania: male impulsiveness to assault women") drains his frenzied gropings of any real enjoyment. The book pushes promiscuity ("It's murder having to screw the same old bodies," says one of Dudley's lady-killing buddies) and a warped view of women (to Dudley, the fact that a girl has had an abortion makes her really attractive). Cornflower's deflowering—he makes a point of not using birth control—is the pits . . . and the epitome of sexploitation.

The thematic opposite of Platt's exercise in mindless coupling, Le Guin's *Very Far Away from Anywhere Else* is a thoughtful, sensitive portrayal of a teenage couple coping with sexual feelings. This is one of the rare positive examples of a book reflecting more than superficial sexual concerns. The teenaged protagonists, who genuinely care about each other, ultimately decide against a sexual relationship in the face of future plans already made that will keep them apart and prevent what is to them a necessary commitment.

Only one of the sexually active characters in the books surveyed asserts control over her body by acquiring a prescription for the Pill from

Planned Parenthood. That's Gail in Peck's *Are You in the House Alone?;* but, ironically, because the author is pointing up society's hang-ups about women who have sexual relations, he shows that her responsible behavior actually works against her (after she's raped by the psychotic scion of the town's leading family, a lawyer advises that protection by the Pill almost precludes protection under the law).

Given the staggering statistics on unwanted teenage pregnancies, one would expect authors of novels for this audience to be stumping for birth control. Quite the opposite is true. Fifteen-year-old Marcia believes it's her natural, God-given right to produce babies—a potentially disastrous position for any teenager. She'll take the Pill, but reluctantly: "I'm gonna defend myself against this sick world by taking birth-control pills every day or sticking some weird rubber thing up my crotch every time I get the hots."

With her wild fears and strange aversion to birth-control devices, Jean, the heroine of Windsor's *Diving for Roses,* makes Marcia look like a spokesperson for Planned Parenthood. Jean sets a horrific example for young readers already prone to overromanticizing the mysteries of sex. For her, a birth-control clinic is a dehumanizing place "where sex is a common everyday job. No need to feel embarrassed here. Sex, spelled S-E-X, fine and dandy, okay, swallow your methods and go out and fuck the world." Small wonder Jean doesn't stick around for the pelvic exam ("I can't discuss my most intimate channels with a rubber finger"), which is how she winds up getting pregnant.

Jean is not the typical heroine of a formula teen-pregnancy novel. She may be unmarried and large with child, but that's not her biggest problem—or the book's. Incurably romantic, she is so self-deluded that she actually believes the backpacker who deflowers her is a wood sprite. She turns up her nose when it turns out that the father of her unborn child is a computer programmer, but elects to keep the baby—a decision, given the state of her mental health, that should give adult readers the shakes. That it might not shake up less experienced teenage readers is even scarier.

The other two novels following the love-'em-and-leave-'em formula are based on wildly improbable propositions. In Minshull's *But I Thought You Really Loved Me,* readers are presented with a Christian shelter for unwed mothers jammed to the rafters with gibbering freaks. The main character, Koral, is a wreck, and she's in good shape compared to three of the featured inmates: a girl who thinks she's the Virgin Mary and attempts suicide when she doesn't deliver on Christmas Day; a gang-bang victim dubbed "Jezebel" by her Bible-thumping parents; and a swinger who flings herself at the school caretaker before taking off, heavily pregnant, with an unidentified man. What Minshull offers is a vision of punishment without supplying any insights into the real roots of the problem (the punishment even extends to having the maternity home double as a foundling home, thereby doubling the guilt of those who are about to give up their babies).

Christman's *A Nice Italian Girl* features a Machiavellian plot in which a handsome, smooth-talking young stud is employed by an illicit adoption ring to impregnate girls to ethnic order. The agency has an Italian couple looking for a bambino and top baby-maker Stephen Albright turns his attention to plain, painfully shy Anne Macarino. She gets wind of the plot, but decides to keep the baby and lead a life the author makes plain will be one of unceasing pain and struggle.

While it's valid for authors to make the impracticality and pressures of teenage parenthood apparent, there's no point in terrifying readers already fearful about sex and its consequences. The simple truth—that most teens who get pregnant are lonely and want to be loved both by the males who make them pregnant and the babies they expect to have—may not make for good book sales. On the other hand, distortions in these novels can only confuse and possibly harm the adolescents they are supposedly trying to help.

In startling contrast are the books written on birth for younger readers, whose very youth apparently makes them a safer audience and enables authors to say affirmative things about sex.

"A man feels awful good up close, so close there's nothing could come between you," Old Ella tells disgruntled twelve-year-old Stacy who, resentful of her pregnant stepmother, has run away from home in Bauer's *Shelter from the Wind*. Stacy stays with Ella long enough to assist in the difficult delivery, graphically detailed, of a German shepherd litter. The hard realities presented here (one of the pups is born deformed and has to be destroyed by Stacy's own hand) are not allowed to sour the birth experience nor diminish the thrilling, awesome power of this lifegiving process.

Human home birth and midwife delivery are rhapsodized over by the flower-child parents of Dragonwagon's *Wind Rose*. (See the review in the November, 1976, *SIECUS Report*.) Not everyone would be at home with the Woodstock Nation trappings, but this picturebook is so warm, so relaxed, so nurturant that any discomfort with its counterculture sensibility is dispelled.

Dealing with the subject of homosexuality for children presents even greater obstacles than does heterosexuality. Most of the authors considered here stumble over them.

Sullivan's *What's This about Pete?* is a transparently contrived setup. Puny Pete is verbally abused by his brawny biker dad and macho school coach, and propositioned by a cruising gay. Helping his mother embroider (he's gaga over satin and sequins) nets him a lot of needling (especially from the swaggering schoolmate he idolizes), but his worries are over when, on the last page, "this gutsy little guy has a date with Barbara." There's nothing inherently wrong with the book that sets itself up to deal with teenage homophobic fear—the fear is real (same-sex crushes are common at Pete's age)—but Sullivan's cheap happy ending won't touch readers whose own sexual-orientation crises can't be as neatly sewn up as her hero's.

The unanswered questions it raises are the sour notes in Wersba's *Tunes for a Small Harmonica.* J. F. McAllister cultivates a butch look with cropped hair and army-surplus attire, and marches in a gay rights parade. However, her sexual ambivalence is never examined. Out of the blue she develops a schoolgirl crush on her ascetic poetry professor to whom she is slavishly devoted in a stereotypically feminine manner.

Boys dress up in women's clothing in Kindred's *Hank and Fred.* While not a picturebook about transvestism, it's hard to tell exactly what it *is* about. By putting Hank in high heels, Kindred may have been trying to one-up Zolotow's *William's Doll* (New York: Harper, 1972), a book about a little boy who fights for his right to own a doll. If so, that's more an exercise in self-consciousness than in consciousness-raising.

Unlike the preceding books which are about *not* being homosexual or about nothing at all, Guy's *Ruby,* a "young adult" novel, is able to confront the subject head-on. It traces the anatomy of an ill-fated lesbian affair, but Guy's overwriting and exaggerated characterizations (Ruby is totally selfless while her lover Daphne is exclusively out for herself) work against anything Guy has to say about women's relationships.

Juvenile books have seldom ventured outside the narrowly understood band of children's sexuality. Nearly all of the books published in 1976 make sexuality the exclusive preserve of adolescence. There is a distinct lack of any attempt to treat the period from preschool to prepuberty, or even to admit to children's awareness of adult sexuality.

A happy exception is Bridger's *Home before Dark,* which sensitively limns a fourteen-year-old's first sexual stirrings but also deals with the love life of her fortyish father. Widowed in the course of the story, he finds a renewed lease on life in the arms of a compassionate middle-aged woman.

Potentially, children's fiction dealing with sexual themes can answer the same questions as nonfiction on the topic, and do so in a more immediate and involving way. Thus it presents a great opportunity not only to provide young people with scientific facts about sex, but also to deal with the emotional and attitudinal concerns that young people have about their own sexuality—and to do it in a form more palatable than some instructional materials, reaching many children who would not turn to formal (nonfiction) sex education books.

This is an opportunity largely ungrasped, a potential largely unfulfilled. Of the eighteen current books discussed here, only five are successful in providing voices of reason and reassurance for the young. Whether this is caused by the inability of adult authors to deal with the sexual concerns of the young in an honest and realistic manner, by the overzealousness of

adult publishers in search of higher profits in the youth market, and/or
by the continuing hang-ups of the adult society at large is not at issue
here. What is at issue is that our young people are being shortchanged.

REFERENCES

Bauer, Marion Dane. *Shelter from the Wind*. New York: Seabury, 1976.
Bawden, Nina. *Devil by the Sea*. Philadelphia: Lippincott, 1976.
Bridgers, Sue Ellen. *Home before Dark*. New York: Knopf, 1976.
Christman, Elizabeth. *A Nice Italian Girl*. New York: Dodd, 1976.
Dizenzo, Patricia. *Why Me? The Story of Jenny*. New York: Avon, 1976.
Dragonwagon, Crescent. *Wind Rose*. New York: Harper, 1976.
Guy, Rosa. *Ruby*. New York: Viking, 1976.
Kindred, Wendy. *Hank and Fred*. Philadelphia: Lippincott, 1976.
Klein, Norma. *Hiding*. New York: Four Winds Press, 1976.
Le Guin, Ursula K. *Very Far Away From Anywhere Else*. New York: Athe-
neum, 1976.
Minshull, Evelyn. *But I Thought You Really Loved Me*. Philadelphia: West-
minster, 1976.
Peck, Richard. *Are You in the House Alone?* New York: Viking, 1976.
Platt, Kin. *The Terrible Love Life of Dudley Cornflower*. Scarsdale, N.Y.:
Bradbury, 1976.
Rosen, Winifred. *Cruisin for a Bruisin*. New York: Knopf, 1976.
Steptoe, John. *Marcia*. New York: Viking, 1976.
Sullivan, Mary W. *What's This about Pete?* New York: Nelson, 1976.
Wersba, Barbara. *Tunes for a Small Harmonica*. New York: Harper, 1976.
Windsor, Patricia. *Diving for Roses*. New York: Harper, 1976.

Can Young Gays Find Happiness in YA Books?

Frances Hanckel and John Cunningham

As many young adult novels suggest, contemporary American society is
a difficult place in which to come of age. Judging from the number of
these novels that focus on problems encountered during adolescence, one
might conclude that the person who struggles through to adulthood without considerable emotional or physical scarring is indeed the exception.

Reprinted by permission from *Wilson Library Bulletin* 50:528-34 (Mar. 1976).
Copyright © 1976 by The H. W. Wilson Company.

Recent YASD "Best Books for Young Adults" booklists were the basis for a quick survey we did of junior novels with major adolescent characters—the survey confirmed this trend in YA fiction.

Librarians also are familiar with which novels are most requested by YAs. Here, too, the pattern holds: Novels that deal with themes of drug abuse, unplanned pregnancy, difficulties in family or peer-group relations, and individual identity struggles are always among the most popular.

The Adolescent Experience

Adolescence is, by definition, a period of transition. It is a time when individual experiences are marked by physical, emotional, and social changes. Such changes often evolve gradually, but may be sometimes precipitated by a crisis or conflict. Through meeting the challenges of adolescence, the individual will, ideally, establish a positive self-identity and develop standards and value systems to guide her or his life. Throughout adolescence the role that both fiction and nonfiction books can play in promoting a healthy discussion of problems is considerable. It is important, therefore, in book selection and recommendation that librarians examine YA books describing adolescent problems to assess their contribution in informing YAs and in aiding their development to responsible adulthood.

On what principles should any critical analysis of young adult literature rest? Honesty and realism in addressing any given circumstance should comprise the base standard in any appraisal. Pregnancies do not just disappear; drug addiction is not easily overcome; poor and minority youth encounter real problems in struggling for equality of opportunity. But librarians and others evaluating YA literature should demand more than a cold rendering of reality. Honesty must be combined with hope, a hope that is life-affirming and encourages the reader to consider and develop a workable moral philosophy.

Books and Social-Sexual Identity

A large portion of YA fiction is devoted to the broad topic of social-sexual identity, with the complacent assumption of heterosexual orientation. But what about adolescents who are gay? A major burden that they carry is the sense of being "different" and somehow outside the norms of ordinary adolescent activity. They are unsure of how to define themselves in their homes and peer groups. Where are the role models for young gays? How do nongay people learn about members of their communities and families who are also gay?

Homosexuality and the life-styles of gay people have recently entered the realm of **YA** literature. Since 1969 four novels have been published in which adolescent homosexual experiences are a major theme: John Donovan's *I'll Get There, It Better Be Worth the Trip;* Isabelle Holland's *The Man without a Face;* Lynn Hall's *Sticks and Stones;* and Sandra Scoppettone's *Trying Hard to Hear You.* Before examining these novels individually and collectively, we should mention the importance of libraries, books, and in particular, novels during the adolescence of gay people.

A Revolution without Communication

In spite of all the talk about the sexual revolution in American society, many adolescents find it difficult to discuss sex frankly with their parents. Sex remains, primarily, a matter of speculation and information sharing within the peer group, aided occasionally by a book or two. When most young people are reluctant to talk with their parents about socially acceptable sexual concerns, imagine the plight of those who suspect or know they are gay.

Can young gays talk openly with their friends? Most young people's ideas about gays come from the media. And in our sexist, homophobic society, the media treats gays as persons to ridicule and/or fear. All adolescents are sensitive about themselves, and thus gay youngsters fear to identify themselves to their friends, who probably will have accepted the stereotype.

In this way social attitudes often force young people with questions about their sexual orientation into personal isolation, into the "closet." Under these circumstances nonpersonal sources of information on sex, sexuality, gay life-styles, and similar concerns become extremely important. Thus many gays head for the library.

If young gays are to understand and react positively to homosexual experiences, then supportive information written specifically for this audience must be available. Similarly if the misconceptions and societal prejudice toward this minority are to be changed, then accurate, positive information on the gay community must exist and be available to all straight readers.

A New and Positive Direction

During the last five years the range and availability of information about gay people has greatly changed. In offering readers advisory services, librarians need to be aware of this redirection in materials. Most libraries now do contain a nuclear collection of positive materials on gay lifestyles.

Two popularly written books which have received the Gay Book Award of the ALA/SRRT Task Force on Gay Liberation are Peter

Fisher's *The Gay Mystique* and Del Martin and Phyllis Lyon's *Lesbian Woman. Woman Plus Woman; Attitudes towards Lesbianism* by Dolores Klaich is another excellent contribution to such popular literature. Directed specifically to YA audiences is Eric Johnson's *Love and Sex in Plain Language* (1974 edition), which contains a fairly written chapter on the experience of being gay.

There remains, however, a large body of written material that is far from supportive. Such information is usually found in psychological studies of "abnormality" or sociological inquiries into "deviance" or "victimless crimes." A catalog search for materials on homosexuality will more than likely turn up a preponderance of these negative books. Librarians aware of this situation can direct patrons to additional literature with an alternative viewpoint.

Also, catalog searches invariably lead only to nonfiction works—works that often are scholarly and contain an abundance of statistical data. Such information can be valuable if it is indirectly supportive: Gay teenagers may find it reassuring to learn that rather than being unique, they are members of a minority numbering perhaps twenty million.

A Search for Authenticity

But rather than scholarly studies, gay adolescents are looking for "flesh and blood" characters. Few adolescents are raised in an environment that includes exposure to the gay community, and so, once interest is aroused in exploring this aspect of identity, young people wonder how others have handled similar experiences. What are gay people *really* like? How and when do they meet each other? Do they find love and lead happy lives? How do straight people react to lesbians and gay men?

Adolescents are looking for answers to their personal questions. They are open and anxious to encounter positive role models, and young adult fiction is a logical place to find some of these models. For most young people the identification and location of such YA fiction is possible only through the active intervention of a librarian. Assuming the availability of the books and the ability to identify them, what kind of information will a young person find?

In order to encourage critical discussion about the perspective of gay life which all adolescents encounter in YA fiction, plot summaries of the previously mentioned four novels follow. They are meant to provide a basis for a critique of the handling of the gay experience in YA fiction as a whole.

I'll Get There, It Better Be Worth the Trip

Davy Ross, age 13, had been raised by his grandmother for the eight years since his parents' divorce. They got along terrifically; she gave Davy his best friend—his dachshund Fred. After his grandmother's death Davy (and Fred) went to New York to live with his mother. Davy visited his father on weekends and gradually came to feel at home in the city. At his new, private day school, he became friends with Altschuler, a classmate who also had divorced parents. One weekend Davy and Altschuler spent a night together. Afterward they were so uncomfortable with each other that Davy's mother suspected something had happened between them and arranged for Davy's father to "talk" to him. While they talked Davy's dog was killed by a car outside the apartment house. Davy felt not only grief over Fred but also guilt, and he blamed himself and Altschuler. Finally the two had a fistfight that allowed them to become regular friends again. Davy came to realize that the accident was not caused by what they had done, and the important thing was not to do it again.

The Man without a Face

Charles Norstadt spent the summer that he was 14 on the island. With him was his mother, who was looking for her fourth husband and with whom he had never been close; his older sister Gloria, with whom he fought constantly; and his younger sister Meg, who was his only real friend, except, of course, for his cat Moxie. Facing a difficult boarding school entrance exam in the fall, Charles was having a hard time studying, until he asked a neighbor, a man known to be a recluse, for tutoring and help.

Initially Charles was afraid of Justin McLeod, "the man without a face." But gradually through their working together, he became the first adult Charles could communicate with and trust. Justin confided to him that the scars on his face were from a car accident in which he had been drunk while driving. In the accident the boy with him was killed.

At the end of the summer Charles had a terrible encounter during which Moxie was killed by Gloria's boyfriend, and she told him that his real father was an alcoholic who had died a bum. Charles fled to Justin. The next morning he was very upset by what happened between the two of them, and Charles went off to his boarding school without seeing Justin again. Two months later Charles tried to find Justin to apologize for treating him badly and learned that Justin had died of a heart attack.

Sticks and Stones

Ward Alexander returned after a year in the army to his small hometown in Iowa to try to write a novel. During the summer he met Tom Naylor, 16, a talented pianist who was also lonely; they often talked about books and music and became good friends. At the beginning of the school year, Tom's classmate Floyd, always envious of his abilities, heard a rumor about Ward, then told his classmates that Tom was queer and that his relationship with Ward proved it. The other students and even the teachers ostracized Tom, who had no idea what was behind their actions.

The reason came into the open when Tom was not allowed to attend the state music competition because the other parents did not want their children staying with a "known" homosexual. Tom was appalled; when he protested that it was not true, he was told that there was no way to prove it or disprove it.

After this he cut himself off from Ward, did not study or play the piano, and by the end of the semester learned that he would have to repeat the year. In shock he started home, offering Floyd a ride. The car crashed—Floyd was killed and Tom critically injured. While in the hospital Tom realized that nothing was the matter with him until he allowed other people to make him doubt himself. At last Ward came to visit, and Tom said he was glad to see him.

Trying Hard to Hear You

Jeff, 18, and Phil, 19, met and became friends through a summer theater company for young people. Shortly afterward their friends began to wonder why they hardly saw them after rehearsals. At a party they did attend one friend, Sam, accused them of being fags and fairies. After much heckling Jeff faced the group and admitted that he and Phil loved each other. The rest, afraid of being considered queer too, at first gave them the silent treatment. Jeff's best friend tried to understand; however, she still could not accept their relationship.

Another group of kids heard about Jeff and Phil and actually attempted to tar and feather them, only to be stopped at the last minute by outsiders. Even after this their friends continued to give the two young men a hard time. Phil finally tried to change the situation by announcing that he had a choice, that he could be straight if he wished. On a subsequently arranged date, he wrecked the car, killing both himself and his date, Penny. Most of the group now admitted how badly they had acted and began to rebuild their friendships with Jeff.

Pioneering Efforts on a Controversial Theme

The preceding plot summaries are useful to establish the major characteristics of each novel. In addition, taken collectively, they enable librarians to make tentative judgments on the validity of criticism leveled against the novels. However, there is no substitute for reading the books themselves. In fairness to the authors, it should be obvious that these short summaries fail to convey forcefully the positive and commendable aspects of each book: The ability of the author as storyteller, the depth of characterization and style, and the degree of the author's success in clarifying complex moral and social questions.

All four novels can be viewed as pioneering efforts in dealing with a controversial theme and, as such, merit inclusion in YA collections. The point of this article, however, is to examine those areas where these novels fail to speak clearly and realistically about the gay experience. The purpose of the following criticism is constructive: The goal is better, more accurate, and more inspiring books for all young adults.

Why Must Gays Pay the Price?

Taken as a group, these novels have two salient characteristics: Being gay has no lasting significance and/or costs someone a terrible price. Not one plot has a happy ending in which the protagonists meet hostile pressures successfully and go on to find fulfillment and a supportive relationship based on love and respect. For gay adolescents the negative impact of these novels cannot be minimized.

The theme of no lasting significance is strongest in the novels by Donovan and Holland. Davy's father and Charles's tutor go to some lengths to tell them that their experience will have no effect on their futures, and that they can grow up straight as a ruler. This may be fine reassurance for insecure straight youths, but it cheats the ones who want to be gay by presenting such experiences as "phases" instead of the first step toward a valid choice. Everyone does, in fact, remember his or her initial sexual experiences and is in some way affected by them. Nor is any concrete support provided to gay adolescents reading Hall's *Sticks and Stones*; the ambiguous ending permits a variety of alternative conclusions.

The theme of gayness exacting a terrible price is so pervasive in all these novels that it needs little further comment. In response to a letter on this point, Sandra Scoppettone wrote: "Phil's death is not because he is gay, but because he tries not to be. That is a very important difference. By trying to be something he is not (heterosexual), he gets drunk and drives his car into a tree. In the other books the characters are punished because they are homosexual. Please don't confuse the death of Phil with punishment for homosexuality."

While Phil may not be punished for being gay, he is forced by peer pressure into a situation where he is killed all the same. Surely the exceptional persons of any race, sex, or persuasion transcend prejudice directed against their being or life-style, but in an open democratic society, why must minorities be expected to withstand extraordinary pressures?

Publishers Turning the Screws?

Indeed external pressure has been applied to one YA writer to insure that the theme of punishment was incorporated into the plot. Lynn Hall wrote:

"I had begun writing the book to show the destructive potential of gossip, but by the time I got well into it, I'm afraid I lost sight of that theme. I wanted Ward and Tom to love each other, to live happily ever after, and that was the way I ended it. But the publishers would not let me do it. In their words, this was showing a homosexual relationship as a possible happy ending and this might be dangerous to young people teetering on the brink. One editor wanted me to kill Tom in a car accident. [!] At least I held out for a friendship at the end, one which might or might not develop into something more, depending on the reader's imagination."

Holland's novel contains one of the most destructive and fallacious stereotypes—the homosexual as child molester. Justin, whose scarred face is noted by the title, is responsible for the death of a boy under unclarified circumstances. In light of such limited coverage of the gay experience in YA fiction, the possible identification of such a major character as a corrupter of children is grossly unfair.

Where Do Women Stand?

Finally, taken as a whole, these novels are generally antifemale. The first obvious point is that none of them is about a lesbian experience. Those women that are portrayed are often negative stereotypes and failures. They are also insensitive or hostile to the young, gay men: Charles's older sister in *Man without a Face* practically drives him from home; in *I'll Get There. . . ,* Davy's mother's negligence is responsible for his dog's death; in *Sticks and Stones,* Tom's mother is so caught up in her own romance that she fails to notice that things are falling apart for her son; in the Scoppettone novel, Phil's friend Penny volunteers herself as a quick test of his "real" masculinity.

As previously stated, each novel does have individual merit and certain aspects do ring true. It can also be said that the young adult genre as a whole tends toward melodrama. One wonders, however, whether any random selection of four YA novels could produce eight central characters with five sets of divorced parents (two of whom are alcoholic) and have plots with three natural deaths and one by violence—plus four car crashes resulting in one mutilation, one head injury, and five fatalities!

Providing Life-Support Systems

Where is there honesty and realism in approaching the gay experience? Where is there a life-affirming hope for a young person who knows or suspects he or she is homosexual? What is the impression left upon young straights who will encounter gays in their schools, families, or communities?

Because the consequences of a homosexual experience in these novels are either irrelevant or grim, not to mention incompatible with the truth of real gay people's lives, the . . . guidelines were designed primarily to assist librarians in evaluating and selecting books with gay themes for children and young adults.* The guidelines also contain suggestions of how to handle those books which do not contain the "ideal" treatment of a gay theme. Finally, the problems inherent in the existing novels (and, fearfully, others to follow) argue for an active, sensitive, and informed reader's advisory service by YA librarians.

It is absolutely essential that all human beings be presented fairly. Gay people only expect to be treated with the awareness and sensitivity now shown to other groups.

---

*The guidelines referred to here were drawn up by the ALA/Social Responsibilities Round Table's Gay Task Force in order to help librarians evaluate the treatment of gay themes in children's and YA literature. A new, eight-page edition of *A Gay Bibliography* by the Gay Task Force covers nonfiction items, audiovisual materials, magazines, and bibliographies. See "What to do Until Utopia Arrives," *Wilson Library Bulletin* 50:532-33 (Mar. 1976). This volume of the *Bulletin* also contains a section of directory information on gay organizations and professional groups (see page 282).

Homosexual Conflicts and Their Resolutions in Five Adolescent Novels: A Psychosocial Inquiry

W. Bernard Lukenbill

Introduction

The previous article by Frances Hanckel and John Cunningham, "Can Young Gays Find Happiness in YA Books," has made a significant contribution to young adult literature.[1] It is important for a number of reasons. First, it introduced the topic of homosexuality into the mainstream of adolescent literary criticism by analyzing the existing four young adult novels having significant homosexual themes: second, it succeeded in interjecting important aspects of gay advocacy ideology into this body

---

of literary criticism; third, in forcefully stating the fundamentals of gay advocacy ideas, it succeeded in disseminating to a new and wider audience much of the philosophy of gay politics and gay psychology; and fourth, it helped raise and pinpoint issues concerning the relationship of adolescent literature to "institutional homosexuality."[2]

Because the Hanckel and Cunningham paper raised these issues and because the authors criticized these adolescent novels for their lack of support for young gay readers, I hope to continue this dialogue by systematically examining these same novels and one other published in 1976 in terms of homosexual conflict situations and to analyze the ways in which these conflict situations were resolved. In addition, I hope to abstract, in sociological and psychological terms, the relationships of these conflicts and resolutions to issues raised by Hanckel and Cunningham regarding gay advocacy, gay psychology, and institutional homosexuality. Because Hanckel and Cunningham saw these novels as a potential source for behavior modeling information for homosexually orientated adolescents, I hope to discuss briefly my perception of the potential of these and other novels like them to act as socializing agents for both young homosexuals and heterosexuals.

But before I discuss my study design and analysis, I feel that I need to give a brief explanation of gay psychology, radical gay therapy, and "institutional homosexuality." This background will perhaps lead to a better understanding of both my findings and conclusions and the comparison I make between these findings and the Hanckel and Cunningham analysis.

Gay Psychology and Therapy

Essentially gay psychology holds that homosexuality is a freely chosen life-style. This is contrary to the traditional view that homosexuality is a symptom of a deep personality dysfunction.

Mark Freedman, a spokesperson for gay psychology, illustrated the tenets of gay psychology when he stated that recent research had demonstrated that homosexual persons are generally less confined to a conventional pattern of sex-role behavior than are heterosexuals and that many homosexual men and women transcend conventional roles and relationship patterns.[3] He further notes that research evidence suggests that gay people are more open in their sexuality than are heterosexuals. It should be remembered that Freedman is referring to studies which speak of homosexuals who have accepted their homosexuality and have established a complementary life-style and are comfortable with it. According to further research which he cites, many homosexuals have "centered"; that is, in responding to social pressures against homosexuality, they have discovered and decided to live by their own values. Freedman says that this process of centering begins as soon as the young homosexual becomes aware of the social pressures in society which are directed against homosexuality.

Freedman also describes the theory and practice of radical gay therapy. Radical gay therapy provides help to individuals with a variety of problems, such as guilt or shame about being gay, irrational fears, and difficulties with close relationships. Another important aspect of gay therapy is the belief that psychotherapy means changes, not adjustment; and that often it is society that needs changing, not the individual. It is claimed that distortions about sexuality come from society, not from the individuals.[4] Many approaches are used in radical gay therapy, including the confrontation of social oppression through individual action. Such actions contribute to the gay person's self-esteem and to the individual's positive identification with being gay. They also contribute to social change by challenging social oppression.

In argument against such research evidence and therapy, Dr. Charles W. Socarides, author of *Beyond Sexual Freedom,* believes that only through traditional psychoanalysis can the true nature of the homosexual encounter and its adverse effects on individuals be truly seen and analyzed.[5] He feels it is only through psychoanalysis that the soul of the individual can be opened and explored. Socarides states that responses gays make to conventional research studies about their homosexuality are invalid because when they are questioned or observed, they are engaged in a face-saving process and are not conscious of their own inner conflicts about their homosexuality.

Institutional Homosexuality

Like many others who write from the perspective of the militant gay movement, Hanckel, Cunningham, and Freedman describe homosexuality in terms of an oppressed minority; and they see homosexuality as being equal with heterosexuality. As stated earlier, they consider it a valid sexual choice and a viable life-style. If they do not completely insist on society's freely making homosexuality a legitimate choice for individuals, they do demand that society not interfere with that choice. By articulating homosexuality in such terms, these spokespersons, in essence, call for the acceptance of homosexuality as a social institution.

Many sexologists and authorities on homosexuality view the whole question of the social institutionalization of homosexuality with alarm. Furthermore, most of these authorities warn that society cannot respond positively to this demand. Authorities such as E. Mansell Pattison, Vice Chairman, Department of Psychiatry and Human Behavior, University of California at Irvine,[6] and Herbert Hendin, believe that society can meet the needs of homosexuals in a humanistic manner by insisting that homosexual behavior be decriminalized by granting gays civil rights and by eliminating social ostracism.[7] However, they hold that society can never abandon its need for a pervasive heterosexuality within society. Pattison writes that society at large is under no obligation to view all forms of behavior with moral indifference nor to take a stand regarding them.[8]

Pattison further notes that a negative social definition of homosexuality is necessary for proper heterosexual gender identification by individuals within a society; and because sexual object choice is a psychosocial learning process, society must continue to provide proper heterosexual response cues for its young people in the form of clearly defined social norms and support systems, such as the family. To further quote Pattison, "neutrality in psychosexual identity may not reflect a humanistic attitude but a failure in psychosexual identity development."

These authorities also claim that another danger in institutionalizing homosexuality or giving it tacit approval is that it makes homosexually prone adolescents further uncertain and confused about meaningful sexual choices and it encourages these young people to accept a homosexual solution to their problem, which, according to traditional interpretation, will generally prove unsatisfactory.[9] Socarides equates institutional homosexuality with gay rights propaganda, and complains that this point-of-view encourages young adolescents to accept homosexuality at an early age without considering the option of seeking early medical help.

Further criticism is that the movement converts what is basically a personal problem into a collective, political statement with the effect of depersonalizing individual emotions.[10] Herbert Hendin warns that such a political movement makes it too easy for individuals to deny the painfulness of homosexual life, to see their problems only in terms of their own "disgust" about their homosexuality, and to encourage young homosexuals to believe that they are part of the new wave.[11] The movement also places a new stress on the individual homosexual man and woman in that he or she must now conform to institutionalized homosexuality. Hendin further says that "openness and politicalization of homosexuality may overcome a sense of isolation, but for many, they substitute the tensions of denial."[12]

Design and Analysis of the Study

These opposing views served as background and catalysts for me as I designed and analyzed five adolescent novels for patterns of homosexual conflicts and resolution. I selected homosexual conflict as the central unit of analysis because it seems that almost all writing on homosexuality deals in some way with the conflict phenomenon.

The sample for this study included five novels which have significant homosexual themes. As indicated earlier, four of these novels were included in the Hanckel and Cunningham study, while the fifth novel was published in 1976, after the study appeared. The novels are: *I'll Get*

There, It Better Be Worth the Trip, by John Donovan (1969); *The Man without a Face,* by Isabelle Holland (1972); *Sticks and Stones,* by Lynn Hall (1972); *Trying Hard to Hear You,* by Sandra Scoppettone (1974); and *Ruby,* by Rosa Guy (1976).[13]

No predetermined schedule or list of conflict situations was developed prior to reading the books included in the sample. Rather, a dictionary definition of conflict was used for general guidance.[14] As each book was read, homosexual conflict episodes were identified and recorded. A homosexual conflict episode in this study is described as a statement of conflict, an action of conflict, or the summation of a series of interactive behaviors comprising a conflict situation growing out of homosexually related incidents. Repeated occurrences of the same basic conflicts were not recorded, although variations and new actions arising from original conflicts were coded. This first analysis resulted in the logging of 351 conflict situations. These episodes were then refined and edited by combining, rewording, separating, or eliminating certain situations thought to be ambiguous. This left 254 conflict statements which required final analysis. The remaining statements were then sorted into thematic units which characterized the conflicts. In this process, eight major conflict areas were identified. I will discuss in some detail the first six of these conflicts. Table 1 below outlines these situations.

Table 1. Major Homosexual Conflict Categories in Five Adolescent Novels

Rank	Areas	Number	Percentage
1	Sexual conflicts	52	20.5
2	Interpersonal conflicts	49	19.3
3	Peer conflicts	41	16.1
4	Intrapersonal conflicts	34	13.4
5	Parental/family conflicts	31	12.2
6	Heterosexual character conflicts	22	8.7
7	Community conflicts	14	5.5
8	Conflicts with authority figures	11	4.3

Sexual Conflicts

Sexual conflicts involving major characters clearly ranked first of all the conflict areas identified. For the purpose of this study, sexual conflicts were defined to mean intrapersonal confusion and defensiveness regarding sexual expression. Subcategories included the fear of sexual attraction to and affection for a member of the same sex; questioning the ability to perform masculine/feminine social roles; questioning the lack of attraction to the opposite sex; indecision about and/or fear of becoming a homosexual; guilt or alarm in finding pleasure in physical contact with the same sex; adverse, defensive reactions to a sexual act with a same-sex person; and expression of concern or anxiety at failure in or displeasure at heterosexual lovemaking. Of these, indecisiveness about homosexuality and the fear of being homosexual predominated as sexual conflict subthemes.

Of these books, *Sticks and Stones, I'll Get There* . . . and *The Man without A Face* displayed the largest number of sexual conflicts, while *Ruby* and *Trying Hard to Hear You* showed the smallest number. The resolutions of these conflicts in the first three titles are rather positive in terms of homosexual identity. In *Sticks and Stones,* the teenage protagonist, Tom Naylor, accepts the friendship of his older homosexual friend, Ward Alexander. This is a friendship and attachment which he had once rejected; and there are implications, although ambiguous, given at the conclusion of the novel that this friendship might develop into a deeper love relationship. In *I'll Get There* . . . , the main teenage character, Davy Ross, rids himself of his guilt about having engaged in a homosexual act and is reunited in friendship with Douglas Altschuler, his co-experimenter in adolescent homosexual lovemaking. There are implications that this was only a passing phase in the boys' development. Nevertheless, the book deals extensively, and perhaps realistically, with the struggle and defensive behavior which thirteen-year-olds may indeed experience in their first encounters with homosexuality. In *The Man without a Face,* fourteen-year-old Charles Norstadt, after much inner torment, accepts the physical attraction to and need for affection from his tutor, Justin McLeod. But the plot of the book prevents the further development of this friendship as McLeod dies of a heart attack before Ross has reached this stage of acceptance. In *Trying Hard to Hear You,* failure to accept one's homosexuality and the need to meet the demands of peer pressure lead to the death of nineteen-year-old Phil, one of the homosexually oriented characters, while in contrast, his lover, Jeff, accepts his homosexuality, learns to handle peer ridicule, develops his own values, and strives to establish new homosexual relationships. Perhaps *Ruby* presents the most unconvincing resolution of sexual conflict of any of the novels analyzed. Although surprisingly free of sexual conflicts regarding the physical expression of love between Ruby and her special friend Daphne, the book's ending has the two women, at the instigation of their parents, turning toward heterosexuality.

Recalling that Hanckel and Cunningham attacked four novels from this group for their failure to provide positive role information to guide young gay people in life-coping needs and to help them develop as socially valuable individuals, it might be hypothesized that the portrayal of conflicts generated by majority society is helpful and necessary if gay individuals are to have the cathartic experience which will prepare them to live as healthy homosexuals in a hostile society. Although the majority of these adolescent novels present a struggle against the acceptance of homosexuality, some of them do conclude with an acceptance of homosexuality and a sympathetic resolution of the sexual conflicts presented.

Many of these resolutions reflect the "centering" characteristics of homo-sexuals described earlier by Freedman.

Interpersonal Conflicts

Interpersonal conflict comprised the second largest area of conflict situa-tions. For this study, "interpersonal conflicts" were defined as those conflicts which primarily occur between two individuals involved in a close personal relationship. Important subcategories included conflicts over accepting the homosexuality of significant others, usually a best friend or teacher; the need for affection, friendship, and sexual expres-sion; feelings or fear of losing self-esteem; conflicts resulting from indi-vidual personality factors such as rigidity, dependency, jealousy; family situational conflicts relating to homosexuality; decisions to "go straight" by one of the parties; and finally, the tendency to express guilt and cast blame on another person for the homosexual situation or involvement.

Of the five titles analyzed, *Ruby* by far displayed the most interpersonal conflicts, accounting for 57 percent of all interpersonal conflict episodes recorded. The most prevalent conflicts in *Ruby* were conflicts within family structures and personality conflicts, such as jealousy, dependency, and personal rigidity.

The novels showing some amount of interpersonal conflict were *I'll Get There . . .* and *Trying Hard to Hear You.* In *I'll Get There . . . ,* the major interpersonal conflict is caused by Davy Ross's defensiveness about his homosexual encounter with his friend Douglas Altschuler and his inclination to blame Douglas for this situation. He also becomes irrational in his assumption of guilt over this situation, and begins to associate the death of his dog, Fred, with punishment for the homosexual actions. On the other hand, in *Trying Hard to Hear You,* the homo-sexual conflict centers on the two homosexual characters and reflects Jeff's and Phil's need for affection from each other and the price they must pay to have it. Although there are other interpersonal conflicts in this novel, they are classified in other categories. For example, in *Trying Hard to Hear You,* an important interpersonal conflict, coded as a heterosexual conflict, involves the struggle of a nongay person, Cam, to come to terms with Jeff's and Phil's homosexuality. Caught between Jeff, her best friend and long-standing neighbor, and Phil, her new boyfriend, Cam slowly accepts Jeff's homosexuality and his right to follow his own destiny. Cam also must deal with her own self-acceptance and ego in trying to under-stand how she came to lose in this triangle.

Intrapersonal Conflicts

Closely allied to interpersonal conflict situations in this study are intra-personal conflicts. Although ranking fourth in terms of frequency of overall conflict situations, intrapersonal conflicts will be discussed here because of the logical relationship to interpersonal conflicts. For definitional purposes, intrapersonal conflicts were considered to occur largely within an individual and to be expressed through private thoughts and emotions. Loneliness, social isolation, self-hate and nonacceptance, considered as one subcategory, predominated as the largest intrapersonal conflict area. This category was followed closely by the internally expressed need for love, affection, and acceptance. Of these novels, *Sticks and Stones, Ruby,* and *The Man without a Face* displayed the highest number of intrapersonal conflicts. In *Sticks and Stones,* Tom Naylor must struggle with his growing need for affection from Ward Alexander, his older friend and a homosexual. The intrapersonal struggle in *Ruby* lies primarily with Ruby and her compulsive and unrewarding need for attention from Daphne. Through this compulsion, Ruby allows herself to be placed at the complete mercy of Daphne's moods and whims.

The Man without a Face largely describes the intense struggle of Charles Norstadt to accept his feelings of affection for Justin McLeod, the tutor who ultimately introduced him to his first physical homosexual experience. Charles must also contend internally with his fear of becoming a homosexual and his guilt over his overt homosexual act with Justin.

Peer Conflicts

Conflicts with peers was the third highest ranking conflict situation identified. As a subcategory, physical abuse and verbal hostility ranked highest in terms of peer conflicts; exclusion of and aloofness toward homosexually identified characters by peers followed closely as additional subcategories. The books *Trying Hard to Hear You* and *Sticks and Stones* were largely responsible for these counts. In *Trying Hard to Hear You,* Jeff and Phil become victims of savage verbal and even physical attacks from their friends after their homosexual involvement becomes known; while in *Sticks and Stones,* Tom Naylor's isolation and loneliness are caused directly by his being deliberately ostracized by school and community.

Family/Parental Conflicts

Oddly enough parental/family conflicts do not enter into the plots of these books to any large extent. Of the titles studied, *Ruby* shows the largest amount of parental/family conflict and this is caused by the struggle between Ruby and her strong-willed father, Calvin. The tenor of the conflicts in *Ruby* is caused by Calvin's interference with Ruby's love affair, his hostility toward her friend, and Daphne and Ruby's desperate but ill-directed struggle to gain independence from him. Ruby's friend, Daphne, uses this weakness in Ruby as a weapon and finally justifies her break with Ruby on the grounds of Ruby's inability to free herself from her father's domination. The other novel which shows some degree of parental conflict is *I'll Get There.* . . . The conflict here arises from Davy's mother and her alarm at finding Davy and Douglas in what she thinks is a compromising sexual situation. She shares her concern with her former husband, Davy's father, who then counsels his son about homosexual involvement in understanding but embarrassed terms. The conflict situation ends with Davy's father assuring him that this one encounter will not set the course for his whole life. The father does express concern about not wanting to see Davy make a mistake and enter into something he will regret.

Ruby's conflict with her own father is resolved largely by his saving her from a suicide attempt caused by Daphne's rejection of her. This traumatic event gives birth to an unspoken understanding between the father and daughter and what appears to be the beginning of a relaxing of Calvin's grip on Ruby's life, ushering in the possibility of a heterosexual life for Ruby.

Novels as Behavior Models

The conflicts in these novels are not pleasant; they are harsh but seemingly realistic. Nevertheless, Hanckel and Cunningham in their paper complained that the books lacked honesty, and they questioned their effect on young homosexuals seeking role models for emulation.

In particular, Hanckel and Cunningham urged that through reading appropriate novels the young homosexual might be introduced to "flesh and blood" characters that could help them learn how to live as healthy homosexuals. They suggested that young homosexuals need model information to tell them: what gay people are really like; how and when [gay people] meet each other; if they find love and lead happy lives; how straight people react to lesbians and gay men.[15]

Hanckel and Cunningham contend that, instead, current novels convey to young homosexuals that being gay has no lasting significance and/or costs someone a terrible price. They also contend that the writers of these novels do a disservice to young adolescents in search of self-confirmation and acceptance as gays. Furthermore, they state that the novels fail to end on a happy note with the "protagonists meeting hostile pressures successfully and going on to find a successful relationship built on love."[16]

In answer to Hanckel and Cunningham's criticism, at least three of these novels might be said to relate positively to gay experience by depicting the successful overcoming of hostile pressure and the further development of successful love relationships. For example, in *Sticks and Stones,* Tom and Ward are reunited in what appears to be a deepening friendship, although the ending is certainly open to reader interpretation, while Floyd, who started the rumor about Tom's homosexuality, which subsequently caused Tom so much unhappiness, is killed. The Hanckel and

Cunningham objections to this particular plot seem to center around the abuse which Tom had to endure in his community and his guilt over Floyd's death. They contend that by this the author equates homosexuality with death and punishment.

In *The Man without a Face,* Charles acknowledges his love for Justin, frees himself of his guilt, and accepts his emotional and physical love for Justin. He realizes that "Justin gave me life . . ."; but Hanckel and Cunningham object to Justin McLeod's death before Charles could reach this level of awareness. They feel that Charles is thereby prevented from responding to Justin within this new consciousness. They also object to early allusions in the book to Justin's past history of pederasty and to what might be interpreted as his punishment for this through the vague references to the earlier death of an unnamed young boy and to Justin's physical disfigurement, loss of a job, and imprisonment as a result of his involvement with this child. They are particularly alarmed that the author chose to use a pederast as a homosexual character in this novel because of the general connotation of evil which pederasty evokes with the American public.

Trying Hard to Hear You seems to come near to what is required in a good novel for gay modeling according to the Hanckel and Cunningham criteria. Jeff accepts his homosexuality almost from the beginning of the plot; he withstands the hostility of his peers, he successfully deals with his grief over the death of Phil, and he goes on to establish a new gay relationship at college. Cam, Phil's heterosexual girlfriend and primary interpreter of the story, experiences personal growth as she becomes aware of the injustice resulting from social hostility and ostracism directed toward those who express their homosexuality; and she comes to accept Jeff's right to be both a gay person and her good friend. Again, Hanckel and Cunningham specifically objected to the negative modeling information provided for gays in this novel by noting Phil's confusion at not being able to accept his gayness; his collapse at public pressure; and his death. Hanckel and Cunningham interpret this as a message to gays that torment and death are the price one pays for being gay in this society. On the other hand, Sandra Scoppettone, the author of *Trying Hard to Hear You,* implies that Phil's death results largely from his weakness at not being able to accept himself as a homosexual.

It is a valid point that these books do not institutionalize homosexual behavior or life-styles as Hanckel and Cunningham and the Gay Task Force of the American Library Association request:[17] but they do present valid portrayals of the homosexual experience. Although the books do portray homosexuality in psychosocial problem and conflict situations, most of these conflicts seem to be resolved in humanistic ways compatible with current social realities. Indeed, it may be unrealistic to expect adolescent novels to institutionalize homosexuality when social expression at large has failed to do this. As Roger Austin notes in his recently published book, *Playing the Game: The Homosexual Novel in America,* even adult gay literature has failed to reach a level of literary and social acceptance due to widespread homophobic feeling in this country.[18] In fact, some observers of society have expressed the feeling that as the boundaries of socially acceptable heterosexual behavior become more confused and ambiguous, those forces within society striving to maintain traditional values will intensify, perhaps even focus, their attacks on homosexuality and those who wish to institutionalize it.

The Influence of Reading on Psychosocial Learning Processes

Throughout this paper, I have referred to Hanckel and Cunningham's concern about the effects of these novels on young homosexuals' psycho-social learning processes in terms of modeling information supplied to them.

Modeling is essentially a form of behaviorism. The works of Albert Bandura, the famous psychologist at Stanford University, well known for his studies in behavior modification, would seem to have application here. Bandura maintains that children learn to behave through imitation of adult behavior in their world as well as from observing adult behavior in the media, particularly television. The acquisition of this adult behavior requires very little rehearsal on the part of the child; and reinforcement for such behavior comes to the child vicariously. In other words, children adopt behavior they see rewarded in life and in the media; and they internalize the rewards which they have observed adults receiving as a consequence of these same behaviors.[19] But can the influence of media as a transmitter of behavior model information be applied to the reading process?

As we are often told, there are too many other competing influences in a reader's social world to make reading a powerful influence on behavior; and Mary Culp in her dissertation study of adolescent readers found that individual factors did play an important part in the effect of reading on behavior. Nevertheless, she discovered that many adolescents are influenced by what they read, especially in terms of attitudes regarding love and sexual mores, family relationships, and the individual and society; but actual changes in behavior are difficult to document. Culp further noted that avid readers, being more open and questioning individuals, tend to be more influenced by what they read than adolescents who are not heavy readers.[20]

Conclusion

The question then remains as to whether the adolescent novel can serve as an effective model for sociopsychological learning in terms of attitudes about homosexuality. It would appear that the adolescent novels just discussed do offer the adolescent reader some degree of modeling information, but the final determinant as to the disposition of that information in terms of interpretation, attitudes, and behavior formation lies with the individual. It goes without saying that this also applies to literary critics who happen to review and analyze these novels.

Whether adolescent novels can present homosexual behavior as accepted, institutionalized behavior is debatable. Social norms are not likely to lend support for such a wholesale endorsement, and there are respected authorities who hold that any institutionalization of homosexuality would be harmful to society. Nevertheless, homosexuality is a social reality; but to encourage the dehumanizing of homosexual persons through attitudes in either society or literature is reprehensible. It seems to me that in final analysis, the homosexual experience must continue to be expressed humanistically in adolescent novels, but this representation will undoubtedly always be in terms of social reality.

NOTES

1. Frances Hanckel and John Cunningham, "Can Young Gays Find Happiness in YA Books?" *Wilson Library Bulletin* 50:528-34 (Mar. 1976).
2. Ibid.
3. Mark Freedman, "Towards a Gay Psychology," in Louie Crew, ed., *The Gay Academic* (Palm Springs, Calif.: ETC Publications, 1978), pp.316-20.
4. Ibid., p.325.
5. Charles W. Socarides, *Beyond Sexual Freedom* (New York: Quadrangle, 1975), pp.96-97.
6. E. Mansell Pattison, "Confusing Concepts about the Concepts of Homosexuality," Psychiatry 37:342 (Nov. 1974).
7. Herbert Handin, *The Age of Sensation* (New York: Norton, 1975), p.118.
8. Pattison, p.342.
9. Socarides, p.92.
10. Hendin, p.105.
11. Ibid., p.114.
12. Ibid., p.115.
13. John Donovan, *I'll Get There, It Better Be Worth the Trip* (New York: Harper, 1969); Isabelle Holland, *The Man without a Face* (Philadelphia: Lippincott, 1972); Lynn Hall, *Sticks and Stones* (Chicago: Follett, 1972); Sandra Scoppettone, *Trying Hard to Hear You* (New York: Harper, 1974); Rosa Guy, *Ruby* (New York: Viking, 1976).
14. "1. A strife for mastery; hostile encounter; a fight; battle; esp., a prolonged struggle. 2. Clash or divergence of opinions, interests, etc.; esp., a mental or moral struggle occasioned by incompatible desires, aims, etc." *Webster's New Collegiate Dictionary* (Springfield, Mass.: Merriam, 1956), p.174.
15. Hanckel and Cunningham, p.529.

16. Ibid., pp.532-533.
17. ALA/Social Responsibilities Round Table's Gay Task Force. ["Evaluating Gay Themes in Children's and Adolescent Novels,"] *Wilson Library Bulletin* 50:532-33 (Mar. 1976).
18. Roger Austin, *Playing the Game: The Homosexual Novel in America* (Indianapolis: Bobbs-Merrill, 1977), p.225.
19. Albert Bandura, *Principles of Behavior Modification* (New York: Holt, 1969).
20. Mary Beth Culp, "A Study of the Influence of Literature on the Attitudes, Values and Behavior of Adolescents" (Ph.D. diss., Florida State Univ., 1975), pp.131-36.

Part 5

Free to Be: Liberation from Stereotypes

Dear God:
Are boys really better than girls? I know you are one, but please try to be fair.

Love,
Sylvia[1]

Vive la différence! the French say, and most of us would agree. Nobody, it seems safe to say, desires a genderless society. However, most sensitive people today recognize that exaggerating the differences between males and females, or falsifying them, inhibits human freedom and stunts the growth of both sexes towards the full realization of their human potentialities.

Someone has said that the women's liberation movement will have succeeded when the woman in the laundry detergent commercial asks her husband why he doesn't wash his neck. The point is well taken, since women are still presented through the media in largely subservient or secondary roles. But again, we must ask, does the fault lie primarily in media and literature—those sometimes distorted mirrors of life? Is it not rather within society itself? We know there are no simple answers; social change is inevitable but slow, and literature and the other media have complex effects, for they operate both in the vanguard of change and as forces for the preservation of the status quo.

Gayle Nelson in "The Double Standard in Adolescent Novels" analyzes five works of fiction in search of nonstereotypical women characters and finds that only one of the central female characters—Julie of *Nobody Waved Goodbye*—"grabs hold of her life" and asserts her selfhood by making her own decisions. Further, Nelson observes that in all of these novels except *Go Ask Alice,* sex for the female is equated with pregnancy, and pregnancy seems to be the punishment for transgressing against society's code of proper behavior for women.

Since 1975, the date of Nelson's article, more novels with nonstereo-typical heroines have appeared—for example Judy Blume's *Forever* and Patricia Windsor's *Diving for Roses.* However, her criticisms are still applicable to a large number of teenage novels. So far, no one has taken up her challenge to create a feminine counterpart of Holden Caulfield.

In "Growing Up Female: The Literary Gaps," Lou Willett Stanek strikes a more positive chord, highlighting the appearance of new, "honest, accurate images of women" in books for young readers. She also notes certain strange omissions, such as the dearth of literature portraying mother-daughter relationships, and she explores, as an intriguing example of this lack, the case of Mary Shelley. Commenting on the "extremes" to which movements for social change can lead us, she points out two serious dangers: censorship from special interest groups (cloaked in the guise of social betterment through the removal of "racist" or "sexist" materials), and the possibility, since our knowledge is fallible, that "gender confusion is dangerous," and that we may err in failing to teach the young clearly defined sex roles. She believes however that we can look forward to more open, honest literature on the theme of mother-daughter relationships.

In "The Cult of Kill in Adolescent Fiction," Jean McClure Kelty takes up the stereotyping of boys. Her central thesis—that "boys are conditioned *via* books to the cult of violence and killing as a part of their initiation into the adult world"—heightens our awareness of our deep-seated, subterranean attitudes towards nature and our assumptions about the means by which a boy grows to manhood. With deep empathy for animals, she examines representative works of fiction, all of them well reputed and widely read by young readers, and analyzes the attitudes towards nature embodied within them. Far too often, she concludes, they employ ". . . the killing of a pet as initiation" into manhood, ". . . the killing of a wild animal as a sign of growing from boyhood to manhood," and they portray "an animal as a symbol of evil or of nature-to-be conquered. . . ." In contrast, she cites one positive example, Hal Borland's *When the Legends Die,* where the central character undergoes the recognition that the "trouble" in his world stems from within, and maturity means accepting this truth, not trying to foist his own guilt "on nature or any of nature's creatures. . . ." Unfortunately, Kelty does not make clear the exact nature or the source of this "trouble within": whether it is indigenous to human nature (is she assuming a belief in "original sin"?), or whether it is caused by conditioning. The philosophical "problem of evil" seems implicit to her argument, but a clearer articulation of her position is needed. She leaves us with a challenge: if we continue to "condition young men to violence and killing as the initiation into manhood," how can we hope they will take seriously our plea for the protection of the fragile ecology of "Spaceship Earth" and our preachments on "reverence for life"? Is not the stereotyping of young men in roles that demand violence and bloodshed even more detrimental and more insidious than the stereotypical limitations we place upon young women?

Not everyone will fully agree with Kelty's interpretations of all of the novels discussed, for at times the examples are somewhat forced and oversimplified, as when the reaction of the men to the weaseling of the dog in *A Day No Pigs Would Die* is said to be one of "delight"—when actually the reactions of the boy and his father are complex and guilt-laden. Nevertheless, Kelty makes an important contribution in leading us to reexamine our most basic assumptions about the meaning of "manhood" and the relationship between humanity and nature.

The reader will notice that the essays in this section are weighted rather heavily towards sexism as it affects women.[2] A search of the literature reveals fewer articles pertaining to sexism as it affects men. This is an imbalance that needs redress. As Robert Unsworth points out in "Holden Caulfield, Where are You?"[3] young men are not being granted "equal time" when it comes to fiction portraying adolescent sexuality and "the problems and joys of the coming-of-age years for boys." He calls upon male writers of young adult books to restore a balance.

W. Bernard Lukenbill's "Fathers in Adolescent Novels: Some Implications for Sex-Role Reinterpretations" is one of the few discussions, in addition to Kelty's and Unsworth's, of men in the context of liberation from sexist stereotypes. In addition to describing the methodology and the results of his study of fathers in fifty adolescent novels, he brings out the uncertainties and complexities surrounding the relationship between literature and real-life behavior patterns and values, and raises two challenging questions: (1) can alternate sex-role patterns in literature significantly change or influence conventional sex-role behavior, and (2) where does a literary reinterpretation of sex roles end and didacticism take over?

NOTES

1. Eric Marshall and Stuart Hample, eds., *Children's Letters to God* (New York: Pocket Books, 1966).
2. For a discussion of sex-role stereotyping from a psychological viewpoint, and a criticism of ways in which psychologists have contributed to such stereotyping, see Inge K. Broverman, et al., "Sex-role Stereotypes and Clinical Judgments of Mental Health" *Journal of Consulting and Clinical Psychology* 34:1-7 (1970).
3. *School Library Journal* 25:40-41 (Jan. 1977).

The Double Standard in Adolescent Novels

Gayle Nelson

One of the many problems facing an adolescent girl who desires a more independent, self-actualized life than the traditional wife/mother role is the lack of positive women models. Television presents women who are concerned with the "ring around the collar" on their husbands' shirts, and most television programs and movies present stereotyped women who merely function as support for the male-dominated program; many cops, doctors, and lawyers are single, and the females are secretaries or nurses. Life itself presents an equally limited supply of positive women models; women work as subordinates to the men who make the decisions and gain the prestige. A third source of women models is the literature adolescents read. Does adolescent literature reinforce the wife/mother model or does it provide alternative models?

In order to analyze how the main women characters are portrayed, I examined the five novels most commonly read by my eleventh- and twelfth-grade women students. These novels were: *My Darling, My Hamburger* by Paul Zindel, *Mr. and Mrs. Bo Jo Jones* by Ann Head, *Phoebe* by Patricia Dizenzo, *Nobody Waved Goodbye* by Elizabeth Haggard, and *Go Ask Alice,* anonymous. All five novels contain stereotyped characters and situations, and specific patterns emerge. The main female character in each comes from a middle class, conventional family with a professional father (banker, professor), a socially-conscious mother, and they are, in general, the type of people labeled "nice." None of the mothers work outside the home, and they're usually depicted serving dinner, washing dishes, or making canapes. Four of the five daughters (Julie in *Nobody Waved Goodbye* is an exception) are in conflict with their parents because they are spending too much time with one boy. Most of the high school girls presented are concerned primarily with weight control, clothes, dates, proms, and whatever makes them more attractive and pleasing to the boys. For example, in *My Darling, My Hamburger,* Maggie is upset because while on a date she ordered popcorn, thereby violating the dictum that it's unfeminine to eat too much. All five heroines submit begrudgingly to a boy's demand for sexual relations and subsequently are bothered by feelings of guilt; they are acted

---

upon and are unable to stand up to their own values. None of the girls uses any kind of contraceptive; four become pregnant; and eventually all are punished for violating the etiquette of womanhood.[1] Many other stereotypes exist (such as single women teachers who are extremely naive about sex and boys concerned primarily with athletics); however, I will focus on the central female character and the pattern that emerges.

Liz, in *My Darling, My Hamburger,* is an attractive, slightly brazen girl who smokes cigarettes and is envied by her friend Maggie because "she could walk into a party and instantly know who was doing what to whom and what they were wearing." Liz and Maggie spend their time talking about their hair, boys, and the prom. Sean, Liz's boyfriend, makes sexual demands on her and although she thinks sexual relations before marriage are wrong, she submits to him and becomes pregnant—her punishment for breaking the rule: a girl should be a virgin on her wedding night. When Sean suggests marriage, she grasps at the opportunity instantly, as though she had no other dreams for her life. Sean, however, changes his mind and Liz has an illegal, messy abortion that keeps her in bed and prevents her from graduating. She is thereby punished further for trying to negate the correlation between sexual intercourse and babies. Sean, on the other hand, graduates and suffers little consequence—the dichotomy proclaiming that what is right for boys is not right for girls.

July, in *Mr. and Mrs. Bo Jo Jones,* resembles Liz in that she too is very attractive, slightly daring and adventurous and believes that it is wrong to make love before marriage. However, she acquiesces to Bo Jo's demands and becomes pregnant. They run away to get married and subsequently drop out of school (it seems as though there must be other alternatives). For a time, July and Bo Jo live with his parents and his mother instructs July in house and husband keeping—how to cook and make beds. When the newlyweds move into their own apartment, July spends her time going to the supermarket and cooking dinner. She does not read, write poetry, visit friends, attend art galleries, or go to movies. When the story ends, July is dutifully working to put Bo Jo through college.

The most interesting character in *Mr. and Mrs. Bo Jo Jones* is Lou Consuela, who wants more out of life than taking care of her husband. She is adventurous, free-thinking, and can make decisions and carry them out. When she discovers she's pregnant, she decides to have an abortion, because children would put an end to her singing career. Like Liz's, her abortion is portrayed as a gruesome and undesirable alternative to pregnancy. After the abortion she says, "It was terrible. It was degradation. . . . It was wrong. I shouldn't have done it." The message: Women are wombs, born to bear children, and if they choose to transgress their natural function, they will be sorely punished.

In *Phoebe,* the heroine appears to be more intelligent and introspective than July or Liz. Phoebe is keenly aware of the possibility of pregnancy and therefore keeps a calendar and practices "rhythm." However, she too becomes pregnant. Unlike the previous heroines, she reflects on the alternatives available to her and searches for applicable data by reading books, visiting a girl who had a baby, and contacting a possible abortion lead. The book clearly points out the need for more sex education among adolescents, but covertly it says that sex and pregnancy are the same thing.

Go Ask Alice is the only novel of the five that does not contain a pregnancy, although the woman-as-womb syndrome is present when Alice writes, "I keep thinking about our teacher in gym teaching us modern dance and always saying that it will make our bodies strong and healthy for child-bearing." Alice is an almost pitifully insecure young woman who during the first part of her diary writes primarily about losing or gaining weight. She does have an adventurous spirit and is intrigued by new experiences; regretfully, most of those experiences are drug-related and she moves from one disaster to another. Alice is a victim, like Liz, July, and Phoebe. She cannot gain control of her life and she is abused sexually, socially, psychologically, and emotionally. When eventually she tries to exercise some strength and withdraw from the drug crowd, she becomes their enemy and they slip her some acid without her knowledge. While recovering from a nightmarish trip, she writes, "The worms are eating away my female parts first. They have almost entirely eaten away my vagina and breasts. . . ." Is she expressing feelings about her sexuality—that sex is evil? Alice dies. She has broken too many codes of moral behavior and must be punished.

The fifth and best of the novels is *Nobody Waved Goodbye*. Julie is an "A" student who is in love with a confused, searching, idealistic young man. Peter skips school, drives without a license, goes to jail, and coaxes Julie into making love. Unlike the other heroines, Julie dates other men, wants to go to college, enjoys studying, and takes the initiative to get birth control pills. It is, however, too late and she is already pregnant. When Peter proposes that they run away, Julie momentarily agrees, but as soon as they're out of town, she realizes how unrealistic they're acting and she hitchhikes home. She is the only heroine who grabs hold of her life and says that regardless of momentary setbacks, she's going ahead with her life and is not merely becoming part of his life. The fact remains though that Julie does get pregnant, further substantiating the hypothesis that sex equals pregnancy.

If we expect our adolescents to function sanely in our complex, pluralistic, ever-changing society, a society having an increasing number of choices for both men and women, we must offer our adolescents more model diversity. A woman no longer has to become a wife and mother. According to the U.S. Department of Labor, the 1970 census showed 17,458,762 single women in the United States. With the exception of the 25 to 34 age group, over half of all women from the ages of 18 to 54 were working.[2] To the extent to which these five novels are representative, adolescent fiction is not meeting the needs of adolescent women, considering the increasing number of working and single women. Young women need to know that they are not merely wombs. They need to learn that their sexuality is an integral part of their being and that it can be positive, healthy, and enjoyable. All high school girls do not talk only about boys and dates. They're thinking about who they are; where they're going; the sort of life they want to lead; the nature of the "good life"; whether or not God exists; whether there is an afterlife; the alternatives which exist for them. Why not a *Catcher in the Rye* with a heroine?

NOTES

1. Marcia R. Lieberman in "Sexism and the Double Standard in Literature" discusses women characters like Anna Karenina, Emma Bovary, Lady Macbeth, Tess Durberfield, Hester Prynne, Mme. de Renal, and Lady Dedlock, who are part of a literary pattern that punishes women for stepping outside the accepted social boundaries, especially if they have committed adultery. Adulterous men, however, such as Stiva Oblonsky in *Anna Karenina,* continue to lead their lives. Suicide, the fate that robs many adulterous women of their lives, would seem an overly dramatic and senseless action to the men.
2. Labor Force Status: 1971, Women's Bureau, U.S. Bureau of the Census.

BIBLIOGRAPHY

Dizenzo, Patricia. *Phoebe.* New York: Bantam, 1970.

Gager, Nancy, ed. *Women's Rights Almanac.* Bethesda, Md.: Elizabeth Cady Stanton Pub. Co., 1974.

Go Ask Alice. New York: Avon, 1972. [Ed.'s note: Published anonymously as a supposed autobiography, but see the review of *Voices* by Beatrice Sparks, *Top of the News* 35:108 (Fall 1978); Alleen Pace Nilsen, "The House That Alice Built," *School Library Journal* 26:109–12 (Oct. 1979); Sparks's reply, *School Library Journal* 26:3 (Feb. 1980).]

Haggard, Elizabeth. *Nobody Waved Goodbye.* New York: Bantam, 1971.

Head, Ann. *Mr. and Mrs. Bo Jo Jones.* New York: Signet, 1968.

Lieberman, Marcia. "Sexism and the Double Standard in Literature." In Susan Koppelman Cornillon, ed., *Images of Women in Fiction.* Bowling Green, Ohio: Bowling Green Univ. Popular Pr., 1973.

Zindel, Paul. *My Darling, My Hamburger.* New York: Bantam, 1969.

Growing Up Female:
The Literary Gaps

Lou Willett Stanek

> As women we have thought so little of ourselves that when the troops
> came to liberate us we rushed into the streets leaving our most valuable
> attributes behind as if they belonged to the enemy. [Ann Roiphe, "Can
> You Have Everything and Still Want Babies?" *(Vogue,* Dec. 1975)]

For a long time so few women novelists wrote about women characters,
especially adolescents, that it was difficult to put together a curriculum
with a counterpart for *Huck Finn, David Copperfield, Catcher in the
Rye, Portrait of an Artist as a Young Man, A Separate Peace,* and that
long list of excellent adolescent boy protagonists. After *Jane Eyre, Wuthering Heights, Pride and Prejudice, Little Women,* and *The Heart is a
Lonely Hunter,* the task became taxing and the selections often tacky.
Nora might have slammed the door on her doll's house in 1879, but
Ibsen—always ahead of his time—did not immediately inspire the creation of heroines for young readers.

Fortunately, all that is changing, especially in adolescent literature.
The 1972 Feminist Press poster challenges: "WHAT ARE LITTLE
GIRLS MADE OF? Mind, Muscle, Bone, Blood . . . Not sugar and
spice. And now that most people realize this, isn't it about time that
honest accurate images of women begin to appear in the books lining our
libraries?"

The junior novel, with a creaky start in the 30s as formula type literature, is growing. The development of female characters in this relatively
young genre appears to be at a stage resembling an adolescent girl's experimentation with makeup: a bit heavy, applied rather thickly, not yet
artistic but showing promise.

Very few of these new, young women characters live on Easy Street in
Virginal White Middle America, and hardly any of them give a damn
about the senior prom. Elizabeth Janeway, commenting on *Little Women,*
has observed that Louisa May Alcott explored the lives of four sisters
and found them—while painfully good at times—to be jealous, mean,
silly, and lazy; and for one hundred years, jealous, mean, silly, and lazy
girls have been ardently grateful for their chance to read about themselves. The cast of *Little Women* has grown to include girls who are
alcoholics, handicapped, dying, fat, cruel, bright, tomboys, cowgirls,

Reprinted by permission from *Media & Methods* 13:46-48 (Sept. 1976).
Copyright © 1976 by North American Publishing Company.

cheerleaders, beauty queens, models, wizards, basketball players, have paper routes, have affairs and babies, love other girls, date boys of other races, defy time, live on their own or with animals, and so on. Unfortunately, there are still gaps, even in this age of plenty.

One of the most serious holes in women's literature involves books that deal seriously with mother-daughter relationships. Abigail Heyman, in *Growing Up Female: A Personal Photo-Journal,* said:

> I have very clear ideas about what a man should be and I've tried to teach my son that, but the reason I didn't want a daughter was I didn't know what I wanted to teach her about being a woman. I've told him he can be strong . . . I don't know if she should be strong. I don't know if that's the right thing to tell her or not.

Ironically, the feminist movement itself might be partially responsible for the scarcity of mother-daughter literary models. Feminist Robin Morgan recently said in an interview:

> I do see certain gaps—for example, poems on motherhood. I think that such poems are being written, but this is not a major theme. And it's understandable why we have not been writing about this . . . It's because these are the subjects the patriarchy has expected us to write about, so we have now refused to do that. . . .

Ann Roiphe, a mother and the author of *Up the Sandbox,* is concerned about this important omission. In her *Vogue* article she wrote:

> It is strange that women novelists do not deal at great length with their feelings about their children. Most women novelists have turned their attention on the sensibilities and anguishes of marriage, love affairs, unfulfilled work hopes, and social ambitions. In a strange way the real experience of mothering, not the picture book one, has suffered from a kind of unspoken taboo, perhaps even stronger than the Victorian one on explicit sexual details. Many women writers never had children at all—for example: Jane Austen, George Eliot, Virginia Woolf, the Brontes and our own Joyce Carol Oates.

Margaret Mead's answer is that mothers have been too busy mothering to write about it. Recently on the "Today" show she said that the population explosion had liberated women, but not the movement. In the past, she has found women in other cultures who have had power, but never domination. That, she said, was because it took men approximately twenty minutes to conceive children, and women the rest of their lives to raise them; she has found no cultures where men had total childcare responsibilities. Now Mead feels that with the social pressure to reproduce the race reduced, only women who really want to be mothers will have children, and many talented women will be freed to make increased contributions to our society.

A revision of Thomas Gray's "Elegy in a Country Churchyard" could surely be inspired by pondering the female writers who might have been;

with traditional cultural values it is miraculous there were any at all. In Jane Austen and the Brontes' day, if a woman did not marry or have a wealthy father, writing or teaching were the only acceptable means of genteel support. And Charlotte Bronte even complained that women writers were considered aberrations, held suspect, and left out of male writers' society. Married women, and most certainly married women with children, just did not work.

A promising exception might have been Mary Shelley and her mother Mary Wollstonecraft whose works included *A Vindication of the Rights of Women*. However, their biographies suggest the plot for a horror story rather than offering a positive mother-daughter literary history. Mary Wollstonecraft died giving birth to her daughter, and Mary Shelley's life was so permeated with birth, tragedy, and death that she wrote only one novel, *Frankenstein*. Even though Shelley was exceptionally well educated and her circle included the most original minds of her age, she was at sixteen pregnant by, but not married to, the poet Percy Shelley, who was married to Harriet, another pregnant teenager. During the following five years, Mary was pregnant most of the time. Harriet, carrying another man's child, drowned herself. Mary's stepsister, Fanny, committed suicide. When Mary eloped with Shelley, she was disowned by her father whom she adored. Of Mary's own children, only one survived.

Ellen Moers, author of *Literary Women* (Doubleday, $8.95), suggests in a provocative chapter entitled "Female Gothic" that *Frankenstein* is a grotesque birth myth subliminally inspired by the traumas Mary Shelley must have suffered as a teenage unwed mother responsible for breaking up the marriage of another woman who was also a young mother. Moers argues that *Frankenstein* is a fantasy of the newborn as both monstrous agent of destruction and piteous victim of parental abandonment.

Although Mary Shelley lived another thirty years after her husband's death, and men like Tolstoy and Zola were beginning to write about pregnancy, birth, and children, she devoted her creative energies to writing about her child-like husband, not about her relationship with her children.

A hundred years have passed, and mother-daughter relationships are still not a popular topic. In many cases, writers who now could easily be both author and mother reject the child-rearing role. Germaine Greer said in *The Female Eunuch* that she might like to have a child one day, but she would immediately send the baby to live in a commune in Italy. Ann Roiphe, one of the few writers who professes her pleasure at being a mother, questions the feminists who have added "a distasteful odor to mothering," and have suggested the maternal instinct is all a male con. She stated in *Vogue:*

> Society seems to swing to extremes, and usually the extremes at either end are disturbing. It is nice to have beautiful feet . . . but it is painful and abusive to bind feet. It is also a good thing for women to have in-

dependence, freedom of choice, movement and opportunity, but I'm not too sure that the current push against mothering will not be another kind of binding of the soul resulting just as certainly in deformities and difficulty in walking.

The swing to the extreme affects school curriculums in two serious ways. Special interest groups, pressuring librarians and English teachers to remove literature that does not project the image fitting their cause, are demonstrating blatant censorship. Professionals who cave into the pressure are more subtle censors, but they tamper with the First Amendment nonetheless. A responsible educator does not recommend sexist or racist literature; neither does he or she make it as inaccessible as Solzhenitsyn in a Russian library. Students cannot miss the message in such behavior.

Secondly, the facts are not yet in on the question, "Do children need sex roles?" Freud assumed that biological nature sets certain limits on male and female sexual identity. Some feel he was the greatest sexist of them all, and that finding one's sexual identity means simply earning a sense of self. Others argue that gender confusion is dangerous, that mothering and fathering are transcultural roles which are rooted in biology and anatomy, and that these nurturing skills should be taught to the young.

Margaret Mead, in an essay for *Women and Analysis: Dialogues on Psychoanalytical Views of Femininity,* says that the path Freud outlined suggests the themes of human development patterned during millions of years. These themes, she states, are ignored at our peril, and if understood give us wisdom. Child psychiatrist Arthur Kornhaber, a strict sexual constructionist, was quoted in *Newsweek* (June 10, 1974) as saying:

> Mothers who don't want to be mothers, and "liberated" women who feel their daughters ought not learn feminine ways, are robbing their daughters of their sexual identities. In extreme cases, these kids are being taught at a crucial stage in their development to hate their wombs, their bodies, the whole idea of having and caring for children.

Since the mother-child relationship is the only irreversible role, it seems that an exploration of this relationship, as one of many options, should be offered to young women. This does not mean that schools should be selling idealized motherhood. The holiest ikon, the Virgin Mary and the Babe—sacred mother and innocent child—has raised as many false expectations as the myth of "and they got married and lived happily ever after." (Pictures perpetuating these images have been collected in *Myth America: Picturing Women, 1865-1945,* by Carol Wald and Judith Papachristou.)

Too many women have looked at their children and dreamed the grandiose unfulfilled dreams of their own adolescence, hoping to remove the scars of their childhoods by the accomplishments of their offspring.

Often they succeed only in raising a stranger, or in refusing to recognize what they've really raised. Nothing, for instance, in Sylvia Plath's life suggests joy, but *Letters Home,* edited by her mother, reveals yet another painful side. Ignoring muted accusations, the mother clings to a line from a letter that says, "You are the most wonderful mommy a girl ever had and I only hope I can continue to lay more laurels at your feet." This was one of the "laurels":

> The Disquieting Muses
> I learned, I learned, I learned elsewhere
> From the muses unhired by you dear mother
> I woke one day to see you, mother,
> Floating above me in bluest air
> On a green balloon bright with a million
> Flowers and bluebirds that never were
> Never, never found anywhere . . .

(Quoted from a review in *The New York Times Book Review,* Dec. 14, 1975)

At a time when women are trying to find more open, honest, rewarding experiences with husbands, lovers, bosses, and friends, ignoring their children would be absurd. Women can divorce a husband, split from a lover, quit a job, and snub a friend, but kids are like fly paper.

With the emergence of adolescent literature, a thematic study of mother-daughter relationships is now possible. There are still more men writers dealing with their own unresolved oedipal complexes, but more women writers—even a few with daughters—are beginning to work in this embryonic genre. Norma Klein, Judy Blume, Betty Miles, and Norma Mazer have girl children. There are probably more. Let's hope so.

PAPERBACK BOOKS ON WOMEN AS MOTHERS

Supportive mothers

Representing Superdoll by Richard Peck.
Forever by Judy Blume.
Mr. & Mrs. Bo Jo Jones by Ann Head.
Seventeenth Summer by Maureen Daly.

Nonsupportive mothers

Lisa, Bright and Dark by John Neufeld.
Songs My Mother Taught Me by Audrey Thomas.
The Pigman by Paul Zindel.
My Darling, My Hamburger by Paul Zindel.

Stepmothers and stepfathers

The Phaedra Complex by Jeannette Eyerly.
The Headless Cupid by Zilpha Snyder.

Surrogate mothers

Up A Road Slowly by Irene Hunt.
I Will Go Barefoot All Summer for You by Katie Letcher Lyle.

Absent fathers

Don't Look Now and It Won't Hurt by Richard Peck.
The Soul Brothers and Sister Lou by Kristin Hunter.

A Room Made of Windows by Eleanor Cameron.
True Grit by Charles Portis.

Divorced mothers

It's Not the End of the World by Judy Blume.
I, Trissy by Norma Mazer.
Leap Before You Look by Mary Stolz.

Unorthodox mothers

Mom, The Wolfman and Me by Norma Klein.
Sunshine by Norma Klein.
Dinky Hocker Shoots Smack by M. E. Kerr.
The Forgotten Beasts of Eld by Patricia McKillip.

Real-life mothers

Flying by Kate Millett.
Young and Female: Turning Points in the Lives of Eight American Women compiled by Pat Ross.
Growing Up Female in America edited by Eve Merriam.

Girls assuming the mother's role

The Heart Is A Lonely Hunter by Carson McCullers.
No More Trains to Tottenville by Hope Campbell.
A Girl Called Al by Constance C. Greene.

The Cult of Kill in Adolescent Fiction

Jean McClure Kelty

Critical attention has recently been directed toward the stereotyping of girls in children's and adolescent fiction. As Diane Gersoni-Stavn points out in "Feminist Criticism: An Overview," "studies show that many more stories have been written about boys than girls. The boys do many more interesting and certainly more physical and fun things and do them in a broader range of geographical settings than do the girls. . . ."[1] But, despite the concentrated research which has been done on this problem, little or no attention is being given to the parallel stereotyping of *boys* within those "fun things," nor to how boys are conditioned *via* books to the cult of violence and killing as a part of their initiation into the adult world. Such stereotyping is, to my mind, far more dangerous than the relegation of the female to passive activity (though indeed the two undoubtedly are philosophically linked). I am, however, most concerned

Reprinted by permission from *English Journal* 64:56-61 (Feb. 1975). Copyright © 1975 by the National Council of Teachers of English.

about the stereotype initiation of the male character who persistently becomes a man when he performs an act of violence against an animal and/or the natural world. Such a pattern is hardly consistent with the ecological revolution of our age. If we are ever to live in harmony with nature, rather than attempting to conquer it as we have done in the past, we must reshape our attitudes toward nature. And an excellent place to begin may be by examining just how boys in fiction are encouraged to regard nature as hostile and alien, something to be overcome.

I am not advocating censorship. Rather, I am trying to create an awareness so that we, as teachers, can help students perceive and judge attitudes and values presented in literature. To that end, I would like to examine some representative fiction which is read by adolescents, in most cases, fiction that has been highly praised and which appears on reading lists for young people all over the country.

I remember reading Marjorie Kinnan Rawlings' *The Yearling* first as a teenager and I remember distinctly that I despised it. Many years later, I discovered why I had reacted to the book as I did and why I believe that we can use *The Yearling* as a base from which to discuss literature which incorporates the cult of the kill. Near the end of the book, Jody, the young boy, is ordered to shoot his pet deer who is destroying the crops by which the family lives. Because he is unable to do it, Jody's mother tries and only wounds the deer. Desperately, the boy pursues the wounded deer and kills it. At the book's end, he accepts his parents' decision and, thereby, we are told, becomes a man. Let us examine the premise contained therein. A boy becomes a man when he reconciles himself to the killing of the thing which he loves most! "He found himself listening for something. It was the sound of the yearling for which he listened. . . . He did not believe he should ever again love anything, man or woman or his own child, as he had loved the yearling. He would be lonely all his life. But *a man took it for his share and went on*" [italics mine].[2] Here then is more than an active denial of reverence for life. Here is a violation of love and feeling and sentiment. A man is not supposed to love.

I am not contending that such a situation is unrealistic; nor am I saying even that the deer need not have been killed. I simply feel that any author who uses such a situation as a base for her character's growing up into manhood is presenting distorted values. To say that we grow by killing something—and that is just what *The Yearling* and other books like it say—is absurd. We probably grow by knowing pain ourselves, and in that part Rawlings is right. But we do not grow by inflicting pain on any living thing, for in doing so we become a little less human. Such acts may be inevitable and inescapable, but Jody, being forced by "life" to accept the killing of the fawn did not "grow" as a result. And, by stating that he does, *The Yearling* fails.

But then the world of *The Yearling* has little respect for life and nature, despite its fine trappings of natural setting. The moral distinction made between the Baxters and the Forresters (the latter kill for the sake of killing, while the Baxters kill only for need) never really comes off. For not even the Baxters consider themselves a part of nature, but feel alien to it: "The Baxters went into the scrub for flesh of deer and hide of wildcat. And the predatory animals and the hungry varmints came into the clearing when they could. The clearing was ringed around with hunger. It was a fortress in the scrub. Baxter's Island was an island of plenty in a hungry sea."[3] For a boy to declare himself a man in such a world, the boy must enjoy killing, and in the end he must kill the thing he loves most and declare it an act of manhood.

Nor does *The Yearling* stand alone in the values which it presents. *Old Yeller* by Fred Gipson, another extremely popular book on reading lists, advances the same curiously twisted values. Old Yeller, the boy's beloved dog, has saved two of the family from the attack of a wolf. Then, because the family is afraid the wolf was rabid and passed the disease on to the dog, Old Yeller must be shot. The boy pleads with the family to tie the dog or shut him up until they can know for sure. "We just can't take the chance," his mother tells him.

> Quickly . . . I left Mama and went to stand in the light of the burning bear grass. I reloaded my gun and called Old Yeller back from the house. I stuck the muzzle of the gun against his head and pulled the trigger.[4]

Later his father tells him: "Now the thing to do is to try to forget it and *go on being a man.*" [italics mine]:

> "How," I asked. "How can you forget a thing like that?" He studied me for a moment, then shook his head. "I guess I don't quite mean that," he said. "It's not a thing you can forget. I don't guess it's a thing that you ought to forget. What I mean is, things like that happen. They may seem mighty cruel and unfair, but that's how life is a part of the time."[5]

And the boy agrees with him. He has become a man now. His solution is to take Arliss (his brother) and the new pup "out for a squirrel hunt."[6] And so again "that's just the way the world is," and a boy "grows up" when he faces the fact that he must kill his loyal dog who has saved mother and brother, because the dog might have rabies and they "just can't take the chance."

A variation on this theme occurs in James Street's *Good-bye, My Lady.* Here the boy is not asked to kill his pet but rather to surrender her for $100 reward money to the rightful owner. To the boy, Lady is a companion, a friend. To the owner (whom she will not allow to touch her) she is breeding stock; he wants her back because she is *valuable.* And because the boy does not fight the return of Lady, because he stoutly leads her to the crate in the man's truck, at the end of the book when asked about coffee for him, Uncle Jesse can say, "Drinks his black, too. Claude does. Black and stout."[7] The boy has become "a man."

An even more vicious example of the theme is the 1972 Robert Newton Peck's *A Day No Pigs Would Die.* The pattern is familiar: The boy becomes a man the day he helps his father kill Pinky, the boy's pet pig, because she is barren. As the boy kisses his father's bloody hands, his father tells him: "That's what being a man is all about, boy. It's just doing what's got to be done."[8] From the opening of the book (which is annoyingly bad English: "I should *of* been in school that April day"[9]) to its conclusion, the book is filled with a cute folksy humor which makes wry asides at the pitiful picture of a young pig being bred for the first time and the reader is expected to see "humor" in the boy helping a calf to be born: "I never hit anybody, boy or beast, as I hit that cow. . . . I kicked her. And stoned her. I kicked her again one last time, so hard in the udder that I thought I heard her grunt."[10] We presume the reader is also supposed to be amused (the characters are) at the weazeling of the dog, until the weazel is dead and the poor dog so brutally injured that it is necessary to shoot him. All this time the men enjoy the activity with the delight of a bear-baiting contest. One wonders what blindness prompted the *New York Times* to observe that this is a "superbly rich and moving novel about boyhood, becoming a man, and love. . . ,"[11] and what further insensitivity prompts teachers to recommend this book to their students as a lesson in growing up.

Perhaps even more popular than the killing of a pet as initiation is the killing of a wild animal as a sign of growing from boyhood to manhood. Books of this type are so familiar that only a few random examples need be chosen to prove the point. Andy in Paul Annixter's *Windigo* comes of age when he kills the bear, Old Boniface Black: "Standing above his quarry, Andy felt no triumph, only wonder and gratitude that this enemy of all the region, hunted so long and so disastrously, was finally dead."[12]

The boy in Ester Wier's *The Loner* is a boy who has devoted himself, by necessity, to taking care of no one but himself. Very little is made of the incident where he takes care of the sheepdog, Jup, by admitting that he, and not the dog, is to blame for stampeding the sheep. Rather, he is accepted as grownup when he kills the bear.

> "You hit his brain, David!" she cried. "One shot and you hit him right in a vital spot!" . . . "I had to do it. I had to kill him—for you, and Tex and Angie. I had to do it myself." . . . She rocked him in her arms and he felt she was crying.[13]

David, the killer, was a man.

A major initiation for the boy in Armstrong Sperry's *Call It Courage* is the killing of the wild boar: "Mafatu was struck dumb. He had killed a wild pig! For a second he could not grasp the wonderful truth of it. Then he leaped wildly into the air, shouting: '. . . Do you hear me, Tavana Nui? I, your son, have killed a boar!' "[14]

Similarly, the killing of whales—mothers and babies alike—constitutes Paul Joplin's education in Christopher Webb's *Quest of the Otter*. He leaves his home a boy and comes home from the whaling expedition a man. At the end of the book he shouts, "Out to the ocean, 'Aye aye, sir! Coming with all hands. All hands and lively.' For the ocean cannot conquer whaling men, nor ever will. And that was what Tom had meant when he had first shouted those words and I had stood beside him, a *wondering boy afraid of reality*" [italics mine].[15] And part of the great reality is the wanton slaughter of whales, which Paul never questions, indeed, thoroughly enjoys.

Less direct, yet perhaps more powerful in their impact, are those books which set up an animal as a symbol of evil of nature-to-be-conquered and then pit a young man against that force, to win or lose. A classic example is *Moby Dick:*

> I, Ishmael, was one of that crew; my shouts had gone up with the rest; my oath had been welded with theirs; and stronger I shouted, and more did I hammer and clinch my oath, because of the dread in my soul. A wild, mystical, sympathetical feeling was in me; Ahab's quenchless feud seemed mine. With greedy ears I learned the history of that murderous monster [the White Whale] against whom I and all the others had taken our oaths of violence and revenge.[16]

The fact that the crew of the *Pequod* goes down with the White Whale at the end and "the great shroud of the sea rolled on as it rolled five thousand years ago"[17] may uphold the irony and perhaps suggest that nature cannot be conquered after all, but it merely reinforces the image of nature, and nature's creatures, as outside of, and alien to, man. Man, like Ahab, can only pit "himself, all mutilated, against it."[18]

In the same vein is Hemingway's *The Old Man and The Sea.* Here the boy is initiated by the old man into the symbolic doing of the impossible—that is, killing the enormous fish. All the boy's sympathy goes to the Old Man and he identifies himself with the killing. The man, having caught the fish, may now dream about lions in peace and the boy, understanding, may now be a man. Both have looked into the heart of life itself: man must pit himself against the forces of nature. Even in the losing at the end, he will nevertheless have tried to do the impossible. He will have killed the fish. As the boy says: "It is what a man must do."[19]

Of the same type, too, is Paul Annixter's *Swiftwater.* Here the animal to be killed is the wolverine, which, according to Dwight L. Burton, "is the symbol of the rendezvous with evil which is the legacy of every adolescent who faces life squarely. . . ."[20] Here again, then, is the tiresome and dangerous repetition of a creature of nature being set up as the foil to man, a *thing* to be conquered in order to be a man.

Nor can adolescent literature apparently escape the ritual slaying, presented vividly in the much acclaimed *Shadow of a Bull* by Maia Wojciechowska. All the details of the bullfight are there, including the sympathy of the author, who apparently agrees with one of the characters who says: "Bullfighting is dying. And it needs someone to make it come alive again."[21] True, the boy, Manolo, who has been chosen to step into his father's shoes and become a great bullfighter, chooses at the end of the book to become a doctor instead. But his choice is conditioned by his desire to be a doctor, not by his condemnation of bullfighting. He leaves bullfighting to his friend, Juan, and at the end of the book he "watched Juan Garcia, fourteen, and the bull 'Castalon the Second,' make bullfighting history. As he watched them, there was a sadness in Manolo, but no jealousy":

> Sadness, for there was much beauty in the sight on the yellow sand and he was not part of that beauty. But there was no jealousy because he was sure what it was he wanted to do with his life. And his father's life, bullfighting, would stay a part of him, as it always had been, but in a different way than anyone had planned.[22]

The initiation of Manolo is complete; he has become his own man. But there is no condemnation of brutality. Apparently Wojciechowska is saying: "Do your own thing. If that be healing, fine. If your own thing be killing, then fine, too. It is all the same."

Not essentially different is the conclusion of Erik in Bryce Walton's *Harpoon Gunner*. Erik, admirably, has begun to question the killing of the whales: "The blue finally gave up and died, but Erik couldn't stop thinking about the baby whale. It had been found still clutched under the mother's dorsal fin. It had been dead from suffocation a long time."[23] Unlike other whaling books, the reader knows that the sympathy of the author is often with the whales, not the men who kill them, and Erik is sickened by the slaughter. He doubts that he will ever go whaling again. But Erik's real chance to be a man passes him by. He is faced with a difficult decision, whether or not to tell the truth which only he knows:

> But should he tell Bornak the truth? If he did, Bornak would take his crew out of the Enderby Sea to safety all right, before it was too late. But Bornak would also know the secret of the hidden sea. If he knew that, he would leave now for safe waters. But he would come back. . . . He would still have his big hunt. It would still mean the final extinction of the blue whales. It was a sad decision to have to make. But Erik hesitated only a moment. If it comes to that, he thought—if it's a choice between our survival or the whales'—it has to be ours.[24]

And Erik has the author's sympathy. By a *deus ex machine* Bornak is killed and, therefore, will not be able to go back. But nonetheless, Erik, when faced with a choice between nobleness and expediency, chooses the latter. Because the author, like Marjorie Kinnan Rawlings, and the others whom we have discussed, would have us believe that such a decision is clearly what makes the difference between a man and a boy. The man will choose expediency. "That's what being a man is all about. . . ."

A review in *The Boston Globe* said of *A Day No Pigs Would Die* that ". . . It isn't trying to move mountains and it has no quarrel with life. . . ." So it can be said of all these books: They have no quarrel with life, no desire to make the world a more compassionate, gentler place. Expediency and practicality are the only yardsticks by which they measure existence, and man's role in the system is all that matters. Because nature and creatures other than man seem often to get in the way of man's desires, then they are enemies to be fought and conquered, or abused and ignored. By way of contrast, let us consider in closing, a much different kind of book: Hal Borland's *When the Legends Die*. Corrupted by the very forces which these other books praise, a young Indian boy has abandoned the legends and the ways of his people to involve himself in the blood sport of rodeo. There, presumably to find himself, he takes it out on the rodeo horses and becomes known as The Killer. He finds neither peace nor himself. It is only when he returns to the place of his past, he begins to discover what he has been searching for all along. Like the other characters we have considered, he too decides to kill the giant bear, which just may be the pet bear of his childhood.

> He closed his eyes, fighting with himself. *I came to kill the bear!* His throbbing pulse asked, *Why?* He answered, *I must!* And again his pulse beat, *Why?* He answered, *To be myself!* And the pulse kept beating the question at him. Angrily he said, *This bear has made trouble!* The question beat back, *To . . . whom?* And his own bitter answer, *To me!* Then the question, as before, *Who . . . are . . . you?* And he, having no answer he could face, said, whispering the words aloud, 'This bear did not make trouble. The trouble is in me." And he lowered the rifle.[25]

For, unlike the other books, *When Legends Die* does have a quarrel with life. It says that for a boy to find himself, to become a man, he must accept that the trouble is in himself; to externalize that trouble and to foist it on nature or any of nature's creatures—to make them the scapegoat, is to remain a boy forever.

I would contend that the books which condition boys to the cult of violence and killing as their initiation into the adult world are untrue to the very deepest meaning of the nature of life itself. It is up to us as teachers to make students aware of the fact—to show them that the true initiation is a recognition that violence and brutality and death, though sometimes necessary, are never praiseworthy, nor do they constitute a *man's* way. To persist in teaching that books like *The Yearling* are a lesson in becoming a man is only to continue in the way of violence for which this century is justifiably famous. The wonderfully profane Norman Mailer would take it all one step further in *Why Are We in Vietnam?* He tells the story of boys conditioned to the glories of sport hunting. They are taught that such is the way of the man. The boys accept their conditioning without questioning because that's the way things are. At the end of the book, the boys are grown; a farewell party is being held for them. We come to know that they are going away. Where, we do not know, until the very end when the one speaks: "Vietnam, hot damn!"[26]

The analogy is an interesting, and, I think, a valid one. So long as we condition young men to violence and killing as the initiation into manhood, so long as we teach them that the enemy is outside themselves, always there to be vanquished, so long as we continue to tell them that "that's the way it is to be a man"—we will go on fighting senseless wars in which everyone loses. Furthermore, we will continue to destroy what little is left of the natural world and to annihilate the myriad creatures with whom we share this fragile planet. It is absurd to preach ecology and reverence for life in the same breath with which we praise *The Yearling* and books like it. For these books are a contradiction of the very foundations of ecology which, if it is to have any meaning for our world, must accept as its base: "Be tolerant, love, understand. The whole universe is but yourself. When you laugh at me, you are laughing at yourself. When you break the stem of a flower, you break your own leg."[27]

The way girls are stereotyped in fiction? Important, yes. But probably not as detrimental to our meaningful survival as the way boys are stereotyped to regard the cult of the kill as a necessary step to manhood and the world of adult reality.

NOTES

1. "Feminist Criticism: An Overview," *Library Journal* 99:182 (Jan. 15, 1974).
2. Marjorie Kinnan Rawlings, *The Yearling* (New York: Scribner, 1939), p.400.
3. Ibid., p.131.
4. (New York: Harper, 1956), p.153.
5. Ibid., p.156.
6. Ibid., p.158.
7. (Philadelphia: Lippincott, 1941), p.222.
8. (New York: Dell, 1972), p.129.
9. Ibid., p.1.
10. Ibid., p.10.
11. Ibid., cover.
12. (New York: Holiday, 1963), p.195.
13. (New York: McKay, 1963), p.147.
14. (New York: Scholastic Book Services, 1963), pp.63-64.
15. (New York: Funk & Wagnalls, 1963), p.180.
16. Herman Melville (New York: Modern Library, 1950), pp.176-77.
17. Ibid., p.565.
18. Ibid., p.183.
19. (New York: Scribner, 1952), p.23.
20. "The Novel for the Adolescent," in Richard A. Meade and Robert C. Small, Jr., eds., *Literature for Adolescents* (Columbus, Ohio: Charles E. Merrill Pub. Co., 1973), p.83.
21. (New York: Atheneum, 1964), p.28.
22. Ibid., p.155.
23. (New York: Crowell, 1968), p.187.
24. Ibid., p.193.
25. (Philadelphia: Lippincott, 1963), p.277.
26. (New York: Putnam, 1967), p.208.
27. John Blofeld, *The Wheel of Life* (Berkeley, Calif.: Shambala Publications, Inc.), p.48.

Fathers in Adolescent Novels: Some Implications for Sex-Role Reinterpretations

W. Bernard Lukenbill

Traditionally, sociologists and psychologists have shown relatively little interest in fatherhood as a topic of research.[1] The same generalization undoubtedly can be extended to research in youth literature (the term "youth literature" will be used in this discussion in reference to literature intended for both children and adolescents). It seems important, then, that those of us who are interested in the content characteristics of media published or produced for youth should begin to seriously analyze the image of the father as presented in contemporary literature for both children and young adults.

Several forces make this analysis imperative now. First, the modern feminist movement has insisted that the rigid, traditionally prescribed roles of the father and mother be altered in society to reflect less differentiation in role patterns. Many writers and reviewers of youth literature have echoed this sentiment and have denounced the image and role of the female as generally projected in literature for children and adolescents. Most of these critics, writing under the assumption that literature has the power to affect behavior patterns of children and adolescents, suggest that new roles must emerge in literature in order to promote nonsexist role patterns in society as a whole. Nevertheless, it may be that the major shortcomings of many of these writings are that they are too emotional, that they editorialize from data rarely gathered through sound, systematic research procedures, and that they often fail to analyze the roles of males and females within a theoretical structure.

A second reason for a careful study of the father in fiction for youth is that, from a sociological standpoint, this literature may well reflect the generally accepted mores of society regarding sex roles and images, regardless of how much at variance they might be with feminist ideology. This, in itself, should be worthy of documentation.

Third, assuming that society is accepting new sex-role patterns, it would seem useful to begin systematic, research-oriented procedures to determine the degree of variation between sex-role patterns in literature

Reprinted by permission of the author from *School Library Journal* 20:26-30 (Feb. 1974).

made available to youth by librarians and teachers and actual sex-role patterns evolving in the real world. Only then can we begin to make sound recommendations for new paradigms of sex-role interpretations in youth literature.

With these questions in mind, I recently completed an analysis of the father image in a body of fiction currently recommended for children and adolescents. Excluding fantasy and science fiction, 227 novels with settings in twentieth-century United States were chosen from the second edition of the *Junior High School Library Catalog* and its 1971 and 1972 supplements. The *Junior High School Library Catalog* was selected as a source reference because it recommends a type of fiction most likely to be made available to older children and adolescents by professional librarians. Fifty titles (a 22 percent random sample) were selected from the 227 novels for reading and analysis. [See list at end of article.]

Although determining the many sociological and psychological interactions of fathers and other family members in these novels was a rather complex process, the following characteristics were isolated for study: (1) *descriptive data,* including occupations, socioeconomic classes, ethnic group memberships, major settings of novels, and, if applicable, reasons for father absences from home; (2) *father-family interpersonal relationships and behavior,* including fathers' socialization patterns; interdependence among fathers and other members of the family unit; the characteristics and organization of the fathers' social position within their family environments; processes of sanction and conformity both initiated by and at work on the fathers within the family structure; work specializations; role performances; tasks performed by fathers within the family setting; the nature and level of children's identification with their fathers; fathers' integration within the family unit; characteristics of fathers' authority; the nature of family stability, as well as the fathers' emotional stability; father-child and father-wife relationships; and finally, instrumental (without emotion)-expressive behavior displayed by the fathers with their children. To ensure a systematic, objective approach to data collection, an analysis instrument was designed, pretested, and used by two coders to analyze and record data from the sample novels. Data presented in this paper represent a consensus of opinion between the coders.

Descriptive Data on Fathers

Sixty-five father characters were identified in the sample. Of these, fifty-six were developed enough for analysis in terms of their behavior patterns and interpersonal relationships. A large majority, 80 percent, of the fifty-six fathers were portrayed as members of the broad middle class, while a smaller number, 16 percent, were from the lower class, and only slightly over three percent were members of the upper class. Division according to ethnic group characteristics showed that a large majority, 84 percent, were white and 13 percent were black, while the remaining three percent came from other ethnic groups.

In terms of the occupations represented, 45 percent of the fathers were engaged in either professional or business-oriented careers, while 31 percent were involved in sales, farm/ranch, skilled, or unskilled occupations. In 21 percent of the cases, the fathers' occupations were not indicated clearly enough in the plot to be determined by the coders. Interestingly enough, 74 percent of the fathers were drawn from rural, suburban, and small-town environments, while only 25 percent came from urban areas. Of the fifty-six father characters analyzed, 18 percent were absent from the home for one of these reasons: death, divorce or separation, and work. Divorce or separation accounted for 50 percent of the father absences.

The Father and Social/Family Control

Through their various roles and authority patterns, fathers act as control agents for society. In current sociological theory, it is hypothesized that, by supporting his family, the father plays a significant part in linking the single family with the larger outside social environment.[2] Indeed, the very social significance of the family is determined by the monetary success with which the father meets his obligations as a provider.[3] When the sample books were examined for father role identity, it was found that his role as head of the household and chief breadwinner was emphasized. In 68 percent of the fictional families analyzed, fathers were heads of households; and in 71 percent of these cases, fathers acted as the sole breadwinner in the family unit. In fact, seldom were fathers pictured as being involved in any other major role activity than that of family breadwinner.

Because he assumes the responsibility of providing materially for his family, the father also acquires the ability to order and control his family. Through this socially important breadwinner position, the father's traditional role of sanctioning, conducting, and ensuring conformity of family members is strengthened and even assured. The sample novels seemed to echo the generally accepted sociological theory that indoctrination and control are indeed universal family and father functions,[4] as 54 percent of all fathers in the study were pictured as having either initiated sanctions or insisted upon conformity from members of their families. On the other hand, almost no sanctions or conformity pressures were exerted on the fathers by members of their families.

While data were not specifically sought on this question, it was noted, nevertheless, that the wives and mothers in this sample were nearly always seen performing the usual tasks of child care and household management. Despite the recent pressure of the feminist movement, the traditional division of labor between mother and father, still rather apparent in society at large, was reflected in the role patterns of wives and mothers.

Looking at the father's breadwinning role from a larger societal perspective, it might be added that historically the father who could not or would not assume the major responsibility for the subsistence of his family has been handicapped as an influential member of the family unit, and, consequently, he has contributed greatly to the dissolution of family stability.[5] On the other hand, in a situation where a wife assumes a major part of the subsistence role along with her husband, the father's participation in family life has not been lost, provided he has acquired a solid self-image of himself as the major family provider.[6] The data from these sample novels may well reinforce these sociological tenets. In these novels, where in a majority of cases the fathers' role was primarily that of family head and provider, 60 percent of the family units were presented as stable, and 80 percent of all fathers were characterized as stable individuals.

Aside from the major breadwinner role, which, as already reported, was performed by 71 percent of the fathers in this sample, only thirty-five specifically home-centered work tasks were found to be performed by fathers. These tasks ranged from driving their children to school and social functions (ten cases) and disciplining children (nine cases) to chopping wood for home use, kindling fires, cooking, and house cleaning (one case each).

Identification with the Father

The father's ability to contribute to social control and stability is further extended to the outside environment through the identification process of his children. Although "identification" is a difficult term to define, it is essentially the mechanism by which persons assume another individual's attitudes, values, and behavior patterns. Theoretically, children should be encouraged to respond to the life-style of their fathers and to identify with them, if for no other reason than for lessening the burden of the mother in the largely father-absent home of the modern, mobile family.[7] However, in the present study, in only 30 percent of the cases did children clearly show patterns of identifying with their fathers. This statistic may indicate either that in adolescent novels, as well as in life, the teenager turns to his peer group or that he uses models provided by the mass media for identification purposes.[8] It may be, too, that authors of these novels did not perceive the father as a figure strong enough to convey significant patterns and attitudes to readers.

Father-Family Socialization

The father's ability to elicit successful behavioral patterns from his children and to exert the proper degree of social control upon them is largely dependent upon the broader concept of the father's successful socialization within his family. Defining "socialized" as behaving willingly in accordance with the prevailing standards of one's culture, a significant 86 percent of all fathers analyzed seemed to accept their father roles within a social context.[9] This does not mean that the families were pictured as being without conflict and that the fathers were always successful in fulfilling the theoretical functions of the father role. Rather, this seems to say only that fathers were portrayed as having accepted their roles and responsibilities as fathers.

Although fathers did exhibit a rather high degree of socialization, the degree of integration of the father within the family structure was decidedly limited. For example, only 46 percent of the fathers were completely integrated within their family units. As "integration" is indicative of establishing and sustaining needed working relationships among individuals within a social system,[10] it would seem that even though most of the fathers in these novels accepted their social responsibilities as fathers and understood the expectations of their roles in a cultural context, in a personal relationship less than half did not maintain positive interactions with members of their families.

Father Authority within the Family

The authority of the father is extended throughout the family in many ways, including his ability to establish sound affective relationships. He exercises this authority through the various roles that he assumes as teacher, censor, promoter.[11] Traditionally, the father's authority has been conceptualized as authoritative and instrumental; but, in the last few decades, social trends have given rise to a more democratic and emotional mode of father behavior. In fact, as the patriarchal family of rural society has decreased in size and influence, the democratic, companionship-oriented father has become more important.[12] Yet, when the sample novels were examined to determine whether the fathers were authoritative or democratic in their behavior, no clear pattern emerged. Thirty-eight percent of the fathers were pictured as democratic; 34 percent, authoritative; 5 percent, democratic/authoritative; and 23 percent displayed ambiguous authority patterns.

It was also noted from the sample that half of all the fathers analyzed performed their fatherly roles in an expressive, emotional way rather than in the manner of the instrumental, impersonal, and remote traditional father. Although authors undoubtedly saw fathers in various degrees of democratic and authoritative behavior patterns, and despite the fathers' inability to fully integrate themselves within their family units, authors tended to characterize fathers as being involved emotionally with members of their families. Fifty-four percent of the fathers were pictured as dependent on their families for emotional support, while 30 percent of the fathers did not display affectional dependency. In addition, 50 percent of the fathers maintained good relationships with their wives, while in only 14 percent of the cases were the relationships between fathers and wives found to be either unsound or conflictive; but, in some 16 percent of the cases, the relationships between fathers and wives were so vague as to be undeterminable.

Relationships between fathers and their sons or daughters, however, were not positive. Only in slightly over one-third of the cases were relations between fathers and sons or fathers and daughters found to be good. Conflictive, unsound, and other negative and undeterminable relationships accounted for the remaining two-thirds of the cases. Yet, despite this rather bleak picture, it should be recalled that the overall family stability pictured in these novels was high, that the fathers' emotional stability was sound, and that fathers were dependent on their families for emotional support. The above findings are not as contradictory as they may appear, for they may well reflect the current situation in the real world. Sociologists maintain that good parental relationships with children are based on democracy, communication, and information;[13] yet, sociological literature also documents the conflicts and alienation between many parents and their children. In the sample novels, although conflicts existed between fathers and children, some authors undoubtedly saw fathers as essentially stable, affectionate, and responsive to family needs despite problems of father-family integration. And the father's inability to be fully integrated within his family was often caused by his authority figure roles as family disciplinarian, provider, and censor.

Summary

It appears, therefore, that fathers in this sample of novels were primarily white, middle class, and professionally or business-career oriented. They and their families resided largely in small towns and rural or suburban areas. When fathers did live away from home, it was largely due to divorce or separation. In terms of family structure and role patterns, fathers were consistently portrayed as the chief breadwinners and heads of their households, while their wives assumed the housekeeping and child-care roles traditionally assigned to women. The fathers' authority in their households was exerted through sanctions and controls imposed on members of their households, while they seldom were the recipients of any sanctions or controls exerted by members of their families. Nevertheless, it was rather difficult to determine any predominantly democratic or autocratic behavior trends on the part of the fathers in the sample. Although the fathers generally were respected in their homes, their children did not overtly identify with them. Nevertheless, for the most part, the fathers were socialized within the famliy units, but problems associated with the integration of the fathers into their family social structures did exist. Often relationships between fathers and their children were either undeterminable or conflictive in nature. Nonetheless, fathers were usually expressive and dependent upon their families for emotional support. Fathers also maintained good relationships with their wives, and the overall family unit was stable. Generally, the fathers in the sample were also found to be emotionally stable.

The implications of these findings for establishing a new paradigm for sex-role interpretations in youth literature seem to relate primarily to the theoretical goals and purposes of this literature that one accepts. Accepting the assumption that literature reflects the society that produces it,[14] it would seem that this sample may have accurately reflected current social values and practices regarding the father and family as revealed in modern sociological theory and research.

The one glaring deficiency seems to be in the portrayal of the mother and her relationship both to the father and the whole family unit. Perhaps in overemphasizing society's custom that the father should be the chief breadwinner and head of the family, the authors of these sample novels inaccurately presented mothers as rather weak, unassuming individuals with little identity outside their homes, and with little real influence on the family environment. One may question this interpretation if for no other reason than that the number of women in the U.S. work force has grown during this century and has had its effects on both the society and home environments.

If one accepts the assumption that literature influences society and is capable of changing behavior patterns and value systems[15]—which seems to be a basic assumption of the women's liberation movement's views concerning youth literature—then we should ask two questions. First, can conventional patterns of sex-role behavior really be changed or influenced by providing alternate sex-role patterns in youth literature? Because youth literature is a rather isolated and elitist medium of expression when compared to other model sources, we can assume that its total effect and influence will be limited and not widely disseminated among the total youth population. Children tend to acquire their sex-role identities and model concepts from many sources, including the family, popularized heroes, and the mass media, sources that often reinforce prevailing mass societal values and behavior patterns. Seemingly, youth literature as a transmission medium may not be able to compete with mass media in this volatile environment. Second, what is the line of demarcation between a literary reinterpretation of sex roles presented in youth literature and an evangelical, didactic interpretation of these roles? It seems that the real danger facing the current feminist ideological volley aimed at youth literature is that it may overplay its hand and usher in an era of contrived, didactic sex-role interpretations.

Nevertheless, we still need more research and correlation with socio-psychological literature and theory regarding this and other questions. Concurrently, we also need to undertake a scientific appraisal of the actual effect of literature on the behavior patterns and sex-role perceptions of children and youth. Hopefully, a new and sociopsychologically sound paradigm for sex-role reinterpretation in youth literature will eventually emerge.

Novels Analyzed

Allen, Elisabeth. *The Loser.* Dutton, 1965.
Annixter, Jane & Paul. *Horns of Plenty.* Holiday, 1960.
Barrett, William E. *The Lilies of the Field.* Doubleday, 1962.
Berry, Barbara J. *Just Don't Bug Me.* Follett, 1970.
Bishop, Curtis. *Field Goal.* Lippincott, 1964.
Bonham, Frank. *Burma Rifles: a Story of Merrill's Marauders,* Crowell, 1960.
———. *Durango Street.* Dutton, 1965.
———. *Viva Chicano.* Dutton, 1970.
Butterworth, W. E. *Wheel of a Fast Car.* Norton, 1969.
Byars, Betsy. *The Summer of the Swans.* Viking, 1970.
Cavanna, Betty, *Jenny Kimura.* Morrow, 1964.
Cleaver, Vera and Bill. *Where the Lilies Bloom.* Lippincott, 1969.
Corcoran, Barbara. *Sam.* Atheneum, 1967.
Daly, Maureen. *Seventeenth Summer.* Dodd, 1942.
Duncan, Lois. *A Gift of Magic.* Little, 1971.
Eyerly, Jeannette. *Drop-Out.* Lippincott, 1963.
———. *The World of Ellen March.* Lippincott, 1964.
Feagles, Anita MacRae. *Me, Cassie.* Dial, 1968.
Fox, Paula. *Blowfish Live in the Sea.* Bradbury, 1970.
Gault, William Campbell. *The Oval Playground.* Dutton, 1968.
Graham, Lorenz. *South Town.* Follett, 1958.
———. *Whose Town?* Crowell, 1969.
Heuman, William. *Fastbreak Rebel.* Dobb, 1971.
Hunter, Kristin. *The Soul Brothers and Sister Lou.* Scribner, 1968.
Jackson, Jesse. *Tessie.* Harper, 1968.
Jordan, June. *His Own Where.* Crowell, 1971.
L'Engle, Madeline. *The Moon by Night.* Ariel: Farrar, 1963.
Lee, Mildred. *The Rock and the Willow.* Lothrop, 1963.
———. *The Skating Rink.* Seabury, 1969.
Maule, Tex. *The Receiver.* McKay, 1968.
O'Hara, Mary. *My Friend Flicka.* Lippincott, 1941.
Olson, Gene. *Fullback Fury.* Dodd, 1964.
Pedersen, Elsa. *Petticoat Fisherman.* Atheneum, 1969.
Pitkin, Dorothy. *Sea Change.* Pantheon, 1964.
Platt, Kin. *The Boy Who Could Make Himself Disappear.* Chilton, 1968.
Richard, Adrienne. *Pistol.* Little, 1969.

Rodman, Bella. *Lions in the Way.* Follett, 1966.
Russ, Lavinia. *Over the Hills and Far Away.* Harcourt, 1968.
Schaefer, Jack. *Old Ramon.* Houghton, 1960.
Scholz, Jackson. *The Big Mitt.* Morrow, 1968.
Sherburne, Zoa. *Jennifer.* Morrow, 1959.
Tarkington, Booth. *Penrod; His Complete Story.* Doubleday, 1931.
Turngren, Ellen. *Listen My Heart.* McKay, 1956.
Viereck, Philip. *The Summer I Was Lost.* John Day, 1965.
Walden, Amelia Elizabeth. *When Love Speaks.* McGraw, 1961.
Walton, Bryce. *Cave of Danger.* Crowell, 1967.
Weber, Leonora Mattingly. *Meet the Malones.* Crowell, 1943.
Wojciechowska, Maia. *Tuned Out.* Harper, 1968.
Wolff, Ruth. *A Crack in the Sidewalk.* John Day, 1965.
Zindel, Paul. *My Darling, My Hamburger.* Harper, 1969.

NOTES

1. Leonard Benson, *Fatherhood: A Sociological Perspective* (New York: Random, 1968), p.6; John Nash, "The Father in Contemporary Culture and Current Psychological Literature," *Child Development* 36:265 (Mar. 1965): Liba Taconis, "The Role of the Contemporary Father in Rearing Young Children," *Educational Research* 11:91-92 (Feb. 1969); E. E. Le Masters, *Parents in Modern America: A Sociological Analysis* (Homewood, Ill.: Dorsey, 1970), p.138.
2. Benson, p.36; Simone De Beauvoir, *The Second Sex* (New York: Bantam, 1961), p.268.
3. Benson, p.47.
4. Benson, pp.47,49; Albert K. Cohen, "The Study of Social Disorganization and Deviant Behavior," in Robert K. Merton and others, eds., *Sociology Today* (New York: Basic Books, 1959), p.471.
5. Benson, p.47.
6. Joan Aldous, "Wives' Employment Status and Lower-Class Men as Husband-Fathers: Support for the Moynihan Thesis," *Journal of Marriage and the Family* 31:475-76 (Aug. 1969).
7. Benson, p.51; Philip E. Slater, "Parental Role Differentiation," *American Journal of Sociology* 67:306 (Nov. 1961).
8. Hans Sebald, *Adolescence: A Sociological Analysis* (New York: Appleton, 1968), p. 193.
9. Thomas Ford Hoult, *Dictionary of Modern Sociology* (Totowa, N.J.: Littlefield, 1969), p.79.
10. Hoult, p.157.
11. Benson, p.49.
12. Ernest Burgess and Harvey Locke, *The Family* (New York: American Bk. Co., 1953), pp.73, 267, 336, 359.
13. Sebald, p.10.
14. Milton C. Albrecht, "The Relationship of Literature to Society," *American Journal of Sociology* 59:425 (Mar. 1954).
15. Albrecht, p.425.

BIBLIOGRAPHY

Albrecht, Milton C. "The Relationship of Literature and Society." *American Journal of Sociology* 59:425-36 (Mar. 1954).

Aldous, Joan. "Wives' Employment Status and Lower-Class Men as Husbands-Fathers: Support for the Moynihan Thesis." *Journal of Marriage and the Family* 31:475-76 (Aug. 1969).

Benson, Leonard. *Fatherhood: A Sociological Perspective.* New York: Random, 1968.

Burgess, Ernest, and Locke, Harvey. *The Family.* New York: American Book Co., 1953.

Cohen, Albert K. "The Study of Social Disorganization and Deviant Behavior." In Robert K. Merton and others, eds., *Sociology Today.* New York: Basic Bks., 1959.

De Beauvoir, Simone. *The Second Sex.* New York: Bantam, 1970.

Hoult, Thomas Ford. *Dictionary of Modern Sociology.* Totowa, N.J.: Littlefield, 1969.

Junior High School Library Catalog. 2nd ed. New York: Wilson, 1970. *Supplements,* 1971 and 1972.

Le Masters, E. E. *Parents in Modern America: A Sociological Analysis.* Homewood, Ill.: Dorsey, 1970.

Nash, John. "The Father in Contemporary Culture and Current Psychological Literature." *Child Development* 36:261-97 (Mar. 1965).

Sebald, Hans. *Adolescence: A Sociological Analysis.* New York: Appleton, 1968.

Slater, Philip E. "Parental Role Differentiation." *American Journal of Sociology* 67:296-308 (Nov. 1961).

Taconis, Liba. "The Role of the Contemporary Father in Rearing Young Children." *Educational Research* 11:83-94 (Feb. 1969).

Part 6

Living in a
Multicultural World

. . . a friend told me of the Korean who died and started on his way to Heaven accompanied by an angel. On the way, he asked for a chance to look at Hell, so that he could appreciate Heaven more fully. The angel agreed.

On their brief visit below, they saw a long table laden with a sumptuous banquet. But the people seated around it were gaunt and emaciated—on the verge of starvation. Looking closely, they saw the reason. The chopsticks supplied all the guests were as long as their arms, making it impossible to feed themselves.

Arriving in Heaven, the Korean saw a similar table, with food and drink galore and the people well-fed, healthy and happy.
As in Hell, the people had chopsticks as long as their arms. But in Heaven they were feeding each other.

Harry Fleischman[1]

The need to understand other cultures becomes increasingly important as one sees more of the world through television and other forms of mass media. In many instances cultural differences among people may be exaggerated to the neglect of their shared humanity. It is important to recognize and accept cultural diversity in a climate of mutual respect and tolerance.

Individuals responsible for the instruction of young people are being encouraged to strengthen their skills and prepare teaching materials that will provide a global understanding. Some state legislatures have adopted position papers urging citizens to become more world-minded.[2]

Yet literature courses fail to reflect a global awareness or even an awareness of cultural diversities within the United States. When one examines American literature as it is taught to adolescents, many of the minorities are seen to be either ignored or misrepresented. In the case of native American literature, Alethea Helbig stresses the importance of understanding the literature that preceded white American literature. The native Americans have a large body of oral literature including stories relating the creation of the world and human beings. The earthdiver tales are simple in structure and assume the existence of water, dirt, and some animals. The creationist stories are similar to Biblical accounts, often with a solitary, powerful, preexistent being who for some reason decides to create a world or a being. Manabozho is a complex character, at times like a buffoon, but also a religious figure and the center of all Woodlands mythology.[3]

Philip D. Ortego and Jose A. Carrasco have strong feelings about the absence of Chicano writings in anthologies of American literature. Hispanic literature is neglected as a part of American literature, and according to Ortego and Carrasco, Spanish language is hardly a reason for not recognizing material as American literature when it is written in the United States. The authors sense that American literature continues a special relationship with England because of the early Puritan settlements, and chooses to ignore the earlier Spanish explorations of the continent. They disavow the "melting pot" theory, calling it a "mould" forcing all non-Anglos to talk about "our founding fathers," et cetera. A reader must be literate in both Spanish and English to understand the lexical arrangement known as "binary phenomenon," where the two languages are mixed, using the syntactic structure of either one.

Leon Hymovitz provides another discussion on the "melting pot" theory and explains how a monolithic culture deprives people of the ability and opportunity to appreciate the benefits of pluralism.[4] He also concludes his article with eleven experiences he believes that schools should provide, so the learner can live more creatively in a bicultural world.

Kai-Hsu and Helen Pablubinskas write that the identity of the Asian American is difficult to define, although writers have analyzed their individual backgrounds in an attempt to find themselves. Virginia Lee feels being a human being is more important than identifying with a specific culture. A writer like C. Y. Lee, who has adopted the United States, writes from a different perspective, because he knows he is Chinese. In contrast to these outlooks is that of Frank Chin, who hates the word "assimilation" and does not feel he is American or Chinese.

Twenty-seven articles published in *English Journal* from February 1968 to May 1973 indicated English teachers thought that a more positive attitude toward blacks could be achieved by teaching black literature.

Ernest R. Page developed a Black Literature Package and devised a method of testing this theory. Unfortunately his results did not indicate a change in negative racial attitudes, and in some instances concentrated exposure may have developed polarized "pro" and "anti" attitudes. The students indicated a preference for black literature to be included as a part of American literature. Readers interested in pursuing this topic should see *Black Literature for High School Students* by Barbara Dodds Stanford and Karima Amin.[5]

Joseph Mersand writes that as a youth growing up he was not exposed to Jewish writers. Their works were not included in anthologies, even though there were many well-established authors by this time. Mersand traces the development of Jewish writing from the 1920s to the present, points out themes used by the writers, and asks what makes a successful Jewish writer. He also contacts some well-known Jewish writers in an attempt to discover what impact Jewish culture has had on them. Irving Malin says he must define himself religiously and confront his heritage whether he believes its religious teachings or not. He thinks Jewish culture must be defined in a specific religious way. Karl Shapiro comments on a conversation he had with a Jewish novelist. Shapiro asked him when he stopped being a minority, and the response was "in the fifties." Shapiro thought the answer was true, because he too no longer feels "Jewish in a literary sense—but fanatically American in a cultural sense."

Other minorities are profiting from the artistic breakthrough of Jewish writers. Certainly the best way to expose young people to these variations in the American "mould" is to incorporate them into American literature. This raises a question—why teach American literature in only one grade in high school?[6] Perhaps literature would be more interesting for the student if studied through a thematic approach, or some other method that would allow all appropriate literature to be used, regardless of the nationality or ethnic origin of the author.[7] An exclusively ethnocentric approach seems undesirable.

Ethnicity in the United States is still a major factor in social thought and numerous groups want to be recognized as unique. Thomas Sowell, in "Ethnicity in a Changing America," however, concludes that all of these groups have contributed to establish an American culture.[8] The concluding paragraph of his essay raises important questions and gives one the impression that the entire concept of ethnicity needs reexamination.

> The very concept of ethnic "minorities" is misleading in the United States; and attempts to generalize about minority problems, or to compare one ethnic group to some national average, are still more misleading. Minority is a meaningful designation in countries where there is an ethnic majority, but in the United States the largest specifically identifiable ethnic group—those of British ancestry—constitute only 15 percent of the population, as compared to 13 percent whose ancestry is German, 11 percent Negro, and 8 percent Irish. No small part of the reason why

American history has been what it has, is that no one group could achieve overwhelming dominance.

Pluralism and toleration were not ideals from which Americans started, but necessities to which they were driven. It was slowest coming in the racial area, where majority-minority lines could be drawn. . . . The assimilation process has been two-way, with the so-called mainstream American culture incorporating many culinary, vernacular, musical, and other features once specifically and exclusively ethnic. Again, the pluralistic mosaic is more descriptive of American social reality than is a simplistic majority-minority dichotomy. What is most clear is that whatever may have determined the past is not inevitably determining the future. There are many objective indications that ethnicity is changing in a changing America. On the whole, and for the present, at least, it is a substantial change for the better.[9]

Thus, what seems to be emerging is "a pluralistic social mosaic" that conforms to no "simplistic majority-minority dichotomy." American society continues to evolve in its own unique way.

NOTES

1. "How to Combat Racism and Bigotry," *Crisis* 82:416 (Dec. 1975).
2. An example of a private global center is The Center for Global Perspectives, 218 East 18th St., New York, NY 10003, and/or Suite 235, Hotel Claremont Office Park, Berkeley, CA 94705.
3. For an analysis of Hiawatha, who is based on Manabozho and other native American literary figures, see Anna Lee Stensland, "The Indian Presence in American Literature," *English Journal* 66:37-41 (Mar. 1977).
4. "Multicultural Education in America: Melting Pot Atonement or At-One-Ment," *English Journal* 66:25-27 (Mar. 1977).
5. (Urbana: National Council of Teachers of English, 1978).
6. See R. Baird Shuman, "World Literature: Toward Global Understanding," *Clearing House* 48:461-67 (Apr. 1974).
7. For bibliographies relating to ethnic experience, G. Robert Carlsen's "The Ethnic Experience in Literature," in his *Books and the Teenage Reader* (rev. ed.; New York: Harper, 1971), pp.208-28, is still a valuable source, though in need of updating. [The 2nd rev. ed., 1980, was unavailable for examination.]
8. ["Ethnicity in a Changing America,"] *Daedalus* 107:232-33; 35 (Winter 1978).
9. *Ibid.,* pp.22-35.

Teaching American Literature from Its Real Beginnings: Native American Stories

Alethea Helbig

American literature—in the sense of literature from the American continents—had its real beginnings long before the settlements of Jamestown and Plymouth. For hundreds of years before the whites came, the Native Americans had a large body of orally transmitted literature consisting of myths, tales, and legends. These old, highly imaginative stories provided entertainment and a way of spending time together for those who told and heard them. They also attempted to answer basic questions about human existence and human nature and were valuable as a means of maintaining the practices of the group by giving advice about the right way to live. Today, these tales offer exciting literary opportunities for young people, who can enjoy them as good stories in their own right. They can discover in these Native American tales dramatic and powerful presentations of universal themes which confront the same sorts of problems with which the young people themselves are attempting to cope in their own lives and which they also meet in the literature which they are studying from white tradition.

The search for group and individual origins has been a continuing concern of Americans as reflected in the works of such writers as Bradford and Byrd all the way down to Alex Haley's *Roots*. So too with Native American literature, where many tribes have legends telling how their people travel long distances in search of a place to settle and about the problems of building their homes and surviving in their new surroundings. Just as white accounts of foundations frequently acknowledge the assistance of the divine, so in Native American traditions the people are often motivated by or actually led by super-human or supernatural forces in locating or establishing their settlements. Leaving behind tension and strife somewhere in the far North, the Choctaw journey for years, guided by a pole which leans in the direction they are to go, until they arrive at their destination in the Southeast, while the Hopis establish and abandon village after village in their efforts to find not only a good place to live in the physical sense but the right way to live in the spiritual sense. Not

Reprinted by permission from *ALAN Newsletter* 6:3-4, 8-9 (Fall 1978).

only do these accounts have to do with clarification of origins and identity, but they are exciting stories of physical ordeal and adventure as well.

While most white American literature reflects the Judeo-Christian accounts in Genesis of the origins of the world and humans, Native Americans have varying traditions about how the world and humans came to be. Although few stories attempt to explain how the earth itself came into being, the tales that exist are of two main types, the creationist and the earthdiver. Of these, the earthdiver is the simpler in structure and the most widespread. Typically in this kind of story, the primary elements consist of a sea, some dirt beneath the waters of the sea, and some animals, the origin of none of which is usually explained. In the story, one of the animals brings up out of the sea a few grains of dirt which then multiply magically to form the earth as we now know it. In a Mono (Calif.) myth, which is a good example of the type, Prairie Falcon and Crow are sitting on a log that projects out over the waters that cover the world. Falcon instructs Duck and Coot successively to dive beneath the surface and to bring up some sand from the bottom. After both try and fail, the little Grebe tries. He dives all the way to the bottom of the waters and gets some sand in each hand. Falcon and Crow take the sand and throw it into the sea, scattering it widely. The amount of sand gradually increases until the earth stretches to the horizon on every side.

Unlike the earthdiver type which always has water, dirt, and some animals already in existence, the creationist type (which strongly recalls the Biblical accounts of creation) often begins with nothing but the creator himself, a solitary, powerful, preexistent being who decides for some reason to create the earth and various features in it. Earthmaker of the Winnebago (Wisc.) Indians is sitting alone in space. He begins to weep—we are not told why—when to his surprise his tears form the seas. After he discovers that everything he wishes for comes into existence, by the power of his will he creates light, the earth, and such features of the earth as trees and grass. As his last act of creation, he makes a man out of clay in his own likeness.

Just as the Indians had different ways of explaining the origin of the world, so they also had various stories telling how human beings came into existence. People may be fashioned from sticks, stones, feathers, dirt, or sweat. They may spring from the soil or hatch from eggs, or they may be transformed from or be the offspring of animals, giants, or some other monstrous beings. Sometimes the trickster, that curiously ambivalent figure, neither good nor evil, has something to do with creating the first humans, and often he botches the job. Of all the many versions of how people came to be, however, few show the warmth of feeling or depth of conception of the Cheyenne and Winnebago tales. In the Cheyenne tradition, Maheo makes the first man and woman from his own ribs. He does this for the express purpose of giving Mother Earth something of himself to keep so that she will never be lonely and will always know that he is near her. The Winnebago tale has Earthmaker fashioning the first man out of clay in his own likeness. After giving the man mind and soul, Earthmaker breathes into the man's mouth, giving him the power of speech so that the man and the creator will be able to talk to each other. For poignancy of detail, not many stories can surpass the Maidu (Calif.) tale of Earth-Initiate who sweats for hours in order to animate his creation. Earth-Initiate takes dark red earth, mixes it with water, and makes two figures, a man and a woman. He puts them inside his house and lies down between them, flat on his back. There he stays, sweating all day and on into the night, until the two people are so thoroughly warmed by the heat emanating from his body that they come to life.

No matter how or when people came to be, a consistent belief in the evolution of the human race appears in Native American stories. The first people are crude and ignorant, lacking common sense. They wear no clothes and sit around doing nothing. They may even eat one another, being too stupid to tell the difference between animals and people. For those who live in the far South, lack of clothing is no great concern, but those in the North worry about keeping warm in the winter. Their problems are variously solved, perhaps by the creator sending a messenger to teach them how to build fires, cook meat, chop wood, and clothe themselves.

Not only were people in the early days not very bright, but they lived in a terrifying world, one that made no sense, one not unlike that confronting the characters of many modern literary works, such as *One Flew over the Cuckoo's Nest, The Big Wave,* or *I Am the Cheese.* The early world of the Native Americans is inhabited by assorted monsters, among them giants, cannibal spirits, huge animals, man-eating owls, walking skeletons, giants that steal the sun, and ogres that drink up all the available water. The work of eliminating these monsters falls to a variety of heroic figures, most of whom, like the heroes of European folktale or of many novels, seem very unlikely to succeed. Opposed to the idea that the world was once filled with many horrible creatures, there seems to have been a common belief that the creator intended that life be easy and comfortable for people and that something happened to thwart his wishes. Sometimes it is the trickster who changes things for the worse. In the Maidu myth of Earth-Initiate, Coyote brings an end to the golden age in which no one worked, got sick, or died.

What lies ahead for us as individuals and for society? Themes of death and ultimate catastrophe dominate many contemporary literary works, among them *Death Be Not Proud, A Separate Peace, Z for Zachariah, Life after Life,* and *Lord of the Flies.* Native Americans also have accounts about the end of the existing order, some of them set in the remote past in which floods, earthquakes, or similar disasters wiped out all life, often because people were behaving badly. Sometimes these disasters were local, sometimes worldwide. There are also stories predicting that the present world will come to an end, possibly being transformed into something quite different by a powerful Changer.

Stories about the origin of death are so numerous that it seems likely that every tribe must have attempted to come to grips with this fact of human existence. Often the story involves a debate between two beings in very early times after the first people have begun to grow old and to die. The argument is usually settled by reasoning, sometimes by chance. One character speaks in favor of having people die, while the other argues that they should live forever. The character who is against death suggests that people be revived after they have been dead for a short period so that they can go on living. The arguments that are advanced in favor of death are usually quite practical: to avoid overpopulation, to give rest to old people who have become tired of living, and to make room for young people. The character who speaks for death wins the argument, a victory which frequently the winner soon regrets, since usually he is the first person to lose a loved one. In a Kiowa story, Saynday would like people to come back to life after four days of being dead, but the ant is adamant in favor of death being a continuing state. "The world will become too full of people," she says. "Where will they all live?" she wonders. Finally, Saynday gives in and lets her have her way. A few days later, ant's son is killed. Griefstricken, she wishes she had thought better of Saynday's plan. However death originates in the tales, they show clearly that Native Americans acknowledged that it brings a deep sense of loss and great sorrow to those involved.

As people today are concerned about the problems and difficulties of everyday life, so too were Native Americans, if one judges by the profusion of tales which have to do with the origin of such essentials as food and fire. Corn stories in particular are numerous, since corn was cultivated over a large part of North America. Perhaps people discover it by chance, or possibly it is the gift of a culture hero, but certain themes are typical of corn stories in general. Often a character in the story dies and comes to life again, perhaps in the form of a corn stalk. Directions for planting, caring for, and storing the corn often appear, and it is evident that corn has been the property of and has come from the divine order. All of these features can be found in an Ojibwa story in which a kind and good Indian youth embarks upon his dreamfast. The youth prays that he be sent a vision of something that will prove to be of benefit not just to himself but also to the other members of his tribe so that they will not have to work so hard. On the third day of his fast, a handsome young man comes down from the sky, dressed richly in garments of green and yellow. On his head the stranger wears a plume of waving greenish feathers. The stranger commands the youth to rise from his fasting and to wrestle with him. The youth grapples with the stranger as hard as he can until he is almost exhausted. This happens for three more days. On the fourth day, at the stranger's command, the youth strips off the stranger's garments and buries his body in the soft, moist earth. Following the stranger's commands, he keeps weeds and grass from the grave, and once each month he sprinkles a little fresh soil over the top so that the grave remains moist and cool. Soon the green plumes the stranger had worn on his head appear, forcing themselves upward through the ground. Later a tall and graceful plant towers over the spot where the body had been placed. In this way, corn, the Indian staple crop, came into the world, the gift of the Great Spirit to the people because an Indian youth was unselfish and persevering.

The Indians had many stories to explain how things important to their lives came to be, such as bows and arrows and tobacco, or about festivals which were regularly held and about customary ways of doing things. These tales, like the others mentioned, are interesting for their own sakes as well as for what they say about Indian life and beliefs as compared to those of the whites.

The stories of the trickster offer still more thought-provoking material about the values and ways of Native Americans. A character not unlike such outcasts or anti-heroes as Holden Caulfield and Willy Loman, the trickster, who combines the elements of mischief-maker, buffoon, and culture hero, is found all over the continent and is the most popular figure in American Indian lore. While sometimes he may in a mischievous way bring discomfort to or make fools of people, he can also be downright evil and cause a great deal of trouble. Sometimes his tricks backfire, and he appears very ridiculous. At other times, he serves as the culture hero, a powerful religious figure who creates and regulates the world and teaches culture habits to the people. Tricksters vary in the degree in which they reveal these contradictory aspects of mischief-maker, fool, and culture hero, but most of them combine these qualities more or less equally, producing a complex and intriguing character.

Manabozho of the North Central Woodlands serves as a good example of a trickster who combines both destructive and benevolent qualities. Widely known under various names, he became the focus of stories so numerous that it was a common saying among Indians that no one person could tell them all. Although the tales varied a little from tribe to tribe, they were consistent enough to be summarized in this way. Manabozho is of miraculous birth, the son of a virgin and the West Wind. Raised by his grandmother, he wages warfare with monsters and performs heroic deeds, experiencing a catastrophe like that of Jonah and a deluge like Noah's. Responsible for cultural necessities, such as fire, he wanders about the recreated earth perpetrating tricks and being tricked. In later life, he develops into a wise man and prophet of whom advice and boons are sought. Eventually, he rejoins the company of the divine order.

Manabozho is often a foolish figure, and frequently the situations in which he finds himself are quite absurd. His lack of common sense and foresight provides the occasion for rollicking tales such as this one. One day he encounters a buffalo cow which he slays for food. As he is butchering the cow, a porcupine comes and asks for a share. Manabozho gives him a hard kick, and the thin, starved creature scampers away. Manabozho hides the prepared meat under some bushes and rushes to get his family to help carry the meat home. While he is gone, the porcupine returns and steals the meat, carrying it into a high pine tree overhanging a river. When Manabozho returns, he finds his cache of meat gone. He and his family scour the area until Manabozho discovers what he thinks is his meat under the water near the bank of the river, with the porcupine sitting nearby, underwater too, guarding it. Manabozho dives repeatedly to recover his meat. Finally, he ties a large stone to his feet to weight himself down so that he can remain underwater long enough to pry loose the supposed cache. To his consternation, he finds he cannot rise back to the surface. With great effort, his lungs almost bursting for lack of air, he manages to untie the rock, but not before he swallows so much water he is bloated to the size of a bear. While resting on the bank, he happens to glance upward and sees his meat in the tree overhead, the porcupine sitting on the branch beside it. To his humiliation, Manabozho realizes that he has almost killed himself diving for a reflection.

On the whole, Manabozho is a careless sort, lacking in prudence, foresight, and self-control. He often overreacts and loses his head. He is a simpleton, and his comic adventures illustrate vividly what will happen if one does not practice certain virtues. The tales caution against being boastful and against being wasteful. They warn against being so naive that one is easily taken advantage of as Manabozho often takes advantage of the creatures around him and against associating with bad companions and consequently getting into trouble. But to cooperate with one's fellows, to use one's common sense, to live with moderation, to look ahead and consider possible courses of action—these are lessons implicitly conveyed by the tales of Manabozho. These are virtues the people of the Woodlands valued and wanted future generations to value.

Although these tales of Manabozho are entertaining and are intended to teach moral values as well, Manabozho is nevertheless primarily a religious figure and as such appears at the very heart of Woodlands mythology. He is not just a rogue and buffoon; he also appears as a leader and demigod who serves as the culture hero who creates and regulates the world. Growing up under the care of his grandmother, Manabozho reveals the qualities of great size, strength, wisdom, and courage by which he is able to achieve worthy ends for which he is later remembered and admired. He kills monsters and evil spirits which are troubling the world, and he brings about features of the landscape and of animal and vegetable life. He is responsible for giving people many good and useful gifts. He invents lances, hatchets, and arrow points and helps people secure tobacco, medicinal herbs, and sugar. In a Promethean tale, a kind of story very widespread among the Indians, he jeopardizes his life in order to steal fire.

The tales go on and on, presenting Manabozho as a kind teacher and helper and as a powerful regulator in nature. Entertaining they are, yes; but they are also much more. Manabozho functioned as a divine role figure to illustrate how people should not behave as well as how they should behave. On still another plane of significance, the Indians could see themselves reflected in the trickster's life and adventures. They could identify with Manabozho's good features and his successes and derive a vicarious satisfaction out of seeing him get his comeuppances. Manabozho served both as a model and as an Indian alter ego as well.

In addition to these tales, there are many other stories which deal with mythological and heroic themes and with historical happenings as transmitted by Indian folk memory from before and after the coming of the whites. The stories discussed here are representative of the main types of American Indian imaginative literature from oral tradition which can readily find a place in the literature curriculum.

Today Native Americans are utilizing white literary forms and the written word to express their views about themselves, life as they see it, and the world around them. In order to understand their writings, students must have some knowledge of the traditional forms and themes. In order, for example, to appreciate such writers as Scott Momaday, James Welch, and Leslie Silko, or the writings of most of the young poets, it is important to know some of the traditional stories and to have in mind how these old tales figured in the lives of the people who made them up and told them. A knowledge of the literature is essential for understanding today's Native American literature.

By the time young people finish high school, we hope they will have some knowledge of important American writers and major works and themes in the white tradition of writing. In the same way, it would be good for them to have some understanding of the literature which preceded that of the whites, of our continent's first literature, the literature of the Native Americans. Not only are these stories of humor, suspense, and conflict dramatic and powerful as literature, but they stand as a verbal record of the literary features, ethical beliefs, and world view of the Native Americans. In addition to gaining pleasure from reading and hearing these tales, students can acquire limited but nevertheless important insights into Indian life and values. By so doing, they will be extending their own view of the world and understanding of life.

Some Selection Aids

Stensland, Anna Lee. *Literature by and about the American Indian: An Annotated Bibliography for Junior and Senior High School Students.* Urbana, Ill.: National Council of Teachers of English, 1973.

Ullom, Judith C. *Folklore of the North American Indians: An Annotated Bibliography.* Washington: Library of Congress, 1969.

SELECTED BIBLIOGRAPHY

Astrov, Margot. *American Indian Prose and Poetry.* New York: Capricorn, 1962.

Barnouw, Victor. *Wisconsin Chippewa Myths and Tales.* Madison: Univ. of Wisconsin Pr., 1977.

Clark, Ella E. *Indian Legends of the Pacific Northwest.* Berkeley: Univ. of California Pr., 1953.

Coffin, Tristram P. *Indian Tales of North America.* Philadelphia: American Folklore Society, Inc., 1961.

Courlander, Harold. *The Fourth World of the Hopis.* Greenwich: Fawcett Pub., Inc., 1971.

Feldmann, Susan. *The Storytelling Stone: Myths and Tales of the American Indians.* New York: Dell, 1965.

Grinnell, George B. *By Cheyenne Campfires.* Lincoln: Univ. of Nebraska Pr., 1971.

Henry, Jeannette. *The American Indian Reader: Literature.* San Francisco: The Indian Historian Pr., 1973.

Johnston, Basil. *Ojibway Heritage.* New York: Columbia Univ. Pr., 1976.

Kroeber, Theodora. *The Inland Whale: Nine Stories Retold from California Indian Legends.* Berkeley: Univ. of California Pr., 1964.

Marriott, Alice, and Rachlin, Carol K. *American Indian Mythology.* New York: New Amer. Lib., 1972.

Sanders, Thomas E., and Peck, Walter W. *Literature of the American Indian.* New York: Glencoe Pr., 1973.

Stevens, James. *Sacred Legends of the Sandy Lake Creek.* Toronto: McClelland and Stewart Limited, 1971.

Thompson, Stith. *Tales of the North American Indians.* Bloomington: Indiana Univ. Pr., 1966.

Chicanos and American Literature

Philip D. Ortego and Jose A. Carrasco

In 1948 Carey McWilliams suggested in the last chapter of *North from Mexico* that the American Southwest had yet "to experience the impact of the first articulate generation of persons of Mexican descent." Moreover, "in the past, Mexicans have been a more or less anonymous, voiceless, expressionless minority." McWilliams pointed out that there had not yet been written "a novel of Southwestern experience by an American-born person of Mexican descent or a significant autobiography by a native-born Mexican." But McWilliams prophesied that "the moment the group begins to achieve this type of expression, a new chapter will be written in the history of the Southwest. For as the Spanish-speaking attain cultural maturity, as they achieve real self-expression, they will exert a profound influence on the culture of the region, and Spanish-Mexican influences that have remained dormant these many years will be revived and infused with new meaning and vigor."[1] Though McWilliams wrote in those prophetic years with a lot of *corazon,* and though *North from Mexico* probably represents the most reliably comprehensive work on Mexican-Americans thus far (despite its date of publication), the fact is that even McWilliams overlooked the literary accomplishments and achievements of Mexican-Americans and their forebears.

There is and has been little in American literature to indicate the full range of the Mexican-American literary experience. For example, in the number of texts examined by the Textbook Review Committee of the National Council of Teachers of English Task Force on Racism and Bias in the Teaching of English, the Mexican-American and the Chicano writer are conspicuously absent. It should be pointed out emphatically that this absence, this blatant omission, is not because there aren't Chicano writers or haven't been Mexican-American writers in the past, but because of ignorance about Mexican-American literature and its writers, and also because of a thoroughly ethnocentric literary point of view that has placed Anglo-American literature and Anglo-American writers at the top of the literary heap in the United States.

Traditionally, American literature has stressed that a *special* literary relationship exists and has existed between the United States and England. There is, of course, no denying this initial relationship between the

Reprinted by permission from *Searching for America,* Ernece B. Kelly, ed. (Urbana: National Council of Teachers of English, 1972), pp.78-94. Copyright © 1972 by the National Council of Teachers of English.

British colonies of the Atlantic frontier and the mother country of England in the days when that relationship was internationally acknowledged. But in the wake and consequence of American independence and the subsequent history of American immigration, that initial relationship between the United States and England was (in actuality) diminished in direct proportion to the changing ratio of the American population: Americans of English ancestry versus Americans of non-English ancestry. When the latter population became preponderant then the Anglo-American relationship should have emerged in its lesser light. But such was not the case, for so strong had the initial relationship been cast and articulated that, despite internecine differences which led to a revolutionary war (a civil war in fact), the idea of a special relationship between the United States and England survived and was institutionalized to the point that the fiction of that relationship was part of the indoctrination received by all newcomers to the United States regardless of their ethnic or national origins. The upshot was that in time *all* non-Anglo-Americans so internalized the idea of that special relationship that the fiction assumed the definitiveness of reality. In time all non-Anglo-Americans were talking about "our" Puritan forebears, "our" founding fathers, and so on. The Anglo-American minority had effectively secured their position and posterity in the United States by the ingenious tactic of pontifical propaganda. The immigrant drones had become what the Anglos said they were: Anglos.

And this was called the "melting pot" theory, except that there never was a melting pot—it was actually a "mould," an Anglo-American mould shaped to turn out German-Anglo-Americans, Italian-Anglo-Americans, French-Anglo-Americans, Mexican-Anglo-Americans, and so on. But in a world shrunk to its true dimensions in an infinite universe, one must come to expect certain kinds of mutations as inevitable. In the assimilist melting pot process the identity factor, once stable and constant, was sufficiently variable to create an entirely new species of American, one cognizant of his ethnic past and heritage yet apprised of the fact that he was politically an American. This has been the situation of the Chicano. For unlike his Mexican-American predecessor, the Chicano is acutely aware of his Mexican cultural-linguistic heritage and of his American political-linguistic context. In some circles of Chicano thought, this situation is regarded as the "next" step in the logical progression of Vasconcelo's theory of the *raza cosmica*. In Hegelian terms, the Chicano is the inevitable synthesis of the Mexican-American cultural conflict, just as the "Mexican" was the inevitable synthesis of the Old and New World cultural conflict.

It is little wonder, therefore, that Chicano literature employs linguistic and cultural elements that pertain to either its Mexican or American facets.[2] The themes of Chicano literature may be either Mexican or American or some combination of both; so too the language of Chicano literature may be either Spanish or English or both in a unique lexical arrangement known as "binary phenomenon," that is, the linguistic symbols of two languages are mixed in utterances using either language's syntactic structure. In the bilingual (Spanish-English) writer this means plugging into either his English or Spanish "idiolect" at will to produce a "stereolect." The phenomenon is very important in order to understand contemporary Chicano literature. For example, the Chicano poet Alurista writes:

> Mis ojos hinchados
>   flooded with lágrimas
> de bronce
> melting on the cheek bones
>   of my concern
>   razgos indígenas
> the scars of history on my face
>   and the veins of my body
> that aches
>   vomito sangre
> y lloro libertad
>   I do not ask for freedom
>   I *am* freedom[3]

Binary phenomenon occurs in Chicano prose too. For example, in Nick Vaca's story of "The Purchase," Doña Lupe exemplifies binary phenomenon as it occurs in the actual speech of Chicanos.

> "Ave Maria Purisíma, I must make another pago hoy or else it'll be too late. Si, too late and then what would I do? Christmas is so close and if I don't hurry con los pagos I'll have nothing to give any of mis hijos. If that should happen it would weigh muy pesado on my mind. Even now, con el pensamiento that I may not be able to give them anything, I have trouble durmiendo en la noche. And, Santo Niño de Atocha, if Christmas should come and catch me sin nada I would never sleep will por el resto de mi vida."[4]

The significance of binary phenomenon in Chicano literature lies in the fact that the parameters of creative expression are extended in each of the languages employed, by the presence of the other and the semantic images made possible by the stereolectic power of the binary line. Apropos of Vaca's story one critic wrote: "Admittedly, Vaca's story requires from the reader a knowledge of a language other than English, but he is writing in an English tradition we can trace to Sterne (with his use of French and Latin) on up to Joyce, who really demands that his reader possess a background of so many languages."[5] Though the parallel may be somewhat stretched in this case, the point is nevertheless valid. For what happens in binary phenomenon as employed in Chicano literature is that the reader must indeed possess more than just "a background of so many languages"; he must be *literate* in both languages involved.

At this point it is important to understand that in Europe or elsewhere binary phenomenon is regarded as a matter of course and hardly viewed as an unusual occurrence.[6] Admittedly, in the United States the phenomenon finds its greatest vogue and outlet in the Chicano experience and Chicano literature reflecting that experience. Why is it, then, that the Chicano experience has been so glaringly disregarded by American literateurs? Why has it been excluded from texts that purport "to provide the reader with the most wide-ranging and generous exposure to the literature of America"? But more importantly, why has the literary heritage of Chicanos been suppressed?

Like the British roots in the new American soil, the Hispanic literary roots yielded a vigorous and dynamic body of literature which, unfortunately for us, has been studied historically as part of a foreign enterprise rather than as part and parcel of our American literary heritage. Indeed, the contributions to American life and literature by the forebears of Mexican-Americans have yet to be fully comprehended and measured. We seldom learn the extent to which the Hispanic literary tradition has influenced American literature.[7] The Hispanic works dealing with the southern and southwestern parts of the United States before 1848 (and later, actually) have become the neglected aspect of the American experience in American literature. The chief factor in this "neglect" has been "language." For all the works of the Spanish and Mexican period of the Southwest were written in Spanish. And many Mexican-Americans continued to write in Spanish from the time of the Mexican-American War to the present, though many of them—like, for example, the descendants of Mariano Vallejo, last of the military governors of Mexican California—acquired English literary styles as well. In fact, contemporary Mexican-American novelists such as Floyd Salas, John Rechy, Richard Vasquez, Antonio Villareal, Raymond Barrio, et al. write chiefly in English, as do most contemporary Mexican-American poets, playwrights, essayists, and short story writers, though most of them are equally capable of writing in Spanish as well. Of course the implication of Chicano and Mexican-American works in Spanish is that such works are not properly within the traditional definition of American literature because they were not written in English.

But language is hardly a logical reason for not recognizing non-English language material as American literature, although it was written in the United States. Furthermore, in the pluralistic cultural and linguistic context of contemporary America, we can no longer consent to the suggestions of American literary historians that American literature properly begins with the arrival of British colonials in America. For in actuality American literature begins with the formation of the United States as a political entity. Thus, the literary period from the founding of the first permanent British settlement at Jamestown, Virginia, in 1607, to the formation of American union represents only the British period of American literature. So, too, the literary period from the first permanent Spanish settlement at Saint Augustine, Florida, 1565, to the dates of acquisition of these Spanish and Mexican lands by the United States, should in fact represent the Hispanic period of American literature. More appropriately, the British and Spanish periods should both be listed under the rubric of "Colonial American Literature." The Mexican period of the Southwest should simply be labeled "The Mexican Period."

But in 1971 Mexican-Americans are ignored in anthologies of American literature save in selections that disparage or denigrate them as a people.[8] The stereotypes of Chicanos in American life and literature present one of the most vicious and distorted images to be found in American society. Their history and background are totally ignored by Anglo society and its literary circles everywhere save for very select aspects. But in general, the Chicano has been dismissed as an entity in all sectors of the Southwest and the midwestern regions, to the extent of being referred to as the "invisible minority."[9] In parts of Louisiana and other southern states Mexicans are thought to be black, while in northern and New England states they are totally undefined as anything other than being from Mexico.

As we have said, within traditional American literature the Chicano writer is totally excluded. The major and minor anthologies of American literature, while pretending to represent the "whole" of American tradition in literature, not only exclude the works of Chicano writers but for the most part exclude dealing with them in any legitimate way. This conscious omission of the Chicano from literary anthologies reflects the unconcern of editors and publishers in truly attempting to represent the "range and style" of literature indigenous to this country. The tragedy is that lack of concern perpetuates and reinforces the ignorance of white America as well as leaves it susceptible to the internalization of the worst stereotypes about Chicanos.

But aside from omission of Chicano writers from the major texts of American literature there is the added problem of misrepresentation. By this we mean the inclusion of works by known authors such as John Steinbeck, Katherine Anne Porter, Ernest Hemingway, and others, who portray the Mexican and Mexican-American from a totally Anglo perspective, thus leaving the image of the Chicano as created by these writers to the naiveté of readers who are unable to distinguish fact from fiction, reality from distortion, and may therefore consider such works as the gospel truth.

Unfortunately, many English teachers think of Mexican-American literature as being rooted firmly in the works of Anglo-American writers such as Harvey Fergusson, J. Frank Dobie, Roy Bedichek, and the like. Quite often, the concept many English teachers have of Mexican-American literature and culture turns out to be the "cowboy" tradition, or the romanticized Hispanic "templar" tradition or the equally romanticized Anglo "pioneer" tradition.[10] What passes for Mexican-American literature and culture at times tends to be material that puts the Mexican-American and his Mexican kinsmen in a bad literary light, as Professor Cecil Robinson pointed out in his work *With the Ears of Strangers*. For like other minority groups, Mexican-Americans were and continue to be inaccurately and superficially represented in literature, movies, television, and other mass media.[11] This situation sometimes has been caused by prejudice, but it has also been caused by those well-meaning romanticists who have seriously distorted the image of the Mexican-American for the sake of their art.

Mexican-Americans have been characterized at both ends of the spectrum of human behavior (seldom in the middle) as untrustworthy, villainous, ruthless, tequila-drinking, and philandering *machos* or else as courteous, devout, and fatalistic peasants who are to be treated more as pets than as people. More often than not Mexican-Americans have been cast either as bandits or as lovable rogues; as hot-blooded, sexually animated creatures or as passive, humble servants.

The result has usually been that Mexican-American youngsters are taught about the cruelty of their Spanish forebears and the savagery of their Mexican-Indian forebears; they have been taught about the Spanish greed for gold, of the infamous Spanish Inquisition, of Aztec human sacrifices, of Mexican bandits, and of the massacre at the Alamo. They seldom, if ever, learn of the other men at the Alamo, their Mexican forebears—unknown and unsung in American history—who were killed fighting on the Texas side. American children probably have never heard of such men as Juan Abamillo, Juan Badillo, Carlos Espalier, Gregorio Esparza, Antonio Fuentes, Jose Maria Guerrero, Toribio Losoya, Andres Nava, and other Texas Mexicans at the Alamo.

Information about the literary accomplishments of Mexican-Americans during the period from the end of the Mexican-American War to the turn of the century, for example, has been negligible. As Américo Paredes has pointed out, "With few exceptions, documents available for study of the region are in English, being for the most part reports made by officials who were, to put it mildly, prejudiced against the people they were trying to pacify."[12] In short, editors of American literary texts have tended to minimize the literary achievement of Mexican-Americans for reasons ranging from jingoism to ignorance.

It should be noted, however, that no sooner had the Spanish established their hold on Mexico than they started a printing press in Mexico City in 1529, more than a century earlier than any established in the British colonies of North America. Indeed, there was a substantial Spanish-reading public in New Spain and Mexico, including the North American states, and after the lands were ceded to the United States in 1848. Spanish literature was read and written in both the Spanish peninsula and in the New World. Such Spanish playwrights as Pedro Calderon de la Barca and Lope de Vega extended their literary influence to Spanish America just as the Mexican-born playwright Juan Ruiz de Alarcon extended his literary influence to Spain. By the time of the Mexican-American War, the Mexican Southwest had been thoroughly nurtured on drama, poetry, and folktales of a literary tradition of several hundred years. Mexicans who became Americans continued the Indo-Hispanic literary tradition, not only by preserving the old literary materials but also by creating new ones in the superimposed American political ambiance.

Nevertheless, Mexican-Americans were poorly regarded by the vast majority of Anglo-Americans who came in contact with them, and many of the literary portraits of Mexican-Americans by Anglo-American writers exerted undue influence on generations of Americans down to our time. The disparaging images of Mexican-Americans were drawn by such American writers as Richard Henry Dana, who, in *Two Years before the Mast,* described Mexican-Americans as "an idle, thriftless people" who could "make nothing for themselves."[13] In 1852, Col. John Monroe reported to Washington:

> The New Mexicans are thoroughly debased and totally incapable of self-government, and there is no latent quality about them that can ever make them respectable. They have more Indian blood than Spanish, and in some respects are below the Pueblo Indians, for they are not as honest or as industrious.[14]

In 1868, the *Overland Monthly* published an article by William V. Wells, "The French in Mexico," in which he wrote that "in the open field, a charge of disciplined troops usually sufficed to put to flight the collection of frowzy-headed mestizos, leperos, mulattoes, Indians, Samboes, and other mongrels now, as in the time of our war with them, composing a Mexican Army."[15] In our own time Walter Prescott Webb characterized the Mexicans as possessing "a cruel streak" that he believes was inherited partly from the Spanish of the Inquisition and partly from their Indian forebears. Webb asserts:

> On the whole, the Mexican warrior . . . was inferior to the Comanche and wholly unequal to Texans, the whine of the leaden slugs stirred in him an irresistible impulse to travel with, rather than against, the music. He won more victories over the Texans partly by parley than by force of arms. For making promises and for breaking them he had no peer.[16]

The glamour and appeal of such noted writers has of course proven destructive to the Mexican in general, but more so to the Mexican-Americans who continue to be victimized by this spurious body of literature.

The early works of Bret Harte, Gertrude Atherton, Jack London, and others popularized the romantic notions of the California of the Dons, the days of the noble land-grant *gachupin* indulging in elaborate Span-ish-European festivities and rodeos, of the Spanish *caballero* mounted upon his excellent steed while señoritas in their silk and embroidered gowns, proud and seemingly uninterested, awaited breathlessly the out-come of horse races. At the same time, some Anglo-American writers took great pains to alert their readers not to mistake the *caballero* for the "greaser," the Mexican male who was undisciplined, uncultured, still savage, and constantly in need of a firm hand and direction. Nor was the "Spanish" señorita to be confused with the "Mexican" wench who was fiery, free-loving, and easily accessible, and who always dressed simply and colorfully to complement her carefree life-style.

In her short story "The Pearls of Loreto," Gertrude Atherton glorifies and romanticizes the California days of the Dons out of focus for the times.[17] While she makes no distinctions between the *criollo* (New World Spaniard) and the *Californio* of mixed blood, the subtlety of her remarks about the latter leave little room for equivocation about her attitudes toward the people she professed to care about. For example, her quick, fleeting references to "heavy-lips" in her descriptions of Mexican men may be read matter-of-factly by Anglo readers, but her mind-set is exposed. Her attitude toward "color" filters through when she describes a strange *caballero* from the south who is fair and with dark-blue eyes. So different is this *caballero* from the local *vaqueros* that all the women are totally enamored by his majestic demeanor: "But the Stranger is so handsome!" "Dios de mi vida! his eyes are like dark blue stars."

The young *caballero* proceeds to fall in love with Ysabel, the rose of California, who, as it turns out, is also light-skinned and green-eyed. We learn from Atherton that when Ysabel looked up as the *caballero* rode past, "his bold profile and thin face were full of power. Such a face was *rare* among the *languid shallow* men of her *race*." (Emphasis added.)

The denigrated character of the Mexican and Mexican-American in American literature changed little toward the end of the nineteenth cen-tury and in the first half of the twentieth century. In fact, strengthened by a plethora of studies by social scientists, the profile of the Mexican-American and Mexican became a motley enumeration of characteristics that have debilitated Mexican-Americans even further. The tragedy (per-haps "crime" is the better word) is that Anglo writers of fiction have shamelessly depicted Mexican-Americans in terms of those utterly per-nicious characteristics. For example, in his short story "The Gambler, the Nun, and the Radio," Ernest Hemingway details the derogation of Mexicans in the dialogue of his characters.[18] And like Atherton, Hem-ingway resorts to a stereotypical English linguistic construction in order to create the aura of a Spanish-speaking environment. What really hap-pens is that the Mexican characters all sound like Puritans speaking Eliza-bethan English. At one point in the story, Frazer responds to one of the Mexican characters: "I thought marijuana was the opium of the poor."

Afterwards he refers to the smaller of the three Mexicans as "that dyspeptic little joint keeper." And later, Hemingway writes:

> The last time [the Mexicans] played Mr. Frazer lay in his room with his door open and listened to the noisy, bad music and could not keep from thinking. When they wanted to know what he wished played, he asked for the Cucaracha, which has the *sinister* lightness and *deftness* of so many of the tunes men have gone to die to. They played noisily and with emotion. [Emphasis ours.]

Frazer is always referred to by name, but Cayetano is most often referred to as "the Mexican."

The perversion and dehumanization of the image of the "Mexican" in American literature has become almost an Anglo-American tradition practiced by the "best" of American writers. In John Steinbeck's story "Flight," the Mexican-American youth, Pepe, is characterized as a naive, knife-wielding farm boy who on his first trip to town kills a man who calls him names.[19] In the end he is hunted down like an animal and killed. Anglo-Americans might argue that the story is a sympathetic portrayal of the Mexican-American experience. That's what Anglo-Americans said about William Styron's *Nat Turner*. "Flight" is one of those gratuitous stories that reaches pretentious heights only because of the fame of its author, not because Steinbeck knew what the Mexican-American experience was all about.

So too Katherine Anne Porter wrote about Mexicans from the perspective that since she was a Texan she knew all about them. Her preferred setting was Mexico, and in her stories she always had a "white Christian intellectual" present to interpret the folkways and mores of the "natives." In "María Concepción," for example, Porter created Given as the American "observer" in Mexico who felt a fatherly indulgence for the "primitive and childish ways" of the Mexicans.[20] Porter attempted to portray the elusive and fictive dynamics of *"machismo"* in "María Concepción," a characteristic all too commonly ascribed to the Mexican male, caricaturizing him as lusty and passionate and philandering. Essentially, *machismo* is defined or depicted as that behavior which is meant to project or defend the *utter* masculinity of the Mexican male. Thus, as a consequence of *machismo*, Pedro Villegas, María Concepción's husband, emerges as a prototypical lovable bastard of the first rank. But what does this do to Mexican-Americans who are regarded via the image of Pedro Villegas?

The pejorations and generalizations about Mexican-Americans are to be deplored, and Mexican-Americans today are beginning to rise up against the perpetuation of such racial clichés. Mexican-Americans have been struggling within the predominantly Anglo-American culture of the United States for over 122 years. Although Mexican-Americans have been writing all that time, the realization of Mexican-American literature as the *élan vital* in the life-styles of the people themselves has come about only within recent years. In the fall of 1967 a cohort of Mexican-American writers at Berkeley, California, formed Quinto Sol Publications in a tiny office over a candy store. Their purpose was "to provide a forum for Mexican-American self-definition and expression on . . . issues of relevance to Mexican-Americans in American society today."

Alternatives is the key word in what has blossomed into the Chicano Renaissance.[21] Mexican-Americans had been completely disenchanted with the plethora of writings about them, writings that depicted them in a variety of literary contexts resorting to the most blatant stereotypes and racial clichés, all of them by "intellectual mercenaries," as the Quinto Sol group called them in the first issue of their literary quarterly magazine, *El Grito: A Journal of Contemporary Mexican American Thought.* The promise of *El Grito* was that it would be the forum for Mexican-Americans to articulate their own sense of identity, a promise which continues to be fulfilled. Even more important in the Chicano Renaissance, the printed word was seen as a very important medium in the Chicano struggle for equality. Hundreds of Chicano literary outlets sprang up after 1967 as Chicanos became increasingly aware of the power of the pen and the persuasiveness of print. And, importantly, in the process Chicanos have discovered their Indian roots and that they were of the Americas before the conquistadores and before the Puritans, and that essentially—despite the overlay of Spanish culture—they are descendants of the great Indian civilizations of Mexico,[22] and they are Montezuma's children more than Coronado's.

Materials for teaching about contemporary Chicano literature and culture in the English classroom are available and increasing daily in quantity as more and more Chicanos turn to writing. The most representative works thus far are *Chicano,* a novel by Richard Vasquez; *The Plum Plum Pickers,* a novel by Raymond Barrio; *Pocho,* a novel by Antonio Villareal; "I Am Joaquin," an epic poem by Rodolfo Gonzales; *Chicano: 25 Pieces of a Chicano Mind,* a collection of poetry by Abelardo Delgado; *Crazy Gypsy,* poetry by Luis Omar Salinas.

Older works representative of the "modern" period are *New Mexico Triptych,* fiction by Angelico Chavez; *With His Pistol in His Hand,* a biographical and folklore treatment of the Mexican-American folk hero Gregorio Cortez by Américo Paredes; *Among the Valiant,* a historical and biographical presentation of the seventeen Mexican-American Medal of Honor winners, by Raul Morin; *We Fed Them Cactus,* a series of reminiscences by Fabiola Cabeza de Baca; *Old Spain in Our Southwest,* a loose history with songs and stories by Nina Otero; *Spanish Tales of Colorado and New Mexico* by Juan B. Rael; *Literary Folklore of the Hispanic Southwest* by Aurora Lucero; *Tough Trip through Paradise,* a Montana journal by Andrew Garcia.

In addition there is fiction by Mexican-Americans in such journals and magazines as the *Arizona Quarterly,* the *New Mexico Quarterly,* the

Southwest Review, and other college and university publications such as *Descant,* published at Texas Christian University. However, the most voluminous publishing of Mexican-American writers of prose, poetry, and fiction has been undertaken by Mexican-American literary magazines such as *El Grito,* mentioned earlier, published quarterly by Quinto Sol: *Regeneracion,* published in Los Angeles; *Aztlan,* published by the Mexican-American Cultural Center at University of California in Los Angeles; *Journal of Mexican American History,* published at Santa Barbara, California; and a host of "little" magazines and newspapers published regularly and intermittently throughout the Southwest and Chicano communities elsewhere.

A modicum of caution should be exercised by the English teacher in selecting Anglo-American material about Mexican-Americans, for so much of it perpetuates wittingly or unwittingly the queer, curious, and quaint notions about Mexican-Americans. For example, Helen Hunt Jackson's *Ramona* should not be exalted as the "true" representation of the Spanish Southwest any more than we should exalt Harriet Beecher Stowe's *Uncle Tom's Cabin* as the "true" representation of blacks in the antebellum South. Indeed, many of the social studies yield a considerable amount of data about Mexican-Americans as they are—beings of two cultures, and as diversely different as Anglo-Americans. English teachers should bear in mind, however, that Mexican-Americans are not misplaced Mexicans, or Puerto Ricans, or Cubans, any more than Anglo-Americans, say, are misplaced Britons, or Scotsmen, or Irishmen.

Just as we study the literary works of the forebears of Anglo-Americans as an essential part of American literature, though it really is British colonial literature, so too we should study the literary works of the forebears of Mexican-Americans. For in truth, the Spanish and Mexican literature of the Southwest is as much a part of American literature as the British literature is of the Atlantic frontier.

There is already a wealth of translated material in this area; and the two works, *Spanish Explorers in the Southern United States: 1528-1543* and *Spanish Exploration in the Southwest: 1542-1706* (Barnes and Noble) make an excellent pair for introducing the "Chronicles of the Southwest" as a unit. Gaspar de Villagra's *The Tragedy of Acoma* (Historia de Nuevo Mexico), written in 1590, should be identified as the *first* American epic. In addition, Herbert E. Bolton's studies on "The Borderlands" are extremely valuable as background material on the Hispanic period of the Southwest. Other equally illuminating works are *North from Mexico* by Carey McWilliams; *Forgotten People* by George Sanchez;[23] *The Decline of the Californios* by Leonard Pitt; *The Mexican American People* by Leo Grebler, et al.; *Mexican Americans in the Southwest* by Ernesto Galarza, et al.; *Mexican Americans: A Brief Look at Their History* by Julian Nava; *South by Southwest* by John Tebell and Ramon Ruiz.

We know the stereotypes of Mexican-Americans are products of historical and sociological circumstances. But the fact that they have survived and have been perpetuated throughout the decades, the fact that they are in our national literature, and all too often whispered furtively in the form of racist jokes leads unerringly to the fact that the American malady of the twentieth century continues to be "racism." Anglo-Americans who have never seen Chicanos lace their conversations with the fugitive images of Chicanos. But the stereotyping of the Mexican-American and Chicano must also be blamed on editors and publishers who select and compile the literature that eventually ends up in waspish American literary anthologies.

If we are truly to overcome the "color" problem, editors and publishers of American literary texts *must* be forced to assume responsibility for the perpetuation of racism towards Chicanos in American society and to take swift and immediate corrective action. By excluding the Mexican-American and Chicano from American literature, publishers and editors have succeeded in keeping the Chicano one of the best-kept secrets in America. Indeed, through biased selection, editors and publishers have perpetuated the slanders, distorted the truth, and perverted their roles with respect to Chicanos who, like the blacks, American Indians, and Asian-Americans, are still looking for America.

NOTES

1. Carey McWilliams, *North from Mexico* (New York: Greenwood Pr., reprint ed., 1968), p.302.
2. Philip D. Ortego, "Mexican American Literature," *Nation* 209:258-59 (Sept. 15, 1969).
3. Alurista, "Mis Ojos Hinchados," *El Espejo—The Mirror: Selected Mexican American Literature* (Berkeley: Quinto Sol Publications, Inc., 1969), p.172.
4. Nicke C. Vaca, "The Purchase," *El Espejo—The Mirror,* p.144
5. Edward Simmen, personal correspondence, May 5, 1970.
6. See Philip D. Ortego, "Some Cultural Implications of a Mexican American Border Dialect of American English," *Studies in Linguistics* 21: 77-84 (1969-70).
7. See Stanley T. Williams, *The Spanish Background of American Literature* 2 vols. (Hamden, Conn.: Shoe String, 1968).
8. For discussions of this point see Edward Simmen, *The Chicano: From Caricature to Self-Portrait* (New York, 1971); Cecil Robinson, *With the Ears of Strangers: The Mexican in American Literature* (Tucson: Univ. of Arizona Pr., 1963); Francisco Rios, "The Mexican in Fact, Fiction and Folklore," *El Grito: A Journal of Contemporary Mexican American Thought,* (Summer 1969).
9. National Education Association Report, "The Invisible Minority" (Tucson, 1966).
10. Philip D. Ortego, "Which Southwestern Literature and Culture in the English Classroom?" *Arizona English Bulletin* 13:15-17 (Apr. 1971).

11. Philip D. Ortego, "Chicago Odyssey," *Transaction* (Apr. 1970), p.82.
12. Américo Paredes, "Folklore and History," in Mody C. Boatwright, Wilson M. Hudson, and Allen Maxwell, eds., *Singers and Storytellers* (Dallas: Southern Methodist Univ. Pr., 1961), pp.162-63.
13. Richard Henry Dana, *Two Years before the Mast* (1840, various eds.).
14. United States Congress, *Congressional Globe*, 32nd Congress, 2nd Session, Jan. 10, 1953, Appendix, p.104.
15. William V. Wells, "The French in Mexico," *Overland Monthly* (Sept. 1868), p.232.
16. Walter Prescott Webb, *The Texas Rangers: A Century of Frontier Defense* (Rev. ed.; Austin: Univ. of Texas Pr., 1965), p.14.
17. Gertrude Atherton, "The Pearls of Loreto," in Angus Burrell and Bennett Cerf, eds., *An Anthology of Famous American Stories* (New York: Modern Library, 1953).
18. Ernest Hemingway, "The Gambler, the Nun, and the Radio," in Burrell and Cerf, eds., *An Anthology of Famous American Stories.*
19. John Steinbeck, "Flight," in Walter Blair et al., eds. *The Literature of the United States: From World War I to the Present,* Book 2 (3rd ed.; Glenview, Ill.: Scott, Foresman, 1969).
20. Katherine Anne Porter, "María Concepción," in Burrell and Cerf, eds. *An Anthology of Famous American Stories.*
21. Philip D. Ortego, "The Chicano Renaissance," *Social Casework* 52:294-307 (May 1971).
22. Philip D. Ortego, "Montezuma's Children," *The Center Magazine* (Nov.-Dec. 1970).
23. See Philip D. Ortego, "The People of Sanchez," *Nation* 206:482-83 (Apr. 8, 1968).

Introduction from *Asian-American Authors*

Kai-ye Hsu and Helen Pablubinskas, editors

An Asian-American is first of all a man, just as a poet has to be human before being poetic. Yes? But no! says Frank Chin, author of "Food for All His Dead," when he disagrees with Virginia Lee, author of *The House that Tai Ming Built,* in an interview on August 2, 1970. Virginia

Lee says that she is not so much concerned about being either Chinese or American or Chinese-American or American-Chinese as she is about being human. That's like saying you are a bean, says Frank Chin, one of the millions and billions of beans in the world, and not even a black or yellow bean at that. Where's your identity, then? snaps Frank in his radio-TV trained voice, clear, sure of his diction, eloquent in his delivery, and very much up-to-date with the slang of the young American—a bit hip, perhaps, but his whole manner communicating self-confidence and freedom from inhibition.

And Virginia cuts a figure in many ways just the opposite, and the contrast goes beyond the difference in sex. She is demure, pretty, feminine, her voice seductively soft with an all-American girl's accent which, if you put her behind a curtain, would suggest a willowy blonde whose every gesture and facial expression is cultivated and well calculated to appeal. I have no identity hang-ups, she declares, after first conceding that she has given some thought to the identity problem at one time or another in her life, but that it no longer bothers her.

But there *is* a problem, and it does bother, in different ways, all Asian-American writers. For that matter, the same problem disturbs all sensitive persons, regardless of their ethnic backgrounds. As Buddha so well recognized some twenty-five hundred years ago, before he reaches wisdom, man is never free from anxiety. He is always anxious to get something, or having gotten it, is worried about losing it. All his anxieties and worries result from his desiring something; he suffers because he has desires. And he has desires because he believes he can get something or hold on to something for *himself*. Buddha's formula for ending man's suffering is clear-cut and simple. The idea about one's self is an illusion, Buddha says, and the moment you can forget about yourself, you are already free. But we, being somewhat less than Buddha, cannot forget our "self"; hence the search—the perpetual search.

In the quiet and contented home of a one-culture family—such as surrounded the young Buddha in Nepal—the search is for an answer to who am I and what am I supposed to do and what does it mean to do and be such-and-such. The bicultural or cross-cultural person's problem is not any more profound, perhaps, but is that much more accentuated and brought to the fore by the dramatic forces, both surface and hidden, that operate on his experience.

To begin with the more obvious, there is the cultural, ethnic, social, and even political confrontation which often painfully victimizes and scars a bicultural person. In his autobiography, *Journey to Washington,* Daniel Inouye witnesses the rape of Pearl Harbor, and it drives him to become fiercely loyal to America, to throw himself repeatedly at the U.S. Army until he is accepted. He leaves an arm behind in the European theater. But he does so with the memory of how the haole (white) American boys at his Hawaiian high school have humiliated him as a "Jap."

Toshio Mori romanticizes the relocation-center experience in his short stories and lives through World War II retaining his faith in this land of opportunity, but a tinge of sentimental nostalgia about his old Japanese village keeps him superimposing the image of Yokohama on his identification with San Leandro, California, where his parents had settled. And there are other vividly told stories about many Japanese-Americans torn between two ethnic, cultural, and political loyalties—so violently torn that it will be a long time before the survivors can feel whether they are alive or dead. For much of them is dead and perhaps can never be revived.

The World War II relocation-camp experience was painful. The United States government ordered thousands of first-, second-, and even third-generation Japanese-Americans to leave their homes, abandon their businesses, and crowd into temporary quarters set up in places like the Tanforan racetrack near San Francisco and at Topaz, Utah, with very little advance warning. No less painful, however, was the earlier immigrants' suffering from racial discrimination at the hands of white Americans—the Bret Hartes, and the Kearneys, and the nondescript and unnamed neighborhood white boys who chanted "Ching Chong Chinaman" and "Fat Jap." [Bret Harte was a poet-journalist who referred to Chinese immigrants of the California gold-rush days as "the yellow heathens." Denis Kearney led a workingmen's protest movement, in the late nineteenth century, which opposed Chinese labor.] Time and gradual sociocultural enlightenment have modified much of the bitter hatred, but the scars are there to remind many Asian-Americans of an identity somehow separate from the mainstream of the white Americans.

In a less damaging but equally provocative way ethnic consciousness continues to be driven home to an Asian-American. When Lawson Inada, a third-generation Japanese-American poet from Fresno, California, courts his brunette wife in Iowa, he is eyed by the ogling townspeople and country people and is frequently gnawed, or perhaps just nibbled, by his memory of the Massachusetts schoolchildren who whispered behind his back, "Look, a Jap teacher, a Jap teacher. . . ." Even a much sweeter sentiment can be provocative. When Jeff Chan, now teaching Asian-American literature at San Francisco State University, marries a white American girl, her folks go out of their way to be nice to him, taking him in as even more than a part of the family, and dote on his first child. But this serves to point up the ironic rejection demonstrated by his father, a totally Americanized and successful dentist who, without meaning to, reduces his communication with Jeff to zero.

On this level an Asian-American is reminded of his difference from a white American. Some Asian-Americans, including Virginia Lee, resent the difference, particularly in those moments when they embrace the American ideal of "regardless of race, religion, or national origin." Others, including Frank Chin, welcome it as something that sets them apart from the amorphous middle-class values of the "average American."

But the problem doesn't end there. Lawson Inada is, culturally, no more Japanese than the black or Chicano living next door to his Fresno home. There is a beautiful culture over there, says Inada, but over there across the Pacific, and some day, not now, he may go to Japan and find out about it (just for a year, perhaps, says his wife Janet). Inada agrees with Frank Chin that the Asian cultures exhibited in Virginia Lee's or Toshio Mori's works are at best Asia's past seen through "white" eyes. They are the Asian images constructed and perpetuated by whites through outdated school textbooks; Chin and Inada have very little to do with them. They are the images of the soft exquisiteness of Chinese jade and the tranquil serenity of a Japanese miniature garden, of the meek, the harmonious, the family-bound and earth-bound, the wise, the introverted, the withdrawn. . . . Virginia Lee says, But aren't these still the majority of the Chinatown inhabitants? The rebellious and discontented, the Chinese hippies, she says, aren't they a very small minority in the minority community? But you are perpetuating the stereotype again, protests Frank Chin, and I want to do just the opposite; I want to torpedo the stereotype.

The rebellion against the stereotype is a real and serious undertaking of these Asian-American writers. They admit that they have responded to the impetus of the black movement, but they recognize that their battle is their own, long overdue. They want Asian-Americans to be liked as they are: human beings with qualities of dignity and beauty, who happen to have skin of different hue, hair darker and straighter, speech accents uniquely their own. They want white Americans to accord respect to these traits without distorting them, coloring them, or romanticizing them. They want white Americans to see beauty in the brown and yellow, and respond to their language, Asian-American language, to its metaphors that may seem quaint or ungrammatical by a white American standard but that sensitively reflect their unique experience and mirror their world.

Above all, they want no more Oriental-houseboy image, no more quaint and exotic curio image, no more conversation-piece image, to be superimposed on them. Asian-American men want their masculinity recognized and responded to, fully and equally, by the white American female, and even more important, recognized and *respected* by the white American male. That's why you see the kind of symbolism developed in my new verses and stories, says Samuel Tagatac, a thirty-year-old Filipino poet brought up in southern California. He wants to reinstate the full-blooded human voice in his writing, the writing of a Filipino-American who has been culturally emasculated along with the Chinese- and Japanese-American for over one hundred years.

Of course, if Frank Chin and Virginia Lee represent two drastically different Asian-American world views, there are also other Asian-Americans whose search for identity has taken varied turns. The refreshing sensitivity in Shawn Wong's poems that speak in quite universal terms of man's joy and sorrow really reveals very little that is Asian-American; but he is writing to isolate blocks of his complex experiences and feelings, hoping to intensify and clarify them through the act of isolating them on paper, and ultimately to see more and know more of himself, an Asian-American. These verses must be me, Shawn Wong says, and if I have not ceased writing them, it means there is still more of me that cries to be written down and perceived, and I sense that there will be more and more of the Asian-American (that's me) emerging from my lines as time goes by.

And Oscar Peñaranda of the Filipino-American literature program at San Francisco State University, having spent more years of his life here than the thirteen he spent in the Philippines, expresses yet another common concern of a bicultural writer. Peñaranda has been trying to write about his Filipino experience in a language acquired in America, but he refuses to be categorized as an "Asian-American." His struggle is not so much one of identity as one of integrating content with form; he knows that the form of his writing is also its content. Like C. Y. Lee (author of *Flower Drum Song,* a novel of the 1950s), Peñaranda feels no identity crisis, although Lee sees the problem in reverse. You people born in this country, says C. Y. Lee, ought to have no problem being assimilated into the American culture. Lee seems to feel that it is people like him who should be living through a perpetual identity crisis because they are Asian, typically and totally Asian, and yet are totally uprooted now in an *alien* country.

But the identity crisis is upon writers like Frank Chin and Lawson Inada, who hate the word *assimilation.* As Frank Chin sees it, C. Y. Lee can write without inhibition because he has adopted the white American medium and he knows he is Chinese, period. While Chin, speaking of himself, declares, "I am neither Chinese nor American; I'm a Chinaman."

BIBLIOGRAPHY

Fiction and poetry

Chang, Diana. *The Frontiers of Love.* New York: Random, 1956.
_____. *A Passion for Life.* New York: Random, 1961.
_____. *A Woman of Thirty.* New York: Random, 1959.
Chu, Louis. *Eat a Bowl of Tea.* New York: Stuart, 1961.
Chuang, Hua. *Crossings.* New York: Dial Pr., 1969.

Gonzalez, N.V.M. *Selected Stories.* Denver: Swallow Pr., 1964.

Inada, Lawson. *Before the War: Poems as They Happened.* New York: Morrow, 1971.

Kim, Richard. *The Innocent.* Boston: Houghton, 1968.

_____. *The Martyred.* New York: Braziller, 1964.

Lee, Virginia. *The House that Tai Ming Built.* New York: Macmillan, 1963.

Li, Chin Y. *Flower Drum Song.* New York: Farrar, 1957.

Mori, Toshio. *Yokohama, California.* Caldwell, Idaho: Caxton, 1949.

Nixon, Lucille, and Tana, Tomoe. *Sounds from the Unknown.* Denver: Swallow Pr., 1963.

Noguchi, Yone. *The Selected Poems of Yone Noguchi.* Somerville, Mass.: Humphries, n.d.

Okada, John. *No-No Boy.* Rutland, Vermont: Tuttle, 1957.

Villa, Jose Garcia. *Selected Poems and New.* New York: Obolensky, 1958.

Yamamoto, Hisaye. Many short stories published in *Kenyon Review, Harper's,* and *Partisan Review.*

Nonfiction

Chin, Frank. "Food for all His Dead." In Susan Cahill and Michele F. Cooper, eds., *The Urban Reader.* Englewood Cliffs, N.J.: Prentice-Hall, 1971.

Chu, Daniel, and Chu, Samuel. *Passage to the Golden Gate.* New York: Zenith Books, 1967.

Girdner, A., and Loftis, A. *The Great Betrayal: The Evacuation of the JapaneseAmericans during World War II.* New York: Macmillan, 1971.

Hosokawa, Bill. *Nisei: The Quiet Americans.* New York: Morrow, 1969.

Inouye, Daniel K. *Journey to Washington.* Englewood Cliffs, N.J.: Prentice-Hall, 1967.

Kitano, Harry H. L. *Japanese Americans: The Evolution of a Subculture.* Englewood Cliffs, N.J.: Prentice-Hall, 1969.

Kitigawa, Diasuke. *Issei and Nisei: The Internment Years.* New York: Seabury, 1967.

Knox, George, and Lawton, Harry, eds. *Analecta: Selected Writings of Sadakichi Hartmann.* New York: Herder and Herder, 1970.

Kung, S. W. *The Chinese in American Life.* Seattle: Univ. of Washington Pr., 1962.

Lasker, Bruno. *Filipino Immigration to Continental United States and to Hawaii.* Chicago: Univ. of Chicago Pr., 1931.

Lee, Rose Hum. *The Chinese in the United States of America.* Hong Kong: Hong Kong Univ. Pr., 1960.

Lowe, Pardee. *Father and Glorious Descendant.* Boston: Little, 1943.

Okimoto, Daniel K. *American in Disguise.* New York: John Weatherhill, 1971.

Okubo, Mine. *Citizen 13660.* New York: AMS Pr., 1946.

Sandmeyer, Elmer Clarence. *The Anti-Chinese Movement in California.* Urbana: Univ. of Illinois Pr., 1939.

Sone, Monica Ito. *Nisei Daughter.* Boston: Atlantic Monthly Pr., 1953.

Spicer, Edward Holland, and others. *Impounded People: Japanese Americans in the Relocation Centers.* Tucson: Univ. of Arizona Pr., 1969.

Sung, Betty Lee. *Mountain of Gold.* New York: Macmillan, 1967. (Also published as *The Story of the Chinese in America.* New York: Collier, 1971.)

Thomas, D. S., and Nishimoto, R. S. *Spoilage: Japanese American Evacuation and Resettlement.* Berkeley: Univ. of California Pr., 1969.

Wong, Jade Snow. *Fifth Chinese Daughter.* New York: Harper, 1945.

Black Literature and Changing Attitudes: Does It Do the Job?

Ernest R. Page

> Whatever else may be said about the relationship of literature to life, so far as the black man is concerned, literature is a weapon, has always been, and will continue to be in the foreseeable future.[1]

In the main, English teachers who purport to change students' negative racial attitudes towards black Americans employ black literature as their catalyst. That is, most English teachers are confident that if black literature is read by students the literature will change or neutralize white students' negative attitudes towards black Americans. Some questions, however, need to be raised. Does black literature, in fact, change the racial attitudes of readers? If so, to what degree? If not, what variables, in relationship to or divorced from black literature, *do* promote a positive metamorphosis in the racial attitudes of students?

Further, what *are* the "negative racial attitudes" that concerned English teachers attempt to change? Most Americans, at one time or another, have heard and even used jokes, stories, sayings, words, dialects, and physical behaviors based in stereotypical, ethnic, and racist thinking, the kind upon which Don Rickles humorously capitalizes and which led to the demise of Earl Butz. A more serious mode of "negative racial attitudes" is reflected in the following interview and is illustrative of what some Americans were thinking and saying about blacks at the end of the last decade, for example. Excerpted from Angus Campbell's sociologically-oriented volume *White Attitudes toward Black People*,[2] the responses, as Campbell qualified, represented the negative extreme in the white population sampled in his 1968 study of fifteen American cities:

> *What do you think was the main cause of these disturbances?*
> Nigger agitators. Martin Luther King and that black bastard Carmichael."
>
> *Have the disturbances helped or hurt the cause of Negro rights?*
> "Hurt. Whites are starting to wise up [to] what a danger these people can be. They are going to be tough from now on. People are fed up with giving in and giving them everything their little black hearts want."

What do you think the city government could do to keep a disturbance from breaking out here?

"Ship them all back to Africa. Lock up all the agitators and show them we mean business."

Would you go along with a program of spending more money for jobs, schooling and housing for Negroes . . . or would you oppose it?

"I'd oppose it. They're getting too much already. If they want something they can damn well work for it. The government would just waste the money anyway."

What is it about Negroes that makes them have worse jobs, education and housing?

"They're lazy and stupid."

Would you say that white people have a right to keep Negroes out of their neighborhoods if they want to or that Negroes have a right to live wherever they can afford?

"Negroes don't have a right to live wherever they want. They would always try to be in with the whites even though they'd be a lot happier by themselves. I'm not against Negroes, mind you, they should have decent housing, good housing as they can afford, just as good as white houses if they can pay for it, but they just shouldn't be in white neighborhoods. It's not fair to either side and would just cause trouble. Whites can make it clear Negroes aren't welcome in the neighborhood. They can make the climate unfriendly and see to it that no one sells to a Negro family. They run down property, make a mess and lots of noise and commotion. The real estate value goes down. Nobody in their right mind would have them in the neighborhood."

That finishes the interview. Is there anything you would like to add to any of the subjects we've discussed?

"I just want to say that I don't have anything against Negroes as long as they don't get pushy and stay in their place. One of my best buddies is a nigger so I don't have anything against them." (pp. 2-3)

Ku Klux Klanner? South Bostonian? Or next door neighbor? Actually, the interviewee was a thirty-one-year-old single male, the son of a North Carolina tobacco sharecropper, who had two years of college and worked as a traveling salesman in California. Peppered with practically every possible negative cliché about blacks, those racial attitudes were not, one hopes, those of the bulk of the white majority in 1968. Like the tip of the iceberg phenomenon, though, maybe there were and still are Americans who, in varying degrees, think, feel, and speak about blacks like the "one of my best buddies is a . . ." spouting salesman.

For those who believe that the extreme in negative racial thinking and speaking has disappeared, the following is taken from the Sunday, November 16, 1975, *Los Angeles Times.* In an article entitled "Blacks, Ethnic Whites Share Common Foes," author Michael Novak cites the following response of a resident of Rosedale, New York, where the home of a black had been recently bombed, to the question of why he and others wanted to keep blacks out. He replied with the following:

> "If you really want to know, they're basically uncivilized. Wherever they go, the crime rate goes up, neighborhoods fall apart, whites have to leave. Well, we don't share their lifestyle and we're not going to live with them. Rosedale is the last white stronghold in this city and nobody's going to push us out. We're going to keep it crime-free, clean and white. If that's racism, make the most of it." (Part VIII, p. 3)

With the emergence of black Americans as an ethnic force following the urban unrest of the middle and late sixties and coupled chronologically, as the movement was, with the increased popularity of English electives and mini-courses, it seemed to make sense that teaching black literature would provoke and promote racial attitude change in readers. Prompted, too, by mandates, legislation, and recommendation, at the international (UNESCO), national (NCTE), and state (Pennsylvania Department of Education) levels, English teachers, as well as social studies teachers, especially in secondary schools, were requested to teach about black Americans through their literature, history, culture, and traditions.

At the global level, for example, UNESCO on June 24, 1968, convened in Paris to discuss the topic and subsequently publish the results of the *Meeting of Experts on Educational Methods Designed to Combat Racial Prejudice*.[3] In the final report, Madeleine Verdière-De Vits of Belgium called for a reform in curricula and related from her own personal teaching experience that it was "perhaps through literature (prose and poetry) that I have had the greatest success in creating a positive attitude towards the combating of racial prejudice in the various continents where I have worked" (p. 55).

At the national level, during a five and a half year period from February 1968 to May 1973, the NCTE, in forty-seven issues of its *English Journal*, published twenty-seven articles centrally and solely focused on the teaching of black literature in English classrooms. Although statements differed quantitatively, qualitatively, and strategically, each writer, to a person, asserted that the teaching of black literature would result in a positive transformation of readers' negative biases and attitudes about black Americans.

At the state level, the Bureau of General and Academic Education of the Pennsylvania Department of Education published a bibliography of resources on racial and ethnic minorities entitled *American Diversity*.[4] In Appendix A of the same publication, David H. Kurtzman, then Superintendent of Public Instruction for Pennsylvania, via a school administrators' memorandum dated August 28, 1968 wrote that:

> These negative stereotypes must be corrected and teachers can no longer pretend that all their students have the common experience and value systems of middle class white Americans.

In order that students may understand the current racial revolution in America, the minority group to receive the most substantial emphasis will be the Afro-American. This content will have immediate relevancy for both black and white. (p. 234)

The three educational agencies cited above agreed that educational materials by and about ethnic groups, particularly blacks, should have proportionate representation in school curricula. If ethnic groups were studied by students, it was assumed that beliefs and concepts which manifest and represent themselves in racism, prejudice, and discrimination would break down and understanding of and compassion for all members of ethnic groups would become more widespread.

In the case of English instructors, naive as many were and still are about blacks, their language, and their literature, teaching *Black Like Me* or *To Sir, with Love* seemed to satisfy those global, national, and statewide dicta. More sophisticated teachers, too, taught under the assumption that if "good" black literature is presented (Baldwin, Cleaver, Cullen, Du Bois, Ellison, Hughes, Toomer, Wright, and many others), negative student feelings and beliefs would change in relation to black Americans.

As a high school teacher of black literature, I believed (and still do believe) that one important function of the school and the English classroom is to expose learners to a variety of cognitive and affective resources that confront and combat ignorance, stereotypical thinking, racism, prejudice, and its correlate, discrimination. It seemed to follow, then, that a rigorous analysis of the ability of black literature to change student negative attitudes towards blacks was fundamental.

Motivated by the need to explore these assumptions, I conducted an experiment which tested whether black literature did, in fact, change students' racial attitudes, at least in this one instance.[5] As a graduate student completing requirements for a Ph.D. degree at the Pennsylvania State University under the tutelage of Professor Edward R. Fagan, I ran a five-week study in a nearly all white high school which involved three "college bound" eleventh-grade classes taught by one female English teacher. Of the three school districts that were asked to permit this experiment to take place in their high schools, only one agreed. The town, with a little over seven thousand inhabitants including a black population of less than eighty, is located in central Pennsylvania.

A Black Literature Package (BLP) consisting of one novel, seven short stories, eight poems, one play, and five portions of autobiographies written by blacks about blacks was created to test whether black literature did change student attitudes (figure 1). Containing twenty-two literary selections in five genres, the BLP was structured as follows: general prefatory note to teacher and students; questions of an introductory nature which prepared the student for the literary piece that followed; directions to the book, page number, and literary selection; questions which focused

Works are listed in the order that students read them. Those selections with an asterisk (*) were deleted if the contents of the package were too numerous for a five-week time span.

NOVEL
Native Son by Richard Wright

SHORT STORIES
"On Being Crazy" by W. E. B. DuBois
"A Summer Tragedy" by Arna Bontemps
"Miss Cynthie" by Rudolph Fisher
"The Only Man on Liberty Street" by William Melvin Kelly
"Bright and Morning Star" from *Uncle Tom's Children* by R. Wright
"In Darkness and Confusion" by Ann Petry
*"Neighbors" by Diane Oliver

POETRY
"We Wear the Mask" by Paul Laurence Dunbar
"The Song of the Smoke" by W. E. B. DuBois
"Yet Do I Marvel" by Countee Cullen
"If We Must Die" by Claude McKay
"Minstrel Man" by Langston Hughes
"Dream Variation" by Langston Hughes
"Birmingham Sunday" by Langston Hughes
*"The Death of Nick Charles" by Imamu Baraka (Leroi Jones)

DRAMA
A Raisin in the Sun by Lorraine Hansberry

AUTOBIOGRAPHY
Narrative of the Life of Frederick Douglass, An American Slave (Chapters I, VI, VII, and X) by Frederick Douglass
"The Ethics of Living Jim Crow: An Autobiographical Sketch" from *Uncle Tom's Children* by Richard Wright
*"Autobiographical Notes" from *Notes of a Native Son* by J. Baldwin
The Autobiography of Malcolm X (Chapter One "Nightmare") by Malcolm X
*"I'll Never Escape the Ghetto" from *Ebony* by Stanley Sanders

The following volumes contain some of the above selections:
On Being Black, edited by Charles T. Davis and Daniel Walden, Fawcett: 1970.
Black Voices, edited by Abraham Chapman, Mentor: 1968.
Native Son by Richard Wright, Harper & Row: 1940.
A Raisin in the Sun by Lorraine Hansberry, Signet: 1958.
NOTE: "On Being Crazy" and "Bright and Morning Star" were presented in mimeograph form.

Fig. 1: Black Literature Package: A Content Listing by Literary Types

the discussion with peers in small groups or guided the teacher to lead large group discussions following the reading of a selection; and three written essay exercises which either preceded or followed a selection.

Black literary works were selected and included in the BLP because they conformed to and coincided with the definitions and dimensions of the Multifactor Racial Attitude Inventory (MRAI), the 120-item instrument used to measure student attitudes in the experiment. Authored by Brigham, Woodmansee, and Cook at the University of Colorado's Institute of Behavioral Science after years of extensive studies and experimentation, the MRAI contains twelve separate subscales which makes the instrument multidimensional in its ability to measure racial attitudes. Stuart W. Cook, one of the three responsible for the MRAI, in a personal telephone conversation with me on March 6, 1974, said that in his own research he used both subscale scores and total scores concomitantly as indicators of racial attitude. In this study, both total and subscale scores were used and analyzed. The twelve MRAI subscales include the following: Integration-Segregation Policy, Gradualism, Local Autonomy, Private Rights, Interracial Marriage, Approaches to Black Progress, Acceptance in Close Personal Relationships, Acceptance in Status-Superior Relationships, Ease in Interracial Contacts, Derogatory Beliefs, Black Inferiority, and Black Superiority.

Without getting into the statistical ramifications of the experiment like Bartlett's test for homogeneity of variance, analysis of variance with repeated measures, the Tukey Wholly Significant Difference test, Cronbach's Coefficient Alpha Index of Reliability, and Pearson Product Moment Correlation Coefficient, I will simply note that this experiment involved one female teacher, sixty-five male and female students, one of whom was black, in three eleventh-grade classes which were equivalent, i. e., not significantly different, in IQ and reading comprehension. To monitor and control the teacher variable and to feature as much as possible the black literature, one class experienced the BLP in a self-paced, individualized manner. That is, the students in this experimental group used the BLP alone or in small groups, but never in conjunction with the teacher. Rarely did the teacher speak to this class in a large group situation. A second class used the BLP in a more "traditional" fashion. Here the teacher gave directions, asked questions, led discussions, made assignments, and generally functioned as she would teaching any unit on literature. In each of the two classes, all materials, activities, and literary content were exactly the same. A third class, the control group, received no black literature treatment. During the five-week experimental period, this class, which contained the only black male student in the study, experienced a "regular course of instruction in language arts." That is, the teacher taught the material the district's curriculum guide recommended in the manner that she normally would teach a homogeneously grouped, "academically able" English class. Along with random, unannounced visits by me to each of the three classes twice and three times a week, the sixty-five students each kept a weekly journal. The reasoning behind student journals was an attempt to determine when attitude change took place or to determine why change did not occur. No specific guidelines were given for the weekly journals. The students were simply told to write honestly about anything that was of concern to them.

Findings, based on the information generated and gathered in this study, suggest that: (1) black literature read by eleventh graders for five weeks either independent of or in conjunction with the teacher did not change negative racial attitudes to positive racial attitudes as measured by the Multifactor Racial Attitude Inventory and its twelve subscales; (2) state legislation which mandated teaching about blacks may have promoted responses in students different from the ones intended; i.e., student attitudes may have become more negative rather than more positive as a result of concentrated instruction and materials about black Americans; (3) students who experienced concentrated exposure to black literature may have developed polarized "anti" and "pro" attitudes about blacks which frustrated the positive effects of the black literature; (4) students in large and small group discussions and in weekly journal entries suggested that black literature should be taught in its chronological, historical, literary, and artistic settings within American literature. (5) Then writers of articles which appear in the *English Journal, College English,* and other English/language arts oriented publications need to temper their promotional recommendations of black literature as an effective agent for changing negative racial attitudes of readers in light of the findings derived from this study.

In fact, the intentions and results of this exercise were not and should not be used to demean, denigrate, and relegate black literature to secondary or tertiary strata within school classrooms and curricula. Black literature, as well as Asian-American, Chicano, Italian-American, Jewish-American, Native-American, Puerto Rican, and other ethnic literatures, must be incorporated within the fabric of the American literary tradition and read by all students because it is effective, stimulating, and insightful reading. However, if ethnic literatures, and especially black literature, continue to be taught using the rationale that the reading of these literatures changes racial and ethnic attitudes of learners, more evidence than is extant supporting such questionable reasoning needs to be developed. If English teachers believe in and wittingly attempt to implement student racial attitude change *via* classroom instruction, it is imperative that materials, methods, media, activities, and strategies of instruction need to be identified, stated, and tested in a rigorous fashion. English teachers will then begin to address themselves and their students to the single most destructive domestic difficulty of the present century, as W. E. B. Du Bois prophetically asserted at the turn of the century, the problem of the color line. Then, and only then, too, will the literature of the black American function truly as a weapon against racist thinking and attitudes.

NOTES

1. D. Alexander Boyd, Charles J. Evans, Ernece B. Kelly, and Sophia P. Nelson, "Literary Sources in Afro-American Literature," in Ernece B. Kelly, ed., *Searching for America* (Urbana, Ill.: National Council of Teachers of English, 1972).
2. Angus Campbell, *White Attitudes toward Black People* (Ann Arbor, Mich.: Institute for Social Research, 1971), pp.2-3.
3. Madeleine Verdière-De Vits, *Meeting of Experts on Educational Methods Designed to Combat Racial Prejudice* (Paris: UNESCO House, 1968).
4. David H. Kurtzman, "Appendix A, School Administrator's Memorandum No. 113," in Elizabeth S. Haller, ed., *American Diversity: A Bibliography* (Philadelphia: Pennsylvania Dept. of Education, 1969).
5. Ernest R. Page, "An Analysis of Racial Attitude Change in Eleventh Grade Students Using a Black Literature Package" (Ph.D. diss., Pennsylvania State Univ., 1974).

The Literary Impact of Jewish Culture

Joseph Mersand

One of the most interesting educational innovations in the last decade on both the secondary and college levels has been the interest in the literary contributions of American writers of Jewish descent. According to *Jewish Studies in American Colleges and Universities,*[1] there are over 250 institutions of higher learning offering such courses. This is a far cry from the turn of the century, when only two institutions—Harvard and Columbia—offered courses dealing with Jews and Judaism after the Biblical period.[2] Of the number of public high schools in America which have introduced Jewish studies in the past few years there is still no accurate count, but it would be safe to say that they probably number in the hundreds and exist in practically every one of our fifty states.[3]

How times have changed from my own high school days in a prestigious Brooklyn high school from 1920-1924! In all those four years I never heard an American-Jewish author mentioned by any of my English teachers (two of whom were Jewish), and we certainly studied no selections

Reprinted by permission from *English Journal* 64:39-46 (Feb. 1975). Copyright © 1975 by the National Council of Teachers of English.

or read as supplementary books any works by such authors. Of the classics we had our full dose: *The Odyssey,* Stevenson's *Treasure Island,* George Eliot's *Silas Marner,* Charles Dickens, *A Tale of Two Cities,* Shakespeare's *Twelfth Night, A Midsummer Night's Dream* and *Macbeth,* Polgrave's *Golden Treasury* (who knew that his grandfather was a Jew named Meyer Cohen?) and a collection of Long's *American Poems* that had not a single poem by an American Jew.

Was this so because there was no literature by American Jews by 1920? Hardly! Emma Lazarus in her *Songs of a Semite* (1882) had won the praise of major American critics, as she had won the praise for her earlier books from Ralph Waldo Emerson for her *Admetus and Other Poems* (1871). This she had dedicated to "My friend, Ralph Waldo Emerson"! Her engaging contemporary, Adah Isaacs Menken, friend of Dickens, Swinburne, Dumas fils, and one of the outstanding actresses on both the American and British stages of the mid-nineteenth century, in her *Infelicia* (1868) expressed her indignation at the indignities of the treatment of Jews in the notorious Mortara affair in Italy in 1858 as well as her kinship with fellow Jews in several other poems.[4]

By 1912 Mary Antin had written her *Promised Land,* one of the most touching evocations of the gratitude of having escaped from the Russian Pole of Settlement and having been reborn in the new world. Abraham Cohen, who had already written two works of fiction in English at the end of the nineteenth century, *Yekl: A Tale of the New York Ghetto* (1896) and *The Imported Bridegroom and Other Stories of the New York Ghetto* (1898), praised highly by William Dean Howells in the same review with Stephen Crane's *The Red Badge of Courage,* saw the publication in 1917 of *The Rise of David Levinsky*—still one of the most perceptive fictional studies of a Jewish immigrant who drops the customs and ideals of the old country to become an American millionaire. But the pleasure was not unalloyed as he realized toward the end of his life how far he had strayed from the ideals of his forefathers in his worship of the golden calf. A recent paperback reprint has won thousands of new readers after almost half a century of comparative neglect.

By 1920 Fannie Hurst had already been acclaimed as one of the greatest living American short story writers. Anzia Yezierska, another Russian Jewish immigrant, had, by 1919, seen her short story, "The Fat of the Land," declared the best short story in the Edward J. O'Brien collection of that year. Her short story, "Hunger," had appeared a few years later in one of the most popular collections of short stories edited for high school students.[5]

Among American dramatists, Manuel Mordecai Noah and Samuel B. Judah had already written successful plays in the early nineteenth century, although none of them had any Jewish content.[6] Isaac Harby had written some of the most penetrating dramatic criticism of the nineteenth century, as well as three plays.

Among the Jewish dramatists of the 1920s who were achieving distinction were the late S. N. Behrman, whose *The Second Man* (1927) was the first of a series of comedies, the excellence of which lasted for almost forty years; Elmer Rice, whose *On Trial* (1914) inaugurated a distinguished career that lasted half a century; George S. Kaufman, whose *Dulcy* (1921) was the first of a series of comedies which raised him to the very front rank of American writers of comedy.

Edna Ferber did not write about Jewish subjects until the publication of *Fanny Herself* (1917), a study of Fanny Brandeis, a Jewish business woman in a midwestern community. She wrote her first novel, *Dawn O'Hara,* in 1911 and for half a century was among America's leading novelists of American life in its great diversity and dimensions.

By 1919, Robert Nathan, that sensitive stylist and charming storyteller, had already published his first of many novels which are still being added to today almost fifty-five years later. His *Road to Asia* (1935), inspired by the Nazi holocaust, seems amazingly contemporary in the light of Israel's provocations at the hands of her hostile Arab neighbors.

By 1919 Louis Untermeyer, that indefatigable octogenarian and author of over 150 books, had already published his *Modern American Poetry,* which even then contained the works of several American Jewish poets. The list could go on and on, and one would be amazed at the output of American writers of Jewish origin by the 1920s.[7] Yet none of this was even brought to my attention by my English teachers between 1920-24 or by my college teachers from 1924-31, when I completed my studies for my doctorate. It was indicative of the times that when I was searching for a topic for specialization for my doctoral thesis, I was discouraged by my friendly German professor from pursuing studies in Yiddish language and literature for two reasons: (1) None were offered in my alma mater; (2) Even if I could pursue such studies in a nearby institution, there would be no one in my alma mater who could advise and guide me. The Jewish professors in American German departments in 1929 could be counted on fewer than the fingers of one's left hand!

American Jewish Writing in the 1930s

When I returned to my own high school in 1931 to begin a teaching career of twelve years there, things had improved somewhat. H. C. Schweiker's *Short Stories* contained at least two stories definitely of Jewish content: Anzia Yezierska's "Hunger," and Fannie Hurst's "Ice Water, Pl_____!", and one by Edna Ferber, "Meadowlark," although not of Jewish interest. A collection of *Representative Plays* by John Galsworthy contained *Loyalties,* a study of subtle anti-Semitism originally written in 1922 and subsequently made into a film with Basil Rathbone as the Jew, Ferdy de Levis, represented by John Galsworthy in a not too complimentary manner. The list of supplementary reading was by now expanded to include novels and plays by American Jewish writers. How could one possibly attend the theatre of the 1930s without seeing plays by Leopold Atlas, George Sklar, Michael Blankfort, Michael Gold, Ben Hecht, S. N. Behrman, George S. Kaufman, Clifford Odets and a veritable host of minor dramatists? Many sons and daughters of East European immigrants of the 1880s and early 1900s were beginning to write about various aspects of American Jewish life in many parts of our vast country.

Meyer Levin, whose first two novels—*Reporter* (1929) and *Frankie and Johnnie* (1930)—had no Jewish content, hit his stride in *Jehuda* (1931) and *The Golden Mountain* (1932) after he had lived in Palestine a while. In *The Old Bunch,* which became a best-seller and won vast critical acclaim in 1937, he pictured with almost Breughel-like verisimilitude a group of young Chicago Jewish men and women, who were beginning to lose their Jewishness as they assumed many of the traits of their gentile neighbors, not always the most commendable ones. Writing exclusively about that section of Brooklyn known as Williamsburg, Daniel Fuchs wrote three novels that might be compared to genre paintings of the Dutch schools: *Summer in Williamsburg* (1939), Homage to Blenholt (1936), and *Low Company* (1937), later filmed as *The Gangster.* Allen Guttmann, a most perceptive critic of American Jewish writers, says of Fuchs, "Daniel Fuchs was the first to take apart the world of Sholom Aleichem's Kasrilevka and to reconstruct it on the sidewalks of New York."[8]

The Generation Gap

As the children of East European immigrants became more assimilated, they clashed inevitably with their parents; and many short stories and novels discussed this theme. Although published in 1934 and hardly noticed for almost a quarter of a century until reissued by Avon Books as a best-selling paperback, Henry Roth's *Call It Sleep* is still the classic study of second-generation childhood. It has been called by Guttmann, "the most Freudian of the great American novels."[9] Isaac Rosenfeld's *Passage from Home* (1946), his only novel, deals with the same theme.

Intermarriage and Jewish Novelists

With assimilation came intermarriage, and quite a few worthy novels were written by Jewish writers on that subject including: Myron Kaufman's *Remember Me to God* (1957); Barbara Probst Solomon's *The Best of Life* (1960); Norman Katkov's *Eagle at My Eyes* (1948); Samuel Yellen's *The Wedding Band* (1961).

Some of them wrote on the insoluble problems due to intermarriage. Others took a more optimistic view, such as Katkov's *Eagle At My Eyes.* Yellen's *The Wedding Band* deals with intermarriage and its results from the point of view of the children.

Jews and the Depression

The depression of 1929-39 stimulated a whole school of Jewish writers to examine the American way of life and to seek both an explanation for our sad state of economic and social affairs and some solutions. Some chose the way of the left in both novels and plays. Michael Gold, an avowed Communist, in *Jews without Money* (1930) presented with merciless reality a set of poor Jewish characters victimized by the depression. Albert Halper, in his *Union Square* (1933), *The Foundry* (1934), and *The Chute* (1937), attempted to depict the effects of the economic chaos upon people in various occupations. Among the Jewish dramatists, George Sklar and Albert Maltz in *Peace on Earth* (1933) and *Stevedore* (1934) portrayed vividly basic problems of their time. Clifford Odets in *Waiting for Lefty* (1935), *Awake and Sing* (1935), and *Paradise Lost* (1935), depicted New York Jewish characters affected by the depression and their attempts to find a way out. (Only recently *Awake and Sing* was given a superb television performance on the stations of the Public Broadcasting System with such stars as Eli Wallach and Sam Groom in important roles.) Many of these works by American Jewish novelists and dramatists had mostly propaganda value but they performed an important function in their own day in making their audiences aware of some of the fundamental causes of the economic collapse and in suggesting some ways out of the economic and social morass.

Jewish Novelists Critical of Jewishness

Beginning in the 1930s, a new type of novel appeared in which the Jewish protagonist was anything but admirable. In fact, such novels were loudly condemned from pulpits and in the journals of American Jewish organizations. One such novel was Jerome Weidman's *I Can Get It for You Wholesale* (1937). It was the saga of a conniving Jew who began as a delivery boy in a cloak and suit business and hustled his way up the financial ladder by stepping on everyone who stood in his way. Budd Schulberg's *What Makes Sammy Run?* (1941) dealt with the same kind of unscrupulous Jewish hustler who reaches the top of the ladder in Hollywood, marries a gorgeous gentile, only to find her and another gentile fornicating in the marriage bed on the wedding night. Philip Roth in his *Portnoy's Complaint* (1969) follows in this tradition, thirty years after *I Can Get It for You Wholesale.*

Jewish Writers on Non-Jewish Topics

Not all writers of Jewish birth have written about Jewish subjects. Franklin P. Adams, in all of his many books, never touched on a Jewish topic although he lived through the pogroms in Eastern Europe following World War I and the Nazi holocaust. George S. Kaufman in his thirty or so plays, written with a dozen collaborators—many of them Jewish like Moss Hart, Louis Teichman, and Edna Ferber—never took up a Jewish theme; nor, to the best of my recollection, did he ever include a Jewish character of major significance. Arthur Guitenman, born in Austria, never wrote on any Jewish subject in a long career as poet. Edna Ferber, whose first book, *Dawn O'Hara,* appeared in 1911, never included a Jewish character in any of her stories and novels until 1917 in *Fanny Herself.* In *Catcher in the Rye*—for a time the bible of the secondary and college student literary elite—J. D. Salinger reveals nothing about his Jewish background, and it does not emerge until his *Franny and Zooey* (1961) stories. S. N. Behrman, perhaps the greatest master of social comedy America produced, never touched a Jewish subject until *Rain From Heaven* (1934), a book which treats of a German Jewish intellectual who has managed to escape to England. However, in his later years he turned to his Jewish background in his *The Worcester Account,* and in his only novel, written at seventy-five, *Through a Glass Darkly.* In his adaptation of Franz Werfel's *Jacabowsky and the Colonel* (1944), written during World War II, he took up the plight of the little European Jew who has to survive by his wits against the arrogance and superior station in life of the Polish colonel.

Robert Nathan is in a class by himself. Descended from one of the earliest American Jewish families, he began writing fiction in 1919 when *Peter Kindred* appeared. For the past fifty-five years he has written over a score of novels and several volumes of poems. His work was not particularly Jewish in content until his *Road of Ages* appeared in 1935, a tragic story of the expulsion of all the Jews from Europe to a homeland in a wilderness in the Gobi desert. Many of his poems are fierce protests against man's inhumanity to man during the Nazi holocaust.

Anti-Semitism

It is only natural that Jewish writers should treat anti-Semitism in America. Before Arthur Miller became perhaps our outstanding American dramatist of the 1940s and 1950s, he had written *Focus,* a novel condemning the bitter anti-Semitism of the followers of the benighted Father Coghlan, who, from his Shrine of the Little Flower in Detroit, was permitted to preach his violent anti-Semitism over the radio to millions of followers. In his play, *Incident at Vichy* (1964), he concerns himself with the plight of some French Jews at the hands of the Nazis in occupied France during World War II. But in his really significant plays, *All My Sons* (1946) and *Death of a Salesman* (1948), there is no Jewish element whatever.

The anti-Semitism that was to be expected when large numbers of

American Jews served in the U.S. Army in World War II was the subject of Irwin Shaw's novel, *The Young Lions* (1948), Arthur Laurents' *Home of the Brave* (1946), Norman Mailer's *The Naked and the Dead,* and many other short stories and novels. A more subtle kind of anti-Semitism is the subject of Laura Z. Hobson's *Gentlemen's Agreement* (1947), which dealt with the discrimination against Jews in posh hotels. (It was made into a successful film with Gregory Peck as the gentile journalist, turned Jew to discover whether such discrimination really took place.) Bruce Jay Friedman's *Stern* (1962) "suggested that the relations between Semite and anti-Semite are a great deal more complicated than those between victim and victimizer."[10]

Anti-Semitism of a more subtle variety is described by Ludwig Lewisohn in his biography, *Upstream* (1922), and his novel, *The Island Within* (1928), which also deals with the topics of intermarriage and rediscovery of one's religious heritage.

Bernard Malamud, the Jewish content of whose novels could be discussed under many categories, dealt with the anti-Semitism engendered by the notorious Mendel Beilis case in Russia in 1912 in his moving novel, *The Fixer* (1966).

If space were available, I could expand upon many other facets of the literary impact of Jewish culture.[11] I have tried to give my own interpretation based on my own experiences and reading in the field for well nigh half a century.[12]

But it seemed to me that it would be valuable to know what impact Jewish culture has had upon some of our leading writers of Jewish origin. Among those I will quote are Bernard Malamud, novelist; Charles Angoff, novelist, editor and critic; Irving Malin, distinguished teacher and author of *Jews as Americans*[13] and *Contemporary American-Jewish Literature;*[14] Allen Guttmann, teacher and author of the *Jewish Writer in America;*[15] Max F. Schulz, teacher and author of *Radical Sophistication: Studies in Contemporary Jewish-American Authors;*[16] Joseph C. Landis, Chairman of the Department of Jewish Studies at Queens College of the City University of New York; Max Nadel, former high school English chairman and now consultant to the American Association for Jewish Education and author of *American Jewish Literature for High School Grades;*[17] Dr. Trude Weiss-Rosmarin, nationally known editor of the *Jewish Spectator* for more than a quarter of a century; the distinguished novelist, Robert Nathan; and last, but not least, the distinguished poet, Karl Shapiro.

Bernard Malamud. As for the matter of "The Literary Impact of Jewish Culture," all I can say as I run off to Europe is that the term, or subject, is so grandiose—and imprecise—that it is almost impossible to comment on. If one were to limit the reference to Jewish-American writers of fiction, perhaps it asks, in essence, what do they take from the cultural heritage. Obviously that differs from writer to writer; yet we are all concerned with the fate of man, a humanistic concern. The Jew and his works thus become a *point d'appui:* From his experiences in history we have learned what is due to all men.[18]

Charles Angoff. I believe we are witnessing a great shift in Jewish-American literature, both on the creative side and on the side of the reading public. Writers are beginning to see the sickness and falsehood of so many of the much touted writings of Philip Roth and even Saul Bellow and Malamud. Writers see in these temporary immortals *kalte neshomes* at best and literary demagogues and hucksters at worst. Even *Commentary* has seen through Philip Roth at last. I believe the time is ripe for writers who practice their art in the glorious manner of Sholem Aleichem and Mendele and Peretz, and who know the difference between criticism arising from love and criticism arising from hatred of one's own people. It could well be that we are about to witness the flowering of Jewish-American literature—its final coming of age.[19]

Irving Malin. I find that I'm slightly written out on the subject of the "literary impact of Jewish culture"—I've said things in print so that any statement now would be "too much"—but I still believe that the literary impact has been as great for modern American literature as has any other "movement." Like the Southern writer who must confront his "special case"—and in doing so, create new images of "the South"—the Jewish writer must recreate (or create) his heritage. His is a more difficult task because he cannot point to any one quality—as can the Southerner—and call it "Jewish." He has to "invent being a Jew"—Roth's idea. I maintain that the Jewish writer must decide whether or not he is really Jewish. He must define himself in religious terms. It is too easy to call anyone born a Jew a *Jewish writer.* Only when a Jewish writer confronts his religious heritage can we say that he partakes of Jewish culture. A Jewish writer, like any Jew, must come to terms with orthodox religion. This is not to say that he must retain the old faith—he can recognize his tensions and non-belief in the process. Unless Jewish culture is defined in a specific, religious way, it becomes a relatively weak, vague term denoting anything from bagels to Hadassah to the synagogue itself.[20]

Allen Guttmann. Although Jewish culture has always played a central role in American literature insofar as the Old and New Testaments can be considered products of Jewish culture—which seems reasonable enough as an assumption—the experience of modern Jews did not play a central role until after the Second World War. Jewish culture was important for Broadway and for the mass media of radio and Hollywood, but American novelists and poets were not strongly influenced by Jewish culture until our own time, when Bellow, Mailer, Malamud, Roth and Ginsberg emerged upon the literary scene. John Updike's novel, *Bech,* can be taken as the symbol of this influence. It should, however, be noted that it has been the most Americanized writers who have had the greatest impact. The interactions of Jewish culture and American culture in general have grown so complex that any attempt to describe them is a dangerous as well as an exhilarating task.[21]

Max F. Schulz. If I were to write *Radical Sophistication* now, I would stress some matters that I paid scant, if any, attention to in the book (which actually consists more of separate essays than of a chronologically developed thesis). At any rate, I would now stress (as a result of my continued teaching occasionally of a course in American-Jewish Fiction):

Jewish literature has raised the level of our urban awareness in the past ten years. We all are more cognizant, I think, of just how completely urban is American experience and unquestionably the novels of men like Malamud and Bellow have been responsible for this.

I also think that they have raised our cultural-ethnic awareness. They, of course, have not been the only influence on this phenomenon but they certainly have contributed their share not only as regards a literate public but also I think as regards practicing artists.

I touch, as I recall, on the next point in my book—contributing to the legitimacy of ethnic experience in America—but I would explore and emphasize this point more now. It seems to me that due to their unself-conscious use of Jewish experience in Jewish materials, the Jewish-American novelists have shown how there is no necessity to apologize for what has normally in the past in American experience been considered narrow and inadequate ethnicity; rather they have shown how one can explore the universals of human experience by way of ethnic materials, without having to focus directly on ethnicity. Black American and Chicano writers surely are profiting from this artistic breakthrough of the Jewish-American experience.

I think I would also be more historical—although this probably is not pertinent to the question you put to me—in showing the literary continuity of Jewish (Yiddish) literary tradition, particularly from Sholem Aleichem through I. J. Singer, drawing especially on the comic tradition and the family saga, as a way of demonstrating contemporary Jewish writing's demonstration that family cohesion and traditional values can still be espoused in the face of deteriorating value systems.

The literary impact of Jewish culture has also clearly demonstrated, as many writers have shown, Leslie Fiedler not the least among them, the Jewish nature of man: pathetic yet heroic, fool yet wise, is a fine definition of man not only for all seasons but particularly for the existentialist world of the twentieth century.

As a follow-up of the above, it seems to me that Jewish-American fiction has taught us how to cope with an alienated situation without losing our humor and sympathy, and without losing our essential humanity.[22]

Joseph C. Landis. With the advent of the postwar, post-Auschwitz world, after the disillusionment with ideologies, after one God had failed and another had died, when the sense of man's abandonment and isolation became, if not the prevailing mood, at least the most prominent awareness, a group of second generation writers appeared who could most sensitively respond to that mood, and that awareness. Having grown up during the thirties and having been caught between two cultures—the immigrant Jewish culture which they left behind and the American whose establishment they could not breach—they had themselves become experts in a kind of alienation. The times they faced and the moods were far different from those in which American culture, vigorous and expanding even if sometimes deeply troubled, an aggressive exponent of Christian values and pieties, had burst with devastating impact upon the immigrant enclaves. The world they saw was one in which the Christian values had themselves broken down, a world in a moral shambles in which the central problem for the individual was to construct for himself a moral guide in a time of the perplexed. To build a new social order—the hope of the thirties—seemed neither feasible nor even pertinent. And the emphasis shifted from the indictment of a destructive and exploiting world to the search for an ethic that could bring meaning, dignity, and humanity in a morally corrupt and bankrupt world. It is in this context that the current group of Jewish writers appeared. And because they began, with varying degrees of conscious intention, to draw upon their own past, to rediscover the traditional Jewish ethical heritage, they seemed to acquire the coherence of a movement. In varying degrees they began to reaffirm that ethic which East-European Jewry had inherited, developed, and to an amazing extent lived, the ethic which saw the moral fulfillment of man in the ideal which it referred to as *mentshlekhkayt*. To rehearse these ethical values is to spell out the moral platform of contemporary Jewish writing and to define its essential Jewishness. In the ethic of mentshlekhkayt these writers discovered a life-giving universality in the midst of a death-dealing world; in the assertion of the necessity for man to be a *mentsh* lies the moral impact of contemporary Jewish writing.[23]

Max Nadel. As I see it, the impact of Jewish culture on American literature has been profound, especially in the last two or three decades, largely as a result of the writings of so many Jewish writers. I think that if we put together the work of American Jewish writers, just those who write about the American Jewish experience, we get a complete picture of the Jew in America with his virtues and faults. The American Jew takes his place alongside the Puritan, Protestant, Catholic, black, Southerner, Western heroes and anti-heroes of current literature, the rich and the poor, the noble and the ignoble, the adjusted and the maladjusted, the exploiter and the exploited, as a familiar and typical figure, and frequently, as a result of the skill and genius of the writer, so universalized that he is Jew only incidentally. He becomes like Oedipus and Hamlet, not Greek nor Elizabethan Dane but representative of Man.

Two unique elements, however, color the relationship of recent American Jewish writers to their characters. These are the holocaust and the establishment of Israel. The two events hover over the telling of so many of the stories in some cases in positive ways; in other cases, in negative ways. It is the Job element, the Jesus element, the Bar Kochba element, and the *luftmensch* element that invade the works. The holocaust is the background of Wallant's *The Pawnbroker* and Bellow's *Mr. Sammler's Planet.* Hugh Nissenson's short stories in a number of instances have their setting in an Israel fighting for independence. In a work I recently read, *St. Urbain's Horseman* by Mordecai Richler, in which the Jew is caricatured as cruelly as he is in *Portnoy's Complaint,* the central character is haunted by the holocaust.

The element of wry, sometimes gentle, sometimes grim, humor and the additional element of sentimentalism that pervaded the work of Yiddish writers and writers like Michael Gold and Charles Angoff have given way frequently to better, often savage satire in the work of writers like Philip Roth and Bruce Jay Friedman. But the best of the writers, men like Saul Bellow and Bernard Malamud, have eschewed the sentimentalism without distorting and caricaturing the Jew and his world.

To me the most profound impact on modern literature was made by the work of Franz Kafka. Though Kafka's characters are not Jewish, they bear the stigmas of the Jew; they are alienated, lost in a hostile and absurd world, seeking a place which can be called home, haven, heaven, and never finding it. So much of current fiction and drama show Kafkaesque influences.[24]

Trude Weiss-Rosmarin. As for "The Literary Impact of Jewish Culture" on American literature, I would say that while it is a recent phenomenon, it is of crucial importance and vast dimensions. I think that this impact is properly referred to as the influence of "the Jew as American culture hero." To me, the most amazing aspect of this impact is manifest in the really enthusiastic response of non-Jews to typical *shtetl* Jewish culture, books, to say nothing of I. J. Singer.[25]

Robert Nathan. You are at liberty to quote whatever you please on the subject of Jewishness, but I am afraid that I've neither the time nor the knowledge to write such an article as you mention: The Literary Impact of Jewish Culture—I suppose you mean in the United States; its impact in Europe and Asia is beyond even my vaguest guess. Your subject certainly is interesting, and deserves an entire book; but one would have to know the work of at least a dozen authors and even more poets—and the effect of that work on such things as publishers, prizes, awards, bestsellerdom and critics, to be able to contribute to it.[26]

Karl Shapiro. Your subject is quite staggering and I don't think I can offer much help, except to suggest a couple of things I have written in the past. One is my poem "Israel" which was commissioned for a mass rally in Baltimore for the founding of modern Israel. It is in my *Selected Poems.* The other is an essay called "The Jewish Writer in America" which is in my book called *In Defense of Ignorance.*

I was speaking with a Jewish (American) novelist about "minorities."

I asked him when Jews had stopped being a "minority." In the fifties, he said. I thought the answer was rather pat but true. For example, I no longer feel Jewish in the literary sense, though more Jewish and perhaps fanatically American in the cultural sense. In my mind I equate Jew and American and do not feel any split about it. Anti-Semites are also aware of this kind of consciousness but place a false emphasis on it.

Of course, the impact of Jewish culture on America is one thing and the impact on the world for millenia is another. It is impossible to calculate. Islam and Christianity are by-products of Jewish culture. Even in this present Russia-inspired war, the Arabs are reluctant to turn anti-Semitic (or rather anti-Jew). We are their fathers.

Well, it is too much for me to take on and I admire your courage. I wish you well with your study and want to thank you for asking my opinion.[27]

NOTES

1. Edited by Rabbi Alfred Jospe, National Director, B'nai B'rith Hillel Foundation (Washington: B'nai B'rith Hillel Foundation, 1972).
2. Ibid., p.1.
3. The latest information can be obtained from Max Nadel, consultant to the American Association for Jewish Education, 114 Fifth Avenue, New York, NY 10010.
4. For a fascinating biography of this most unusually talented lady who died young and is buried in Pere Lachaise Cemetery in Paris, see Allen Lesser's *Enchanting Rebel* (Port Washington, N.Y.: Kennikat Pr., 1972).
5. H. C. Schweikert, ed., *Short Stories* (New York: Harcourt, 1936). Originally published in 1925.
6. Noah wrote the *Fortress of Sorrento* and four other plays in 1808 and Judah wrote the *Mountain Torrent* (1830).
7. See the writer's *Traditions in American Literature: A Study of Jewish Authors and Portraits* (1939; reprint ed., Port Washington, N.Y.: Kennikat Pr., 1966).
8. Allen Guttmann, *The Jewish Writer in America: Assimilation and the Crisis of Identity* (New York: Oxford Univ. Pr., 1971), p.45.
9. Ibid., p.50.
10. Ibid., p.100.
11. Joseph Mersand and Frank Griffith, eds., *Eight American Ethnic Plays* (New York: Scribner, 1974).
12. Scripts for four of these programs and study guides, under my editorship, may be ordered from *Anti-Defamation League of B'nai B'rith,* 114 Lexington Avenue, New York, NY 10017.
13. Published in 1965 by the Southern Illinois Univ. Pr.
14. Published in 1973 by the Indiana Univ. Pr.
15. Published in 1972 by the Oxford Univ. Pr.
16. Published in 1969 by the Ohio Univ. Pr.

17. Published in 1973 by the Board of Jewish Education of New York City.
18. Personal letter from Mr. Malamud, dated 6 October 1973.
19. Personal letter from Mr. Angoff dated 3 October 1973.
20. Personal letter from Professor Malin, dated 3 October 1973.
21. Personal letter from Professor Guttmann, dated 13 October 1973.
22. Personal letter from Professor Schulz, dated 12 October 1973.
23. Quoted from the article, "Reflections on American Jewish Writers." by Professor Joseph C. Landis, originally published in the 25th Anniversary *Jewish Book Annual,* pp.144-45, and reprinted with permission of Professor Landis and the editors of the *Jewish Book Annual.*
24. Personal letter from Mr. Nadel, dated 3 October 1973.
25. Personal letter from Dr. Trude Weiss-Rosmarin, dated 7 November 1973.
26. Personal letter from Robert Nathan, dated 31 October 1973.
27. Personal letter from Mr. Shapiro, dated 15 October 1973.

ADDITIONAL READINGS ABOUT JEWS AND THEIR CONTRIBUTIONS TO AMERICAN LITERATURE

Alter, Robert. *After the Tradition: Essays on Modern Jewish Writing.* New York: Dutton, 1969.
Balakian, Nona and Simmons, Charles. *The Creative Present: Notes on Contemporary American Fiction.* Garden City, N.Y.: Doubleday, 1963.
Bambaugh, Jonathan. *The Landscape of Nightmare: Studies in the Contemporary American Novel.* New York: New York Univ. Pr., 1965.
Bryant, Jerry H. *The Open Decision—The Contemporary American Novel and Its Intellectual Background.* New York: Free Pr., 1970.
Burgess, Anthony. *The Novel Now—A Student's Guide to Contemporary Fiction.* London: Faber and Faber, 1967.
Fiedler, Leslie A. *The New in the American Novel.* New York: Henzl Pr., 1959.
French, Warren, ed. *The Fifties: Fiction, Poetry, Drama.* DeLand, Fla.: Everett/Edwards, 1971.
Guttmann, Allen. *The Jewish Writer in America—Assimilation and the Crisis of Identity.* New York: Oxford Univ. Pr., 1971.
Hassan, Ihab. *Radical Innocence: Studies in the Contemporary American Novel.* Princeton, N.J.: Princeton Univ. Pr., 1961.
Liptzin, Solomon. *The Jew in American Literature.* New York: Bloch, 1966.
Malin, Irving. *Jews and Americans.* Carbondale: Southern Illinois Univ. Pr., 1965.
———. *Contemporary American-Jewish Literature.* Bloomington, Ind.: Indiana Univ. Pr., 1973.
Schulz, Max F. *Radical Sophistication: Studies in Contemporary Jewish American Novelists.* Athens, Ohio: Ohio Univ. Pr., 1969.
Sherman, Bernard. *The Invention of the Jew—Jewish American Education Novels (1916-1964).* New York: Yoseloff, 1969.
Teller, Judd L. *Strangers and Natives—The Evolution of the American Jew from 1921 to the Prsent.* New York: Doubleday, 1968.

Part 7

Media in the Global Village

As electrically contracted, the globe is no more than a village. Electric speed in bringing all social and political functions together in a sudden implosion has heightened human awareness of responsibility to an intense degree. It is this implosive factor that alters the position of the Negro, the teenager, and some other groups. They can no longer be *contained,* in the political sense of limited association. They are now *involved* in our lives, as we in theirs, thanks to the electric media.

The young people who have experienced a decade of TV have naturally imbibed an urge toward involvement in depth that makes all the remote visualized goals of usual culture seem not only unreal but irrelevant. . . . It is the total involvement in all-inclusive *nowness* that occurs in young lives via TV's mosaic image. . . . The TV child cannot see ahead because he wants involvement, and he cannot accept a fragmentary and merely visualized goal or destiny in learning or in life.

Marshall McLuhan[1]

It is impossible to assess precisely the full impact of the electronic media upon the world of today's teenagers. In the passage quoted above, McLuhan stresses the role television has played in creating a desire for involvement in what he terms an "all-inclusive nowness." Countless others have seen television in a more negative light, as the villain responsible for creating a nation of nonverbal "videots." Surely the progressive and steady declines in verbal and quantitative test scores of entering college freshmen testify to a decline in the analytic intellectual powers of the young, and many are convinced that this decline reflects their involvement in nonprint media to the neglect of reading. Those of us who grew up in a print-oriented culture must lament this loss, at the same time realizing it is fruitless to blame the media for society's collective failure to make intelligent use of their immense power as educational tools.

In "Zen and the Art of English Teaching," G. Lynn Nelson draws upon the research of Robert Ornstein into the specialized functions of the left and right hemispheres of the brain as a basis for criticizing our culture's "almost exclusively left-brained approach to perception" and consequent failure to develop the "intuitive, imaginative, artistic perceptions" of the right side. He describes in detail some teaching techniques designed to help cultivate "right-brain" potentialities. His emphasis on developing right-hemisphere capacities almost eclipses his closing observation that the goal of education is "the meaningful merging of both right- and left-hemisphere modes of perception." As a more recent researcher has observed, ". . . there is thinking that exists without language, thinking that precedes language, and thinking that surpasses it," but the whole brain is involved in such processes.[2]

Turning from the topic of media in general to the particular medium of the comic strip, "Spider-Man: Superhero in the Liberal Tradition" by Salvatore Mondello demonstrates how this comic superhero has "helped to shape and reflect the American character. . . ." Mondello draws a rather startling parallel between the influence of the Spider-Man comics and that of the McGuffey readers and the *New England Primer* of earlier times. He also explores why Spider-Man has appealed so strongly to the young and why he has been able to master technology. Remembering Stevenson's essay on "Constructing Useful Realities," readers may want to consider how Mondello's thoughts relate to Stevenson's ideas on the uses of popular culture.

William Blake Tyrrell in " 'Star Trek' as Myth and Television as Myth Maker" speculates on the phenomenon of "Star Trek" as it illustrates the power of television. He explains how "Star Trek" adopts the "Western myth" of the frontier, transposing it to space. After defining myth and expressing its power, he shows how the program was able, by using the "intimate" quality of television, to bring "revitalized mythic narratives . . . directly to the emotional needs of the viewer. . . ." One of these needs was for "the confidence and triumph of the American past," which "Star Trek" satisfied "by disguising our past as our future. . . ." His detailed exposition of the mythic theme of paradise lends credence to his conclusion that " 'Star Trek' offers the comfort of religion" to a generation much in need of it.

Many threads of thought in previous essays are echoed in *"Star Wars:*

Nostalgia in Hyperdrive" by Peter Schillaci. Schillaci seeks to discover "the significance of the event" by probing into the reasons *why* the film "works," and he highlights three: it is fun, it "tames" technology, and it is "rooted in folklore media," chiefly comic strips and old movies. Like Tyrrell in the previous essay, Schillaci discusses the power of myth and concludes that although "there are no established myths for a technological civilization" [has he forgotten Frankenstein?], "some are being created which draw their energy from timeless sources in human experience." This, he believes, *Star Wars* does, and it is not difficult to agree with him. His final image of "a substantial world of myth" condensing from "this manufactured cloud of trivia" once again may remind us of Stevenson's uses of popular culture. Schillaci's essay, like the film he analyzes, leaves us feeling good about life and humanity's future.

Schillaci's second essay, "Where Have All the Heroes Gone?" explores the possibility that the world of current movies might supply our need for heroes and heroines. Schillaci believes the recent films based on Vietnam and Watergate, surprisingly, have "come closest to generating new heroes. . . ." Recognizing that we are in a period of "sloughing off sexual stereotypes," he devotes much of the latter part of his article to illuminating the new movie "heroine" who is still in the process of being created. *Coming Home* may presage, with its portrayal of a "truce" in the battle of the sexes, "a new heroism rising out of the ruins of the traditional American war myth."

The final essay in this section, Jeanne Betancourt's "The 16mm Treatment: A Prescription for Passive Viewers," describes techniques for helping students "integrate" the powers of the left and right brain hemispheres. Her many imaginative and yet practical ideas will be of value to all those who share her aim of encouraging young people to "study media with an inquiring tone that fosters investigation."

NOTES

1. *Understanding Media: The Extensions of Man* (New York: McGraw-Hill, 1964), pp.5, 335.
2. Francois Lhermitte, "Thinking Without Language," *Réalités* No. 4 (Apr. 1979), p.63.

Zen and the Art of English Teaching

G. Lynn Nelson

The psychology of human consciousness is currently in a period of new formation; we are reconsidering our thoughts about thinking, our perceptions of perceiving, our knowledge of knowing. The seeds for such a change have been lying around for a long time. Even before the turn of the century, William James said in *The Varieties of Religious Experience,* "Our normal waking consciousness, rational consciousness as we call it, is but one special type of consciousness, whilst all about it, parted from it by the filmiest of screens, *there lie potential forms of consciousness entirely different"* (italics mine). These seeds of change have been a long time sprouting in the difficult soil of the generally Western and typically American obsession with the linear, the left-brained, the logical.

Now it seems that a right-brained reformation of some sort is at last upon us. In the street, for example, there is a growing interest in such things as acupuncture, meditation, mysticism, Zen, consciousness-altering drugs, new and old religions, etc. And in the ivory towers above the streets, the scientists, psychologists, psychiatrists, and others of the academic world can no longer ignore these "forms of consciousness entirely different." In his recently edited book on *The Nature of Human Consciousness,* for example, research psychologist Robert Ornstein refers to the generally growing interest in "other" modes of perception, declaring his belief that "there is a cultural and scientific evolution, if not revolution, in process." And in the May 1973 issue of *Psychology Today*—an issue especially concerned with nonanalytic modes of perception—editor T. George Harris expresses the observation that "a rightheaded rebellion is now in full swing" in our country.

Such statements may sound a bit more wishful than emphatic (in a society so totally geared for acquisition, analysis, and material progress, any voices speaking for imagination and intuition must inevitably sound small). Still they—and the voice of my own intuition—give me cause to hope. And to wonder. . . .

Being an English teacher involved in the training of other English teachers, I wonder, for example, how long (if ever) it will take the new attitudes toward learning and consciousness to reach into our institutional system of education. And once there, how much longer to reach the English classroom. And once there, what the implications might be for the teaching of English.

It is, after all, well past the time that education—and *especially* English education—concerned itself with more than just the left half of the human brain. For despite the great predilection of our culture toward this left-brained approach to life, there is no denying a strong movement toward other more right-brained and intuitive approaches—and this, largely because our analytical perception of life has brought us quite abruptly into a spiritual and technological corner. Consciously or subconsciously, we are all looking for ways out of that corner.

In education we still prefer to drag our feet and to look, one-eyed, in the other direction. For this right-brained thing is messy stuff and somehow smacks of muddy romanticism rather than hard, clean science—and how many times did our mothers tell us not to get dirty.

But all this will soon be difficult for us to ignore. It is that very hard, clean science that is now amassing the evidence of our cultural blindness. Robert Ornstein, in that same issue of *Psychology Today* referred to earlier, has an article entitled "Right and Left Thinking." In it he discusses the research being done with split-brain patients (patients in whom the corpus callosum connecting the right and left hemispheres of their brain has been severed as a treatment for epilepsy). The article is but a brief synopsis of Ornstein's other book, *The Psychology of Consciousness,* in which he elaborates on such research and shows that the human brain has indeed developed a bi-modal consciousness in which the left side has become the repository of primarily logical, linear, analytical perception while the right side houses the intuitive, imaginative, artistic perception. Ornstein goes on to show how our culture (as opposed, say, to the American Indian culture or many Eastern cultures) has developed an almost exclusively left-brained approach to perception and how it has given almost no recognition or credence to the perceptions of the right half of the brain.

While Ornstein has been the leader or at least the primary voice in such research, he has not been alone; the evidence is growing daily. In other words, modern, scientific, linear research is now telling the left side of our brain what the right side knew all along: that as human beings our perceptions are *not* exclusively logical and analytical, that there is another dimension to human consciousness which has been largely ignored and buried under our Western obsession with left-brained perception.

With the exposure of this new dimension of human perception (or rather with our emerging cultural acknowledgment of it), comes a growing awareness of the need for a new dimension in the teaching of English and in the preparation of English teachers. While the full ramifications of all this and the full extent of the possibilities for the teaching of language and languaging are yet to be discovered, one thing is certain: we must no longer be content (as we never should have been) to send teachers out prepared to work with only half of the student's mind.

For example, when we experience a work of literature, a great part of our response—whether we acknowledge it or not—is nonlogical, nonintellectual, right-brained, sub- or semi-conscious and initially nonverbal (the left brain houses the language faculty). In the classroom, we have never known quite what to do with this aspect of the human response; for the most part, we have ignored it. Granted, at least since the days of the Dartmouth Conference, we have given lip service to what came to be called the "affective domain"—but even this we have done in a largely condescending and half-hearted manner. For in truth, the beep of that first Russian Sputnik and the ghost of McNamara still haunt us, and in the humanities we still feel apologetic about anything that lacks the crispness of an algebraic formula.

Now, however, with *scientific* evidence that human consciousness is indeed bi-modal, this "other" kind of response takes on a new validity. And if we cannot yet imagine how all this might change our teaching techniques, some speculation is in order. I would like briefly to suggest three alternatives to our present generally accepted and generally left-brain oriented methods. None of these alternatives is new; but in light of this recent research, all now have a new credence and cry out for new emphasis.

The first alternative is the use of creative projects in place of (or at the very least in addition to) tests. Tests—especially objective tests, but even essay tests—almost exclusively measure left-brain response. Creative projects allow students to use both sides of their brain: they use their cognitive understanding of, say, a short story or a poem as the basis for another creation—their own—through which they reveal (and *discover*) a deeper, more intuitive, more emotional understanding.

I am thinking of things my own students have done (many of them very memorable and meaningful for me—and I can't think of a single test that was either memorable or meaningful). I am thinking, for example, of an art major who did an elaborate pencil sketch of four figures (the main characters in four novels) arranged in different relationships to a glass bowl which symbolized society. The project, as she explained it, revealed a deep and intricate and *creative* (rather than passive) understanding of the novels we had read—something that would not have been revealed by a conventional test, *and* something that she might not have discovered if she had not done the project.

Not all projects, of course, are this impressive. Not all students are art majors. But projects like rewriting a part of a short story, or doing a photography study of the imagery in a poem, or even just creating a collage from magazine pictures and explaining how it represents one's reactions to and feelings about a short story, these are things that all students can do and that involve the student's mind more creatively and comprehensively than taking a test.

In education, we have traditionally concentrated on left-brained response partly because we thought it to be the *only* valid response, but also because it is more amenable to institutionalized education, i.e., more packageable, more measureable, more quantifiable, less messy. In short, because Big Nurse liked it better. But we now have laboratory evidence (and Big Nurse respects *that*) to support our moving away from purely left-brained evaluation. Having students do creative projects instead of taking tests is a good way to begin that move.

A second alternative which supports bi-modal consciousness is emphasizing the importance of discussion over lecture, of "languaging with" rather than being "languaged at." Lectures are inevitably aimed at the left side of the brain. Lectures involve note-taking and rote memorization. Discussion, however (and I am not talking about Socratic, teacher-led, guess-what-I'm-thinking-of discussion) allows for active, imaginative, bi-modal response; it is process-oriented; it can lead to individual, creative, meaningful discovery and learning.

For many years I conducted Socratic-type discussions with my students, carefully and patiently leading them toward my preconceived "answers." I thought this was much better than lecturing. In reality, it was almost the same—it just took longer. The problem was that the students were always "getting off the trail" and I was always having to herd them back. It took a long time for me to realize that there are many trails.

The process of discussion, of oral languaging, is necessary for discovering what one already knows. Now this is a little tricky, but I think it makes sense. Researchers working with persons who have had "split-brain" operations discovered that when information is fed only into the right half of the brain, that half can "know" the information without the left half "knowing" it. And since the left half houses the language faculty, the person is unable to articulate what is "known." For example, Michael S. Gazzaniga, in "The Split Brain in Man" (*Scientific American,* Aug. 1967), reports that a patient holding an object in the left hand (which is controlled by the right half of the brain) and out of view, was unable to name or describe it, though the patient was later able to point to a card on which the name of the object was written. Numerous such experiments have been performed, and the conclusion seems to be that the two sides of our brain can "know" different things and can "know" them in different ways. The important thing for English teachers to realize, then, is that discussion now takes on a new dimension: it becomes a potential process of discovery, i.e., of using the language of the left brain to discover—articulate—the knowledge of the right brain.

Let me relate a personal example. A couple of years ago, I went with my wife and another couple to see Bergman's *Cries and Whispers.* I came away from the movie feeling very disturbed, but unable to articulate almost anything about the film except that it was disturbing. The others, I think, felt much the same way because we stopped for a drink and for quite a while no one ventured more than very tentative and general reactions to the film. But slowly we got going on it, and as one person would articulate a particular observation or response, someone else would pick up on it. Two hours later as we left the bar I felt much more comfortable with Bergman's film. (I know what you're thinking—but I only had *two* drinks.) I felt I "knew" much more about the film than I had "known" two hours before. But no "expert" had come into the bar and lectured to us on the movie. We had simply languaged about it and, I suspect, transferred a good deal of what our right brain had already "known" about it to the left brain where it could be articulated, shared, and used to trigger additional transfer. And that is what discussion in the class-room should be about: discovering and sharing and enlarging what we *already* know.

The third alternative is closely related to the second, only it involves talking to oneself to discover what one already knows. I'm referring to the use of the informal languaging journal in place of (or at least in addition to) the formal report and/or the research paper. The principle is the same as the lecture-discussion antithesis: the formal report is primarily left-brain oriented. Imagination and intuition are taboo; there is usually very little merging of the two modes into meaningful "seeing." In journal writing, however, one can language about one's feelings and reactions to the works of literature freely and "unscientifically." The idea is to explore one's own reactions, emotional as well as intellectual; to develop a dia-logue with oneself; to range the whole spectrum of responses and mean-ings rather than to be limited to one narrow area of linear response.

I encourage my students not to worry a great deal in their journal writ-ing about mechanics, logic, unity, etc. but to relate themselves in a per-sonal way to the work of literature and to explore those relationships and reactions. I tell them when they get on the track of something to fol-low it as far as they can and when it gives out to drop it and try to pick it up again later. And when I read the journals, I try to respond with both sides of my own brain; I try to encourage them (and most of them need a lot of this) to quit worrying about structure and order and to let the words flow easily.

I have come to these methods largely intuitively, led by the persistent whispers of the right side of my brain. But I have been greatly encour-aged, of late, by the research which now helps support such approaches. And I see that there is still a long way to go, that we will need to "see" with both eyes if we ever hope to find our way out of our cultural corner. In the classroom, we must begin this journey by ceasing to teach to only half of our students' minds with only half of our own minds. Pirsig de-scribes it beautifully:

> The reason why, if he were not more than two thousand years dead, [Phaedrus] would have gladly rubbed [Aristotle] out is that he saw him as a prototype for the many millions of self-satisfied and truly ignorant teachers throughout history who have smugly and callously killed the

creative spirit of their students with this dumb ritual of analysis, this blind, rote, eternal naming of things. Walk into any of a hundred thousand classrooms today and hear the teachers divide and subdivide and interrelate and establish 'principles' and study 'methods' and what you will hear is the ghost of Aristotle speaking down through the centuries—the desiccating lifeless voice of dualistic reason. (*Zen and the Art of Motorcycle Maintenance,* pp. 354-55)

The goal is not *either* the left brain *or* the right brain, not *either* the intellect *or* the imagination, not *either* classicism *or* romanticism. The goal is the meaningful merging of both modes of perception.

BIBLIOGRAPHY

Blackburn, Thomas R. "Sensuous-Intellectual Complementarity in Science." *Science* 172:1003-07 (June 4, 1971).

Brown, Barbara B. "New Mind, New Body." *Psychology Today* 8:45-56; 74-112 (Aug. 1974).

Bruner, Jerome. *On Knowing: Essays for the Left Hand.* New York: Atheneum, 1965.

Deikman, Arthur J. "Bimodal Consciousness." *Archives of General Psychiatry* 25:481-89 (Dec. 1971).

Gazzaniga, Michael S. "The Split Brain in Man." *Scientific American* 217: 24-29 (Aug. 1967).

James, William. *Principles of Psychology.* 2 vols. New York: Dover, 1950. (Original copyright 1890).

———. *The Varieties of Religious Experience.* New York: New American Library, n.d.

Lee, Dorothy. "Codifications of Reality: Lineal and Nonlineal." *Psychosomatic Medicine* 12:89-97 (Mar.-Apr. 1950).

Maslow, Abraham. *The Psychology of Science: A Reconnaissance.* South Bend, Ind.: Gateway Editions, Ltd., 1969.

Pirsig, Robert M. *Zen and the Art of Motorcycle Maintenance.* New York: Bantam, 1975.

Ornstein, Robert, ed. *The Nature of Human Consciousness.* San Francisco: W. H. Freeman, 1973.

———. *The Psychology of Consciousness.* New York: Penguin, 1975.

———. "Right and Left Thinking." *Psychology Today* 6:86-92 (May 1973).

Samples, Robert. "The Intuitive Mode: Completing the Educational Process." *Media & Methods* 11:24-25 + (May/June 1975).

Sohn, David. "A Talk with James Moffett." *Media & Methods* 11:22-24 + (Feb. 1975).

Spider-Man: Superhero in the Liberal Tradition

Salvatore Mondello

The cover of *The Mighty Marvel Bicentennial Calendar* shows Spider-Man, the Hulk, and Captain America as imposing members of a fife and drum corps. Behind the superheroes are soldiers of the American Revolution. Like his two companions, Spider-Man has become an important fictional hero and is entitled to be represented as an American patriot on such a calendar celebrating American independence. Yet, in the beginning, his days as a superhero—like his country's first years of freedom—seemed numbered.

Even Stan Lee, Spider-Man's creator, saw little hope of success for his new comic book superhero when he introduced him to the public in Marvel's *Amazing Fantasy* #15 for August 1962. That publication had become a financial liability, couldn't compete for readership with other Marvel titles, and was scheduled for cancellation with the August issue.[1]

Written by Lee and illustrated by Steve Ditko, the original tale stuck closely to time-tested formulas used by comic book writers and artists since the late 1930s. Shy, studious, and introspective, Peter Parker, a student first at Midtown High School and later at Empire State University, is ridiculed by his classmates. While attending a science lecture and demonstration, he is bitten by a radioactive spider and acquires its characteristics. Using his knowledge of science and technology, Peter adds to his already considerable powers by inventing a web-shooter for each hand, enabling him to swing easily from one rooftop to another. He creates for himself a costume of red and blue and decides to embark upon a career as a television entertainer, hoping thereby to repay his Aunt May and Uncle Ben for the love, care, and affection they have given their orphaned nephew over the years. At the television studio, Spider-Man refuses to assist a security guard pursuing a thief, the very robber who later invades the Parker residence and kills Uncle Ben. Capturing the murderer in an abandoned warehouse, blaming himself for his uncle's death, Spider-Man swears to avenge the crime by waging relentless war against the forces of evil.

Teenage superheroes, such as Airboy, Robin, and Bucky, appeared

---

Reprinted by permission from *Journal of Popular Culture* 10:232-38 (Summer 1976). Copyright © 1976 by Ray B. Browne.

years before Spider-Man; arachnids, like the Spider, feared by both the police and the underworld, were staple fictional characters in the old pulp magazines and movie serials; revenge following the murder of loved ones was a gambit used by countless comic book heroes, such as Batman and Blackhawk to name two of the most famous; and orphaned kids who became superheroes abounded in the comics, with Superman leading the pack.[2]

Granted all this, Spider-Man *did* become the comic book superstar of the sixties, entitled to his own magazine, *The Amazing Spider-Man,* as early as March 1963. Why did Spider-Man merit such a large, diverse, and enthusiastic audience, including many college students? From the start, Spider-Man was given unique characteristics for a superhero, human characteristics and problems with which readers could identify. He always finds it hard to make ends meet and even tries to sell his services as a crime fighter to the Fantastic Four, only to learn that they are a non-profit organization. He offers to pose for bubble gum cards, but is turned down by the card manufacturer who tells him he is a has-been. So, as Peter Parker, he must work for a pittance as a part-time photographer for *The Daily Bugle.* That newspaper's publisher, J. Jonah Jameson, pays him little for his action-filled photographs of Spider-Man in deadly combat with supervillains. And, to add insult to injury, Jameson detests Spider-Man, considering him a glory-hound and criminal.

The Amazing Spider-Man has found an enthusiastic young audience because it deals fundamentally with titanic battles between a teenage superhero and middle-aged supervillains—an impressive rogues' gallery which includes such memorable knaves and grotesques as the Vulture, Doc Ock, the Sandman, Kraven the Hunter, Electro, the Evil Enforcers, Mysterio, the Green Goblin, the Scorpion, the Rino, the Shocker, the Kingpin, the Lizard, Hammerhead, and the Jackal, names which shake the very soul of every True Believer. With each battle between Spider-Man and one of his tormentors, we enter the realm of high adventure, knowing full well that the hero's victory will only be temporary, for the villain will return time and again to haunt and pursue him.

Many of the supervillains degenerate into knaves as a result of scientific accidents. Some examples will suffice here. Doc Ock was working at an atomic research center, designing a contraption with four metal tentacles which would enable him to conduct all sorts of nuclear experiments. An accident occurred, causing brain damage to Ock and causing his mechanical device to adhere to his body. Flint Marko, escaping from a maximum security prison, finds himself in an atomic devices testing center; a nuclear test takes place and the molecules of his body fuse with the molecules of sand under his feet—ergo, Sandman, capable of assuming many shapes. (Once, Spidey captured Sandman by sucking him up with a vacuum cleaner.) Dr. Curtis Conners, a brilliant surgeon and devoted family man, lost his right arm in war. He studies lizard life, discovering a serum which restores his arm but changes him into a giant lizard whose only interest is to destroy mankind.

Now Spider-Man himself is the result of a scientific mishap. But what is incontrovertible is that the accident brought out Peter's best attributes, including his willingness to question power and to assume public responsibilities, while the accidents which befell the others brought out their evil side. We must especially ask why the sensitive Dr. Connors becomes a misanthropic grotesque while the less sophisticated Peter Parker becomes a crusader for social justice.

The answer is found in the age of the protagonists. *The Amazing Spider-Man* appeals to the young. As Peter Parker, he must accept abuse from Jameson, must not miss any more classes or his teacher will fail him, must call his cloying Aunt May to assure her he will take his vitamin pills. And what has he gained from all this? An ulcer. But as Spider-Man, he is the superior of any middle-aged person. He can swing freely with his webbing from rooftop to rooftop without giving his aunt a second thought, or he can playfully suspend himself on his webbing outside Jameson's office window and taunt him mercilessly. Through Spider-Man, Stan Lee has brought redemption to America's Peter Parkers.

But Lee tried to do more than that, and *The Amazing Spider-Man* was used skillfully to bridge the generation gap which was tearing the nation apart in the late sixties and early seventies. He introduced Captain George Stacy, a retired policeman who understood teenagers, all this at a time when our more radical youth were calling cops "fascist pigs." He introduced Joe Robertson, a black journalist, who also tried to relate to young people and who fought for responsible reporting of the news at a time when many Americans believed our journalists were concerned only with sensational headlines calculated more to sell newspapers than to report events accurately. *The Amazing Spider-Man* was intended to find an irenic solution to the challenges facing America.

While many novelists have bemoaned the growing pervasiveness of urbanization and technology upon American society, *The Amazing Spider-Man* treats these as controllable forces.[3] Spider-Man does not work in some fictionalized urban centers like Metropolis or Gotham City, but lives and goes to school in New York City. He is New York's Tarzan swinging from rooftop to rooftop as the Lord of the Jungle swings from tree to tree. Spider-Man seems less agile when pursuing adversaries in New York's suburbs, for buildings there are too low for him to leap with ease from place to place.

Spider-Man deals with supervillains possessing considerable technological skills. He manages to more than hold his own against their mechanical devices. On occasion, he uses technology to fight technology. Discovering that the Vulture can fly because he has harnessed magnetic power, Spider-Man invents an anti-magnetic inverter. At other times, he relies on Yankee ingenuity or just plain common sense to thwart the nefarious designs of his enemies. He once defeated the mighty Electro by spraying him with a water hose. And when all else fails, Spider-Man, like John Wayne, still knows what to do with his fists. He once floored Doc Ock with a smashing right to the jaw. In this case, human, not super-human powers, triumphed over the mechanical tentacles of his opponent. Morally superior to his adversaries, Spider-Man can always beat them even when they match his scientific genius. Even the Shocker's two vibro-smashers are unequal to Spider-Man's powers, which are not artificial but an integral part of his very being.

Spider-Man has mastered his technology and crippled that of his opponents because he has learned to control his emotions. If this were not the case, Spider-Man would have long been driven to insanity by the diabolical Mysterio, who fights him by creating illusions. In 1965, Mysterio, disguised as Dr. Ludwig Rinehart, visited Jameson and told him that Spider-Man is a human who wants to be a spider. Hence, he should eventually suffer a mental breakdown. Jameson printed Rinehart's views in *The Daily Bugle,* and Peter, after reading the account, began to fear the possibility of having a nervous collapse. Using his scientific skills, Mysterio creates visions of Doc Ock, Sandman, and the Vulture, but when Spider-Man attempts to fight them, they vanish. Utterly bewildered, Spider-Man goes to see Rinehart, hoping he can save him from the horrors of madness. Entering his office, he finds that the entire room and its furniture, including Rinehart sitting at his desk, are upside down. He finally learns that Mysterio actually constructed the room that way, even nailing the furnishings to the ceiling, in order to drive Spider-Man insane.

Mysterio has never been able to understand how Spider-Man manages to maintain his equilibrium. But the Mindworm knows. Born a freak, the Mindworm drove both of his parents to madness and then to death. In 1974, the Mindworm placed hundreds of people in a trance in Far Rockaway, New York; he is forced to do this, for his mind feeds upon controlling the will of others. He yearns to dominate Spider-Man's mind. This would represent his greatest victory. He tells Spider-Man: "You're not like them. You feel things . . . you're more involved . . . your emotions are so deep, they intoxicate me. . . ."[4] With this incisive statement, the Mindworm gives us the key to Spider-Man's greatness—his ability to control his emotions, his ability to dominate himself. Since Spider-Man has mastered himself, he can master the technology around him.

The Amazing Spider-Man is an historic document that reflects three periods from our recent past. From 1962 to 1967, Spider-Man mirrored an era still dominated by Cold War diplomacy and a citizenry still concerned more with personal gratification than public service. In 1963, Spider-Man foiled the Chameleon's attempt to turn over secret documents from an American defense installation to the Communists. In that same year, he fought the Vulture for personal gain—to pay his aunt's mortgage—not to rid society of a public menace. The July 1967, issue of *The Amaz-*

ing Spider-Man is an important historical document, for it marks a significant turning point in the development of the superhero and perhaps of his nation. Peter decides to abandon his career as a crime fighter. As he throws away his costume in a garbage can, he says to himself: "Can I be sure my only motive was the conquest of crime? Or was it the heady thrill of battle . . . the precious taste of triumph . . . the paranoic thirst for power which can never be quenched?" When the Kingpin learns that Spider-Man has become inactive, he unleashes a reign of terror upon New York City. Peter, rescuing a security guard who is being manhandled by two thugs, realizes that he must continue as Spider-Man as long as people need his assistance.

From 1967 to 1973, Spider-Man addressed himself to every important issue confronting American society. He fought drug abuse and drug pushers, organized crime, pollution, and racial bigotry. It was in this period that superheroines made their appearance in the periodical, compelling Spider-Man to deal with the feminist movement. In 1970, he battled the glamorous Black Widow, who at first wanted to imitate his style as a superhero but finally decided against it, noting that she had her own special destiny to fulfill.

In an era demanding relevance, few magazines were more typical or current than Lee's comic book. It was in this period that *The Amazing Spider-Man* became popular on college campuses throughout the United States. Once contemporary issues were discussed, *The Amazing Spider-Man* became a subtle persuader, fashioning and reflecting public and popular attitudes under the rubric of entertainment. During World War II, comic book superheroes, such as Superman, Batman, and Captain America, to name only the most celebrated, had come to the assistance of our government and its armed forces as we engaged the Germans, Japanese, and Italians in combat. At that time, comics were doing more than simply entertaining the young. But our early superheroes were presiding over a united people, all intent upon defeating the Axis powers. Spider-Man's stand on crucial issues during the late sixties and early seventies could bring him not only supporters but critics, for America was divided on every public question. Superman came to us in a period of consensus; Spider-Man had to find consensus in an era of conflict.

In 1971, Stan Lee was quoted as saying that he was neither a hippie nor a conservative.[5] The same may be said for Spider-Man. During the late sixties and early seventies, we learned that the young man behind the mask was a resolute defender of traditional American liberalism, especially the liberalism fashioned by Franklin D. Roosevelt and other New Dealers.

Let us study the record. Peter Parker believes in equal justice for black Americans, but he has never joined a protest movement to defend that principle. Like his fellow liberals, he feels that blacks will attain full social and political parity with whites by working in the system. In 1968, he was asked to participate in a student protest, and the issue for which his classmates were demonstrating was abundantly clear. The petrified clay tablet—with its inscribed hieroglyphics revealing the secret of eternal youth to anyone capable of deciphering the symbols—was being displayed at Exhibition Hall of Empire State University. After the show, the university planned to convert Exhibition Hall into a private dormitory for visiting alumni. Among the protesting students who wanted the place to become a low-rent dormitory for needy students were two black youths, Josh, and Robertson's son Randy. When the protestors invited Peter to join in the rally, he refused, telling them he wanted to hear the Dean's position on this matter. Secretly, he sympathized with their demands but felt further consultations between the students and administrators would break the impasse. (It eventually did in favor of the protesters.) When the demonstrators entered Exhibition Hall, one of the security guards nervously reached for his gun but the other guard restrained him, showing that not all policemen were intent upon shooting young college protesters. During the ensuing commotion, the Kingpin entered the building and made off with the tablet, proving that protest rallies benefited only the criminal elements in American society.

In the late sixties and early seventies, Spider-Man confronted the problem of drug abuse as energetically as Captain battled the Red Skull during World War II. Spidey was so moved upon seeing a black youth, under the influence of drugs, jump off a roof thinking he could walk on air that he remarked: "My life as Spider-Man is probably as dangerous as any . . . but I'd rather face a hundred super-villains than toss it away by getting hooked on hard drugs! . . . cause that's one fight you can't win!"[6] When his rich friend Harry Osborn began taking drugs, Peter recognized that drug addiction had reached epidemic proportions, not restricted solely to ghetto youngsters. He became so enraged that as Peter Parker, he beat to a pulp three drug pushers.

At the very moment America was experiencing the tragedy of Attica, Peter was sent by Jameson to photograph a riot at city prison. He discovered that most of the inmates were only trying to improve living conditions at the jail. Shortly thereafter, Spider-Man made a television appearance and gave a talk on the need to better prison life.[7]

As Peter Parker, he was deeply troubled by the American involvement in the war in Vietnam. Like most middle-class young men, he never talked about it. But after saying farewell to his friend Flash Thompson, who is leaving for a tour of duty in Vietnam, Peter thinks to himself: "Which is worse . . . ? Staying behind while other guys are doing the fighting . . . ? Or fighting in a war that nobody wants . . . against an enemy you don't even hate?"[8]

By 1970, Spider-Man seemed worried about political extremism, especially from the right. He was suspicious of a law-and-order spokesman, Sam Bullit, a former policeman running for district attorney. Bullit, who made pronouncements against "left-wing anarchists," employed thugs to threaten or assault his opponents. When Robertson uncovered evidence exposing him as a fraud, Bullit had him kidnapped. While Jameson had initially lent Bullit full support, Peter and Robertson had viewed the law-and-order candidate as a fake from the very beginning. The danger from the extreme right to America's freedoms was as evident to Spider-Man as it was to Pogo.

Since 1973, Spider-Man has been locked in combat with such villains as the Jackal, Tarantula, the Cyclone, and the ever popular Doc Ock, among others. Occult themes have become popular. But, Spider-Man as an embattled defender of American liberalism, as a hero trying to update and revise that political ideology, ended with the termination of our involvement in the war in Southeast Asia. By the mid-1970s, Americans, Spider-Man included, had grown weary of crusades and crusaders.

Since 1962, *The Amazing Spider-Man* has helped to shape and reflect the American character and deserves special attention from students of American history because it has enjoyed a popularity and thus an influence second to no other comic book. Like the McGuffey readers and the *New-England Primer* of earlier times, *The Amazing Spider-Man* has helped to educate America's young people. During the 1960s, many older Americans feared the teenagers in their midst, stereotyping them as flag burners, pot smokers, and police baiters. By the mid-1970s, however, most of our young adults—former members of the so-called lost generation of the sixties—were responsible, moderate men and women, bringing up families, putting in a full day of work at the office, taking their children on patriotic pilgrimages to Philadelphia and Washington, D.C., to celebrate their country's two-hundredth birthday. Such behavior was only natural from a generation that had been educated by super-heroes like Spider-Man. During the late sixties and early seventies, Spider-Man had helped to keep alive American liberalism among the young, a tradition stressing cooperation among individuals and minorities rather than conflict, moderation in politics rather than extremism, and the right of each American to social recognition and economic opportunity.

After Watergate and Vietnam, Americans found themselves plagued by serious economic ills. Little wonder that they wanted Spider-Man to take them away from harsh social realities and transport them into the world of fantasy, circuses, and the occult. But a people and a superhero who had confronted the great social problems of the sixties with courage and decisiveness may have been so changed by that experience that they could hardly be expected to dwell in a fantasy world for very long.

NOTES

1. For an inside view of how Spider-Man was created, see Stan Lee, *Origin of Marvel Comics* (New York: Simon & Schuster, 1974), pp.131-38.

2. The superheroes of the "Golden Age" of comics are discussed in James Steranko's *History of Comics* I (Reading: Supergraphics, 1970).
3. For an analysis of the relationship between technology and the Fantastic Four, see Arthur Asa Berger, *The Comic-Stripped American* (Baltimore: Penguin, 1973), pp.197-207.
4. "Madness Means the Mindworm," *The Amazing Spider-Man, Marvel* no.138:30 (Nov. 1974).
5. Robin Green, "Face Front: Clap Your Hands! You're on the Winning Team," *Rolling Stone* (Sept. 16, 1971), p.34.
6. "And Now the Goblin," *The Amazing Spider-Man, Marvel* no.96:14 (May 1971).
7. "Panic in the Prison," *Ibid.*, no.99:18-19 (Aug. 1971).
8. "The Schemer," *Ibid.*, no.83:10 (Apr. 1970).

"Star Trek" as Myth and Television as Mythmaker

William Blake Tyrrell

The phenomenon of "Star Trek" is unique in television. More popular now than its first run in the late 60s, it has spawned books of adapted scripts and of fandom as well as countless fanzines. "Star Trek" realia extend to complete blueprints of the *Enterprise* and code of conduct for its personnel. Fan clubs have led to conventions where attendance must be limited. All this is the result of something beyond the dramatic spectacle. "Star Trek" is consistent but often childish science fiction, engaging but often belabored drama. I wish to propose a reason for the phenomenon of "Star Trek" as a contribution to our understanding of the power of television.

"Star Trek" never had high ratings; it did have in science fiction an intriguing format. By inventing a believable world, "Star Trek" provided the viewer with material for his own imagination. He could elaborate upon the sets and equipment, bandy arcane knowledge, even write his own scripts. That the format had the potential to involve the viewer beyond one hour each week is the initial basis for the phenomenon. "Star Trek" s' format created a world alive, turning viewers into fans.

Reprinted by permission from *Journal of Popular Culture* 10:711-19 (Spring 1977). Copyright © 1977 by Ray B. Browne.

Gene Roddenberry, creator of the series, referred to it, if only in jest, as " 'Wagon Train' to the stars,"[1] and the similarity between groups journeying toward the unknown is evident. Movement is a prominent motif of both Western and "Star Trek," where it is made visual in the flyby of the gliding starship. But the similarity goes deeper. The Western story is the only indigenous mythic narrative of the white American. "The isolation of a vast unexplored continent, the slow growth of social forms, the impact of an unremitting New England Puritanism obsessed with the cosmic struggle of good and evil, of the elect and the damned, the clash of allegiances to Mother Country and New World, these factors," as Jim Kitses says in *Focus on the Western,* "are the crucible in which the American consciousness was formed."[2] Since the publication in 1893 of Frederick J. Turner's essay "The Significance of the Frontier in American History," the dominant symbol of the Western myth has been the frontier.[3] "Star Trek" views space as "the final frontier."[4] Despite its format "Star Trek" is not speculative fiction in the way of written science fiction or even of "Space 1999" in its first season. It is American myths clothed in the garb of science fiction. "Space—the final frontier" is conceptualized through the same motifs and themes as the Western frontier. A brief example:

The heart of the Western myth is the encounter with the Indian. The myth-making imagination has contained the Indian's alienness in two types: Chingachgook, the noble warrior ever outside White Man's world, and Magua, sly, perfidious, fallen and by that fall, bound to the white world. Both types are found in "Star Trek." The Romulans, whose name recalls the heroic founder of Rome, are aggressive, militaristic aliens. Nonetheless they are "hard to hate," *The Making of Star Trek* explains, "as they often display enormous courage." The Klingons, a name as low as Cooper's Magua, are ruled by the principle "that rules are made to be broken by shrewdness, deceit, or power."[5] There is nothing admirable about them and with them in time, one episode predicts,[6] the White Man of the *Enterprise* is destined to unite. Though apparently distinct figures in the series (and perhaps in their creator's imagination), their dark, satanic visages reveal Romulans and Klingons as aspects of a whole, the Indian reborn.

Yet "Star Trek" is more than the transposing of visuals and motifs, more than the shifting from one metaphor to another. Myths are narratives with the power to move our psychic energies toward integration of self and of self with the cosmos. Myths define an image of the world within and without and relate us to it emotionally. Myths put in narrative form the unconscious assumptions that constitute the spirit of a culture. They can inspire and direct those energies to monumental achievements of good or ill. During the 60s, American myths and the values they supported, after a brief sojourn in Camelot, began coming apart, not to be replaced by those of the counter culture. "Star Trek" revitalizes American myths by displacing them into a futuristic, quasi-scientific setting.[7] In effect, "Star Trek" takes our roots and disguises them as branches for some of us to cling to. Moreover, "Star Trek" put them on television.

Television is the medium of immediate, personal communication. No willed suspension of disbelief occurs; television speaks not to the intelligence or to its pilot, the will. It works through the emotions on a non-reasoning level and is thus the medium best suited to the emotional word, *mythos*.[8] "Star Trek" exploits television's intimate communication. Things on "Star Trek" look right. The family of the *Enterprise* is closely knit, appealing, and calmly efficient. The men are men, and the women are endowed. (Though set in the twenty-third century, sexual roles are those of the 50s.) Kirk, broadly played by William Shatner, projects emotion, strength, and unthreatening paternalism. Leonard Nimoy's Spock surpasses him by striving not to emote at all. The result was that "Star Trek's" message of revitalized mythic narratives, brought directly to the emotional needs of the viewer, engendered the feeling that the shows were more than escapist entertainment. They had meaning. That feeling transformed the forty-eight-minute episodes into rituals, and rituals, being group-creating, led to clubs and to the convention. This feeling and the power to generate it are, I believe, what is unique about "Star Trek" and the reason for the phenomenon.

"Star Trek" is a product of the dreams and nightmares of the 60s. It came to those who needed the confidence and triumph of the American past, while fearing a present that forebode the disappearance of the American way. The need has become stronger in the diffident 70s. "Star Trek"'s vision, as Roddenberry and the authors of *Star Trek Lives!* maintain, is "of a brighter future of man, of a world characterized by hope, achievement and understanding."[9] But "Star Trek"'s impact transcends simple optimism for a tomorrow we may never see. "Star Trek" creates a future world where the glories of the past are pristine and the failures and doubts of the present have been overcome. It gives us our past as our future, while making our present the past which, like any historical event for the future-oriented American, is safely over and forgotten. One way that myths function, particularly those of creation, is to anchor the present to the past and place the worshipper in the time of first beginnings.[10] Something similar is the source of "Star Trek"'s power. Myths no longer link us to the past, since we know the past is gone and is of historical, not immediate, relevance to the present. Bicentennialism recalls the past. On the other hand, any science fiction can link us to the future. But the future, even that imagined in books, is uncertain. "Star Trek," by disguising our past as our future, puts us in it—not the historical past but the mythic past of our first beginnings. There ensues a feeling of permanence, stability, and renewed confidence. This is what's different about "Star Trek."

I wish now to illustrate this view by looking at one mythic theme of "Star Trek"—that of paradise, whose role in mythicizing America began before the Puritans touched its shores.[11]

Paradise is a fundamental theme of the series, the subject of at least thirteen of seventy-nine episodes.[12] It is imagined as the lost Eden of Genesis or as the garden of the New World that lies just beyond the Western frontier. Paradise is destroyed, the victim of "Star Trek" 's unquestioned identification of tranquility with stagnation. In "The Apple," for instance, the crew of the *Enterprise* have happened upon a planet controlled in weather, food supply, everything by a computer named Vaal.[13] The inhabitants are humanoids living in a state of nature. Their single task is to feed Vaal with rocks. Watching the fueling process, McCoy, Spock, and Kirk are speaking together:

> McCoy: What's going on, Jim?
> Kirk: Mess call.
> Spock: In my view a splendid example of reciprocity.
> McCoy: It would take a computerized Vulcan mind such as yours to make that kind of a statement.
> Spock: Doctor, you insist on applying human standards to non-human cultures. I remind you that humans are only a tiny minority in this galaxy.
> McCoy: There are certain absolutes, Mr. Spock, and one of them is the right of humanoids to a free and unchained environment. The right to have conditions which permit growth.
> Spock: Another is their right to choose a system which seems to work for them.
> McCoy: Jim, you're not just going to stand by and be blinded to what's going on here. These are humanoids. Intelligent. They need to advance and grow. Don't you understand what my readings indicate. There's been no change or progress here in at least ten thousand years. This isn't life. It's stagnation.
> Spock: Doctor, these people are healthy, and they are happy. Whatever you choose to call it, this system works despite your emotional reaction to it.
> McCoy: It might for you, Mr. Spock, but it doesn't work for me. Humanoids living so they can service a hunk of tin.
> Kirk: Gentlemen, I think this philosophical argument can wait until our ship's out of danger.

For the men of "Star Trek" as for the pioneers paradise is to be exploited. Open land beckons the plow, way to the new beginning that brings rebirth. It is the dream our ancestors followed westward; it launches our descendants into space. Inseparable with rebirth is death: natives of paradise too contented to appreciate the virtues of progress and advancement are reeducated. Kirk violently inflicts Federation enterprise upon them by destroying Vaal. Despite the nagging of its conscience, Spock, the series subscribes to McCoy's benevolent imperialism. At the time of the first airing of "The Apple," the belief in America as

World Peacemaker and Liberator, a belief which is surely an aspect of the myth of the frontier, was coming apart in Vietnam and in Washington, D.C.[14] "Star Trek" assures us of its validity by showing it as the unquestioned truth of the twenty-third century. Near propagandizing, to be sure, but "Star Trek" gives out the message to those who want to believe in a way that they can believe.

In one episode the theme of paradise is treated quite differently. The tensions inherent in the myth are relieved, not by the dogmatic destruction of one pole, but by the device of the mediator. Although not typical of the paradise-theme, "This Side of Paradise" is a microcosm for the way the series generates its impact.[15] The plot is as follows.

The *Enterprise* arrives on Omicron Ceti III expecting to find the members of an agricultural colony dead. The planet is bombarded by Berthold radiation that disintegrates human tissue. Yet they are greeted by the colonists. They have survived because of their symbiosis with spores that absorb the radiation. These spores are a group organism; they cause their hosts to lose the sense of self and of self-advancement. No progress has been made toward the goals of the colony. The crew succumbs to the spores and abandons the *Enterprise*. Included are McCoy and Spock, the latter experiencing the only painful conversion. While under the spores Spock falls in love with an old admirer who happens to be on the planet. Captain Kirk is overcome by the spores while on the ship, but becomes so angered at the thought of leaving it, that he is released from their influence. He later discovers that violent emotions dissolve the spores. He provokes Spock to a fight in the Transporter Room, and the ensuing violence dissolves his spores.[16] Together they bring the crew to its senses and the *Enterprise* to order.

A mediator is a third between two opposites that shares something of the nature of each. Being anomalous, it may function to overcome the opposition. In Genesis the Serpent mediates between man and God as well as between man and woman.[17] In the myth of the frontier the trapper, hunter, or scout is the anomaly between White and Red. Fundamental to the psychology informing the myth is the tension between the longing for paradise and the knowledge of its passing. But both paradise myths, Genesis and the Frontier, link this tension with others—social, sexual, and moral. Such is the way paradise is treated in "This Side of Paradise." Paradise as an idea, desirable but manifestly impossible, is mediated by the alien Spock. Paradise as a place lost yet sought after is mediated by the *Enterprise*. These tensions are connected with those over drugs and the differences between generations which had become polarized because of drugs. The structure of the story may be diagrammed:

Reading down the columns . . . McCoy accepts the spores painlessly. Forgetting his duty, he loses his self in the group induced by the spores. He gains peace and contentment, marked by the return of his Southern

Paradise	Mediation	Paradise Lost
I. Paradise as an Idea		
a. McCoy	Spock	Kirk
b. Spores	Spores then violent emotions	Violent emotions
c. Painless acceptance	Painful acceptance	[Painless rejection]
d. Abdication of duty	Return to duty	Unquestioned duty
e. Loss of self	Sacrifice of self	Self as all
f. Stagnation	Friendship	Ambition
II. Paradise as a Place		
a. Omicron Ceti III	*Enterprise* with crew	*Enterprise* empty
b. down	Transporter Room	except for Kirk up

accent and the evoking in the viewer's mind of the opening scenes of *Gone with the Wind,* that is, the plantation as paradise.[18] Kirk, his opposite, is briefly affected. Because of his anger, he rejects the spores painlessly and without regret. Though he says he realizes their meaning, his sense of duty is too strong for them. Kirk is left by himself—literally, alone with his self. Spock, the middle ground between them, accepts the spores but painfully. For him, as for Kirk, they are unnatural; like McCoy, he experiences their effect, wants it, and regrets its passing. Spock breaks continuity with the group by asserting his individuality; he fights back when Kirk insults his parentage and logical outlook. When he returns to duty, he does so knowing his loss. He sacrifices the happiness of the spores to his responsibility to others. The cost of the sacrifice is made real through the love affair with Leila. The spores suppress Spock's Vulcan side. Fully human, he can love. Once returned to normal, he can not even speak of his regard for her. Given the characterization of Spock as a constant struggle against emotions and the sexual feelings that he has aroused in viewers, the affair expresses poignantly the pain of paradise lost.[19]

"Star Trek" is committed to technological progress as the answer to our problems. Roddenberry reiterated in a *Penthouse* interview (March 1976) his reasons for the series' popularity, one of which is:

> First of all, we live in a time in which everyone, and particularly young minds, are aware that we face huge troubles ahead. There are many people saying, "I doubt if we'll make it through the next twenty or thirty years." And indeed, if you read the newspapers it seems so. "Star Trek" was a rare show that said, "Hey, it's not all over. It hasn't all been invented. If we're wise, why the human adventure is just beginning." And this is a powerful statement to young-minded people, to think that the explorations and discoveries and challenges ahead of us are greater than anything in the past.

For such an attitude, Roddenberry's paradise, a state of wholeness, of unity, can only be stagnation, for paradise denies the need for the quest. Sandoval, head of the colony, says after his release from the spores:

> We've done nothing here. No accomplishments. No progress. Three years wasted. We wanted to make this planet a garden.

Kirk pronounces the moral of the episode:

> Maybe we weren't meant for paradise. Maybe we were meant to fight our way through. Struggle. Claw our way up. Scratch for every inch of the way. Maybe we can't stroll to the music of the lute. We must march to the sound of the drums.

Edifying but unpleasant. There is a third way, one suggested by the structure of the story: responsibility to others. Spock tells Leila:

> I have a responsibility. To this ship. To that man on the bridge. I am what I am, Leila. If there are self-made purgatories, then we all have to live in them. Mine can be no worse than someone else's.

Paradise is knowingly and willingly sacrificed for love of others and for duty.

Omicron Ceti III is depicted as rural America, and the *Enterprise* without its crew as a helpless hulk. The one place expresses the simplicity of the past. Alone on the ship, Kirk, whose vast technological capabilities are a repeated theme of the series, expresses the loneliness of those who have left the past for the uncertainty of the future. Between them is the *Enterprise* with crew. The struggle between Kirk and Spock that determines Spock's role as a mediator occurs in the Transporter Room, the intersecting point of the "down" of the planet and the "up" of the ship. Here the conflict over the idea of paradise is resolved, for here on the ship the sacrifice is ever made.

The authors intend for us to see the story in the context of the drug culture of the 60s. Their intended message is found in the pontifications of Kirk. But the meaning coming from the story's structure is very different: friendship and the self-sacrifice and responsibility it demands offer a middle way between the dropping out of the Flower Children and the rat race of their parents. The episode ends—the last thing we see—with the three friends reunited in the common mission of the *Enterprise*. This mission, stated after the teaser of every show, is never questioned (or questioned in order to be reaffirmed) in this or any episode. The bitter conflict over life-styles of the 60s, as worked out through the mediator Spock, is relieved by a third: being with friends on a mission whose undoubted worth confers upon existence ready-made meaning and purpose.

In a similar fashion the series itself mediates the tension between the past and the present by establishing a third time, that of first beginnings. It is a time with the anticipation and wonder of the future without the anxieties of the present, with the glory and security of the past without its remoteness. By transcending in an ultimately inexplicable way the sum of message and medium, "Star Trek" puts the fan-become-believer in that time. As an indication of what I am saying I quote the following poem from a "Star Trek" fanzine:[20]

Gliding swiftly through the dark,
Sailing now in starry space,
Silently and free you fly,
Traveling midst time and place.

Like a quiet thing, alive,
Though your engines hum and roar,
Faster than the speed of light,
High above the sky you soar.

Oh! To be aboard you now
As between the stars you roam,
To be once more upon your decks,
The Enterprise — my home.

For the believer, "Star Trek Lives" is more than the slogan of a television show that would not die. It is the ritual cry to a world where he belongs, where he has it all together. "Star Trek" offers the comfort of religion.

Notes

1. Stephen E. Whitfield and Gene Roddenberry, *The Making of Star Trek* (New York: Ballantine, 1968), p.22. The context of Roddenberry's remark is one of throwing sand into the network's eyes in order to get the show on the air. But see Robert L. Shayon's comment in *Saturday Review* 50:46 (June 17, 1967): *Star Trek* is a space version of *Wagon Train*. There's the crew, there's the encountered. The problems arise now from the in-group, now from the out. The future is not without its counterpart of violence in the past and present.
2. Jim Kitses, "The Western: Ideology and Archetype," in Jack Nachbar, ed., *Focus on the Western* (Englewood Cliffs: Prentice-Hall, 1974), p.66.
3. Frederick J. Turner, "The Significance of the Frontier in American History," *Annual Report of the American Historical Association for the Year 1893* (Washington, D.C.: The Association, 1894), pp.199-207. For a more convenient source see Ray A. Billington, *Frontier and Section: Selected Essays of Frederick Jackson Turner* (Englewood Cliffs: Prentice-Hall, 1961).
4. Stated after the teaser of every episode is the series' continuing theme: Space—the final frontier. These are voyages of the Star Ship *Enterprise*. Its five year mission: to explore strange new worlds, to seek out new civilizations, to boldly go where no man has gone before.
5. Whitfield, *The Making of Star Trek*, p.257.
6. Gene L. Coon, *Errand of Mercy*, first shown on March 23, 1967. An adaptation of the script has been published by James Blish, *Star*

Trek 2 (New York: Bantam, 1968), pp.41-54. Although many writers contributed to "Star Trek," Coon along with D. C. Fontana (see note 15 below) and Roddenberry maintained consistency and provided the series with its best, most characteristic episodes.

7. The term is from Northrup Frye's *Anatomy of Criticism* (Princeton: Princeton Univ. Pr., 1957), pp.136-37: Myth, then, is one extreme of literary design; naturalism is the other, and in between lies the whole area of romance, using that term to mean . . . the tendency . . . to displace myth in a human direction and yet, in contrast to "realism," to conventionalize content in an idealized direction. The central principle of displacement is that what can be metaphorically identified in a myth can only be linked in romance by some form of simile: analogy, significant association, incidental accompanying imagery, and the like.

8. For the intimate communication of television see Mawry Green, "The Mythology of Television," *Television Quarterly* 9:5-15 (Spring 1970); Robert C. O'Hara, *Media for the Millions* (New York: Random, 1961), pp.286-306; Horace Newcomb, *TV: The Most Popular Art* (Garden City: Anchor Press, 1974), pp.154-60; 243-64. Ernest Cassirer [*Essay on Man* (New Haven: Yale Univ. Pr., 1944; reprint: New York: Bantam, 1970), p.89] has suggested that myth has "not a substratum of thought but of feeling. Myth and primitive religion are by no means entirely incoherent, they are not bereft of sense or reason. But their coherence depends much more upon unity of feeling than upon logical rules."

9. Jacqueline Lichtenberg, Sondra Marshak, and Joan Winston, *Star Trek Lives* (New York: Bantam, 1975), pp.107-8. More revealing of "Star Trek's" appeal, I believe, is the authors' comment on what the reader may gain from their book: "Most of all, perhaps, we hope you will find that *you are not alone.*" (Authors' italics)

10. Mircea Eliade, *The Sacred and the Profane*, trans. Willard Trask (New York Harcourt, 1961), pp.80-113.

11. Arthur K. Moore, *The Frontier Mind, A Cultural Analysis of the Kentucky Frontiersman* (Lexington: Univ. of Kentucky Pr., 1957), pp.25-37. See also Henry Smith, *Virgin Land* (Cambridge: Harvard Univ. Pr., 1950).

12. The theme of paradise appears in order of airing in: "The Menagarie" (two-part episode), "Shore Leave," "This Side of Paradise," "Who Mourns for Adonais?" "The Apple," "Metamorphosis," "Paradise Syndrome," "For the World is Hollow and I Have Touched the Sky," "Mark of Gideon," and "The Way to Eden."

13. Max Ehrlick, "The Apple." All quotations from the episodes are taken from the televised version of the script. There is an adaptation of "The Apple" by James Blish in *Star Trek 6* (New York: Bantam, 1972), pp.49-68. Blish takes too many liberties with the scripts for his adaptations to be useful for the study of "Star Trek."

14. "The Apple" was first shown on October 13, 1967. On October 21 and 22 demonstrations took place in Washington, and in particular at the Pentagon, protesting the number of those killed in Vietnam.

15. Nathan Butler and D. C. Fontana, "This Side of Paradise," first shown on March 2, 1967, and adapted by James Blish in *Star Trek 5* (New York: Bantam, 1972), pp.58-72.

16. The transporter is a "device for converting matter temporarily into energy, beaming that energy to a predetermined point, and reconverting it back to its original pattern and structure." (Whitfield, *The Making of Star Trek*, p.192). It is the usual means of access to and from the ship.
17. Edmund R. Leach, "Genesis as Myth," in John Middleton, ed., *Myth and Cosmos* (Garden City, Natural History Pr., 1967), pp.1-13.
18. Smith, *Virgin Land*, pp.145-54.
19. See Lichtenberg, *Star Trek Lives*, pp.71-105, for a discussion of Spock from the fan's point of view.
20. J. Clinkenbeard, "Love Poem to a Ship," *Warped Space*, fanzine of the Star Trek Club of Michigan State University, Oct. 31, 1974.

Star Wars: Nostalgia in Hyperdrive

Peter Schillaci

On a black background dusted with distant galaxies, rebel fighters trail angry rocket exhausts as they swarm up at the Death Star. In the futuristic foreground, a young warrior holds a star-beam saber—its white light challenging the dark brooding presence of Evil's helmeted visage. Poised with the youth, a Princess, whose menacing ray gun belies her flowing robe and sensual form, while two gleaming metallic androids stand ready to help. And beneath it all, the two words that sum up this galactic fantasy: *Star Wars.*

This is the stuff that myth is made of, and the poster by Hildebrandt says it all. Filmmaker George Lucas has taken the artistic mode of the moment—the collage—and merged comic strip and old movies, radio serials and pulp sci-fi, rocket models and computerized cameras. The result is a mythical structure as swift (and improbable) as its spaceship creation, the Millennium Falcon. In only a few months it has shuttled millions of earthlings back to "a long time ago, in a galaxy far, far away," where they recapture their youth, a period when everything seems possible and the only limit is the curve of space turning back on itself eternally.

Reprinted by permission from *Media & Methods* 14:18-21; 62-68 (Nov. 1977).

Phenomenon

The cultural phenomenon of *Star Wars* is just beginning to take shape and dimension, and the early reports read like discoveries of new worlds. *Variety,* showing marvelous restraint by shunning the word "stellar," reports $140 million gross by September, and sees the space vehicle gaining on the mechanical fish, with *Star Wars* expected to outgross the record-holding *Jaws* on its first run, heading for a predicted $200 million total. Twentieth Century Fox's foresight (audacity?) has further been rewarded by a rise in its stock, on which *Star Wars* exercised an antigravity pull from 10⅝ to 22½ per share in only a few weeks. More remarkable—people seem to be actually buying a piece of *Star Wars* rather than a piece of Fox.

Meanwhile, the media blitz is in hyperdrive. Marvel Comics (Spiderman, etc.) has six editions of *Star Wars* planned, and thirty newspapers are syndicating a strip. Kids too broke to see the film for the twentieth time can listen to the soundtrack album all they want (1.3 million sold, at $8.89 each). Ballantine Books, chirping and gurgling like R2D2 over its three million copy sales of the paperback, is busy preparing millions more of producer Gary Kurtz's *Making of Star Wars*. Trunks of *Star Wars* calendars, T-shirts, lunch boxes, and vinyl pools are being prepared for time capsules and future trivia collectors. And among last Halloween's ghosts and witches was a respectable sampling of Wookies and Darth Vaders.

There's a real danger of media overkill in writing about *Star Wars*. Already, a sequel is in preparation, with a first draft completed by science fiction writer Alan Dean Foster. Other studios are jamming their production machines to ride in the wake of SW-1. Steven *(Jaws)* Spielberg is preparing his UFO epic, *Close Encounters of the Third Kind;* a feature *Star Trek* is on-again/off-again at Paramount; and two studios are racing productions of *When Worlds Collide*. Too much has already been written about the *Star Wars* trip, and yet the verbal din has mostly served to drown out the significance of the event with a barrage of trivial statistics. It may be time to analyze the facts from a broader perspective of interest to alert educators and other people who like to think and talk about media.

It Works

Star Wars is a "head" film, a trip for all ages, a blast-off (drug-assisted or not) from the mundane. Audiences gasp as the Millennium Falcon "goes hyper," sucking every star in the viewer screen into the vortex of its wake as the souped-up space freighter quads the speed of light and escapes the Emperor's minions. They haven't felt such exhilaration since Keir Dullea entered the atmosphere of Jupiter in *Space Odyssey*. We pause on lyrical shots of a golden 'droid wandering the sandy wastes of twin-sunned Tatooine, muttering all the while like Edward Everett Horton playing Jeeves. With barely enough time to fasten our seatbelts, we are precipitated into crises and climaxes, neatly paced with touches of campy humor. The spaceport bar on Tatooine is a masterpiece of latex makeup—mutants from a thousand galaxies, the scum of the known universe, and yet "no androids served here."

All of this would be enough to justify the existence of any film, and yet, far from being "mere" escape (the adjective is a trap), there are ideas behind the plot and action of *Star Wars*. Lucas shows a galaxy we can recognize from our own past: a democracy deteriorated into a brutal Empire whose prime creation is the massive, oppressive Death Star (the term itself conjures up delicious contradictions of a life source perverted to an instrument of destruction). Machines such as space stations and satellites, androids and robots are in fine shape, but living things are a mess. Genetic mutants clutter up the corners of the galaxy, while deformed creatures such as the pathetic Jawas and savage Sand People scavenge the ravaged surface of planets like Tatooine, where moisture farms fight back encroaching deserts. Even the faces of the Imperial Storm Troopers are permanently sheathed in rigid reptilian armor of high-impact plastic.

Reason and technology have created this chaotic cosmos, and only romance and intuition can redeem it. A handful of humans join the Rebel Alliance and, armed with laser swords and a mythic code—the semi-religious Force of the Jedi knights—they set out to destroy Darth Vader, the fallen angel who masterminds the engines of destruction.

Hokey? Yes, but in the very way that myth transmutes the dross of everyday life problems into the spun gold cotton candy of fantasy.

Why It Works—It's Fun

Pondering the effectiveness of *Star Wars* is important. While audiences need not ask why it works, the answer is crucial to educators and thinking people. Cruising over the surface of the film as if encased in Luke Skywalker's landspeeder, we should note, first of all, that *Star Wars* is (need we say it?) a fun film. Director George Lucas has said "the word for this movie is fun," and audience participation is so full of contagious good feeling that we can believe him. Art is always a form of play, and this film invites everyone to share the fun.

The pace of the film keeps the plot from going maudlin: fast cuts, wipes, and dissolves leave you wanting just a bit more of each shot or scene. We want more because the images have style. Production designer John Barry can put together a space bar or a Death Star just the way we want to imagine it should look. British photography director Gilbert Taylor chooses the action angles that work, while John Mollo's costumes are exotic enough to feed our famished inner eyes.

The linear narrative is simplified to reach the kid in each of us—just as Lucas planned it. There are no complex side plots, issues or pauses, not even a full-blown romance to interrupt the action-packed story which, in the manner of radio serials and comic strips, begins in the middle and works both ways to its end, giving us a television-paced climax every fifteen minutes.

Star Wars is an "upper." Good overcomes Evil without explicit sex, sloppy violence (all deaths are highly stylized), or pessimistic musings about the plight of modern man/woman—even the sober moralizing of *Planet of the Apes* is spared. The result is fun without guilt. The difference between this kind of romantic innocence and escapism is that, while both take us out of our everyday mindset, escapism makes the return a trauma of guilt. *Star Wars* makes us feel good.

Why It Works—It Tames Technology

Star Wars audiences have been doing the unprecedented—cheering the technical credits at the end of the film, the more than three hundred technicians who helped create the fun. Although some critics feel the technical achievements overwhelm the fragile screenplay, the two are actually much too integral to compete, since they appear both on the screen and behind the scenes.

An essential ingredient of space fiction is its ability to create wonder and awe, to stimulate and satisfy our enormous curiosity about the space environment: other worlds with different time/space parameters; other creatures with whom we may learn to communicate. Unlike science fiction as such, there is little inclination for space epics to fear science, no mad scientists whose experiments take them where no one was intended to trod, creating Frankenstein monsters or Jekyll/Hyde transformations. The demons of space fiction are not the preternatural nightmares of horror films, the Draculas and werewolves, the mummies and devils which come from the past. Space fiction looks to the future, extrapolating from the hints which existing technology gives us, and conjecturing on human life and behavior in space, in other worlds, with other intelligences. The demon one finds in space is, as always, oneself, whether mirrored in neurotic computers like Hal with its programmed lie, or rising up in creatures that represent a distorted or isolated aspect of our own nature.

The technology-packed scenes of *Star Wars* are all the more effective because they are not laboriously explained—they're just there. The landspeeders antigrav float is as authentic as a forties flivver's chugging progress. The Millennium Falcon's beat-up look is somehow more reassuring than the gleaming perfection of Cape Kennedy's creations. When R2D2 finally delivers Princess Leia's desperate message to Ben Kenobi, he projects her holographic image to make the plea. Even the Death Star's deadly destructive power appears convincingly as a blasphemous imitation of a planetary moon.

Star Wars has a way of radically changing attitudes toward technology, particularly through those excellent emissaries R2D2 and C3PO. These "metallic megastars" are not only more human than most of the humans, but they allay fears of technology by their "human" failings. We come to expect the prissy fussiness of C3PO, a Tin Woodsman still creaky, but *with* a heart—especially for R2D2. This latter 'droid is a walking computer, totally loyal to Princess Leia, spunky, and, to the voluble exasperation of the devoted C3PO, continually in trouble. R2D2's language is a marvel of improvised sound technology. We are soon convinced we can understand his combination of bleeps, whistles, clicks, and sighs as well as we did the horns and whistles of the more libidinous Harpo Marx—both are the language of pure emotion.

R2D2 and C3PO generate a perfect complementarity of skills, talents, personalities, and emotions, a factor which causes many to liken them to Abbot and Costello or Laurel and Hardy. In reality they are more like Don Quixote and Sancho Panza, tall and short, idealist and pragmatist, computer and public relations robot, each needing the other to fill out the integral image of the human nature which they mirror. Unlike the lascivious computer of *Demon Seed* or the power-mad Colossus, they wanted to help. Young people, even those reared on the antitechnology of the sixties, *want* to feel good about technology. Jesse Kornbluth, who once held a Dow Chemical college recruiter hostage, admits in his *New Times* piece on the film, "*Star Wars* cured me . . . of a lifelong fear that computers might run wild and take over the world." R2D2 would chirp happily at the remark, even if C3PO is more likely to sniff at its patronizing tone. Just compare the two with the Six Million Dollar Man, Woman and Bionic Dog, and you'll know the difference. The technological virtuosity of *Star Wars* goes further than the delighted youngster's mastery of terms like "going hyper," laser swords and blasters, energy bolts and deflector shields. The action created *behind* the screen by photography and mechanical effects directors John Dykstra and John Stears is an equally effective interface between art and technique, human and machine. *Star Wars* boasts some 360 special effects, as opposed to 35 in *Space Odyssey,* a feat made possible by giant steps in technology during the ten years or less since Kubrick's film was made. Going beyond simple matte photography, the special effects recreate the three-dimensional motion of outer space by combining multiple moving objects and backgrounds, as in the attack on the Death Star. Computers attached to cameras made a hopelessly complex editing job possible by giving instant access to each take for selection and combination. The sound in *Star Wars* is an auditory marvel, from the asthmatic rum-

ble of Darth Vader to Chewbacca's expressive roar. There are an estimated 2000 snippets of processed sound used to distort even a door
slam into an "authentic" other-galaxy sound. Even the subtitled tongues
of the space-bar conversation are a computerized scrambling of 30 to
40 actual earthly languages. The standards for technological excellence
set by *Star Wars* will be hard to meet for future films in science fiction
and other genres.

Even as we admire the imaginative creations of Jawas and Wookies,
Tusken Raiders riding Banthas, and the mutants in the space-bar, we
have to note the traditional science fiction ambivalence toward technology which is manifest in *Star Wars*. All technology is subject to the Force.
Technology alone leads to such hideous creations as the Death Star,
which can vaporize a planet with a simple bolt of incredible energy. Unless technology is accompanied by the intuitive Force—the field of human energy and aspiration flowing from the deity or the collective unconscious—it destroys. Han Solo can argue cynically, "Hokey religions
and archaic weapons are no substitute for a good blaster at your side,"
but he himself is saved by the Force, as is the Rebel Alliance. When
Luke goes in for his final bombing run on the planetoid's nuclear center, Kenobi's voice persuades him to act by instinct and not by the computerized bombsight. Only then is the Death Star destroyed.

Star Wars restores the romance which our space program successes
have unwittingly taken from space exploration. I recall a night sail this
summer in which the sight of two orbiting satellites careening through
a maze of fixed stars briefly reminded me of what I had missed. The
NASA moon shots were vastly impressive, but they tended to reduce
space to a deadening banality, a technical achievement by managerial
types whose mundane reactions cheapened the experience. The reality
tended to stultify the imaginative advance of space fiction—until a simple fantasy restored us to our original, intuitive expectations of space exploration. Hostile critic Richard Corliss summed it up with grudging
admiration in *New Times:* "[*Star Wars*] is more than the sum of its parts.
It's a marriage of creative and mechanical virtuosity which is the American Capitalist ideal. *Star Wars* is that rare multimillion dollar epic that
can be called the vision of one man; it's also the most impressive kind
of collaborative effort." The astronaut/entrepreneurs took away the Man
in the Moon. We needed an Arthur Clarke and a George Lucas to bring
back the romantic sense that we are not alone, and to teach us once
again to Look to the Skies.

Why It Works—It's Rooted in Folklore Media

Fun film and technological marvel may be easily accessible reasons why
Star Wars works, but to get close to its conceptual heart we must explore
the film's roots in folklore and myth.

Prior to *Star Wars,* George Lucas scored as director with a meticulously detailed and tonally accurate return to his adolescence in *American Graffiti*. One of a new breed of young filmmakers coming out of film *schools* instead of studios, Lucas (along with Martin Scorsese, Francis Ford Coppola, and Steven Spielberg) is part of the first generation of filmmakers to share a past completely dominated by media. The result is that the personal history they draw upon for creative inspiration is the folklore and popular culture contained in old movies and radio serials, comic strips and pulp fiction, rock music and early television. What appears to be an incestuous "movie-movie" trend or a preference for media over reality is, instead, an awareness of how completely our folklore is dominated by the fables and fantasies of mass media.

Star Wars is a richly complex collage of not-so-old media experiences, sucked dry by the shallow but vigorous young roots of a media-bred director. Of all the sources used, two stand out: comic strips and old movies.

Anyone who can recall hours of adolescent oblivion buried in Marvel Comics will appreciate George Lucas' return to the comic strip. *Star Wars* is like a Sunday paper with a year's adventures all delivered at once, in color and motion, on a wide screen. Before conceiving *Star Wars,* Lucas sought the rights to *Flash Gordon*. But when the King Features price ran too high, he did something better—he created his own comic strip space epic. *Flash Gordon* was a blonde god, a futuristic Siegfried on an interstellar Rhine Journey to carry the Aryan ethic to alien worlds. After a long success as a comic strip, the story was serialized by Universal Films and became its second best hit of 1936, billed above the feature film on the marquees. With Olympic swimmer Buster Crabbe as Flash, the serial was given an unprecedented $350 million budget with which to generate twelve episodes of space adventure.

The parallels between *Star Wars* and *Flash Gordon* are obvious— Vader as Ming the Merciless, whose planet Mongo hurtled toward earth like the planetoid Death Star. But the similarities of technique are even more important than those of content. As one of many who have taught filmmaking by use of comic strips, I can think of much that *Star Wars* owes to that form. The use of a simple, direct narrative, accelerated by fast-cut images of colorful action, following each other in an effective rhythm of long, medium, and close shots is the first trait. Add to this the dramatic camera angles, minimal dialogue and carryover sound, and a series of climaxes at regular intervals before the grand crescendo of To Be Continued, and the likeness is almost complete. All that is missing is a preference of action over ideas, clearly defined hero/villain types in a simple morality play, and you have the stylistic structure of the old serial/strip. Audiences could not resist the opulent resurrection of their juiciest adolescent fantasies so faithfully rendered by *Star Wars.*

The second media source tapped by Lucas was the motion picture, a form just beginning to have a "history." From the old films we all enjoyed, *Star Wars* mined characters and situations, plots and ideas. The point here, however, is that the old films did not create the types, but drew them from the culture into the myth-making factory which was Hollywood in its Golden Age. Much has been made of George Lucas' use of dozens of old war movie aerial battle scenes for his inspiration in shooting and cutting the grand battle of the Alliance's X and Y rocket ships with the fighters of the Empire. Even more significant than this is the composite portrait of the American Hero taken from old movies ranging from *Wings* to *The Bridges at Toko-Ri.* Luke Skywalker (the name betrays the director's Icarus complex) is Andy Hardy, growing into a man under the guidance of Ben Kenobi standing in for Lewis Stone. This innocent hero is backed up by a more familiar type with the symbolic name of Solo: the rugged individuals, the private eyes, the cowboys and soldiers of fortune played by Bogart, Wayne, and a dozen other actors—characters who begin as cynics uninvolved in causes, but end up heroes in the thick of the fray. From the Western, Lucas borrowed the revenge motif and perhaps the old warrior (Samurai?) Ben Kenobi, who resurrects his Force in one last effort to overcome evil.

There are specific scenes duly noted—Luke's discovery of his aunt and uncle's burned-out moisture farm is a direct tribute to a scene from John Ford's *The Searchers. Forbidden Planet,* one of the best space fiction classics, gets a nod for its friendly Robby the Robot, and for the vast underground powerhouse of the vanished Krel civilization ("Man is unfit as yet to receive such power," says Dr. Morbius). Fritz Lang's *Metropolis* and any number of monster epics are similarly honored. Other media can also claim their share. The Shadow's "power to cloud the minds of men" is surely part of Kenobi's clever evasion of the Imperial Troopers. What is more, the very manner in which movies such as these personalized vast conflicts—focusing on individuals in a world at war—helped to generate the conviction that one person *can* make a difference, as only a hero can in myth. The Death Star considered itself invulnerable to single-piloted fighters; Luke proved otherwise.

New Myths for Old

The deepest response to *Star Wars* is on the level of myth, taken here to mean the human creative effort to make sense of oneself and the universe by stories, epics, and all the arts. The old myths helped us deal with fearsome, capricious natural forces—*The Iliad* and *The Odyssey,* for example, personifying the elements and "explaining" their interactions and relationships to humans in epic tales of a hero's adventures. There are no established myths for a technological civilization, and yet some are being created which draw their energy from timeless sources in human experience. It was no accident that Stanley Kubrick subtitled his film "A Space Odyssey." In a sense, we have been on but one journey throughout our entire history, and that is the exploration of our own ultimate identity and destiny. Is *Star Wars* part of that search?

Giambattista Vico some two hundred years ago saw myths as a way of conceiving and ordering the world, a means to generate the concepts and categories which govern our vision. Out of the natural, spontaneous expression of myth comes art, the attempt to embody, in ever more concrete, beautiful forms, that vision of society which unifies its structure. Cassirer adds to this notion the role of myth in objectifying inner states by isolating everyday phenomena and intensifying them until their objective form, their "demon," bursts forth in concrete, metaphorical image. Film performs an identical function in our society, crystallizing vague desires and social trends, giving them experiential forms that satisfy the needs of that society.

Star Wars, in a crazy, pop art way, touches a deep chord in the culture. Situated in the myth-structure of space/science fiction, it sets up an uneasy balance between technology and humanity, combining them in the timeless ritual we need to experience over and over again: the restoration of order in the universe by good overcoming evil. In this Manichean struggle, the Force comes down strongly on the side of the intuitive and irrational over the reasoned and the practical, the emotional over the planned and pragmatic. We might say that *Star Wars* opts for the right hemisphere of the brain, plugging into the sensibilities that send millions into TM, I Ching, T-groups, and even the new sects and renascent evangelist churches.

The symbolism of *Star Wars* is ultimately religious. The Force may have overtones of the "élan vital" of Bergson and the collective unconscious of Jung, but it appears concretely in Obi Wan Kenobi. Dressed like a medieval friar, Kenobi wields a sword that recalls the legend of King Arthur and the Knights of the Round Table seeking the Holy Grail. His prefix Ben ties him to Old Testament traditions, while his sacrificial "death" so that others may live places him in a generalized Christian frame of reference. Life, death, and resurrection form part of a ritual as old as the seasons of earth and the rise of organic life. What movie myths like *Star Wars* do with these eternal myths is to apply them to the modern culture, mediated by a colorful tradition of folk art and pop culture.

Conclusion

Star Wars exercises its own Force upon young people, many of whom have seen it dozens of times and memorized its images and words. Their response to the film is, in a sense, more important than the film itself, since the power of *Star Wars* comes from its audience. Like all successful films, it draws its ideas and feelings from the culture and returns them to the people refined as myth. How we read popular responses to the film is of great significance for education. If it merely precipitates a sudden surge of science fiction courses, it will have generated too narrow a reaction. What it can do is direct young people to other works for an even deeper individual (if not collective) experience of the awe and wonder of the universe. After viewing other science fiction film classics, there are books ranging from Burroughs, through H. G. Wells, to the theology fiction of C. S. Lewis and beyond into Heinlein, Clarke, and a dozen other masters. But we must not stop there. The values orientation of the search must ultimately end in philosophy if we are careful not to limit the range of application of *Star Wars.*

At the same time, educators and aware people must assimilate the experience of *Star Wars* for themselves. The film shows us a way to understand popular culture through the arts. Moreover, this technologically supersophisticated but simple film proves that no myth can be generated for our age without the use of applied technology working closely with a creative imagination. Furthermore, the work of young artists such as George Lucas reveals that media—even trashy pop media—*are* the only past the young have known, their roots, the common matrix of their youthful sensibilities. This *is* their history. Whether this small segment of the past relates to the history of the race depends largely on us. For this reason, *Star Wars* deserves more analysis than eulogizing, but an analysis which does not deteriorate into a deadening chapter-and-verse exegesis. Let the Force of *Star Wars* be with you by giving an entree to all the arts in the educational process, and not by merely placing a science fiction course in the curriculum.

George Lucas said he intended to give young people "an honest, wholesome fantasy life, the kind my generation had." *Star Wars,* with its computerized succession of action-filled images, does what its young creator envisioned. From this collage of comic strips and old movies, of radio serials and pulp sci-fi, from this manufactured cloud of trivia, there may one day condense, like galactic gases and cosmic debris, a substantial world of Myth.

Where Have All the Heroes Gone?

Peter Schillaci

A casual glance at the movie screen marks the seventies as the decade in which the hero became an endangered species. Wistfully peering through the San Francisco fog for Humphrey Bogart, we stumble, instead, into Peter Falk as *The Cheap Detective*. The more "experienced" among us long for Rudolf Valentino's sighs, but all we hear is nervous giggles from Gene Wilder's *The World's Greatest Lover*. With our heroes reduced to Campy Spoofs, the great genres are fair game for the sophomoric satirist—*Blazing Saddles* demolishes the Western, and *Young Frankenstein* does the same for Horror. The appearance of *Rocky* and *Star Wars* does not reverse the trend—these are comic book heroes who can amuse but not inspire. Perhaps the movie hero is not endangered, but already extinct?

It is too facile to explain the hero's abrupt exit by describing ours as an Antiheroic Age. Even antiheroes such as Dustin Hoffman (*The Graduate*) and Jack Nicholson (*One Flew over the Cuckoo's Nest*) were heroes of a sort in their attack on institutions, but we find no equivalent of their roles today. Our age seems to be as weary of causes as dog soldier Ray Hicks in *Who'll Stop the Rain?* Like him, we have had too many heroes in the hyped-up mode of the sixties. What is interesting, however, is the cluster of reasons for our suspicion. They may give us a clue to the untimely demise of the hero.

The demythologizing of the American hero began, as did the apotheosis, with actual persons in historical events. The hero is an individual who performs a brave and significant deed which helps restore the balance of good and evil in the universe. But the problems we face in the Global Village are either too massive for an individual to overcome, or of a nature which we consider unsusceptible to heroics. We can admire a Ralph Nader taking on the auto industry, the American Medical Association, and other institutions, but (for all that) he does not become a folk hero . . . the stuff that myth is made of. Neither does the middle management type at the General Services Administration who blows the whistle on waste. No one individual is likely to solve the problems of world hunger, energy, cancer, the arms race, genocide, racism, pollution, *or* the decline of traditional values.

Furthermore, those individuals who do seize the popular imagination seldom stand up under the scrutiny of the media. Our emergent heroes are as short-lived as nightblooming cactus. No sooner do they rise up in the public eye than they are cut down by relentless reporting, over-exposure, and a suffocating blizzard of information which leaves little for our imaginations. The late Hubert Humphrey or any living sports star are cases in point. We know too much about them—their injuries, their investments, their lives. Our media-focus on Humphrey's campaign funds and Joe Namath's knees distracts from their heroic personae. Even F.D.R. and Winston Churchill are unlikely to have survived today's media spotlight, which inspires blandness and makes public figures as vulnerable as a flasher. Our heroes are as often shot down by mistresses and mob connections, by financial statements and psychiatric histories, as they are by assassins' bullets.

Can we seriously ask, then, "Where have all the heroes gone?" The disappearance of the American Hero has followed upon the demise of the American Dream, with a sour cynicism gradually replacing youthful optimism. In a process culminating in the twin events of Vietnam and Watergate, mirror images of domestic and foreign decay became one.

Vietnam did more than spoil the dream of international altruism which, since World War II, characterized our self-image as a world power. There died in Indochina one of the prototypical heroes, the soldier, second only to the Western hero in influence on our culture. The war movie as a genre began to die in Korea, in films etched with bitterness (*Pork Chop Hill, Steel Helmet*). By the time the truth was out on Vietnam, only one film attempted (unsuccessfully) to mythologize the conflict—*The Green Berets,* produced and acted by John Wayne, who had a "hero's" reputation invested in the war.

Watergate, in turn, did for our domestic innocence what Vietnam had done for our international naivete. The crime and the coverup shook our political processes, toppled a president, and even threatened the democratic system itself. The FBI and (to a lesser extent) the CIA spy heroes stood exposed as willing to sacrifice law in the enforcement of order, viewing American dissenters as their most dangerous enemy. With these ideals died all the traditional lawman heroes of film history. The Good Cop myth, like the Western before it, was shunted to the fantasy world of television, where it was anesthetized in an endless outpouring of mindless series. Some "realists" welcome the dissolution of myth and the disappearance of the hero as signs of our culture's maturity, a leaving aside of the toys of its childhood. But as educators with a sense of history we know that a culture cannot exist without myth, taken here not as an escape *from reality,* but *into* reality under all its aspects—objective and subjective, actual and potential, logical and imaginative. Art is the primary mode by which a culture adapts to its environment. As that environment becomes subject to accelerated change, the adaptation becomes critically necessary, and myths must be developed which are at once a reaction to and a control of rapid change. The Western myth arose as a reaction to the revolutionary change of the American Frontier. It telescoped history from the Civil War to the transcontinental railroad, and incorporated the virtues and values of half a dozen American folk heroes under the towering image of the Western hero. The crime film performed the same service for the complex sociopolitical arena of the great urban centers under the impact of mass immigration, industrialization, and the rise of the large corporations. Our image of the Great Depression and Prohibition, like that of the American West, was formed on the movie screens of America. It is the image of ourselves.

What are current films doing to generate a myth for our times, a hero capable of ordering the complexity of our troubled environment?

In chaotic times the first resort is to metaphor, fantasy, and the occult. Disaster films, for example, not only articulate our fear of our own technological advances (*Towering Inferno, Airport*), but of their impact on the natural environment as well (*Earthquake*). In the disaster film (a controlled *Ship of Fools* situation) personal problems are solved, and one or a few individuals can cooperate to save the rest. In *Jaws,* the evil in the world is reduced in metaphor to a force outside ourselves, a transferral which becomes diabolical influence in occult films such as *Exorcist* and *Omen*. The "heroes" of these films symbolically restore the balance between good and evil . . . the sheriff and scientist in *Jaws,* the exorcist in the other film. But the gesture of heroism is symbolic, an escapist ploy to avoid facing the evil within, and largely unrooted in myth.

Another recourse taken in the face of complex. radical change is the comic book heroics of *Rocky* and *Star Wars*. The comic book has long served as our lowest-common-denominator morality play, delivering the message with liberal doses of zippy action, heavy violence and sophomoric sexiness. Television has adapted the comic book creatures (*The Incredible Hulk* and *Wonder Woman*) and after the success of its own creations has come up with the technological equivalent of the Tarzan menage: the Bionic Man, Woman, Boy, and Dog. Meanwhile, a spectacular film version of *Superman* is in the works. *Star Wars* epitomizes the trend, but handles the form with more originality—a reconstruction which amounts to recreating the form, an achievement which television's *Battlestar Galactica* has thus far been unable to duplicate. *Rocky*'s hero is also a comic book creation, but with a special mission to shore up the sagging American Dream of the poor boy making it to the top. *Rocky* was also a shade more conscious of what it was doing than the others. None of these attempts, however popular, amounts to mythmaking.

Surprisingly enough, we have come closest to generating new heroes in films which come to grips with Vietnam and Watergate . . . the hero rising out of the ashes of the previous myth, as it were. In *All the President's Men,* Woodward and Bernstein are first incorporated into the movie personae of Robert Redford and Dustin Hoffman, teaming the Wasp western with the ethnic urban image, and then melded into the venerable genre of American journalism films such as *The Front Page.* The result is the revival of the investigative journalist hero myth in which two individuals successfully buck the enormous machinery of government and bring out the truth which a democracy needs to function. *All the President's Men* says that the system works. The tens of thousands of young people packing journalism schools seem to believe it.

The Hero Redivivus is much more complex in recent films coming out of the Vietnam experience. Whereas *The Green Berets* merely reran the World War II movie myth in Indochina, the Vietnam films are closer to *All Quiet on the Western Front.* The standard for films attempting to get the monkey of Vietnam off our backs has been set by *Coming Home*—at once an apologia and a manifesto on that event. A returned paraplegic is an improbable hero. He cannot undo the Vietnam war, but he can see it as it was. Moreover, he can help high school kids by telling it like it is, breaking down as he talks of "all that shit we did in 'Nam." His decision to keep living, to use his fragmented strength to fight the ongoing war, is in the tradition of heroic courage. His mutual effect on Jane Fonda is an upbeat contemporary love story which further fits the tradition. To his role as Luke Martin, Jon Voight brings the qualities of the hero who must first overcome his own fears before performing the symbolic heroic act. In this film, disowning the Vietnam war is the first step toward helping the culture to deal with it. We have not yet had the honesty to explore in films the military hospitals in which the thousands who will never graduate to a wheelchair are carefully kept out of sight.

Who'll Stop the Rain? is another returned-veteran film which continues the exorcising process of revelations. As Ray Hicks, Nick Nolte represents the fundamentally decent person trying to live with the horrors of his Vietnam experiences. His refusal to be pushed around by the corrupt narcs is a sign that, unlike Converse, the burned-out war journalist, he is still able to act, to incorporate his sixties consciousness into one last futile gesture of courage in a questionable cause.

There are, then, new heroes and myths in formation. But how can we limit our inquiry to "heroes" and ignore "heroines"? Complicating the slow and painful process of reconstructing the American Dream in an age of cynicism is the revolutionary realignment of sexual roles in America. We need to find a new definition of hero which will incorporate the redeployment of sexual roles and the purging of sexual stereotypes now in progress. The most immediate change comes from the forthright demand by women to be allowed heroics, the demand for a woman who is a heroine in her own right as a person, and not simply in reference to a hero. One pertinent answer to the question, "where have all the heroes gone?" is the creative artist's negotiations with women fighting for a place in the heroic spotlight. This is a transitional period in which we are trying to build new myths along the lines of an evolving sexuality in which human persons representing the full range of personality (including their sex) are equally represented.

The obvious inclination to tone down sexual differences does not make for exciting myths. There is no such thing as a "Unisex Hero." We demand that hero/heroine be fully man and fully woman. But as our perception of the meaning of these terms changes, we find it difficult to delineate the heroic mode with an appropriate sexual orientation. Is it possible to define the male hero without falling into the macho image? And can we liberate the heroine without making her appear a man in drag? Are we doomed to the comical compromise of *Charlie's Angels,* which both patronizes and exploits its "liberated" women?

The dilemma just posed is operative in some phenomenally popular recent films which are searching (however tentatively) for a new heroic mode. The films starring males are trying to shake the macho image and still preserve masculinity . . . (whatever that is). And the vehicles for women feature them in various stages of liberation (whatever that is), trying to reconcile liberation with commitment. Several examples will illustrate the trend.

Saturday Night Fever made John Travolta a star . . . but did it create a hero out of Tony Manero, the disco king? The answer is unclear. His heroic act comes, not in his victory amid the pulsing strobes of the disco floor (as less perceptive audiences imagined), but on a lonely subway car ride after the elusive Karen Lynn Gorney opens his eyes to a new life-style. Will he give up the rumbles and the back-seat sex, the tiresome trade-off of tepid days in the hardware store for a few hours of feverish Saturday night action? The film makes no easy guarantees, but at least this emergent hero is thinking about his life and his masculinity. Under the candy-colored gloss of *Grease* there lurks a similar theme, a taming-the-male-rogue formula with a new twist. Travolta must leave the T-Birds and Pink Ladies for Sandy and a life of genteel sexuality because he is turned off by her tight-pants sexpot act. On a different level but a related one, a young boy's cynicism over the nurturing stability of his foster father is summed up in the title, *A Hero Ain't Nothin' but a Sandwich.* The common denominator of these film heroes is the search for a new way to be a man, and in each case the woman shows the way.

While the male hero is shedding the macho image like an old skin, the emerging woman is busy trying to reconcile her liberation with commitment. There is nothing new about this reconciliation, except that it is usually the man who wrestles with his "loss of freedom" in our traditionally male-dominated society. Now the surrender of freedom is the woman's problem, and the choice is all the more dramatic in that it is made from a position of limited power and restricted opportunity. Some of the most interesting recent films treat this theme of liberation.

The first area to be liberated by the so-called women's films is that of feminine friendships. It may or may not be true that the desperate competition for the male made all women enemies. What is certain, however, is that (in comparison to the male-bonding films like *Butch Cassidy and the Sundance Kid*) the role of friendship among women has remained underdeveloped. Claudia Weill's flawed first feature film, *Girlfriends,* portrays friendship as an interim commitment, one which would allow a woman to develop autonomy without falling into premature dependency. When aspiring poet Anne marries for security, the betrayal felt by photographer Susan is acute. For her, a common experiment has been abandoned. Susan's life may be uneasy and insecure, but she, at least, has had the courage to reject a tender trap—Eric's invitation to live with him. The friendship between the women is in danger, and yet both women feel they need it in order to "survive."

The friendship in *Turning Point* allows Shirley MacLaine and Anne Bancroft to be friends *and* competitors. Each has taken a dramatically different direction within their common commitment to dance: one raising a family and continuing to teach dance, the other pursuing her long career through a dwindling repertoire of roles. They meet in the crisis of midlife, realize they've come by different routes to the same problem, and physically fight out their differences. Bursting into laughter, they finally understand that both careers are completely fulfilling and totally frustrating. They remain friends.

In *Julia,* the friendship between socialist reformer Vanessa Redgrave and writer/observer Jane Fonda is played against a backdrop of historical conflict which deepens their friendship *and* their individual growth. Each woman is strong, each a tough competitor in dangerous situations: Julia mutilated and killed helping Jews escape Nazi Germany; Lillian making it in the man's world of literature and drama. Unfortunately, certain ambiguities in their relationship, which provided the subject of Hellman's play, *The Children's Hour,* were left unexamined by the film. Nevertheless, for each of them their friendship gave an autonomy which made commitment possible.

The risks of liberation are evident in a film such as *Looking for Mr. Goodbar,* where the abrupt transition from repressed abstinence to free sexual experimentation proves self-destructive. The innocence which Diane Keaton brought to this role made her death sacrificial, in a sense, but not heroic. That quality *is* found, however, in Jill Clayburgh's portrait of *An Unmarried Woman.* The negative title tells us what odds Erica faces when her Wall Street workaholic husband leaves her after twelve years of an apparently ideal marriage. Although she lives amidst marital chaos (her women friends are either unhappily married, divorced, or sleeping around), Erica is unprepared for the split and almost goes to pieces. Her heroism, however, consists not so much in carrying on, but in refusing to accept a new relationship until she has made it on her own as a person. We may be skeptical at how easily she meets Mr. Right—artist Saul Kaplan (played irresistibly by Alan Bates)—after a few one-night stands. But given the sincerity of his love, we can only admire her courage in not taking his offer of a summer idyll. The contemporary heroine's grand gesture is to refuse a commitment, with or without marriage, until she has inner freedom; otherwise it's only a "liberated dependency."

The heroics of sexual liberation may appear to be small potatoes. The drama of men freeing themselves of macho prerogatives and liberated women refusing premature commitment is hardly mythical in stature. Compared to the rousing action and sexual clashes of past movies, today's thoughtful films make it appear that Hollywood has undergone a sex-change operation. But in reality, it is the society which is changing, and films are searching for a way to "control" this radical change by incorporating it into a mythological structure.

This period of sloughing off sexual stereotypes may leave us uncomfortable and disorientated, especially since it will take some time before the new myths take shape. But in the transition, we can take comfort from several films which point symbolically to the future.

Coming Home is the most coherent filmic prognostication of things to come. Its hero comes from where we've been—the masterpiece of machismo which was the Vietnam war. He returns paralyzed from the waist down, "half a man," as we once would say, and yet whole, in spite of the symbolic suspension of a destructive sexuality. His maddening rage is subdued by Jane Fonda, and their love scenes are a moving discovery of the sensuality of reversed sex roles. Jon Voight's presence gives the new heroic role provocative resonances. As a "midnight cowboy," Voight changed from strutting stud to caring for his buddy, Ratzo Rizzo. In the sleeper, *Conrack,* Voight brought to his teacher's role a strength of nurturing gentility which we would call "feminine" only if we still believed in the parceling out of human characteristics to each sex for the distortions of exclusivity. And in *Deliverance,* it was Voight's fearful courage which saved his friends, in contrast to the "fearless" machismo and recklessness of Burt Reynolds. *Coming Home* also portrays the conversion of the woman from doting housewife to dedicated political radical. Here the sexes meet each other half way and proclaim a truce in the war which for centuries has been parceling out human virtues and vices as weapons to one sex or the other, but not to both. Fonda's husband, his psyche unhinged by the failure of his masculine code and the "violation" of his wife, walks into the sea, metaphorically destroying the macho image. In *Coming Home,* then, we can discern the hope of a new heroism rising out of the ruins of the traditional American war myth.

Educators can render young people a service by showing them how to keep alive the human need for heroics without souring it with cynicism or inflating it by escapist fantasizing. We live in an age of pop culture "stars," from the Fonz to Travolta, idols who are ultimately going to disappoint a generation of worshipping youngsters. These junk food heroes should be compared with the great human models provided by literature and drama. By showing the past as continuing to give meaning to the present, we establish a continuity, a matrix out of which new, humanizing myths, with their heroes and heroines, can grow.

For all their endangerment through the collapse of the American Dream, the hero and heroine are not extinct. If we have the sensitivity to perceive their presence in the film medium, we may be stimulated to form a new definition of heroics. We may come to recognize the heroine in *An Unmarried Woman* who sets about liberating herself from the worst subjugation of all—a limiting concept of her own potential. And we may also come to recognize the hero in the telephone linesman of *Close Encounters of the Third Kind,* the unprepossessing Richard Dreyfuss, who single-mindedly pursues a vision all the way. In a gesture of spiritual courage, he joins the aliens, a gracious encounter staged as an almost religious ritual. We the audience, in turn, are welcomed by him into the heroic movie myth, a world of ecstatic devotion to an ideal, a belief in worlds beyond this world, and an acceptance of extraterrestrial beings whose benevolence brings peace.

This is the world of movies, a world which offers, in its controlled environment, heroic scale and total experience, our last, brave hope for the hero and heroine we need so desperately.

The 16mm Treatment: A Prescription for Passive Viewers

Jeanne Betancourt

Much of my work with young people and media requires logical and ordered, in fact, linear thinking. Visual media themselves are nonlinear, holistic, or, as currently theorized, use the right hemisphere of the brain. As a high school teacher, I develop lessons in media to encourage kids to exercise the *left hemisphere*—the school side—on stuff they more frequently experience in nonschool life. To help them integrate the two areas of their growing experience, I ask them to apply some rational, critical skills to their out-of-school viewing and to bring some of the intuitive, sensual stuff into school.

In this article I would like to share certain techniques for using film studies in the high school classroom which can also work in public library and museum settings. I have organized these strategies into: Film Logs, Feature Film, Independent Film, Filmmaker-Speakers, and Activities.

Film Logs

Film Logs (see figure 1) are designed to help students react to their individual movie-viewing experiences. Most teenagers don't spend much time in movie theaters. The number of films I saw at Saturday afternoon double-features and, later, on Saturday night movie dates far outnumber the four or five popular films they see each year. I often wonder which will be their "last picture show." But they do see a lot of movies—on television. Therefore, in their film logs students have the choice of using a movie that is replayed on television or one shown in a theater. Daily postings in my class (on a student-run bulletin board) announce good reruns on television and we also discuss what is playing in local movie houses.

Early in the course we learn the vocabulary film people use. I find "my kids" already react to camera distance, angle, transition, timing, et cetera. I just help them label these phenomena in order to facilitate our mutual exploration of film. We also analyze the differences between a screening on television or at a movie house, and the relationship between

Reprinted by permission of the author and publisher from *Film Library Quarterly* 10:4-11; 66-69 (No. 3 & 4, 1977). Copyright © 1977 by Film Library Information Council.

the sociological content of films and the era that produced them. The movies shown on television embrace a range of genre and eras—this is one of television's advantages. In a two-week period this fall in New York they could see Flash Gordon shorts, *Birth of a Nation* by D. W. Griffith, *Strike* by Eisenstein, *That's Entertainment Part II, The Return of the Pink Panther, The Longest Yard,* and the beginning of a Katherine Hepburn retrospective—a real smorgasbord!

For the first several weeks in my class students use a general log form that can be applied to most movie experiences. Later they use different forms for contemporary films, older films, and documentaries. Each includes a classification which goes from simple reporting skills (plot summary), through analytic thinking (shot-by-shot analysis), to creative thinking (other media experiences on the topic). These film logs have produced encouraging results. Whole families get involved in the log and in answering the questions—"We can't just watch a movie anymore" is a typical complaint I get from parents. Obviously completing the log integrates out-of-school experiences with classroom experiences. Another positive result is that kids are introduced to whole areas of film they had not previously considered. Sometimes this happens through the classroom postings, what they see in their friends' logs, the kind of film log they are working on, or because they put the assignment off and have to catch whatever is on the tube the night before a deadline. Log questions are open-ended and require both analytic and creative thinking.

Title: **Date Of Screening:**
Year: **Channel Or Theater:**
Director: **Genre:**
Stars:

1. **Plot Summary:** What happened in this film?

2. **Memorable Shots**
   What was happening? what you saw the effect on you
   (shot by shot)

3. **Transitions** (How the filmmaker got from one shot or sequence to another —visual and/or audio.)
   Shot Transition Shot Effect

4. **Soundtrack**
   What was happening? What did you hear? The effect on you

5. **Set**

6. Describe another media experience that you have had on the same topic, story, or theme of this film.

7. **Rating: ★★★★** (one to four stars)

Fig. 1 Film log form

This allows motivated students to go as far as their interest and ability take them. And occasionally students who start out with little interest will pick up self-confidence and skills through working with the logs, leaving the course with more thorough and creative responses than when they began.

Feature Length Films

The log is one way of "using" the feature length film. Another way of working with feature length films without showing them in the classroom is by analyzing films most kids have seen on their own (*Rocky, Jaws, Star Wars, Wizard of Oz,* etc.) in reference to technique and so on. When I take class time to screen feature length films I use less accessible works, showing their place in film history and using them as a frame of reference for more recent commercial and/or independent films. My favorites include films from Russia in the twenties, particularly Eisenstein and Vertov for their inventive technique, their effect on film history, and their exploration of the relationship between form and content. In 1976 when there was so much discussion about violence in film and on television we studied Fritz Lang's *M*. For an introduction we described the techniques in contemporary film for showing violence—both visually and aurally. Lang's indirect techniques suggesting violence—all off-screen and symbolic—contrast strongly with the techniques employed in recent films such as *Taxi Driver* or television's *Starsky and Hutch*. It helps kids develop a sense of the varied ways people have expressed themselves through film when they can see the connections between early works (Eisenstein, Lang, etc.) and current productions.

Independent Films

My major film source for classroom viewing is the work of independent filmmakers—works that are often less than thirty minutes long. All films can't be approached in the same way. Different energies and skills are required for watching a commercial Disney film and for viewing an independent documentary on Mid-East politics. These independent works introduce students to a range of visual experiences and encourage them to develop viewing competency. If we are going to help kids adapt to the ever-changing and expanding media of today's fast-paced world, we need to find alternatives to the economically motivated and controlled commercial media. Since independent filmmakers are not restricted to commercial formats, many of their works involve creative explorations in form. Moreover, much independent work attempts to share, with some depths, the filmmaker behind-the-camera and permits the viewer to learn something about the subject as well as the artist's attitude toward it.

The independent or alternate filmmaker often explores both new and old ideas from points of view that are refreshingly honest. For example *Chris and Bernie* (Bonnie Friedman and Deborah Shaffer, New Day Films) documents the lives of two women and their children without the laugh-a-minute or evangelizing moralisms of situation comedies. After viewing *Chris and Bernie* my classes analyze how Chris and Bernie would be treated as subjects of a situation comedy, a soap opera, or as the guest stars of one week's episode in a police or hospital drama.

Working with alternate media sends kids back to more available media with an aroused critical consciousness.

Filmmaker Speakers

I find it a great help to introduce kids to independent film by inviting filmmakers to visit the class. Filmmakers are made available through Film Bureau, a project supported by public funds from the New York State Council on the Arts, and from Lincoln Center.

I have evolved a number of guidelines in trying to make the most out of their visits.

Give the class some background on the artist and remind them that he or she is coming. If possible show another work by the filmmaker before the visit/screening.

Place the films logically within the curriculum, connecting them with other work.

Prepare the filmmaker for what the students have experienced and where the curriculum is going.

When the filmmaker leaves, it is not over. The class is responsible for a worksheet, letter, or arts actively related to the visit. I let them know in advance that there will be a follow-up activity.

If a filmmaker works out really well with the class—I often have him/her back the next year to visit a new group or to present new works to the same group.

Have an alternate lesson/film in case there is a snowstorm, power failure, flood, epidemic, or transit strike and the filmmaker can't make it.

Susan Sussman recently brought her film *Eugenie* to my class, and we developed a lesson to integrate her visit with the curriculum. *Eugenie* is the story of a twelve-year-old sometimes girl, sometimes woman, who lives with her divorced mother and younger sister. Eugenie is taunted by the local teenage boys who cruise her neighborhood in an old convertible, taught by the babysitter who seems more knowing about sex, and troubled by her attractive mother who appears more concerned with her beauty and her boyfriend than her children (16 min., Phoenix, 1977). After the screening, she discussed the steps she followed to produce her film. Since I wanted to contrast the representation of the young teen in this independent work with the more stereotyped images of teens in commercial works, I had students make a chart on the image of teens in film and television. This list was a warm-up exercise providing a basis for a personal essay on their opinion of how teens are represented in commercial media. After Sussman's visit we discussed the representation of the young teen in *Eugenie* in relationship to those they listed. One student said:

> The only believable experience I've had with teen portrayal has not been through television but through film. *Eugenie* was a story about a twelve-year-old girl who was in fact twelve years old . . . I could believe Eugenie and also as important, her entire living situation. I felt things and people were done honestly so I could relate my own similar experiences to Eugenie's.
>
> —Laurie Benjamin.

When Susan Sussman visited my "Novel To Film" class with the same film, I preceded her visit by reading them the short story by Christine Shutt that was the basis for the *Eugenie* script. Sussman followed the screening with a discussion on the process of writing a script from a short story and translating it to the screen. We followed this by creating story-boarded scenes from short fiction works.

Activities

For openers. Like strangers at a party, films should be introduced. I present films to my class with a few words, a motivating activity, or an assignment the students do the night before. *String Bean,* a short narrative by Edmund Sechan, and *Yudie,* a documentary by Mirra Bank, both deal with older women. A comfortable way to introduce either of these films is to have the class write a word association list on "old age." Then I ask them to write a paragraph describing themselves in fifty or sixty years, and we share these before the screening.

The word association that begins this exercise prepares students to meet a new person or idea, to interact with the film, and to personalize the experience. It takes little time and sets an inviting tone. Ask the participants to write the first five to ten words they think of on the subject of the film, e.g. war, love, death, drugs, parenting. Next, create a "living poem." Have them imagine they are at a slide show with pictures flashing all over the walls and ceiling that visualize the topic. Now *they* are the soundtrack for that experience. Each person says a word from their list. Sometimes I repeat this exercise with new words after the screening in order to demonstrate the effect of the film. Questionnaires also help personalize a screening experience. *Men's Lives* (Josh Hanig and Will Roberts, New Day Films) documents, through interviews, cinema verité footage, and narration, the demands and expectations of the American male from childhood through adulthood. To introduce the film I have students

complete a rather lengthy questionnaire about their own stages of maturation: What was your favorite toy (at 5)? What was your favorite television
show (at 11)? How did what your parents, teachers, and/or peers expect
of you connect with the fact that you were male or female? And so on.
While these motivators are not necessarily filmic they help students deal
with content, particularly of nontheatrical films, that might otherwise be
difficult for them to understand. I find it easier to deal with form after
the screening if we work with aspects of the content before viewing the
film.

Worksheets. Worksheets, very much like film logs, follow a similar classification—going from simple recall to analysis and ending with creative
thinking. In worksheets, however, the questions are designed around a
specific film and placed in such a way as to demand an increasing range
of skills. For the film *Yudie,* mentioned earlier, I asked them to list at
least seven things they learned from the film about the life of the Jewish
community on the lower East side in the early 1900s. Next, I ask them
to write Yudie's life history in chronological order. (It is not in the film).
These content/recall questions are followed by more analytical ones:
when were stills used?; how did you react to them?; analyze memorable
shots and soundtrack for effect; what was the filmmaker's point of view?;
how does the relationship between the subject and the filmmaker affect
the film? Finally I ask creative questions. How would this material have
been handled in a situation comedy or a soap? Describe a film you would
like to see made about someone you care for—be specific about the
soundtrack; what would be shot and how would it be edited to express
what you feel about your subject?

Comparison. I ask students to compare films—an exercise which develops their analytic skills. We divide comparisons into two major sections:
content (what the film says), and *form* (how it says what it says). Through
thinking about form, students realize what makes film distinct from other
art forms. Content analysis helps them isolate what each film is trying to
say—hopefully sharpening their critical awareness of what films deliver.
Frequently, they will compare a fiction film with a documentary on the
same topic, or two films with a similar theme, one they liked and one
they didn't. The comparison chart helps them to understand their reasons
for favoring or disliking a particular film. After some instruction on ordering ideas and the use of transitional devices, students can use these
technical tools to develop their comparison chart into an essay.

Critical Essays. Just as the comparison chart provides the material for
comparative essays, the worksheets and film logs provide the basis for
writing a critical paper. Many students discover, to their surprise, that
they have the outline for several paragraphs about a film in the answers
on their film log or worksheet. We discuss topic sentences, transition,
order, introduction, and conclusion in class and they take it home and

go to it. The essays are developed in the later part of the course so kids can choose their "best" worksheet or log as their source. This allows a stimulating diversity. They don't all write about *Star Wars*—and the final product lends itself to either large or small group sharing.

Conclusion

None of the work we do with media in schools replaces the students' experience of individual film or television programs. Certainly everything we educators do *around* the screening is relevant, but each work has its own particular moment. Just as a poem by e.e. cummings communicates, independent of the study of alliteration or analysis of its meaning, so a film by Eisenstein communicates without studying montage or analyzing the film's relation to politics.

At times I design a section in film studies on a thematic base: short curricula on the theme "Ages of Women," a series on war and peace, and so on. I enjoy watching how the content of one film informs the others. Now, when I think thematically, I am interested in grouping films that can help kids deal with social situations—family life, adult role models, youth and identity. Grouping films along themes is useful in setting up mini-courses and organizing community or library screenings. Thematically structured filmographies can be helpful to people in other disciplines—e.g., sociology and anthropology. Since you may work with kids and film in single meetings and not in consecutive classes as I do, you will obviously have to adapt my suggestions to your own situation.

I don't presume to know what is "good" or "bad" for kids in contemporary media. My students study media with an inquiring tone that fosters investigation. Their questions and their viewing experiences help them become analytical, critical, and creative in their responses. This prepares them to make choices for their viewing from an informed base. This is especially important since their choices affect the quality of broadcasting both today and in the future; but perhaps even more so because they will help to create the content of television, film, and as yet undiscovered media to come.

Student Answers to Film Log Questions

Compare this film with other media experiences that you have had on the same topic.

High Noon

I would compare this film with the Spiderman cartoons in the Daily News. Each character has to fight evil to save the townspeople alone. The people don't want to help them and don't even thank them. Each man is pitted against his foe in a suicide mission and the people don't even care. Both stories show that when trouble comes you can't depend on anyone but yourself.   —Eric Wilck

A Night in Casablanca

This comedy murder situation in a detective style is very similar to the format of the TV serial *Get Smart*. Agent 89 is looking out for the murderer with his fellow agents and on the way is confronted by many outrageous situations which make this a comedy too. The two are extremely similar but the Marx Brothers win me over any day.   —Shifra Teitelbaum

What contemporary values are reflected in this film?

Network

The apparent lack of morals in the corporate structures was taken for granted. Violence was also taken for granted. Sex was completely open. There was no restriction on language. People were a product of television. The media molded people, but business molded the media. According to this film business is the real power. . . . Values are warped by the corporations' desires.   —Anita Karl

In this film the main value was to show how far people will go to win others over to their side. Another value reflected was the man leaving his wife of twenty-five years for a younger woman. Actually this whole film reflected the "now" time.   —Alisa Yalan

What values of that time are reflected in the film?

On the Waterfront

During the 1950s Americans were interested in finding out the truth behind many things. This is evidenced by the popularity of the televised Kefauver and Army-McCarthy hearings. This film values honesty at any cost. At the time Director Kazan had testified against others at the House UnAmerican Activities Committee.

What new ideas did this film introduce to you?

Cuba: The Castro Generation

This film introduced me to the idea of one day meeting my cousins, aunts, uncles and other relatives still in Cuba and to be the first American to interview Castro and to find out what he is really like.

—Yvonne Ambersley

Describe this topic as it might be experienced in another form (situation comedy, feature-length film, news item, etc.).

The Miracle Months

If this topic was in the form of a doctor show, some true-to-life experiences would have been changed for the sake of drama. Instead of showing and explaining the normal gestation period and what went wrong for these three mothers, their stories would have been exploited, and it would be hard to understand what was happening and why. Also, at least one of the babies would have died.   —Eric Sherman

The Mysterious Monsters
If this documentary was a feature length film, they would have to make the Bigfoot attack people and kill to make the film have more appeal to the public. The film would have more action and adventure.

Lure of the Dolphins
A Dolphin magazine could be created. This monthly would include updates on all scientific research and new achievements on dolphins. . . . It could include announcements of all dolphin television programs, films, and books that could be coming out. It could even include a fictional article each week on dolphins—maybe science fiction or even a rescue story . . . the photographs would have to be an essential part of the magazine.

Describe the reaction of the audience that was with you in the theater. What did it tell you?

Airport '77
The audience was restless at times and excited at the action at other times. They laughed when a man in pain was stepped on. This showed me that these people came to the movie to see violence and death. When the movie dragged they wanted it to pick up. But when Jack Lemmon escaped and called for help they applauded. This showed me that even though they like danger, they were glad to see him escape death.

—Robert Coiro

BIBLIOGRAPHY

Amelio, Ralph J. *Film in the Classroom*. Fairfield, N. J.: Pflaum/Standard, 1971.

Armes, Roy. *Film & Reality, An Historical Survey*. New York: Penguin, 1974. (Good as text for high interest/ability.)

Bobker, Lee. *Elements of Film*. 2nd ed. New York: Harcourt, 1974.

Brown, Roland G. *The Bookless Curriculum*. Fairfield, N. J.: Pflaum/Standard, 1972.

Johnson, Ron and Bone, Jan. *Understanding the Film*. New York: Amphoto, 1976. (High School text with guides.)

Knight, Arthur. *The Liveliest Art*. rev. ed. New York: New American Library, 1971.

Kuhns, William, and Stanley, Robert. *Exploring the Film*. Fairfield, N. J.: Pflaum/Standard, 1969. (High School text with guides.)

Kuhns, William. *Movies in America*. Fairfield, N. J.: Pflaum/Standard, 1973. (Text with guide entitled *Teaching in the Dark*.)

————. *The Moving Picture Book*. Fairfield, N. J.: Pflaum/Standard, 1975. (High School text.)

Lacy, Richard A. *Seeing with Feeling — Film in the Classroom*. Philadelphia: Saunders, 1972.

Lindgren, Ernest. *The Art of Film*. New York: Macmillan, 1970. (College text.)

Maynard, Richard. *The Celluloid Curriculum*. Rochelle Park, N. J.: Hayden, 1971.

Wigal, Donald, and Murphy, Sharon F., eds. *Screen Experience*: *An Approach to Film*. rev. ed. Fairfield, N. J.: Pflaum/Standard, 1975. (Broad coverage of the field.)

Focus on Alternatives: A Filmography of
Adult Role Models for Teens

Films about adults who cope with change in nonstereotypical ways:
Angel and Big Joe. 27 min., Learning Corporation, 1975. (Bert Salzman) A middle-aged telephone lineman, Joe, and Angel, a young migrant worker, become close friends. In helping Angel make a difficult decision, Joe shares some of his own experiences as a young man. Their friendship is marked by fun and respect.
Chris and Bernie. 25 min., New Day, 1974. (Bonnie Friedman, Deborah Shaffer) Chris and Bernie, divorcees with young children, combine their resources and for a time raise their children together. This documentary film explores the texture of their daily lives.
Clorae and Albie. 36 min., EDC, 1975. (Joyce Chopra) This documentary illustrates that adulthood is a time of change. Clorae, divorced, with three young children, is going back to high school and Albie is putting herself through college after many false starts.
Joyce at 34. 28 min., New Day, 1972. (Joyce Chopra, Claudia Weill) Joyce Chopra and Tom Cole experience joy and difficulty as they juggle parenting with their careers.
Luke Was There. 32 min., LCA, 1977. (Richard Marquand) Young Julius struggles with feelings of abandonment when he is temporarily placed in a children's shelter. Luke, his counselor, reveals an admirable commitment, love and maturity in dealing with the explosive emotional situations that Julius faces.
Men's Lives. 43 min., New Day, 1975. (Josh Hanig and Will Roberts) Interviews and cinema verité footage explore the influences that define masculinity for American men from childhood through middle age. A barber is particularly clear about the limitations imposed by the "male myth."
Portrait of Grandpa Doc. 32 min., Phoenix, 1977. (Randal Kleiser) As a young painter prepares for an exhibition he remembers summer holidays with his grandfather through stills, home movies, and re-created dramatic sequences. The film explores the effect the sensitive grandfather, now dead, still has on the artist, his work, and his relationship with his mother.
Ruth Stout's Garden. 23 min., Arthur Mokin Productions, 1976. (Arthur Mokin) From a perspective of more than ninety years, Ruth Stout shares her philosophy of gardening, politics, aging, and self-reliance—all highlighted by her joy in life.

Part 8

Confession, Celebration, Illumination: Poetry Power

Anne Sexton, in her poem "With Mercy for the Greedy," speaks of her process of writing poetry as a sacramental rite: ". . . I was born/ doing reference work in sin, and born/ confessing it. This is what poems are: / with mercy / for the greedy, . . ."[1] Poetry here is seen as confessional, providing a means of grace for a human nature saturated with *cupiditas,* a view that has deep roots in the Puritan tradition; and as Al Poulin, Jr. tells us in his essay on "Contemporary American Poetry," this is a tradition still very much alive, though metamorphosed into contemporary dress.

The idea that poetry provides newness of life in some form or another, that it is charismatic and revelatory, would seem to be universal. That rich language, enhanced by metaphor and rhythm, has life-giving power is an ancient idea, whereas wordlessness signifies negation. Maya Angelou has expressed a similar idea by remarking that "to persist in being inarticulate is to align yourself with your own death." Someone else has said, in a lighter vein, "impression without expression equals depression." Perhaps we could borrow a metaphor from the Old English poem, "The Phoenix," to express the recreative power of poetry and the poet's experience of transformation: ". . . Yet life is always wonderfully/ Awakened, stirred back from bones and ashes . . . ./ he never forgets/ That for him the flames cool into life."[2] Traditionally representative of Christ, the phoenix might be seen as a symbol for the resurrection of life in spiritual and psychological terms.

Poetry by its very nature is in all eras close to the pulse of a people's life and full of portent for their life in the future. Poulin's essay provides an historical perspective for the understanding of the poets of the present, whose "adventure," "somewhat anarchic but abundantly fresh," nonetheless has roots in the past, links to the Puritan and Whitman traditions, as well as to the tradition represented by the New Critics.

Contemporary poetry, as Poulin stresses, is complex, diverse, reflective of the discordancy of life in our century—intimate, personal-confessional, "committed" or activist, ethnic, exploratory; above all, it is a mirror for the experience of the "brutalized self" of our century and its quest for expression of a sometimes profoundly individual religious sense that has not found satisfaction within institutionalized religions.

The alienation that forms so constant a theme in contemporary poetry and the related metaphor of the wasteland have an especially strong appeal to young people who feel "outside" the mainstream of life (a feeling spurred by the heightened sensitivities of adolescence) and who are keenly aware of the perils of spiritual poverty and sterility in a materialistically abundant society.

The poetry of rock music and "pop" lyrics is related to the despair that young people so keenly feel. Larrick uses this perspective to show the importance of these lyrics to youth. She surveys themes of rock lyrics of the early seventies and observes the effect of music in turning youth on to poetry. Adults can gain from Larrick's article insight into how listening to pop/rock lyrics can help in guiding teens to pleasure from print, serving as another road to learning through the medium of popular culture.

The recreative power of poetry that the confessional mode makes possible is characteristic of feminist poetry. Sandra Gilbert focusses on "the self-defining confessional genre" as perhaps "a distinctly female poetic mode" and copes with the peculiar difficulty encountered by the female poet who, in contrast to the male, must forge for herself "a self . . . a tradition," and to resist being cast in the role of muse when she desires instead the role of mythmaker. Gilbert's essay closes on the insight that individual women poets (e.g., Levertov) may be on the verge of finding a way to spiritual unity, a successful means of incorporating their "second," "supernatural" selves into their "natural," bread-eating selves. Levertov's image in the final quotation gives hope that the poet's second self can be not burdensome but nurturing: ". . . a basket/ of bread . . ." perhaps symbolic of the wellspring of creativity itself.

Black poetry forms the subject of an essay not included in this volume, Alan Lomax and Raoul Abdul's "Introduction" to *3000 Years of Black Poetry*.[3] To read of the extroverted, communal praise songs of the black tradition is to be transported away from the introspective, self-searching, self-defining poetry emphasized by Poulin and Gilbert into another poetic world, wherein the central values are "the erotic, the procreative, the social . . ."—a poetic world that shares the celebrative approach to life that we find in American poetry in the Whitman tradition. The centrality of music to traditional African poetry and its ties to the oral tradition suggest comparison with the bardic poetry of the medieval northern Europeans and the ancient Greeks. Heroic poetry, brimming with self-confidence and pride and faith in human potentialities, contrasts starkly with the uncertainty, self-doubt, and "wasteland" atmosphere of contemporary American poetry and makes us conscious of another perhaps more innocent and surely more joyful way of perceiving the world and human experience of it.

Rushing helps us to recognize the various ways that black women have been imaged forth in black poetry, and to realize that the often stereotypical images fail to portray "the multifaceted nature of the black woman in America." Her essay forms a most interesting contrast in its concerns to Gilbert's—Rushing being concerned with how black women are perceived by poets, Gilbert with how women poets perceive themselves. Both however feel the need for a greater range of images or myths to, in Rushing's words, "reflect our myriad realities."

Stensland's essay leads us into another poetic realm, the universe of the Indian ("Native American," the preferred term, might have been a more fortuitous choice of words). It is a realm where spirituality permeates every aspect of existence, where all is interrelated and, hence, every detail of nature and life is freighted with meaning. In this poetic realm we are far removed from self-absorption, self-definition, and we sense a feeling that might be called numinous—an experience of the holiness of all life. (But here again, are we not back to something akin to the Whitman tradition?) Uppermost in Native American poetry is the strong appreciation of the incantatory power of language, of words as carriers of a spell, and repetition of words (exact, formulaic repetition) as generating "accumulated power" rather than boredom.

Poulin gives us a basic, insightful overview of the mainstream of primarily white, primarily male American contemporary poetry and its uses of and departures from tradition. The other essayists—Gilbert, Rushing, and Stensland—supplement and complement Poulin's ideas; each, in turn, carves out a smaller territory for examination, giving a "minority" report, one might say, which we can fruitfully compare and contrast to the "majority" report of the opening essay. So doing, we must come away with a sense of wonder at the omnivorousness of contemporary poets (in the variety of human experiences they can digest), and a feeling of the vitality, richness, and excitement of the poetry which draws upon its newly discovered—or rediscovered—wellsprings, whether they lie in Europe, remote Africa, in native soil, or wherever else in creation our kinship may reach.

NOTES

1. Quoted in Al Poulin, Jr., ed., *Contemporary American Poetry* (Boston: Houghton, 1971), pp. 294-95.
2. *Poems from the Old English,* tr. Burton Raffel. 2nd ed. (Lincoln: Univ. of Nebraska Pr., 1964), p. 118.
3. (New York: Dodd, 1970), pp. xix-xxvi.

Contemporary American Poetry: The Radical Tradition

Al Poulin, Jr.

American poetry since 1945 may be viewed as the product of the dialectics of generations. A recurrent phenomenon in literary (as well as in much of human) history, the pattern of one generation's revolt against another is familiar indeed. That rebellion, however, is usually not so much against the generation as against its excesses: principle atrophied into prejudice, freshness of thought and sensibility petrified into cliché, discipline forged into tyranny. The revolution also doesn't always succeed in realizing a clean break with the immediate or distant past; the blood, the genes remain camouflaged by a radical façade.

Emphasizing the freshness of contemporary poetry, poets and critics have argued that it reflects a violent break with modernist poetry, if not with all of tradition. In the introduction to his anthology of contemporary American poetry (1962), Donald Hall announced that the orthodoxy of T. S. Eliot and the New Critics had ceased: "In modern art anarchy has proved preferable to the restrictions of a benevolent tyranny." The modern artist, Hall wrote, "has acted as if restlessness were a conviction and has destroyed his own past in order to create a future." In *The Poem in Its Skin* (1968), Paul Carroll argues that today's poets have attempted "to write poems either alien or hostile to the poem as defined and explored by Eliot and leading writers dominating the scene ten or fifteen years ago." Later he asserts: "this generation of American poets is on the high, happy adventure of creating and innovating a complex of new ways in which to view our common condition—an adventure which in its abundance, freshness and originality is . . . as interesting as any since the Olympians of 1917."

That the adventure of today's poets is somewhat anarchic but abundantly fresh is unquestionable. That it has produced poems entirely alien to modernist poetry is open to much debate. But the notion that the contemporary poet has destroyed his own past, for whatever reasons, is hogwash. Admittedly, T. S. Eliot may have been poetically, temperamentally, and constitutionally incapable of writing a poem like Sylvia Plath's "Daddy" or Frank O'Hara's campy poem to Lana Turner. And the New Critics may not quite know what to make of such poems. (When confronted by the poems in *Life Studies,* Allen Tate reportedly turned to Lowell and agonizingly blurted "But, *Cal,* it's not *poetry!*") Nevertheless, although the dicta of the New Critics have not been regarded as sacred commandments by contemporary poets, they haven't been ignored altogether either. Nor have the older and more profound Whitman and Puritan traditions; they are still active and vital, influencing the formal and thematic directions of much contemporary poetry. If today's poets have achieved a unique vitality, they have done so by making full use of the past, immediate and distant, personal and communal, while simultaneously contributing new and exciting elements of their own.

The characteristics of the modernist poem are obviously vital elements in the work of such poets as Richard Wilbur, John Berryman, and Robert Lowell, the younger poets of the modernist generation whose sensibilities were shaped by new criticism. Commenting on his own poetry in *Poets on Poetry,* Wilbur said: "Most American poets of my generation were taught to admire the English Metaphysical poets of the seventeenth century and such contemporary masters of irony as John Crowe Ransom. We were led by our teachers and by the critics whom we read to feel that the most adequate and convincing poetry is that which accommodates mixed feelings, clashing ideas and incongruous images. Poetry could not be honest, we thought, unless it began by acknowledging the full discordancy of modern life and consciousness. I still believe that to be a true view of poetry. . . ." Written under the tutelage of John Crowe Ransom and Allen Tate, Robert Lowell's early work was immediately hailed as a model of what the modernist poem should and could be. And even for his recent monumental series of dream songs, John Berryman clearly employed the basic techniques of modernist poetry, including inventing a multidimensional persona, Henry Pussycat.

The major difference between modernist and contemporary poetry is that the latter is more intimate and personal. The elements of the modernist poem worked toward assuring a distance between the poet and his subject, the poet and his poem. From persona to tradition, each was a formal, emotional, and intellectual means for the poet's objectification of his subject, emotion, and medium. The unique personality of the poet, his more intimate experiences and emotions were not only absent, indeed they were virtually taboo, and in the hands of lesser poets such an attitude resulted in a depersonalized and inhuman versification.

In contemporary poetry, although means of objectification remain, the person is more vibrant than the persona; "he" [or "she"] is replaced by "I." The speaker of the poem and the poet are often one in the same person, and the subjects are [one's] own personal, at times intimate, experiences. Full appreciation of some contemporary poems hinges on the reader's knowledge of biographical information about the poet's life:

Robert Lowell was in fact jailed as a C.O., as he says in "Memories of West Street and Lepke"; Sylvia Plath's father was a German emigrant and, reputedly, "Pure Aryan, pure Nazi," as she implies in "Daddy." With the poet's private self as both subject and speaker of the poem, the interaction between the work of art and the reader becomes proportionately more intimate: the poet speaks directly to the reader, as if he were father confessor, psychiatrist, intimate friend, or lover.

The personalization of poetry has evolved in various ways. In the work of Robert Bly, James Wright, and W. S. Merwin a personal poetry occurs as a result of the exploration of and response to the most inner reaches of the poet's self below the rational and conscious levels. Poems grow out of images discovered in the depths of human darkness; they are spoken by the voice of that most profound silence in a man. The poems of Allen Ginsberg and Frank O'Hara, on the other hand, although they contain moments of private joy and grief, depend primarily on the self's discovery of the outer world and response to it. The reader hears with O'Hara's ears or touches with Ginsberg's hands.

The personalization of poetry is most obvious in the work of those poets who reveal elements of their personality, events in their personal lives usually considered intimate, private, or confidential. When the sexual deviance of some of this century's great poets remains among the best kept secrets in literary history, Allen Ginsberg's repeated avowal of his own deviance can be somewhat startling, albeit refreshing. Illness, madness, failure, a propensity for self-destruction—these are some of the re-occurring subjects of personal-confessional poets like Lowell, Plath, Sexton, and Snodgrass.

Today's poets, then, have succeeded in making poetry often radically personal; but under closer scrutiny factors come into focus to temper that judgment. Subject and voice paradoxically work toward making even the most intimate poetry less personal than it first seems and toward erecting another kind of persona, i.e., that part of the poet's private self which he wishes to make public. Because they have been primarily concerned with physical and psychic limitations, the personal-confessional poets have written a poetry which to a large extent reveals only the deteriorating self speaking in a chosen voice, ranging from the modulated whine of W. D. Snodgrass to the near hysteria of Sylvia Plath. Moreover, in the work of some poets, technique and craftsmanship cause more doubt as to just how personal poetry can be; for by drawing formal attention, even the most personal poem reminds the reader that it is a fabrication. Like any art, personal poetry is a selective, calculated and public gesture, a formal utterance for which the poet selects a voice, one which is as approximate to his own as is manageable.

Irony and paradox are also present in the work of today's poets. Confronted by the quality of our common condition, the sensitive and mature human being may not survive without a strong ironic sense; for although irony may thwart all genuine emotion, its absence also makes genuine emotion virtually impossible. The range and uses of irony in contemporary poetry can be seen in the work of two rather different poets: Sylvia Plath and Frank O'Hara. In Sylvia Plath's poetry, especially her later poems, the presence of irony serves to temper the intensity of emotion and suffering by undercutting the vehement and often near-gothic imagery and emotion. Indeed, many of Sylvia Plath's more intense poems survive *as poems* because her sharp ironic sense is also at play. For example, "Lady Lazarus" is protected from bathos by the ironic sense of humor which not only views the would-be suicide as "The big strip tease" in a three-ring circus of horrors, but also through intonation and line break which begin the poem by suggesting that it is spoken by some rich Jewish lady coming out of a beauty spa like Maine Chance. . . .

If the contemporary poet is more drawn toward existential experience, he is also less inclined to use what Eliot called "the mythical method" to organize and present his experience. Indeed, myth, except as a subconscious, elemental, and perhaps inevitable ritualistic pattern of human response, is virtually absent from the work of post-War poets. However, if the traditional mythic method at this moment in history is not viable, the mythical vision and the need for it remains an active force in contemporary poetry. Poets increasingly sense the necessity to be not simply myth users, but myth makers. Both as persons and as poets they reflect "the instinct that their work-a-day world is interpenetrated with a superrational or extra-rational activity in which they can and do share." If the pattern of such more-than-human activity is not immediately accessible, then they must dig it out of the accumulation of their experience and create myths that are closer to the contemporary experience than those inherited from myth makers of the past. . . .

Other poets have discovered myth in other contemporary dramas and figures. For an age of violence Sylvia Plath has turned away from ancient mythology (the Colossus of Rhodes) and toward more recent history (Hiroshima and Hitler's concentration camps) for the mythic background against and in which her personal suffering occurs. For an age of media Frank O'Hara has recognized the mythic dimensions of those "stars" whose personal and public lives determine the rhythm and quality of this civilization just as surely and profoundly as did the fabricated gods of other mythologies. In Henry Pussycat, Berryman has erected a myth out of and for the tortured and suffering, middle-aged, white "human American man." But throughout contemporary poetry one also senses that the isolated self, the multifaceted and complex "I" rises above communal, historical and extrarational events and assumes mythic proportions of its own. The collective impact of contemporary poetry seems to say: I am my own myth.

The blood and genes inherited by contemporary poetry, however, are not merely the formal demands of new criticism, but the full tradition

of American (and British) poetry. Muted, modified, transformed—
nonetheless, the spirit and energy of that tradition continue as vital
forces in today's poetry. And it is not simply an aesthetic heritage, but a
complex of formal and thematic (moral) stances which constitute the
polarities, not only of our art, but also of our national psychic and
mythic life. The polarized stances (toward man, his history and his art)
constituting the mainstream of American poetry are the Puritan tradition and the Whitman tradition. Of course, other less powerful currents,
occasional springs and pools have also contributed to the evolution of
American poetry. But the life and energy of American poetry, especially
in the twentieth century, spring primarily from the tension, balance,
and occasional reconciliation between the microcosmic and macrocosmic
vision and art of the Puritans and, for lack of a more felicitous term, the
Whitmanians.

Whether written by Edward Taylor or Robert Lowell, Puritan poetry
arises out of the fundamental view of man as the heir of and participant
in the specific history of the fallen Adam. It views man as essentially
corrupt, seeking the contours of his life in an equally corrupt universe,
incapable of personal salvation. Characteristically intellectual and highly
personal, seeking the speaker's place in history, it focuses primarily on
his spiritual and physical limitations and deterioration. Its structure is
usually complex, emblematic, and metaphysical, the texture of its language intricate. Because contemporary Puritan poets have rejected the
possibility of the traditional concept of Christian salvation, that one
thread of light which sustained the original Puritan, sin is symbolically
replaced by mental and emotional imbalance and, lacking the hope of
salvation, the poet is threatened by madness and tempted to self-destruction. Robert Lowell's "Skunk Hour" and Sylvia Plath's "Lady Lazarus"
are among the best examples of the Puritan tradition in contemporary
American poetry.

The Whitman tradition stands in stark contrast to its predecessor. Refusing to submit man to the bonds of history, sacred or secular, it asserts
the holiness of the Adamic man, inside and out, and celebrates the grace
of purely human and physical activity in an equally holy universe. Im-
patient with and often scornful of intellectualization, it focuses on the
unique and separate self's place and role in the day and points to that
self's limitless potential for transcendence. Open, loose, often the product of emotion rather than of intellect and conscious craftsmanship, its
language also tends to be more recognizably "American" and earthy.
However, because the tradition is more specifically "literary," Whitman
the *poet,* his vision and his poems often serve as the basis for lament;
and the contemporary poet decries the betrayal of history since Whitman's prophetic songs. Allen Ginsberg's "Howl" and Lawrence Ferlinghetti's "Starting from San Francisco" are rather obvious examples.

As critics have noted, however, American poetry has also experienced a large measure of internationalization and reflects the presence of other traditions. The influence of the French symbolists persists. Pound's "discovery" of the East is expanded through the influence of Zen Buddhism and Japanese poetry on the work of Gary Snyder, and Spanish surrealists have had a profound effect on the poetry of such poets as Robert Bly and W. S. Merwin.

Clearly, then, the vitality of contemporary American poetry depends in large part on its full participation in and transformation of a broad and rich tradition of poetry. And yet, after having posited this participation, one must also recognize the contemporary poets' measure of dissatisfaction and restlessness—not only with that tradition, but also with their specific art and medium—which also accounts for the vitality and diversity of today's poetry.

The poet's restlessness with their medium is largely evident in the number of those who for various reasons have changed their styles radically in the course of their careers; these stylistic transformations in turn reflect equally radical shifts in their basic assumptions about the nature and function of their art. From compact and trippingly anapestic poems dealing with somewhat private experience, James Dickey's poems have grown more expansive, looser, public, and charged by a kind of revivalist energy. On the other hand, W. S. Merwin's poems have moved from technical and structural complexity toward an imaginative and emotional density which is almost hermetic. At times savagely personal, Merwin's poems seem to refuse all further human contact. For reasons which ultimately may not be far removed from Merwin's, LeRoi Jones's style and attitude have also undergone a radical shift, moving from a projectivist (literary) poetics informed by a sense of the black heritage and an awareness of the political situation toward a more emphatic and indeed ethnic and political poetics of activism. Other poets have shown their restlessness with their medium in other ways by attempting the techniques of other media. Some of John Ashbery's poems, for example, clearly reflect the influence of action painting, while Lawrence Ferlinghetti's poems explore the possibilities of poetry as jazz. Underlying these stylistic transformations and experiments, however, is not merely an obsession with originality, but rather the more profound need of the poet to shape the structures and rhythms and to explore the timbre of the voice of the individual man and his day.

Each age discovers or fabricates one or two encompassing metaphors for the quality of human experience which it affords or seeks. It was T. S. Eliot, of course, who fabricated the first encompassing metaphor for the twentieth century: the waste land was the image of man's spiritual and cultural sterility, an image which, after Hiroshima and Nagasaki, proved to be frighteningly precise in its prophetic implications. To date no single poet seems to have fabricated the central metaphor for the quality of our experience since World War II. However, this is what seems to have happened. "The Waste Land" was a powerful *mise en scène* of the modern situation, but to a large extent its characters were composite ghosts, unreal men and women in an unreal city. Eliot was describing "the human condition" and not the individual condition. In other words, Eliot set the scene, but contemporary poets have peopled that waste land, mostly with themselves. They have described the deterioration and sterility of the individual self and, having done so, have fabricated a cumulative metaphor for our own age.

The language of that metaphor is as stark, brutal, and familiar as the experience. More often than not it is the language of experience and emotion—and not recollected in tranquillity. The brutalized self responds neither in pentameters nor in euphemisms, nor, at times, even in metaphor. In the midst of unbearable suffering, Sylvia Plath, as do most of us, utters clichés. At the peak of emotion and frustration John Logan utters obscenities at "this fucking war." And the language in LeRoi Jones's later poems not only reflects the poet's fierce emotion but indeed brutalizes the reader. In differing ways, today's poets have followed the advice and example of Walt Whitman and later William Carlos Williams and agree with George Starbuck's remark: "We've got language we haven't yet used." And it is the language of today's poetry which immediately strikes us as vitally contemporary and fresh. By making poetry out of the full range of everyday speech, including obscenity, vulgarity, and slang, contemporary poets have returned to poetry a richness of expression and experience which has been lacking probably since the Renaissance.

A healthy respect for the living language of the tribe and for its potential is in part responsible for an equally healthy respect for the full spectrum of that tribe's experiences. Perhaps just the opposite is truer. At any rate, contemporary poets have managed to reinstate in poetry a directness and honesty toward that tribe's sexual experience and all its ramifications. The range is broad: menstruation, masturbation, love making, adultery, homosexuality, sodomy, abortion. Moreover, whether the cause for celebration or lamentation or both, sexuality in today's poetry is neither a programmatic metaphor, a consciously Freudian exploration, or a mystical Lawrencian-Victorianism. Although clearly an essential element of the poet's theme, first and foremost it is an existential human experience, capable of being simultaneously ugly and the source of grace, tender and brutal, and, as John Berryman suggests, lyrical and vulgar: "like the memory of a lovely fuck."

An imagination of commitment which recognizes and responds directly, honestly, and morally to everyday political realities is also one of the distinguishing elements of today's poetry. The political climate has become a crucial arena within which contemporary poets have exercised their talents, and the conflict in Vietnam has generated an enormous amount of antiwar poetry which reflects the contemporary poets' belief in poetry *engagé*. The political consciousness of the contemporary poets has returned poetry to a long and vital tradition in the life of poetry. That tradition was virtually ignored during the first half of this century, especially when the notion of art for art's sake virtually prohibited poetry from being anything but hermetic, when political concern had to be masked with myth, clothed with wit, and moved by indirection. But the contemporary poet agrees with Sartre and Camus that art must be committed if it is to survive. As Ferlinghetti said: "Only the dead are disengaged." . . .

The poets' moral stance against the war is only part of their more inclusive ethical and spiritual concerns. Although to date none has publicly proclaimed allegiance to any formal ethical, or religious system, and although some have been members of the Catholic church, for example, and later quietly left it, nevertheless there is a diversity of profound religious experience in the work of most of them. In some of Richard Wilbur's poems ("A Dubious Night," for example) the existence of God is at best irrelevant, at worst a handicap to the discovery of that more profound salvation found through human activity. The ending of Lawrence Ferlinghetti's "Sometime during eternity" affirms (but implicitly laments) the contemporary theological stance that God is dead, while "I Am Waiting" humorously reveals the poet's quest for and anticipation of a measure of salvation. His profound mystical sense is also acutely felt in "Assassination Raga," as is Allen Ginsberg's in "Wichita Vortex Sutra." In "Medusa" Sylvia Plath rejects the formal religion of the Vatican, and yet in "Mary's Song" she sees the cycle of Christian salvation present in contemporary history's need for sacrificial victims. Moreover, in much of her poetry one senses the ancient mysticism which affirms salvation through suffering: "The fire makes it precious." And whereas the existence of God or the possibility of human grace seems either irrelevant or impossible in most of Merwin's poems, "Lemuel's Blessing" is probably the most powerful prayer-poem of the century.

To a large extent, then, most contemporary poets, like many of their modern predecessors, view traditional, formal, and established religious belief and experience as impossible. Rather, they affirm a personal and vital religious or mystical or spiritual sense. John Berryman is one of the few who use the traditional Judaic-Christian mythology, complete with God, Saint Peter, and Satan, as at least a potentially legitimate (and, in his poems, credible) framework for religious experience. However, the work of John Logan, perhaps one of the most truly religious poets of the generation, is more exemplary of the contemporary poet's evolution from a formal and established to a personal religious affirmation. Logan's early work, such as "On a Prize Crucifix by a Student

Sculptor," relied primarily on what James Dickey called an "orthodox symbology" and religious sense. His more recent work, however, having shed the formal accoutrements of religion, has also gained intensity of fervor tempered by a greater human complexity. The mystery of salvation is its human incarnation. Grace is discovered and given and received specifically through human and incarnate acts. Thus, "The White Pass Ski Patrol" is a secular and sporty account of the ascension. The member of the ski patrol continually rises and then caroms down—speeding, dancing, balancing, taking all human risks and ministering to others, even in danger. And he rises again, "vanishes in air!" But only after he has come down, after he has learned what the body can do, what grace the body can realize on its own. And finally, like Teilhard de Chardin's fully evolved man, he moves through the final process into pure light.

Politics, sex, and religion, the outdated taboos of polite conversation, are only a few of the many concerns to which today's poets have addressed themselves. They are also only a few of the themes which contribute to the freshness and especially the "relevance" of contemporary poetry. Alive with the blood and genes of the immediate and distant tradition of poetry, rebelling against all that is petrified and dead in that heritage, and affirming their fierce personal response to all that is demanded of a human being at this moment of history, contemporary American poets repeatedly affirm with Louis Simpson that American poetry,

> Whatever it is, . . . must have
> A stomach that can digest
> Rubber, coal, uranium, moons, poems. . . .
>
> It must swim for miles through the desert
> Uttering cries that are almost human.

Pop/Rock Lyrics, Poetry and Reading

Nancy Larrick

When Elvis Presley became a national figure in the early fifties, teenagers collapsed in adoration of the youth from Tupelo, Mississippi. Those over thirty-five looked down upon Presley as a passing phenomenon not worth a serious thought. In the first six months of 1956, Presley sold eight million records; at year's end he had become a $20-million-a-year industry. The kids did it.

Ten years and uncounted millions of records later, the Beatles landed to exploit the youth culture which had sprung up with Elvis and flourished on the rock songs of Chuck Berry, the fury of the twist, and the dark passion of soul. By that time, the early disciples of Elvis had children of their own. But these young parents were still part of the rock cult which today includes almost everyone under thirty. With the advent of the Beatles, pop exploded all over. Hundreds of musical groups were soon seeking portions of the glory and the money.

In the meanwhile a new generation of folksingers had emerged. Bob Dylan, Phil Ochs, Joan Baez, and Tom Paxton were passionately political, demonstrating that lyrics could be as important as sound. Rock groups began to sharpen their lines until they said something.

The music of youth was a boon to the management of civic auditoriums that had been subsisting on prestige rather than profit. The record industry struck a Comstock lode. Today no less than 85 percent of all single records are bought by persons under twenty-five. "The kids will go without food to buy records," one critic remarked.

Who are the favorite composers, poets, and spokesmen of America's young? Don Roberts of the State University of New York made inquiries from coast to coast and reported "you hear the names Simon and Garfunkel, the Beatles, Mick Jagger, Bob Dylan, Judy Collins, and others over and over again" (Roberts, 1970). Bob Dylan and Leonard Cohen are the most popular poets. All are part of the oral literature of our time, exalted by the young but—until recently—brushed aside by teachers and librarians.

Reprinted by permission of the author and publisher from *Journal of Reading* 14:184-90 (Dec. 1971). Copyright © 1971 by International Reading Association.

One of the most persuasive rock commentators is Nik Cohn, whose book, *Rock from the Beginning,* came out in 1969. "I was ten when it started," he says of rock music. "I'm twenty-two now, and it has bossed my life. It has surrounded me always, cut me off, and it has given me heroes, it has made my myths. Almost, it has done my living for me. Six hours of trash every day, and it's meant more to me than anything else" (Cohn, 1969).

I am of the generation that tilted its nose at the Presley frenzy. The songs that he and his followers shouted and screamed were both tuneless and meaningless to me. The Beatles struck me as more of the same, plus hair.

Bridge over Troubled Years

But my isolation was not impenetrable. Several members of the teeny-bopper set (six to sixteen) spent some time at our house and immediately switched our radio from the classical music station to one that blasted the loudest rock music I ever tried not to hear. These youngsters knew all the words of songs I had never heard of. "But it's the sound that counts," one of them told me. "Sound is everything." It was everything, all right, and at times I was ready to flee to the woods.

I was saved by a book: *Favorite Pop/Rock Lyrics,* a Scholastic paperback by Dr. Jerry L. Walker, Professor of Secondary and Continuing Education at the University of Illinois (Walker, 1969). For the first time I read the words of "Mrs. Robinson," "The Unknown Soldier," and "Jennifer Juniper." I read every lyric in the book. I found that I was opening my mind to some new ideas, to some fresh pictures of the society I belong to. And once I had opened my mind, I no longer had to close my ears.

I took this slender book to my poetry workshop at Lehigh University and dropped it into the circulating collection, which ranged from Lewis Carroll and Walter de la Mare to Eve Merriam. The book became the most popular title of the lot. My students are all inservice teachers, some first-year interns. Two-thirds of these teachers are twenty-five or younger. No wonder they went for *Favorite Pop/Rock Lyrics,* a collection that grew out of their own generation—the generation of Nik Cohn, who had said that rock "meant more to me than anything else."

Four students chose pop/rock lyrics as a project for a report to the class. They converted an adjoining room into a discotheque with psychedelic lights, posters, record player, records, and copies of the lyrics. As the music blared and beat in the changing light, I tried to follow the words to "Nowhere Man," by John Lennon and Paul McCartney.

The record ended. "Let's hear it again!" came the cry. The 23-year-old teacher in charge swung the needle over. The young teachers listened with heads back, eyes closed, feet tapping the rhythm. The words and music of rock were part of them.

Discussion was vigorous. Who is the Nowhere Man? Where is Nowhere Land? At first the teachers seemed to equate Nowhere with a low social or economic status: the guy without a job, the school dropout, the failure. But could the president of a great corporation ever become a Nowhere Man? Yes, if he got fired, someone said. And he could be so tied into the rat race that he wouldn't know where he was heading, said another.

"We better listen again," the chairman said. "How is he 'a bit like you and me'? When have you and I been in Nowhere Land?"

"When I'm worrying about whether the draft will get me," a young man said.

"And will my kids ever grow up in our fouled-up environment?" another suggested.

"I feel like a Nowhere Man in these foundation courses we have to take," said a conscientious objector to regimented education.

Why does our society produce so many nowhere men? Many of the answers came from students who had not been involved in discussions before. Every comment was deeply personal, and some were quite provocative.

Does this lyric suggest any poems you know? Someone replied, "What about Richard Cory?" referring to the rock title. This led to Edward Arlington Robinson's poem of the same title and then to Edgar Lee Masters' poem "William Goode" and Edwin Markham's "The Man with the Hoe." Thus the teachers were drawn into a discussion much broader than the pop/rock lyrics they had begun with.

Months later the young teacher who had planned the session wrote to me: "I was a business major in college. I never did dig poetry, and I guess you thought I was a misfit in the Poetry Workshop. But when you let us bring in pop/rock lyrics, I found myself."

He is now teaching fifth and sixth graders in the worn-out coal country of eastern Pennsylvania. Recently he sent me a book of poems his pupils had written—beautiful and sensitive work. "It's not rock stuff," the teacher said. "But it took rock music and rock lyrics to get us going."

Another teacher showed us a film his sixth graders had made for "Nowhere Man." "It was their idea," he said. "I think it's their favorite poem."

The Sound of It All

Why do these kids move to pop/rock like iron filings to a magnet? After many hours of discussion, observation, and listening, I am convinced that the great appeal is sound. My friends of under twenty-five get things better by ear than by eye, probably because they have grown up in a constant bombardment of words from radio, television, and records. I usually say, "Let me see the words," but they say, "Let me hear it again"—even when the printed words are right in front of them.

Much of the music is, to me, a jangling discord with frequent explosive effects that make me almost as uncomfortable as the audience that first heard Stravinsky's *Le Sacre du Printemps* in 1913. But I can't deny that the insidious beat of rock whams away at my complacency. No one can remain the same after a thorough exposure.

The lyrics reinforce the rhythm with an abundance of monosyllabic words in a conversational pattern that repeats, backs up, and repeats again. It's the modern jargon which drops subjects, slurs syllables, and spices the lines with long drawn-out *ohs, nos,* and *uh-hums.*

Furthermore, rock lyric writers use first and second person pronouns to enfold the listener in the song. Thus the Vogues sing:

> There is someone, walking behind you
> Turn around, look at me.

And the Isley Brothers say:

> Let me hear you say, "It's my thing:
> I do what I wanna do."

They sing primarily about the concerns and anxieties which haunt those of us who are lonely, unsure, frustrated, and groping for solutions we can live with. This is poetry of feeling—deeply personal feeling. As the Youngbloods sing:

> . . . say what you're feelin', feelin' inside . . .
> Don't keep your feelin's locked up inside ya
> Tear down your walls, don't let 'em hide ya
> Reach out your hand, now
> Can't you understand?

The issues tackled by these song writers come from the hearts of the young: school with its meaningless routines (*Twenty years of schoolin' / And they put you on the day shift*—Bob Dylan); the generation gap (*People try to put us down / Just because we get around*—Peter Townsend for the Who); pollution and destruction of the environment (*They took all the trees and put them in a tree museum / And they charged all the people a dollar and a half to see 'em*—Joni Mitchell); never-ending war *(It's all over for the unknown soldier*—the Doors); the agony of loneliness *(All the lonely people / Where do they all belong?*—the Beatles); and the enigma of love (*Love is but the song we sing and fear's the way we die*—Chet Powers for the Youngbloods).

These topics are not usually studied in school. They seldom show up in anthologies, certainly not in the context of the here and now. But the fact is that pop/rock is going to school in spite of the curriculum—and it is getting an enthusiastic welcome. In many classrooms, students bring their own records to introduce reading lessons based on pop/rock lyrics. Even the dullest exercise in reading skills takes on life with this approach.

The Beat Goes In

One teacher, Bud Scoppa, asked seventh- and eighth-grade students to listen to records by the Beatles and by the Rolling Stones and to sketch their spontaneous responses to the two groups. "I had suggested," he wrote in *Scholastic Teacher* (Scoppa, 1970), "that they avoid trying to figure out the songs' meaning and instead simply 'feel' the music." The drawings led to a discussion of the theme and mood of each song. When the teacher duplicated the words of a song so the comments could be more specific, the kids called for the music again. Apparently the sound of words was more comfortable for them and more comprehensible than the sight of words.

Young people have shown unprecedented interest in poetry during the past few years. They have been listening, chanting, singing, writing, and reading as never before. I think the prevailing passion for the sounds and content of pop/rock has turned them to poetry.

Writing poetry used to be an assignment, and seldom was it enjoyed. Today's children are writing poetry because they want to. Older youngsters are meeting in writers' workshops held in church basements and storefront centers when schools are locked. In Upward Bound groups, even in classes for slow learners, poetry has become a medium for the message of the young.

Much of this new poetry is unrhymed and conversational in tone. Once these youngsters feel free to express themselves, they pour forth their anxieties much as the pop/rock people do.

The Sound of the City

The poems of city children are particularly poignant. What child—or what adult—could write gaily about poverty, pollution, deception, injustice, corruption, and violence? A year ago, when I was compiling my anthology, *I Heard a Scream in the Street* (Larrick, 1970), I read more than five thousand poems by children in cities all around the country. Again and again I found cries of loneliness and despair, but never any tributes to parents, friends, or teachers. School has evidently been a bitter experience for many of these children. If any of them had an inspiring teacher, or even a kind one, this individual was overlooked. What troubled the poets was the nagging "worry about being a fool."

> I look at these dark
> heated green walls
> that make me feel
> like a rat

wrote Deborah Jones of Forest Park High School in Baltimore. Then, as though speaking to herself, she added:

> Run, jump, leap, creep
> but free yourself
> before you become
> beat.

Her feeling of panic is shared by many young people. Listen to Lucia Martin, once a student in Benjamin Franklin High School, New York, now lost in a maze of school transfers and dropouts:

> Oh God! I don't want to die in
> Harlem
> Yet living here is hell . . . (Larrick, 1970)

Ron Chafetz of Mather High School, Chicago, asks, "If I get out now, what then?" and adds:

> . . . here I stand near this post
> between my past and my future
> God damn it! I'm scared. (Larrick, 1970)

Right now there is a dark and lovely rock-folk musical playing on Broadway, *The Me Nobody Knows*. It grew out of an anthology of children's poetry and prose collected by a New York City teacher and published, uncensored, as a mass-market paperback (Joseph, 1969). The twelve youngsters who make up the cast of the musical—eight black and four white—talk and sing about their world of poverty and desperation. Their language is simple and harsh and strangely beautiful. Who could easily forget the cry of the seventeen-year-old Clorox who rejoices at his little brother's death because he knows that the youngster will thus not have to suffer the pain of life as Clorox knows it.

Clorox lives in a squalid world, but his compassion is beautiful. The audience which cheered his performance was cheering the triumph of the human spirit—the heroism of "the me nobody knows."

There may not be a Clorox in every class, but in every youngster there is a search for hope, an effort to reach the world inside. For these boys and girls poetry is the key through which experiences are recreated, values are sharpened, and dreams are brought into focus.

Since these poets are part of the pop/rock generation, they have special demands when they meet poetry in print. They say it must be real; nothing phoney will pass. And nothing too sweet, which is perhaps the most damning judgment of the modern youngster.

Above all there must be feeling. One fourth grader explained at the Lehigh Poetry Festival of 1969: "You like the poet who feels. I mean, poets seem to be just like me. They feel . . . ."

One reason for children's response to Aileen Fisher's *Listen Rabbit* is that the poet's sensitivity shows. Her narrative poem stirs the feelings of each listener or reader.

When a fourth grader reads "This Is My Rock" by David McCord, I can almost hear him thinking, "This is me. It's my rock, my very own."

Young readers in the middle and upper grades warm to the poetry of Carl Sandburg and Langston Hughes. Many are keen about such moderns as Ferlinghetti and Gregory Corso and Eve Merriam. The new black poetry of protest has an enthusiastic following. Anyone who reads June Jordan, Nikki Giovanni, and LeRoi Jones—to name only three —will feel the emotional ferment. Some of these poems remind me of the comment of a young pop/rock fan to Myra Cohn Livingston, the poet, when she expressed uncertainty about the meaning of a pop/rock song. "No meaning," he said. "Just feel. You can read anything in it you want or no meaning at all" (Larrick, 1971).

One More Time

That's a very different approach to reading from the traditional one. It's a very different kind of reading material, too. But the pop/rock syndrome is tremendously significant in understanding our children and guiding them to pleasure from print. Here is the one great factor in our culture which is youth-centered. It screams out the importance of sound over sight, and it shows us that listening is the road to reading. It illustrates the power of first-person commentary in a rhythmical, conversational style. It exacts an emotional commitment that young people long for. It puts feeling above meaning and invites each listener to sing from his own senses.

Pop/rock culture is not what many of us grew up with, and most of us still feel strange about a development which our children take for granted. But we can't turn back the wheels of time and make now into then. We can't recycle the children to fit the old patterns, although some adults are making that foolish effort.

Our only choice—and it is actually an opportunity—is to become so immersed in the sounds of our children's language and in the sense of their feelings that we can sing and listen with them.

REFERENCES

Cohn, Nik. *Rock from the Beginning*. New York: Stein and Day, 1969; Pocket Books, 1970.

Joseph, Stephen M. *The Me Nobody Knows: Children's Voices from the Ghetto*. New York: Avon, 1969.

Larrick, Nancy, ed. *I Heard a Scream in the Street*. New York: M. Evans, 1970.

————, ed. *Somebody Turned On a Tap in These Kids: Poetry and Young People Today*. New York: Delacorte Pr., 1971.

Roberts, Don. "Listen, Miss, Mrs., Mr. Librarian," *School Library Journal* 17:30-32 (Nov. 1970).

Scoppa, Bud. "Discovery through Rock," *Scholastic Teacher* (Oct. 5, 1970) pp.14-15.

Walker, Jerry L., ed. *Favorite Pop/Rock Lyrics*. New York: Scholastic Book Services, 1969.

"My Name Is Darkness": The Poetry of Self-Definition

Sandra M. Gilbert

"Something hangs in back of me," wrote Denise Levertov in "The Wings," a poem published in the middle sixties. "I can't see it, can't move it. / / I know it's black, / a hump on my back. . . . black / / inimical power."[1] A few years later, in 1972, Anne Sexton published a poem called "The Ambition Bird" that made a similar point:

> I would like a simple life
> yet all night I am laying
> poems away in a long box.
>
> All night dark wings
> flopping in my heart.
> Each an ambition bird.[2]

Reprinted by permission from *Contemporary Literature* 18:443-57 (Autumn 1977). Copyright © 1977 by the Board of Regents of the University of Wisconsin System.

Both poets, whether consciously or not, seem to have been echoing the terrified and yet triumphantly self-defining metaphors of Sylvia Plath's "Stings":

> I stand in a column
> Of winged, unmiraculous women,
>
>   but I
>
> Have a self to recover, a queen.
> Is she dead, is she sleeping?
> Where has she been,
> With her lion-red body, her wings of glass?
>
> Now she is flying
> More terrible than she ever was. . . .[3]

And all three women—Plath, Levertov, Sexton—are writing in a vein of self-definition that has also been worked by other recent women poets as diverse as Adrienne Rich, Diane Wakoski, Muriel Rukeyser, Ruth Stone, Gwendolyn Brooks, Erica Jong, and Margaret Atwood. In fact, I'd like to speculate here that the self-defining confessional genre, with its persistent assertions of identity and its emphasis on a central mythology of the self, may be (at least for our own time) a distinctively female poetic mode.

"Confessional" poetry has, of course, been generally associated with a number of contemporary male poets, most notably Berryman, Lowell, and Snodgrass. A tradition of such writing, moreover, can easily be traced back through such male mythologists of the self as Whitman and Yeats to Wordsworth and Byron, those romantic patriarchs whose self-examinations and self-dramatizations probably fathered not only the poetry of what Keats called the egotistical sublime, but also the more recent ironic mode we might call the egotistical ridiculous. Most male poets, however, have been able to move beyond the self-deprecations and self-assertions of confessional writing to larger, more objectively formulated appraisals of God, humanity, society. Writers like Bly and Snyder, though they, too, are descendants of Whitman and Wordsworth, cannot by any stretch of the vocabulary be called confessional. Such obviously confessional male poets as Lowell and Berryman write verse in which (as M. L. Rosenthal's definition of confessional poetry puts it) "the private life of the poet himself . . . often becomes a major theme." Yet they manage to be "at once private and public, lyrical and rhetorical" (as Rosenthal also notes) because the personal crisis of the male poet "is felt at the same time as a symbolic embodiment of national and cultural crisis."[4] Thus, just as the growth of Wordsworth's mind stands for the growth of all self-fulfilling human minds, so "the 'myth' that Lowell creates is that of an America . . . whose history and present predicament are embodied in those of his own family and epitomized in his own psychological experience."[5]

The male confessional poet, in other words, even while romantically exploring his own psyche, observes himself as a representative specimen with a sort of scientific exactitude. Alienated, he's nevertheless an ironic sociologist of his own alienation because he considers his analytic perspective on himself a civilized, normative point of view. Lowell, describing his own mental illness with desperate intensity, is still able to note with detachment the "hackneyed speech" and "homicidal eye" of "the kingdom of the mad," and, recalling an impassioned past, to describe his younger self with surgical precision as "boiled and shy / and poker-faced."[6] Like other modern male *poètes maudits,* in short, he has a cool faith in his own ability to classify his own exemplary sufferings, a curious, calm confidence that even in madness he is in some sense at the intellectual center of things. Can it be (at least in part) that because he's a man, he can readily picture himself as Everyman?

Certainly, by contrast, the female confessional poet seems to feel no such paradoxical ease with her own anxieties. Even when she observes herself with amused irony, as Plath does in "Lady Lazarus" ("What a trash / To annihilate each decade. . . . It's the theatrical / / Comeback in broad day. . . . That knocks me out"—*Ariel,* pp.6-9), she enacts as well as dissects her suffering, her rage, her anxiety:

> Herr God, Herr Lucifer
> Beware
> Beware.
>
> Out of the ash
> I rise with my red hair
> And I eat men like air. (*Ariel,* p.9)

The detached irony of a Lowell or a Berryman—the irony possible for a self-assured, normative sensibility—is totally unavailable to her, unavailable because even at her most objective she feels eccentric, not representative; peripheral, not central. More, she struggles with her suffering, grapples with it in bewilderment, writing what Plath (who is again paradigmatic here) called "sweating, heaving poems," because she cannot easily classify either herself or her problem. To define her suffering would be to define her identity, and such self-definition is her goal, rather than her starting point.

The male confessional poet—Lowell, Berryman, Yeats—writes in the certainty that he is the inheritor of major traditions, the grandson of history, whose very anxieties, as Harold Bloom has noted, are defined by the ambiguities of the past that has shaped him as it shaped his fathers.[7] The female poet, however, even when she is not consciously confessional like Plath or Sexton, writes in the hope of discovering or defining a self, a certainty, a tradition. Striving for self-knowledge, she experiments with different propositions about her own nature, never cool or comfortable enough to be (like her male counterparts) an ironic sociologist; always, instead, a desperate Galileo, a passionate empiricist who sees herself founding a new science rather than extending the techniques and discoveries of an old one. It is for this reason, I believe, that otherwise radically different poets like Plath, Sexton, Rich, Wakoski, and Levertov all write verse characterized by such recurrent self-defining statements—hypotheses, really—as the following:

"I am your opus, / I am your valuable."
"I am a nun now. . . ."
"I am not a nurse. . . . I am not a smile."
"I am dark-suited and still, a member of the party."
"I am the arrow, / The dew that flies / Suicidal. . . ."
"I am a miner."
"I am a letter in this slot. . . ."
"I / Am a pure acetylene / Virgin."
"I think I may well be a Jew."
"I am not a Caesar."
"I am the magician's girl."
"I am no source of honey."
"I am no drudge. . . ."
"O God, I am not like you. . . ."[8]

"I am a tree gypsy: you can't shake me out of your branches."
"Here I am. . . . a strange combination of images."
"I am like the guerrilla fighter
   who must sleep with one eye
   open for attack."
"I am blue,
   I am blue as a blues singer, / I am blue in the face. . . ."
"My body dries out / and becomes a bone sceptre. . . ."
"I am the sword with / the starry hilt. . . ."
"I am ringless, ringless. . . ."
"I am a blackbird."
"I am / also a ruler of the sun, I am / the woman / whose hair
   lights up a dark room, whose words are matches. . . ."
"I am solitary, / like the owls I never see. . . ."[9]

"I'm . . . a naked man fleeing / across the roofs. . . ."
"I am a galactic cloud . . . / I am an instrument in the shape of
   a woman. . . ."
"I am a woman in the prime of life, with certain powers. . . ."

"I am the androgyne / I am the living mind you fail to describe. . . ."

"I am she: I am he / Whose drowned face sleeps with open eyes. . . ."

"I am an American woman, / my body a hollow ship. . . . / I am not the wheatfield / nor the virgin forest."[10]

"Everyone in me is a bird, / I am beating all my wings."

"I am no different from Emily Goering."

"I am a watercolor. / I wash off."

"I'm Ethan Frome's wife. I'll move when I'm able."

"I am no longer the suicide / with her raft and paddle."

"I am not an idler, / am I?"

"Yes! I am still the criminal. . . ."

"I have become a tree, / I have become a vase. . . ."

"I am an ocean-going vessel. . . ."

"I am a small handful. . . ."

"I am not immortal. Faustus and I are the also-ran."[11]

"The moon is a sow / . . . . and I a pig and a poet."

"Am I a pier, / half-in, half-out of the water?"

"I am faithful to
  ebb and flow . . .
I hold steady / in the black sky. . . . / There is no savor
more sweet, more salt / than to be glad to be
what, woman,
and who, myself
I am, a shadow / that grows longer as the sun
moves, drawn out
on a thread of wonder."[12]

Though they were taken out of context, you probably recognized many of these lines. In order of appearance, they were by Plath, Wakoski, Rich, Sexton, and Levertov. But they might all have been by one, anxiously experimental, modern Everywoman, so strikingly similar are they in structure and intention. Considering and discarding different metaphors, different propositions of identity, each of these five writers seems to be straining to formulate an ontology of selfhood, some irreducible and essential truth about her own nature. While the male poet, even at his most wretched and alienated, can at least solace himself with his open or secret creativity, his mythmaking power, the female poet must come to terms with the fact that as a female she is that which is mythologized, the incarnation of otherness (to use de Beauvoir's terminology) and hence the object of anthologies full of male metaphors. Many of her hypotheses about herself are therefore in one way or

another replies to prevalent definitions of her femininity, replies expressing either her distress at the disparity between male myths about her
and her own sense of herself, or else her triumphant repudiation of those
myths. Men tell her that she is a muse. Yet she knows that she is not
a muse, she *has* a muse (and what is its sex?). Men tell her she is
the "angel in the house," yet she doesn't *feel* angelic, and wonders,
therefore, if she is a devil, a witch, an animal, a criminal. Men tell her
that she is Molly Bloom, Mother Earth, Ishtar, a fertility goddess, a
thing whose periodicity expresses the divine order (or is it the *dis*order?)
of seasons, skies, stars. They tell her, echoing Archibald MacLeish's
definition of a poem, that she should not mean but be. Yet meanings
delight her, along with seemings, games, plays, costumes, and ideas of
order, as they delight male poets. But perhaps, she speculates, her
rage for order is mistaken, presumptuous?

"Alas!" complained Anne Finch, Countess of Winchilsea, in the
late seventeenth century,

> a woman that attempts the pen,
> Such an intruder on the rights of men,
> Such a presumptuous Creature, is esteem'd,
> The fault, can by no vertue be redeem'd.
> They tell us we mistake our sex and way;
> Good breeding, fassion, dancing, dressing, play
> Are the accomplishments we shou'd desire;
> To write, or read, or think, or to enquire
> Wou'd cloud our beauty, and exaust our time.
> And interrupt the Conquests of our prime;
> Whilst the dull mannage, of a servile house
> Is held by some, our outmost art, and use.

Given these disadvantages, she admonished herself to "Be caution'd
then . . . and still retir'd . . . / Conscious of wants, still with contracted
wing, / To some few freinds [*sic*], and to thy sorrows sing. . . ."[13]
Nevertheless, this modest poetess of "Spleen" and sorrow, contending
against a sense of her own contracted wing, pioneered a poetic mode
for other women, a mode of reticence conquered by assertion and self-
examination, a mode of self-definition *within* and *against* the context
of prevailing male definitions of women.

Today, doubting her likeness to crops and fields, the woman poet asks
herself, with Adrienne Rich, "Has Nature shown / her household books
to you, daughter-in-law, / that her sons never saw?" ("Snapshots of a
Daughter-in-Law," *Poems,* p.49), and, refusing to be "a woman in the
shape of a monster," she defines herself instead as "an instrument in
the shape / of a woman trying to translate pulsations / into images
for the relief of the body / and the reconstruction of the mind ("Plane-

tarium," *Poems,* p.148). With Esther Greenwood in *The Bell Jar* she denies that she is the passive "place an arrow shoots off from" and proposes, rather, to "shoot off in all directions" herself, to be as active and full of intentions as "the colored arrows from a Fourth of July rocket."[14] Yet all the while, limited and defined by others, enclosed in cells of history, she perceives that she is supposed to be living quietly in her kitchen, adhering, as Plath wrathfully wrote, "to rules, to rules, to rules" ("A Birthday Present," *Ariel,* p.42). And so she wonders if she is, after all, a monster like Spenser's Duessa. "A thinking woman sleeps with monsters," notes Adrienne Rich. "The beak that grips her, she becomes" ("Snapshots," *Poems,* p.48). And Plath asks, "What am I / That these late mouths"—the dissenting mouths of her mind — "cry open . . .?" ("Poppies in October," *Ariel,* p.19).

What am I? Who am I? What shall I call myself? Another aspect of the woman poet's struggle toward self-definition is her search for a name. Significantly, the problems and possibilities of naming recur throughout the poetry of such writers as Plath, Rich, Sexton, Levertov, and Wakoski. Perhaps even more significantly, however, where the male confessional poet uses the real names of real people to authenticate his ironic sociology, the self-defining female poet uses names as symbolic motifs, as mythic ideas. Robert Lowell, for instance, entitles one of his books *For Lizzie and Harriet,* and confesses that "hand on glass / and heart in mouth [I] / outdrank the Rahvs in the heat / of Greenwich Village . . . ,"[15] while Dewitt Snodgrass sardonically insists that "Snodgrass is walking through the universe."[16] But Levertov gives herself a generic name, reconciling herself with deep serenity to "what, woman, / and who, myself, / I am."[17] And Plath, trapped in the identity crisis Levertov appears to have transcended, relinquishes her name, symbolic of a mistaken identity, with intense relief: "I am nobody; I have nothing to do with explosions. / I have given my name and my day-clothes up to the nurses . . ." ("Tulips," *Ariel,* p.10).

Even Sexton, who seems at first to be playing with her name as Snodgrass toys with his, invents an imaginary Christopher to go with the reality of Anne and sets the two names in the context of a series of psalms outlining a private myth of origins: "For Anne and Christopher were born in my head as I howled at the grave of the roses. . . ."[18] Adrienne Rich goes further still, defining herself as a participant in a mysterious universal reality—"The Stranger," "the androgyne"—and noting, therefore, that "the letters of my name are written under the lids / of the newborn child."[19] Finally, Diane Wakoski, perhaps the most obsessed with names of all these poets, mythologizes one aspect of herself by emphasizing the various implications of her name: "If you know my name, / you know Diane comes across diamond in the word book," she writes in "The Diamond Merchant," "crossing my life . . .

leaving me incomplete . . ." (*Dancing,* p.118). Elsewhere she adds: "There is / an ancient priestess / whose tears make the spiderlilies grow. / She knows my name is darkness" ("The Mirror of a Day Chiming Marigold," *Dancing,* p.23). And she reveals a crucial tension between her name and her real identity: "Feeling the loneliness / of my cold name, / I live in a secret place, / behind a carved door. / My house is a diamond and my life / is unspoken" ("In the Secret Room, East of the Sun, West of the Moon," *Dancing,* p.22).

This tension between the woman's name and the reality that it may not after all represent suggests, however, a central problem that shadows all the attempts at self-definition made by the female poets discussed here. For as she struggles to define herself, to reconcile male myths about her with her own sense of herself, to find some connection between the name the world has given her and the secret name she has given herself, the woman poet inevitably postulates that perhaps she has not one but two (or more) selves, making her task of self-definition bewilderingly complex. The first of these selves is usually public and social, defined by circumstance and by the names the world calls her—daughter, wife, mother, Miss, Mrs., Mademoiselle—a self that seems, in the context of the poet's cultural conditioning, to be her natural personality (in the sense of being both physiologically inevitable and morally proper or appropriate). The female poet's second self, however, is associated with her secret name, her rebellious longings, her rage against imposed definitions, her creative passions, her anxiety, and—yes—her art. And it is this *Doppelgänger* of a second self which, generating the woman's uneasiness with male myths of femininity, gives energy as well as complexity to her struggle toward self-definition.

For if the first self is public, rational, social, and therefore seems somehow "natural," this dark, other, second self is private, irrational, antisocial, and therefore—in the best romantic tradition—associated with the supernatural. Denise Levertov's poem "In Mind" outlines the dichotomy between the two selves better than any prose analysis could. Noting that the poet's mind contains two radically opposite (but implicitly complementary) selves, Levertov describes the first of these as "a woman / of innocence," a woman who is "unadorned" but sweet-smelling and "fair-featured." She wears

> a utopian smock or shift, her hair
> is light brown and smooth, and she
>
> is kind and very clean without
> ostentation—
>   but she has
> no imagination.

Shadowing this kindly public woman, however, the poet imagines a

> turbulent moon-ridden girl
> or old woman, or both,
> dressed in opals and rags, feathers
>
> and torn taffeta,
> who knows strange songs —
>
> but she is not kind.[20]

Innumerable male writers have also, of course, spoken in ways similar to this of doubles and otherness, imagining second supernatural selves ranging from good wizards like Superman to bad alter egos like Mr. Hyde. But the exploration of inner alterity is only one of many modes of self-analysis available to the modern male confessional poet, whereas all the women whose poetry has been discussed here seem to share a real obsession with the second, supernatural self. "The Other" and "Again and Again and Again" are just two of many poems by Sexton that deal with this phenomenon of otherness. In the first, interestingly, she describes her supernatural self—her "other"—as masculine, an early avatar, I suppose, of Christopher, the imaginary twin she associates (in *The Death Notebooks*) with the mad eighteenth-century poet Christopher Smart:

> Under my bowels, yellow with smoke,
> it waits.
> Under my eyes, those milk bunnies,
> it waits.
> It is waiting.
> It is waiting.
> Mr. Doppelgänger. My brother. My spouse.
> Mr. Doppelgänger. My enemy. My lover.

Like Levertov's second self, Sexton's is unkind and therefore unfeminine, aggressive, masculine. My "other," she writes, "swallows Lysol."

> When the child is soothed and resting on the breast
> My other beats a tin drum in my heart.
>
> It cries and cries and cries
> until I put on a painted mask
> and leer at Jesus in His passion.
> Then it giggles.
> It is a thumbscrew.
> Its hatred makes it clairvoyant.
> I can only sign over everything,

the house, the dog, the ladders, the jewels,
the soul, the family tree, the mailbox.

Then I can sleep.

Maybe.[21]

Inhabited by such rage, it is no wonder that the woman poet often struggles, with a kind of feverish panic, to define herself, frantically clearing away the debris of alternative selves like "old whore petticoats" —to quote Sylvia Plath—in the hope of reattaining the blazing chastity, the unviolated singleness, of a "pure acetylene/Virgin" ("Fever 103°," *Ariel,* pp.54-55). For, inhabiting her, the second self is a cry that keeps her awake—to go on quoting Plath—flapping out nightly and "looking, with its hooks, for something to love." Yet she can define it no more precisely, can define instead only her own pain, her fear of its otherness. "I am terrified by this dark thing / That sleeps in me . . . ," Plath continues in "Elm." "All day I feel its soft, feathery turnings, its malignity" (*Ariel,* p.16). In "Again and Again and Again" Sexton notes: "I have a black look I do not / like. It is a mask I try on. / . . . its frog / sits on my lips and defecates."[22] Even Adrienne Rich, usually affirmative in her definition of a second, supernatural self, acknowledges the awful anxiety associated with such experiences of interior otherness: "A pair of eyes imprisoned for years inside my skull / is burning its way outward, the headaches are terrible" ("Ghazals: Homage to Ghalib," *Poems,* p.125). Diane Wakoski, who writes of wanting "to smash through the fortified walls of myself / with a sledge," describes, in heavily sexual terms, "the anger of my own hair, / which is long / and wants to tie knots, / strangle, avenge this face of mine . . ." ("This King: The Tombed Egyptian One," "Water Shapes," *Inside,* pp.23, 33). Inhabited by this cry of fury, these self-assertive, witch-dark wings that flap inside so many women poets, she feels a sort of supernatural electricity "dripping" from her "like cream" and perceives the whole world as transformed, seething with magical dangerous blue phenomena: "blue trains rush by in my sleep. / Blue herons fly overhead. . . . / Blue liquid pours down my poisoned throat and blue veins / rip open my breast. Blue daggers tip / and are juggled in my palms. / Blue death lives in my fingernails" ("Blue Monday," *Inside,* pp.10-11). "The Eye altering alters all," as Blake observed so long ago, and the woman poet who defines herself as possessor of (or possessed by) a deadly second self inevitably begins to imagine that she's lost in a universe of death.

Where is the way out of such a universe? What kind of self-definition is possible to someone who feels herself imprisoned there, her back humped with black inimical power, black wings flapping in her heart? —to go back to the poems with which I began these speculations. One answer, the one Sylvia Plath most often chooses, is for the woman poet to completely reject the "natural" self—the public, outer self of roles and names—and instead to identify entirely with her supernatural self. "Mrs. Hughes," for instance, is clearly one of Plath's old whore petticoats, as are "Otto Plath's daughter" and "the Guest Managing Editor of *Mademoiselle.*" Her real self, she insists, is "no drudge" but a queen, unleashed and flying, more terrible than she ever was. Yet here the terror is not a cause of anxiety but a sign of life and triumph. Become celestial like Rich's woman-as-galactic-cloud, healing the wounds of self-division, Plath's supernatural self appears at last as a "red / Scar in the sky, red comet," flying "Over the engine that killed her— / The mausoleum, the wax house" of the dying "natural" self ("Stings," *Ariel,* p.63).

Denise Levertov, on the other hand, opts in "The Wings" for a very different solution to the problem of her black inimical power, speculating that she may have *two* wings, two second selves, both equally supernatural but "one / feathered in soot, the other // . . . pale / flare-pinions." "Well—" she asks, repudiating the rage of Plath's terrible flying scar, "Could I go / on one wing, // the white one?"[23] Perhaps, she implies, the second self is not witch, devil, animal, but in the best, Blakean sense, goddess, angel, spirit.

But, of course, to go on only one wing is a compromise, an admission of defeat and fragmentation akin to Anne Finch's sorrowful presentation of her "contracted wing." And Adrienne Rich, determined "to save the skein" of "this trailing knitted thing, this cloth of darkness, / this woman's garment" of enigmatic selfhood, refuses to compromise ("When We Dead Awaken," *Poems,* p.187). Like both Plath and Levertov, however, she identifies primarily with a supernatural self, a self flying "lonely and level" as "a plane . . . / on its radio beam, aiming / across the Rockies" ("Song," *Diving,* p.20). But unlike Plath in "Stings" or Levertov in "The Wings," she's untroubled by questions about the morality of this second self. Neither black nor white, neither terrible nor blessed, it exists, Rich suggests, because it has to, for the sake of the survival of all women. Thus, the second pair of eyes, which gave the poet headaches in the 1968 "Ghazals," reappears later in "From the Prison House" as a single, healthy, visionary, third eye that is impervious to pain, pure, objective, an instrument of accurate perception:

> Underneath my lids another eye has opened
> it looks nakedly
> at the light
>
> that soaks in from the world of pain
> even when I sleep
>
> This eye
> is not for weeping
> its vision must be unblurred

though tears are on my face

its intent is clarity
it must forget
nothing.
     ("From the Prison House," *Diving,* pp.17-18)

Despite this affirmation of the justice and inevitability of her visionary anger, it's plain that Rich, too, sees herself as fragmented. Displacing her poetic vision onto a supernatural third eye and leaving the eyes of her outer, natural self merely for weeping, she implicitly concedes—at least in this poem—the difficulty of achieving a wholeness, a single, entirely adequate self-definition. And to be honest, very few women poets, from Anne Finch to the present, have in fact managed a definitive statement of self-assertion, a complete self-definition. Yet I hope that these preliminary speculations have at least partly recorded what I think women poets themselves have fully recorded: a difficult process of self-discovery that is in full progress, moving all women continually forward toward what D. H. Lawrence (for whom the problem was considerably simpler) called "self-accomplishment."[24]

Like Lawrence, W. B. Yeats was an heir of the romantic movement's egotistical sublime, so it was natural for him to imagine a woman singing, " 'I am I, am I; / The greater grows my light / The further that I fly,' " and to note, "All creation shivers / With that sweet cry."[25] But soon, perhaps, such self-assertive imaginings will be equally natural for women poets. Already Muriel Rukeyser, in one of her most famous passages, has envisioned a radiant union of inner and outer selves, a first jubilant joining of the fragments into a true creative whole: "No more masks! No more mythologies! / Now, for the first time, the god lifts his hand, / the fragments join in me with their own music."[26] And Denise Levertov, transcending her divided self of black and white wings, has proclaimed: "There is no savor / more sweet, more salt / than to be glad to be / what, woman, / and who, myself, / I am. . . ." As for the hump of black inimical power on her back, the burden of her wings, that other self can be assimilated, she suggests, into a force that nourishes her wholeness:

\
    If I bear burdens
    they begin to be remembered
    as gifts, goods, a basket

    of bread that hurts
    my shoulders but closes me

    in fragrance. I can
    eat as I go.[27]

NOTES

1. Denise Levertov, *The Sorrow Dance* (1963; reprint ed., New York: New Directions, 1966), p.11. The double slash (/ /) indicates the break between stanzas.
2. Anne Sexton, *The Book of Folly* (Boston: Houghton, 1972), p.3.
3. Sylvia Plath, *Ariel* (New York: Harper, 1966), pp.61-63. Parenthetical page references in the text, preceded by *Ariel,* will be to this edition.
4. *The New Poets: American and British Poetry Since World War II* (New York: Oxford Univ. Pr., 1967), p.15.
5. Ibid., p.61.
6. Robert Lowell, "Man and Wife," *Life Studies, and for the Union Dead* (New York: Farrar, 1967), p.87.
7. Harold Bloom, *The Anxiety of Influence* (New York: Oxford Univ. Pr., 1973), especially "Introduction: A Meditation upon Priority," pp.5-16.
8. All from Plath, *Ariel.*
9. All from Diane Wakoski, *Inside the Blood Factory* (New York: Doubleday, 1968), and *Dancing on the Grave of a Son of a Bitch* (Los Angeles: Black Sparrow Pr., 1975). Parenthetical page references in the text, preceded by *Inside* or *Dancing,* will be to these editions.
10. All from Adrienne Rich, *Poems: Selected and New, 1950-1974* (New York: Norton, 1974). Parenthetical page references in the text, preceded by *Poems,* will be to this edition.
11. All from Anne Sexton, *Love Poems* (Boston: Houghton, 1969), *The Book of Folly,* and *The Death Notebooks* (Boston: Houghton, 1974).
12. All from Denise Levertov, *O Taste and See* (New York: New Directions, 1964), and *The Sorrow Dance.*
13. "The Introduction," *The Poems of Anne Countess of Winchilsea,* ed. Myra Reynolds (Chicago: Univ. of Chicago Pr., 1903), pp.4-6.
14. Sylvia Plath, *The Bell Jar* (New York: Bantam, 1972), p.68.
15. "Man and Wife," *Life Studies,* p.87.
16. "These Trees Stand . . . ," *Heart's Needle* (New York: Knopf, 1961), p.36.
17. "Stepping Westward," *The Sorrow Dance,* p.15.
18. "Third Psalm," *The Death Notebooks,* p.82.
19. Adrienne Rich, "The Stranger," *Diving into the Wreck: Poems 1971-1972* (New York: Norton, 1973), p.19. Parenthetical page references in the text, preceded by *Diving,* will be to this edition.
20. *O Taste and See,* p.71.
21. "The Other," *The Book of Folly,* pp.30-31. On Anne Sexton's use of Christopher Smart, see my "Jubilate Anne," *Nation* 219:214-16 (Sept. 14, 1974).
22. *Love Poems,* p.29.
23. "The Wings," *The Sorrow Dance,* p.12.
24. "Humiliation," in Vivian Pinto and Warren Roberts, eds., *The Complete Poems of D. H. Lawrence,* vol. 1 (New York: Viking, 1964), p.215.
25. "He and She," from "Supernatural Songs," *The Collected Poems of W. B. Yeats* (New York: Macmillan, 1956), p.285.

26. "The Poem as Mask," *The Speed of Darkness* (New York: Random, 1968), p.3.
27. "Stepping Westward," *The Sorrow Dance*, pp.15-16.

Images of Black Women in Afro-American Poetry

Andrea Benton Rushing

> first
> a woman should
> be
> a woman *first,*
> but
> if she's *black,* really black
> and a woman
> that's special, that's real special.[1]

"The Negro," Richard Wright said, "is America's metaphor." In a way, black women function as metaphors for salient aspects of the black experience in this strange and terrible land. The symbolism which surrounds them creates a paradox: images of black women in Afro-American poetry are both varied and narrow. They afford a greater range of types than the two-stop Mammy-Sapphire syndrome of films, but, except on rare occasions, they fail to portray the multifaceted nature of the black woman in America. Although audience, the author's sex, and the prevailing literary conventions are all contributing factors, the main reason we do not see the richness and variety of black women reflected in Afro-American poetry is that women often symbolize aspects of black life that are valued by the race. As Dunbar says:

Reprinted by permission from Sharon Harley and Rosalyn Terborg-Penn, eds., *The Afro-American Woman: Struggles and Images* (National University Series in American Studies [Port Washington, N. Y.: Kennikat Pr., 1978]), pp.74-84. Based on an article which originally appeared in *Black World,* Sept. 1975, pp.18-30.

> The women of a race should be its pride;
>   We glory in the strength our mothers had,
> We glory that this strength was not denied
>   To labor bravely, nobly, and be glad.[2]

That usually unconscious symbolic thrust has been something of a straitjacket. It is not so much that there are, in Waring Cuney's words, "No Images," but rather that the images only rarely reflect the full reality.

The most prevalent image of black women in Afro-American poetry is the image of mother. We find it in early poetry like Frances Harper's "Eliza Harris" and "The Slave Auction," in Helene Johnson's "The Mother's Rock," in John Wesley Holloway's "Black Mammies," and in Jessie Fauset's "Oriflamme." We also find it in recent poetry like Ed Sprigg's "my beige mom." Almost all the images of mother revolve around her strength under stress. This is in contrast to African literature, where, according to Wilfred Cartey, the West Indian Africanist, mother and the earth of Africa are one symbol, and mother is the cushion from troubled and chaotic conditions who manifests affection, possessiveness, and shrewd practicality: an emblem of strength and support.[3] Cartey cites the Guinean author Camara Laye: "She was Mother. She belonged to me. With her everything was always all right."[4] It is rare to find an Afro-American mother likened to the earth; this may be because we are not still a peasant people or because, after the agonies of slavery and Reconstruction, we are too bitter about the land to use it as a nurturing metaphor. In the Afro-American tradition, mother is not a cushion but the impetus and example for perseverance in a hostile world. (There are, though, suffering mothers like the one portrayed in Sterling Brown's "Maumee Ruth," where the dying woman has lost her children to the city, cocaine, and gin.) Langston Hughes's "Mother to Son," with its brilliant staircase metaphor, is the best-known example of this.

The most extensive treatment of mother in black poetry comes from master poet Gwendolyn Brooks, whose gallery includes Emmett Till's strangely passive mother; Mrs. Sallie Smith, the "prudent partridge" mother of nine;[5] Mrs. Martin, who disowns her son when he makes Rosa Brown pregnant; and Jessie Mitchell's vindictive yellow mother, who, ill, comforts herself comparing her "exquisite yellow youth" to the hard fate she predicts for her black daughter.[6] Two of Brooks's most memorable figures are the dazed and doomed speaker of "the mother," recalling the children her abortions deprived her of, and the figure in "What shall I give my children who are poor?" lamenting her inability to give her children access to rich life. Other mothers include the tough one in Betty Gates's "Mamma Settles the Dropout Problem":

Umgoing up side yo head
Wit my big fiss
An' when I swings
I don aim to miss[7]

and the boldly eccentric mother in Lucille Clifton's "Admonitions":

children
when they ask you
why is your mama so funny
say
she is a poet
she don't have no sense.[8]

Often, as in poems like Sterling Brown's "When the Saints Go Ma'chin In" and Owen Dodson's "Black Mother Praying," a poet combines mother and religion to express deep emotion. This is effective because both are still points in the turning world of black experience both in Africa and in the diaspora, so combining them provides emotional resonance.

Afro-American attitudes toward mother are extremely complex, but in almost all the mother poems, mother is above criticism, the almost perfect symbol of black struggle, suffering, and endurance. Reading about her, we know where Sterling Brown's strong men come from, for she says:

You must keep going
You can't stop there; World will
waive; will be
facetious, angry. You can't stop there
You have to keep on going.[9]

Black women singers are our culture heroes. More durable than movie stars, the giants among them endure and symbolize both transcendent beauty and deeply experienced pain. The images of black women singers alternate between expressing what they share with other black people and what makes them extraordinary. The African proverb says, "The spirit will not descend without a song,"[10] and black women singers (there is no comparable body of poems by male singers) express, manage, modulate the pain we sustain. Treatment of this subject goes back as far as Dunbar's "When Malindy Sings" and comes right up to Don Lee's dedication in *We Walk the Way of the New World:* "To those who helped create a New Consciousness . . . Miriam Makeba, Nina Simone: two internationally known black women entertainers that are consistently black and relevant, can u name me two brothers/ blackmen that are as. . . ."[11]

Dunbar establishes the humble Malindy as a symbol by deflecting from details of her appearance and personality and emphasizing her naturalness (as opposed to Miss Lucy's studied art), which is in concord with and even surpasses nature, so that birds are awed by her singing. She is also a bridge, a conduit making the transcendent imminent in the lives of singers. Langston Hughes in "Jazzonia" and Claude McKay in "The Harlem Dancer" illustrate the Negro Renaissance use of black women entertainers. The significance is apparent in three lines of McKay's poem:

> Grown lovelier for passing through a storm
>
> But looking at her falsely-smiling face,
>
> I knew her self was not in that strange place.[12]

Two all-important poems about black women singers are "Ma Rainey" and "Poem to Aretha." The first contrasts Ma Rainey's little and low appearance with her ability to articulate her listeners' experience. Sterling Brown stresses the nexus of shared life between the singer, a priestess, and those she sings for:

> O Ma Rainey
> Sing yo' song;
> Now you's back
> Whah you belong,
> Git way inside us,
> Keep us strong . . .
> O Ma Rainey
> Li'l and low;
> Sing us 'bout de hard luck
> Round our do';
> Sing us 'bout de lonesome road
> We mus' go . . .
>
> Dere wasn't much more de fellow say:
> She jes' gits hold of us dataway.[13]

Another important poem about a woman singer begins linking the singing Aretha to mother images, moves through the pedestrian in her life, refers back to Dinah Washington and Billie Holiday; then Giovanni gives Aretha a scepter of blackness making her the impetus for steps toward the essence of black life and art:

> the blacks songs started coming from the singers on stage and
> the dancers in the streets.

Finally, she ascribes political potential to Aretha's songs:

> aretha was the riot was the leader if she had said "come
> let's do it" it would have been done.[14]

Although very early Afro-American poetry (like Phillis Wheatley's), under the influence of neoclassical models that stressed elegance and formality, shunned self-revelation[15] and cherished the universal rather than the racial, Afro-American poetry is replete with examples of our attempts to translate the beauty of black women into language. In the face of the mass of cultural support for the beauty of white women, black poets move to create the uncreated consciousness of their race. An early poem like Holloway's "Miss Melerlee" pictures a black woman:

> Sof' brown cheek, an' smilin' face,
> An' willowy form chuck full o' grace—
>
> Pearly teef, an' shinin' hair,
> An' silky arm so plump and bare![16]

Later Gwendolyn Bennett's "To a Dark Girl" links black women to their historical antecedents by mentioning "old forgotten queens" and suggesting that "something of the shackled slave/sobs in the rhythm of your talk."[17] Langston Hughes also reflects a history-tuned sense of black women in "When Sue Wears Red" with references to "ancient cameo/Turned brown by the ages" and "A queen from some time-dead Egyptian night."[18]

Gwendolyn Brooks, writing before the 1960s black-is-beautiful wave, provides a window on our perverse preoccupation with color, hair, noses, and lips. A woman asks for an upsweep with humpteen baby curls:

> Got Madam C. J. Walker's first
> Got Poro Grower next
> Ain't none of 'em worked with me . . .
> But I ain't vexed
> Long hair's out of style anyhow, aint it?[19]

In "the ballad of chocolate Mabbie," a seven-year-old girl's boy friend prefers "a lemon-hued lynx/with sand-waves loving her brow."[20] Annie Allen's husband takes up with a "maple banshee" and thinks of his wife:

> Not that woman! (Not that room!
> Not that dusted demi-gloom!)
> Nothing limpid, nothing meek,
> But a gorgeous and gold shriek.[21]

And, in an extremely unusual poem, Pearl Mae Lee sings a crazed song after her lover is lynched for making love with a white woman who cries rape to cover her acquiescence:

> At school, your girls were the bright little girls.
> You couldn't abide dark meat.
> Yellow was for to look at
> Black for the famished to eat . . .
>
> You grew up with bright skins on the brain
> And me in your black folks' bed.[22]

Contemporary Afro-American poetry often glories in details of black beauty. Ishmael Reed mentions "juicy Ethiopian art/Lips,"[23] Michael Harper uses "nutmeg reflection"[24] and "raisin skin."[25] Emmett Till's mother's face has the "tint of pulled taffy."[26] Mrs. Sallie Smith is a "lowbrown butterball,"[27] Dougherty Long has a gingerbread mama "all sweet and brown" valued above collard greens, candied yams, and new watermelon.[28] Black breasts against a windowpane are blackbirds for Lucille Clifton;[29] Carolyn Rodgers refers to ashy skin and nappy hair;[30] Dudley Randall likens lips to cherries in their curve, grapes in their fullness, and blackberries in their sweetness.[31] Hoagland starts with "honeystain," compares breasts to "african gourds" and "american pumpkins," and calls his woman "night interpreted";[32] and he pulls out all stops in the rash of food imagery in "love Child—a black aesthetic": "sweet baked apple dappled cinnamon speckled," "nutmeg freckled peach brandy and amber wine woman," african pepper pot, coffee flowing with cream, brown sugar, cocoa, candied yams, sweet-potato pie, raisins, blackberry pie, and honey love syrup.[33]

Note that the audience for black poetry has historically been white and distanced from black standards, and the poetry reflects that in the shift from the general descriptions of early poetry to the specificity of the poetry, for a changed audience, for the 1960s and 1970s. Also, black women can look so many different ways, there is so much intra-racial variation, that poetry cannot show an "ideal." Finally, much recent poetry, despite the interest in the physical represented by black-is-beautiful, considers moral, intellectual, and political stances more critical than physical beauty.

In 1918, when William Stanley Braithwaite wrote an introduction to Georgia Douglas Johnson's *The Heart of a Woman,* he emphasized the short time (less than fifty years) that women had spoken or acted with a sense of freedom; he went on to say:

> Sadness is a kind of felicity with woman, paradoxical as it may seem; and it is so because through this inexplicable felicity *they* touched, intuitionally caress reality . . . Mrs. Johnson creates just that reality of woman's heart and experience with astonishing raptures. It is a kind of privilege to know so much about the secrets of woman's nature, a privilege all the more to be cherished when given, as in these poems, with exquisite utterance, with such lyric sensibility.[34]

Du Bois wrote the foreword to Johnson's 1922 *Bronze*. He starts by mentioning her blackness, which Braithwaite had omitted and which the poet herself had downplayed in her earlier volume. "Her work is simple, sometimes trite, but it is singularly sincere and true, and as a revelation of the soul struggle of the women of a race, it is invaluable."[35] In his 1970 introduction to June Jordan's *Some Changes,* Julius Lester wrote:

> June Jordan is a black poet, a black woman poet. That's a devastating combination. To be black and to be a woman. To be a double outsider, to be twice oppressed, to be more than invisible. That's a triple vision. June Jordan is faithful to the three primary aspects of her being.[36]

In recent years the image of black women in Afro-American poetry has become more autobiographical (more in keeping with the assertive mood of the race than with the confessional trends in Euro-American poetry). It is as if the younger women poets see themselves as similes of their sisters. Poems in this category include Mari Evans's "To Mother and Steve" with its search for love and struggle against the thrall of drugs. Her "into blackness softly" is like both Audre Lorde's "Naturally" and Johari Amini's "Identity (For Don L. Lee)" in registering the poet's new black consciousness. Carolyn Rodger's "Me, In Kulu Se & Karma" is autobiographical, as is Nikki Giovanni's "Nikki-Rosa." Sonia Sanchez's "poem for my father," "poem for etheridge," and "why I don't get high on shit" are all autobiographical, and the whole section "In these Dissenting . . . Surrounding Ground and Autobiography" in *Revolutionary Petunias* is autobiographical.

White women are, as part of their new consciousness, fighting stereotypes. No student of this movement, I use Mary Ellmann's categories (formlessness, passivity, instability, confinement, piety, materiality, spirituality, irrationality, compliancy, the shrew, and the witch) as a gauge.[37] Few of these seem appropriate to Afro-American images of black women because they are rarely seen as weak or frivolous or incompetent. As Faulkner said of Dilsey, black women in Afro-American poerty have "endured." They have had, given their economic and political powerlessness, and their social status, no other choice. Passivity, for example, is inapplicable. Except for examples like Emmett Till's mother (but it may just be that we cannot see the "chaos" in her "red prairie"),[38] the women are action-oriented: aggressiveness is part of the matriarch stereotype black women labor under. Passivity had a certain vogue under the 1960s influence of Muslim ideology, which elevated black men—often at the expense of black women:

> blackwoman:
> is an
> in and out
> rightsideup

action-image
of her man . . .
in other
(blacker) words:
she's together
if
he
bes[39]

though Kay Lindsey says:

. . . But now that the revolution needs numbers
Mothers got a new position
Five steps behind manhood.

And I thought sittin' in the back of the bus
Went out with Martin Luther King.[40]

All the examples of irrationality I found in my survey of Afro-American poetry were in the blues tradition of loving a man who doesn't love you; but who *does* love wisely? Compliancy doesn't apply: black women are not portrayed as compliant to their men, their children, or their white employers. Ellman's spirituality means refining or ennobling the man who loves one;[41] for black women it means strengthening, centering black men, being keepers of the flame of black culture (as seen in the coalescence of women and the integrity of Africa in the poetry of the 1960s).

Molly Means, "Chile of the devil, the dark, and witch,"[42] who changes a young bride into a howling dog, is the only explicit witch my research revealed—though Saint Louis woman, who enchants a man with diamond rings, power, and store-bought hair,[43] is perhaps an urbane, urban witch.

The most common stereotypes of black women are tragic mulatto, hot-blooded exotic whore, and matriarch.[44] I found no examples of tragic mulatto in the poetry. I found several street women (Gwendolyn Brooks's Sadie, Countee Cullen's "Black Magdelens," and Fenton Johnson's "The Scarlet Woman"), but none of them were exotic. Sapphire is another stereotype in black life, but she is nowhere visible in formal Afro-American poetry, where the relations between black women and black men are usually tender, desperate, or tragic, but never angry, domineering or aggressive. The strong black mammy, "bad-talking, ball-busting, strong enough to sustain her family and herself through the hardest conditions,"[45] does exist in the literature, but she is humanized by being scaled down as Gwendolyn Brooks does Mrs. Sallie Smith, Emmett Till's mother, Mrs. Small, and Big Bessie, who "throws" her son into the street. Washington says:

> To outsiders, she is the one-dimensional Rock of Gibraltar—strong of back, long of arm, invincible. But to those writers whose perceptions are shaped by their own black womanhood, who can take us into the dark recesses of the soul, she is an individual—profound, tragic, mysterious, sacred, and unfathomable—strong in many ways, but not all.[46]

While this may be true of fiction, few of the images in Afro-American poetry reveal the complexity she describes.

The epic (heroic, archetypal) is an aspect of many of the images of black women in Afro-American poetry, though few poems, and most of them are recent, have only this thread:

> and the breath of your life
> sustains us . . .
> the female in the middle passage,
> you endure
> we endured through you[47]

and

> i am a blk/woo OOMAN
> my face
>   my brown
>   bamboo/colored
> black/berry/face
> will spread itself over
> this western hemisphere and
> be remembered
>   be sunnnnnNNGG
> for i will be called
>   QUEEN
> walk/move in
>   blk/queenly ways.
> and the world
>   shaken by
> my blkness
>   will channnnnNNGGGEEE
> colors. and be
>   reborn.
>   blk. again.[48]

and

> I
> am a black woman
> tall as a cypress
> strong

> beyond all definition still
> defying place
> and time
> and circumstance
>   assailed
>   impervious
>   indestructible
> Look
>   on me and be
> renewed.[49]

Usually, however, the heroic is a strand in a poem about a mother or a singer. Consider Helene Johnson's "The Mother's Rock" or Imamu Baraka's "leroy," where the mother is seen as the transmitter and interpreter of "our life from our ancestors/and knowledge, and the strong nigger feeling," with Baraka picturing his mother with "black angels straining above her head,"[50] a bridge between old and new blues. Mari Evans handles the epic this way:

> and the old women gathered
> and sang His praises
> standing
> resolutely together
> like supply sergeants who
> have seen
> everything
> and are still
> Regular Army: It
> was fierce and
> not melodic and
> although we ran
> the sound of it
> stayed in our ears . . .[51]

Robert Hayden's "Runagate, Runagate" provides a magnificent example of the epic black woman:

> Rises from their anguish and their power,
>
>   Harriet Tubman
>
>   woman of earth, whipscarred,
>   a summoning, a shining
>
>   Mean to be free

. . . .

and fear starts a-murbling, Never make it,
we'll never make it. *Hush that now,*
and she's turned upon us, levelled pistol
glinting in the moonlight;
Dead folks can't jaybird-talk, she says;
you keep on going now or die, she says.

Wanted . . . Harriet Tubman   alias The General
alias Moses   Stealer of Slaves

In league with Garrison   Alcott   Emerson
Garrett   Douglass   Thoreau   John Brown

Armed and known to be Dangerous

Wanted   Reward   Dead or Alive

. . . .

Mean mean mean to be free.[52]

Images of black women in Afro-American poetry come very close to
what Ellison said about the blues: "Their attraction lies in this, that
they at once express the agony of life and the possibility of conquering
it through sheer toughness of spirit."[53] The limitation is that the intensely symbolic nature of the images has often limited both the range
of women we see and the ways in which they are presented. We need,
now, poems to reflect our myriad realities.

NOTES

1. Don L. Lee, *We Walk the Way of the New World* (Detroit: Broadside,
   1970), p.39.
2. Paul Laurence Dunbar, *The Complete Poems* (New York: Dodd,
   1913), p.214.
3. Wilfred Cartey, *Whispers from a Continent* (New York: Vintage,
   1969), pp.3-4.
4. Ibid., p.38.
5. Gwendolyn Brooks, *The World of Gwendolyn Brooks* (New York:
   Random, 1971), p.377.
6. Ibid., p.329.
7. Betty Gates, "Mamma Settles the Dropout Problem," *Understanding
   the New Black Poetry* (New York: Morrow, 1973), p.309.
8. Lucille Clifton, "Admonitions," *The Black Poets* (New York: Bantam,
   1971), p.251.
9. Brooks, p.381.
10. LeRoi Jones, *Blues People* (New York: Morrow, 1963), p.41.
11. Lee, p.5.
12. Claude McKay, "The Harlem Dancer," *The Book of American Negro
   Poetry* (New York: Harcourt, 1949), p.170.

13. Sterling Brown, "Ma Rainey," *Southern Road* (Boston: Beacon, 1974), pp.63-64.
14. Nikki Giovanni, "Poem for Aretha," *Black Poets*, p.329.
15. Robert Hayden, ed., *Kaleidoscope* (New York: Harcourt, 1967), p.xx.
16. John Wesley Holloway, "Miss Melerlee," *Book of American Negro Poetry*, pp.134-35.
17. Gwendolyn Bennett, "To a Dark Girl," *Book of American Negro Poetry*, p.243.
18. Langston Hughes, "When Sue Wears Red," *Understanding the New Black Poetry*, p.126.
19. Brooks, p.37.
20. Ibid., p.14.
21. Ibid., p.88.
22. Ibid., p.45.
23. Ishmael Reed, "To a Daughter of Isaiah," *Chattanooga* (New York: Random, 1972), p.35.
24. Michael Harper, "Echoes: One," *Dear John, Dear Coltrane* (Univ. of Pittsburgh Pr., 1970), p.24.
25. Ibid., p.69.
26. Brooks, p.324.
27. Ibid., p.377.
28. Dougherty Long, "Ginger Bread Mamma," *Black Poets*, p.310.
29. Lucille Clifton, "If I Stand in My Window," *Black Poets*, p.251.
30. Carolyn Rodgers, "Me, in Kulu Se & Karma," *Understanding the New Black Poetry*, p.345.
31. Dudley Randall, "Blackberry Sweet," *The New Black Poetry* (New York: International, 1969), p.103.
32. Everett Hoagland, "The Anti-Semanticist," *Black Poets*, pp.314-15.
33. Ibid., p.312.
34. Georgia Douglas Johnson, *The Heart of a Woman* (Freeport, N. Y.: Books for Libraries Pr., 1971), p.xx.
35. Georgia Douglas Johnson, *Bronze* (Boston: B. J. Brimmer, 1922), p.7.
36. June Jordan, *Some Changes* (New York: Dutton, 1971), p.ix.
37. Mary Ellmann, *Thinking About Women* (New York: Harcourt, 1968), p.55.
38. Brooks, p.324.
39. Don L. Lee, "blackwoman:" *Don't Cry, Scream* (Detroit: Broadside, 1969), p.51.
40. Kay Lindsey, "Poem," *The Black Woman* (New York: New American Library, 1970), p.17.
41. Ellmann, p.102.
42. Margaret Walker, "Molly Means," *Book of Negro Folklore* (New York: Dodd, 1958), p.545.
43. W. C. Handy, "St. Louis Blues," *The Negro Caravan* (New York: Amo, 1969), p.473.
44. Mary Helen Washington, "Black Women Image Makers," *Black World*, 23:10 (Aug. 1974).
45. Ibid., p.11.
46. Ibid., p.13.
47. Larry Neal, "For Our Women," *Black Fire* (New York: Morrow, 1968), p.311.

48. Sonia Sanchez, *We a BaddDDD People* (Detroit: Broadside, 1970), p.6.
49. Mari Evans, *I Am a Black Woman* (New York: Morrow, 1970), p.12.
50. Imamu Amiri Baraka, "leroy," *Black Poets*, pp.215-16.
51. Mari Evans, ". . . And the Old Women Gathered (The Gospel Singers)," *New Negro Poets: U.S.A.* (Bloomington: Univ. of Indiana Pr., 1964), p.79.
52. Robert Hayden, "Runagate, Runagate," *Understanding the New Black Poetry*, pp.158-59.
53. Ralph Ellison, *Shadow and Act* (New York: Vintage, 1972), p.94.

Traditional Poetry of the American Indian

Anna Lee Stensland

Teachers in every country in the world accept the necessity of teaching the culture and heritage of the people of that country. In the United States we have seen our heritage as British-American, with literary roots in such British giants as Chaucer, Shakespeare, and Milton, as well as in American masters like Emerson, Hawthorne, and Mark Twain. Very few literary critics have bothered to separate the two and to ask, "What makes our American heritage different from that of the British?" One answer to that question has to be our contact with the American Indian. Examine, for example, the names of our states: Wisconsin, Minnesota, Dakota, Missouri, Iowa—all Indian names; the names of cities—Omaha, Bemidji, Shakopee, Peoria, Seattle—and the names of some of our lakes along the Canadian border—Saganaga, Kabetogema, Namakon, Winnibigoshish. Note the food, so common on our tables, all plants which were first cultivated by Indians: corn, beans, sweet potatoes, strawberries, tomatoes, peanuts, and squash. Politically, Benjamin Franklin gave credit to the League of the Iroquois when preparing his proposals for the union of the colonies in 1754, ideas which later found their way into the United States Constitution. And in our American literature, authors from Philip Freneau to William Faulkner have used Indian themes: Bryant, Whittier, Cooper, Longfellow, Thoreau, Willa Cather, to mention only a few.

Reprinted by permission from *English Journal* 64:41-47 (Sept. 1975). Copyright © 1975 by the National Council of Teachers of English.

Unfortunately, too often our American literary masters were inaccurate or prejudiced in their knowledge of the American Indian.

Thomas Sanders and Walter Peek, two modern Indian collectors of the works of Indian authors, write, "If you would seek to know a people, look to their poetry. It is there in the most intense, controlled but emotionally honest statements that the natural eloquence of the group reveals itself in unguarded expression of unveiled needs and desires, passions, aspirations, and dreams. The rhythms of the people's poetry indicate the nature of their response to the rhythms of the world in which they live."[1] In no place is the spiritual nature of the Indian more evident than in his traditional poetry or songs, those works which have come to us from the distant past and the names of whose authors have been lost.

If the non-Indian teacher is to introduce students to this very important corpus of American literature, he should acquaint himself with certain Indian characteristics, ideas, and concepts which are divergent from his own, or there is danger of misunderstanding and ethnocentrism in his interpretations of the material. Natalie Curtis, who was recording Indian music around the beginning of this century when it was against the law for Indians to sing their native songs in government schools, wrote, "Indian thought presents material absolutely unique. . . ."[2] This poetry must be read and understood in the context of the tribal society and the uses that society made of songs and chants.

Most traditional songs had religious significance. In some tribes no secular poetry at all has been recorded. Consequently, the concept of the Great Mystery, which is one quite unfamiliar to those of Judeo-Christian backgrounds, is crucial to understanding. The Great Mystery is not a god which created man in his own image. This concept is most important, because horrendous Indian stereotypes created by the white man have pictured the Indian as one who worshipped the sun, rocks, coyotes, rabbits, and all manner of objects. Charles Eastman, Sioux Indian medical doctor, writes, ". . . the Indian no more worshiped the Sun than the Christian adores the Cross."[3] Gitchi Manito or Wah'kon-tah, whatever the term a particular tribe used for the Great Mystery, is invisible and immaterial, a spirit without a man-like personality. All things are in and of this spirit. The Indian does not divide the cosmos into the natural and the supernatural, nor his life into the physical and the spiritual as the modern Christian tends to do. Man does not hold some special place on a great chain of being suspended between the natural and the supernatural, as he does in the Christian view. The Indian view of the cosmos is that of one great circle of being to which all things belong: thunder, wind, rain, snow, animals, man, rocks and plants. Again Eastman explains, "We believed that the spirit pervades all creation and that every creature possesses a soul in some degree, though not necessarily a soul conscious of itself. The tree, the waterfall, the grizzly bear, each is an embodied Force, and as such an object of reverence."[4] Sanders and Peek tell us that Emerson's concept of the Oversoul has some similarities to the Great Mystery.

For this reason the Indian can speak through intermediaries which share equally with him in the Mystery. Notice the following Arapaho song:

> Our father, the Whirlwind,
> Our father, the Whirlwind—
> By its aid I am running swiftly,
> By its aid I am running swiftly,
> By which means I saw our father,
> By which means I saw our father.[5]

A Papago hunter puts himself into the skin of the deer in the following:

> Here I come forth.
> On the earth I fall over:
> The snapping bow made me dizzy.
>
> Here I come forth.
> On the mountain I slipped:
> The humming arrow made me dizzy.[6]

Because they share in the Great Mystery, animals, rocks, and clouds can talk to man. It is not the specific buffalo or bear to which the Indian speaks; it is to Buffalo, Bear, or Loon, the spiritual essence of the animal or bird. In the introduction to Natalie Curtis' book, a Cheyenne chief explains:

> There are birds of many colors—red, blue, green, yellow—yet it is all one bird. There are horses of many colors—brown, black, yellow, white —yet it is all one horse. So cattle, so all living things—animals, flowers, trees. So men: in this land where once were only Indians are now men of every color—white, black, yellow, red—yet all one people. That this should come to pass was in the heart of the Great Mystery. It is right thus. And everywhere there shall be peace.[7]

This concept of the Great Mystery can cause difficulty for the translator of a song. The much-translated Ojibwa "Chant to the Firefly" is an example. William Brandon's free version, adapted from Henry Rowe Schoolcraft, goes like this:

> Flickering firefly
>   give me light
>   light
>   once more before I sleep
>
> Dancing firefly
>   Wandering firefly

>   light
>   once more before I sleep
>
>   White light sailing
>   white light winking
>   just once more before I sleep.[8]

Such words as *bug* and *insect,* which appeared in Schoolcraft's original translation, have a connotation which places man in a superior position to the firefly and therefore are inappropriate to the Indian view of things. Gandhi's respect for all life when he refused to kill a mosquito or roach is closer to the Indian's view. The magic and power which "Chant to the Firefly" is intended to invoke defies translation into English; it is the Indian's prayer for power and wisdom which the firefly has to give him.

Songs and chants were part of all of Indian life, because every act was a religious act. A song always had a purpose. The Indian sang for power: when he hunted, fished or planted; when he went to battle or faced other dangers; when he mourned and when he celebrated great events. Games, dances, work and ceremonies all had sacred meanings. For this reason, every Indian was a poet or singer; this was not limited to the cultured few. The artistic effects of his song were irrelevant; its purpose was communication between himself and the Great Mystery. This does not mean, of course, that some people, because of experiences, did not sing with more power—the elders of some tribes or the Navajo Night Chanters, for example. Some of the great ceremonial cycles do not belong to everyone; their mysteries are known and understood only by very specialized persons. But everyone sang his own songs.

One can, for example, picture a Papago on his arid land longing for a harvest and looking toward the west singing for rain:

> Close to the west the great ocean is singing.
> The waves are rolling toward me, covered
>   with many clouds.
> Even here I catch the sound
> The earth is shaking beneath me
>   and I hear the deep rumbling.[9]

The warrior, who was frightened, sang in order to keep up his courage, as in this song from the Omahas:

> I shall vanish and be no more,
> But the land over which I roam
> Shall remain and change not.[10]

Most personal and cherished of all songs by the male of the tribe was that song he received when vision-seeking. In many tribes, the young man, after preparing himself ceremoniously, went out, often to a mountain top, where for days he would fast, without food or water, until he received a vision or dream which would determine his future. Considered messages from the spirit world, some songs often could not be shared, lest their power be lost, so such songs were never recorded. But under other conditions, the owner might share his song with a friend or give it to his tribe. Such a song is the following:

> Where the wind is blowing
> The wind is roaring
> I stand.
>
> Westward the wind is blowing
> The wind is roaring
> I stand.[11]

Women, too, had songs—for the safe journey of a husband, for brave husbands or sons fighting for the tribe, for presenting a newborn child to the cosmos, or for charming a loved one. The often-sung Indian love call is a creation of the white man, as are such romanticized ideas as maiden's leaps, where a young Indian maid is supposed to have leaped to her death because her love was scorned. But the use of song to place a charm on the object of one's love was common. Sanders and Peek quote such an Ojibwa love charm poem:

> What are you saying to me?
> I am arrayed like the roses
> And beautiful as they.[12]

The type of lyrical love or nature poem which English-speaking peoples associate with Romanticism and such poets as Wordsworth, Keats, or Bryant, is almost unknown among traditional Indian poetry. The Indian did not sing in order to celebrate his own feelings. To do that would be absurd, since in his view of the world, anyone could do it. The Indian sang in order to bring himself into harmony with his tribe, Nature, and the Great Mystery. In fact, the singer usually did not consider himself the author, but rather merely the messenger from the Great Spirit. Black Elk, the late nineteenth and early twentieth century Sioux holy man, looked upon the dictating of his autobiography in this way: ". . . if it were only my story I think I would not tell it; for what is one man that he should make much of his winters, even when they bend him like a heavy snow? . . . It is the story of all life that is holy and it is good to tell, and of us two-leggeds sharing it with the four-leggeds and the wings of the air and all green things; for these are the children of one mother and their father is one Spirit."[13]

Rather than an expression of the impassioned poet, or the innermost feelings of the author, the purpose of the Indian poem is power to exert influence on the cosmos. This was possible in the Indian world because of the magic and wonder of the *word*. The modern Pulitzer Prize Kiowa author, N. Scott Momaday, writes, "A word has power in and of itself. It comes from nothing into sound and meaning; it gives origin to all things. By means of words can a man deal with the world on equal terms. The word is sacred."[14]

Some tribes, in fact, believed that the *word* existed before anything else. Since the thought or the dream came before Creation, the word which was the manifestation of thought also preceded Creation. Whether or not the *word* came before the Great Mystery is not always clear. Consequently, words were sacred and carried power. They enabled the singer to control the universe and therefore could not be profaned or used casually or falsely. The Indian treated words with a respect which is alien to non-Indian people. In many tribes the individual's name had such power that he never spoke it. Theodora Kroeber tells us that in 1911 when Ishi, the last of his Yahi tribe, came out of the mountains there was great difficulty finding out his name. Reporters kept pressing for it as they wrote their stories of the "last wild Indian in North America." Finally, Alfred Kroeber, California anthropologist and Ishi's friend, said that he should be known as *Ishi,* a word which simply meant "man" in the Yahi language. Mrs. Kroeber explains, "He *never* revealed his own private Yahi name. It was as though it had been consumed in the funeral pyre of the last of his beloved ones. He accepted the new name, answering to it unreluctantly. But once it was bestowed it took on enough of his true name's mystic identification with himself, his soul, whatever inner essence of a man it is which a name shares, that he was never again heard to pronounce it."[15]

Such reverence for words leads often to characteristics in poetry which are unfamiliar to modern readers. Words in the Indian world are used ritually. Washington Matthews told of a Navajo priest who before he was to tell a Creation story always began with these words:

> I am never out of sight.
> Therefore I must tell the truth
> I hold my word tight to my breast.[16]

Stories of the Kiowa's trickster, Old Saynday, always begin with "Saynday was coming along. . . ." Among Indian people, many stories, poems, even jokes must be told or sung exactly, with the same gestures, pauses, and expressions each time they are presented. Otherwise, the spell which the words should cast will be broken. Some songs can be understood only because of a belief in the *word's* power to bring about a desired result.

Repetition is part of this mystery. A magic and powerful line might be repeated and repeated until the request or power is granted. Fear, loneliness, illness can be carried away by words. This repetition has, of course, caused difficulty for translators. For the Indian, alone with

Nature, repetition accumulated power; for the modern reader, alone with his printed page, repetition accumulates boredom.

One of the most impressive examples of complete faith in the mysticism of the word, music and dance, repeated for days, was the messianic Ghost Dance movement which ended tragically at Wounded Knee in 1890. It was the religion of the peaceful prophet, Wovoka, which was misinterpreted by desperate and unhappy people into a belief that all Indians who had died, as well as the buffalo which had gone, would return to save the land and the old way of life for the Indian and that magic shirts could stop bullets. Each tribe which received and accepted the word from Wovoka developed its own doctrines and sequences of songs. These sequences were incantations sung over and over for days, while the people danced. One of the songs from the Kiowa will illustrate the style.

> The spirit army is approaching,
> The spirit army is approaching.
> The whole world is moving onward
> The whole world is moving onward.
> See! Everyone is standing watching,
> See! Everyone is standing watching.
> Let us all pray,
> Let us all pray.[17]

Because they were chants which were repeated over and over, many of the traditional Indian poems as they are printed are very short. The bases for all poetry and song were found in the various rhythms of nature—the sound of the water on the shore, breathing, the pounding of rain and the beat of a human heart. Melody came from the songs of birds, the blowing of the wind and the sound of the brook. All of these sounds tend to be brief and repetitious, and so is much Indian poetry. It must be explained, however, that there are some very long poems, especially those which are parts of ceremonials: the Navajo Night Chant, for example, which has 324 songs, is recited over a succession of days and nights.

Another reason Indian songs tend to be very short is the tribal knowledge which all members know and have in common. Such information may be implied rather than explained in a song. A Papago woman once told anthropologist Ruth Underhill, "The song is very short because we understand so much."[18] Everyone growing up and living with the tribe knows mythological and ceremonial characters, tribal events and beliefs so well that a word or phrase suggests a whole series of ideas. One Chippewa poem is only two words long: One word means warrior, the other the name of the hero. People in the tribe know his brave deeds, so it is not necessary to say more.

The deep symbolism understood by tribal members often makes what seems like a simple nature poem into a kind of prayer when the reader understands:

> the first to come
> epithet among the birds
> bringing the rain
> Crow is my name.[19]

As Gerald Vizenor, Chippewa poet, explains it, the Ojibwa believed that black crows arrive early in the spring to bring the first rain and also that the crow is a symbol of wisdom.

The symbolism, the conciseness, the repetition and the traditional tribal knowledge, which is often implied, all make translations of traditional songs difficult and literal translation impossible. If a teacher is free to choose paperback collections of traditional Indian poetry for his class to use, he needs to be aware of some of the problems. The earliest collections of Indian poetry were done by anthropologists or ethnologists, often published originally in Bureau of American Ethnology reports. Most of these field workers tried to keep the poem as much like the original song as possible, but often the poem, when translated literally into English, was absurd. Since many of these ethnologists knew the Indian languages they were dealing with, they talked to the Indian reporting the song and then added to their translations certain hidden meanings known to the Indian but not expressed in the literal translation. More recently as self-styled poets, not knowing the languages or having contact with the original singer, having worked with the poems, their primary concern has been a good English poem, not a truly Indian one. The thought and perhaps the emotion of an Indian poem can be translated, but the very phenomenon of an Indian poem in print is alien to it. The personal ownership of it, the oral tradition with its background in nature, and the singing and body movements which went with the song, all are missing for the modern reader. But it is questionable that "modern interpretations" are the answer. Some critic-scholars are beginning to examine new editions of English poetry to describe the kinds of changes free translators are making.[20] There is nothing wrong with good, free translations so long as the teacher and the reader know when they are reading quite literal translations, when they are free translations and when they are "interpretations."

Some of the most accessible collections of works from many tribes are the following, all in paperback:

Astrov, Margot. *American Indian Prose and Poetry: an Anthology*. Berkeley: Capricorn Press, 1962. (Originally published in 1946 under the title *The Winged Serpent*.)

Although it contains both prose and poetry and has been criticized by some as being mainly the work of anthropologists, the translations are quite literal and close to the original Indian. The book is divided into ten area sections by geographical, cultural areas. It also has a good introduction about Indian poetry.

Bierhorst, John. *In the Trail of the Wind: American Indian Poems and Ritual Orations.* New York: Farrar, Straus and Giroux, 1972.

The arrangement here is thematic rather than geographical. Translations are chosen from well-known Indian specialists, using mainly rather literal translations. The beauty of the book is enhanced by carefully chosen period engravings.

Brandon, William. *The Magic World: American Indian Songs and Poems.* New York: William Morrow, 1971.

The editor says that his only criterion for inclusion of a poem was "do the lines feel good, moving?" The result is some very free translations taken from the original, more literal translations. (See the William Bevis article for the kinds of changes Brandon has made.) The book is organized geographically by tribes.

Cronyn, George W. *American Indian Poetry: an Anthology of Songs and Chants.* New York: Liveright, 1970. (Originally published in 1918 under the title *The Path on the Rainbow.*)

This is the earliest of collections. It has been much criticized because of certain errors: The author assumes that the Ojibwa and Chippewa are different tribes; the writer of the introduction praises an alleged Indian poem, which had years before proved to be a fraud; and the section of "interpretations" turns out to be quite non-Indian. For its time, however, the work is important.

Day, A. Grove. *The Sky Clears: Poetry of the American Indians.* Lincoln: University of Nebraska Press, 1964.

This is a book *about* Indian poetry more than an anthology of poems, but it does contain more than 200 poems from about forty Indian tribes as examples of points the author is making. The book is organized geographically by tribes. It is a useful reference book for teachers to have.

Rothenburg, Jerome. *Shaking the Pumpkin: Traditional Poetry of the Indian North Americas.* Garden City, New York: Doubleday, 1972. The editor in this case has been quite free in his translations. He sees the translator as one who "attempts to restore what has been torn apart." The vulgarity and lust which were part of Indian life are in these translations.

The recent popularity of ethnic courses in high school has given students opportunities to study cultures quite different from their own, opportunities to see themselves and their world through other eyes. As English majors we know the importance of understanding the literature we teach. Consequently, we should not teach these ethnic courses or units casually without preparation and study. Traditional Indian poetry, often difficult because it is so unlike poetry we know, is worth the effort because it will give students a different perspective on life and correct fragmentary and erroneous ideas about the First Americans.

NOTES

1. Thomas E. Sanders and Walter W. Peek, *Literature of the American Indian* (Beverly Hills: Glencoe Pr., 1973), p.103.
2. Natalie Curtis, *The Indians' Book* (New York: Dover, 1968), p.xxix.
3. Charles Eastman, *The Soul of the Indian* (Rapid City, S. D.: Fenwyn Pr., 1970), p.13.
4. Ibid., pp.14-15.
5. John Bierhorst, *In the Trail of the Wind* (New York: Farrar, 1971), p.24.
6. Ibid., p.56.
7. Curtis, p.x.
8. William Brandon, *The Magic World* (New York: Morrow, 1971), p.97.
9. Frances Densmore, *Papago Music* (Washington, D. C.: Bureau of American Ethnology Bulletin 90, 1929), p.140.
10. Margot Astrov, *American Indian Prose and Poetry: An Anthology* (New York: Capricorn, 1962), p.133.
11. Ibid., p.121.
12. Sanders and Peek, p.151.
13. John Neihardt, *Black Elk Speaks* (Lincoln: Univ. of Nebraska Pr., 1961), p.1.
14. N. Scott Momaday, *The Way to Rainy Mountain* (New York: Ballantine, 1969), p.42.
15. Theodora Kroeber, *Ishi in Two Worlds* (Berkeley: Univ. of California Pr., 1971), p.128.
16. Astrov, p.3.
17. Sanders and Peek, p.346.
18. Ruth Underhill, *The Autobiography of a Papago Woman* (Menasha: American Anthropological Assn., 1936), p.11.
19. Gerald Vizenor, *Anishinabe Nagamon: Songs of the People* (Minneapolis: Nodin Pr., 1965), p.43.
20. See, for example, William Bevis, "American Indian Verse Translations," *College English* 35:693-703 (Mar. 1974).

BIBLIOGRAPHY

Astrov, Margot. *American Indian Prose and Poetry: An Anthology.* New York: Capricorn, 1962.
Bevis, William. "American Indian Verse Translations," *College English* 35:693-703 (Mar. 1974).
Bierhorst, John. *In the Trail of the Wind.* New York: Farrar, 1971.
Brandon, William. *The Magic World.* New York: Morrow, 1971.
Cronyn, George W. *American Indian Poetry: An Anthology of Songs and Chants.* New York: Liveright, 1970.
Curtis, Natalie. *The Indian's Book.* New York: Dover, 1968.
Day, A. Grove. *The Sky Clears: Poetry of the American Indians.* Lincoln: Univ. of Nebraska Pr., 1964.
Densmore, Frances. *Papago Music.* Washington, D. C.: Bureau of American Ethnology Bulletin 90, 1929.

Kroeber, Theodora. *Ishi in Two Worlds*. Berkeley: Univ. of California Pr., 1971.

Momaday, N. Scott. *The Way to Rainy Mountain*. New York: Ballantine, 1969.

Neihardt, John. *Black Elk Speaks*. Lincoln: Univ. of Nebraska Pr., 1961.

Rothenburg, Jerome. *Shaking the Pumpkin: Traditional Poetry of the Indian North Americas*. Garden City, N. Y.: Doubleday, 1972.

Sanders, Thomas E. and Walter W. Peek. *Literature of the American Indian*. Beverly Hills: Glencoe Pr., 1972.

Underhill, Ruth. *The Autobiography of a Papago Woman*. Menasha: American Anthropological Assn., 1936.

Vizenor, Gerald. *Anishinabe Nagamon: Songs of the People*. Minneapolis: Nodin Pr., 1965.

Part 9

Alternate Worlds and a Multiplicity of Futures

We have come from God, and inevitably the myths woven by us, though they contain error, will also reflect a splintered fragment of the true light, the eternal truth that is with God.

J. R. R. Tolkien, speaking to
C. S. Lewis[1]

Shared visions are transmitted from generation to generation through the telling of stories that provide a common mythological structure for belief and confidence in the future. The central problem confronting Western civilization may be that we have lost our capacity for shared stories.

Robert Bundy[2]

Lloyd Alexander has said that the ability to fantasize is the ability to survive. In this time when survival seems uppermost in the thoughts of all the people of our planet, fantasy serves to express the quest for a new order. Fantasy has been described as "a mode of knowing . . . a profound literature," appealing because it answers to some basic human needs, above all, perhaps, the need for "a new vision . . ." for "seeing the Primary World in new ways."[3] The allusion is to Tolkien's distinction in "On Fairy Stories" between the "Primary World" of everyday reality and the "Secondary World" fashioned by the creator of fantasy. Tolkien explains how the storymaker, when successful as "sub-creator," "makes a Secondary World which your mind can enter. Inside it, what he relates is 'true': it accords with the laws of that world. You therefore believe it, while you are, as it were, inside. The moment disbelief arises, the spell is broken; the magic, or rather art, has failed. You are then out in the Primary World again . . . ."[4] Well-fashioned fantasy elicits the response that Tolkien calls "literary belief," to the end of imparting a fresh vision of truth. At its finest, fantasy offers not escape, but encounter with psychological and spiritual realities.

Robert Sklar's essay on Tolkien and Hesse takes as its thesis the belief that the visions of life found in the works of these two writers "accord with the contemporary visions of youth." Convincingly, he maintains that the young see in Tolkien's hobbits a reflection of their own situation; they too feel "called upon to leave behind a way of life equally self-serving and as oblivious to social truths." True, Tolkien's mood is one of Spenglerian doom (echoing the Germanic *Götterdämmerung*), but young people can identify this present age with the era of apocalypse, and they yearn for involvement, for readiness to "inherit the future" that must follow upon the demise of civilization as we know it.

Whereas Tolkien concerns himself with the cosmic struggle between good and evil as it is manifested in individual, everyday lives (and ignores the conventional "issues of adolescence," such as "Who am I?"), Hesse spotlights ontological questions. Both *Siddhartha* and *Demian* are "quest" books, and the object of the quest is the Self; yet ultimately, Hesse recognizes, after searching within, one must seek the answer to one's identity through action in the world. Sklar sees in the popularity of Tolkien and Hesse a basis for optimism about the young, a token of their "new delight in human mysteries, in life's possibilities, in the power of will and the pleasures of imagination."

Science fiction has been defined variously as "fantasy projected into the future," as "what is found on the library shelves under the sign, 'science fiction,' " and in a host of other ways. One of the finest definitions comes from Lloyd Alexander's lecture, "Fantasy and the Human Condition."[5] The elements distinguishing science fiction from fantasy for Alexander are three: a scientific or pseudo-scientific rationale to explain events; extrapolation from existing technology; and an emphasis on the play of intellect rather than on emotion.

Sylvia Engdahl, as a writer of science fiction herself, discusses her reasons for expressing herself through this genre: a fascination with the future, a belief in the necessity of space exploration to the survival of humanity, and a conviction that teenagers desire "a broader view than our present society offers them"—and need the inner security that a perspective on the future can provide. She further believes the young are refusing to accept the "fashionable" notion that the universe is "patternless and absurd." The nonfiction book she refers to, on the topic of "an infinity of worlds," has since appeared: her *The Planet-Girded Suns: Man's View of Other Solar Systems*.[6] Engdahl finds no dichotomy between scientific progress and the spiritual well-being of humanity; on the contrary she believes science enhances life, and science fiction, in turn, enriches literature.

In "Reason and Mysticism in Fantasy and Science Fiction," Joseph E. Milosh, Jr. gives an historical overview of the two ways of knowing—reason and intuition—as manifested in well-known works of literature from medieval times to the present. His insights into the link between the concerns of contemporary fantasy/science fiction and those of certain representative classics of the Middle Ages provide a rich background for the discussion of the topics of the limits of human knowledge and the "necessary complexity" of the human quest for truth—particularly as these topics relate to the young person's search for certainties. (Readers may wish to compare and contrast the two modes of knowing as viewed here with the two modes of consciousness as discussed in G. Lynn Nelson's "Zen and the Art of English Teaching.")

Margaret P. Esmonde's article reviews with acute perception fifteen "postcataclysmic" novels produced between 1973 and 1976. These "dystopian" works all share the theme of humanity facing the end of the world or at least of civilization as we know it.[7] She identifies certain patterns in these novels, for example, a focus in one group upon "the overthrow of our way of life through socioeconomic breakdown" or, in another, on "man's longing for peace and his struggle to free himself from the curse of violence" through cultivating his psychic powers. Several of the novels reviewed are found wanting in literary quality, and the incisive criticisms deftly separate the wheat from the chaff that too often contaminates this genre. In closing, Esmonde stresses the universal, unwavering truth, embodied in the finest of these books, that survival hinges ultimately upon the life-sustaining power of love.

NOTES

1. As quoted in Humphrey Carpenter, *Tolkien: A Biography* (Boston: Houghton, 1977), p.147.
2. In Robert Bundy, ed., *Images of the Future: The Twenty-first Century and Beyond* (Buffalo: Prometheus, 1976), p.35.
3. *The CEA Critic* 40:2-3 (Jan. 1978).
4. In his *Tree and Leaf* (Boston: Houghton, 1965), p.37.
5. Cassette tape, from *Prelude: Mini-Seminars on Using Books Creatively,* Series 2. (New York: Children's Book Council, 1976).
6. (New York: Atheneum, 1974). Those who wish to explore further the idea touched upon by Engdahl—the necessity to mankind's survival of the colonization of space—will want to read Kenneth Brower's fascinating study of physicist Freeman Dyson and his son, George Dyson, *The Starship and the Canoe* (New York: Holt, 1978). The elder Dyson believes we must colonize the stars, or at least the comets, if we are to survive as a race. The book creates a dialectic between his ideas and those of his son, who has been drawn to the simple life of earlier times,

and whose aspiration is to build not a starship but a canoe—a great, ocean-navigating kayak.

7. "Dystopian" novels depict an imaginary "dystopia"—that is, "bad place," an anti-utopia, "marked by extreme mechanization or authoritarianism" —e.g. George Orwell's *1984* (1949) or Aldous Huxley's *Brave New World* (1932). From Karl E. Beckson and Arthur Ganz, *Literary Terms: A Dictionary* (New York: Farrar, 1975), p.266.

Tolkien and Hesse: Top of the Pops

Robert Sklar

Even for those who believe strongly, as I do, that the present-day young generation differs significantly from any that has come before, there are moments when the whole concept of a new and distinctive young generation threatens to collapse into a concoction of advertising actuaries and slick-magazine moralists. These are the moments when their taste in literature—if nothing else—redeems the young. Books are commodities as much as underarm deodorants, but as yet no monopolies limit the brands and no market research has come up with a package sure to sell. You can lead students to books, as any teacher can tell you, but they can't be forced to drink. Reading remains, like dying, a task most people have to do alone. The immense popularity of J. R. R. Tolkien's fantasies and the growing interest in Hermann Hesse's novels are better guides than most to the styles and moods of young people today.

The Tolkien fad began just at the time when young people sensed their own identity as a generation, when SNCC was breaking off from older civil rights groups, and the Free Speech Movement at Berkeley passed on the word: "You can't trust anyone over 30." But Tolkien himself, a retired professor of Anglo-Saxon, was in his seventies when students began to mine nicknames, epithets, slogans, and even complete languages from his books. And Hesse, a German writer born in the Bismarck era, who had been popular among the young before Marconi invented the wireless, had died at 85 in 1962. Neither in poetry, nor in prophecy, nor in any other sphere of imagination or

Reprinted by permission from *Nation* 204:598-601 (May 8, 1967). Copyright © 1967 by The Nation Associates.

intellect have the young taken so readily to guides and entertainers ancient enough to be their great-grandfathers.

There are enough sociological, psychological and literary hypotheses readily at hand to produce an explanation as scholarly and detailed as Tolkien's genealogies. But let us rest content with a simple truth: Tolkien and Hesse's visions of life accord with the contemporary visions of youth. In the same way, Salinger's *The Catcher in the Rye* and Golding's *Lord of the Flies* mirrored the youthful imagination of the past decade. And now that their popularity belongs to history we can see how blessedly far we have come. *The Catcher in the Rye* and *Lord of the Flies* reflected the fear young people felt in that era of McCarthy and the bomb, their helplessness, their hopelessness. Their tone matched the cynical style of those years, and raised to the level of art the bitter compromises youth managed then to make with such ease. Even the most pessimistic critics of long hair and sexual freedom would not want to return us to that.

One is tempted to add another hypothesis because it reflects a little credit on adults. Parents who panicked after Sputnik may find proof in the popularity of Tolkien and Hesse that our schools have brought about a whole new range of literacy. The best extracurricular reading students could manage fifteen years ago usually reached its peak at *The Fountainhead.* Salinger and Golding at least marked a step up to good writing; with Tolkien and Hesse we have attained an astonishing goal, with implications we have yet to grasp: youngsters reading as their favorites, by their own free choice, great works of literature.

You may not bridle to hear the works of a Nobel Prize winner called great. But what of *The Lord of the Rings* trilogy, with its enormous bulk, strange creatures, and stranger scholarly paraphernalia, language grammars, tables of dates, genealogies? I can say only this: initially I was put off by the cults and fetishes which surround it, by the crescendo of praise coming from hands grown gnarled with the beating of drums. But reading it won me over. I found *The Lord of the Rings* a work of immense narrative power that can sweep the unresisting reader up and hold him enthralled for days and weeks as he lives the story through.

Everyone must have heard by now a little of the ringbearer's tale. The ring first appeared in Tolkien's earlier, simpler story, *The Hobbit,* where Bilbo, the plump three-foot-high creature after whom the book is named, finds it in a mountain cave. The ring makes its wearer invisible, and Bilbo uses it to good advantage during his adventures with the wizard Gandalf and a band of dwarfs. But by the first book of the trilogy, when the ring is owned by Frodo, Bilbo's nephew and heir, it has been revealed as the One Ring, key to supreme power over all Middle Earth.

Evil Sauron had forged the ring. In his first bid for power, when his forces were defeated, he had lost it. But in his desolate land, Mordor, he prepares for a new attempt to conquer Middle Earth. With the ring he would be invincible; and though his opponents possess the ring it does them little good, for its powers work only for evil.

The one way to defeat Sauron is to destroy the ring, and the only way to destroy it is to throw it into the Crack of Doom, the fiery cauldron at the heart of Mordor where it was forged. This is the appalling task Frodo undertakes, with a small company of hobbits, men, an elf, a dwarf, and Gandalf the wizard. What happens to them on their journeys is the story Tolkien tells in *The Lord of the Rings,* with a vigor of language, a complexity of history and character and, above all, a pace and drive of action, adventure and excitement that make the reader feel he sits at the feet of an ancient bard.

Tolkien's trilogy indeed resembles the Anglo-Saxon chronicles he studied as a scholar. *The Lord of the Rings* is a work of art but it is also history—even if invented history—and it bears comparison to works of Gibbon or Parkman more readily than it does to other novels. The great historians are equally artists and builders of worlds. Gibbon's Rome and Parkman's French America are worlds as strange and distant from our own as Tolkien's Middle Earth. On the level of great historical narrative it matters little whether the events described can be absolutely verified; what matters far more is the historian's attitude toward his world and his treatment of it.

As a work of history *The Lord of the Rings* is distinctly Spenglerian in tone. Tolkien has created an historical world with a comprehensive erudition and a philosophical audacity few historians since Spengler have been able to match—and with a sense of tragic destiny nearly equal to Spengler's.

For at its core *The Lord of the Rings* is the story of civilization's decline. Good may finally triumph over evil, but good is never unalloyed—in men or in hobbits or in cultures. The Third Age of Middle Earth, which the trilogy brings to a close, was founded on the powers of lesser rings, rings for dwarfs, elves and men. But the One Ring rules them all. Were Sauron to recover the ring he could only subjugate Middle Earth; when Frodo succeeds in destroying it the other rings must lose their power, too. Frodo and his company know from the start, whether they should succeed or fail, that a three-thousand-year era is doomed to end.

In many ways the Third Age had been a time of peace and beauty. Yet Tolkien's historical panorama is too vast to allow mourning over the passing of an age. The elves had "attempted nothing new, living in memory of the past." The dwarfs selfishly hoarded their treasures. Their time now was passed, and they were fated to depart, leaving Middle Earth to men.

For the hobbits, too, time in Middle Earth is drawing to an end. But these little people, with their provincial narrowness, their agelong inconsequence, their simple love of beer and pipe smoking, provide the moral center and the humor of Tolkien's trilogy, and the deep recognition young people feel when they read it. Ignored and underrated by others; hedonistic and isolationist by choice—suddenly a handful of them, Frodo and Samwise, Pippin and Merry, are chosen; or choose themselves. Their moment on the great stage of history has come: to act, to dare, to be brave, to endure hardship, risk their lives, and lose forever their comfort and anonymity. This challenge, and their response, is the true moral drama in *The Lord of the Rings.*

If young people identify more with the hobbits than with the warriors and kings of men in Tolkien's tale, surely one reason—though of course Tolkien could not have envisioned such a remarkable coincidence—lies in the resemblance of the hobbits' situation to their own. Many in the present generation of American youth see themselves as just such a chosen band, called upon to leave behind a way of life equally as self-serving and as oblivious to social truths.

This represents in part a vast metaphor for coming of age—*The Lord of the Rings* provides a most dramatic and mythic analogy for the rite of passage to maturity. But it also suggests a distinctive attitude toward the present. Young people are not so saddened by the Third Age's passing, perhaps because they envision the present as a time when another outmoded era is being left behind—an era when humans are as selfish as dwarfs and as self-satisfied as elves. Like the hobbit band, they can rise above the limitations of their own society and thus prepare themselves to inherit the future.

Above all, what matters is the act of choosing to take part, of participating in company with others. This is a significant distinguishing feature of the present generation of youth—not to take refuge in private life, or in institutions, or in dogmas but to become involved in life. This impulse finds expression just as much among hippies or dropouts or acid heads—drugs too are an aspect of the desire to tune in on life, not to retreat from it—as it does in more conventional forms of political or social action. And the hobbits perfectly reflect their concern, not with the power of kings or knights or presidents or generals but with the power that resides in simple lives and everyday people.

The fantasy and imagination and other-worldliness of Tolkien's work are all important, but what is most important is not that it serves as an escape, or leads to contemplation, or makes for livelier dreams but that it provides a paradigm for action. It asks not who you are, or your pedigree, or your past associations but simply states: this is the task; are you willing to carry it through?

None of the enormous enthusiasm for Tolkien has spilled over onto other fantasy writers or into science fiction. Rather, the young have taken up the novels of Hermann Hesse, where fantasy plays a role strikingly similar to Tolkien's; instead of dreams or separation, fantasy provides new mysteries for our normal state of consciousness and creates new possibilities in the quotidian world.

The most unusual aspect of Tolkien's popularity is his complete un-concern with the traditional and conventional issues of adolescence, particularly that ontological stumper, "who am I?" In the trilogy, charac-ters may change their names and identities several times over, but they are the last ones to stew over it. They know who they are and what they must do, and if they use disguises or pseudonyms it is simply part of the job. Young people do not miss the usual questions in Tolkien because the immediacy of action cancels out all Hamlet-like musings on the self. But in Hesse's novels they find contemplation and a goodly share of action, too.

Hesse's recent popularity rests primarily on one work, *Siddhartha*. Any seeker of self who has looked into Zen or Oriental mysticism is likely to have read it. A paperback edition of *Demian* came out last fall and was boosted to immediate success in no little part by its roman-tically evocative, mystical cover drawing (artist unidentified). *Steppen-wolf* and *Magister Ludi,* the two novels which established Hesse's liter-ary reputation, as well as *The Journey to the East* are also available in inexpensive editions; so far, though, Hesse appeals to the young through *Siddhartha* and *Demian*.

Siddhartha and *Demian,* like *The Lord of the Rings,* are quest books. But their quests turn far away from the battlefields of Middle Earth, the deserts and mountain peaks of Mordor, turn and tunnel deep down into "the innermost, the Self." Why Hesse, one may ask, among so many competing versions of peering at the looking glass? Precisely because wherever one ends when the search is done, whatever dark tunnels and winding corridors have been traversed, there, at the end, Hesse provides a door into the world.

Siddhartha is a simple story, told in the limpid prose of an oral tale. A handsome boy, son of wealthy Brahmins, Siddhartha is yet unhappy. In his religion and his social position he cannot find the True, the Eter-nal. "One must find the source within one's own Self," he thinks, "one must possess it." He wants to overcome the Self and find the mystery deep within. Self-denial provides no solution, either. He must discover his Self by bringing it to life in the world. However, the moment comes when he is satiated by life in the world as he was by self-denial. He leaves all behind, and again wanders, seeking. In the end, Siddhartha concludes that "love is the most important thing in the world. It may be important to great thinkers to examine the world, to explain and despise it. But I think it is only important to love the world, not to despise it, not for us to hate each other, but to be able to regard the world and ourselves and all beings with love, admiration, and respect."

Demian appeared in 1919, three years before *Siddhartha*. While the story of *Siddhartha* is a parable for all individual and historical ages, a resolution for Hesse of the active and the contemplative life, of seeking and of knowing, the earlier story of the German youth is a work intensely involved with a particular generation and a particular time, resolved not so much by art as by the intervention of catastrophe.

Hesse had been a pacifist during the First World War and had spent the war years in Switzerland. Reviled by his own countrymen, he suffered through the breakup of his marriage and the breakdown of his health. It was a time of personal crisis, a crisis of loyalty and identity we call adolescence, though in an independent, questioning life it may occur several times. *Demian* is the product of that crisis, a novel for and about German youth. Published under a pseudonym, it became a great success. Its author was then 42 years old.

Demian is "the story of Emil Sinclair's youth." Narrating his own story, Sinclair describes how his conventional middle-class youth fell apart when he told a boastful lie and left himself open to blackmail and humiliation by an evil youth, Kromer. But he is unexpectedly rescued by Max Demian, an older boy who lives mysteriously with his widowed mother. Sinclair first notices Demian when he takes Cain's side in a Biblical discussion. Later Demian talks to Sinclair about persons who bear the mark of Cain on their foreheads.

Those who wear the sign of Cain, like Tolkien's Fellowship of the Ring, are a chosen band. "We represented the will of Nature to something new, to the individualism of the future," says Sinclair, while "the others sought to perpetuate the status quo." Humanity was not something to be maintained and protected; it "was a distant goal toward which all men were moving, whose image no one knew, whose laws were nowhere written down." *Demian* ends with the World War, marking an end to the old, and a new beginning.

Hesse's Freudian and Jungian symbolism is clangorous and ultimately opaque. His treatment of the war is equivocal enough to be acceptable both to those who loved it and those who deplored it—a secret of the book's widespread success. Nevertheless, in the prologue to *Demian,* Hesse sharply outlined his own nonviolent humanism. If men truly knew the value of a living human being, he wrote, they would not shoot one another wholesale. We must love all, good or bad, Siddhartha says; all-pervading love surely will create more good than bad.

To the question, "who am I?" *Demian* and *Siddhartha* say: you must look only within your innermost self, but you will find an answer only in the midst of life. To many of the young this is precisely the answer fashioned by their own call, their desire for personal authenticity, separate from, yet expressed through, common action. Each of the chosen chooses himself; the whole is exactly the sum of its parts.

For those young people who heed this call, who seek their selves in the world, word of Tolkien's trilogy and Hesse's novels is passed from mouth to ear. *The Lord of the Rings, Siddhartha,* and now *Demian* have become their guides, their expression, their pleasure. Delight in Tolkien and Hesse signifies a new delight in human mysteries, in life's possibilities, in the power of will and the pleasures of imagination. Life imitates art; may the taste of the young, and our luck, hold.

WORKS OF J. R. R. TOLKIEN

The Adventures of Tom Bombadil. Boston: Houghton, 1963.
Farmer Giles of Ham. Boston: Houghton, 1978.
The Hobbit, or There and Back Again. Boston: Houghton, 1938. New York: Ballantine, 1976.
The Lord of the Rings. 3 vols. *The Fellowship of the Ring; The Two Towers; The Return of the King.* Boston: Houghton, 1974. New York: Ballantine, 1975.
The Tolkien Reader: The Homecoming of Beorhtnoth Beorhthelm's Son; Tree and Leaf; Farmer Giles of Ham; The Adventures of Tom Bombadil. New York: Ballantine, 1976.
Tree and Leaf. Boston: Houghton, 1965.

HERMANN HESSE IN PAPERBACK

Demian: The Story of Emil Sinclair's Youth. Translated by Michael Roloff and Michael Lebeck. New York: Bantam, 1966.
The Journey to the East. Translated by Hilda Rosner. New York: Noonday Pr., 1956.
Magister Ludi. Translated by Mervyn Savill. New York: Ungar, 1957.
Siddhartha. Translated by Hilda Rosner. New York: New Directions, 1951.
Steppenwolf. Translated by Basil Creighton. New York: Holt, 1963.

Perspective on the Future: The Quest of Space Age Young People

Sylvia Engdahl

Those of us who work with literature for youth have many things in common, whether we are writers, librarians, or teachers—and I believe that one of them is a very strong and basic interest in the future. I have been fascinated by ideas about the future, and particularly about space exploration, since I myself was in my teens; for the past five years I have devoted my full time to writing about it. While educators may not have such specific enthusiasm for the subject of the distant future, all are deeply concerned with preparing young people to live in the world of tomorrow. None of us can predict just what that world is going to be like, but I think there is much we can do to equip the next generation to cope with whatever tomorrow brings.

I suppose every author is asked how he came to write what he writes, but I think the question is raised more frequently with authors of science fiction than with others. People are always curious about why anyone would choose to write about imaginary things instead of the things we know. Each author has his own reasons, and mine are not really typical; perhaps an explanation of them will make clear why I feel that stories that deal with the future are important, and are of interest even to those for whom neither science fiction nor science itself has any special appeal.

First of all, I should mention that my books are more for a general audience than for science fiction fans. Although I think science fiction fans will enjoy them, I aim them principally toward people—especially girls—who normally do not read science fiction, and I avoid using esoteric terminology that only established fans can understand. Actually I am not what one would call a fan myself, at least not in the sense of keeping up with the adult science fiction genre. I use the science fiction form simply because my ideas about man's place in the universe can best be expressed in the context of future or hypothetical worlds.

This is not to say that my books are wholly allegorical. I have been rather dismayed to find that some people interpret them that way, be-

Reprinted by permission of the author from *School Media Quarterly* 1:27-35 (Fall 1972). Copyright © 1972 by Sylvia Louise Engdahl.

cause although there is indeed a good deal of allegory in them, they also have a literal level. For instance, what is said in *Enchantress from the Stars* and *The Far Side of Evil* about how a truly mature civilization would view peoples of lesser advancement is meant to be taken literally; scientists are beginning to ask why, if civilizations more advanced than ours do exist in other solar systems, they haven't contacted us, and that is my answer as to why.

Of course, one of my main reasons for writing science fiction is that I believe very strongly in the importance of space exploration to the survival of mankind. I have held this belief since the days when all space travel was considered fantastic, and indeed I developed the theory of the "Critical Stage," on which my book *The Far Side of Evil* is based, in unpublished work that I did before the first artificial satellite was launched. I am entirely serious about the choice between expansion into space and human self-destruction being a normal and inevitable stage of evolution; the fact that when I came to write the book, our establishment of a space program had made it impossible for the story's setting to be Earth, as it was in my original version, is to me the most encouraging sign of our era. In the early fifties I had been afraid that the Space Age would not begin soon enough.

But apart from my commitment to the cause of space exploration, I think there is good reason to set stories in the future when writing for teenagers. Today's young people identify with the future. Many of them find it a more pertinent concept than that of the past. If we are going to make any generalization about the human condition, any convincing statement that evolution is a continuous process in which the *now* that seems all-important to them is only a small link, we stand a better chance of communicating when we speak of the future than when we describe past ages that—however mistakenly—the young have dismissed as dead and irrelevant. Teenagers are far more serious-minded than they used to be, yet they don't consider anything worth serious attention unless they see its relationship to problems they have experienced or can envision.

This has become more and more evident during the past few years. It so happened that I began writing in a period when young people's involvement with matters once thought too deep for them was increasing. I was not at all sure that there would be a place for the kind of novels I wanted to write, because they were too optimistic to fit the gloomy mold of contemporary adult fiction, yet too philosophical, I thought, to be published as junior fiction. Fortunately I directed them to young people anyway, and quite a few seem to like them. I don't think this would be the case were it not that the boys and girls now growing up are more mature in their interests than those of former generations.

It is apparent today that the young people of our time are searching desperately for something that they are not getting in the course of a standard education. They are searching in all directions: some through political activism; some through "dropping out"; some through renewed interest in religion in both traditional and novel forms, or even in the occult; and all too many through drugs or violence. Misguided though some of these attempts may be, I feel that they all reflect a genuine and growing concern on the part of our youth for a broader view of the universe than our present society offers them. Some can find meaning in the values of their elders; others cannot. There would seem to be a wide gulf between the two attitudes. There is a great deal of talk about polarization. Yet underneath, whatever their immediate and conscious goals, I believe that all young people are seeking the same thing: they are seeking a perspective on the future.

The need for such perspective is not new. It is a basic and universal human characteristic. What is different now is that the perspective inherent in the culture passed automatically from one generation to the next is no longer enough. Perspective implies a framework, a firm base from which to look ahead, and in this age of rapid change the old framework is not firm. Many of its components are still true and sound, but it has become so complex that as a whole it must necessarily invite question, if only because of the contradictions it contains. Scarcely anyone today is so naive as to suppose that all aspects of our current outlook are valid. There is much controversy, however, as to which are valid and which are not, and among free people the controversy will continue, for we live in an era when man's outlook is constantly shifting and expanding.

Whether this is occurring because—as I believe—the time of our first steps beyond our native planet is the most crucial period in mankind's history, or whether its basic cause is something else, the fact remains that it is happening. It is a confusing time for all of us, but especially for our young people, the members of the first Space Age generation, who are so aware of change and of the need for change that they can find nothing solid to hold to. They haven't the background to know that problems have been solved in the past, that present and future problems will in turn be solved, that the existence of problems is not in itself grounds for bitterness. They hear their disillusioned elders speak of the future with despair and they have no basis for disbelief. Yet instinctively, they do disbelieve—and I wonder if this, as much as the world's obvious lack of perfection, may not be why they find it so hard to believe anything else their elders tell them. They cannot accept the now-fashionable notion that the universe is patternless and absurd; they are looking for answers. Inside, they know that those answers must exist.

Young people cannot be blamed for thinking the answers are simple. Earlier generations have thought the same. But nowadays one's faith in a simple answer cannot survive very long; what the Space Age generation needs is awareness that one must not expect simple answers, and that man's progress toward solutions is a long, slow process that extends not merely over years, but over centuries. Knowledge of past history alone does not give such awareness because most of today's teenagers just don't care about the past. Significance, to them, lies not in what has been, but in what is to come. I believe that only by pointing out relationships between past, present, and future can we help them to gain the perspective that is the true object of their search.

One might wonder how I can consider this need for perspective so fundamental when for years psychologists have been saying that people's basic need is for security. Yet I think our young people are showing over and over again that they do not want security, at least not security as it has commonly been defined. A great deal of effort has been devoted to making them secure, yet many turn their backs and deliberately seek out something dangerous to do. The security they need cannot come from outside; it must come from within, from experiences through which each person proves that he is capable of handling himself in an indisputably insecure world. But no one can handle a situation in which he sees no pattern, no meaning. There can be no security without direction. Thus a perspective on the future is implicit in the very concept of inner security.

One's view of the future is, of course, a highly personal thing. Our beliefs can differ greatly as to the direction we are going, or ought to go. In my books I naturally present my own opinions, and I don't expect all readers to agree with them. But I hope that even those who do not agree will gain something by being encouraged to develop their private thoughts about the topics I deal with. I hope that they will be convinced that we are going *somewhere,* and that this will help to counter the all-too-prevalent feeling that human evolution is over and done with. It is this, more than anything else, that I try to put across: the idea that there is continuity to history, that progress—however slow—does occur, and that whatever happens to us on this planet is part of some overall pattern that encompasses the entire universe. We are not in a position to see the pattern. We can only make guesses about it, and many of those guesses are bound to be wrong. Still, I do not believe that guessing, either in fantasy or in serious speculation, is a futile task; for when we ignore the issue, we are apt to forget that the pattern exists whether we see it or not. That, I think, is the root of many young people's turmoil. They have no conviction that there is any pattern.

A common reaction to the space flights so far undertaken seems to be that we had better appreciate Earth because it's the only good planet there is. It is quite true that it is the only one in this solar system that is suitable for us to live on at present, and that those of this system are the only ones we have any immediate prospect of reaching. But the attitude that no other planet is worth anything strikes me as a new form of provincialism. Our solar system is merely a small part of a vast universe that contains billions upon billions of stars. People sometimes ask me if I really believe that there are habitable planets circling those other stars; the answer is that I do, and that most scientists now do also. Not everyone seems to realize this; several acquaintances have told me rather shamefacedly that they themselves think that there is life in other solar systems, although they are sure that scientists would laugh at them. As a result, I am now writing a nonfiction book that will explain to young people not only what modern scientists do believe, but what many philosophers of past ages believed about an infinity of worlds. The idea is not new, and it has not been confined to science fiction. Giordano Bruno was burned at the stake in the year 1600 for holding it.

Of course, I do not believe that the inhabitants of other solar systems are as much like us in the physical and cultural sense as I have depicted them in my novels. Most serious science fiction does not make them so similar, and I think that many potential readers are thereby turned away. They are put off by the weird element inherent in any attempt to imagine what sentient species other than ours would be like. I feel that this is distracting. Since we don't know what they are like and my aim is to show essentially identical spiritual qualities, it seems to me best to portray them in our terms, just as I have to make them speak in our language. Also, in *Enchantress from the Stars,* I wanted to leave open the question of which, if any, of the people were from Earth. Only in that way could I make my point about various levels of advancement.

This point, which is further developed in *The Far Side of Evil,* concerns evolutionary advancement, not mere cultural advancement. My intent was to comment upon relationships between eras of history, and between peoples at different stages of evolution, not relationships between societies here on Earth. We of Earth, whatever our nationality or our color, are all members of the same human race. We are one people, one species. Someday, generations hence, we may encounter other sentient species. It is not too soon for us to begin thinking about our identity as a people, our place in a universe inhabited by many; the young are better aware of that than most adults.

To those who do not believe that there will ever be contact between the stars, I would like to suggest that as far as contemporary youth's perspective is concerned, it makes no difference whether there is or not. The mere idea is, in itself, of consequence. I am troubled by science fiction's usual portrayal of advanced aliens either as hostile, or as presumptuous meddlers who take it upon themselves to interfere with the evolutionary process. The dangers of the first attitude are obvious; those of the second are perhaps less so. Maybe the whole issue seems remote and insignificant when we have so much else to worry about. Yet if young people acquire the idea that some extrasolar civilization could solve our problems for us if its starships happened to come here, or that it would consider our failings evidence that our whole human race is wicked instead of merely immature, will that not add to their already-great sense of futility? Will it not interfere with whatever perspective on human history they have managed to absorb? I think it will; and furthermore, whether there really are any alien civilizations is immaterial. Science fiction may be fantasy, but that young people like it and are affected by it is fact. It is also a fact that the Jupiter probe recently launched by NASA carried a plaque designed to communicate its origin to any intelligent beings who recover it after it passes out of our solar system. It may be that no aliens will ever see that plaque, but our children saw it on television; their attitude toward its hypothetical viewers is bound to influence their attitude toward our own civilization.

Their view of civilization is already confused and inconsistent enough. On one hand, many believe that only scientific knowledge is factual, and that advancement is merely a matter of inventions and technical skill. On the other, during the past few years some people, especially the young, have come to distrust science, to blame it for our problems and even to question the value of technological advance—which, I believe, is the greatest distortion of perspective I have yet seen.

Today, in their quest for meaning, young people are challenging the materialistic outlook many scientists have held in the past—and rightly so. At the same time, however, some of them are rejecting not only inadequate theories, but the whole idea of scientific progress. They seem to feel that in so doing they are defending spiritual values against some implacable enemy. They imagine that they seek a wider truth. Yet actually this viewpoint is equally narrow and in fact self-contradictory, for truth is precisely what science seeks, and has always sought from its very beginnings. There has never been any conflict between the real scientific attitude and spiritual values; where there appears to be, the trouble is with the particular theory involved and not with science as such. Truth is truth; science is simply the name given to the part we have attempted to organize and verify.

I think the current misunderstanding is the result of our tendency over the past hundred years or so to compartmentalize science, to separate it from the rest of life in the same way that some people separate religion. There was a time when the major scientific thought of an era could be understood by every educated person; but for many years now specialization has been necessary, and this has led to an unfortunate conception of what science is. Nonscientists have gotten the idea that it is some kind of esoteric cult that stands apart from other human endeavors, while both they and the scientists themselves have felt that its realms have been charted and need only to be conquered. When young people observe that there are things worth investigating outside these realms, and that some of our current scientific theories are questionable, it often doesn't occur to them that the answer lies not in abandoning science but in expanding it: refuting its dogmatic portions as dogma has been refuted countless times in the past. This, perhaps, is why some of them are turning in desperation to supernaturalism, astrology, and the like. Yet science is distinguished from superstition not by the subject matter with which it deals, but by the maturity of its explanations; it is distinguished from philosophy not by content, but by the availability of data to which objective scientific methods can be applied. All the phenomena now dealt with by science were once explained by superstition and, as an intermediate step, all our sciences were once divisions of philosophy. For that matter, there are advanced theories in all fields that are philosophic in that they are not yet subject to empirical proof. Because nowadays the men who hold such theories are called scientists and not philosophers, we get the impression that the theories are authoritative; but actually some are no more so than theories of the Middle Ages that have been disproven.

The point to be made is that this process of progression is by no means finished or complete. There is no area of truth that is outside the province of science in principle, though there are many that science lacks the practical means to investigate at its present stage of development. It is thus a great mistake to identify science with materialism, and to assume that it inherently deals only with the material aspects of the universe, when the fact is merely that these aspects can be more readily studied than other aspects that we are just beginning to rescue from the realms of the "supernatural." There is no such thing as the supernatural, since "natural," by definition, includes all aspects of reality. But too many of us have shut out parts of reality. We have discarded not only superstition, but also the areas with which superstition presently deals, forgetting that the superstition of today is merely an immature explanation of the science of tomorrow. We have failed to recognize that there are natural laws that cannot be explained in terms of the ones we know because they are, in themselves, equally basic.

Worse, our society has tended to assume that there is a firm line between science and religion. It has outgrown trust in superstition, and many have identified faith with superstition, discarding that also. Yet the fact that the physical aspects of natural law are the most readily analyzed does not mean that there isn't a spiritual reality that is just as real, just as much a part of the universe, as the material reality that science has so far studied objectively. I don't wonder that young people have difficulty in viewing the world with perspective when they have been led to feel that it is necessary to reject one or the other. The young today sense that moral and spiritual values are important, though they will not accept dogma in religion any more than in any other field, and it is understandably hard for them to reconcile their innate idealism with a science that is seemingly opposed.

To me, science itself can never be opposed to truth in any form whatsoever, no matter how many specific theories may be mistaken, and no matter how dogmatic certain scientists may be in support of their own era's belief's. This is how I have viewed it in *Enchantress from the Stars,* and I think one of the book's appeals for young people is that it does take seriously certain things outside the traditional bounds of science, such as extrasensory perception, without putting a materialistic interpretation on them. I hope readers notice that nowhere have I suggested that advanced peoples, in progressing beyond a materialistic orientation, would give up any of their technology; because I feel strongly that as they matured, they would improve their technology and learn to put it to better use.

I am convinced, therefore, that the solution to future problems lies not in de-emphasizing science, but in advancing it, as well as in an outlook that recognizes that the science of any given age is imperfect and incomplete. For instance, I believe that while there is much that can and should be done now to slow the rate of population growth, the only permanent answer to overpopulation is the colonization of new worlds. I have been asked how I can approve of our colonizing planets in other solar systems if other sentient species exist. Certainly I don't think we should colonize planets that are already occupied; I trust my books make that very clear. What I do think is that there are many worlds on which no intelligent life has evolved that can be made livable by advanced technology, and that in the normal course of a sentient species' evolution, it expands and utilizes such worlds. There is nothing less natural in that than in our ancestors building the ships and other equipment needed to colonize America. Pioneering is a basic human activity; that's the comparison I have tried to draw in *Journey between Worlds.*

This question of what is natural for us seems to need a good deal of examination right now. There is a feeling prevalent today, particularly among young people, that we ought to get "back to nature." Insofar as this means preserving and enjoying the beauties of our world, it is a good thing. But those who say that we as a species should *live* in a more "natural" way are, I think, overlooking what "natural" means as applied to human beings. It is the nature of animal species to remain the same from generation to generation, evolving only as adaptation to physical environment may demand. It is the nature of man, however—and of whatever other sentient races may inhabit this universe—to learn, to change, and to progress. There is no point at which it is "natural" to stop, for to cease changing is contrary to the mental instincts that are uniquely human. If it were not so, all learning, from the discovery of fire to the conquest of disease, would be unnatural, and I don't think anyone believes that—least of all the young, who are more eager for change than their elders. It is the nature of man to solve problems. It is the nature of man to grope continuously toward an understanding of truth. There may be disagreement as to means, disagreement as to what is true and what is not, but never on the principle that to search for truth is an inherent attribute of mankind.

In my most recent novel *This Star Shall Abide* and its forthcoming second volume *Beyond the Tomorrow Mountains,* I have said quite a bit about the search for truth, from both the scientific and the religious standpoints; and I have also tried to say something about the importance of faith. Yet the people of these stories are stranded in a desperate situation where only advanced technology, and an eventual major advance in scientific theory, can prevent their extinction. To achieve this advance, they are dependent on the kind of creative inspiration that has underlain all human progress since the beginning of time. Their religion is central to their culture, and it is in no way a materialistic religion; but the hope it offers them can be fulfilled only through faith in the ultimate success of their scientific research.

I wrote a description of the books not long ago in which I defined science as the portion of truth that no longer demands faith for acceptance. That's the way I look at science: it is part of a larger truth. I believe that if we can give young people that sort of attitude toward it —if they can be helped to view its failure to provide all the answers overnight with neither hostility nor despair, but with the willingness to keep on searching—we will go a long way toward building their perspective on the future. And I believe that it is such perspective, more than anything else, that will fit them to take their place in tomorrow's world.

Reason and Mysticism in Fantasy and Science Fiction

Joseph E. Milosh, Jr.

In certain ages and geographical areas Truth appears to have been a relatively simple matter. In the Middle Ages in England, despite controversies about refinements in doctrine and severe abuses of power at all levels in the ecclesiastical hierarchy, certain basic beliefs are societal givens, like "Jesus Christ is the son of God." In Chaucer's *Miller's Tale* the old carpenter whose young wife is going to cuckold him with the boarder-student Nicholas discovers Nicholas apparently in a daze, really a part of Nicholas's plot. The carpenter immediately concludes that the madness results from Nicholas's study of the stars and flatters himself

Used by permission of the author.

on the simplicity of his own faith: "Ye, blessed be alwey [ignorant] man / That noght but only his bileve kan [knows]!"[1] No matter what we or Chaucer or Nicholas may think of the carpenter's ironic proud ignorance, the carpenter is at least certain that ignorance is bliss.

Today's young reader has very frequently come to distrust or even reject out of hand anything resembling comprehensive societal truth. Many have argued that the disillusionment has followed Watergate, after the idealism of the Kennedy days. Equally possible is the realization of the threats of scientific advance, after the success and romance of moon walks. Whether bound to politics or science or economics or all of these, or bound to large cycles rather than the topical, this disillusionment will no doubt remain a pervasive factor for many young and perhaps not so young in our society. On the negative side, the disillusionment can be painful for the person needing stability; in excess, it can be suicidal. On the positive side the disillusionment can lead to the personal, individual quest, a quest which rewards in the seeking even when there is not complete confidence in the finding. This quest the teacher can nurture and the young reader can explore in the learning processes in science fiction and fantasy. Historical backgrounds for this particular aspect of the quest can add another dimension, giving the younger reader a perspective for his or her immediate and troubling concerns and a basis for examining larger, universal questions with intensely personal ramifications. As Ira Progoff has observed, ". . . underneath the seemingly vast differences between the medieval and modern images of the universe, we find an underlying sameness of searching and experience that can significantly enlarge our areas of awareness."[2]

For the Middle Ages, reasoning is an imperative for those who have the talent, while at the same time a potentially misleading and therefore dangerous activity when not properly confined. With the seven liberal arts the medieval clerk can better understand the Bible, and with debate skills sharpened on exercises questioning how many angels can dance on the head of a pin (never a serious theological topic), he can defend the faith. Further, reason can endeavor to explain many of the ways of God to man, exploring topics like predestination, free will, and fortune: the great popularity of Boethius' *Consolation of Philosophy,* translated in Anglo-Saxon times and later in the Middle Ages by Chaucer, stems unquestionably from its treatment of man's relationship to his universe and how much he can know about the micro/macrocosm. But the satisfactions of reason are only partial. The really interesting questions often go beyond revelation or the categories of logic to God's deliberate mysteries, unattainable by mere finite reason though sometimes sought after audaciously and blasphemously by Faustian characters. And even that reason which deals with purely human concerns, like sorrow, may end up as its own exercise and no more: while it analyzes skillfully, whether the *Consolation of Philosophy* successfully consoles by lessening human grief is another matter altogether. For the hierarchical Middle Ages, then, the limitations of human reason upward are God's mysteries and sideways—for man himself, that is—the gulf between reasoning as an enclosed system and all the rest of human experience and response.

Without the particular limitations of reasoning is a different access to knowledge. In the Middle Ages it was achieved by the mystic and was sometimes described by phrases like "felt knowledge"; today we might suggest this knowledge—ineffable at any rate—with reference to emotional knowledge or intuition or nonlogical perception. But this knowledge also has its limitations, though different from those of reasoning. First, it is incomplete. Walter Hilton, a fourteenth-century contemplative, uses a very nice image to demonstrate the partiality of this experience. A person of reason alone, with absolutely no such felt knowledge of heaven, is like a blind man standing in the sun, who knows he is in the sun only because an honest man tells him so, that is, by faith. At the other extreme, with full experience of heaven, is the soul after death, like a person with full, undistorted sight of the sun. In between the extremes is the living mystic with partial felt knowledge, likened to the seeing man looking directly at the full sun, squinting, eyelids even closing: "But he seeth through the lid of his eyes a glimmering of great light. . . ."[3] Along with recognizing the incompleteness of the highest experience, the mystic must also deal with a second problem and limitation, the veridicality or truthfulness of the experience.[4] There is always the chance that an experience is diabolically inspired, intended to mislead immediately or ultimately. The felt knowledge of the mystic, though different in kind from and superior to the reasoned knowledge of the clerk, requires its own caveats and does not remove the final question. Given the limitations in the ways of knowing, what actions can finite man, mystic or clerk or both, legitimately take based on them?

Chaucer deals with the problem of translating knowledge into action with much wit in *The Nun's Priest's Tale,* the mock tragedy in which the fox almost dines on the proud rooster Chauntecleer. At the beginning of the tale Chauntecleer has a dream warning him of danger, a vision of great importance. To the vision he applies reason through an extended debate, coming to the conclusion, via both methods of knowing, that he should be cautious of the barnyard. But while he refuses to take the laxatives prescribed for his nightmares by Pertelote, his favorite wife, he does allow her to pressure him into putting aside his vision and his reason, neglecting the most obvious danger, the flattering fox. *The Nun's Priest's Tale* draws on several medieval traditions and provides several delightful levels of sophistication for the reader, but certainly one question Chaucer emphasizes throughout: Why do we not act on what we apparently know? At the popular level of a society there is usually much conventional wisdom, such as proverbs, though here translating knowledge into action entails choosing the right proverbs, frequently very difficult except in retrospect. Hesitating to act on one's personal knowledge, felt or reasoned, requires other explanations. One might be that despite the persuasive force of strong intuition or indisputable logic, doubts about total truth preclude that confidence which makes action easy.

The contemporary reader often finds in his or her literature many of these same difficulties with processes of knowing, frequently much intensified by the personal searching and extra frustrations of the adolescent reader. Despite its certain value for particular procedures or problems, reason is incomplete and therefore alone inadequate for many human situations, especially when approximately equal options present themselves. Felt knowledge, whether labeled intuition or emotion, often demanding attention more vigorously than reason, will often be in conflict with it. But where reason is incomplete, felt knowledge is "unscientific." Yet the desire to know about the world and one's individual place in its and how to act accordingly remains the paramount feature in the personal thinking time of most adolescents; for some of us beyond adolescence that desire never relinquishes its importance. Unlike the medieval thinker who could return to commonly accepted hierarchical models of the universe to sort out truths satisfactorily, today's adolescent may strive to devise his or her own rough models, weighting proportionately or disproportionately what he or she knows either in the head or in the heart. Determining how to act on this mixed knowledge can produce the most painful decisions in one's life.

In American education the two modes of knowing have been evident in commonly read fantastic literature, if not taught specifically for themselves. In the first paragraph of Edgar Allan Poe's "The Fall of the House of Usher" the narrator arrives at his destination:

> I know not how it was—but, with the first glimpse of the building, a sense of insufferable gloom pervaded my spirit. I say insufferable; for the feeling was unrelieved by any of that half-pleasurable, because poetic, sentiment, with which the mind usually receives even the sternest natural images of the desolate or terrible. . . . What was it—I paused to think—what was it that so unnerved me in the contemplation of the House of Usher? It was a mystery all insoluble; nor could I grapple with the shadowy fancies that crowded upon me as I pondered. I was forced to fall back upon the unsatisfactory conclusion, that while, beyond doubt, there *are* combinations of very simple natural objects which have the power of thus affecting us, still the analysis of this power lies among considerations beyond our depth. It was possible, I reflected, that a mere different arrangement of the particulars of the scene, of the details of the picture, would be sufficient to modify, or perhaps to annihilate its capacity for sorrowful impression; . . .[5]

The felt knowledge here is somehow suspect and requires the application of reason, the analysis, at this time to no satisfactory conclusion.

The gloom is so much the more terrible for being only partially understood. Despite the ominous, the narrator is obliged to proceed, Poe thereby establishing the felt knowledge and reasoned inquiry for the tale, as well as a situation which, if real, most might choose to avoid. The reader, assured of safety of course, can pursue the fantastic to test the truthfulness of the narrator's early perceptions.

A contemporary work which has intrigued many young readers with its treatment of the dual processes of learning is John Gardner's *Grendel*.[6] The monster—sensitive, introspective, humorous—begins with the very human desire for love, and is much confused by warriors' immediate hostile reactions to him, merely curious and earlier guilty of no evil whatsoever. Much of this short book, advertised humbly enough as "The Beowulf Legend Retold from the Monster's Point of View," traces Grendel's growth from naiveté and an acceptance of conventional wisdom to the questioning of authority and a cynicism about the noble.[7] Reasoned knowledge and felt knowledge play strong roles in creating tensions and the ultimate frustrations, paralleling the pains of growth frequently examined in adolescent literature. The humor, mock heroic, and debunking of *Grendel* all contribute to its popularity, of course. But the fantasy of a monster with human qualities, honestly desiring to know by feeling and by reason and to act properly, sharing our delicate problems despite his powers of body and mind, pleases particularly. Amusing beast fables have long been respectable teaching techniques, and *Grendel* shares in this tradition of fantasy.

In science fiction the two processes of learning with their frustrations can be explored with the same freedom found in Gardner's fantastic *Grendel* and Chaucer's tale of the cock and the fox. In each tradition the unreal as a given permits devising new models for illustrating differently points of view about very old human concerns. In each tradition the wildest speculations, images, and settings of an author can be entertained by the most thoughtful reader, at least for the duration of the tale and sometimes, by analogy, much after that. Poul Anderson's "Goat Song" is a superb example of the potential of science fiction for such inquiry.

The plot of "Goat Song" deliberately recalls the Orpheus myth. The narrator's love has died, and he wishes SUM, the highly logical mastermachine evolved from being humanity's servant, to return her. With the aid of the Dark Lady, an exceptional, periodically recreated mortal working with SUM, the narrator enters SUM's world, convinces SUM to let his lover return, but cancels the agreement and return by looking back. But the simple plot, like the plot of Chaucer's *Nun's Priest's Tale,* becomes a vehicle for extraordinary embellishment. As a literary piece "Goat Song" is rich with allusions and employs striking techniques like imitating Anglo-Saxon alliterative lines: want of literary quality could never be an excuse for not recommending the story. But more to purpose here, among the themes developed is learning through reason and nonreason.

Though not perfect in knowledge and reason, SUM is advanced enough to manipulate successfully, usually without being questioned, as if it were irrefutable logic. When it speaks, it exudes an arrogance, assuming that what it does not know it will certainly conclude with its experiments. Unlike the study of the liberal arts in the Middle Ages, subordinate to a higher spiritual goal, SUM's intellectuality feeds only itself. "SUM's ordered universe," as the narrator-poet describes it, asserts much about itself through its very name, whatever interpretation the reader prefers:[8] SUM translated as "I am" suggests essence, presumably in contrast to all that is not SUM; SUM as "sum" represents totality, the whole that has absorbed its parts. In either case, the machine gone beyond its creators' intentions becomes a demi-god.

Felt knowledge is the prerogative of the narrator-poet, whose songs can "trouble" despite SUM's logic.[9] The troubling awakens that other part of man, the nonrational or mystical, and Anderson uses several times a medieval commonplace to suggest both cause and effect. *Timor mortis conturbat me* is not only the refrain of many a Middle English passage quoted, but an expanding theme, like a song with incremental repetition.[10] The narrator, driven by the developed force of the troubling and awakening, finally responds to SUM's demand for proof for anything beyond its mechanical self:

> "No," I say. "Prove to me instead, beyond any doubt, that there is not something we cannot understand with words and equations. Prove to me likewise that I have no right to seek for it.
> "The burden of proof is on You Two, so often have You lied to us. In the name of rationality, You resurrected myth. The better to control us! In the name of service, You bound and blinkered us. In the name of achievement, You held us to a narrower round than any swine in its pen. In the name of beneficence, You created pain, and horror, and darkness beyond darkness."[11]

The conflict is clear, but Anderson does not conclude simplistically. Rejecting the arrogance and suppression of unrestrained mechanical logic does not mean rejecting all reason, just as restoring the mystical does not guarantee ineffable happiness. "The wholeness of mankind, which I am bringing back, has its horrors," the narrator sadly knows.[12] The use of both ways of knowing is not easy, but a necessary complexity if man is to seek truth.

The young reader can ask about and learn much in such tales. The question of human universals, approached through a few specific works, can be startling. Is the searching of Chaucer's vain rooster, of Gardner's philosophical monster Grendel, and of Anderson's narrator-poet essentially one and the same? Is there in fact nothing new under the sun? How much do contemporary writers treat old questions by inventing new models for investigating them, or even new genres, like science fiction? Or why do authors in various ages choose vehicles like the animal fable, the fantastic story, or the science fiction tale to express observations and give warnings to humans on a real planet?

Certain questions about literary tradition can be equally interesting, again if related to specific texts rather than to handbook abstractions. What major variations occur in the Orpheus story told in the classical version, a retelling from the Middle Ages, and a tale like "Goat Song"? Individualized reading projects or reports from students, stemming from an exciting theme in an appealing contemporary story, can lead backwards to an appreciation of literary history which, while narrow, may be surprisingly intense.

Finally—and far more significant for the majority of younger readers—there is the value of considering processes of learning directly affecting them. In a world of advertisers with quick, easy answers to any problem and romantic literature with facile happy endings suggesting permanent fulfillment, real knowledge based even somewhat securely on reason and intuition stands as a very different, complex commodity. A story like "Goat Song" can encourage a search, reinforcing the reader frustrated by his or her own doubts about a difficult personal decision but aware that canned advice is simplistic. The complex way to solve questions about man, his personal relations to others, and his universe is the hard way, to be sure; and reason and intuition at their very complementary best are still limited and potentially dangerous. But they are all man has, so he might as well grow accustomed to using them, with all their pleasure and pain.

NOTES

1. *The Works of Geoffrey Chaucer,* ed. F. N. Robinson (2nd ed.; Boston: Houghton, 1957), p.51, lines 3455-56.
2. *The Cloud of Unknowing,* trans. Ira Progoff (New York: Dell, 1957), p.3.
3. *The Scale of Perfection,* ed. Evelyn Underhill (London: John Watkins, 1948), p.372.
4. A recent collection of essays, *Mysticism and Philosophical Analysis,* ed. Steven T. Katz (New York: Oxford Univ. Pr., 1978), deals with determining veridicality as well as other important related matters. Most of the essays can be read well enough without a specialist's background in philosophy or mysticism; examples are clear and interesting.
5. As reprinted in *The Norton Anthology of Short Fiction,* ed. R. V. Cassill (New York: Norton, 1978), p.1126.
6. High-school teachers at the national meeting of the Conference on English Education and Secondary School English (March, 1979) reported real successes with *Grendel,* as did two-year college teachers

at the annual Illinois College English Association meeting (May, 1979). Interest in *Grendel* was not confined to advanced students or honors classes, and it generated excitement for the study of *Beowulf.*

7. John Gardner, *Grendel* (New York: Ballatine, 1972), front cover.
8. Poul Anderson, "Goat Song," as reprinted in *Science Fiction: Contemporary Mythology,* ed. Patricia Warrick, Martin Harry Greenberg, and Joseph Olander (New York: Harper, 1978), p.19. This anthology, published under the auspices of the Science Fiction Research Associates and Science Fiction Writers of America, contains ten sections with stories illustrating various themes. The very valuable introductions will be helpful to readers wanting to pursue particular interests as well as to teachers preparing units.
9. Ibid., p.15.
10. Ibid., pp.16, 17, 21.
11. Ibid., p.36.
12. Ibid., p.38.

After Armageddon: The Postcataclysmic Novel for Young Readers

Margaret P. Esmonde

Whether we trace its origin to Plato's *Critias,* More's *Utopia,* or Wells's *The Time Machine,* the best science fiction has always provided an excellent medium for social criticism and speculation about man's possible future. Though contemporary science fiction writers generally avoid the mantle of prophet, their works are often quite consciously didactic and reflect the anxieties of the society in which they live, especially the growing disbelief that technology will save the world and the growing acceptance of the fact that, one way or another, the destruction of our society, and perhaps our world, is inevitable. These repressed fears have given rise to a special type of science fiction—the postcataclysmic novel—an unusual number of which are being published in the United States and Great Britain.

Reprinted from *Children's Literature* 6:211-20 (1977) by permission of the author and of *Children's Literature: An International Journal,* Inc. Copyright © 1977 by Francelia Butler.

Though atomic warfare and alien invasion were once the most popular way to accomplish the end of the world, the majority of disaster novels for young readers produced between 1973 and 1976 predict the overthrow of our way of life through socioeconomic breakdown—often coupled with ecological disaster. Included in this first category are John Rowe Townsend's *Noah's Castle,* Simon Watson's *No Man's Land,* G. R. Kestevan's *The Pale Invaders,* Elizabeth Mace's *Ransome Revisited,* William Sleator's *House of Stairs,* Ben Bova's *City of Darkness,* and John Christopher's *Wild Jack.*

Most realistic of these dystopian novels is Townsend's *Noah's Castle,* which is set in England "two or three years after the time you are reading it." The novel's protagonist tells the story of his father, Norman, the manager of a shoe store, who purchases an old Victorian mansion which he fortifies and provisions to carry his family through the period of chaos he sees looming as the pound sterling becomes worthless and England experiences economic collapse. Using the unsympathetic viewpoint of the teenage son, Townsend characterizes the father with psychological acuity. Lower class in background because *his* father drank away the family's money, forced to leave school without a diploma at the age of fourteen, Mr. Mortimer nonetheless rose through the ranks to become an officer in World War II, only to find himself relegated shortly thereafter to the status of a shopkeeper by the British class system. A martinet, he runs his family like an Army regiment, demanding unquestioning obedience from all. His obsession with providing for his family alienates all of them in the end, as they choose to endure the hardships of the famine rather than the guilt of hoarding while others starve. Though one might observe that his description of the suffering lacks full impact because the central characters do not experience physical privation, the great strengths of the book—the characterization of the father and the presentation of the moral dilemma of hoarding—overshadow this weakness.

On the dedication page of *No Man's Land,* another British author, Simon Watson, writes: "This story takes place in a possible future." In this future, not much further away than Townsend's, his dystopian vision sees man regimented, depersonalized, separated from nature, encased in concrete "campuses," which are described as gigantic units "housing over three-thousand people, containing all the shops and services that anyone could require. . . ." The countryside has been "rationalized," carefully cleared of all living things, by the science-fiction device of the novel "Giant," the ultimate machine—"Man's first invention to have a mind of its own." Pitted against this technological Frankenstein are thirteen-year-old Alan; his friend Jay, an adamant nonconformist; the sixty-five-year-old "General," who hides to avoid the compulsory welfare home; and his female counterpart, an escapee from such a home, where she was "waited on night and day, never allowed out, no chores to do . . . built-in television and scented bedlinen, breakfast in bed—a gilded cage indeed." Watson's real monster—the ultimate, depersonalized welfare state—the gilded cage—is more insidious in some ways than Orwell's Big Brother, for the government sincerely believes itself to be the benefactor of its citizens. Watson keeps the reader off-balance by presenting the government as logical, efficient, progressive, and well-intentioned—opposed only by the ignorant youths and the eccentric old people. He hurls some challenging ideas at his readers, subtly underscoring the choice men have to make in governing themselves—the Hobson's choice of the ennui of total security versus the risks of individual freedom. Watson's England has chosen security and material comfort, and the government discourages all variety in people and in nature. The defeat of the science fiction *bete noire,* the supermachine, by the boy, Alan, is merely camouflage for this larger issue which remains unresolved. Though Watson pays lip service to qualified conformity, he does allow Jay to reach an island refuge where he can find a new life, "not comfortable" but "interesting." The reader is left to consider for himself which life is preferable.

A third Briitsh novel, *The Pale Invaders* by G. R. Kestevan, takes place in England eighty years after "the Upheaval," a time of social and economic breakdown. A small group of people takes refuge in a mountain valley on the Welsh border and remains totally isolated, living in virtually a Stone Age culture. Two of the more imaginative young people begin to suspect that the wild stories told by Old Carz, one of the original settlers, are based in truth. At this point, the village is discovered by pale-faced men who want to open the old coal mines in the region to provide energy for the slowly recovering society. The confrontation between this isolated community and a more sophisticated society is realistically treated and makes a very effective, low-key statement about today's situation, as our oil-hungry world probes remote areas for new energy supplies. Perhaps more pointedly, it observes that man is not as far from his Stone Age ancestors as he may think.

One of the bleakest of these postcatastrophe novels is Elizabeth Mace's existential nightmare, *Ransome Revisited.* A "Great War," followed by pestilence and natural catastrophes, reduces Britain's population to a few thousand people. The children, "pale, thin, and sadly dressed," have numbers instead of names, and they look forward to going "Out There" to earn their names and, perhaps, help to regain the "secret of flight to the glorious stars." Instead of the stars, the young protagonist and several others are assigned to work in a quarry, doing pointless labor under the direction of a brutal supervisor who drives them to escape by his cruelty. A pathetic group of misfits—the boy, his retarded brother, a little orphan girl, and enigmatic Susannah, whose one treasure from before the "Terrible Disaster" is an old copy of Arthur Ransome's *Swallowdale*—travels north in search of a legendary place where people are free. After an arduous trek, trailed by Will, a ruthless, amoral young man who has killed the supervisor and caused the death of the retarded brother, they reach Scotland only to discover that "the Colony" is an island which lies some three-days journey across the sea. Too tired to continue, Susannah remains in Scotland; Will goes on to seek "the place in the far North where clever men work to find the way back to the stars." The boy and the orphan girl undertake the last journey and reach their goal. Mace paints a surrealistic nightmare filled with pointless cruelty and characters too exhausted to experience emotion, even grief for the dead. What the author intends by her story is hard to say for certain. The amoral Will (perhaps a symbolic name) pursues the stars, representing technological knowledge, while Susannah longs for the past of Ransome's novel. Neither crosses into the Promised Land. Only the two innocents achieve the vision: "Swallowdale sheep waiting like white stars . . . on the green universe, the mountain."

Perhaps because economic problems are not as threatening, American writers examine a variety of tensions. In the *House of Stairs,* William Sleator creates a nightmare of behavioral psychology. Five sixteen-year-old orphans—Lola, the nonconformist; Peter, the dreamer; Abigail, who just wants to be liked; Oliver, the self-centered; and fat, vicious Blossom—find themselves imprisoned in a strange building that consists of a maze of intersecting staircases. Unaware that they are human guinea pigs in a psychological experiment in conditioned human response, the five teenagers quickly become dependent on a machine as their only food supply. As time passes, they determine that cruelty and physical abuse are the keys to the operation of the machine. Lola and Peter are appalled by this knowledge and refuse to take part, resisting to the point of starvation. In a chilling concluding chapter, the doctor in charge of the experiment reveals the full purpose and the extent of the conditioning. Sleator's novel sustains the feelings of suspense and horror which are only increased as explanations of the house of stairs are made. Set in what might possibly be our near future, the *House of Stairs* is a chilling glimpse of man's inhumanity as well as a vision of man's indomitable will to resist the darker side of his nature.

Well-known science fiction writer Ben Bova chooses as his theme racial prejudice, coupled with ecological disaster, to present a grim look at the future of our large cities. A domed New York City, supposedly evacuated because of killing pollution, is opened up each summer as a vacation resort to prosperous tourists from the Tracts, the endless suburbia of conformity and upper-middle-class white ambition. The young protagonist, Ron Morgan, is trapped inside when the city closes on Labor Day because his ID pass has been stolen. During his enforced stay, Ron discovers that, when the city was originally evacuated, some people were left behind. Trapped, they survived by forming ethnic gangs which wage incessant warfare. The black gangs, under the leadership of the Black Muslims, have united and are planning to break out and seize a decent life, by force if necessary. By the book's end, Ron has recovered his ID card; and in a confrontation with the Black Muslim leader, he learns to his horror that the government had forcibly prevented the blacks and Puerto Ricans from leaving New York City, sentencing them "to starve, to freeze, to be rat bait." Ron is permitted to exit and returns to the Tracts vowing "to change things." Though no one can quarrel with Bova's message, the thinly disguised social criticism remains just that. His characters are one-dimensional and his science fiction device, a domed, doomed New York, where people come for a summer holiday, seems as implausible as does Ron's enforced detainment in that city. The grim warning to complacent suburban whites is so obtrusive that the book scarcely deserves the label "fiction."

A similar plot serves British author John Christopher in *Wild Jack,* though the conflict is one of class prejudice rather than racial prejudice. No stranger to this particular type of science fiction, Christopher is off and running in this novel, reversing the theme of his previous work, *The Guardians. Wild Jack* takes place in twenty-third-century England, after "the Breakdown"; the population of London and other English cities is limited to a few-thousand people each, living in luxury thanks to their "energy towers." Outside the walled cities in the Outlands live the Savages, descendants of the people who had been expelled generations before. The protagonist, Clive Anderson, son of a London councillor, is an overprivileged young man who accepts without question the status quo until a political maneuver against his father results in the son's deportation to a prison island for social deviants. His escape in the company of an American and a Japanese boy seems rather contrived, but never mind that. The trio find their way back to the English Outlands and live among the Savages, whose leader is a Robin Hood figure called "Wild Jack." In the Outlands Clive learns to appreciate the more demanding life outside the walls. This is quite obviously the first book of a series and is Christopher's usual fast-paced adventure story about courageous and resourceful boys who regain long-lost freedom for England. But Christopher's standard plot, reworked again and again, is getting a bit threadbare; his latest story seems rather perfunctory.

A second major pattern in the postcataclysmic novel can be found in the six books which focus on man's longing for peace and his struggle to free himself from the curse of violence. In each book in this group, the survivors of earth's ruin develop psychic powers which help them cope. This group includes Andre Norton's *No Night without Stars,* H. M. Hoover's *Children of Morrow* and *Treasures of Morrow,*

Jay Williams's *The People of the Ax,* and Zilpha K. Snyder's *Below the Root* and *And All Between.*

In her usual capable fashion Andre Norton, who might well be considered the originator of this type of science fiction novel, offers *No Night without Stars.* In a North America largely destroyed by volcanic eruption, tidal waves, and pollution, Sander, a young metalsmith of Jak's Mob, a clan of nomadic herdsmen, sets forth to discover the lost metallurgic knowledge of the Before Time in order to regain his rightful place in the tribe. In his wanderings, he encounters Fanyi, a young shaman whose people have been slaughtered during her absence. She too seeks the secret stronghold of the Before People to gain knowledge which will enlarge her psychic powers so that she may revenge her people. After encountering a number of standard mutated horrors, the pair confront an evil master computer which seeks, in its endless hatred of its creators, to eliminate all life from earth. When Fanyi's mental powers fail in the contest, Sander succeeds in badly crippling the malevolent machine. At the conclusion, Fanyi voices Norton's understated message: "There is no night without a star, so the blackness of our night can be lighted by our own efforts. We are ourselves, not the Before Ones. Therefore, we must learn for ourselves, not try to revive what was known by those we might not even want to call kin were we to meet them. . . ."

H. M. Hoover's novels, *Children of Morrow* and its sequel *Treasures of Morrow,* deal with the adventures of Tia and Rabbit, young misfits in a harsh, primitive society comprised of descendants of survivors of an army-missile-base shelter. Hoover's world has been destroyed by "The Death of the Seas," which diminished the world's oxygen supply and ultimately resulted in the death of 93 percent of all living creatures by simple suffocation. The children's unusual appearance and telepathic power draw down upon them the wrath of the chief, and they flee toward the Pacific Ocean, encouraged and advised by the highly intelligent members of another survival community named Morrow, with whom the children have inadvertently established telepathic contact. Hoover maintains the suspense of the chase nicely with a last-minute rescue which will satisfy young readers.

In the sequel, the chldren learn that their grandfather was a Morrowan scientist who, on a field trip to the San Francisco area, had artificially inseminated one of the women of the Base. The Morrowans, who have developed telepathic abilities through genetic mutation, return to the Base taking the children with them—though the reasons for the return seem contrived. It appears that Hoover is leading up to a choice for the children: to return to the idyllic existence of Morrow Hall or to stay at the Base and try to raise the people from savagery. But, no. Tia is glad to see how savage the people are because if they "were anything more, then I couldn't leave again." Interesting enough as escape tales, Ms. Hoover's books fail to offer insight into the human condition. The enlightened Morrowans display a surprisingly inhuman attitude toward their debased fellow men. Smug in their own superiority, the Morrowans' solution is to leave them to their misery and ignorance. One finishes the second book wondering: was this trip really necessary?

Similar in general theme but superior to Hoover's books is Jay Williams's *The People of the Ax*. In an Iron Age culture, Arne and Frey, young initiates into the People of the Ax, are sent by the village council to Osan, the wise woman of the mountains, to learn how the hairy, apelike Crom have suddenly acquired iron clubs. Arne's discovery of mysterious writing in the caverns beneath Osan's mountains gives the reader the first intimation that this novel is science fiction not fantasy. Arne learns from Osan that he possesses "tendo," the psychic power to manipulate matter and, as he comes into his full power, he proposes that the Crom are not bestial but "unfinished people" to whom souls may be given. In the course of a council, Osan tells of atomic holocaust coupled with volcanic action which destroyed the materialistic civilization of the forefathers of the Crom, who are now systematically eradicated so they cannot regain control. Repelled by this heartlessness, Arne risks his life to prove that the hapless Crom are people like themselves who can be rehabilitated. Though reminiscent of LeGuin and Boule, Williams's simple but powerful style and deft handling of plot enhance the thought-provoking examination of man's inhumanity to man.

In her books, *Below the Root* and *And All Between*, Zilpha K. Snyder chooses to examine man's inhumanity to fellow man arising out of the abuse of power. She sets her story on a planet called Greensky to which, long ago, the people came after "a desperate flight from a far distant planet, which had been totally destroyed by the terrible curse of war." The Kindar, as they called themselves, built their cities in the giant trees of the planet and, through rituals of joy and peace, developed remarkable mental powers of psychokinesis and telepathy. The only shadow in this utopia is the Pash-shan, vicious monsters who dwell below the impenetrable roots of the forest floor waiting to kill Kindar, unwise enough to descend from the trees. After rescuing a little Pash-shan girl, three young initiates into the priestly ruling class discover that the Pash-shan are not monsters but only imprisoned Kindar who had disagreed with the Ol-zhaan, the ruling caste. *Below the Root* ends with the promise to "rekindle the light of the dream for all Green-sky." In her sequel *And All Between*, Snyder attempts an interesting literary experiment. The same story told in the first book is now told from the point of view of Teera, the rescued girl. Snyder repeats the identical dialogue expanding only Teera's part of the story. The first reaction to the technique is "what an easy way to write a second novel," but a fairer assessment of Snyder's attempt to provide a dual point of view must be made. The dual narration is an interesting innovation, but it would have been more effective if the two points of view could have been integrated into one novel to avoid the repetition of so much of the dialogue. In this second book, the plot is carried beyond the conclusion of the first book to a confrontation between the power factions of Green-sky. Snyder poses the age-old question: should one submit to evil, or use evil methods to oppose it? Her thought-provoking portrait of a society seeking to escape the curse of violence and her experiment in narrative technique make these books stimulating reading.

In this abundance of postcataclysmic novels, even the old standard catastrophes—the atomic war and the alien invasion—are given new vitality by contemporary authors. Utilizing the atomic holocaust popular in the 1950s, Newbery medalist Robert C. O'Brien presents his novel [Z for Zachariah] as the diary of teenage Ann Burden, who escapes death from atomic cataclysm because atmospheric inversion protects the small valley in which she dwells. Having lost her family to radiation, she lives alone with her dog and a few farm animals until the arrival of a chemist from Cornell, who escaped by wearing a radiation "safe suit." She nurses him through a bout of radiation sickness and even dreams that together they will be a new Adam and Eve. This daydream of a new Eden is ruthlessly shattered by the chemist when he recovers and demands that Ann serve him with unquestioning obedience. The new Eve chooses to go out into the unknown world without Adam, having refused to repeat the old mistakes. O'Brien does not soften the edges of his apocalyptic vision by providing a happy ending for Ann. As in real life, he gives her only hope and faith that someone might be out there to give life purpose and meaning.

Last, and perhaps the most creative of all the postcataclysmic novels, is Atheneum editor Jean Karl's The Turning Place. In a dazzling display of imagination, Ms. Karl takes as her starting point that old chestnut, the alien death ray. In the first episode, Ms. Karl eradicates most of the world's population by means of the "Clordian Sweep," and in the eight subsequent sections, she spans thousands of years of the development of a new mankind, taking us eventually out into the vast reaches of space. Never consciously didactic, the taut stories read like abstracts from some future history, giving a tantalizing view of the millenia. Like poetry, her compressed narratives run the risk of obscurity, which she seeks to alleviate by means of "Some Notes on Sources." These "notes" not only provide additional information but also lend an air of historical authenticity to her work. The reader finishes the book hoping that Ms. Karl will expand each of her stories into a novel.

The Turning Place sums up the mood of the 1970s. We are at a turning point; the good old days are gone, and we must find a new course. As her space traveler says at the novel's close: "There are always problems. They change. Patterns change. And sometimes things get worse, sometimes better. But no matter what happens, problems remain." A large part of the appeal of contemporary science fiction for the young reader is its ability to delineate these eternal problems and to suggest that their answers lie within each man's grasp—love of fellow man.

REFERENCES

Bova, Ben. *City of Darkness*. New York: Scribner, 1976.
Christopher, John. *Wild Jack*. New York: Macmillan, 1974.
Hoover, H. M. *Children of Morrow*. New York: Four Winds Pr., 1973.
———. *Treasures of Morrow*. New York: Four Winds Pr., 1976.
Karl, Jean E. *The Turning Place: Stories of a Future Past*. New York: Dutton, 1976.
Kestevan, G. R. *The Pale Invaders*. New York: Atheneum, 1976.
Mace, Elisabeth. *Ransome Revisited*. London: Andre Deutsch, 1975.
Norton, Andre. *No Night without Stars*. A Margaret McElderry Book. New York: Atheneum, 1975.
O'Brien, Robert C. *Z for Zachariah*. New York: Atheneum, 1975.
Sleator, William. *House of Stairs*. New York: Dutton, 1974.
Snyder, Zilpha K. *And All Between*. New York: Atheneum, 1976.
———. *Below the Root*. New York: Atheneum, 1975.
Townsend, John Rowe. *Noah's Castle*. Philadelphia: Lippincott, 1976.
Watson, Simon. *No Man's Land*. New York: Greenwillow Books, 1976.
Williams, Jay. *The People of the Ax*. New York: Walck, 1974.

Part 10

Unshackling the Mind

Minds are like parachutes; they function only when open.

Anonymous

Anyone who has read that delightful classic, *The Censored Mother Goose,* knows that even the most innocent of texts can assume lascivious connotations if strategic words are blotted out, indicating that prurience, like beauty, is the brainchild of the beholder. Consider, for instance, this censored nursery rhyme:

> He that would thrive
> Must / / / / / / at five;
> He that hath thriven
> May / / / / / / till seven.[1]

The censored-out terms make it impossible for even the least jaded of adults to read the rhyme without bawdy imaginings, bearing out the author's insight that the censors, to whom the book is dedicated, "have taught us to read naughty meanings into harmless words."

Out of the reams that have been written on the topic of intellectual freedom versus censorship, certain classic essays come to mind whenever the topic is broached, as for instance John Milton's *Areopagitica,* D. H. Lawrence's "Pornography and Obscenity," and Lester Asheim's "Not Censorship, But Selection."[2] All of these present inexhaustible materials for discussion, but with this topic—as with the home in the folktale, "there is always room for one more" perspective. Here the focus will be upon censorship as it affects young adult literature.

In his article on "The Most Censored Materials in the U. S.," L. B. Woods notes that J. D. Salinger's *The Catcher in the Rye* distinguished itself as "the most censored item" in educational institutions in the years between 1966 and 1975. This is astonishing enough, but even more astounding is his revelation that "A number of objectors admitted they had never read the book, but 'were objecting on the grounds of the book's reputation.' "[3]

"Censorship from ignorance" abounds, and what makes it even more insidious is that it often comes masked with good intentions, most usually the intent of "protecting" the young from the viciousness of a corrupt world. Richard Lettis, in "The Book is Not for Burning" brings out the ironic dimension of Holden Caulfield's desire to protect the innocence of Phoebe and the other children; Holden is redeemed from being a censor only by his recognition that "the alternative to life in a dangerous and sordid adult world" is self-extinction: to cling to innocence is to lose the chance of achieving moral maturity. In the words of Robert Frost, in a fallen world, "Nothing Gold Can Stay." Adults need the kind of love for the young which knows when to "let go with the hands . . . ," and allows the young person to grow towards autonomy, which can be found only through exercising his own moral judgment.

Readers are not the only ones who stand to be impoverished by the attempts of censors to control the content of literature, or to establish guidelines for judging literature, not primarily on its literary quality, but on its adherence to certain social values, didactically conceived. Writers are also deeply affected, as Nat Hentoff makes clear in "Any Writer Who Follows Anyone Else's Guidelines Should Be in Advertising." He points up the tendency for literature to "stiffen into propaganda" unless it can be "freely conceived" in an act of imaginative vision. To impose guidelines is to strangle the imagination, and the resulting productions, while perhaps harmless enough, can scarcely avoid being simplistic, bland, and boring. Hentoff urges the Council on Interracial Books for Children to reaffirm and work anew towards its original goals—"to really open up opportunities for black [and other minority] writers, illustrators, publishers, and minority-owned bookstores"—"honestly political ends"—and to trust literature to the imaginations of the writers and their young audiences.

Jerzy Kosinski presents the perspective of another writer, one who has "been there," for he has seen his book *Being There* banned from school shelves in New Jersey on the basis of parental claims against its "objectionable passages." He accurately analyzes the attempts of "the typical anti-literary mind" to "sanitize the classroom (or the living room) . . . oblivious to the student's need to understand the wider world and to grow socially and emotionally." Growth of this sort can be enhanced by books that fire the imagination in a way that only books can, but such growth is impossible if the only books left on the shelves are the innocuous variety that no one could find offensive. Education can and must amount to more than "the bland leading the bland" if the school is to fulfill its mission as the last stronghold for the nurturing of critical intelligence.

A philosophy which affirms the nurturance of critical intelligence in the young is expressed by Dorothy Broderick in "Censorship: A Family Affair." She explains her perspective of youth advocacy, defined as believing "in creating the conditions under which young people can make decisions about their own lives." It is the adult's (and the librarian's) role not to impose choices upon youth, but to make the range of choices known to them. Her keen insight into the reasons underlying the "protectionist philosophy" of many adults (librarians included) are illuminated through her discussion of the "sociology of morality." A person's value system is not rationally conceived, but represents an "emotional commitment"; hence, factual, rational arguments against censorship are invariably ineffectual. The content of media constitutes a kind of "public behavior," and when this "behavior" goes against the conventional, public morality (however much it may reflect "private" morality), it *does* undermine society's claim that the public moral position is the only "correct" one. One of the most striking features of the essay is the analogy Broderick draws between dysfunctional families and censors. She follows this with a statement of the positive values that uphold freedom (which she finds woefully lacking among both librarians and society in general), plus an examination of the tactics of the enemy, using its attacks upon *Our Bodies, Ourselves* as evidence. She closes with a challenge to the library profession to make a real, active "commitment to youth's rights." This provocative essay offers a stimulating topic for classroom debate—"Resolved: that young adult librarianship by its very nature demands a commitment offensively to undermine society by making accessible materials that are at odds with the publically professed, 'official' morality."

One of the other questions raised by a thoughtful reading of Broderick's essay has to do with the nature of literature itself. Unless literature is to be merely derivative or trivial, it inevitably will find itself in conflict with "*official* morality"—especially whenever such morality "has degenerated into mere respectability, Pharisaism, and hypocrisy."[4] Thus great writers traditionally have found themselves in the eye of the storm over the conflict between the "morality" to which society may give lip-service and their individual visions of a higher, truer way of life. Because the values of the young are never, in any generation, exactly in tune with the professed, publically embraced values of their elders, serious young adult literature is bound to find itself embroiled in controversy. The very controversy may be itself a sign of the strength and authenticity of the literature concerned.

NOTES

1. Kendall Banning, *The Censored Mother Goose* (New York: Mother Goose, 1926), unp.
2. Merritt Y. Hughes, ed., *John Milton: Complete Poems and Major Prose* (New York: Odyssey, 1957), pp.716-49; Anthony Beal, ed., *D. H. Lawrence: Selected Literary Criticism* (New York: Viking, 1956), pp.32-51; *Wilson Library Bulletin* 28:63-67 (Sept. 1953).
3. *Library Journal* 103:2170-71 (Nov. 1, 1978).
4. Arvid Shulenberger, "The Orthodox Poetic" (Lawrence: Univ. of Kansas, 1962).

The Book Is Not for Burning

Richard Lettis

Censorship has of late acquired such a bad reputation that it is almost impossible to practice it without first repudiating it. "I'm no censor," the would-be censor hotly argues, "but—." Despite our growing conviction that books should be consumed by eyes, not flames, there are still a few burning "buts" left to be put out.

By far the most popular, successful and unchallenged negative conjunction now scorching our literature is the argument that children need to be protected. Perhaps few of us will be inflamed these days by the thought of adults wading through filth, but who can keep his cool when he thinks of exposing kids to such stuff?

Such a book, the fiery censors of Long Island's Trees School Board have repeatedly argued, is J. D. Salinger's novel, *The Catcher in the Rye*. It has foul language. One of it characters is a prostitute. It openly describes and discusses sexual perversion. Worst of all, it tells the story of a teenager, a boy our children may identify with, who does all sorts of objectionable things like drinking and dropping out of school and disobeying his parents and all. We're not censors, but obviously such things are not good for our children, and we object heatedly when we find that book in our school library.

The astonishing thing is that the young boy of the novel agrees with us. He's no censor, either, but he asserts with considerable warmth that certain words and ideas are dangerous for children. In one scene,

Reprinted by permission of the author from *Journal of Reading* 21:106-8 (Nov. 1977). Copyright © 1977 by Richard Lettis.

for example, while searching for his beloved young sister Phoebe, he sees the English-speaking world's classic four-letter word written on her school wall and tries to rub it out.

Holden's desire to protect children from bad words is but a part of his conviction that they must in all ways be sheltered from an evil world. In thinking about what he himself would like to do as an adult, he imagines a huge field of rye in which thousands of children are playing. The field is on the edge of a "crazy cliff," and the children in their play are in danger of falling off. Holden thinks he would like to be the one to save them: "I mean if they're running and they don't look where they're going I have to come out from somewhere and *catch* them. That's all I'd do all day. I'd just be the catcher in the rye. . . ."

Why is it that the hero of the book we all want to censor is himself a kind of a censor? Why has Salinger put into his objectionable book a character who rejects the objectionable? The answer lies in what Holden learns about "catching" children, in what he finds is the cost of keeping them from falling. The "fall" they are in danger of taking is the inevitable departure from the garden of innocence, through experience into adulthood. Like us, Holden dreads this terrible step, for he sees the adult world as a shabby and corrupting place. But he comes to realize that there is only one method for preventing children from taking this fall, only one way to catch them. Only one child in Holden's story will never be contaminated by adulthood: his other beloved sibling, Allie. Allie is dead.

To be the catcher in the rye, one has to be a kind of a killer; there is no other way to keep children from growing up. The alternative to life in a dangerous and sordid adult world is no life at all. When Holden has come to understand this, he takes his sister Phoebe for a ride on a carousel, and watches her reach for the gold ring. Though he is afraid she may fall and injure herself, he decides that he must not try to stop her. It is not that Holden has become less concerned for children, or less anguished by their fall. It is simply that he has come to understand the alternative.

When children reach out for the golden ring, it is time for them to get off the merry-go-round, and we have to let them do it. When children are ready to encounter the larger world of adult experience, we must not inhibit them, no matter how much it hurts us to watch them hurt. To the extent that we do prevent them, we prevent them from growing, that is, living.

One of the surest ways of growing is to read. But often it is that very kind of reading which makes us most fearful for the welfare of our children—reading about controversial things like violence and rebellion and nonconformity and rejection of traditional values, reading about sex—which will do the most to help them grow. The "safe" books in the library, of which we comfortably approve, are frequently the ones which keep young minds on the merry-go-round, repeating the same limited values and simplified concepts which were right for their childish comprehension but are insufficient for, and even damaging to, their expanding intellects.

The point is not that children should be steeped in sex, inundated with immorality or pressed to abandon their early beliefs. But if the convictions youngsters have been given are to become truly theirs, they must make them so by refining, modifying, developing and testing them. To do this, they must read books which are sometimes troublesome, challenging, controversial, argumentative.

The child who reaches for the ring of gold may wind up with brass, or worse: he or she may adopt wrong ideas, acquire reprehensible tastes, become confirmed in immoral behavior, develop a way of life that is repugnant to us. But that is the chance we (and they) have to take. While they were children we gave them all we could to help them choose well: a sense of our concept of right, a sense of their own dignity, a sense of mutual love. We can still advise them, urge our way of life upon them, love them. But we must not keep them from reaching out. When they do, they will inevitably and perhaps fortunately fall, and we must steel ourselves not to catch. It should not be too difficult to refrain, not if we remember the cost of catching, not if we remember the alternative of the fall.

Any Writer Who Follows Anyone Else's Guidelines Ought to Be in Advertising

Nat Hentoff

In the early 1960s, Ursula Nordstrom asked if I'd be interested in writing a book for children. The notion had never occurred to me, but what proved tempting was Ursula's statement that, of course, I would have total freedom to write what I imagined. The result was

Reprinted by permission of the author from *School Library Journal* 24:27-29 (Nov. 1977). R. R. Bowker Company/A Xerox Corporation.

Jazz Country, a novel about black music and the dues white boys have to pay to get inside that perilous land of marvels. The book has been read by black, white, Danish, Japanese—all kinds of kids. And for a time, I am delighted to say, it was stolen from a number of libraries more often than almost any other book.

That experience, for which I remain grateful to Ursula, was so much fun and so satisfying (because of all the letters I received from kids) that I have been writing novels for children ever since.

On the other hand, let us suppose that in the early 60s, I had been told by Ursula—or by a librarians' group—that as I wrote, I would have to remember that my book was going to be judged by the following guidelines:

> antiracist/nonracist/racist (by omission/commission)
> antisexist/nonsexist/sexist
> antielitist/nonelitist/elitist
> antimaterialist/nonmaterialist/materialist
> antiindividualist/nonindividualist/individualist
> antiageist/nonageist/ageist
> anticonformist/nonconformist/conformist
> antiescapist/nonescapist/escapist
> builds positive images of females/minorities
> builds negative images of females/minorities
> inspires action vs. oppression/culturally authentic

And then down in the corner, almost as an afterthought:

> literary quality/art quality.

Had anyone actually shown me such a set of guidelines, my first reaction would have been that I had suddenly been transported to Czechoslovakia or some such utterly stifling state. My second reaction would have been to ignore these externally dictated "standards" entirely, because any writer who follows anyone else's guidelines ought to be in advertising.

Yet I did not invent that list. Those are the criteria by which children's books are judged by the Council on Interracial Books for Children, Inc. (CIBC) in their 1976 volume, *Human (and Anti-Human) Values in Children's Books: a Content Rating Instrument for Educators and Concerned Parents.*

Furthermore, these and similar criteria permeate the council's *Bulletin* and their public statements. To what end? Not only to sensitize parents, educators, and librarians to books that are "harmful" to children, but also to mount campaigns to censor those books.

Like certain Orwellian characters, the sepulchral representatives of the council deny that they are censors. For instance, in a letter to *School Library Journal* (January 1977, p.4), Bradford Chambers, director of CIBC—that Watch and Ward Society—declares that he is encouraged at the realization "by many librarians that enlightened weeding and selection policies aimed at reducing racism and sexism do not constitute 'censoring.' "

One librarian's act of weeding can be a writer's shock of recognition that his or her books are being censored off the shelves. That is, if the weeding is not part of the normal process of making room for new books by removing those that kids no longer read but is rather a yielding to such slippery "guidelines" as those of CIBC. The latter is censorship, as even a child can tell you.

Let me stipulate my agreement with the political goals of the council as they are stated on page 4 of *Human (and Anti-Human) Values. . . .* "We are advocates of a society which will be free of racism, sexism, ageism, classism, materialism, elitism, and other negative values." (Such other negative values as censorship, I would add.) I can make this stipulation not out of piety but on the basis of some thirty years of rather dogged if unspectacular work toward these ends as a democratic socialist involved in all kinds of movements to redistribute power in this land.

Politics, however, is not literature. And children ought to have access to the freest literature we can write for them. And literature must be freely conceived or it stiffens into propaganda (no matter how nobly intended) or into some other form of narrowing didacticism.

The council, however, is quite openly working toward the end of having "children's literature become a tool for the conscious promotion of human values that will help lead to greater human liberation" *(Human (and Anti-Human) Values . . .* p.4). I apologize for being obvious, but literature cannot breathe if it is forced to be utilitarian in this or any other sense. The council fundamentally misunderstands the act of imagination.

Recently, an internationally renowned writer for children commented about the council to me: "Of course, we should all be more tender and understanding toward the aged and we should work to shrive ourselves of racism and sexism, but when you impose guidelines like theirs on writing, you're strangling the imagination. And that means that you're limiting the ability of children to imagine. If all books for them were 'cleansed' according to these criteria, it would be the equivalent of giving them nothing to eat but white bread.

"To write according to such guidelines," this storyteller continued, "is to take the life out of what you do. Also the complexity, the ambivalence. And thereby the young reader gets no real sense of the wonders and terrors and unpredictabilities of living. Paradoxically, censors like the council clamor for 'truth' but are actually working to flatten children's reading experiences into the most misleading, simplistic kinds of untruth."

The writer quoted has never been attacked by CIBC but nonetheless asked me not to disclose his or her identity. "Otherwise," the writer said, "they'll go after me. And that, of course, is another chilling effect of their work." In fact, no writer of books for children whom I spoke to in connection with this piece was willing to be identified, for all were fearful of the council.

I also talked—for nonattribution—to several former members of the council who supported CIBC in its early days but who left when the organization began to move toward its current function of righteous vigilanteism. "At the beginning," one of them, a black librarian, said, "the idea was to really open up opportunities for black writers, illustrators, publishers, and minority-owned bookstores. God knows, that needed to be done then, as it needs to be done now. But then the council changed course and turned into censors. That's when I left. I know damn well that if everybody doesn't have the freedom to express himself or herself, I'm going to be one of the first to lose mine."

Yet the council has a ready, if rather devious, rejoinder to such talk of indivisible freedoms. Their contention is that the publishing industry has long practiced "covert censorship." By that, Bradford Chambers says he means the kinds of venerable publishing criteria that result in an "underexposure of the views of women and Third World people." And he's right. For all the belated eagerness of many houses to publish books expressing just such views, the book industry as a whole is certainly still white-dominated. (By the way, that eagerness has so far led to an excess of virtuous pap and scarcely any literature. In the rush to repent, publishers have not sufficiently searched out truly creative tellers of tales who cannot be fitted into neat, sanitized, newly "proper" molds.)

However, the answer to what the council calls "covert censorship" is hardly the council's kind of book "elimination." At base, whatever the reasons of the expungers, all censorship is the same. It is suppression of speech and creates a climate in which creative imagination, the writer's and the child's, must hide to survive.

That the council does not understand the necessarily free ambience for children's literature is regularly evident in its *Bulletin* as well as in its procrustean rating systems for "worthy" books. For instance, in a recent issue of the *Bulletin* (vol. 8, no. 3) there is an article about the books that East German children are reading in grades one to six ("What Children Are Reading in GDR Schools" by Donna Garund-Sletack). The author focuses mainly on the "messages" these books convey about sex roles. For the most part, the books get high grades. Women are shown in a wider range of careers than in comparable American readers; children of both sexes exercise real responsibility; individualism is downplayed (no kidding!); all sorts of positive values are inculcated (such as helpfulness); respect for older people is "promoted"; there are plentiful tales of racial discrimination (the East Germans are against it); and by God, "an analysis of poverty and inequality is offered as early as in the first grade reader."

Nowhere in the article is there a hint that East German writers (whether their audiences are adults or children) who offend the state do not get published any more. Some are even given a chance to reflect on their "anti-human values" in prison.

Freedom of expression, however, is clearly not a focal passion of CIBC. Correctness of perspective and attitude are its driving priorities as is stated in the council's pamphlet *10 Quick Ways to Analyze Children's Books for Racism and Sexism*:

No. 7: "Consider the Author's or Illustrator's Background." Look at the biographical material on the jacket. "A book that deals with the feelings and insights of women should be more carefully examined if it is written by a man." If it's written by Phyllis Schlafly, it also ought to be carefully examined. Obviously, blacks are likely to bring more to black themes, as Jews are to Jewish themes. But why not judge each book for itself, rather than order a lineup before you read?

No. 9: "Watch for Loaded Words." Like what? "Chairman" instead of "chairperson." I would take twenty lashes rather than be forced to use so utterly graceless a word as "chairperson." And what does that make me, according to the council? A stone sexist, that's what.

And so it goes—"Check the Story Line," "Look at the Lifestyles," "Weigh the Relationships Between People," and so on. Fine for East Germany, if that's where you want to write, but no different here from the John Birch Society trying to hammer *its* values into books for children. Such groups are the enemies of any writer with self-respect.

Another dulling, constricting effect of the council's ardent work is that when successful, it produces its own stereotypes. During an appearance by representatives of the council at a February 1977 meeting in New York of the National Coalition against Censorship, Mary K. Chelton, consultant on young adult services for the Westchester County Library System, made a good point about the council's addiction to labeling groups. She said that the council's view of racial minorities and women makes the groups emerge as monolithic, with each member of these groups in total accord on any matter that affects them. Describing herself as a feminist, she pointed out that she knows from personal experience that there is no unified perspective among feminists about what is most important to women now, or how best to achieve feminist ends, or even what the term "feminist" means.

The same is true of blacks, Chicanos, and all other so-called "Third World" people. It is no wonder the council considers "individualism" highly suspicious.

Yet there can be no literature without individualism—uncategorizable individualism—sometimes flaky, sometimes complexly rebellious, sometimes so stubbornly unassimilable as to make the child shout in recognition of himself. (Or herself. Or the chair he/she is personing.)

Collectivism is for politics. And if the council were to marshall its energies and foundation-financed resources for honestly political ends, I'd join it. Organize, bring pressure to greatly increase the numbers of "Third World" editors who will then find more nonwhite writers than white editors are likely to. (If only because they know a lot more.) Organize support for "Third World" publishing firms and bookstores. And by all means, hold sessions for librarians and editors on ways in which the children's booklists ought to be expanded (without censoring other books). There is still so little of value for children on the jazz life. Or on the turbulent, desperately complicated history of Puerto Rican independence movements. The list is huge.

But then leave the authors alone. Always leave authors alone. I'm not talking about editing for grammar and grace. But stay out of authors' quirkily individualistic heads in terms of what they write.

I am currently making notes for a novel, a successor to *This School Is Driving Me Crazy*. I am trying to imagine Sam, the maddeningly unregimentable hero, two years older. And there is a cohero, who is black. There are always blacks in my novels, and not once have I checked any of them out with the Council on Interracial Books for Children. I am trying to imagine the many intersecting reasons this black youngster, while witty, is also angry. Is he angry at the council because he is torn between collective and individual imperatives? That's a possibility. Maybe I'll be able to incorporate Bradford Chambers into the book. That's a real possibility.

And I am thinking of how the weather will be in certain scenes and trying to remember what it was like, in my teens, to be paralyzed at meeting a certain girl unexpectedly on the street. There will also be music in the book, and I am listening for those sounds. And there are voices I am after, rhythms, timbres. How do you put those into words? The council's guidelines do not tell me.

During this preliminary process and then as I write, I will have one of the council's precepts in mind: "It is the final *product* that counts—not the intent. We must be concerned above all with the effects of a book on the children who read it."

Exactly. Except that the council's concern with children is expressed through guarding them against any thoughts, characters, plot lines, words, and art work that might "harm" them. The council, of course, considers itself the arbiter of all that, having discovered, by innate virtue, the sole and correct party line.

My concern with children, on the other hand, is that they find in a book what they had never quite expected to see in print—elements of themselves, dreams they're not sure but what they too may have dreamed. And a chance, as many chances as I can give them, to play with their imagination. To stretch it and bend it and peer through and around it and make whatever connections are natural between the book and themselves, the life in the book and the life outside. And I want to make them care about the people in the book, and dig their foolishness, and maybe cry a little (I loved to cry over books when I was a kid.) And I hope to get letters from readers. I will start a correspondence, as has happened after all the books before. And my correspondents will ask me all kinds of things, as I will them—none of which can be fitted into those grimly symmetrical checklist boxes so beloved by CIBC.

Later, probably in a library, I will meet some of the readers of this new book, and will be astonished again at how marvelously, though sometimes hesitantly, different each one is. Whether they're all black, as in Brooklyn's Ocean Hill-Brownsville, or a motley, as in Tulsa. And I will look at them and think how truly stupid and destructive it is for anyone to stand guard over the ideas that may be offered to their lively minds.

What it comes down to is that CIBC not only distrusts individualism ("should be discouraged as a highly negative force"), but it also greatly distrusts children.

And that is reason enough why the council should not be messing with children's literature.

Against Book Censorship

Jerzy Kosinski

If properly learned, reading can prepare students to deal perceptively with the complexities of society. But it cannot be properly learned if self-appointed censors are permitted to force the exclusion from the schools of any literary work which they label as "objectionable." Such action, however lofty its stated motives, undermines one of the basic reasons for teaching contemporary literature: to present the students with hypothetical situations—emotional, moral, political, religious, sex-

Reprinted by permission of the author and publisher from *Media & Methods* 12:21-24 (Jan. 1976). Copyright © 1976 by Jerzy Kosinski.

ual—which they are likely to face once they leave the protective structures of school, family, or community, or which they may be struggling
to face already.

Zealots of the book-banning persuasion invariably confuse the literary
work with the instructional manual, ascribing the same purpose to these
two very different kinds of writing: to control the reader's behavior.
Thus they see the reader reduced to a robot, destined to imitate the
events portrayed in whatever book he or she happens to be reading.

Furthermore, the typical antiliterary mind perceives the student as
an ideal, isolated being removed from the myriad influences that mass
media, violence, social unrest, and commercialism bring to bear in contemporary society. Yet students today are anything but uncontaminated
mentally. These forces reach them despite all attempts to sanitize the
classroom (or the living room) and quarantine its occupants. Still, the
zealot, locked in a past of fictitious purity, tends to see the studentt as
inviolable, a perpetual child, and will stress his or her "immaturity,"
remaining oblivious to the student's need to understand the wider world
and to grow socially and emotionally.

One source of this growth can be the confrontation between a student
and a book. Exposure to various forms of fiction usually teaches students that they can (and *must* if they are to enjoy reading) recreate the
text's situations within their own mind's eye. This ability to visualize,
to know that one can shape and control images triggered by the printed
word, is invaluable. Its presence or absence will color every aspect of
an individual's life—as a member of the community, as a spouse or
parent, as a participant in professional activities.

In this act of imaginative projection, readers remain aware that, however involved they may be in the act of reading, they nevertheless stand
outside the depicted events. Such forced separation between reading
and imagining can act as a catalyst for a formative realization: that the
reader is a mediator, able to distinguish between false and true images,
between appropriate and inappropriate responses. This goes beyond
mental or aesthetic ability; it implies the power to judge, to see a novel's
people and events in moral terms. And such judgment demands that
the reader develop—or have already developed—a working ethical
code. This is the irony of censorship, that it thwarts the very ethical
development that its proponents see threatened by access to diverse literary works.

Of course, the actual process by which students come to terms with
their complex role as readers is a highly personal, internal one that cannot be taught. But students can be led to read correctly, to appreciate
unfamiliar literary terrain and to choose books which will challenge their
minds and continually demand new responses, new ethical judgments.
As their reading skills develop, so too does their imagination—not to
conjure up deviant spectacles and behaviors, but to project themselves

into complexities of life which are yet beyond their present experiential perimeters.

Banning fiction of a certain type from the classroom is one of the surest ways to keep students from exercising and expanding their imaginations. Denied the opportunity to learn how to respond to all literature imaginatively—instead of simply accepting it—a student can lose the ability to handle real and potentially damaging events. The tragic outcome is that the myopia which characterizes the zealot's outlook may become reincarnated in the life of the student who is barred from a literary work because it contains an "objectionable passage."

Clearly, life in contemporary American society is not easy for most people, including the young. Suicide is the second most frequent cause of death among persons between the ages of fifteen and twenty-four. (The most frequent cause, accidental death, includes many drug-induced, *de facto* suicides.) A recent national survey of prosperous American business executives indicates that more than half of them feel too pressured to enjoy life; one third admit that the strain and tension of their jobs have hurt their health; over half say that their work is at best unrewarding; nearly half have changed or considered changing their professions; and about seventy percent admit they have been expected to compromise personal principles in order to conform to standards established by their superiors within the corporate structure.

One of the bulwarks against this increasing sense of personal frustration is a strengthening of the intellectual life. Yet Americans seem to be growing further and further away from such a life. And what is worse, they are abandoning the very tools upon which this life is built—a major one of which is reading. One fifth of all Americans are known to be functionally illiterate. During the past few years the verbal aptitude of American high school graduates has consistently declined—hardly surprising since that same graduate has logged eighteen thousand hours of television viewing, the equivalent of nine years of full-time employment. Only now are we recognizing the intellectual destruction that this unreflective pastime can produce. (See my comments in "A Nation of Videots," *Media & Methods,* April 1975.)

As this trend toward depression, passivity, and isolation becomes increasingly irreversible, schools are among the few remaining institutions that can help tomorrow's adults become thinking individuals, able to judge and function in a world of pressures, conflicting values, and moral ambiguities. The classroom experience in general, and the reading experience in particular, are two of the few demanding mental activities left in modern society. And both must be allowed to flourish freely— without arbitrary restrictions on what is taught and what is read—if we are to keep at least some small part of the student population from becoming emotionally and intellectually crippled.

Of course, ours is a free society and zealots are at liberty to suppress what they consider wrong and alien, just as teachers are at liberty to defend their authority and knowledge in the selection of material to be read. Yet there is a difference: professional training and the rights vested in teachers by the community should confer a special authority. But, at the hands of the small-minded traditionalists, teachers are often exposed to prejudice and attack. They are cast as scapegoats and forced to present time-consuming, humiliating defenses. They may be called upon to testify on behalf of a literary work they have selected for a course, or to justify such a choice as if *they* were the proponent of an outlandish vision of life, rather than being the victim of a handful of hysterical parents.

Since the specter of book censorship can emerge anywhere in America, a general play for counterattack must be drawn up. When the book-banners gather together, the teacher—in addition to alerting the teachers' association, the school, the library, and (if he or she is involved as an individual) the Civil Liberties Union—should promptly notify the novel's author, publishers, and regional and local book distributors. Some or all of these parties will no doubt be interested in providing assistance by furnishing materials (reviews from mass media and religious publications, scholarly analyses, and other pertinent opinions) that can assist the teacher in making a stand.

Teachers constrained from discharging their responsibilities must notify the community at large, and the larger the better. This is a national as well as a local issue; the entire country should be kept aware of every student's right to have access to all forms of art. So the national media should be alerted, in addition to local television and radio stations, magazines, and newspapers.

Embattled teachers might also consider occasional visits to local magazine and newspaper stands where they can find materials which make the "objectionable passages" in school texts seem ridiculous. The students, whose protection is so earnestly invoked, have free access to these sources. A cursory review of local theaters will turn up films which portray violence and human destruction on a much more impressive scale than the "objectionable" passages in some school readings. Many a local supermarket offers boudoir confessional accounts in publications of questionable character, lubricously illustrated, and placed conveniently near the check-outs for casual perusal if not actual purchase.

It is argued that such materials, though available, do not have any official sanction, that the schools are the guardians of public morals and thus should be more selective about what is approved for student use. This opinion undermines the more vital function of education, which is to help students cope with life by exploring with them the realities and ambiguities expressed in recognized literary works. The school offers one of the few structured forums for analyzing such situations—an opportunity to critically evaluate the human condition within the guidelines of literary value and human interchange. If students are exposed to a situation which departs from their ethical sense, better that this occur within the school context than behind some magazine rack. But the question is not one of exposure—that will occur no matter how protective the local citizenry might be. The question is rather one of analysis and evaluation—a function which the school is established to provide.

Finally, local boards of education as well as other community organizations would do well to recognize the importance of teachers who make their students aware of personal and world events, particularly at a time of political polarization, economic turmoil, and general unpredictability. These teachers, who want to prepare their students for various contingencies, deserve considerable respect. They are often attacked as "experimentalists," but they play a vital role in ensuring that schools will produce responsible individuals, men and women without fear of the world around them.

Editor's Note

The impetus for Jerzy Kosinski's article on book censorship in the schools was a report that the Woodbridge, New Jersey, School District, under pressure from a local citizens' group, had banned his novel, *Being There*.

Media & Methods contacted the Woodbridge School District, and obtained the following information:

The Kosinski book was being used as a supplementary title in a high school course on mass media. A group of parents, claiming that *Being There* contained "objectionable passages," prevailed on the school officials to have the work removed from the reading list for the course. This was done, and *Being There* is no longer available in the Woodbridge schools.

While the Kosinski article obviously reflects the particulars of the Woodbridge action, its scope is much broader. At issue is the overall danger that school censorship of books poses and what educators can do when confronted by demands that a book be banned.

Postscript

The compilers of the present volume contacted the Woodbridge School District to determine the current status of *Being There* in the schools. Estelle Marks, Supervisor, Libraries and Media, stated, "We have never banned *Being There* from the Woodbridge, New Jersey, school libraries. It has always been available in the library collections for students who want to read it." She indicated, however, that inclusion of the book as required reading for a course was another matter, to be decided by those who plan curriculum.

Censorship: A Family Affair?

Dorothy M. Broderick

This is written from my perspective as a youth advocate, so it is best to begin by defining that phrase. A youth advocate is a person who believes in creating the conditions under which young people can make decisions about their own lives. The position stems from accepting the following basic assumptions: (1) decisions affecting behavior cannot be imposed externally on young adults but must be arrived at from within the person; (2) most young adults, when given accurate information reflecting the wide range of choices available in most areas of life, will make wise decisions; and (3) conversely, bad decisions are more often the result of ignorance than of perversity. I use the word *wise* to mean a decision that is good for the individual youth, even though it may run contrary to the decision the adults in that youth's life would prefer seeing made.

These assumptions have been arrived at through reading in the literature of family systems health research. Researchers in this field agree that the family is the unit of health and/or disease. Psychologically healthy young people live in families where the parents have attained a degree of emotional stability in their own lives and work to create the conditions under which their children will grow to be autonomous adults.[1]

The importance of becoming an autonomous person is well stated by Willard Gaylin in *Doing Good: The Limits of Benevolence:*

> Whenever a person's sense of control over his own life is expanded; whenever he sees himself as the source of his own pleasures and security, his pride increases, his self-esteem increases, and his capacity for caring and concern is enhanced with it. The opportunity to sense one's self as a competent, independent, coping person allows one the generosity, unavailable in the humiliation of dependence, of sharing one's self with others and of exposing one's self to the vulnerability that loving inevitably implies. When an individual can be more self-reliant, fewer of his relationships have to be centered around the rather unreciprocal fulfillment of his own personal needs. He can proceed to service, to participation, to self-sacrifice, to love, to creativity, and to the caring for the intrinsically helpless.[2]

While there are major differences between human beings and other animals on earth, a characteristic we all share is that the good parent(s) brings its offspring up to be independent and able to function without the presence of the parent. A bird who stays too long in the nest is kicked out; a kitten wanting to suckle too long is physically assaulted by its mother; larger animals, such as bears, teach their offspring how to hunt and avoid danger and then walk away from them. For human beings the process takes longer—years instead of a season or months— and is complicated by the fact that the ideal is independence of the offspring coupled with an ongoing loving relationship with the parents and siblings, if any.

This process of separation from parents for humans is further complicated by the fact that we face choices. The mother bear knows that her cub will grow up to be a bear and do what all the other bears do who manage to survive. Excluding those children who later become transsexuals, the only thing human parents can be sure of is that their child will grow up to be either male or female. All else is open to question (and worry). Will the children be straight, gay, bisexual, or asexual? Will they be doctors, plumbers, or thieves? Will they marry and be happy or will they marry and become part of the divorce statistics? Will they live long enough to become adults or will they join the ever-growing number of teenagers who commit suicide or die in automobile accidents (many of which are now assumed to be suicides)? Will they be alcoholics or junkies by age twelve? If female, will they be mothers before they cease being children?

These and a thousand similar questions have very real application in our world, and all adults, not just parents, have a right to be concerned about the future of the younger generation. Under such circumstances, it strikes me as very human to be more inclined to protect than to free young people. The problem is that, if we admit the truth, there is very little protection we can provide for the important areas of life. We can hope that today's young people will have sound economic futures, but unemployment, inflation, worldwide depression cannot be coped with by individuals, only by governments. We can dream that today's young people will have productive careers, but the big jobs of the future may not exist today.

Human beings *need* to feel in control, and, since we live in a world where the large issues are beyond our control, we search for ways to prove to ourselves that we have some measure of control over our existence. We vote for a Proposition 13; we join a group dedicated to removing books from libraries and courses of study from schools. We form groups to pressure the television industry or to close "adult book-stores." We cannot protect our youth from the great threats of society, so we turn to protecting them in the only areas in which we have any sense of control at all—we direct our energies at censoring what young people will be allowed to read, hear, and view. And because we so often attack the things that are indigenous to *their* culture (which is different from *our* culture), we lose their trust. They see us not as protectors but as adversaries.

Librarians engage in this protectionist philosophy by nonselection of materials and lofty pronouncements about our mission as transmitters of our cultural heritage. Other adults form groups and mobilize to attack materials in schools and libraries, and they are labeled censors. But the only difference between them and *most* librarians is that the range of materials and topics they find offensive is broader than ours, so inadvertently we occasionally buy items that will cause trouble. (There are *some* librarians in this country who conscientiously and systematically buy a wide range of materials reflecting all available standards of taste and viewpoints, but they are so few as not to warrant consideration here.)

What Upsets Adults and Why

There are two ways in which this dicussion can proceed: we can ask what is there about the word *fuck* that upsets so many people; why does a poem like "The City to a Young Girl"[3] arouse such intense reaction by a school board; why does a sentence saying "If you have never masturbated, we invite you to try"[4] inspire a nationwide letter-writing campaign? I hope that before I am through, some insight into those questions will be given. But the second way in which we can proceed, the one I want to deal with now, is to examine the "sociology of morality" so that we have a shared background of philosophical approaches against which to evaluate the specifics and perhaps place them in some kind of perspective.

In *The Legislation of Morality,* a book I feel all librarians should read, Troy Duster analyzes how a particular behavior pattern becomes a moral issue. While Duster is talking about how heroin addiction changed from being an acceptable behavior pattern to a crime, many of his statements are analogous for all issues we label moral. He says:

> As every social philosopher and theoretician of social order has noted in some form, men grow up in communities learning what is appropriate and inappropriate behavior, then become emotionally committed to those things considered most appropriate.[5]

It is important for us to understand that our value system is not arrived at, generally speaking, through abstract intellectualization but rather represents an emotional commitment. This is why logic plays little or no role in arguments between people holding opposite views. This fact cannot be stated too strongly, since librarians tend to feel that all they must do is marshal the facts in favor of an attacked book, film, or phonodisc, and the opposition will fade away. Equally important to understand is that the emotional commitment is to the world in which we grew up and not to the one in which we are presently living.

Liberals tend to dismiss as so much rhetoric the statements by conservative groups that conservatives are fighting to preserve a way of life. In fact, they are stating the truth, for as Duster points out:

> So long as a small minority of a community engage in immoral behavior *publicly,* [emphasis in original] then moral control of that behavior is effective. However, when there is public knowledge that even a sizable minority (one fourth or one third) are behaving publicly contrary to a community's "moral" principles, then those principles cannot long persist.[6]

Librarians must understand that the content of books and other media constitutes public behavior in the sense in which Duster uses it, and when that content differs from the public morality, it *is* an undermining factor in society. For example, not too long ago all sex education materials stressed that sexual intercourse occurred only between opposite sexes within marriage (and basically to have children, not pleasure). Except for an occasional individual who objected to a discussion of sex *per se,* there were no attacks on these materials. Now, with so many sex education materials placing sexual intercourse within a framework of situational ethics, the attacks are numerous and ongoing. The attackers understand, correctly, that each time a book (or other medium) describing alternatives in sexual relationships is bought by a school or public library, another step has been taken that will undermine their determination to maintain as the community standard their opinion that the older, traditional view of sex is the only correct one. A key word in the preceding sentence is *describing* because authors need not advocate a point of view, merely describe it, to be subject to attack.

It is obvious, I hope, that this situation applies to the presence of language deemed offensive, to social issues such as abortion and gay rights, and to all areas of personal behavior from the length of hair appropriate for males to females wearing trousers. Many of us have lived through the battle over boys' hair, and, in the early days when it was a small minority wearing long hair, the boys were subject to harassment by school officials and by their peers. The moment the number grew, harassment was no longer possible, and, once the harassment stopped, more boys chose to let their hair grow and for a time, at least, the deviate was the boy with short hair.

If, then, as I have tried to demonstrate, the censorship groups have a sound theoretical position underlying their actions, why is there so much controversy? Why do we not all subscribe to this position; why do we not all rally to defend "the erosion of values" occurring in our society?

Perceptions of the Present

It is my opinion that the answer to those questions rests in how people perceive the world in which they live. Those perceptions, in turn, are related to the degree of mental health existing within the family units.

I want to share with you some characteristics of family mental health as identified by researchers at the Timberlawn Psychiatric Foundation in Dallas, Texas. These researchers, under the leadership of Dr. Jerry M. Lewis, are engaged in identifying what constitutes sound psychological family health. It is important to keep in mind that, at this point in time, all families in the sample are white and middle-class, both parents are present, the oldest child is in mid-adolescence and has never been in trouble with the law or needed psychological counseling of any sort. All families are members of a local Protestant church. (Whether the characteristics of family health will be found to differ in other religious, ethnic, racial groups or single-parent families, the remarried, et al., remains to be seen.)

I became fascinated by this research when I heard Lewis deliver a paper at the 1977 annual conference of the Society for Adolescent Medicine (SAM). As I listened to Lewis describe the characteristics that contribute to a family's *incompetence,* I could not help thinking that these characteristics sounded very much like those I have identified (admittedly unscientifically) as belonging to members of censorship groups. I strongly believe that were Lewis and his associates to study members of these groups, they would conclude that these people are part of dysfunctional families. This strikes me as of vital importance to us because the rallying cry of the censors of our society is "Save the Family." Whether they are cleaning up the school's curriculum, weeding libraries of noxious materials, or attacking television, it is all done in the name of preserving family life and protecting children. In my view, the family these people want to preserve is basically an unhealthy unit, and it is time the library community used some of the excellent resource materials on our shelves to mount a public information campaign that tells the world that censors are basically unhealthy people who are in need of a good family therapist. And that goes for the censors among *us* as well as those from the general community.

I cannot possibly summarize all or even most of Lewis' research, but a general idea of what he is up to is necessary. And I can recommend his very fine book *No Single Thread* (Bruner & Mazel, 1976).

Lewis and his associates measure family competency by the degree to which "it provides for the stabilization of the adults' personality and for the development of autonomous children." Basically this means that the adults (father and mother) enjoy each other and are themselves fulfilled enough so that they have no need to live vicariously through their children. Since they have no great psychic need to have their children fulfill their frustrated dreams, they are willing to let their children develop in their own way, free of sex stereotyping or preconceived ideas of what the children are to become as personalities. Children within healthy families are allowed to differ from each other without parental prejudice causing favoritism of one type of personality over another.

As with everything else in life, there are degrees of family competency. At this time, the Timberlawn group has identified four types on a continuum: (1) optimal; (2) competent, but pained; (3) midrange dysfunctional; and (4) severely dysfunctional. There are twelve characteristics that go into evaluating a family, all of them so interwined that the title *No Single Thread* thoughtfully reflects this concept.

Obviously, I cannot go into all twelve, or even one of them in detail, but let me explore just a few of the characteristics of a healthy family and talk a bit about their implications. I am assuming that family characteristics carry over into the outer world—that people do not behave one way at home and another out in the world.

In optimal families each member is first and foremost an individual "with private feelings and thoughts which may either agree or disagree with those of other family members." This respect for individuality allows for negotiation when problems arise, and optimal families "habitually deal with problems as they arise, spend time making certain the problem is clearly defined and agreed upon, then they explore possible solutions. They can come to general agreement on the best answer, discover there is no general agreement and thus agree to compromise, or, if compromise doesn't prove feasible, they can usually agree to disagree in a way that is acceptable to each member."[7]

Members of optimal families say what they mean and are "heard" by other members; it is assumed that individuals are responsible for their own thoughts, feelings, and behavior, and they can express a broad range of emotions. There is a high level of tolerance for ambiguity and a belief in complex motivations. Optimal families have a small central core of deeply held beliefs, but there are a minimum of "shoulds" and "oughts" in their value system.

Let's look at those characteristics and ask some questions. Is it possible to have respect for the individual's thoughts and feelings and be the kind of person who says, "I don't want to read this, so you can't"? Is it possible to believe in agreeing to disagree and constantly provoke the win-lose situations censors specialize in? Is it possible to have a high tolerance for ambiguity and proceed to divide the world up into either-ors: good, evil, black, white, we, they, etc.? Can one believe in complex motivations and feel that there is a single cause for juvenile delinquency, sexual activity, or anything else in life?

Now one does not have to get to midrange and severely dysfunctional family characteristics to begin to spot the attitudes that lay the groundwork for becoming a censor. In their descriptions of "competent but pained" families, the Timberlawn group makes the following observations:

> There was some fear of people's inner impulses and, therefore, an effort to preach and shape behavior. As one result, this family was not high on the variable of respect for the subjective world view of one's self and others.
>
> The family was restricted in receptivity to the outside world and they had successfully trained the children to ignore ideas not stamped "approved."
>
> One technique unhappy families have of minimizing their own pain is "scapegoating."
>
> Few degrees of freedom were allowed — the watchword was not growth, but stability, and heightened anxiety attended any family member's getting out of line.
>
> This family group showed little respect for individual viewpoints or feelings. Their concern was with form: proper words were considered important and the reality behind those words was not given much consideration.
>
> "Oughts" and "shoulds" abounded in the family dialogue with attendant anxiety and resentment.[8]

All these characteristics are found to a greater degree in midrange and severely dysfunctional families, so they are worth analyzing.

Let's begin with "fear of people's inner impulses." The censorious person does believe that people are basically evil; that unless they are kept under rigid control, they will misbehave ("misbehave" being defined as anything unacceptable to that person's value system). I am willing to bet that everyone who is a censor mistrusts him- or herself so much that he or she cannot believe other people can be trusted to do the right thing without severe threats of punishment. According to Kohlberg's theory of moral development, the lowest stage of such development is behavior based on fear of punishment.

Lack of respect for the subjective world view of one's self and others is a natural accompaniment to this fear of inner impulses. It also goes hand in hand with training children to ignore ideas not approved by the family. However, for the censors, it is not enough to have trained their own children to behave this way—they are willing crusaders to eliminate the unapproved ideas entirely.

But the statement that has the greatest implication for us, in my opinion, is that "proper words were considered important and the reality behind those words was not given much consideration." Form over substance is clearly the root of our problem with language. Unable to hear people's feelings or respect their right to view the world differently, we zero in on the form the expression takes. By objecting to words, we are spared the need to deal with feelings and ideas. This valuing of form over substance is a major characteristic of librarians, and as long as it governs our behavior, we will be, in our own way, every bit as censorious as the groups we decry.

What Must We Do?

Let me now turn my attention to just a few of the values I feel we must have if we are to fight the good fight in favor of freedom.

We must believe that the more information adolescents have, the more responsible will be their decision making.

We must believe that adolescents deserve to be trusted and treated with respect and are entitled to make their wishes known and have their needs met.

We must value the potential for growth over the stability that, at its worst, encourages the creation of mental clones.

We must value individuality over stereotypic labeling.

Most of all, we must believe that whatever dangers accompany freedom, they are fewer and less destructive than the dangers of authoritarianism.

I do not find these values widely held within librarianship (or society as a whole). You may feel that that is okay and disagree with me when I say that we are in big trouble if we cannot bring ourselves to build these values into our programs of library service. You may feel, for example, that while it is okay for adolescents to have access to *most* information, there are areas where you prefer to restrict that access. The problem with this selective approach is that it leaves us vulnerable to the organized censorship groups who hold rigid opinions on everything. And, believe me, an organized group of twenty that believes passionately can defeat one hundred thousand people who aren't sure what they believe.

Know the Enemy

The most attacked book in the country at the moment is *Our Bodies, Ourselves.* The attack is well organized, systematic, and nationwide, and I want to quote from a couple of letters objecting to it; but before I do, let's suppose that you personally don't approve of the book (there are librarians who don't, you know) and can't get very excited about people wanting it removed from those libraries dumb enough to have bought it. Why should you bother defending a book you find offensive?

I have never believed in the domino theory—I didn't when it was applied to foreign policy, and I don't when it comes to removing a book from the library shelf—but let me say that the range of issues objected to by right-wing groups in this country is frightening enough to make me think twice before I would give in to them on any issue. Let me share with you some items from a newsletter published by the Coalition for Children in Prince George's County, Maryland, so that you can begin to see that there is no end to the potential problems for librarians.

It is estimated that up to one million teenagers run away from home every year. The coalition's view on this complex subject: "Through advertising literature, which was distributed in schools and community centers and libraries, the kids were encouraged to 'runaway' from home at the least provocation and were promised shelter . . . Kids, who at one time were picked up by the police and kicked back home where they belonged, now became wards of the State and parents had to go to court to get them back, sometimes having to agree to undergo 'group or family therapy.' " Hotlines and shelters encourage kids to run away so they can keep getting federal money. The coalition's solution? "Cut off the funding."

This is such a perfect example of the coalition's mind-set that I hope you'll forgive me if I belabor it just a bit. Would it help if you pointed out to these people that the National Runaways Network was set up in answer to a pressing problem and did not create the problem? No, because if kids run away, they deserve to suffer and should not be pampered. Notice the attitude toward kids—"kicked back home." The assumption that all homes are healthy places for young people to be underlies much of the coalition's approach to life, as does the idea that parents own their children. Don't try telling such people that one-third of the runaways leave home because they are systematically physically or sexually abused: information that does not fit the coalition's preconceived opinions is rejected. Now, any well-stocked library has three to four dozen good books on runaways. After *Our Bodies, Ourselves,* will runaway literature be the next to go?

Perhaps. But in a paragraph labeled "Self-Awareness and the Mushy Brains Set," the following subjects are all found objectionable: "sensitivity training, transactional analysis, transcendental meditation, assertiveness training, parent/teacher effectiveness, management by objectives, group therapy, rap sessions, and all the others too numerous to mention." Our library collection is getting smaller, isn't it?

It goes without saying that the coalition disapproves of both abortion and sex education. The price for sex should always be paid; and if you feel that abortion could be greatly eliminated by better birth control information, forget it: Califano is just another one out to destroy the family.

The ERA is a no-no, and so is the Panama Canal Treaty.

Norma Klein is the queen of kiddie porn (eat your heart out, Judy Blume) and *Grendel* is "raunchy."

I could go on and on. The coalition is able to find an enemy of the family under every federal program, behind every library stack, and within every classroom. What emerges is the picture of a group of adults who find themselves living in a hostile world, surrounded by enemies "out to get them." They are people whose world is filled with "oughts" and "shoulds" and any indication that other people are freer in their decision-making processes arouses in them severe feelings of anxiety and resentment. One feels this most strongly when noting the zeal with which they excerpt the juiciest parts of *Our Bodies, Ourselves,* ostensibly quoting for horror purposes but more likely with more than a touch of envy.

After *Our Bodies, Ourselves* was placed on the "Best Books for Young Adults 1977" list, both the YASD Office and *Today's Education* (where the list was printed) received innumerable letters protesting the book's inclusion. Writers said things like, "This is a feminist book. This book will produce sick people." Others used the word "filth," and it becomes clear that filth and feminism are synonyms in their minds. Others spoke as "women who want to be women," and as "Christian homemakers."

Here again we have a fine example of how our perceptions of the world influence our attitudes. For these women, there is nothing seriously wrong with the status of women in society, and those who are discontented with their roles as mothers, wives, homemakers are clearly weird.

We are in for some very hard times in the immediate future. The right wing is organized and geared for action. And the library profession, which has never made a real commitment to youth's rights, is going to find that either it marshals its resources to defend the rights of adolescents to the information they need and want, or we will find our libraries under the "pall of orthodoxy" as preached by people who are looking for scapegoats to ease their own pain, people who view the world as hostile and see human nature as basically evil. Are those really the values we want to see guiding us?

It is not enough that each of us answers the question individually, whether that answer be yes or no. The commitment to youth's rights must permeate the profession, and we must also take the offensive in telling the library story. Personally, I would like to see National Library Week get off its butt and design posters that read, "This library has something offensive to everyone," or, "If you aren't offended by something we own, please complain." Instead of cowering in corners hoping the censors won't notice us, why not launch a massive education campaign to tell people that an inoffensive library collection is a waste of money; that libraries exist to provide the materials that will allow those people who want to grow to do so? Dare we be that bold? If enough of us do not answer yes, the time to begin thinking about a new career is right now, because the libraries the censors of the world want to create will disintegrate under the sheer weight of boredom. Think about it.

NOTES

1. For a review of research in family health systems, see chapter 1 in Jerry M. Lewis and others, *No Single Thread* (New York: Bruner & Mazel, 1976).
2. (New York: Pantheon, 1978), pp.30-31.
3. "The City to a Young Girl" is the poem in Nancy Larrick and Eve Merriam, eds., *Male & Female under 18* (New York: Discus Books, 1973), p.95, that inspired the Chelsea, Massachusetts, court case.
4. *Our Bodies, Ourselves* (New York: Simon & Schuster, 1976), p.47.
5. *The Legislation of Morality; Law, Drugs, and Moral Judgment* (New York: Free Pr., 1970), p.86.
6. Ibid. pp.99-100.
7. Jerry M. Lewis, *"Evaluating Family Competence"* (speech delivered at the Society for Adolescent Medicine, Nov. 1977).
8. Lewis, *No Single Thread*, pp.117; 119; 122; 131; 132; 127.

Part 11

Turning Teens On to Books

School can be more than just a place to endure and pass through.

From the film *Foxfire*

The closing section is concerned with selecting books for reluctant readers and suggestions for showing them reading can be fun, and it concludes with an article on booktalking.

Eliot Wigginton, originator of the ideas that resulted in the Foxfire books, tells of his personal experience with less-than-eager high school students, and reveals how he worked a transformation upon them by opening up the opportunity for creative involvement in the production of a magazine, and ultimately, a series of books. His story should be an inspiration to all those who face the same "distress signals" that he, in his own phrase, "came perilously close to ignoring." Readers may wish to see also his more recent article, "The Foxfire Approach: It Can Work for You."[1]

Lance M. Gentile and Merna M. McMillan, in "Why Won't Teenagers Read?" and "Humor and the Reading Program," supply some sound practical ideas for reaching the nonreader and/or the slow or reluctant reader. Their ideas, aimed primarily at reading teachers, should also interest all librarians who feel a need to strengthen their collections with lively, attractive, yet easy and fun-to-read materials. It is noteworthy that, despite the lipservice given to the idea that reading can be fun, a search of the literature reveals very little to support the conclusion that teachers and librarians are aware of humor as a genre. The article on humor presented here is especially welcome because of the rarity of discussions of this topic.

In "Identifying High Interest/Low Reading Level Books," Barbara S. Bates presents a rationale for the need for early identification of books of this type—during the initial reviewing process—so that they may reach their ultimate audience sooner and more effectively. Her clearly defined criteria are exceedingly helpful towards achieving this goal.

The final article, Mary K. Chelton's "Booktalking: You Can Do It," offers a smorgasbord of practical and provocative ideas for "promoting the love of reading for pleasure . . . ." Alongside the current emphasis on the need for cultivating the use of nonprint materials, it is refreshing to renew our dedication to the time-honored activity of talking about books. Readers may also wish to see "Booktalks: What, Why and How-To," by Joni Bodart.[2]

Space limitations have not allowed the inclusion of other useful articles. For ideas on involving young adults in "selling" books to each other, see Catherine Monnin's "YAs Sell Paperbacks to YAs," a description of slide-tape presentations of book talks by high school students.[3] Those desiring help in locating reviews of young adult books will want to consult "The Young Adult Book Review Media" by Audrey B. Eaglen.[4]

NOTES

1. *Media & Methods* 14:49-52 (Nov. 1977).
2. *Top of the News* 35:273-77 (Spring 1979).
3. —— 34:85-86 (Fall 1977).
4. —— 35:143-45 (Winter 1979).

Introduction to *The Foxfire Book*

Eliot Wigginton

The contents of this book need little introduction; they stand on their own as helpful instructions and enjoyable reading. But what is not immediately apparent is that the material here was collected and put together almost entirely by high school students. And that makes the book a little special—for me at least, since they were kids I was supposed to be teaching.

It was 1966, and I had just finished five years at Cornell. I had an A.B. in English and an M.A. in Teaching, and I thought I was a big deal—a force to be reckoned with. So I went to Georgia and took a job at the 240-pupil Rabun Gap-Nacoochee School where I taught ninth and tenth grade English, geography, and had about ten other side responsibilities. Rabun Gap is right in the Appalachians. God's country, as they say here, and I'll go along with that.

About six weeks later, I surveyed the wreckage. My lecturn (that's a protective device a teacher cowers behind while giving a lecture nobody's listening to) was scorched from the time Tommy Green tried to set it on fire with his lighter—during class. Charles Henslee had already broken off the blade of his Barlow knife in the floorboards. Every desk was decorated with graffiti. My box of yellow chalk was gone, and so were the thumbtacks that had held up the chart of the Globe Theatre. The nine water pistols I had confiscated that very afternoon had been reconfiscated from under my nose.

And it was with a deep sigh that, as I launched one of several paper airplanes within easy reach, I began to ponder greener pastures. Either that or start all over.

The answer was obvious. If I were to finish out the year honorably, it would be necessary to reassert my authority. No teenagers were going to push me around. Besides, my course was too important. First offense would be an "X" in the grade book. Second, a paddling. Third, to the principal. Fourth, out of class for two weeks.

It frightens me to think how close I came to making another stupid mistake. First, I had bored them unmercifully. Now I was about to impose a welcome punishment. Two weeks out of that class would have been more pleasure than pain.

Those who cannot remember the past not only relive it; they tend to impose it, mistakes and all, on others. My own high school—monumentally boring texts and lectures, all forgotten; punishments and regulations and slights that only filled a reservoir of bitterness; and three blessed teachers who let me make things, helped me make them, and praised the results.

Luckily, it took only a few rewards to keep me going. How many students were denied even those few scraps of self-esteem from anyone other than their peers? And how many was I now denying?

I am not sure what the magic formula is or whether I have it pegged yet, but it involves a chemistry that allows us to believe we may have worth after all. Someone says, "You've done well," and we hunger to make that happen again and again. Too often we, as teachers, slip, and that first flush of success our students get comes after they've survived a night of drinking Colt 45, stuck up the local gas station, or taken two tabs of acid and made it out the other side alive.

We could catch some of those if we would.

The next day I walked into class and said, "How would you like to throw away the text and start a magazine?" And that's how *Foxfire* began.

From the beginning, the idea was to involve everyone. (It hasn't always worked, but we try.) We decided to print one issue put together by all of us as a class and during class time. If that issue did what I hoped it would do for my ailing classes, we might try to make it a regular thing. But for the time being, one issue only.

The contents? There were lots of possibilities. Many older people in this area, for example, still plant today by the signs of the zodiac and the stages of the moon. I had heard them mention it, but I didn't know what it meant. Rather than interrupt a conversation to find out, I figured I'd get my students to tell me. They'd probably know since it was mostly their parents and grandparents who were doing it. But my kids didn't really know what it was either, and soon they were as curious as I was. Why not find out and turn the information into an article?

So they went home and talked—really talked—to their own relatives, some of them for the first time. From those conversations came superstitions, old home remedies, weather signs, a story about a hog hunt, a taped interview with the retired sheriff about the time the local bank was robbed—and directions for planting by the signs. It was looking good.

Another possibility was poetry. Many of my students hated the stuff. I suspect one of the reasons was that they were forced to read pages of sentimental greeting card verse before they ever got to high school. In any case, working with poetry from an editor's point of view might be one way to overcome an already deeply rooted bias, and they were willing to try. So we added poetry too. Some was from our school (and some was from notably bad students in an effort to give them a boost they were hungry for). Some of it was from students in other schools in the state. And some was even from practicing poets. As we said in the first issue, "We hoped that they would remember their own beginnings and their own battles to be recognized and not be too proud to provide us with examples to follow—pieces we could aspire to in our own work."

The name? Each student submitted three choices. Duplications were eliminated, a master list was mimeographed and passed out, the obviously unworkable ones were dropped, and the kids voted from among those left. They chose "foxfire," a tiny organism that glows in the dark and is frequently seen in the shaded coves of these mountains.

And money? The school could provide no support at all. Any financial obligations would be my problem—not theirs. Looking back, I can see what a blessing in disguise that was. It meant the magazine had to sell, and that literally forced us to emphasize folklore rather than poetry, for magazines devoted to verse almost never survive for very long on the market. It also meant the kids had to find the money for that first issue themselves, and that made them more determined to see the magazine go than anything I could have said.

And so they hit the streets after school. Any donor, no matter how small his gift, would be listed in the issue, and he would receive a free copy signed by all the kids.

They collected four hundred fifty dollars. The local printer said that was enough to print six hundred copies photo-offset. So we printed six hundred copies, sold out in a week, and printed six hundred more.

It sounds simple doesn't it? I can promise there were times we almost chucked the whole thing and went back to *Silas Marner*. In our total ignorance we made some colossal blunders. We went broke a couple of times, for one. People like John Dyson and groups like the Coordinating Council of Literary Magazines came along and pulled us out of the mud, brushed us off, and wound us up again.

And each time we flopped, we got up a little stronger. Now, in Rabun Gap, there exists a magazine that has subscribers in all fifty states and a dozen foreign countries. It has been written about in magazines like *Saturday Review, New Republic, National Geographic School Bulletin, Scholastic Scope,* and *Whole Earth Catalogue.* It has received two grants from the National Endowment for the Humanities, one of them for $10,000. But most important, it is run by high school students—students who are going on to college knowing that they can be forces for constructive change; knowing that they can *act* responsibly and effectively rather than being always *acted upon.*

Looking beyond Rabun Gap and *Foxfire,* I can't get over the feeling that similar projects could be duplicated successfully in many other areas of the country, and to the genuine benefit of almost everyone involved.

Daily our grandparents are moving out of our lives, taking with them, irreparably, the kind of information contained in this book. They are taking it, not because they want to, but because they think we don't care. And it isn't happening just in Appalachia. I think, for example, of numerous Indian reservations, black cultures near the southern coasts, Ozark mountain communities, and a hundred others.

The big problem, of course, is that since these grandparents were primarily an oral civilization, information being passed through the generations by word of mouth and demonstration, little of it is written down. When they're gone, the magnificent hunting tales, the ghost stories that kept a thousand children sleepless, the intricate tricks of self-sufficiency acquired through years of trial and error, the eloquent and haunting stories of suffering and sharing and building and healing and planting and harvesting—all these go with them, and what a loss.

If this information is to be saved at all, for whatever reason, it must be saved now; and the logical researchers are the grandchildren, not university researchers from the outside. In the process, these grandchildren (and we) gain an invaluable, unique knowledge about their own roots, heritage, and culture. Suddenly they discover their families—previously people to be ignored in the face of the seventies—as pretelevision, preautomobile, preflight individuals who endured and survived the incredible task of total self-sufficiency, and came out of it all with a perspective on ourselves as a country that we are not likely to see again. They have something to tell us about self-reliance, human interdependence, and the human spirit that we would do well to listen to.

Is the subject, English, ignored in the process? Hardly. In fact, the opposite is true. English, in its simplest definition, is communication—reaching out and touching people with words, sounds, and visual images. We are in the business of improving students' prowess in these areas. In their work with photography (which must tell the story with as much impact and clarity as the words), text (which must be grammatically correct except in the use of pure dialect from tapes that they transcribe), lay-out, make-up, correspondence, art and cover design, and selection of manuscripts from outside poets and writers—to say nothing of related skills such as fund raising, typing, retailing, advertising, and speaking at conferences and public meetings—they learn more about English than from any other curriculum I could devise. Moreover, this curriculum has built-in motivations and immediate and tangible rewards.

The project also has benefits for the community at large. The collection of artifacts, tapes, and photographs is a valuable addition to any community museum. Furthermore, many still culturally distinctive areas, cut off from the main thrust of our country, are also economically and educationally deprived. Articles about local craftsmen and craft cooperatives, to give only one small example, can result in a welcome flow of income from a population grown weary of a plastic world. And the education the students can acquire in the process can be a welcome supplement to their ordinary routine.

And the whole thing doesn't cost that much. In pure business terms, you can get a staggering return from a relatively small investment.

The kid who scorched my lecturn had been trying to tell me something. He and his classmates, through their boredom and restlessness, were sending out distress signals—signals that I came perilously close to ignoring.

It's the same old story. The answer to student boredom and restlessness (manifested in everything from paper airplanes to dope) maybe—just maybe—is not stricter penalties, innumerable suspensions, and bathroom monitors. How many schools (mine included) have dealt with those students that still have fire and spirit, *not* by channeling that fire in constructive, creative directions, but by pouring water on the very flames that could make them great? And it's not *necessarily* that the rules are wrong. It's the arrogant way we tend to enforce them. Until we can *inspire* rather than babysit, we're in big trouble. Don't believe me. Just watch and see what happens. We think drugs and turnover rates and dropouts are a problem now. We haven't seen anything yet.

Foxfire obviously isn't the whole answer. But maybe it's a tiny part of it. If this book is worth anything at all, it's because every piece of it was put together and handled and squeezed and shaped and touched by teenagers.

And it's been a long time since I found a paper airplane under my desk.

Why Won't Teenagers Read?

Lance M. Gentile
Merna M. McMillan

One of the more disconcerting problems facing teachers in the secondary schools today is not only their students' inability to read, but students' general lack of interest, indifference, or sheer rejection of reading. These pupils are asking, "Why read at all?" Frequently a sense of acquiescent numbness overcomes these youngsters when reading assignments are made.

Part of the problem of developing students' interest in reading is a direct result of persistently posing the question, "Why *can't* they read?" Corrective programs have focused on diagnosing deficits and prescribing remediation. Following the medical model of treating the symptoms and not the disease, major efforts are launched to determine the intellectual or physiological basis of a student's reading deficiency. This diagnostic/prescriptive approach is not altogether without success, but it fails drastically to promote an individual's desire to read.

To understand why many teenagers will not read is to take the first

Reprinted by permission from *Journal of Reading* 20:649-54 (May 1977). Copyright © 1977 by International Reading Association.

step toward sound instructional methods and materials. The following list presents ten factors that contribute heavily to this reluctant reader syndrome. These are supplemented with a number of practical instructional alternatives designed for use by the teacher of reading or the content area teacher at the secondary level.

(1) By the time many students reach high school they may equate reading with ridicule, failure, or exclusively school-related tasks. Often these youngsters have never experienced joy in reading.

These students might profit from exposure to a wide variety of reading material, from which they may select or reject on the basis of personal interest. They really will read difficult articles and books with high levels of comprehension and appreciation while rejecting very simple material that bores them. A recent survey at the University of Iowa revealed that most adolescents between fifteen and nineteen prefer:

Science fiction
The supernatural
Mystery and intrigue
Love stories or books dealing with various forms of terminal illness
Factual crime cases

Many of the titles they rated highly were adult best-sellers—*Jaws* (Benchley, 1974), *Eric* (Lund, 1975), *All Things Bright and Beautiful* (Herriot, 1975), and *Sunshine* (Klein, 1975). For the first time in the three-year history of the University of Iowa's "Most Popular Young Adult's Book List," a book of poetry was included—*Poems by Richard Thomas* (1974), television's John Boy of *The Waltons*.

(2) Some pupils are not excited by ideas. Many are driven to experience life directly rather than through reading.

They must understand that this limits their experiences. Adolescents are drawn to a myriad of vicarious experiences through television—reading experiences can be equally rewarding:

Deep sea diving
Piloting or jumping out of an airplane
Becoming a fire fighter, detective, or police officer
Being a jockey or other professional athlete
Sailing around the world
Driving Formula I race cars
Competing in the Olympics
Fighting in a war
Being president or other elected official

The individual's real and vicarious experiences are inextricable and often serve to elevate and intensify one another.

(3) A great number of adolescents do not want to sit, and in some cases are incapable of sitting, for prolonged periods.

Get these pupils out of their seats and involve them in doing something "active" that requires reading. Implement material found in various "how to" sources like *Popular Mechanics, Popular Science, Decorating and Craft Ideas, Favorite Recipes for Home Economics Teachers*. Have youngsters work with short stories: *Teen-Age Tales* (Strang and Roberts, 1954), *Short Story Masterpieces* (Warren and Erskine, 1971), or *Two Minute Mysteries* (Sobal, 1973), and its sequel *More Two Minute Mysteries* (Sobal, 1974).

Other material, easily adapted to classroom dramatizations, role-playing, and pantomime activities, includes:

Teen-Age Ghost Stories (Furman, 1961)
Teen-Age Outer Space Stories (Furman, 1962)
Teen-Age Underwater Adventures (Thomas, 1962)
Teen-Age Suspense Stories (Elam, 1963)
Teen-Age Party Time Stories (Furman, 1966)
Teen-Age Wild Animal Stories (Thomas, 1966)
Teen-Age Secret Agent Stories (Furman, 1970)
Teen-Age Plays for Classroom Reading (Durrell, 1971)
Teen-Age Spy Stories (Furman, 1972)
Teen-Age Mexican Stories (Witton, 1973)

Allow young people opportunities to act out a character role or a specific situation from these narratives. Give them a story to read with an important part missing—with written clues to the precise location of the missing part. Have members of the class assemble recipes for cooking and preparing various "cultural" dishes or home favorites that play up the relationship between their own lives and an out-of-your-seat activity that requires reading.

(4) Adolescence is a time of intense egocentrism. Teenagers are preoccupied with themselves, their problems, families, sexual roles, and material possessions.

During this period of development, youngsters experience tremendous "growing pains" in their effort to come to terms with demands made of them by parents, teachers, and peers. Three sources for appropriate books are:

Books for You (Wilson, 1971). Two thousand titles in forty-five categories and subcategories, including indexes by title and author, and a complete list of the publishers' addresses.

Books, Young People, and Reading Guidance (Pilgrim and Mc-Allister, 1968). This entire work is devoted to reading and adolescence but chapter five contains lists of books that relate directly to the sundry needs of youth. It is an invaluable aid in relating reading experiences to the following teenage problems and concerns:

The need to be like others
The need for emotional independence from adults
The need for wholesome family relationships
The need to learn adult roles
The need for peer status
The need to understand the physical world
The need for success
The need for assuming social responsibility
The need for a philosophy of life
The need for beauty
The need for fun and relaxation

Books and the Teen-Age Reader (Carlsen, 1971), revised and updated, contains all new bibliographies and a special chapter on ethnic literature.

> (5) Many young people demand to be entertained. They have developed little understanding or appreciation of intrinsic rewards, such as the sense of personal accomplishment that comes about through prolonged effort.

These motives leave many teachers and parents at a loss as to why or how reading instruction should be presented. Students' interests in other media cannot be overlooked. Critical reading skills can be developed through them—the same "thinking processes" are required to interpret and analyze a speech delivered by a politician before the television cameras as would be employed to read an account written in the newspaper. Though the viewer has the advantage of watching facial and gesticular movements and responding to the differences in tone and vocal expression, the reader has the opportunity to make up his own mind as to precisely what the candidate "might" have said, as opposed to being told what he really "meant" to say by one of the network's political analysts.

In terms of the number of hours devoted to a particular activity, next to sleep, watching television predominates in a youngster's life. Teenagers should realize how controlled they allow themselves to be by the program schedules of the television industry. Reading offers a personal selection and a variety not available to a captive viewing audience.

> (6) A lot of these students are pressured at home as well as in high school to read! read! read! Persistent stress proves counterproductive.

Parents and teachers are most effective as models. Pressuring anyone to read can lead to a loss of inclination. A graduate student (herself a teacher of reading) testified: "We pressured our younger boy to read and almost turned him against reading altogether. When the pressure was lifted we discovered that Randy, like most teenagers, read what he wanted to read. At present, he's involved with plants and constructing his own greenhouse—his reading interests have been absorbed by botany. Swimming has become a major athletic attraction for him. On weekends he has been teaching several younger children, and he has several books from which he studies the proper techniques for teaching swimming."

(7) Many young people grow up in an atmosphere void of reading material. The "significant people" in their lives may not read or have any appreciation for learning by reading. These values are handed down.

Values can be altered! If reading material is not available and parents do not provide models, the school must serve as the example. Paperback books, newspapers, comic books, magazines are essential: *Newsweek, People, Time, Horse and Rider, National Geographic, National Geographic World, Field and Stream, Sports Illustrated, Outdoor Life, Seventeen, Glamour, Vogue, Woman's Day, Ms., Motorcycle World, Hot Rod, Reader's Digest, Mad, National Lampoon.* These "soft" materials should be available to students on a check out basis, even to take home and share with the family.

(8) Reading may be considered an "antisocial" activity.

Because most teenagers seek peer approval, they sometimes forego their own individual needs and interests in an effort to become part of the "in" crowd. Group reading activities should emphasize interaction and discussion. There is tremendous potential for growth and development through the sharing of ideas and experiences with the teacher and other members of the class. Material can be adapted to include group practice in word recognition, comprehension, and critical reading activities.

By involving himself or herself in these group activities and by reading to the class, the reading teacher underscores the importance and the beauty of reading. Too much emphasis on programmed reading materials or "individual" work in reading tends to depersonalize it.

(9) Many classroom texts and supplementary reading materials are dull to look at.

If texts are not illustrated or designed to attract the reader, young people can collect pictures and photographs or create drawings of their own. They can fashion collages to represent specific concepts presented in the text. Ask the students to pictorialize poetry, modern songs, short stories, or television programs and motion pictures.

Ask the group to develop an ideal mini-text highlighting a particular unit, including varied typographical styles and illustrations. As an example, the class might decide to underline the main idea(s) in red or italicize them. The significant or subordinate details might appear in various colored type. Abstract or difficult vocabulary could be defined in page margins.

Designing multicolored charts and graphs would help students understand technical data. Pictures or illustrations ought to be interspersed throughout the text's pages or regularly presented among the printed subdivisions.

(10) Some adolescents view reading as a part of the adult world and automatically reject it.

Give students many opportunities to develop materials of their own. Encourage them to create and dramatize plays based on their personal experiences. Urging them to pantomime short stories, songs, or literary articles and commentaries forces them to interpret the material with a personal touch. Plans might be developed to direct their own television and radio broadcasts (including sound effects and background music). Episodes might consist of some of their current favorites such as "Welcome Back, Kotter," "Sanford and Son," or "Happy Days." They can be stimulated to write their own newspapers or news articles, to originate a magazine, or to produce humorous material such as cartoons or comics detailing ludicrous events and utilizing witty or cant language.

A wide range of students reject reading because of these ten factors as well as because of visual, auditory, or physiological disorders that create discomfort when they try to read. An ideal program must include what we know about human learning and habit formation. A total effort in the classroom is needed to provide pupils with reading experiences that fully engage their emotions as well as their intellects. Hard evidence must be presented to youth that reading is not something only certain people can do or can enjoy doing.

REFERENCES

Benchley, Peter. *Jaws*. New York: Doubleday, 1974.

Carlsen, G. Robert. *Books and the Teen-Age Reader*. 2nd rev. ed. New York: Harper, 1980.

Dreikurs, Rudolph; Grunwald, Bernice B.; and Pepper, Floyd C. *Maintaining Sanity in the Classroom*. New York: Harper, 1971.

Durrell, Donald D., and Crossley, Alice B. *Teen-Age Plays for Classroom Reading*. Boston: Plays, Inc., 1971.

Elam, Richard M. *Teen-Age Suspense Stories*. Mt. Vernon, N.Y.: Lantern Pr., 1963.

Fader, Daniel N. *The New Hooked on Books*. New York: Putnam, 1977.

Furman, Abraham L. *Teen-Age Ghost Stories*. Mt. Vernon, N.Y.: Lantern Pr., 1961.
——. *Teen-Age Outer Space Stories*. Mt. Vernon, N.Y.: Lantern Pr., 1962.
——. *Teen-Age Party Time Stories*. Mt. Vernon, N.Y.: Lantern Pr., 1966.
——. *Teen-Age Secret Agent Stories*. Mt. Vernon, N.Y.: Lantern Pr., 1970.
——. *Teen-Age Spy Stories*. Mt. Vernon, N.Y.: Lantern Pr., 1972.
Herriot, James. *All Things Bright and Beautiful*. New York: Bantam, 1975.
Klein, Norma. *Sunshine*. New York: Holt, 1975.
Lund, Doris. *Eric*. New York: Dell, 1975.
Pilgrim, Geneva H., and McAllister, Mariana K. *Books, Young People and Reading Guidance*. New York: Harper, 1968.
Sobal, Donald. *Two Minute Mysteries*. New York: Scholastic, 1973.
——. *More Two Minute Mysteries*. New York: Scholastic, 1974.
Strang, Ruth and Roberts, R. *Teen-Age Tales*. Lexington, MA.: Heath, 1954.
Thomas, P. *Teen-Age Underwater Adventures*. Mt. Vernon, N.Y.: Lantern Pr., 1962.
——. *Teen-Age Wild Animal Stories*. Mt. Vernon, N.Y.: Lantern Pr., 1966.
Thomas, Richard. *Poems by Richard Thomas*. New York: Avon, 1974.
Vidal, Gore. *A Novel: 1876*. New York: Random, 1976.
Warren, Robert P. and Erskine, Albert. *Short Story Masterpieces*. New York: Dell, 1971.
Wilson, Jean A. *Books for You*. New York: Pocket Books, 1971.
Witton, Dorothy. *Teen-Age Mexican Stories*. Mt. Vernon, N.Y.: Lantern Pr., 1973.

Humor and the Reading Program

Lance M. Gentile
Merna M. McMillan

A brief glance at the history of the United States reveals a nation born of revolution and violence. Unfortunately, not only do these elements continue to defile life in this country, but today a person must cope with the innumerable problems of a highly technological and "pressure packed" environment. Therefore, in addition to acquiring specific skills to earn a living, it is vital that people develop a sense of humor to sustain them in times of stress. Durrell (1956, p. 320) stated:

Reprinted by permission of the authors and publisher from *Journal of Reading* 21:343-49 (Jan. 1978). Copyright © 1978 by the International Reading Association.

Humor is a highly important characteristic of the American tradition and an extremely useful part of social intercourse. It provides balance, encourages cooperation, reduces emotional pressure, relieves dullness and opens conversation.

The current "back to basics" movement and mounting concern about the reading difficulties of so many young people portend an overly serious direction in education. While school, and the reading program in particular, provide ideal opportunities to deal with humorous or witty material, quite often this aspect is overlooked or viewed as being "out of place" in the standard curriculum. Many individuals contend that school is a place where people prepare to make a living rather than a life.

Laughter and mirth are more visible among young people away from the classroom. Hallways, gymnasiums, playgrounds, restrooms, and cafeterias are the "acceptable" places to show emotion, but a return to the pupil's desk from any of these areas is generally a signal to "straighten up."

In his book, *The Atrocity of Education,* Arthur Pearl (1972) deplored the lack of humor and affect in most of what students are asked to read. In particular he criticized readings describing work functions for their gross distortions. Pearl said (pp. 69-71):

> The reader is unable to share the humor—or the heartache—that is part of all work activities. There is an absence of detail. No children's book writer of today is doing for the truck-driver or any other occupation what Mark Twain did in the nineteenth century for the riverboat pilot.

Pearl cited a section from Twain's *Life on the Mississippi* detailing the manner in which a pilot directed landsmen in moving a gangplank. This passage is so vivid, it could be reenacted as a play, or students might model its style, language, or characterization through role-playing activities. Mark Twain's writing comes alive; it has substance, whereas so much of what is written for today's students is contrived. Small wonder most youngsters are not excited or "turned on" by their reading experiences and greatly prefer watching endless hours of violent television.

In earlier years television accentuated humor and comedy through shows like Sid Ceasar and Imogene Coca's "Your Show of Shows," "The Colgate Comedy Hour," Jackie Gleason's "Cavalcade of Stars," Art Linkletter's "People Are Funny," and so on. Comedians such as Danny Thomas, Red Buttons, Jack Benny, George Gobel, and George Burns and Gracie Allen dominated prime time viewing.

Today these programs and people have been replaced by "cops and robbers" series whose themes are violence, perversion, and emotional trauma. This damaging influence may well contribute to an absence of humor and lightheartedness among young people.

Corcoran (1976, p.22) described a week-long experience at the International Platform Association's Convention in Washington, D.C., where he observed a teenagers' speech contest:

> It has been a solemn performance all around. When William Howard Taft III comes forward to present the winner's trophy, he appears stunned. He turns to the contestants and says: "I've never heard such seriousness from those so young. I just hope they cheer up as life goes forward." He asks the teens, who are now fidgeting nervously, "I wonder if there are any light stories each of you could tell?" Silence and uncomprehending glances. "Is there *one* light story among you?" More silence. "I've proved my point," Taft sighs.

It is essential that reading programs provide ample opportunities for students to experience life's whimsical, preposterous, zany, and nonsensical characters and events. For purposes of inner harmony and peace, no single human phenomenon is as healthy, spontaneous, honest, and soothing as laughter.

Notwithstanding the salubrious side effects of funny material, reading at this level often demands critical thinking and great insight. The development of the latter constitutes one of the most crucial comprehension skills. It affords individuals a much purer and more amusing view of themselves and their surroundings. Out of the overflow of good humor and comedy comes a healthy sense of proportion or sanity. People who have balanced their personal qualities and fondest values readily perceive their incongruities and absurdities. Allport (1961, p. 292) noted:

> Perhaps the most striking correlate of insight is the sense of humor. In one unpublished study where subjects rated one another on a large number of traits, the correlation between ratings on insight and humor turned out to be .88. Such a high coefficient means either that personalities with marked insight are also high in humor, or else that the raters were not able to distinguish between the two qualities. In either case the result is important.

A sense of humor develops among people in rather distinct stages. Its growth is dependent on age and experience. Gessell, Ilg, and Ames (1956, pp. 343-46) summarized this development from 10 years of age and above. An awareness of this successive progression will help the reading teacher provide materials and design humorously appealing experiences for each age group. For each phase we provide a partial bibliography as a starter.

Age 10: Humor is of the literal or obvious type and quite often not funny to adults. Some of it is slapstick, but much of it is a reaction to anything unexpected.

TRADE MATERIALS

Alexander, Lloyd. *The Marvelous Misadventures of Sebastian.* New York, N.Y.: Dutton, 1970.

Brewton, Sara and John Brewton. *Laughable Limericks.* New York, N.Y.: Crowell, 1965.

Fast, Howard. *Tony and the Wonderful Door.* New York, N.Y.: Knopf, 1968.

Hoke, Helen. *Jokes, Jokes, Jokes.* New York, N.Y.: Grolier, 1963.

Masin, Herman. *For Laughing Out Loud.* Englewood Cliffs, N.J.: Scholastic Book Services, 1974.

Wilson, Dagmar. *Jokes, Riddles, and Funny Stories.* New York, N.Y.: Grosset & Dunlap, 1959.

COMICS AND CARTOONS

Aragones, Sergio. *Mad as the Devil.* New York, N.Y.: Warner Books, 1975; *Mad about Mad.* New York, N.Y.: New American Library, 1970.

Archie Comics Ed. *Everything's Archie.* New York, N.Y.: Bantam Books, 1972.

Debartolo, Dick. *Mad Look at Old Movies.* New York, N.Y.: Warner Books, 1973.

Ketcham, Hank. *Dennis the Menace: Short Swinger,* 1976; *Dennis the Menace: Who Me?,* 1976. New York, N.Y.: Fawcett World Library.

Mad Libs, no. 1, 1958; no. 5, 1968; no. 6, 1970; no. 7, 1974. Los Angeles, Calif.: Price/Stern/Sloan.

Schulz, Charles. *Peanuts,* 1952; *Peanuts Classics,* 1970. New York, N.Y.: Holt, Rinehart & Winston.

Walker, Mort. *Beetle Bailey #9: Shape Up or Ship Out.* New York, N.Y.: Grossett & Dunlap, 1974.

Age 11: Humor is "corny" and often smutty, with much laughing at misbehavior and minor accidents. The child can understand a little adult humor, but his/her own humor is of a different type and still based at a literal, concrete level.

TRADE MATERIALS

Clark, David. *Jokes, Puns, and Riddles.* New York, N.Y.: Doubleday, 1968.

Cole, William. *Humorous Poetry for Children.* Cleveland, Ohio: Collins-World, 1955.

Fox, Sonny. *Jokes and How to Tell Them.* New York, N.Y.: Putnam, 1965.

Haskins, James. *Jokes from Black Folks.* New York, N.Y.: Doubleday, 1973.

Malone, Mary. *Here's Howie.* New York, N.Y.: Dodd, 1962.

Preston, Edna. *Barrel of Chuckles,* 1972; *Barrel of Fun,* 1973; *Barrel of Laughs,* 1974. Englewood Cliffs, N.J.: Scholastic Book Services.

COMICS AND CARTOONS

Debartolo, D. and J. Torres. *Mad Look at TV.* New York, N.Y.: Warner Books, 1974.

Ketcham, Hank. *Dennis the Menace: Just for Fun.* New York, N.Y.: Faw-
cett World Library, 1976.
Mad Magazine Ed. *Mad at You.* New York, N.Y.: Warner Books, 1975.
Martin, Don. *Mad Adventures of Captain Klutz.* New York, N.Y.: New
American Library, 1974.
Schulz, Charles. *Peanuts Revisited,* 1970. New York, N.Y.: Holt, Rinehart
& Winston. *Snoopy and His Sopwith Camel,* 1974; *Snoopy and the Red
Baron,* 1976. New York, N.Y.: Fawcett World Library.
The World's Worst Knock-Knock Jokes, 1974; . . . *Doctor Jokes,* 1974; . . .
Riddles, 1974; . . . *Jokes,* 1974; . . . *Moron Jokes,* 1974; . . . *Monster
Jokes,* 1974; . . . *Psychiatrist Jokes,* 1974; . . . *Golf Jokes,* 1974. Los
Angeles, Calif.: Price/Stern/Sloan.

Age 12: This stage is marked by many practical jokes of an obvious
kind, teasing and some exchange of banter with adults.

TRADE MATERIALS

Adler, Bill. *Hip Kids' Letters from Camp.* New York, N.Y.: New American
Library, 1973.
Byfield, Barbara. *Book of Weird.* New York, N.Y.: Doubleday, 1973.
Cahn, Victor. *Disrespectful Dictionary.* Los Angeles, Calif.: Price/Stern/
Sloan, 1974.
Gerles, Bill. *Jokes, Riddles and Other Funny Things.* New York, N.Y.: Western
Publications, 1975.
Insult Dictionary: How to Snarl Back in Five Languages. Los Angeles, Calif.:
Price/Stern/Sloan, 1970.
Lewis, George. *Dictionary of Bloopers and Boners.* Englewood Cliffs, N.J.:
Scholastic Book Services, 1974.
Roylance, William. *Complete Book of Insults, Boasts and Riddles.* Engle-
wood Cliffs, N.J.: Prentice-Hall, 1970.

COMICS AND CARTOONS

Jacobs, F. and B. Richard. *Mad about Sports.* New York, N.Y.: Warner
Books, 1972.
Jaffee, Al. *Mad Book of Magic and Other Dirty Tricks.* New York, N.Y.:
New American Library, 1970.
Lear, Ed. *Ed Lear's Nonsense Coloring Book.* New York, N.Y.: Dover, 1971.
Mad Magazine Ed. *Mad Strikes Back.* New York, N.Y.: Ballantine, 1975.
Prohias, Antonio. *Fourth Mad Declassified Papers on Spy vs. Spy.* New York,
N.Y.: Warner Books, 1974.
Schulz, Charles. *Snoopy,* 1958; *Peanuts Every Sunday,* 1961. New York,
N.Y.: Holt, Rinehart & Winston.

Age 13: Humor is rather less obvious and more reserved than at
earlier or later stages; the beginnings of sarcasm mark this stage of
development.

Trade Materials

Anobile, Richard. *Drat: W.C. Fields.* New York, N.Y.: New American Library, 1973.

Blair, Dike. *Books and Bedlam.* Middlebury, Vt.: Vermont Books, 1962.

Garagiola, Joe. *Baseball is a Funny Game.* New York, N.Y.: Bantam, 1974.

Heller, Jack. *Jokesmith's Jubilee.* New York, N.Y.: Scholastic Book Services, 1971.

Kearne, Bill. *Just in Pun.* New York, N.Y.: Scholastic Book Services, 1969.

Lauber, Pat. *Jokes and More Jokes.* New York, N.Y.: Scholastic Book Services, 1967.

Lewis, Martin. *The Quotations of W.C. Fields.* New York, N.Y.: Drake, 1976.

Masin, Herman. *Baseball Laughs.* Englewood Cliffs, N.J.: Scholastic Book Services, 1969.

Comics and Cartoons

Brandel, Max. *Mad Book of Word Power.* New York, N.Y.: Warner Books, 1976.

Friedman, Les. *Eggbert: The Fun Born,* 1976; *Belly Laughs,* 1975; *Funny Side Up,* 1975. New York, N.Y.: Pocket Books.

Ketcham, Hank. *Dennis the Menace: Dennis Power,* 1975; *Dennis the Menace: Where the Action Is,* 1975. New York, N.Y.: Fawcett World Library.

Lariar, Lawrence. *The Teen-Scene.* New York, N.Y.: Dodd, 1966.

Mad Magazine Ed. *Fighting Mad,* 1974; *Boiling Mad,* 1973. New York, N.Y.: Warner Books.

Walker, Mort. *Beetle Bailey #1: Beetle Bailey,* 1968; *Beetle Bailey #4,* 1970; *Beetle Bailey #7,* 1973; *Beetle Bailey #11,* 1975. New York, N.Y.: Grossett & Dunlap.

Age 14: Humor is used against parents or others in authority; smutty jokes among members of one's own sex and dislike of parents' jokes are characteristic of this age group.

Trade Materials·

Armour, Richard. *It All Started with Columbus,* 1976; . . . *with Eve,* 1963; . . . *with Europa,* 1955; . . . *with Hippocrates,* 1966; . . . *with Freshman English,* 1973; . . . *with Marx,* 1958; . . . *with Stones and Clubs,* 1967; *Golf is a Four-Letter Word,* 1964. New York, N.Y.: McGraw-Hill.

Behrens, Frank. *Dante's Infernal Guide to Your School.* New York, N.Y.: Simon & Schuster, 1971.

Critchfield, J. and J. Hopkins. *You Were Born on a Rotten Day.* Los Angeles, Calif.: Price/Stern/Sloan, 1975.

Everhart, Jim. *The Illustrated Texas Dictionary of the English Language,* vols. 1, 2, 3, 4. Lincoln, Neb.: Cliff's Notes, 1973.

Everhart, Jim. *CB Language.* Lincoln, Neb.: Centennial Press, 1976.

Ferrell, T. *Sneaky Feats,* 1975; *More Sneaky Feats,* 1976. Mission, Kan.:
Sheed & Ward.
Fidell, Jeanette. *Jokes, Jokes, Jokes.* New York, N.Y.: Scholastic Book
Services, 1976.

COMICS AND CARTOONS

Schulz, Charles. *Peanuts Double,* vol. 1 and 2, 1976; *Peanuts for Everybody:
Selected Cartoons,* 1975. New York, N.Y.: Fawcett World Library. *Pea-
nuts Jubilee: My Life and Art with Charlie Brown,* 1976. New York,
N.Y.: Ballantine Books.

Age 15: Evident at this stage are the beginnings of the ability to laugh
at oneself and to see something funny when teased or "kidded." Also
emerging at this time is the understanding of irony as a form of humor.

TRADE MATERIALS

Buchwald, Art. *I Never Danced at the White House.* New York, N.Y.: Faw-
cett World Library, 1976.
Elliott, B. and R. Goulding. *Write If You Get Work: The Best of Bob and
Ray.* New York, N.Y.: Random House, 1975.
Harron, D. *K.O.R.N. Allmynack.* Buffalo, N.Y.: Gage Publications, 1976.
McGeachy, D. P. *Gospel According to Andy Capp.* Atlanta, Ga.: John Knox
Press, 1973.
Stokes, Jack. *Mind Your A's and Q's: Useless Questions to Dumb Answers.*
Garden City, N.Y.: Doubleday, 1977.
Wilde, Larry. *The Official Democrat/Republican Joke Book.* New York,
N.Y.: Pinnacle Books, 1976.
Wood, Rob. *The Book of Blunders.* Kansas City, Mo.: Hallmark Cards, Inc.,
1974.

COMICS AND CARTOONS

Hart, Johnny. *B.C.: Big Wheel,* 1976; *B.C.: Dip in Road,* 1976; *B.C.: Great
Zot I'm Beautiful,* 1976; *B.C.: It's a Funny World,* 1976. New York,
N.Y.: Fawcett World Library.
Kelley, Walt. *Pogo's Body Politic,* 1976; *Pogo Revisited,* 1974. New York,
N.Y.: Simon & Schuster.
Parker, Brant and Johnny Hart. *Wizard of Id: "Long Live the King,"* 1975;
Wizard of Id: No. 8, 1976. New York, N.Y.: Fawcett World Library.
Schulz, Charles. *Peanuts for Everybody.* New York, N.Y.: Fawcett World
Library, 1975.

Age 16 and above: Ability to understand more subtle forms of humor,
such as satire, for example, participation in adult jokes, and the beginnings of spontaneous humor on an adult level mark this stage of
development.

TRADE MATERIALS

Adler, Bill. *How to Be Funny in Your Own Lifetime*. Chicago, Ill.: Playboy Press, 1973.

Busch, Wilhelm. *Bushel of Merry Thoughts,* W.H. Rogers, trans. New York, N.Y.: Dover Publications, 1971.

Hughes, Langston. *Book of Negro Humor*. New York, N.Y.: Dodd, 1965.

Johnson, Charles. *Black Humor*. Chicago, Ill.: Johnson Publications, 1970.

McKenzie, E.C. *Eighteen Hundred Quippable Quotes*. Grand Rapids, Iowa: Baker Books, 1973.

Nash, Ogden. *I Couldn't Help Laughing*. Philadelphia, Pa.: Lippincott, 1957.

Reit, Seymour, ed. *America Laughs: A Treasury of Great Humor*. New York, N.Y.: Crowell-Collier Press, 1966.

Rosenberg, Marvin, ed. *The Best Cartoons from Punch*. New York, N.Y.: Simon & Schuster, 1952.

Schirmer, Mathilda. *The Bedside Book of Humor*. Chicago, Ill.; People's Book Club, 1948.

Scoggin, Margaret. *More Chucklebait*. New York, N.Y.: Knopf, 1949.

Untermeyer, Louis. *Treasury of Great Humor*. New York, N.Y.: McGraw-Hill, 1972.

MAGAZINES (samples sent on request)

Dublin Opinion: The National Humorous Journal of Ireland, Gordon Clark, ed. First published in 1922. Dublin Opinion Ltd., 193 Pearse St., Dublin, L, Ireland.

Funny Funny World, Martin A. Ragaway, ed. First published in 1971. 407 Commercial Center St., Beverly Hills, Calif. 90201.

Harvard Lampoon, James H. Siegelman, ed. First published in 1876. 44 Bow St., Cambridge, Mass. 02138.

Journal of Irreproducible Results, Alexander Kohn, ed. First published in 1955. Society for Basic Irreproducible Research, Box 234, Chicago Heights, Ill. 60411.

Mad, William Gaines and Albert B. Feldstein, eds. First published in 1953. E.C. Publications, Inc., 485 Madison Avenue, New York, N.Y. 10022

National Lampoon, Douglas C. Kenney, ed. First published in 1970. Twentieth Century Publications, 635 Madison Avenue, New York, N.Y. 10022.

Private Eye. Richard Ingrams, ed. First published in 1961. Pressdam Ltd., 34 Greek St., London W1, England.

Worm Runner's Digest and Journal of Biological Psychology, James V. McConnel, ed. First published in 1959. Box 644, Ann Arbor, Mich. 48107.

REFERENCES

Allport, G. W. *Pattern and Growth in Personality*. New York: Holt, 1961.

Corcoran, John H., Jr. "At Last a (Slim) Chance to Make the Big-Time." *The National Observer* (Oct. 23, 1976), p.22.

Durrell, Donald D. *Improving Reading Instruction*. New York: Harcourt, 1956.

Gessell, A.; Ilg, F. L.; and Ames, L. B. *Youth: The Years from Ten to Sixteen.* New York: Harper, 1956.
Pearl, Arthur. *The Atrocity of Education.* New York: Dutton, 1972.

Identifying High Interest/Low Reading Level Books

Barbara S. Bates

"How can you keep putting out easy-to-read books?" a librarian asked an editor at the 1977 ALA Conference in Detroit. "You're pandering to lazy readers. Soon we'll have no real literature any more!" Such a reaction reflects a panicky fear that familiar literary standards may be changing for the worse.

But what happens to new readers who have struggled through a long and painful process of diagnosis and special instruction to learn a skill most of their classmates acquired more easily and much earlier? No skill, from guitar playing to reading, can be maintained without practice. But older students just beginning to read have been hurt by constant failure, by teasing and rejection, by the very effort that reading demands. Martin Haberman, in his article "The Reading Movement Has Gone Too Far," says, "The overemphasis on formal reading instruction is turning large numbers off reading. They are not learning to love literature."[1]

As the clamor for easy reading material grows, librarians need to look at new standards and adopt creative approaches to reading. Judith Goldberger of *Booklist* spelled out the first boundaries when she divided easier reading books into three distinct categories—*beginning-to-read* books: readable at the earliest elementary school level; *easy-to-read* books: slightly more difficult than beginning-to-read books and geared toward early learning experiences, with special attention to slow learners; and *high interest/low-reading level* (HILRL) books: designed for or useful to reluctant, retarded, or problem readers among older students who need books with reading levels below their interest levels.[2]

Within the last two decades publishers have contributed some excellent books in the first two categories but it is the third category, HILRL

Reprinted by permission of the author from *School Library Journal* 24:19-21 (Nov. 1977). R. R. Bowker Company/A Xerox Corporation.

books, that poses a problem. Goldberger pleads, "There is a crying need for all [types of] materials written three or more reading levels below interest level."[3] I suggest that a book should not be recommended for purchase as an HILRL book unless this three-year divergence of reading level and interest level is present and valid.

Two subjective tests will help reviewers and librarians distinguish easy-to-read literature from "written-to-assignment, composed-by-formula" kinds of writing. First, do you yourself find the book gripping and memorable—enjoyable to read? Second, does it read aloud well? A good reviewer can sense creativity, especially in beginning-to-read and easy-to-read books. But, finding books of value for beginning readers who are age eleven or older presents a real problem.

George D. Spache states, "Books that are high in interest may be reacted to as appropriate in difficulty even though they are actually two or more grade levels above the pupils' reading levels. At the same time, books are often rated by children as too hard even though below the pupil's reading level when interest is low."[4]

Editors of HILRL books in series tend to choose subject matter of interest to readers who are economically or socially disadvantaged or of educational value to these readers. Yet, Josette Frank reminds us that there is a "vast group of children whose interests and sophistication outrun their reading ability."[5]

More often than not, book editors who have worked to help produce novels and nonfiction that are attractive to older new readers find that (unless the books are blatantly labeled as HILRL's) reviewers dismiss them as "too easy" or "too simplistic," or as "deadlevel storytelling." Rather than work at the early identification of books that may prove satisfying for the reading levels attained by young teens who have had reading problems, reviewers tend to rush past some of the obvious signals that indicate books with potential for recommendation to these readers. This is as true for review agencies serving libraries as it is for review columns in the general press, despite the fact that librarians serving young teens have been calling for just such books to be published in greater numbers!

Instead, what has happened is that HILRL books are usually discovered by the problem readers themselves. After librarians and teachers have observed this phenomenon, only then are the books recognized for their value to those youngsters with reading difficulties.

In sharp contrast, the early identification of good books to call to the attention of youngsters reading at their own grade levels or beyond is considered a matter of professional skill.

To speed the process of early identification of good HILRL books, what's needed is a clear and agreed upon set of criteria for spotting—in advance of experience with the ultimate audience—books with possibilities for HILRL youngsters.

From my discussions with teachers, librarians, writers, and other book editors concerned about presenting a variety of reading material for young people who are still in the process of learning to read, as well as from my analysis of the studies of experts on remedial reading, the following criteria emerge for identifying some of the factors common to HILRL books that provide satisfying reading experiences for older new readers.

Appearance

1. Pocket-size paperbacks are the least formidable and most congenial to all teenage readers, but library hardbacks are still the forerunners of paperback titles and creative librarians can make these attractive too.
2. The book must look thin or "easy" but not babyish. Those readers who are just beginning to select their own books will choose one that looks short.

Phyliss Wood, working with adolescents in "Last Chance High" reading lab in south San Francisco, discovered that if a book is interesting enough to hook new readers and easy enough for them to read, they will not want it to end too soon. Eleanor Scott, reading specialist in the Lansdowne-Aldan school system outside of Philadelphia, reports that new readers like short stories, but are bewildered by collections that do not have distinct divisions between stories. Once readers have become familiar with one subject or set of characters they are bewildered when suddenly confronted with different characters.

3. Oversize pages, a photo format, and a "reading series" look may be acceptable in remedial reading classrooms, but not for new readers using library collections.
4. The appearance of a page can look easy without looking babyish, as editors of adult "self-improvement" books have found in designing them to seem accessible to adults. The following design elements are recommended:

Wide margins.

Extra leading (space) between lines—but not so much as to make eye motions from line to line difficult.

Short chapters—with a lot of space at beginning and end, and/or frequent "breaks" or space gaps dividing the text into sections. These must come at logical pauses in the story, as at the end of a scene, or when time or place changes. In nonfiction, such breaks can be made with subheads or photos. But subheads under subheads are confusing for readers who are reading through books of their own choice for the first time. Breaking up the text into small segments of type provides frequent places to pause along with an accompanying sense of achievement.

Type style that looks easy to read—type must be black, crisp and clean. The gray look of much offset printing is a deterrent. Print must not be oversized or babyish. (HILRL readers scorn books designed for readers with sight problems.) An easy look creates a good psychological effect. Properly chosen 11-point type with optimum word and line spacing may appear much more readable than a 12-point type with lines too close together or words that are not well spaced.

Paper must be of good quality—opaque enough to prevent "see-through." Print or pictures that show through from the back of the page confuse and distract readers besides creating a negative impression on tentative browsers. Off-white or light cream seem pleasantest to most readers. Strong buff can make a book look "old." A sharp contrast between type and page increases reading difficulty, as does paper with a high-glare finish.

Content: Fiction

Narrative line. Should be direct and simple and events should be related in chronological order. Flashbacks, stories within stories, and incidents reported by letter or conversation make plots hard to follow. In fiction, the time span should be brief—a day, a week, or at most a year—so that transitions, time gaps, and summarizing do not add to readers' problems.

Story line. Best developed mainly through dialogue and action. Moving readers forward with conversations and actions creates a participatory and visual appeal. The technique is almost that of a television script. Readers are on stage with the characters. Writers must have the skill to set scenes, moods, and backgrounds of characters by weaving some deftly chosen words and phrases into the action and dialogue, and should not indulge in chunks of description.

Point of view. Should follow one person only, seeing everything through his or her eyes. Multiple or shifting points of view create comprehension blocks and prevent the satisfaction of reader identification with the main character.

Characters. Should be few and strongly identified. Creative writers characterize through suggestion and selectivity of detail rather than complexity of analysis and dense description. Characters become real through their speech and actions, not by what the author says about them.

Cast. Should include only the persons whom the main character meets face-to-face and who are important to him. Sketching in the paperboy, school classmates, the people on the street and in stores only confuses those readers who have trouble building images out of words and phrases.

Situations. Should be familiar to the readers or easy for them to project themselves into. An historical tale or an Eskimo adventure needs uncommon immediacy to make it accessible to new readers.

Emotional appeal. A prime element for youngsters who are discovering books. Involve them deeply, in a familiar or anticipated crisis—rejection, fear, loss of a loved person, and the printed page comes alive for them.

Mood. Important to tentative readers. If they have just read a book that ends on a positive, reassuring note, they are more likely to move on to another. Problems and failures may be the meat of the story, but an upbeat ending is important to young people who have already had a lifetime of unhappy experiences with trying to learn to read.

A good opening sentence. Page one can make or break a book. Dubious readers must be plunged immediately and irretrievably into a story. There must be a sense of stepping right into someone's life and being grabbed by his or her concerns.

Content: Nonfiction

Scope. The subject should be carefully limited to allow thorough description and explanation.

Organization. Direct and progressive presentation is easiest to follow. Referring backward or forward to facts in the text adds problems. Each item or point should be made clear by using familiar terms or comparisons with familiar objects, or by combining clear and simple concepts. Summarizing and putting new information into perspective helps.

Technique. Includes the use of writing devices that add life and color to facts—enumeration, anecdote, example, summary, personalization, comparison. The books of Jeanne Bendick are an excellent example of writing that makes facts come alive.

Illustration. Should be copious and well distributed throughout the text to supplement it. Pictures should be used to tempt readers into the text rather than as devices for telling the story independently as a substitute for reading. Fans of the *National Geographic* take note! Visual appeal goes a long way toward "selling" a simple nonfiction book and making the contents seem real and relevant. Photography is most appealing to older children and helps avoid the "picture-book look." *Underground* and other books by David Macaulay are among the notable exceptions because his drawings look adult.

Subject matter. How-to ideas, sports, current biography, popular subjects appearing on television or in the news appeal to slow readers. Physical achievement is often a compensation for academic failure. Books on topics that appeal to older readers such as body building and individual sports (white-water canoeing, riding, and golf) seem to be losing out to team and spectator sports in the easy-to-read arena.

Style

Vocabulary should be simple. [Words should be] used naturally rather than tailored to a word list. The concrete word is always preferable to the abstract, the specific to the general. Reader interest and motivation have a strong effect on comprehension. A story about sports car racing may be sprinkled with multisyllabic automotive words but readers who are turned on to auto mechanics already know these terms by ear and probably have seen them on labels and directions. They may be able to assimilate the difficult words with ease, though a reading formula might grade the book well above their customary reading level. An occasional long word that is familiar keeps readers stretching and makes a book seem adult.

Sentences should vary in length. They should not run over two and a half printed lines. Simplicity of grammatical construction is best. Inversions are mannered and confusing ("Down the street he hurried" has no advantage over "He hurried down the street," except to show an inept writer struggling for variety). Subordinate clauses and phrases ought not to be piled one on another.

Paragraphs need to be short. [They should be] consistent with thought units. Terse, natural dialogue gives an open, easy look to the text.

Concepts must be simple. Avoid allegory and symbolism. Figures of speech are acceptable if they are specific and concrete. Similes are easier to comprehend than metaphors and other stylistic devices.

Sensory appeal is important. Descriptions of smells and tastes, textures, sounds, and colors create an impression of reality.

Good rhythm and pace. These can be attained with the simplest structure and vocabulary, as poets and skilled prose writers show us. But pace should be appropriate to content. The slow cadence and poetic mood that suits a nature scene or a love scene is not the right literary style for a motorcycle race, which demands abrupt, choppy, fast-paced combinations of words.

The presence of any or even all of these factors cannot guarantee a book's success with individual youngsters who have a history of difficulties in reading anymore than the agreement of adults about the outstanding qualities of an award-winning children's book can guarantee the popularity of that book with all children. However, if these factors are employed with regularity by reviewers and selectors, I believe that many more and much better HILRL books will be readily available to the young people who need such books to help them become readers.

The highest accolade an HILRL book can receive is to be shared eagerly by problem readers and their reading friends. Books that are accessible to slow readers and just as absorbing for proficient readers have claim to being classified as literature.

The challenge is clear. Writers, publishers, editors, and librarians must provide books for turned-off or reluctant older readers who are searching for books on their level—we may yet turn them into enthusiastic readers.

Notes

1. Martin Haberman, "The Reading Movement Has Gone Too Far," *Today's Education* 65:38 (Mar.-Apr. 1976).
2. Judith M. Goldberger, "Easy to Read: Hard to Review," *Booklist:* 73:480 (Nov. 15, 1976).
3. Ibid., p.481.
4. George D. Spache, *Good Reading for Poor Readers* (Rev. ed.; New Canaan, Conn.: Garrard, 1974), p.2.
5. Josette Frank, *Your Children's Reading Today* (New York: Doubleday, 1969), p.50.

Booktalking: You Can Do It

Mary K. Chelton

Skill in booktalking remains one of the most valuable promotional devices YA librarians can have at hand to interest teenagers in the library. Once acquired, this skill can be adapted to floor work with individual readers, radio spots, booklist annotations, and class visits in the library or in the classroom. It can be combined with slide-tape, film, or musical presentations, and with outreach skills. Its limitations are set by YA librarians who either refuse to learn the technique, have never learned it (and judge it valueless even after learning it), or who remain inflexible in chosen methods of doing it. The best young adult librarians I have known, whether they see their book selection role as one of expanding horizons and literary tastes or of just giving kids what they want (and most of us usually fall somewhere in between), have a "hidden agenda" for promoting the love of reading for pleasure, and have found booktalks a superb way of doing that.

It should be said here that booktalking skills do not preempt professional abilities in programming, information and referral, traditional reference work, audiovisual collection building, or community outreach, as is often unjustly assumed of the YA specialty. It is my contention, however, that the public still assumes that libraries deal in books and our nonbook related skills and materials will win us no friends or financial support for other information or enrichment media unless librarians do traditional reader's advisory work very well.

Reprinted by permission of the author from *School Library Journal* 22:39-43 (Apr. 1976). R. R. Bowker Company/A Xerox Corp.

In my opinion, the two simplest definitions of booktalks are Amelia Munson's, "The booktalk falls into place between storytelling and book reviewing, partakes of both and is unlike either," taken from *An Ample Field* (American Library Assn., 1950); the other is my own "A booktalk is a formal or informal presentation about a book or group of books designed to entice the listener into reading them."

Elaine Simpson, in her YA course at Rutgers, describes a booktalk as "That part of a librarian's visit to a classroom or during a class visit to the library devoted to presenting two or more books to the group. It is an art and a device by which the librarian tries to interest young people in all books in general and in some books in particular through a talk so carefully prepared as to seem spontaneous, in which he or she gives the subject, the flavor, and the appeal of each book presented." Simpson adds, "Indirectly through book talks we are able to show the teenager that he or she is welcome in the school or public library, and that he or she has a place there. We are also able to identify ourselves as friends . . . ."

One of the axiomatic things about booktalking is that the talk is not to reveal everything about the book. This is a common beginner's mistake. Doris M. Cole's suggestion in "The Book Talk" in *Junior Plots* (Bowker, 1967) is that booktalks should give only an "enticing sample of the book's contents." In the same article, Margaret Edwards calls the sample "a little piece of pie so good that it tempts one to consume the whole concoction." Learning how to find and then how to present just the right sample is the essence of learning to booktalk. In her book, *The Fair Garden and the Swarm of Beasts* (Hawthorn, 1974), Edwards states that the objectives of booktalks are "to sell the idea of reading for pleasure; to introduce new ideas and new fields of reading; to develop an appreciation of style and character portrayal; lift the level of reading by introducing the best books the audience can read with pleasure; to humanize books, the library and the librarian."

To all of these objectives, I would add that booktalks keep librarians from becoming hypocrites who despair of their patrons' reading tastes while never reading for themselves or for their patrons.

There are probably as many types of booktalks as there are librarians doing them, but roughly they fall into long or short talks with interesting combinations of the two. A short talk, and the one which should be mastered first, usually presents only one title and lasts from thirty seconds to one minute. In it, the librarian tells listeners about something happening to someone in the book, without either divulging the entire plot or stringing along a variety of superlatives. Examples:

> When BoJo was 17 and July was 16 and they'd been going steady all through high school, July got pregnant and they ran away and got married, even though both sets of parents were disgusted; July had to drop out of school; and BoJo gave up his college football scholarship. *Mr.*

and Mrs. Bo Jo Jones will tell you how they made a go of a teenage marriage with three strikes against them.

Even though Harold Krents went totally blind as a child, his parents refused to send him to special schools, and in *To Race the Wind,* he tells his true life story about how he played football, became a lawyer, got drafted into the army, and inspired the writing of *Butterflies Are Free.*

As a baby, she had been fried alive by alcoholic parents. By the time Laura was twelve and Dr. D'Ambrosio discovered her in an institution, she had been diagnosed as schizophrenic (the severest form of mental illness), had a long list of physical problems, and had never spoken a word. *No Language but a Cry* is about how he helped her.

It is obvious in these examples how easily short talks can be adapted to floor work, when a teen asks what the book's about, to annotated booklists, and to prerecorded radio spots. Depending on the use or situation, the booktalks can be shortened further or lengthened. "Booktalk" is probably too formal a word, but these short talks do demand that YA librarians discipline themselves to think constantly about the books they've read in terms of plot and the teen audience rather than literary quality or a strictly personal reaction. Kids want to know what happens in a book, what is so exciting about it that they should want to read it. Keeping out your own adjectives lets them feel that they make the decision to read the book, despite your predilection, rather than that the librarian is just pushing either personal favorites or some sort of "literary spinach" down their throats. In other words, let the book sell itself.

A long booktalk lasts ten to fifteen minutes and usually emphasizes one particular section of one particular title, whether memorized or told in your own words but not read aloud. Some examples of good sections of books to use are the dead horse scene in *Red Sky at Morning,* the first day on the tubercular ward in *I'm Done Crying,* Albert Scully meeting Mrs. Woodfin for the first time and getting drunk in *The Dreamwatcher,* being fitted for braces and shoes in *Easy Walking,* the race at Riverside with no clutch in *Parnelli,* discovering that Madek has left him naked to die in the desert in *Death Watch,* or Capt. Lebrun's escape in *Escape from Colditz.* Long talks are more formal than short talks and are best used to follow up several short ones on the same theme or as a break in the middle of a variety of unrelated shorts.

Typing out a long talk, double-spaced, helps both with editing it and learning it, because no matter how closely you follow the author's words, there's usually a sentence or two which can be eliminated for an oral presentation. It also helps you incorporate an introduction, ending, and transitions from short talks into one coherent, packaged talk, rather than relying on your own memory. Typed talks can also be kept on file and used repeatedly by the same person or for training new talkers. It is possible to get stale or become dependent on out-of-date talks or, worse still, to forget all other sections of the book except the typed talk, but I have found that because a much-used talk is new to the audience it also remains fresh for the librarian, unless the subject matter is no longer relevant.

The major disagreement among the YA service experts is whether to memorize the long talk or not. Some feel the preparation is too hard, that it is too easy to forget a memorized talk in public, or that such talks are not adaptable enough for all types of audience situations. Some feel the kids will not be interested in so formal an approach or that the librarian will get stale and sound wooden if the same talk is given repeatedly. Others feel that memorization, at least once during a training session, is the only way new booktalkers can learn delivery and talk-cutting techniques against which to evolve their own individual styles later. Having been trained and having trained people by the memorization method, I find the latter to be true, for myself and for most beginners. I do believe, however, that there is no *one* way to do booktalks and that you should do what is comfortable for you—within the guidelines of experience outlined here—and what gets kids to read the books you talk about. It does seem illogical to reject a method just because it is difficult without trying it to see the results or how you might improve upon it.

The combination booktalk presentation can mean a combination of types of talks, librarians, books, genres, or media, and should generally not run more than twenty-five to thirty minutes. It is the most common type of presentation done for a teenage audience and is usually pre-arranged with the teacher or group leader to allow time for browsing, card registration, a film, discussion, questions, or just relaxing afterward. Examples would be interspersing poetry, cassette folk-rock lyrics, and short talks on a loneliness theme, or using themes like overcoming handicaps, teenagers in trouble, the future, love, etc.

Short talks could alternate with related slides of the books or the situations described, or of the library itself. Talks can be woven into a creative dramatic presentation or improvisation. If the theme is related to a particular curriculum unit, the combination of readable fun books with magazines, pamphlets, and reference works is valuable. With a little imagination, short talks can even be combined with a lesson on using the catalog. The combinations are limited only by your time, talent, ingenuity, and the audience response. It is always important to remember that your ultimate object in booktalking is to get the kids interested in reading the books you talk about. So if you get so AV-oriented that you are no longer connected with books or so entertaining that only your dramatic ability dazzles your audience, you may be missing the point.

Elaine Simpson further differentiates booktalks into the resource talk done by school librarians, which "is a supplement to a particular unit of work being done in a class, and its purpose is to show the useful, inter-

esting, unusual materials available in the library on the subject"—done
at the request of the teacher concerned—and the public library booktalk,
which "is to show the great variety of materials and services available for
all library users" and is not directed toward a specific subject. This distinction seems arbitrary to me with some of the popular curriculum topics
now taught. It does seem unfair to ask public YA librarians to do only
curriculum-related resource talks (which are extremely popular with
teachers when they discover them) when a school librarian is available,
but priorities must be decided by school and public YA librarians based
on local circumstances, time, and talent, and should always be a fully
cooperative, courteous, joint effort. The teenagers are the ultimate losers
in territorial feuds between school and public librarians.

To prepare for booktalks and the accompanying reader's advisory floor
work, YA librarians should read widely all types of books and subjects
of interest to their teen patrons and keep track of what they have read.
Writing a short talk on every title read on a 3″ x 5″ card is a good way
to discipline yourself to think of books in terms of how you would present a particular title to a particular teenager. This also helps you keep
the names of the characters straight—an eternal problem with teen novels—and the cards can be filed according to themes, which then helps
train you in associating similar titles for talks, lists, and reader's advisory
service.

The next step is to master talk delivery techniques in private, prefer-
ably in a formal training session where the rest of the group is as nervous
as you are, and where videotape playback and group criticism are encouraged. The horrible shock of seeing your unconscious mannerisms on a
television monitor corrects them faster than any other method I know,
and addressing any audience will give you practice in pitching your voice
properly.

If you are in a small, isolated library, have no one more experienced
to work with you, and have not learned the technique in library school—
an all too common problem among YA librarians—practice on your
family or clerical staff and use a full-length mirror and a tape recorder if
you have no access to videotaping. A tape recorder can help you memorize a talk in addition to correcting mistakes, but there is a danger that
learning your booktalk this way will make you bored with it before you
ever give it for the first time. Since a formal group training workshop is
so valuable in learning to booktalk, I feel isolated YA librarians should
pressure local library schools to provide this as continuing education in
extension programs and pressure library associations to give regional
workshops and create videotapes of different booktalks which can be
borrowed.

Once you feel you have mastered the cutting and delivery of a talk in
the abstract and have read widely enough so that you won't be undone
because a kid has already read one of the books you're prepared to talk

about and you can't suggest another one, announce your availability to do this (with a prior agreement with your supervisors as to how often you'll be available) by letters and/or visits to teachers, curriculum supervisors and department heads, school librarians, principals, reading specialists, and youth workers. Be sure to state in the letter what you *will* and *will not* do, and I suggest that you always insist that the teacher or leader remain with the class or group. You are a guest, not a substitute, and it is extremely hard to be an entertaining booktalker as well as an authority figure at the same time. Classes are notorious for going berserk when they think an inexperienced substitute is on the scene, and teachers who have never had booktalkers before are equally notorious for disappearing the whole period.

Be sure to state how long you will talk, usually twenty-five to thirty minutes and what you will do in any leftover time. If you will not do curriculum related talks, this is the place to say so, or to list which subjects or books you are prepared to talk about so they can be chosen in advance. English teachers will sometimes want you to discuss the literary merits of the books you talk about to reinforce their classroom objectives, and since it usually is disastrous to do this with booktalks, you can state this in your letter or in person as arrangements are finalized.

Another way to advertise yourself is to demonstrate the technique at faculty and department meetings and to invite teachers of other classes to observe you while you talk to a particular class.

Some schools assume that once you talk there you will never return and they will hit you with double classes and assemblies. So it is wise to state whether you will stay all day and talk to single classes successively or return at another convenient time. While I feel that assemblies are an awkward way to booktalk because of projection problems and the lack of personal eye contact, the Free Library of Philadelphia has perfected "On Your Own," a thirty minute multimedia assembly program featuring short films, slides, a tape of music and narration, and three librarians who present five short one-minute bookspots in person.

Ideally, the school librarian is the contact for the public YA librarian in neighboring schools and booktalk efforts should be coordinated through the school librarian.

A day or two before you are to appear, call to remind the person who invited you and check to see if circumstances have remained the same, and, if you're depending on school AV equipment, to make sure that the equipment is working and will be there when you need it. One piece of equipment you may need is some sort of podium if you're tall, and you can improvise with a dictionary stand or a pile of encyclopedias if necessary, on the spot, or carry a portable one with you. It's a useful crutch, and I suspect short people or those with photographic memories may scorn the use of such props.

You will find, as you booktalk more often, that the sheer public relations value of being so visible in the adolescent community makes rapport with them much easier because they remember you. "Hey, Miss, didn't I see you in my school the other day?" "Hey, what're you doing here?" Other youth service professionals will remember you also as a friendly helpful ally and often reciprocate with help at programs and recommend you as a resource person to others. Your own self-confidence grows immeasurably and you soon find that you're really not scared to talk to anybody anymore.

Best of all, though, is the immediate and immensely gratifying feedback from the kids who truly appreciate your presentation and will charge back to the library to get "the book about the guy who drank the blood" or say, in wonder, "Have you *really* read *all these books?*" or as one teen recently said, "that was a nice thing you did for us the other day."

There is almost no better way to let them know you're on their side than good booktalking, and I can only agree with Doris Cole who said, "Young people are the best, the most responsive audience in the world."

A Guide for Booktalkers

Don't wait until the eleventh hour to prepare, nor be unduly concerned by preliminary nervousness.

Make sure you know how to get where you're going to speak, unless the audience is coming to you. If the latter is true, make sure the room is reserved and set up in advance. If you are a librarian going to a school, always check in at the main office first to introduce yourself and announce the purpose of your visit.

Organize your books and equipment. Set them up in the order in which you'll talk about them and have chosen passages marked with a clip at the bottom of the page. Hold your notes up if you have to, use a podium, or clip them to the inside or back of the book.

Do not begin to speak until the audience is ready to listen, and wait for attention with good humor, unobtrusively. Introduce yourself or allow your host to introduce you and any other team members at the beginning of the period and be sure everyone in the room can hear all that is said and understands why you are there.

State clearly the author and title of each book you talk about. Sometimes it is wise to have a list of your talk titles prepared in advance you can distribute and let the audience keep and check off as you speak. This is especially good if your charging system or the circumstances don't allow you to circulate the books on the spot at the end of the period or visit.

Speak slowly and clearly, trying not to think too far ahead so you don't forget what you're saying. Talk to the back of the room and don't be afraid to smile occasionally or to laugh with the kids at a funny spot. Avoid any gestures or tones which do not enhance the story and call attention to yourself, and don't try to be hip or you'll be very embarrassing to the audience. On the other hand, don't talk down to them using phrases like "boys and girls" or "you young people," or you'll alienate them.

Try not to be monotonal, a quality which can be discovered and corrected if you have practiced with a tape recorder prior to your appearance and change the pace of your speaking as well as your loudness occasionally. Don't be dramatic unless it comes naturally or you've been coached by more experienced people.

Stand firmly without rocking and try not to lean, or play with rubber bands or paper clips. It looks terrible and distracts the audience. If you hold a book up so they can see it or show illustrations, hold it firmly and consciously and pan slowly so everyone can see it. A book held at an unconsciously lopsided, impossible viewing angle is an all too common fault among beginning booktalkers trying to remember everything at once, and it is very annoying to an audience.

Don't illustrate a book with an example or incident applicable to a class member. I once introduced *Slipping Down Life* to a class saying, "Evie Decker was the second fattest kid in her whole high school," only to see the entire class, to my horror, turn in unison to stare at an overweight member. It was awful, and I never used it again. Try to learn from your own mistakes.

Try to know the characters' names, especially in teen novels, or they all sound alike out loud, and don't frustrate the audience by making every talk a cliff-hanger or they'll tune you out as the tease you are in such a case. Don't get nervous and tell the whole story or no one will read the books. This is avoided by careful preparation and discipline on the spot if the kids beg you to tell them the ending.

Be flexible enough to wind up quickly and go on to another title or activity if the group seems restless or bored, and whatever you do, don't scold the audience for not being fascinated with you. It backfires every time.

Try not to use difficult words they may not understand. Don't be nonplussed if they say, "Hey, what's that mean?" Beware of rhetorical questions. Someone may answer them. Don't use dialect unless it's natural to you or you'll be ridiculed or will unwittingly insult the kids by making them feel you're making fun of them. And avoid profanity and *double entendres* because the kids usually either think it's hilarious from you and go into phony gales of shocked laughter or are actually shocked and forget what else you're saying. There are some exceptions to the *double entendres* like *Night to Remember,* which always got asked about without fail by an unwitting teen who thought it was a torrid love story. One of those is usually enough because tricking the unknowing audience is hardly the point.

Don't oversell average books. There's no bigger bore than a librarian who gushes over every teen or sports story as if each is equal to *War and Peace.* The kids will peg you as a phony each time and you are guaranteed to bore them to death. Be sure of your terms and facts in technical and sports books and do not use explicit factual books on physical or sexual development unless you're sure of both community reactions and your own ability to speak without embarrassment.

Set up the books or give out the lists and, if you've gained enough experience, let the audience call out titles they want to hear about or ask them to tell you any they've already read so that you can match them with a similar story. On the other hand, always be honest and admit when they've stumped you, and never pretend to have read a book you haven't. You'll need to have a talk prepared in case you meet only stolid indifference despite your most artful efforts to stimulate comment.

Be prepared for interruptions by the kids saying "Oooo!" at scary spots and laughing at funny ones. The school PA system usually broadcasts daily announcements once or twice each day and finding out just when can save you much grief so you're not in the middle of a talk when these come on. There is no way to avoid the more dramatic interruptions, but knowing that they do happen will keep you reasonably calm in all circumstances.

Try never to read to the audience unless in the material you are presenting the author's style is the important thing and can be communicated in no other way: poetry, some essays, fine writing in general. Even then then you would do well to quote rather than to read or know the book so well that you are not bound to it—your eyes can still rove over the group and take cognizance of their enjoyment. Be watchful for signs of disinterest.

Go on to pre-arranged announcements of upcoming library events after you have finished talking. Tell how to get a card or check out a book, invite questions or browsing, distribute additional lists, etc.

Keep track of every class or group you've spoken to for periodic statistical reports which may help justify more staff assistance for your service specialty. Write a brief narrative report so there is a record of what you have done, both for your supervisor and for any possible successors.

Evaluate your success as a booktalker primarily by noting how many people read the books you discussed or come to the library asking for them or to get a card for the first time. You are often successful even when the audience seems indifferent, asleep, or incredibly itchy, although continual responses like these should make you alter your technique.

Perhaps the selection wasn't right, or you spoke too long, or over the heads of your audience, or were too monotonal or too dramatic.

REFERENCES

Bradford, Richard. *Red Sky at Morning.* New York: Lippincott, 1968.

Carr, John D. *Death Watch.* New York: Macmillan, 1963.

D'Ambrosio, Richard. *No Language but a Cry.* New York: Doubleday, 1970.

Ferris, Louanne. *I'm Done Crying,* ed. Beth Day. New York: Evans, 1969.

Gershe, Leonard. *Butterflies Are Free.* New York: Random, 1970.

Head, Ann. *Mr. and Mrs. Bo Jo Jones.* New York: Putnam, 1967.

Krents, Harold. *To Race the Wind: An Autobiography.* New York: Putnam, 1972.

Libby, Bill. *Parnelli: A Story of Auto-Racing.* New York: Dutton, 1969.

Lord, Walter. *Night to Remember.* New York: Holt, 1955.

Nasaw, Jonathan. *Easy Walking.* New York: Lippincott, 1975.

Reid, P. R. *Escape from Colditz.* New York: Lippincott, 1973.

Tolstoy, Leo. *War and Peace.* New York: Modern Library, 1931.

Tyler, Anne. *Slipping Down Life.* New York: Knopf, 1970.

Contributors

(Unless more current information was available, contributors have been described as of the date of publications included.)

Barbara S. Bates is editor, Juvenile Books, Westminster Press, Philadelphia.

Joanne E. Bernstein, associate professor, School of Education, Brooklyn College, is the author of *Books to Help Children Cope with Separation and Loss* (Bowker, 1977).

Jeanne Betancourt has developed and taught media studies courses in high schools and is on the Media Studies graduate faculty of the New School for Research in New York City. She is the author of *Women in Focus* (distr. EFLA) and Director of Development for commercial television projects at MedCom, Inc.

Dorothy M. Broderick is the author of *The Image of the Black in Children's Fiction* (Bowker, 1973), plus numerous articles on children's and young adult literature. She is an editor of *VOYA (Voice of Youth Advocates)* and an associate professor of Library Service, University of Alabama.

Mary S. Calderone is president of SIECUS (Sex Information and Education Council of the U.S., Inc.).

Jose A. Carrasco is an assistant professor of Mexican American Graduate Studies at San Jose State College and department coordinator of the community college and field placement interns and of the Bilingual Studio-Laboratory sponsored by the John Hay Whitney Foundation.

Mary K. Chelton is a coadjutant professor of Library Service, University of Alabama, and editor of *VOYA (Voice of Youth Advocates)*.

John Cunningham is the Girard Avenue Branch (Philadelphia Free Library) YA librarian and is active in the Social Responsibilities Round Table's Gay Task Force.

Kenneth L. Donelson, a prolific author of articles on young adult literature, is a professor of English at Arizona State University, Tempe. With Alleen Pace Nilsen, he is the author of *Literature for Today's Young Adults* (Scott, Foresman, 1980).

Sylvia Engdahl is an author of science fiction novels for young people, including *Beyond the Tomorrow Mountains* (Atheneum, 1973) and *This Star Shall Abide* (Atheneum, 1972).

Margaret P. Esmonde is an assistant professor of English at Villanova University and a past president of the Children's Literature Association.

Dana L. Farnsworth is Henry K. Oliver Professor of Hygiene, Emeritus, Harvard University, and consultant on Psychiatry, Harvard School of Public Health.

Lance M. Gentile, a specialist in elementary and secondary reading and bilingual education, is on the faculty of the College of Education, North Texas State University, Denton.

Sandra M. Gilbert is an associate professor of English at the University of California, Davis, and the author of *Act of Attention: The Poems of D. H. Lawrence* (Cornell Univ. Pr., 1972).

James S. Gordon is a research psychiatrist and consultant on alternative forms of service at the Center for Studies of Child and Family Mental Health, National Institute of Mental Health.

Armin Grams is head of the Human Development Program, The Merrill-Palmer Institute, Detroit.

Frances Hanckel is the administrator and technical coordinator for a univerversity hospital cardiology unit in Philadelphia and is active in the Social Responsibilities Round Table's Gay Task Force.

Alethea Helbig teaches English at Eastern Michigan University.

James T. Henke is associate professor of English at Youngstown State University, Ohio.

Natt Hentoff is a prolific author, well known for *Jazz Country* (Harper & Row, 1965) and *This School Is Driving Me Crazy* (Delacorte, 1976).

Isabelle Holland is the author of *Of Love and Death and Other Journeys* and *The Man without a Face* (Lippincott, 1975, 1972), as well as numerous other books and articles.

Kai-ye Hsu is a professor of Comparative Literature at San Francisco State University. His publications include *Twentieth Century Chinese Poetry* (Cornell Univ. Pr., 1970) and *The Chinese Literary Scene: A Writer's Visit to the People's Republic* (Random, 1975).

Jean McClure Kelty teaches at Youngstown State University, Ohio.

Jerzy Kosinski, born in Poland, has become a noted American novelist, whose works include *Steps, Painted Bird, Being There,* and *The Devil Tree* (Bantam, 1969, 1972, 1972, and 1974, resp.). He has taught English prose at Yale and Princeton and received the National Book Award for *Steps.* He is also a past president of P. E. N. International, a writers' association pledged to oppose the suppression of freedom of expression.

Nancy Larrick is a free-lance writer and adjunct professor of Education and director of Poetry Workshop at Lehigh University, Bethlehem, Pennsylvania.

Richard Lettis is a professor of English, C. W. Post College, Long Island University, Greenvale, New York.

W. Bernard Lukenbill is an assistant professor, Graduate School of Library Science, University of Texas at Austin.

Mary Lystad is special assistant to the director, Division of Special Mental Health Programs, National Institute of Mental Health.

Merna M. McMillan is director of Mental Health Services for the San Luis Obispo Community Mental Services, San Luis Obispo, California.

Joseph Mersand, former president of the National Council of Teachers of English, teaches in the Department of English at York College, Jamaica, New York.

Joseph E. Milosh, Jr., author of *The Scale of Perfection and the English Mystical Tradition* (Univ. of Wisconsin Pr., 1966) and *Teaching the History of the English Language in the Secondary School* (NCTE, 1972), has taught medieval English literature at the University of Wisconsin and Northern Illinois University. He is now chairman, Department of English, Mississippi State University.

Salvatore Mondello is a professor of American Popular Culture and Ethnic History at the Rochester Institute of Technology.

G. Lynn Nelson is an assistant professor of English, Arizona State University, Tempe.

Gayle Nelson is a member of the English faculty at Edison High School, Minneapolis.

Philip D. Ortego is a professor of English and executive director of the Chicano Affairs Program at the University of Texas at El Paso. His prose, poetry, and fiction have appeared in leading scholarly and literary publications, such as *Nation, Saturday Review, Chaucer Review, Ecology Today,* and *El Grito.*

Helen Pablubinskas has studied Chinese language and culture at National Chengchi University, Taipei, and at the University of Hawaii and the University of California, Berkeley. Since 1962, she has taught creative writing to young Asian-American students in San Francisco.

Ernest R. Page is an assistant professor of English Education, West Georgia College, Carrollton.

Pamela D. Pollack is an Associate Book Review Editor, *School Library Journal,* New York City.

Al Poulin, Jr., teaches English at St. Francis College, Biddeford, Maine. He is the translator of Rainer M. Rilke's *Duino Elegies & Sonnets to Orpheus* (Houghton Mifflin, 1977).

Lawrence Rakow is a secondary schools specialist, Cuyahoga County Public Library, Cleveland, Ohio.

Gerald Rosen teaches at California State University, Sonoma, and is the author of *Zen in the Art of J. D. Salinger* (Creative Arts Book Co., 1977).

Mel Rosenberg is coordinator, Young Adult Services, Los Angeles Public Library.

Steve Roxburgh is a doctoral student in English at the State University of New York at Stony Brook, where he has taught courses in children's literature. He is currently writing a dissertation on children's literature and is a member of the Children's Book Department of Farrar, Straus and Giroux, Inc.

Andrea Benton Rushing teaches in the Department of Black Studies, Amherst College, Amherst, Massachusetts.

Peter Scharf is an assistant professor, Program in Social Ecology, University of California at Irvine.

Peter Schillaci, a consultant in educational media, is currently doing research on the relationship between cinema and myth.

Robert Sklar teaches American studies at the University of Michigan. He is the author of *F. Scott Fitzgerald, The Last Laocoon* (Oxford Univ. Pr., 1967) and *Movie-Made America* (Random, 1975).

Lou Willett Stanek, a free-lance writer and critic, and formerly director of the M.A.T. program at the University of Chicago, is on the faculty of Marymount Manhattan College, New York City.

Anna Lee Stensland is a professor of English, University of Minnesota, Duluth.

Gordon Stevenson is an associate professor, School of Library and Information Science, State University of New York at Albany.

Marvin B. Sussman is UNIDELL Professor of Human Behavior, University of Delaware.

William Blake Tyrrell is an associate professor of classics at Michigan State University.

Eliot Wigginton teaches high school English in Rabun Gap, Georgia. In 1966, he helped his students found a quarterly magazine which they named *Foxfire.* This led to *The Foxfire Book* (Doubleday) which was followed by *Foxfire 2, Foxfire 3,* and *Foxfire 4.* Other student projects include Foxfire Video, Foxfire Records, The Foxfire Press, and Foxfire Furniture.

W. Cody Wilson is a professor of behaviorial sciences in the Graduate School of Social Work, Adelphi University, Garden City, New York, and a member of Sex Health and Education Associates, New York City.

Gary K. Wolfe teaches in the Department of the Humanities at Roosevelt University, Chicago.

Kary K. Wolfe is associated with the University of Chicago.

Designed by Will Gallagher
Composed by FM Typesetting Company in Linotype
    Times Roman and Optima with Optima display type
Printed on Warren's 50# 1854, a pH neutral stock,
and bound by Braun-Brumfield, Inc.

DATE DUE

fai 5-81			
4-25-87			
NOV. 1 2 1990			